Chinese Aerospace Power

Chinese Aerospace Power

Evolving Maritime Roles

Edited by Andrew S. Erickson and Lyle J. Goldstein

NAVAL INSTITUTE PRESS
Annapolis, Maryland

Naval Institute Press
291 Wood Road
Annapolis, MD 21402

Library of Congress Cataloging-in-Publication Data
Chinese aerospace power : evolving maritime roles / edited by Andrew S. Erickson
and Lyle J. Goldstein.
    p. cm.
  Includes bibliographical references and index.
    ISBN 978-1-59114-241-6 (hardcover : alk. paper) 1. Air-power—China. 2. Sea-
power—China. 3. Aeronautics, Military—China. 4. China—Military policy. 5.
Aerospace engineering—China. 6. Aerospace industries—China. I. Erickson,
Andrew S. II. Goldstein, Lyle.
  UG635.C6C483 2011
  359.9'40951—dc22
                              2011008727

Printed in the United States of America.

19 18 17 16 15 14 13 12 11   9 8 7 6 5 4 3 2 1
First printing

Contents

Foreword

IT HAS BEEN MORE than thirty years since the United States established formal diplomatic relations with the People's Republic of China (PRC), yet those relations remain ambiguous and perplexing. The U.S. government seeks to encourage the PRC's evolution into a responsible stakeholder on the world stage, especially in the Pacific, while the Department of Defense strives to balance military-to-military interaction with the PLA and yet still maintain credible deterrence against China's rapidly increasing military capability.

The chapters that follow address the reality of the emergence of the People's Liberation Army (and People's Liberation Army Navy) as a modern, complex military. They are not intended to assuage either hawks or doves on the controversial issue of China; rather, they provide a broad and objective assessment of Chinese aerospace and maritime power by professional researchers who take their analyses with the utmost seriousness. This is important work.

Is war with China possible? Regrettably, yes. Acknowledging that unfortunate fact and ensuring that the United States is sufficiently prepared to prevent and deter such a conflict is what this volume is about. The most essential work being done today is the broad effort to avoid conflict with the PRC without compromising our national principles. Global economic challenges are daunting, but the threat of a nuclear-enabled Iran and North Korea, or terrorists with weapons of mass destruction, pale in comparison to the potential devastation that might occur if war erupts between the United States and China. Beyond imperiling the survival of Taiwan, war with China would cause broader physical and economic destruction and could very well spiral into a lengthy global conflict.

The surest way to limit that potential is to mature the relationship between the United States and China, which is currently stuck in the molasses of its modern origins. It is an elaborate ballet of protocol and protest, pirouetting around the status of Taiwan. We must find a way beyond the false formalities of our special relationship with the PRC. To build on the hopeful signs of the first year of the Ma Ying-jeou government and PRC–Taiwan interaction, I suggest the following: the United States government should stress at every turn that U.S. involvement with Taiwan is good for the PRC. During the government of Chen Shui-bian, U.S. pressure on Chen was key to keeping his actions away from PRC red lines. My experience in dealing with Beijing suggests that a candid and direct approach to diplomacy can yield practical solutions to the delicate problems in U.S.–China relations.

Most fundamentally, we should assess PRC military modernization in objective terms for what we know it is—a significant build up in capability well beyond defensive requirements. Special attention needs to be focused on China's undersea capabilities and also its new prowess in the domain of electronic warfare. Moreover, it is crucial that we avoid the presumption that we can know Beijing's intent. We do not know, and we cannot. We must assess the quality of China's hand without trying to predict how Beijing will ultimately play its cards. We are duty bound to continuously evaluate the military balance, considerations of readiness and risk, and the potential for engagement and deterrence.

Those who ignore the lessons of history may be condemned to repeat it, but those who turn a blind eye to the realities of the present, for example by underestimating China's dramatically enhanced aerospace and maritime power, are assuming irresponsible risks for our nation.

LIEUTENANT GENERAL DANIEL P. LEAF, USAF (RET.)

Lyle J. Goldstein

Introduction

CHINA'S AIRCRAFT CARRIER program is making major waves well before the first ship is completed. Undoubtedly, this development heralds a new era in Chinese national security policy. While the present volume presents substantial new insights on that particular question, its focus is decidedly broader in scope. This book instead aspires to offer a comprehensive survey of Chinese aerospace developments, with a focus particularly on areas of potential strategic significance previously unexplored in Western scholarship. It then seeks to link these developments to the vast maritime battle space of the Asia-Pacific region and consequent implications for the U.S. military, particularly the Navy.

Whether some hypothetical future Chinese expeditionary force operating off Africa a decade or two from now does so under the protective umbrella of carrier aircraft is not without consequence for the global strategic balance. But a relatively simpler set of aerospace systems, from microsatellites to unmanned aerial vehicles to ballistic and cruise missiles, are challenging U.S. maritime dominance in East Asia today. Cumulatively, progress in all major aerospace dimensions by various elements of the People's Liberation Army (PLA) heralds a new period in which Chinese forces are now decidedly altering the complexion of the military balance in the East Asian littoral.

Faced with such rapid developments in Chinese aerospace development, the U.S. Naval War College's China Maritime Studies Institute (CMSI) assembled a group of technical specialists—U.S. Air Force (USAF) and U.S.

Navy operators, and regional experts on—10–11 December 2008 for its fourth annual conference, "Evolving Maritime Roles for Chinese Aerospace Power." Most of the chapters herein were presented initially as papers at that conference, and were subsequently revised substantially to address recent events. A select group of chapters was added to take advantage of the authors' cutting-edge knowledge of key subject areas. The chapters are designed to offer a wide range of perspectives because constructive academic dialogue and debate is at the heart of CMSI's analytical philosophy. They may be read sequentially or individually, depending on the reader's interest.

CMSI is the first undertaking of its kind outside of China. Established in 2006 to increase knowledge and understanding of the maritime dimensions of China's rise, it supports the research needs of the U.S. Navy. Based at the Naval War College in Newport, Rhode Island, CMSI is located at the nexus of academic, policy, and operational communities. In addition to an annual conference and regular research seminars at the college, the institute focuses on intensive research into China's future maritime development, based principally on the ever-growing array of Chinese-language primary sources.

CMSI has developed a record of discussing and analyzing in depth the most advanced areas of Chinese naval development; CMSI's 2005 conference, for example, discussed "China's Future Nuclear Submarine Force." The institute has also been at the forefront of developing a positive working relationship between the U.S. and Chinese navies, hosting in 2007 a conference on "Defining a Maritime Partnership with China." At every step, CMSI has striven to add objectivity and data-based analysis to inform the U.S. Navy's approach to China. In that spirit, this volume, like its four predecessors, contains many chapters that draw extensively on original Chinese-language sources, many not previously cited outside China. Numerous articles and books have been written on Chinese aerospace development, and many more discuss future U.S. naval strategy in the Asia-Pacific region. But no other volume connects the two issues, simultaneously evaluating the Chinese aerospace challenge and its implications for U.S. naval strategy.

This volume is divided into six thematic sections. The first section establishes the maritime context for China's rapid aerospace development. Andrew S. Erickson leads off with a survey of current developments and concludes that "Chinese aerospace capabilities are improving in a rapid, broad-based fashion that can properly be described as a 'revolution.'" Mark A. Stokes and Ian Easton follow with an in-depth analysis of both the organizational underpinnings of China's aerospace development and its regional implications. They find that, "largely driven by a Taiwan scenario, mainland China's capacity to conduct a successful aerospace campaign to swiftly gain a decisive air advantage is surpassing defenses that its neighbors, including Taiwan, Japan, perhaps India, and even U.S. forces operating in the Western Pacific, can field." Wayne A. Ulman reveals that "all indicators point to the continued improvement of both the PLAAF and PLA naval aviation over the next decade, to the point where China will have one of the world's foremost air forces by 2020." Kevin Pollpeter concludes the section by exploring Chinese writings that reveal "an ambitious plan to fully integrate space into Chinese warfighting," with an understanding that this approach could "hold an [adversary's] economy hostage and . . . undermine an opponent's will."

The second section surveys the roles for Chinese aerospace assets in promoting Chinese intelligence, surveillance, and reconnaissance (ISR) and in denying these capabilities to China's potential adversaries in conflict, as well as corresponding maritime implications. Anthony J. Mastalir surveys China's space development, including especially its 11 January 2007 antisatellite (ASAT) test, and concludes that if Beijing's approach in this sensitive domain is not to become the twenty-first century equivalent of the destabilizing German dreadnoughts, then Washington requires a more comprehensive approach to space policy regarding China. Peter A. Dutton discusses China's new initiative to restrict military operations in the airspace over its exclusive economic zone (EEZ), concluding that such efforts must be strongly contested because "information is inherently stabilizing," so that such operations are actually very much in China's own national interest. Richard D. Fisher Jr.'s analysis reveals yet another Chinese ISR capability, noting that "the PLA has apparently committed to investing in a world-class unmanned [aerial vehicle] systems capability," as suggested by the more than twenty-five prototypes or major projects that were unveiled at China's 2010 Zhuhai Airshow. Garth Hekler's extensive research in Chinese sources reveals a similarly robust Chinese effort in the areas of both defensive and offensive airborne electronic warfare—another key element of the evolving ISR environment along the East Asian littoral.

The third section considers prospective maritime missions that might develop further in the future as the result of advances in Chinese aerospace. Dennis J. Blasko investigates helicopter development in the PLA and finds that this process is "still in the rudimentary phase" though the "force is expanding in size and scope of its missions." Lyle J. Goldstein, Miguel Martinez, and William S. Murray address a related theme, Chinese airborne antisubmarine warfare (ASW), and likewise conclude that Chinese capabilities are not robust—with the caveat that China's navy seems to be prioritizing airborne ASW given the amount of ongoing research in this area evident in Chinese sources. Similar limitations are evident in the development of China's aerial refueling capabilities, according to the chapter by Gabriel Collins, Michael McGauvran, and Timothy White, who conclude that "even major AR [aerial refueling] improvements over the next ten to fifteen years will not give the PLA a capacity resembling the global power projection capability the United States has with its more than four hundred tankers." Nan Li and Christopher Weuve take up the issue of Chinese aircraft carrier development. Noting the possible options that Beijing might pursue, they determine that various necessary conditions appear to have been met, including endorsement by the central leadership, affordability, a concise naval strategy incorporating the new platforms, and the availability of the requisite technologies. Daniel J. Kostecka surveys the potential spectrum of Chinese deck aviation development. He concludes that "between now and 2020, the acquisition of aircraft carriers will afford the PLAN the capacity to conduct force projection operations in East Asia."

Section four of this volume examines the emerging threat from Chinese prowess in fielding advanced cruise missiles. Roger Cliff begins by surveying the latest developments in capabilities, doctrine, and missions for China's air forces. He finds that "China's air forces have made substantial strides over the past decade" and "have the potential to present a significant obstacle to U.S. success in such a conflict." Kevin Lanzit and David Chen evaluate the maritime strike mission among China's air forces and note that China already has 570 strike aircraft, which are armed with lethal antiship cruise missiles and capable of operating 1,200 km or more from China's coast. Andrew S. Erickson and Jingdong Yuan describe these missiles in detail, observing that China is no longer reliant on Russia to deploy these advanced weapons. Michael S. Chase focuses on the latest dimension of the cruise missile threat, arguing that major progress in Chinese land-attack cruise missiles could allow Beijing "to at least partially address the asymmetry in conventional strategic warfare capabilities that currently prevents the PLA from retaliating in kind if the United States launches conventional attacks against targets on the Chinese mainland."

First among Chinese antiaccess/area denial systems in potential strategic significance is China's DF-21D antiship ballistic missile (ASBM), which Admiral Robert Willard, commander, U.S. Pacific Command, declared in December 2010 to have reached the equivalent of initial operational capability.[1] The vital issue of Chinese ASBM development is addressed in section five of the present volume. Ron Christman describes the conventional force of the PLA Second Artillery Corps as seven times larger than the nuclear forces component of the service. Andrew S. Erickson and David D. Yang probe the writings of Chinese analysts concerning China's emerging ASBM capability and conclude that this concept has a long and well-developed history in Chinese strategic thought. Toshi Yoshihara examines Chinese perspectives on the ballistic missile defense architecture and finds that China views Aegis missile defense systems as a highly lucrative target for striking U.S. Navy carrier strike groups (CSGs) in a conflict scenario. Paul S. Giarra then evaluates the implications of Chinese ASBM development for the U.S. Navy and comes to the stark conclusion that the deployment of an effective ASBM by China could alter naval warfare to an extraordinary extent, comparable to the introduction of aircraft and submarines in the twentieth century.

Concluding chapters in section six develop more comprehensive assessments. Eric Hagt develops the sobering assessment that "time (and money) appears to be on China's side. Although the United States will remain the dominant military power at the global scale for decades to come, in the regional context of Taiwan, China's near seas, or even within the second island chain, the demands for power projection are far less onerous for China." James R. Holmes posits that "since the dawn of carrier warfare, U.S. naval strategy has viewed command of the air as a prerequisite for surface fleet operations" and asserts that this assumption is increasingly questionable regarding any possible conflict in the East Asian littoral. Larry M. Wortzel judges that the "U.S. Navy and Air Force . . . will likely be hindered in carrying out some . . . missions in the Western Pacific, particularly within proximity of China." Xiaoming Zhang and Sean D. McClung argue that much improvement is needed in U.S. studies of Chinese air and space power, which is "being transformed." They demonstrate that the PLAAF faces challenges both in upgrading its own forces and in competing with the General Armament Department and the Second Artillery Corps for ownership of space-based platforms: "Given the PLAAF's limited ownership and control of space assets, Chinese military theorists have recommended that the service concentrate on building facilitie s and institutions to receive satellite services for communication, weather, navigation, and global positioning." Jeff Hagen evaluates the implications of China's growing aerospace capabilities on U.S. influence in the Asia-Pacific region, and suggests a variety of countermeasures, including "increas[ing] the number of air bases and their hardness; solidify[ing] regional basing arrangements; improv[ing] long-range strike capability; increas[ing] operational coordination between the U.S. Air Force and U.S. Navy; continu[ing] modernization of [the] fighter force; [and,] to the greatest extent possible, encourag[ing] Taiwan and other partners to pursue defensive systems that are more survivable and effective against attack." In his concluding chapter, Eric A. McVadon carefully weighs the motivations behind, and implications of, Beijing's aerospace development.

While he is careful to note the substantial areas in which the United States and China share interests and may build on them further, he also emphasizes that the U.S. Navy and fellow services should make substantial, "innovative" preparations to ensure that their forces do not become outmoded. For instance, "the pending development of maritime UAVs such as the land-based broad-area maritime surveillance (BAMS) UAV- and carrier-based unmanned combat air system (UCAS)" can ameliorate the risk to the CSG or other units posed by the MaRVed MRBMs under development by China.

For now, it is hardly controversial to conclude that revolutionary change is under way in the skies above the East Asian littoral. China's space technology prowess, as demonstrated by its 2007 ASAT test and suggested by rapid progress in microsatellite development, poses a major challenge to heavy U.S. reliance on space capabilities. China's growing inventory of strike aircraft is complemented by newly advanced weaponry and ISR capabilities to support those aircraft. The breadth of this effort is demonstrated by Beijing's efforts in the legal arena to establish greater control of the airspace in its EEZ. The potential deployment of ASBMs is most troubling, however, since this weapon has the potential to render surface forces in the region all but obsolete in a single stroke.

At the same time, this balanced assessment acknowledges that certain real limitations continue to hinder China's aspirations in the aerospace domain, especially as they pertain to the maritime strategic balance. For example, Chinese aircraft have to date lacked reliable, indigenously built jet engines. Moreover, it should be noted that certain Chinese advances in aerospace technologies, processes, and systems (e.g., aerial refueling, as it gradually advances; and increasing reliance on such space-based assets as the emerging Compass satellite navigation-positioning system) may also open up new vulnerabilities to adversary countermeasures. Most fundamentally, the point is made by many contributors that China's naval air arm, like Chinese aviation in general, remains the "poor cousin" of Chinese aerospace, and progress has been moderate or even slow in developing key areas (e.g., doctrine for integrated aerospace operations in the maritime domain).

A key finding of this volume and also the December 2008 conference is that the U.S. armed forces as a whole must come to grips with enhanced Chinese long-range precision-strike capabilities that are now coming to fruition and that pose a significant threat to forces in the Western Pacific theater. The development of such capabilities as the ASBM strongly suggest that America's future fleet must reduce its vulnerability to long-range strike, with an emphasis on undersea capabilities as well as unmanned systems in order to preserve survivability in a more challenging threat environment. Additionally, evolving Chinese aerospace capabilities raise the salience of deterrence initiatives as well as the imperative to develop effective crisis-management mechanisms, not to mention a robust, long-term cooperative engagement strategy. Although American and Chinese aspirations for the twenty-first century are not so different, creativity and determination are nevertheless required to find ways to cooperate in meaningful ways on the seas and in the air and space above them. Indeed, many at the 2008 conference suggested that enhanced military-to-military engagement could reduce the mistrust that might fuel arms racing in the aerospace dimension.

The editors of this volume wish to thank, above all, the researchers who have contributed to it. Here it must be emphasized that all opinions expressed in this book are those of the authors and editors alone and in no way represent the policies or estimates of the U.S. Navy or any other organization of the U.S. government. We also are tremendously grateful to those who helped to organize the December 2008 conference, including especially Dalton Alexander, Leah Averitt, Gigi Davis, Julia Gage, Christina Hartley, Albert Lawton, Jim Lewis, Debbie Maddix, Brian Pagel, and Michael Sherlock. CMSI wishes to thank Raytheon Integrated Defense Systems for its support of the conference through a generous gift to the Naval War College Foundation. Timely and thorough assistance from key members of the Naval War College's Information Resources Department, including Mike Carroll, Neil Davis, Luke Desrochers, Dave Fields, Kerrie Hull, John Neves, and Rodham Smith, was essential to enabling Andrew S. Erickson to edit the manuscript from Seoul, South Korea; as were facilities generously provided there by Major Christopher M. Heber, USAF, and Major Cheree S. Kochen, USAF. The support of Naval War College leadership has been critical to the success of CMSI and in enabling the creation of research products such as the present volume. Finally, we wish to thank Naval Institute Press for its professionalism and dedication in publication of the series "Studies in Chinese Maritime Development," of which this is the fifth volume.

Notes

1. Andrew S. Erickson, "China's Anti-Ship Ballistic Missile (ASBM) Reaches Equivalent of 'Initial Operational Capability' (IOC)—Where It's Going and What it Means," *China Analysis from Original Sources*, 4 January 2011, http://www.andrewerickson .com/2011/01/china%E2%80%99s-anti-ship-ballistic-missile-asbm-reaches-equivalent- of-%E2%80%9Cinitial-operational-capability%E2%80%9D-ioc%E2%80%94where- it%E2%80%99s-going-and-what-it-means/.

PART I

Chinese Aerospace Development

Emerging Maritime Roles

Andrew S. Erickson

Beijing's Aerospace Revolution
Short-Range Opportunities, Long-Range Challenges

CHINA HAS ENTERED the second decade of the twenty-first century as a global economic and political power with growing regional military capabilities. Of all great powers, China has both the most uncertain political future and the greatest potential to influence global affairs. To support power projection overseas, both for national prestige and for limited missions beyond Taiwan, China must continue military growth and extend the range of its aerospace power. A major uncertainty remains: how far will China's military operate beyond its shores?

To probe the implications of China's progress in air and space, this chapter will begin by establishing the importance of aerospace development, followed by highlighting the most significant developments in China's aerospace revolution. It will subsequently examine Chinese theories of aerospace and their relevance to naval warfare. Finally, it will offer implications for China's maritime development and its significance for the U.S. Navy.

Major findings of the chapter include the following:

- China is achieving a rapid, if uneven, revolution in aerospace capabilities.

- These capabilities are mainly divided among China's Second Artillery, air force, and navy. There is likely to be competition among the services for control of new forces (e.g., space) as they emerge. China has methodically developed and acquired technologies that target limitations in the physics of high-technology warfare, placing high-end competitors (e.g., the U.S. Navy) on the costly end of an asymmetric arms race.

- In addition to widespread incremental improvements, China is on the verge of achieving several potentially "game changing" breakthroughs (particularly antiship ballistic missiles, or ASBMs, but also streaming cruise missile attacks and the application of satellite navigation).

- Such achievements will radically improve the People's Liberation Army's (PLA) antiaccess/area denial (A2/AD) capabilities by allowing it to hold at risk a wide variety of enemy surface- and air-based assets were they to enter strategically vital zones on China's contested maritime periphery in the event of conflict.

- Ongoing challenges include deficiencies in human capital; realism of training, hardware, and operations; and C4ISR (command, control, communications, computers, intelligence, surveillance, and reconnaissance).

- China can mitigate these limitations for kinetic operations around Taiwan and in its maritime periphery, and potentially for nonkinetic peacetime operations further afield.

- Conducting high-intensity wartime operations in contested environments beyond Taiwan would require major qualitative and quantitative improvements, particularly in aerospace.

- The biggest strategic question for U.S. military planners is whether China will choose to develop the aerospace capabilities to support major kinetic force projection beyond the first island chain, and if so, how.

Why Aerospace?

Since the end of World War II, full-spectrum aerospace development has been an objective indicator of comprehensive national power among great powers. Aerospace development may be defined as the production, integration, and utilization of military and civilian devices for both aviation and spaceflight. While air and space systems have their respective fundamental differences, a nation's overall attainment of comprehensive aerospace capability requires mastery of both aspects, which are increasingly interrelated.

China's methodical, relatively comprehensive aerospace development is proportionate to its rising comprehensive national power, and thus serves as a useful indicator of its future trajectory in the international system. China offers a prime example of differential aerospace development: its aerospace performance, while significant in aggregate, has thus far been lopsided. Lopsided aerospace achievement means military gaps and missed economic and strategic technological opportunities, neither of which supports great power status.

While it shares certain commonalities, Beijing's aerospace development trajectory differs from the experiences of many other aspiring and established powers (see tables 1 and 2). By the Cold War's end, China had already become the first developing nation to achieve some form of full-spectrum aerospace development. In several areas, China has achieved capabilities of great strategic significance, such as advanced ballistic and cruise missiles and increasingly advanced satellites. Taken together, these developments can be properly termed a "revolution" because, in aggregate, they significantly boost China's technological level, military capabilities, and international position.

Table 1: China's Full-Spectrum Aerospace Development

Aerospace Aspirant	Missile/SLV Success	Satellite Success	Military/Commercial Aircraft Success
1. USA	High	High	High
2. EU	High	High	High
3. Russia/USSR	High	High	High
4. China	High	High	Medium, rising
5. India	Moderate	Moderate	Low
6. Brazil	Low	Low	High

Table 2: Subcomponents of China's Differential Aerospace Development

Sector	Resources	Activity	Technology	Incentives	Institutions
Rockets	High	High	High	Medium	High
Satellites	High	Medium	Medium–High	Medium	High
Aircraft	Medium, rising	Medium, rising	Medium, rising	Medium, rising	Medium, rising

Revolution or Evolution?

The amount of sophisticated Western scholarship focused on China's aerospace development is small, and works tend to be specialized. Most significantly, despite the importance of the interrelation between Beijing's efforts in the critical aerospace and maritime spheres, there has never been a large-scale attempt to consider this nexus. An updated, comprehensive study of China's aerospace development and its maritime implications is in order, in part because the tremendous changes of the past few years have eclipsed many existing studies, as well as U.S. government estimates. According to Vice Admiral David Dorsett, deputy chief of naval operations for information dominance, "we have been pretty consistent in underestimating the delivery and IOC [initial operational capability] of Chinese technology, weapons systems." And that outpacing of respected analysis by recent developments is itself a sign of revolutionary, not evolutionary, change.

Defining Revolution

According to Eliot Cohen's criteria, a military revolution would

- "change the appearance of combat;
- [change] the structure of armies;
- lead to the rise of new military elites; [and]
- alter countries' power position."[1]

Equally important is what is *not* required to realize a military revolution. According to Cohen and Andrew F. Krepinevich, there is

- no need for comprehensive cutting-edge aerospace capacity;
- no need to be a superpower;
- no need to be symmetric; and
- no need to do it all at once.[2]

Let us now analyze the Chinese case. As Barry Posen contends, America's preeminent position in the international system hinges on its ability to command the global commons by dominating and exploiting the sea, air, and space for military purposes.[3] This prevents regional powers from denying the U.S. military access to any economically or strategically important maritime spaces.[4] However, recent Chinese aerospace improvements may allow Beijing to deny Washington the military use of critical areas in the Western Pacific and the South China Sea, which the United States and its regional allies have long conceived as part of the global commons. The PLA—long unable to engage in many military activities because of serious aerospace technology limitations—is now poised to promote China's interests beyond its immediate shores.

Key Chinese Aerospace Trends

It is worth highlighting strategically significant trends in Chinese aerospace development. When projecting possible trajectories for future Chinese capabilities, rate of change and scope of effort is more important than extant capabilities (which are limited in some cases). Table 3 offers a visual representation of this effort.

Hardware

Over the past decade China has developed, acquired, and upgraded platforms, weapons systems, and supporting architecture. While progress is uneven, it is beginning to acquire significant—and even unique—capabilities in selected areas and to achieve breakthroughs that have surprised many observers.

Ballistic and Cruise Missiles

According to the Department of Defense (DoD), "China has the most active land-based ballistic and cruise missile program in the world."[5] As its earliest area of aerospace development, dating from the late 1950s, and arguably its most organized and capable, China has produced a full range of missiles. Three emerging types of ballistic missiles stand out in particular. In 2007 China demonstrated a direct ascent antisatellite (ASAT) capability; in 2010 it demonstrated an antiballistic missile (ABM) capability. China is also developing the capability to target U.S. ships with ASBMs, which could be difficult to defend against. China's DF-21D ASBM reached the equivalent of initial operational capability (IOC) in December 2010 and is supported by a broad-based, sophisticated ISR architecture.[6] According to China's *Global Times*, an estimated intermediate-range conventional missile with a range of roughly 4,000 km is under development (scheduled for deployment in 2015). This would enable the Second Artillery to launch conventional strikes against targets as far away as Guam.

China's 1,050–1,150 CSS-6/DF-15 and CSS-7/DF-11 SRBMs deployed opposite Taiwan offer a precision-guided munitions (PGM) capability without the costly investment in more-complex manned aircraft.[7] Short-range ballistic missiles (SRBMs) can render Taiwan's airfields inoperable and destroy infrastructure nodes, disrupting Taiwan's ability to support its economy and military. Land-attack cruise missiles (LACMs) such as the indigenous DH-10 also

Table 3: Notional Direction and Rate of Change in Selected Hardware, Software, and Systems Capabilities

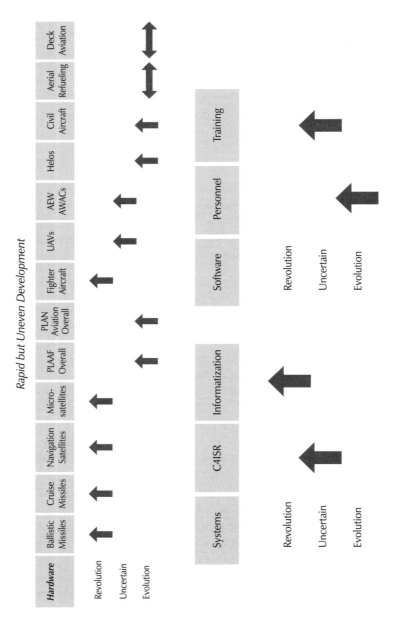

have the potential to complicate Taiwan's capacity to use its previously superior air force to thwart Chinese attack options. China has also developed anti-ship cruise missiles (ASCMs) with improved guidance and satellite navigation capabilities, providing multiaxis firepower against targets at sea.

Navigation, Maritime Surveillance, and Microsatellites

Beijing's satellite capabilities, while far from cutting edge in many respects, are improving rapidly due to standardization and quality control. The achievement of reliable indigenous satellite navigation, high-quality real-time satellite imagery and target-locating data, and microsatellites with space control capabilities would enhance Chinese intelligence, surveillance, and reconnaissance (ISR) capabilities and be significant "game changers" for the PLA.

Satellite navigation differentiates friendly and enemy forces by offering reliable positioning signals. China is developing its own indigenous Beidou satellite navigation system; three are currently deployed to support operations on China's immediate maritime periphery. Within the next ten years, China will deploy a thirty-five-satellite (five geostationary, thirty medium earth orbit) constellation—called Beidou-2/Compass—to provide much-improved accuracy and support broader operations; seven have been launched thus far.

China launched its first maritime observation satellite, Haiyang-1A, in 2002, which monitored ocean water color and temperature. In 2007 China launched a follow-on satellite, HY-1B, with double its predecessor's data capacity, to survey its maritime periphery, including the East and South China seas. A total of fifteen additional Haiyang satellites are planned in three sets to be launched in 2012, 2017, and 2022. Likewise relevant to maritime surveillance will be China's Huanjing disaster/environmental monitoring constellation, envisioned to contain eight satellites capable of visible, infrared, multispectral, and synthetic aperture radar imaging.

China produces increasingly sophisticated micro (10–100 kg) and small (100–500 kg) satellites. Mission-optimized standardized platforms ("buses") will quite literally constitute the backbone of China's future microsatellites, thereby reducing costs and enhancing quality control and reliability—part of a larger trend in China's dual-use military technological projects.

PLAAF and PLAN Aviation

China has begun to achieve comprehensive domestic aviation production capabilities by focusing on "informatizing" (improving with information technology and networks) its air force by upgrading to modern avionics and developing new systems for future-generation fighters. China's military aircraft are outfitted with a variety of increasingly advanced weapons systems, although the country still relies heavily on imports from Russia and technological challenges still remain, particularly mastery of modern engine technology.

People's Liberation Army Air Force (PLAAF) and People's Liberation Army Navy (PLAN) aviation forces currently possess twenty-three hundred operational combat aircraft.[8] Efforts to render the PLAAF more capable of offensive missions include an aggressive procurement program, refit and modernization of the air force bomber fleet, and renewed domestic defense industrial renovation to assemble a stable of advanced fighter aircraft, including the imported Su-27 and Su-30; the domestically produced J-11; the domestically developed J-10 and J-20; and advanced air-defense systems.

Recent equipment upgrades and improved doctrine and training will improve China's prospects for conducting effective joint operations between PLAAF and PLAN aviation. For instance, Sukhoi has developed an improved naval aviation–specialized variant of its Su-30 for the PLAN. The twenty-four received by the PLAN so far have improved engines and combat radius, new radar, antiship strike capability, and an improved electronic warfare and countermeasures suite.[9] Maritime strike missions are increasing in importance and China's fifth-generation J-20 stealth fighter, first flight-tested on 11 January 2011, may have an important role to play. The resulting inventory of modern aircraft and associated weapons are increasing China's ability to achieve air superiority over the Taiwan Strait and permanently shift the balance of military power toward the PRC.

Helicopters

In contrast to recent improvements in fixed-wing aviation, helicopters remain an area of evolution, not revolution. Most platforms in China's disproportionately small but growing fleet (roughly seven hundred to eight hundred in the PLA and more than one hundred in the PLAN) are either imports or copies of foreign models. China Helicopter Research and Development Institute has developed an indigenous WZ-10 advanced attack helicopter, with possible army and transport variants.

Unmanned Aerial Vehicles (UAVs)

Having observed the U.S. military's use of UAVs and drones, China is purchasing foreign models, transforming former piloted aircraft into unmanned combat aerial vehicles (UCAVs), and developing indigenous variants.

Deck Aviation Developments

Aircraft carriers are likely needed for the PLAN to move "beyond Taiwan" to genuine maritime power projection capabilities. The U.S. Office of Naval Intelligence estimates that "the PRC will likely have an operational, domestically produced carrier sometime after 2015."[10] Hull construction is likely to begin earlier, and China's ex-Ukrainian *Varyag* is already being refitted as a training platform. Scott Bray, senior intelligence officer-China, ONI, predicts that China will use deck aviation to "protect Chinese sea lanes, shipping, and enforc[e] maritime claims."[11] To date, however, Beijing has made greater progress in analyzing and targeting enemy carriers than in building its own.

Software

Chinese planners realize that rapidly improving equipment is useless without corresponding improvement in human performance. Aerospace success requires highly skilled and educated personnel, particularly with specific technical capabilities. But building human capital takes much more time, investment, and careful management than does platform acquisition.

Personnel and Training

Since the 1990s, increasingly realistic training and organizational reforms (including downsizing of personnel, streamlining of bureaucratic structures, and reconfiguration of logistics and maintenance) facilitate modernization of China's aerospace forces. Facilities, faculty, curricula, and research at PLA educational institutions are being improved, in part through increased funding and even monetary rewards.

Officers of unprecedented caliber are being recruited. Increasing the number of civilian-college-graduated officers through the National Defense Student Program is raising technical capabilities and may permit consolidation and merger of other PLAAF and PLAN aviation institutions (while raising new service culture challenges). The enlisted corps is being similarly improved. Pilots with a greater level of higher education (military and civilian) are being recruited, and higher performance in challenging situations is already being attributed to their higher theoretical and technical knowledge. The quality and education level of noncommissioned officers remains a problem, however, necessitating remedial education. Cultivating sufficient numbers of experienced combat pilots remains challenging.

The PLA has gradually increased its technological research and development, military and educational exchanges, attaché offices abroad (though few have PLAAF attachés), and has conducted a variety of joint exercises with Russia and Western nations. Aerospace-relevant services (e.g., the PLAAF and Second Artillery) are receiving a larger proportion of PLA personnel and funding as the PLA is transformed into a leaner, more technology-intensive force through successive personnel reductions (particularly of the ground forces).

C4ISR

China's emerging ISR network promises to radically improve the targeting and information processing capabilities of the PLAN. This critical linchpin, according to Larry Wortzel, promises to give the PLA unprecedented ability to "provide real-time support for joint military operations" on or near China's territory "with communications and data relay satellites" but still "lacks a comprehensive set of data transfer systems."[12]

The Aerospace-Maritime Theoretical Connection

Strategists in the West and in China have developed a relatively coherent theory of sea power, reinforced by top naval and military leadership. In recent years a broadly analogous but far less developed set of theories has emerged among Chinese aerospace thinkers. This doctrinal theorizing connects future air and sea warfare but often in a rather superficial manner that fails to explore potential contradictions and may still be largely aspirational in nature.

Central Military Commission (CMC) chairman Hu Jintao requires the PLA "to not only pay close attention to the interests of national survival, but also national development interests; not only safeguard the security of national territory, territorial waters, and airspace, but also safeguard electromagnetic space, outer space, the ocean, and other aspects of national security."[13] But sea, air, and space power theories and their prospects for more sophisticated linkage remain effectively subordinate to a PLA legacy that, while changing rapidly, retains strong ground force roots.

Aerospace capabilities underpin China's current military capabilities. According to DoD, "PLA doctrine does not appear to contemplate space operations as an operational 'campaign' on its own; rather, space operations form an integral component of all campaigns."[14] To some extent, the relative immaturity of Chinese aerospace theory can be traced to the PLAAF's slowness to be granted its own strategy. Whereas the PLA's overarching "active defense" strategy was implemented in the 1930s and the CMC approved a subordinate "off-shore defense" strategy for the PLAN in 1985, the PLAAF's "空天一体化，攻防兼备 [integrated air and space, simultaneous offensive and defensive operations]" equivalent was not approved until 2004 (when PLAAF, PLAN, and Second Artillery representatives joined the CMC), even though it had been proposed as early as 1987. This, and lingering resistance by ground force elements, has complicated the PLAAF's efforts to transcend its historical missions of air defense and supporting ground forces.

To meet Beijing's military objectives with its new, increasingly sophisticated platforms, the PLAAF is undergoing a doctrinal and institutional revolution, setting itself up to be the best placed of all services to assume authority over China's growing military space assets. On the doctrinal front, there is an unprecedented focus on offensive operations, based in part on ongoing improvements in long-range "air strike, air and missile defense, early warning and reconnaissance, and strategic projection."[15] Jointness is increasingly emphasized (though actual results appear to lag).

There is not yet any clear evidence in open publications that the PLA has formally adopted space theory, doctrine, missions, or regulations in the informatization process. Even the "integrated air and space" component of its strategy has generated little public clarification, with one CMC general office member stating that "there is no consensus on what 'integrated' means in China."[16] It would appear that China has moved beyond the traditional land-sea-air warfare zone demarcation to think in a more sophisticated fashion about how to integrate zones of warfare and how to achieve superiority in each—but not necessarily in a kinetic fashion.

Strategic Context: Implications for the U.S. Navy

The Chinese aerospace revolution outlined here has different implications in three geographic areas: (1) It is most relevant in the Taiwan Strait, where it has already reversed the balance of military power. (2) It is very significant in China's "near seas" (the Yellow Sea and East and South China seas), where it is shifting the regional balance of power. (3) It has some significance in the global maritime and aerospace commons, where its direct and indirect effects will be felt in years to come.

Sea Denial: Taiwan and Maritime Periphery

In the event of a Taiwan Strait crisis, China seeks to deny the United States and any regional allies access to the East Asian littoral to ensure its ability to influence Taiwan militarily. The East China Sea is an important part of this equation, but it presents particular challenges for China because existing capabilities and alliances (e.g., that between the United States and Japan) complicate antiaccess efforts. The South China Sea, at least until recently, has been a more permissive environment for China.

At present, China's submarine-focused navy and still-limited air and naval aviation forces can only support a more limited strategy of sea denial and offensive counterair as opposed to outright control. This access denial strategy is ever-more potent, however, thanks to a vast and growing inventory of short-range ballistic and cruise missiles deployed in coastal units and on a variety of air, surface, and undersea platforms. Long-range ballistic missiles, which already undergird China's increasingly diverse and sophisticated land- and sea-based nuclear deterrent, may greatly strengthen the antiaccess equation if a conventional version can be made to target surface vessels successfully. Additionally, the Second Artillery and airborne platforms controlled by the other services have a wide range of missiles capable of either threatening or striking Taiwan and surrounding areas.

Overall, U.S. qualitative and even numerical superiority in advanced platforms and systems is of limited relevance for two reasons. First, the platforms most likely to be employed are those that are based within immediate striking distance at the outbreak of war; here China inherently enjoys theater concentration while U.S. platforms are dispersed globally. Second, aircraft sent to the theater need airfields from which to operate; here U.S. regional options are limited and vulnerable to Chinese missile attack. Guam is almost 2,600 km from Taiwan. Okinawa is closer, but there is no guarantee that Japan would allow tactical aircraft to be operated from its airfields, which in any case are within range of China's SRBM forces.

Here it must be emphasized that antiaccess affords China a strategic defensive posture along interior lines. The PLA can mitigate ongoing challenges in command and control and target deconfliction by employing landlines, high-power line-of-sight communications, advanced planning, and geographic and temporal segregation. Its strength is relative to its objective, and here China may be capable of achieving its goals. China need not keep pace with the United States technologically for its incremental developments to have disproportionate impact and potentially deny U.S. access to portions of the global commons. The United States is inherently exposed because it operates offensively on exterior lines and must maintain technological superiority to reduce this vulnerability.

Beyond Taiwan? A Question of Aerospace Power Projection

A fundamental question for U.S. military planners today is whether (and if so, when) the PLA will project power beyond the East Asian littoral. Given its lack of overseas bases and limited unrefueled range of its aircraft, the PLA is far from such a capability. In DoD's estimation, "while remaining focused on Taiwan as a primary mission, China will, by 2020, lay the foundation for a force able to accomplish broader regional and global objectives. By the latter half of this decade, it is likely that China will be able to project and sustain a modest sized force . . . in low-intensity operations far from China."[17]

As a growing number of Chinese military analysts advocate, Beijing may gradually change its policy against overseas military facilities. If China acquires or builds sufficient aircraft carriers and escort vessels to maintain an operationally relevant presence at sea, this might indicate an ambition to conduct some form of regional operations. The PLAN would face a steep learning curve in carrier operations, however, since air operations are particularly dependent on effective C4ISR, which may be difficult to attain far from China's territory, where information assurance is more elusive.

The PLA might also use air and space power to support ocean surveillance and targeting (e.g., antisubmarine warfare), particularly over the horizon. This would require mastering the developments in air- and space-based platforms and C4ISR needed to support significant military operations far from the many facilities on or near China's shores. These very systems might become more vulnerable to electronic, computer network, and kinetic attacks; satellite communications and long-range signals might be jammed or geolocated. This might finally place PLA forces at the costly end of some of the very asymmetric arms races from which they are benefitting closer to mainland China.

It remains unclear what future PLA aerospace-enabled power projection might look like. Will it focus on kinetic destruction (actual kill) or merely nonkinetic denial of use (mission kill)? Space is itself a potential battle space but also a potential enabler of nonkinetic power projection in the electromagnetic, cyber, and public opinion realms. It is possible that China is developing a concept of power projection very different from that of the United States.

Key Factors

China's maritime military posture is currently based on A2/AD and appears to have well-thought-out acquisition programs to achieve antiaccess in the near seas and perhaps eventually beyond. In attempting to consolidate its regional position, China is engaging in activities that threaten to marginalize U.S. power there and make it particularly difficult and costly for the United States to intervene militarily, particularly at a time when the United States is committed geostrategically in the Middle East and Southwest Asia and faces increasing budgetary challenges at home.

Much will depend on how Chinese decision makers decide to use the potent capabilities that aerospace affords, however. Space-based information assets are increasingly linked to shooting assets (e.g., aircraft, surface, and undersea vessels). Aerospace capabilities thus give military and civilian leaders more flexible deterrent options and the ability to fine tune operations—capabilities valuable to any leaders and perhaps especially those of China. While aerospace capabilities have the potential to enable more sophisticated decision making, it is unclear to what extent this will actually occur. This is because China has yet to reform fundamentally its government decision-making system, which is particularly unsuited to responding rapidly to crises.

Conclusion

Beijing's emphasis on, and partial success in, aerospace development are in keeping with its substantial, rising comprehensive national power. Chinese aerospace capabilities are improving in a rapid, broad-based fashion that can properly be described as a "revolution"—albeit from a low baseline and uneven in present realization. Translating new hardware into operational capabilities is a complex process. We are likely to witness a larger pattern in which China rapidly deploys hardware that is formidable in technical parameters but whose actual combat performance, while improving quickly, remains unclear. China's mastery of critical components of many processes will have significant implications for Beijing's ability to manage its maritime periphery and to challenge U.S. hegemony.

Since successful aerospace development requires sustained government support, any future political instability could threaten China's present aerospace development trajectory. This aspect of China's future hinges on too many variables to allow for accurate prediction. What is clear is that China's current leadership appears determined to pursue aerospace development consistent with its increasing national power. Just as China was not dissuaded from naval development (e.g., of submarines) in the recent past by American dominance in that area, Beijing also seems determined to develop a major presence in air and space.

While conflict is not foreordained and interaction and cooperation should be pursued as feasible, this challenge cannot be ignored. Given the extended period through which carrier strike groups (CSGs) have served as the nucleus of U.S. military power projection, the appearance of credible threats to the CSG will force a significant rethinking of U.S. approaches to warfare and might even end seven decades of carrier-centrism in the Navy. That some experts have minimized the latter possibly would only increase the impact on U.S. planning should such a change come materialize.

To the extent that the United States fails to deploy adequate countermeasures, China's growing aerospace capabilities will improve substantially the PLA's ability to hold at risk and potentially destabilize U.S. naval platforms in the Western Pacific. However, as China's military becomes increasingly reliant on satellites, and the United States further develops relevant countermeasures, its own vulnerabilities increase. A resulting increase in bilateral surveillance and early warning as well as strategic symmetry could thus ultimately enhance the great and growing chances that the two great powers avoid devastating conflict.

This volume probes how Beijing's aerospace revolution will impact the U.S. Navy and other services, including

- Beijing's aerospace strategy and how it relates to its maritime strategy;
- the respective strategic and commercial payoffs to investing resources in various aerospace areas;
- key technological hurdles and how to surmount them;
- services that might control China's various aerospace capabilities; and
- analysis of what China needs to support and use advanced aerospace systems.

The United States must closely study China's aerospace trajectory and plan accordingly.

Notes

The views expressed in this article are those of the author alone. They do not represent the estimates or policies of the U.S. Navy or any other element of the U.S. government. The author is indebted to Amy Chang for her invaluable editorial suggestions, as well as to Kenneth Allen, Dean Cheng, Craig Covault, Peter Dutton, Lyle Goldstein, Hank Kamradt, Craig Koerner, Nan Li, Donald Marin, William Murray, Robert Rubel, and Christopher Weuve for their incisive comments.

1. Eliot A. Cohen, "A Revolution in Warfare," *Foreign Affairs* 75, no. 2 (March–April 1996): 37–54.

2. Andrew F. Krepinevich, "Cavalry to Computer: The Pattern of Military Revolutions," *The National Interest*, Fall 1993–1994; and Cohen, "Revolution in Warfare."

3. Barry R. Posen, "Command of the Commons: The Military Foundation of U.S. Hegemony," *International Security* 28, no. 1 (Summer 2003): 21.

4. Andrew F. Krepinevich, "Why AirSea Battle?" Center for Strategic and Budgetary Assessments, 19 February 2010, http://www.csbaonline.org/4Publications/PubLibrary/R.20100219.Why_AirSea_Battle/R.20100219.Why_AirSea_Battle.pdf.

5. Office of the Secretary of Defense (DoD), *Military and Security Developments Involving the People's Republic of China 2010*, Annual Report to Congress (Washington, DC: Office of the Secretary of Defense, 16 August 2010), 1, http://www.defense.gov/pubs/pdfs/2010_CMPR_Final.pdf.

6. Andrew S. Erickson, "China's Anti-Ship Ballistic Missile (ASBM) Reaches Equivalent of 'Initial Operational Capability' (IOC)—Where It's Going and What It Means," *China Analysis from Original Sources*, 4 January 2011, http://www.andrewerickson.com/2011/01/china%E2%80%99s-anti-ship-ballistic-missile-asbm-reaches-equivalent-of-%E2%80%9Cinitial-operational-capability%E2%80%9D-ioc%E2%80%94where-it%E2%80%99s-going-and-what-it-means/.

7. DoD, *Military and Security Developments*, 1.

8. Ibid., 62.

9. See "Su-30MKK Multirole Fighter Aircraft," Sinodefence.com, http://www.sinodefence.com/airforce/fighter/su30.asp.

10. "The People's Liberation Army Navy: A Modern Navy with Chinese Characteristics" (Suitland, Md.: Office of Naval Intelligence, July 2009), 19.

11. Quotation obtained from ONI Public Affairs Office.

12. Larry M. Wortzel, "PLA Command, Control, and Targeting Architectures: Theory, Doctrine, and Warfighting Applications," in *Right-Sizing the People's Liberation Army: Exploring the Contours of China's Military*, ed. Roy Kamphausen and Andrew Scobell (Carlisle, PA: Army War College, 2007), 192, 217–19.

13. 刘明福, 程钢, 孙学富 [Liu Mingfu, Cheng Gang, and Sun Xuefu], "人民军队历史使命的又一次与时俱进" ["The Historical Mission of the People's Army Once Again Advances with the Times"], 解放军报 [*Liberation Army Daily*], 8 December 2005, 6.

14. DoD, *Military and Security Developments*, 36.

15. "China's National Defense in 2006," Information Office of the State Council, People's Republic of China, 29 December 2006, http://www.fas.org/nuke/guide/china/doctrine/wp2006.html.

16. Liu Jiangjia, "一体化联合作战价值论" ["Discussion on the Value of Integrated Joint Operations"], 中国军事科学 [*China Military Science*] 1 (2006): 1–33.

17. DoD, *Military and Security Developments*, 29.

Mark A. Stokes and Ian Easton

Evolving Chinese Aerospace Trends
Regional Maritime Implications

AEROSPACE POWER IS EMERGING as a key instrument of Chinese statecraft. Informed by universal air campaign theory and spurred by a global diffusion of technology, the People's Republic of China (PRC) is developing capabilities that could alter the strategic landscape well beyond the Asia-Pacific region. Aerospace power is already defining the future strategic environment in the Asia-Pacific region, whose vast distances place a premium on speed and agility that defy the laws of gravity.

In this theater, aerospace power is the key to gaining strategic advantages by application of military force via platforms operating in or passing through air and space. Control of the skies is a critical enabler for dominance on the earth's surface and is often a vital determinant of success or defeat in a conflict. Gaining and maintaining air superiority provides a political and military leadership with the operational freedom needed to coerce an opponent to make concessions in political disputes or gain a decisive edge on the surface.

The rise of China as a major economic, technological, military, and political player is changing the dynamics within the Asia-Pacific region and the world at large. Uncertainty over Chinese intentions is creating anxieties. As the Brookings Institution's Richard Bush notes, "a rising power poses a challenge to the prevailing international system and to the states that guard that system, because the new power's intentions are usually unclear."[1] Against the backdrop of ambiguity and uncertainty of the future, China's aerospace developments merit further examination.

The People's Liberation Army (PLA) is rapidly advancing its capacity to apply aerospace power to defend against perceived threats to national sovereignty and territorial integrity. Constrained by a relatively underdeveloped aviation establishment, the PLA is investing in aerospace capabilities that may offset shortcomings in the face of a more technologically advanced adversary. Whoever dominates the skies over a given area (such as Taiwan, disputed territories in northern India or Japan, or the South China Sea) has a decisive advantage on the surface.

Most significant is the expansion of, and growing reliance on, conventional ballistic and ground-launched cruise missiles (GLCMs) as the centerpiece of the PRC's political and military strategy. Large-scale theater missile raids combined with other enablers such as an electronic attack, directed against selected critical nodes within an opponent's command and control structure or air-defense system, can enable conventional air operations to be carried out at reduced risk and cost.

Barring the fielding of effective countermeasures, Chinese conventional theater missiles, specifically short- and medium-range ballistic and extended-range land-attack cruise missiles (LACMs), may over time give the PLA a decisive advantage in future conflicts around China's periphery. Ballistic and ground-launched land-attack cruise missiles are an attractive means of delivering lethal payloads due to the inherent difficulties in defending against them. Ballistic missiles themselves have a strong coercive effect as potential adversaries around the PRC's periphery have limited defensive countermeasures.

The PRC is also focused on developing the means to deny or complicate the ability of the United States to intervene in a regional crisis. Authoritative Chinese writings indicate research into and development of increasingly accurate and longer-range conventional strategic strike systems that could be launched from Chinese territory against land- and sea-based targets throughout the Asia-Pacific region in a crisis situation.

Extended-range conventional precision-strike assets could be used to suppress U.S. operations from forward bases in Japan, from U.S. aircraft carrier strike groups operating in the Western Pacific, and perhaps over the next five to ten years from U.S. bases on Guam. Development and eventual deployment of an antiship ballistic missile (ASBM) is an example of an emerging capability. China's research and development community also is expanding the nation's capacity for regional maritime surveillance. Most noteworthy is the apparent ongoing development of slow-moving flight vehicles that operate in near space—the domain above where conventional aircraft fly yet below orbiting satellites.

Beijing's theater missile-centric strategy presents challenges that transcend the operational realm. Beijing's large infrastructure of short-range ballistic missiles opposite Taiwan fosters mistrust and discourages meaningful political dialogue that could lead toward a resolution of differences in a manner acceptable to people on Taiwan and in the international community.

Beyond Taiwan, the conventional theater missile build-up has the potential to catalyze strategic competitions that increase the risks of conflict in the future. The PRC's growing capacity to exercise its aerospace power around its periphery provides an incentive for neighbors to shore up defenses as well as develop similar capabilities. The most effective and efficient means of defending against theater missiles is neutralizing the missile infrastructure on the ground. In the absence of a common set of norms governing the horizontal and vertical proliferation of ballistic missiles and GLCMs, countries throughout the region, including the United States and India, are by necessity increasing investment in long-range precision-strike systems to maintain a conventional deterrent and ensure effective defense, should deterrence fail.

China's successes in designing, developing, and producing the world's largest and most sophisticated arsenal of medium- and intermediate-range ballistic missiles creates a demand for similar capabilities around the world. Thus, the PLA's conventional theater missile-centric strategy potentially weakens international efforts to curb the proliferation of the means of delivery for weapons of mass destruction.

This chapter addresses trends in PRC force modernization, strategy, and doctrine intended to exploit weaknesses in regional air defenses, including a growing ability to maintain persistent surveillance out to a range of 3,000 km. Included is a detailed overview of China's expanding short- and medium-range ballistic missile and GLCM infrastructure. The subsequent section outlines trends in conventional air force, air and missile defense, and long-range precision-strike modernization in Taiwan, Japan, India, and the United States. The final section addresses options for countering the coercive utility of evolving PRC aerospace power, including cooperative threat reduction initiatives.

Aerospace Campaign Theory

Unimpeded access to skies over a region is a significant demonstration of power. As a key architect of modern U.S. air doctrine, retired colonel John Warden once observed, "No country has won a war in the face of enemy air superiority, no major offensive has succeeded against an opponent who controlled the air, and no defense has sustained itself against an enemy who had air superiority."[2] Success in a campaign for sea control, an amphibious invasion, a ground campaign, or a coercive air campaign depends upon air superiority because air superiority significantly reduces the risk of surface operations. In a conflict, the side that first wins air superiority will gain an overwhelming advantage.

Aerospace power can serve political as well as military objectives. Coercive aerospace power is the integrated application of information operations and weapon systems through the medium of air against strategic and operational-level targets to influence an adversary to act in a manner that it may not otherwise. Therefore, strikes are not only mounted or threatened against key infrastructure and installations but are also intended to change the target entity's policy. Hence, the effectiveness of a coercive air campaign is measured by strategic outcomes, notably attainment of political goals, rather than on tactical effectiveness (e.g., the effects that bombs, missiles, and electronic attack have on their intended targets).[3]

Chinese Force Modernization

Influenced by U.S. campaign theory, aerospace power is emerging as a key instrument of PRC statecraft. Like most defense establishments, the PLA characterizes its modernization efforts as defensive in nature. To this end, aerospace power is viewed as a vital element of territorial air defense with offensive air operations as a key capability. Over the years the PLA has made significant advances in developing a force capable of applying aerospace power in a joint environment. PLA analysts view aerospace campaigns as an integral component of "firepower warfare," which involves the coordinated use of PLA Air Force (PLAAF) strike aviation assets, Second Artillery conventional theater missiles, and information warfare.

Today, the PLA leadership depends on its ballistic missile and GLCM force—the Second Artillery—to deter potential adversaries and defend against perceived threats to national sovereignty and territorial integrity. Increasingly accurate conventional ballistic missiles and GLCMs are the optimal means for suppressing enemy air defense and creating a more permissive environment for subsequent conventional air operations due to their relative immunity to defense systems. In addition, space-based, airborne, and ground-based sensors can facilitate command and control and can provide crucial strategic intelligence, theater awareness, targeting, and battle damage assessment information.

Together the joint application of aerospace forces creates a synergy that could have significant military and political effects. Looking beyond traditional ballistic and land-attack cruise missiles, China currently views the realm between the atmosphere and space as a new area of global competition. This has compelled its research and development community to conduct feasibility studies into a new generation of flight vehicles and sensor systems.

The Centerpiece of China's Coercive Aerospace Power: Conventional Ballistic and Land-Attack Cruise Missiles

The PRC's growing arsenal of increasingly accurate and lethal conventional ballistic and land-attack cruise missiles has rapidly emerged as a cornerstone of PLA warfighting capability. Since the official establishment of the PLA's first SRBM brigade in 1993, ballistic missiles have been not only a primary instrument of psychological and political intimidation but also a potentially devastating tool of military utility. Over the last two decades, the Second Artillery's conventional ballistic and land-attack cruise missile force—a form of aerospace power that will be critical for achievement of information dominance and air superiority in the opening phase of a conflict—has expanded significantly. Reporting directly to the Central Military Commission, Second Artillery headquarters oversees one central nuclear warhead storage base and six missile bases that operate throughout the vast expanse of China:

- Headquartered in Shenyang, Base 51 consists of five brigades extended across five provinces in north and northeastern China.

- From the Anhui city of Huangshan, Base 52 oversees five SRBM brigades and as many as three medium-range ballistic missile (MRBM) brigades in southeast China.

- Headquartered in Kunming, Base 53 manages two MRBM brigades in Yunnan and two ground-launched cruise missile (GLCM) brigades located in the provinces of Guangxi and Guizhou.

- Luoyang's Base 54 commands three intercontinental ballistic missile (ICBM) brigades concentrated in Henan.

- Headquartered in the western Hunan city of Huaihua, Base 55 consists of three ICBM brigades in Hunan and one GLCM brigade in neighboring Jiangxi Province.

- From the Qinghai city of Xining, Base 56 oversees four brigades operating in Qinghai, Xinjiang, and Gansu.

- The Second Artillery stores most of the country's nuclear warheads centrally in Taibai County, deep in the Qinling Mountains of Shaanxi Province.

Second Artillery headquarters also oversee a number of direct reporting operational support units. For example, a regiment-sized unit north of Beijing specializes in all-source intelligence and would likely be deployed to a theater command center as the intelligence cell.[4] At least one, and probably two, electronic countermeasures (ECM) regiments would support the Second Artillery component commander within a Joint Theater Command. A central depot north of Beijing stores nonmission essential supplies for the entire force.[5]

Short-Range Ballistic Missile Infrastructure

The Second Artillery's SRBM infrastructure is a central component of the PRC's coercive political and military strategy. In 2000 China's SRBM force was limited to one "regimental-sized unit" in southeastern China. Today the force has grown to at least seven SRBM brigades. Among these, five are subordinate to the Second Artillery's Base 52 and the remaining two units report directly to military regions. The number of missiles in the Second Artillery, widely cited as exceeding 1,300 (inclusive of tactical missiles assigned to ground forces), may be less relevant than how they are organized and prepared for deployment.

A standard SRBM brigade consists of six battalions; each including two companies, with at least two or three launchers assigned to each company. Therefore, a combined force of five brigades could theoretically leverage between 120 and 180 mobile launchers to carry out salvos fired from multiple axes to saturate missile defenses, paralyze airbases by damaging runways, and attack other military infrastructure. In addition to the launch battalions, a brigade headquarters oversees a command post, a technical battalion, a communications battalion, an ECM group, and an established rail transfer point. Arrayed against Taiwan are at least five SRBM brigades subordinate to the Second Artillery, the PLA's primary strategic strike force.

Medium-Range Ballistic Missiles

Having established a solid foundation in conventional SRBMs, the PLA has begun to extend and diversify the warfighting capacity of the Second Artillery's ballistic missile force. The centerpiece of the Second Artillery's regional capability is the two-stage solid-fueled DF-21 MRBM. The first DF-21 system, with a dedicated nuclear mission, entered the Second Artillery's operational inventory in 1991 and gradually replaced older liquid-fueled DF-3A intermediate-range ballistic missile systems.

Over the next five to ten years, the centerpiece of the Second Artillery's extended range conventional strike capability will be the DF-21C MRBM. Capable of "both conventional and nuclear missions" (*hechang jianbei*; 核常 兼备), the DF-21C's guidance, navigation, and control system is modeled after the U.S. Pershing II. The terminally guided DF-21C can deliver a 2,000 kg warhead to a range of at least 1,750 km with a circular error probable of less than 50 m. The system could be used for conventional strikes against targets throughout Japan from east and northeast China, in New Delhi if based in Xinjiang, and in western India if based in Yunnan.

The Second Artillery has an operational force structure of at least eight, and possibly as many as ten, brigades equipped with a DF-21 variant. Trends indicate that conventionally capable variants are gradually replacing at least a portion of the force's DF-21A inventory. Standard DF-21C force structure appears to mirror that of SRBM brigades with each brigade having six launch battalions with two companies each. Assuming that a single launcher is assigned to each company, a DF-21C brigade could be equipped initially with twelve launchers.

Ground-Launched Cruise Missiles

To augment its ballistic missile arsenal, Second Artillery is steadily expanding its ground-launched LACM infrastructure. GLCMs are powerful instruments of military and political utility due to the inherent difficulty in defending against them. Within only a few years of initial deployments, the PRC today has the world's largest inventory of extended-range GLCMs. Able to penetrate defenses and strike critical targets on land, out to a range of more than 1,500 km, the Second Artillery's DH-10 LACMs appear to have enjoyed a relatively high acquisition priority. Home-based in south-central and southwestern China and highly mobile via rail, cruise missiles are able to strike from any direction, presenting a challenge for the defender with their low-altitude trajectories. The DH-10 is deployed on a three-tube road mobile launcher, and approximately one hundred LACMs are reportedly entering the operational inventory each year.[6]

In short, the PRC has the fastest-growing and most sophisticated extended-range ground-launched LACM infrastructure in the world. Based in south-central and southwest China, two or possibly three Second Artillery GLCM brigades would be able to forward deploy rapidly in a crisis.

Antiship Ballistic Missiles and Beyond

Authoritative Chinese writings indicate research into and the development of increasingly accurate and longer-range conventional strategic strike systems that could be launched from Chinese territory against land- and sea-based targets throughout the Asia-Pacific. An imminent manifestation of long-term intent would be the deployment of conventional medium-range ballistic missiles capable of engaging naval combatants, including aircraft carrier strike groups, in the western Pacific Ocean.

Many of the basic technologies needed for a rudimentary ASBM capability have been in development for more than twenty years. At the core of this capability is an advanced missile-borne sensing and data processing system supported by strategic cueing from a dual-use maritime surveillance network. Building on the successes of the terminally guided DF-21C and DF-15C programs, development of an ASBM program is centered on advanced microelectronics and an upgraded guidance, navigation, and control (GNC) package.[7]

Technical studies address a wide range of GNC issues, including the need for some form of midcourse update, missile-borne synthetic aperture radar (SAR), automated target recognition, terminal guidance, thermal protection, and radiofrequency blackout associated with a flight vehicle traveling at hypersonic speeds in the upper atmosphere. Manufacturing facilities for solid rocket motors associated with an initial ASBM variant, designated as the DF-21D, appear to have been constructed in 2009. Some form of "testing," likely flight testing of a new motor and airframe, is under way.[8] Integrated flight testing of the airframe, motor, guidance, navigation, and control systems against a target at sea will likely be the final step in the design certification process.

Barring deployment of effective defenses, an initial ASBM would give the PLA a precision-strike capability against aircraft carriers and other U.S. and allied ships operating within 1,500–2,000 km of China's coast. Chinese technical writings indicate the preliminary conceptual development of a conventional global precision-strike capability. The accuracy and range of the PLA's conventional ballistic missile force is also expected to improve significantly over the next ten to fifteen years as missiles incorporate more advanced inertial and satellite aided navigation systems, sophisticated terminal guidance systems, and increasingly powerful solid rocket motors.

Conventional Air Modernization

While the Second Artillery has expanded significantly, PLAAF modernization has progressed at a more modest pace. The PLAAF has been diversifying its roles and missions, moving away from a force responsible exclusively for air defense, interdiction, and close-air support for ground forces toward a service whose primary mission is deterrence and strategic attack. The PLAAF's diversification is grounded in a body of theory that stipulates that a firepower warfare campaign could independently support national objectives. The predominant operational focus of the Air Force is denial—paralyzing an adversary's capabilities to the extent that further resistance appears futile and the costs of continued resistance outweigh surrender. However, the PLAAF envisions its future role as an independent service capable of conducting strategic strike missions at extended ranges in support of national objectives.

Given resource constraints and the overlap in the core mission of strategic strike, the rapid rise of the conventional Second Artillery may have contributed to the slow pace of PLAAF modernization. The rapid deployment of ballistic missiles and GLCMs has dampened the requirement for an offensive-oriented air force. Another possible constraint has been the limitations of China's aviation industry and its corresponding reliance on foreign procurement of key systems. Nevertheless, over the coming decade, a capable, technologically advancing domestic aviation industry may be positioned to better support the PLAAF's vision of becoming a world-class service capable of conducting air campaigns independent of the Second Artillery.

To close the gap between its doctrinal aspirations and capabilities, senior PLAAF representatives have outlined general requirements for meeting expected strategic challenges. Guided by the development strategy of "integrated air and space, and combined offense and defense [空天一体, 攻防兼备]," senior PLAAF leadership note that required capabilities include the capacity to carry out long-range precision strike and an ability to attain local or limited air superiority, stealth, "full spectrum" air and missile defense, new "trump card" (撒手锏) weapons systems, long-range airlift (远程投送), and unmanned aerial vehicles.[9] According to one detailed Taiwanese assessment, the PLAAF had set a goal to be able to conduct an air campaign within a 1,000 km radius of China's periphery by 2010—one that it has yet to realize fully—and to extend the range to 3,000 km by 2030.[10]

In sum, the PLAAF is making modest progress in developing advanced capabilities with an eye toward expanding its operational range. The ability to carry out strategic strike missions at ranges of 3,000 km or more is viewed as the key to becoming a truly independent service, rather than one dependent on Second Artillery or a supporting player to the ground forces. Despite the PLAAF's aspirations to develop a force capable of an independent air campaign around China's periphery, senior PRC political and military authorities will likely continue to rely on the established capabilities of the Second Artillery for coercion, strategic strike missions, and suppression of enemy air defenses for some time to come.

Sensor Architecture and Integrated Air and Space Defense

The PLA's ability to conduct strategic and operational strike missions is likely to be restricted by the range of its persistent surveillance. To expand its battle space awareness, the PLA is investing in at least four capabilities that could enable it to monitor activities in the Western Pacific, South China Sea, and Indian Ocean.

Persistent near-space surveillance.

Chinese analysts view the realm between the atmosphere and space—"near space"—as an area of future strategic competition.[11] Over the decade, near-space flight vehicles (*jinkongjian feixingqi*; 近空间飞行器) may emerge as a dominant platform for a persistent region-wide surveillance capability during crisis situations. Near space is generally characterized as the region between 20 and 100 km (65,000–328,000 feet) above the earth's surface.

While technical challenges exist, the Second Artillery and China's defense research and development community have become increasingly interested in near-space flight vehicles for reconnaissance, communications relay, electronic countermeasures, and precision-strike operations.[12] To overcome technical challenges, China's aerospace industry, specifically CASC and CASIC, have established new research institutes dedicated to the design, development, and manufacturing of near-space flight vehicles. The establishment of two dedicated research institutes, one within CASC and one within CASIC, for leveraging the unique characteristics of near space signifies the importance that China places on this domain.[13]

Space-based surveillance.

Increasingly sophisticated space-based systems would expand PLA battle space awareness and support strike operations further from Chinese shores. Space assets enable the monitoring of naval activities in surrounding waters and the tracking of air force deployments into the region. Space-based reconnaissance systems also provide imagery necessary for mission planning functions, such as navigation and terminal guidance for LACMs. Satellite communications also offer a survivable means of transmission that will become particularly important as the PLA operates further from its territory.

A regional strike capability would rely partly on high-resolution, dual-use, space-based SAR, electro-optical, and possibly electronic intelligence (ELINT) satellites for surveillance and targeting. China's space industry is reportedly nearing completion of its second-generation SAR satellite, and its electro-optical capabilities have been steadily progressing. While information is sparse, indications exist that at least some funding has been dedicated toward developing a space-based ELINT capability. In a crisis, China may have the option of augmenting existing space-based assets with microsatellites launched on solid-fueled launch vehicles. Existing and future data relay satellites and other beyond-line-of-sight communications systems could transmit targeting data to and from the theater and/or Second Artillery's operational-level command center.[14]

Over-the-horizon radar.

In addition to space-based, near-space, and airborne sensors, over-the-horizon (OTH) backscatter radar systems would be a central element of an extended range air and maritime surveillance architecture. Managed by the PLAAF, an OTH radar system could define the range of China's maritime precision-strike capability. Skywave OTH radar systems emit a pulse in the lower part of the frequency spectrum (3–30 MHz) that bounces off the ionosphere to illuminate a target—either air or surface—from the top down. As a result, detection ranges for wide area surveillance can extend out to 1,000–4,000 km.[15]

In summary, a PLA aerospace campaign intended to coerce an adversary would emphasize preemption, surprise, and concentration of its most advanced assets to achieve a measure of shock. To effectively guide a campaign, command and control would be centrally planned and executed by the Joint Theater Command. It would also be supported by other joint command systems, including a joint Firepower Coordination Center as well as command centers that oversee component operations of the PLAAF and the Second Artillery. The PLAAF, while technologically behind the U.S. Air Force and others, is evolving into a force capable of dominating the skies around its periphery, with support from the Second Artillery and information warfare assets.

Regional Scenarios

The PRC's expanding capacity for conducting an aerospace campaign in the Asia-Pacific region would likely be a variable of its territorial disputes with states around its periphery. As its military strength increases relative to those of its neighbors, the PRC could feasibly become more assertive in its claims.

Along this trajectory, miscalculations, accidents, sovereignty disputes, or other unforeseen events have the potential to escalate into armed conflict between the PRC and its neighbors. Each defense establishment in the region appears to be approaching the challenges differently, although most are attempting to balance interests in maintaining healthy relations with Beijing while at the same time hedging in the event of a future conflict.

Taiwan

Taiwan serves as the principle coalescing driver for mainland China's development of capabilities that seek to dominate the skies around its periphery. Beijing is steadily broadening its military options, including the ability to use force at reduced cost in terms of PLA lives, equipment, and diminished overall effects on the country's longer-term development goals. Beyond simply expanding military options against Taiwan, the PRC is also is developing the means to deny or complicate the ability or willingness of the United States to intervene in response to its use of force.

A fundamental PLA guiding concept is to compel a political concession swiftly, using only the minimal force necessary. However, most analyses of the cross-strait military balance are based upon the worst-case, least-likely scenario involving a PLA amphibious invasion and physical occupation of Taiwan. In these scenarios, air dominance is a necessary precondition. It is envisioned that large-scale SRBM salvos would be carried out against ground-based air defenses, airbases, and other critical military infrastructure, and would be followed up by conventional PLAAF strikes to ensure that air defenses remain suppressed. The Second Artillery's ability to overwhelm ground-based air defenses and damage runways would give the PLAAF the necessary advantage to attain air superiority over the Taiwan Strait. If indeed able to operate in the skies over Taiwan with impunity, PLAAF interdiction missions could support an amphibious invasion effectively.

A relative erosion of Taiwan's military capabilities, especially in aerospace power, could create opportunities and incentives for Beijing's political and military leadership to assume greater risk in cross-Strait relations, including resorting to force to resolve political differences. Among the most significant aspects of Taiwan's aerospace power are its conventional air force assets, missile defenses, and strategic strike capabilities.

Responsible for ensuring air sovereignty, the Republic of China Air Force (ROCAF) has traditionally sought to maintain a fleet of approximately 400 fighters. Its inventory today includes 56 Mirage-2000, 145 F-16 A/B, 126 Indigenous Defense Fighters (IDFs), and 60 F-5E/F fighters. With its F-5s reaching the end of their operational life and the entire Mirage, IDF, and F-16 fleet all having entered service in 1997, the ROCAF began long-range planning for procurement of new fighters as early as 1999. Evaluating a range of options, including the AV-8B and F-35/Joint Strike Fighter, the ROCAF's first preference has been a vertical/short takeoff and landing (V/STOL) airframe.

As the ROCAF's F-5 fleet gradually retires over the next five years, planners foresee a widening fighter gap between now and 2020, which is the earliest that a V/STOL airframe could enter its operational inventory. To bridge the gap, the ROCAF has pursued acquisition of an additional 66 F-16 fighters.

The primary challenge that the ROCAF faces is not its counterpart, the PLAAF, but rather the Second Artillery's potential ability to ground ROCAF fighters by damaging runways and other airbase infrastructure. As a result, the ROCAF has been evaluating how best to maximize its ability to sustain flight operations after initial strikes.[16] Taiwan is also investing in early-warning and terminal missile defenses to undercut the coercive utility of Second Artillery theater missiles.

To counter PRC coercion, Taiwan stresses maintenance of the necessary military strength, the ability to survive a first-strike attack, and an ability to carry out a second-strike retaliation. The ROCAF has traditionally designated a limited portion of its fighter fleets for strike missions, should a decision be made to do so. However, with PLA air defenses growing increasingly sophisticated, Taiwan has been diversifying its operational options, including enabling an antiship cruise missile to conduct land-attack missions.[17]

Japan

Unlike Taiwan, Japan's security concerns are primarily directed at North Korea. The chances for armed conflict between the PRC and Japan are slim, despite historical animosity and budding nationalist sentiments. However, unresolved territorial disputes and a more assertive China could lead to a crisis in the future. With North Korea serving as the most-immediate concern, Japan has been modernizing its defenses. Although a shift in the strategic environment could alter its direction, Japan has maintained an operationally defensive strategy and relies on its alliance partner, the United States, for operations outside its territory. As a result, it places a premium on early warning and engagement of inbound threats. Therefore, Tokyo's priorities include the procurement of next-generation fighters, integrated air and missile defenses, intelligence, surveillance, and reconnaissance systems.[18]

In light of the PRC's ambitious force modernization, the Japanese Maritime Self-Defense Force (JMSDF) faces a number of challenges in the years ahead.

Given the PRC's impressive advancements in ballistic and cruise missile technology; electronic, cyber, and antisatellite capabilities; C4ISR developments; and conventional air modernization programs, prevailing trends suggest that improving PLA capabilities relative to those of the JMSDF could enable the former to attain local air superiority over competing territorial claims at the outset of any future conflict. Japan's vulnerabilities include the lack of hardening at key airbases and command-and-control facilities, deficiencies in cruise missile defense, and uncertainties surrounding procurement of a suitable next-generation fighter. Of the aforementioned vulnerabilities, loss of command-and-control facilities appears to be a particular shortcoming.

As time goes on, the Japan Air Self-Defense Force's requirement for a low-observable air-superiority fighter, preferably one able to interoperate with U.S. Air Force counterparts, will grow. Furthermore, should the U.S.–Japan alliance prove incapable of deterring PRC military action over a territorial dispute, an inability to defend against conventional MRBMs and GLCMs could prompt a future political leadership in Tokyo to rethink self-imposed restrictions on the development of offensive strike systems. Past media reporting indicates Tokyo has at least considered the procurement of strike systems such as Tomahawks.[19]

India

While India and China today maintain cordial official relations, tensions simmer under the surface. The PRC's territorial dispute with India is over two tracts of land in the eastern and northern India—Aksai Chin, which is currently administered by the PRC under the Xinjiang Uighur Autonomous Region; and Arunachal Pradesh, which is currently administered by India. While competing claims are unlikely to erupt in conflict, it is worth noting that New Delhi and Beijing did go to war over this in 1962 and that the experience has severely conditioned Indian threat perceptions of China. For all the PRC's attempts to resolve border disputes with its neighbors, the one with India is still outstanding. India is enhancing its aerospace power with significant investment in air force, theater missile, and missile defense modernization.

With declared security interests extending from the Persian Gulf to the Strait of Malacca, the Indian Air Force (IAF) is modernizing rapidly to address the country's security interests. The IAF is in the process of upgrading its older fighter fleet. In response to Chinese and Pakistani theater missile-development programs, India's Defence Research and Development Organization also has been diversifying the Indian Army's ballistic and land-attack cruise missile inventory.

PRC Aerospace Modernization and Regional Stability

The Asia-Pacific region is in the midst of fundamental change, with significant implications for long-term strategic stability. The gradual expansion of China's long-range precision-strike capabilities, especially its increasingly sophisticated conventional ballistic and GLCM infrastructure, is altering the regional strategic landscape. Due to their speed, precision, and difficulties in fielding viable defenses, these systems—if deployed in sufficient numbers—have the potential to provide the PRC with a decisive military edge in the event of conflict over territorial or sovereignty claims. Reliance on ballistic missiles and extended-range LACMs also incentivizes other militaries to develop similar capabilities. The PRC's expansion of its aerospace capabilities is also driving a modest shift in U.S. defense policies.

The PLA's expanding capacity to deny U.S. forces access to bases and the ability to project power into the region figured prominently in the 2010 Quadrennial Defense Review (QDR). Augmenting the QDR are a number of analyses outlining ways to manage the dynamic shifts under way in the region. With concerns mounting over the antiaccess challenge to using bases in the Western Pacific and area denial capabilities that could restrict U.S. naval operations, pressure to reduce the U.S. footprint in Japan and relocate further from China's periphery could grow.[20] As an alternative, one detailed study suggests investing in the ability to withstand initial strikes and limit damage to U.S. and allied forces and bases; neutralizing PLA command and control networks; suppressing the PLA's theater sensor architecture and theater strike systems; and sustaining initiative in the air, on the sea, in space, and within the cyber domain.[21]

In short, the PRC's expanding aerospace capabilities are influencing the development of similar capabilities in other defense establishments, including that of the United States. However, they may also have another effect. PLA successes in fielding advanced long-range precision-strike systems dilutes international efforts to stem proliferation of the means of delivery for weapons of mass destruction. This may encourage other countries to follow suit, especially as China's global leadership and standing increases. In particular, GLCMs have emerged as a proliferation concern.

Conclusion

Largely driven by a Taiwan scenario, mainland China's capacity to conduct a successful aerospace campaign to swiftly gain a decisive air advantage is surpassing defenses that its neighbors, including Taiwan, Japan, perhaps India, and even U.S. forces operating in the Western Pacific, can field. Among the most significant capabilities that are contributing to an imbalance are the PLA's long-range precision-strike systems, primarily its conventional ballistic and land-attack cruise missiles. Perhaps equally important, however, is an evolving sensor network that would be needed to cue strike assets and offer situation awareness around China's periphery. Other factors include China's growing ability to defend its strike assets from interdiction on the ground and the redundancy in its command-and-control system.

Over time, an expansion of its theater missile infrastructure, conventional air power, and sensor systems could give China a decisive edge in securing control over the skies around its periphery, should territorial disputes erupt into conflict. The ability to dominate the airspace over a given geographic domain has the potential to create instability, should political disagreements flare up. The more confident that a country is of military success, the greater the chance that force could be assertively applied in pursuit of political demands. Balance and stability require that no single power be assured of air superiority.

Over the next fifteen years, the PRC may be increasingly confident of its ability to dominate the skies around its periphery. If thus confident, Beijing could become more assertive in its dealings with others in the region. A strategic shift in the regional aerospace balance also may increasingly unravel the fabric of U.S. alliances and prompt allies and friends to consider use of weapons of mass destruction and means of delivery as a way to achieve security.

Addressing these challenges requires maintaining or developing the means to undercut the political and military utility of the PRC's theater missile-centric strategy and striving for a balance that could deter PRC recourse to force or other means of coercion. However, alternative approaches could offer initiatives for moderating PLA force postures and address underlying security dilemmas through cooperative threat reduction programs.

Rolling back the missile problem starts with Taiwan. The potential for PRC coercive use of force to resolve political differences with Taiwan has been and likely will remain the primary flash point in the region. It is also the contingency that most likely would bring the United States and mainland China, as well as others in the region, into armed conflict. With the aforementioned in mind, a relative erosion of Taiwan's military capabilities could create opportunities and incentives for Beijing's political and military leadership to assume greater risk in cross-strait relations, including resorting to force to resolve political differences.

The PRC's emphasis on ballistic missiles and LACMs also provides an impetus for others to develop similar capabilities. Chinese restraint in the development, production, and deployment of extended-range, land-based conventional ballistic and cruise missiles would build confidence among its neighbors and reduce incentives to develop and field countermeasures.

China's conventional ballistic missile and GLCM build-up has taken place within the vacuum created by the Intermediate-Range Nuclear Forces (INF) Treaty. The treaty, signed in December 1987, had called for the elimination of all U.S. and Soviet land-based ballistic and cruise missiles with ranges between 500 and 5,500 km within three years. By May 1991 the United States and Soviet Union had dismantled the last of more than 2,500 GLCMs and ground-launched ballistic missiles along with their support equipment as covered under the INF Treaty. More recently, Washington and Moscow have sought to strengthen the INF Treaty by encouraging other countries to join the accord.[22]

How PRC aerospace-related capabilities will evolve over the next fifteen years is still unclear, particularly in relation to those of the United States and Taiwan as well as U.S. allies and friends such as Japan, the Republic of Korea, Australia, and India. Over time, the same capabilities arrayed against Taiwan could support the pursuit of other sovereignty claims around its periphery. The PLA's short-range ballistic missile infrastructure is the centerpiece of Beijing's political and military coercive strategy toward Taiwan today. The size and form of the Second Artillery's extended-range ballistic and ground-launched cruise missile infrastructure could be a metric of China's intent toward others in the future.

An international or regional agreement restricting land-based theater missiles is worth considering. Barring progress, being underprepared could prove to be detrimental to long-term U.S. interests. Developments to watch closely include improvements in the range and payload of PLA aircraft; increases in the lethality, accuracy, and numbers of PLA conventional ballistic and land-attack cruise missiles; and an expansion of China's regional persistent surveillance network. These indicators have profound strategic implications for the United States. Given the centrality of the Asia-Pacific to U.S. global interests, China's aerospace development certainly warrants further attention.

Notes

1. Richard C. Bush III, "China and the U.S.-Japan Alliance," *Yomiuri Shimbun*, 6 June 2009.

2. John A. Warden, *The Air Campaign: Planning for Combat* (Washington, DC: National Defense University Press, 1988), 13–24.

3. See, for example, John A. Warden, "The Enemy as a System," *Airpower Journal* (Spring 1995): 40–45.

4. See, for example, Liu Feng and Wang Bingjun, "第二炮兵96637部队营造"尚武"文化" ["Second Artillery 96637 Unit Establishes 'Warrior Culture'"], *Worker's Daily*, 3 August 2006.

5. Among various sources, see "第二炮兵后勤部某综合仓库育人经验谈" ["Experience in Personnel Education in the Second Artillery Logistics Department Integrated Depot"], *China Youth Daily*, 30 November 2000.

6. For an illustrative overview of a cruise missile leader, see "陆基巡航导弹方队长苟翼" ["Ground Launched Cruise Missile Group Commander Gou Yi"], *Xinhua*, 1 October 2009.

7. See Zhang Yiguang and Zhou Chengping, "地地弹道导弹实现远程精确打击的技术途径" ("Technological Trends Associated with Surface-to-Surface Ballistic Missile Precision Guidance"), *Tactical Missile Control Technology* (*Zhanshu daodan kongzhi jishu*) (2004): 58–60.

8. "Statement of Admiral Robert F. Willard, U.S. Navy, Commander, U.S. Pacific Command, before the House Armed Services Committee on the U.S. Pacific Command Posture," 23 March 2010, http://www.pacom.mil/web/pacom_resources/pdf/Willard_Statement_HASC_032510.pdf.

9. See Liu Yalou, "在新的历史起点上推进空军现代化建设" ["New Historical Starting Point in the Modernizing the Air Force"], *Qiushi* [*Seeking Truth*], 17 January 2008.

10. Wang Changhe, "中共空军20年的回顧與展望" ["PLA Air Force 20 Year Review and Outlook"], in 戰爭哲學與中共戰略研究 [*The Philosophy of War and the Study on PRC's Strategy*], ed. Li Chentong, Zhu Chuanzhi, Le Yijun, Wang Zhimin, Peng Zhengjun, Li Hengwen, Gao Zhengwei, and Jiang Chunwang (Taipei: National Defense University War Academy, 2008), 96–97.

11. See Li Yiyong and Shen Huairong, "发展近空间飞行器系统的关键技术" ["Key Technologies for Developing Near Space Flight Vehicles"], *Journal of the Academy of Equipment Command and Technology* (October 2006): 52–55.

12. For a representative Second Artillery overview, see Li Chao, Luo Chuanyong, and Wang Hongli, "近空间飞行器在第二炮兵部队的应用研究" ["Research into Near Space Flight Vehicle Applications for the Second Artillery"], *Journal of Projectiles and Guidance* (January 2009).

13. See Yang Jian, "航天一院10所揭牌成立" ["CASC First Academy 10th Research Institute Established"], *China Space News*, 24 October 2008.

14. See "China Blasts off First Data Relay Satellite," *Xinhua*, 26 April 2008.

15. See Tang Xiaodong, Han Yunjie, and Zhou Wenyu, "Skywave Over-the-Horizon Backscatter Radar," 2001 CIE International Radar Conference Proceedings, Beijing, China, 2 January 2001.

16. For discussions of the airbase survivability issue, see Tsai Ming-Yen, "Air Base Defense: China's Missile Attacks and Taiwan's Defensive Responses," *Taiwan Defense Review* 3, no. 2 (Winter 2002–2003).

17. See "传台湾将试射可攻大陆雄2E导弹年底产80套" ["Taiwan to Produce at Least 80 Hsiungfeng-2E Cruise Missiles That Can Hit Mainland China"], *Global Times*, 25 March 2010.

18. Ministry of Defense, *Defense of Japan 2009*, ch. 1, sec. 3, p. 212, http://www.mod.go .jp/e/publ/w_paper/2009.html.

19. Nao Shimoyachi, "Japan Mulled Buying Cruise Missiles for Pre-Emptive Self-Defense: Ishiba," *Japan Times*, 25 January 2005.

20. Robert D. Kaplan, "The Geography of Chinese Power: How Far Can Beijing Reach on Land and at Sea?" *Foreign Affairs* (May–June 2010).

21. See Jan van Tol, Mark Gunzinger, Andrew Krepinevich, and Jim Thomas, *AirSea Battle: A Point-of-Departure Operational Concept* (Washington, DC: Center for Strategic and Budgetary Assessments, 2010), xiii.

22. Luke Harding, "Putin Threatens Withdrawal from Cold War Nuclear Treaty," *The Guardian*, 12 October 2007.

Wayne A. Ulman

China's Military Aviation Forces

MUCH LIKE CHINA as a whole, the air forces of the People's Liberation Army (PLA) have been undergoing transformational change over the past decade. These air forces have transformed from poorly equipped and poorly trained organizations into increasingly capable fighting forces. Dramatic changes have occurred in the areas of mission, personnel, training, and equipment. From an overly large, technologically inferior force, the PLA Air Force (PLAAF) is emerging as a well-equipped and increasingly well-trained force that still exhibits some identifiable shortcomings and weaknesses. All indicators point to the continued improvement of both the PLAAF and PLA naval aviation over the next decade, to the point that China will have one of the world's foremost air forces by 2020. It should be noted, however, that no discussion of Chinese concepts for air power would be complete without consideration of China's ballistic missile forces, known as the Second Artillery Corps. Chinese strategies for achieving air superiority rely on cooperation between missile and aviation forces to disrupt and defeat adversary air and air-defense operations.

Evolving PLA Missions

Over the past twenty years, the PLA's overall doctrine has evolved rapidly.[1] The highest level of PLA doctrine is known as the Military-Strategic Guidelines.

These guidelines define the fundamental nature of warfare as viewed by the PLA and describe the types of wars that the PLA must be prepared to fight. New Military-Strategic Guidelines were issued in 1993 to reflect a major shift in the view of the nature of modern warfare. Based on world events and PLA analysis of U.S. military operations, the PLA was instructed to prepare to fight "Local Wars under High-Tech Conditions." In essence, the PLA was told to prepare to fight the type of high-tech war conducted by the U.S. military in the 1991 Persian Gulf War.

These guidelines were updated when President Hu Jintao, in 2002, proposed modifying them to reflect the importance of information in modern warfare. This resulted in the guidelines being reissued as "Local Wars under Informatized Conditions." The PLA was thus charged with improving its use of information, denying the adversary the use of information, and controlling the electromagnetic spectrum. Efforts to enhance PLA use of information include improving all aspects of information, surveillance, and reconnaissance (ISR), increasing capabilities for cyber operations, and strengthening joint communications. Efforts to deny enemy information include growing capabilities in electronic warfare, counter space, denial and deception, and secure communications.

The final major driver for the development of PLA forces and doctrine was President Hu's desire for the PLA to begin preparations for nontraditional security operations and operations beyond Taiwan. This desire was articulated in 2004 by Hu as "The Historic Missions of Our Military in the New Period of the New Century." In light of China's growing global interests and influence, the PLA has been asked to protect and support the interests of the People's Republic of China (PRC) worldwide.

Emergence of PLAAF Strategy

The PLA has historically been a ground-centric military with all branches and services being part of the greater People's Liberation Army. Whereas the PLA Navy (PLAN) has had its own service-specific strategy, known as "Near Seas Defense" since 1987, the PLAAF has struggled to emerge from the shadow of the greater army. The PLAAF was long considered a primarily defensive force tasked with defending mainland China and supporting the ground forces. From an equipment perspective, the PLAAF had little capability to project force until nearly the year 2000—being equipped primarily with short-range air-defense fighters and B-6 (H-6) bombers equipped with gravity bombs. The PLAAF had been in the process of developing its own service-specific strategy for quite some time, but it was not until 2004 that "Integrated Air and Space Operations, Simultaneous Offensive and Defensive Operations" was finally announced. This new strategy mandates that the PLAAF prepare for various offensive missions in addition to maintaining its long-standing defensive missions. The PLAAF is increasingly equipped with multirole fighters and now trains for both offensive and defensive operations.

Of greater uncertainty is the phrase "integrated air and space operations." PLAAF writings seem to indicate a desire by the PLAAF to integrate the use of space into its air operations. PLAAF writings indicate that the PLAAF assumes that it will naturally use space-based capabilities; however, it is uncertain what role the PLAAF sees for itself in managing such capabilities. Space and counter-space capabilities are still relatively new to the PLA, and a variety of writings indicate that there remains uncertainty about who will ultimately manage and operate space capabilities.

As its missions and capabilities have changed, the PLAAF has taken on an increasing number of offensive missions in addition to its traditional defensive missions. These missions require the PLAAF to operate at greater distances from home bases and increasingly entail overwater operations. As the PLA prepares for combat in the information and electromagnetic domains, the PLAAF is undergoing a transformation to an informatized force with improved sensors, ISR, communications, and electronic warfare capabilities.

Under the heading of "New Historic Missions," the PLA has been directed to prepare for a wide range of nontraditional missions (e.g., protecting PRC economic interests, preventing hegemony, protecting sea lines of communication, and participating in peacekeeping operations). The service-specific details of these missions do not yet seem to be fully defined, and the resulting equipment requirements may likewise remain unclear. China's 12th Five-Year Plan, which began in 2011, will likely address the equipment requirements supporting the PLA's New Historic Missions.

PLAAF writings have referred to this ongoing transformation as an evolution from a "traditional" air force (with primarily defensive missions) into a "strategic" air force (with global missions such as ISR, strike, and lift). Certainly the development of a strategic projection capability is an area of emphasis for the PLAAF. Currently the PLAAF cannot effectively conduct strikes out to the second island chain;[2] however, systems under development should give the PLAAF the capability to strike targets throughout the Western Pacific and South China Sea.

Campaigns for Air Superiority

The ability of China's air forces to execute their assigned missions is largely dependent on the scenario and adversary, and should be examined in the context of overall military campaigns. The PLA has a construct of both single-service and joint-service campaigns designed for implementation during major military conflict. These campaigns seem to reflect doctrinal planning for a wide range of possible military contingencies including military options regarding Taiwan and the possibility of U.S. military intervention. China's air forces have crucial roles in several doctrinal campaigns with implications for Taiwan, including the Joint Fire Strike Campaign, the Joint Blockade Campaign, and the Airborne Landing Campaign; the Joint Anti-Air Raid Campaign is designed specifically to counter the intervention of a strong adversary such as the United States.

Joint Fire Strike Campaign

The Joint Fire Strike Campaign is designed to be implemented against targets either on the island of Taiwan or on the Taiwan offshore islands. Doctrine calls for the Second Artillery Corps and the PLAAF to conduct these operations jointly. Missile forces would likely comprise the initial strike, followed by PLAAF forces. Enemy command, control, computers, and communications (C4); air defenses; and air capabilities would be included in the initial strikes in order to achieve air superiority and to allow for follow-on air strikes by the PLAAF. Critical to the success of this effort would also be electronic warfare and cyber operations aimed at gaining superiority in the information and electromagnetic domains.

Both the Second Artillery Corps and the PLAAF are well equipped to conduct strike operations against Taiwan and the Taiwan offshore islands. Strike-capable aircraft constitute a significant portion of the new equipment added to PLAAF inventories since the late 1990s. In addition, the Second Artillery Corps is equipped with well over one thousand short-range ballistic missiles (SRBMs) for use against Taiwan. The PLAAF and Second Artillery Corps are well equipped and trained to conduct initial jointly planned strikes. Their ability to react dynamically and to sustain operations over an extended period remains unclear, however.

Joint Blockade Campaign

One of the doctrinally defined military options developed for use against Taiwan is a joint air and naval blockade of Taiwan. PLAAF missions would include enforcing the air blockade in conjunction with missile forces from the Second Artillery Corps. The PLAAF would also provide support to the PLAN as it conducted the naval portion of the Joint Blockade. PLA doctrine on the joint blockade indicates that this operation would be planned as a much more destructive operation than a simple quarantine or embargo. Enforcing the joint blockade would likely involve kinetic strikes against at least ports, airfields, and air-defense assets.

The PLAAF is well equipped to conduct the air blockade and to support PLAN in the naval blockade. The ability of the PLAAF to enforce a blockade over an extended period and the effectiveness of PLAAF–PLAN joint operations remain uncertain.

Airborne Landing Campaign

Within the PLA, airborne forces belong to the PLAAF. As part of any larger campaign to land forces on the island of Taiwan or against off-shore islands, the PLAAF would have the mission of conducting airborne landing operations. Airborne forces do train regularly, but an overall shortage of heavy-lift transport within the PLAAF would likely limit the scale of any airborne landing operations.

Joint Anti-Air Raid Campaign

The Joint Anti-Air Raid Campaign is designed as the cornerstone for countering U.S. military intervention and draws heavily on PLA observations of U.S. war-fighting tendencies as demonstrated in numerous conflicts including the 1991 Gulf War and 1999 Operation Allied Force. The Joint Anti-Air Raid Campaign has both defensive and offensive components.

Defensively, the PLAAF is responsible for air defense of the mainland, including Beijing and other critical civil and military targets. This mission is accomplished primarily using its surface-to-air (SAM) and fighter forces, but other PLA services contribute to the effort with electronic warfare, civil air defense, denial and deception, and other measures aimed at resisting precision strike operations.

The offensive component involves attacking adversary airpower at its source by striking airbases, carrier strike groups (CSGs), and support elements such as logistics, communications, and ISR (including space assets). PLAAF missions include conducting strike operations, primarily in conjunction with the Second Artillery Corps' conventional cruise missile and ballistic missile forces. Against a base such as Japan's Kadena, the missile forces would likely conduct the initial strike—targeting air defenses, airfields, and C4 nodes. This would be followed closely by PLAAF antiradiation unmanned aerial vehicles (UAVs) jamming aircraft and strike aircraft armed with precision-guided weapons. The Chinese goal would be to reduce the effectiveness of enemy strike forces by shutting down air operations. Against CSGs, the PLAAF has primarily a role of supporting and protecting PLAN forces. The actual strikes against naval targets would likely be left to the PLAN, which would use aircraft, surface ships and submarines—all armed with antiship cruise missiles.

The PLAAF is well equipped and relatively well trained to execute an air-defense mission. Offensively, the PLAAF and Second Artillery Corps are equipped to execute strike operations against bases such as Kadena—including multirole fighters with precision strike weapons and SRBMs and medium-range ballistic missile (MRBMs) with tailored warheads. The success of these operations would depend on many variables, including the ability of the PLA to effectively coordinate operations between services, the preparations and actions of any adversary, and the actual situation at the time of combat. Less certain is the PLAAF's ability to operate effectively in a dynamic combat environment or after the initial stages of a conflict. It's ability to sustain operations over an extended period is also uncertain. The PLAAF and Second Artillery Corps currently have only limited capabilities to threaten U.S. facilities on Guam due to their distance from mainland China. However, the PLA appears to be working toward longer-range strike systems to rectify this shortcoming. For example, PLAAF is developing a longer-range version of its B-6 (H-6) bomber, which will be armed with long-range land-attack cruise missiles. When operational, this system will have the capability to strike targets throughout the region, including Guam.

Professionalization, Education, and Training

Accomplishing this growing set of missions is only possible with professional and well-trained personnel. Since the late 1990s the entire PLA has placed a much greater emphasis on professionalization. Prior to the mid-1990s, the PLA was not only greatly oversized, it was also heavily involved in money-making endeavors (both legal and illegal). By the late 1990s, the PLA had been forcibly divested of most of its commercial activity and was undergoing a series of major personnel reductions. These reforms resulted in a smaller, less corrupt, more professional PLA with a greater focus on soldiering.

The late 1990s also saw the creation of a professional Noncommissioned Officer (NCO) Corps in the PLA. The increasing use of complex, high-technology systems in the PLAAF, PLAN, and Second Artillery Corps were not well suited to the high rate of personnel turnover that resulted from the enlisted conscription process. The professional NCO Corps has quickly grown in size and importance in these services; some 60 percent of PLAAF enlisted personnel are now professional NCOs (serving voluntarily beyond their initial conscription). But the relatively short time the NCO programs have been in place means there are still shortages of the most experienced NCOs.

The PLAAF has likewise sought to increase the number of college-educated officers. According to the PLAAF, some 40 percent of its officers have bachelor's degrees while 3 percent have postgraduate degrees. However, only about 30 percent of these bachelor's degrees are from full-time university study. Formal education is a top priority for the PLAAF, but it is expected to remain below that of the U.S. Air Force in terms of officer education for the foreseeable future.

Pilot training in the PLAAF and PLAN aviation has been progressing from a relatively low level since the mid-1990s. Up until that time, the PLAAF completely lacked any fourth-generation fighter aircraft. With the introduction of the Russian Su-27, the PLAAF for the first time had fighters with beyond-visual-range radar and weapons, and relatively modern communication. It was only with the introduction of these capabilities that the PLAAF was able to begin to develop and train with modern air combat tactics. The number of these modern fighters remained small throughout the 1990s, and it was not until after 2000 that a significant number of units received modern fighters.

Since that time, the PLAAF and PLAN have worked diligently to improve the caliber of their aircrews. Compared to other air forces worldwide, the PLAAF is now considered to be professional and well trained. In terms of flight hours, safety standards, night-time flying, debriefing, and overall training subjects, the PLAAF is likely approaching NATO standards. PLAAF pilots regularly fly one hundred to two hundred hours per year, depending on aircraft. Transport and bomber pilots are typically at the upper end of this range, as are the pilots for the most modern fighters. Pilots in units equipped with older aircraft are typically near the lower end of this range. In addition, the PLAAF has worked to increase the amount of simulator training time available to all pilots. PLAAF pilots train more extensively for defensive operations and should be considered more proficient in these areas. Offensive strike training seems to be conducted less regularly and is probably rather inflexible in execution.

Since 2007 the entire PLA has placed an emphasis on joint training and on training to fight in a complex electromagnetic environment (CEME). Consistent with the overall Military-Strategic Guidelines of preparing to fight local wars under informatized conditions, the PLA believes that any future combat environment will be conducted in a cluttered electromagnetic environment containing emissions from commercial and military systems, in addition to significant amounts of jamming. The PLA is preparing units to operate in this electromagnetically dense environment. As a result, some level of adversary electronic warfare and cyber operations are represented in nearly all training and exercise events. Within the PLAAF, electronic warfare and jamming are important elements in most tactical training.

In 2009 the PLA implemented a new revision of its Outline of Military Training and Evaluation (OMTE)—a regulation guiding how training will be organized, implemented, and evaluated. Emphasized in this OMTE were joint training, training in CEME, and improved realism in training, including increased use of opposition forces (known as Blue Forces). Within the PLAAF, most tactical training and exercises now seem to contain some level of opposition force participation. Also appearing in this OMTE were new requirements for training in antiterrorism operations, international peacekeeping, and military operations other than war.

Finally, the PLAAF is increasingly seeking opportunities to train with pilots from other countries—particularly with air forces that also train with the U.S. Air Force. The PLA has been conducting annual training exercises with the Russian military since 2005, but the last two years have seen an increase in PLAAF engagement with Western air forces. This joint training offers the opportunity to test equipment, procedures, and pilot skills with dissimilar air forces. It can also help to mitigate the PLAAF's lack of actual combat experience over the past three decades.

Equipment Modernization

Since 2000 China's air forces have shrunk significantly in size while greatly increasing their number of modern aircraft. In 2000 the combined PLAAF and PLAN aviation had more than three thousand fighters, almost all of which were antiquated F-6 (J-6) and F-7 (J-7) variants (modeled after Soviet MiG-19 and MiG-21). Of this number, only the approximately fifty Su-27 would be considered modern fighters (fourth generation). Today total fighters have been reduced to approximately two thousand aircraft, nearly five hundred of which are modern fourth-generation aircraft. The PLAAF has also brought online critical force multiplying aircraft for airborne early warning and control (AEW&C), electronic warfare, and ISR.

The PLAAF has likewise made a tremendous investment in ground-based air defenses. By 2000 the PLAAF had begun to modernize its SAM forces with the purchase of advanced Russian SAMs. Since then the PLA has purchased additional units of the Russian SA-20. China has also begun the deployment of the domestically produced HQ-9, a SAM comparable to the SA-20.

Within the PLAAF, the introduction of modern systems began in the early 1990s with the purchase of Su-27 fighters and SA-10 SAMs from Russia. At that time China's aviation and aerospace industries were not yet able to produce modern systems of this class. By the mid-1990s, China signed a licensed production agreement with Russia for production of two hundred Su-27s. The domestic F-10 (J-10) was under development but was not yet ready for production. Although the PLAAF was aware of the need to modernize its force, national priorities were focused on economic modernization, so military modernization progressed at a measured pace.

In 1999 the combination of independence-minded comments by Taiwan president Lee Teng-hui, coupled with U.S.–NATO military involvement in Kosovo (without a UN mandate), quickly raised concerns in Beijing. The PRC's leadership perceived that Taiwan was moving more rapidly toward independence than previously anticipated while the United States was demonstrating an increasing willingness to become militarily involved in the internal affairs of other countries. China's leadership decided that increased prioritization of military development was needed to prepare for possible military contingencies for Taiwan, and for the likelihood of U.S. intervention therein.

As a result, China increased its arms purchases from Russia over the next few years. For the PLAAF, this included the procurement of Su-30MKK multirole fighters, SA-20 advanced SAMs, and additional Su-27s. For the PLAN, this included purchase of Su-30MK2s, advanced destroyers, and *Kilo*-class submarines. Despite these large purchases of entire systems, the PRC retained its long-term goal of becoming independent in the development and production of arms. So while China bought arms from Russia, it simultaneously pursued domestic production of weapon systems such as the F-10 (J-10) fighter and SRBMs.

Over the past ten years the PRC has continued to purchase weapon systems, subsystems, technology, and expertise from Russia and elsewhere; however, the trend has moved away from the purchase of entire systems. Meanwhile, China's defense industries have demonstrated an increasing ability to develop and produce advanced weapon systems. The F-10 (J-10) is currently in production, upgraded versions of F-10 (J-10) and F-11 (J-11, a Chinese produced version of Su-27) have both been developed, and a next-generation fighter (referred to as the XXJ or F-20/J-20) was first flight tested on 11 January 2011 and should be operational around 2018.

The PLAAF is working to develop effective counterstealth capabilities. China has been working on technologies, systems, and procedures to detect, track, and engage stealth aircraft and cruise missiles. It is developing a network-centric kill chain to fuse data from an extensive and diverse sensor network. It is also working to reduce the signature of current aircraft designs and on developing a low-observable fighter. As the PLAAF gains access to reduced-signature systems, it will allow the development of tactics, training, and procedures for use against low-observable threat systems.

The PLA is working on a comprehensive approach to information superiority. It seeks to integrate electronic warfare, cyber operations, psychological operations, denial and deception, and kinetic attack to defeat adversary information systems. The PLA seems intent on integrating electronic warfare with cyber operations. Chinese efforts to develop counter-space capabilities are also an important element of this effort to achieve information superiority by denying or degrading adversary ISR, C4, and navigational capabilities. Overall, the PLA considers itself at a fairly early stage of informatization, with a goal of achieving a fully informatized PLA by 2050.

The PLA is also expected to continue development of antiaccess (or what China would refer to as "counterintervention") capabilities. Long-range aerodynamic systems, longer-range conventional ballistic missiles, and antiship ballistic missiles are all under development. Over time, the ISR, the C4, and the procedures will be developed and refined to give PLA the ability to hold at risk all classes of targets in the Western Pacific and South China Sea.

Because of the complex nature of modern weapons, coupled with the global market for arms, technology, and components, it may never be practical or desirable for the PRC to be fully independent in producing all military systems. China continues to lag behind world standards in some areas of military technology, though it is near world-class in many others.

The Final Verdict

Improvements in PLA capabilities over the past decade are undeniably tied to improvements in weapons systems over that time span. The PLA can now boast fourth-generation fighters equipped with modern jammers, communications systems, and weapons. However, improvements in military capabilities should also be credited to advances in other key areas. Since the late 1990s, the

PLA has implemented new doctrine and strategies more suitable for twenty-first-century warfare. It has placed an increased emphasis on training and operationalizing its military forces. Great strides have been made in streamlining and professionalizing the PLA. Lastly, the PLA has developed a clear sense of mission and purpose. These factors all contribute to a greatly improved and capable PLA, which shows every sign of becoming a truly modern military with a small but growing ability to influence global events.

Specific strengths of China's air forces include the following:

- Nearly five hundred fourth-generation fighters can be considered at a technical parity with U.S. legacy fighters.

- Internal lines of communication and redundant infrastructure for basing and C4 are well suited for any Taiwan-related contingency.

- Its air-defense network is one of the world's most advanced and robust.

- A limited set of well-defined missions associated with a very specific set of contingencies allows the PLAAF to allocate a greater amount of its time and focus to the tasks that it believes are most important.

- History and PLA writings demonstrate a willingness to plan for and accept extensive losses.

- PLAAF willingness to be self-critical and increasing willingness to implement change indicates a strong motivation to improve.

China's air forces also have weaknesses:

- It is difficult to recruit and retain the number of technologically proficient officers and enlisted troops needed to operate a technologically advanced military.

- Pilot training, experience, and the development of tactics still fall short of the best Western militaries.

- Many of the key supporting aircraft are not yet operational, or are not yet deployed in sufficient numbers. The KJ-200 and KJ-2000 AEW&C aircraft may just be reaching operational status and have not yet been built in large numbers. Tanker aircraft are in short supply (although few of the missions directly related to a Taiwan military contingency require extensive tanker support). The PLA does not yet have sufficient numbers of large transport aircraft for missions such as strategic lift, aerial refueling, and AEW&C.

- The PLA lacks corporate experience with modern combat. Although the PLAAF and PLAN aviation strategists and personnel have studied modern combat extensively, the most recent campaign for the PLA was the Sino-Vietnam conflict in 1979, a campaign in which the PLAAF played almost no part and in which PLAN aviation was not involved. This lack of live experience presents difficulties in validating tactics, procedures, and concepts and can lead to misjudgments.

- The PLAAF and other PLA services appear proficient in conducting detailed planning, but there is significant uncertainty about their ability to react effectively to a very fluid, dynamic military situation.

- The PLA will likely continue to rely on a fairly inflexible command-and-control structure, and the PLAAF, specifically, on a ground-based command architecture. This may only be a weakness if it can be exploited by an adversary.

Notes

1. Technically, the PLA does not use the term "doctrine"; however, it does possess a well-developed body of official views regarding the conduct of war. For purposes of discussion, this chapter will use "doctrine" to refer to the wide range of PLA literature that serves this purpose.

2. The second island chain, as conceptualized by Admiral Liu Huaqing, PLAN commander 1982–88, runs from the Japanese archipelago south through the Bonins, the Marianas (including Guam), the Carolines, and Indonesia. See 刘华清 [Liu Huaqing], 刘华清回忆录 [*The Memoirs of Liu Huaqing*] (Beijing: Liberation Army Press, 2004), 437.

Kevin Pollpeter

PLA Space Doctrine

SINCE THE 11 JANUARY 2007 Chinese antisatellite (ASAT) test, increasing attention has been focused on China's counter-space intentions and the role that counter space may play in People's Liberation Army (PLA) operations. China's space program, however, has made marked progress in nearly all areas since 2001. While its manned and lunar orbiting missions have garnered international attention, it has also launched more satellites than at any other time in its history. China has also developed several new types of satellites, including a regional satellite navigation constellation, ocean-monitoring satellites, a data-relay satellite, and synthetic aperture radar (SAR) satellites, and has improved satellite communication and remote sensing satellites. China has also managed to resurrect its failing launch industry from the disasters of the mid-1990s to achieve a launch success rate equal to international counterparts.

Chinese advances in space technology not only represent China's ambitions to become a leading world power, they also represent a determined effort to make space an integral part of PLA operations. Despite Chinese efforts to portray their space program as nonmilitary, Chinese doctrinal and technical writings indicate that while China's space program is used for civil and commercial applications, an overriding motive for the development of space technology is military applications. This not only includes the much publicized counter-space capabilities but also a variety of force enhancement applications that can better enable terrestrial forces strike enemy targets. Consequently,

China's entire space program must be considered when assessing its military space doctrine.

This chapter evaluates Chinese writings on the characterization and use of space in military operations. It finds that while China has laid a technological foundation for space-enabled and counter-space operations, it has yet to define an official space doctrine. In fact, most writings on the use of space in military operations are aspirational. These writings serve as guides for the development of the PLA as an informatized force, with space playing a critical role in this effort. They advance the proposition that space will be the preeminent battlefield in future wars. Chinese writers argue that space is critical to forming an integrated command, control, communications, computers, intelligence, surveillance, and reconnaissance (C4ISR) network that can enable Chinese forces to increase the speed, efficiency, and precision of terrestrial strikes. They also argue that because the strength of modern militaries is derived from space, China must develop ASAT weapons to paralyze an adversary by debilitating its C4ISR network. As a consequence of this conclusion, these analysts argue that the PLA should fully integrate space into operations and that the PLA should strive for space control—the ability to freely use space and deny its use to adversaries.

Despite the aspirational nature of these writings, the near unanimity of Chinese writings on this topic is clear. Through the course of completing this chapter, seven books on space operations, three books on information warfare, and seventy-eight doctrinal and technical articles were consulted. All except one either supported the need to achieve space control or expressed no opposition. Moreover, Chinese writings on the military use of space appear to have made a transition from advocacy by a small but vocal core of "space cadets" to a larger and more professional body of work that merits attention. Authors spanned a range of organizations within the PLA, the defense industry, and civilian schools. The role of space in military operations is also beginning to be researched by the larger community of information warfare researchers, some of whom have come to the same conclusions as their space warfare counterparts. Consequently, these writings may portend the direction of the wartime application of China's space program and the future development of Chinese space technologies.

Chinese military operations aimed at achieving space supremacy could have important consequences for the U.S. Navy. If successful, Chinese space operations could play a critical role in the C4ISR architecture necessary for long-range precision strikes against aircraft carriers using antiship cruise or ballistic missiles. Chinese counter-space operations, conversely, could imperil the ability of the U.S. Navy to conduct operations. The degradation of satellite communications, for example, could deprive the Navy of vital communications. The loss of the global positioning system signal could limit precision strikes to laser-guided munitions and increase aircraft sortie rates due to a heavier reliance on so-called dumb bombs. The loss of space-based intelligence, surveillance, and reconnaissance (ISR) assets would threaten the ability of the U.S. Navy to collect intelligence on the disposition of the PLA and conduct battle damage assessments. Chinese control of space could thus seriously affect the way the U.S. Navy currently conducts war and could force it to fight wars as it did during the 1991 Gulf War or the Vietnam War.

Characterization and Definitions of Space

Chinese writings acknowledge that there is no clear boundary defining the beginning of space. However, the majority of Chinese analysts define space as starting at an altitude of 100 km, although some refer to space starting at an altitude of 120 km.[1] The altitude of 100 km, known as the Kármán Line, indicates the approximate altitude at which air becomes too thin for aeronautic purposes and is officially recognized by the Fédération Aéronautique Internationale as the boundary of space. The altitude of 120 km cited by some Chinese researchers is where atmospheric drag becomes noticeable on reentering spacecraft.

Definitions of Space Warfare

Chinese sources use two terms for space warfare: *kongjian zhan* (空间战) and *taikong zhan* (太空战). The meanings of both terms appear to be synonymous and have evolved over the years. For example, the 1993 *China Military Encyclopedia* defines space warfare as a type of warfare conducted against China: "The enemy conducting military strikes against our country in outer space. It is called *kongjian zhan* or *taikong zhan*. It includes military offensive and defensive operations in outer space, operations to strike air and ground targets from outer space as well as ground and airborne strikes against targets in space. The purpose is to destroy or disable space systems."[2] The definition provided in 1997 *Chinese PLA Military Encyclopedia* offers a more neutral definition: "Military confrontations conducted in outer space between rival countries. . . . It includes offensive and defensive operations in outer space, operations conducted to engage targets in air, space or on the ground from outer space, as well as operations conducted from the ground or in airspace aimed at destroying or incapacitating space systems."[3] These more official definitions are not universally used by individual researchers, who often provide their own definitions. Often these definitions expand the definition of space warfare to include nonspace operations that use space-based force enhancement methods, such as satellite navigation and positioning for precision strikes. For example:

> Space Warfare: . . . offensive and defensive operations employed or aimed at military space forces. There are two main types of operations: First, operations conducted to gain space dominance. The objectives are to damage enemy space systems in order to protect one's own space systems and freedom of actions in space. Operations include confrontations between military space forces of the two parties at war, as well as operations conducted by the party that sets to attack rival military space targets using non-space military forces. Second, actions meant to achieve the goal of joint military operations by means of military space forces. Both sides will use space forces to provide their own war systems with surveillance, navigation, communications, command and control support, among others, as well as to engage ground targets via space-based weapons systems.[4]

Based on these definitions, the widest Chinese conceptions of space war involve military offensive and defensive operations in space; attacks against targets in air, ground, sea, or space from space; attacks against targets in space from air, ground, sea, or space; and force enhancement measures to enable attack targets against air, ground, and sea. Consequently, when Chinese writers discuss space warfare, it is frequently the case that satellites providing support to military operations may be characterized as space weapons, whereas in the United States this term is reserved for technologies that directly attack satellites. Such definitional ambiguities may be lessened as Chinese researchers associate space less as a tool of a "hegemon" and more as a tool that the PLA itself must exploit.

Importance of Space

Chinese analysts describe space as a future source of wealth that countries will compete for and may engage in armed conflict over. They argue that guaranteeing access to space and having the ability to deny access to space will become imperative to ensuring national security.[5] Chinese writings also propose that space is a principal source of economic growth and an important part of national security. In fact, some even argue that space is a major resource for a country's strength and prosperity. Modern economies and the ability of countries to compete globally will increasingly rely not only on the ability to transmit and process information but also on the ability to sell the goods and services involved in information technologies.[6] As a result, space assumes a much more strategic character than its military operational and tactical applications alone reveal.[7] China, therefore, in order to become a secure major power, must develop the ability to achieve space control—the ability to access space freely and deny its use to others.

Information Warfare and the Importance of Space in Military Operations

The importance of space in military operations is linked to the PLA's view of the role of information in modern war. The PLA is tasked with winning "local wars under conditions of informatization," and the major criterion for evaluating PLA performance is its level of informatization.[8] Chinese writings regard information collection, processing, and transmission and the denial of those capabilities to an adversary as vital to the successful prosecution of a modern high-tech war. According to Chinese writings, information supremacy is the precondition for achieving supremacy in the air, at sea, and on the ground, and is critical to achieving and maintaining battlefield supremacy. Consequently, information operations are the most important operational method of modern wars.[9] As a result, the PLA has focused on the development of a modern C4ISR system to enhance its ability to conduct strikes against an enemy as well as the development of offensive technologies to deny those same capabilities to an adversary.

C4ISR Development

The PLA's concept of a modern C4ISR system is heavily influenced by the U.S. concept of network centric warfare (NCW). Proponents of NCW believe that networks can enable the military to achieve improved situational awareness using sensors, networks, display technology, and modeling and simulation capabilities, and can increase the speed of command by enabling decisions to be made at the lowest levels possible.

Chinese writings argue that NCW is the basis for informatized warfare. According to the PLA's vision for its C4ISR system, improvements in sensor, communication, and guidance technologies will allow the PLA to gather and use information about the battlefield more rapidly and effectively than before. C4ISR systems will be networked and linked at every level of command, every unit will have access to the same information, and the needs of each service and command organization will be met.[10]

Offensive Information Operations

For information warfare to be successful, the PLA must not only collect and use information, it must also deny that same ability to an adversary. Information warfare is not characterized by attacks aimed at complete annihilation of the enemy. Instead, information warfare is focused on attacks against enemy command centers, communication systems, and ISR systems. In particular, it is directed against targets whose loss can lead to the paralysis of the entire system.[11]

This goal is particularly important to the PLA, which would prefer to fight "quick wars with quick resolutions." Chinese analysts have indicated that bringing a war to a rapid conclusion benefits the PLA due to the ability of a more strongly armed opponent, such as the United States, to eventually bring the full might of its military to bear. Indeed, in prosecuting a war against a "strong enemy" the PLA cannot afford to get into a war of attrition with the United States. Even though the PLA is larger than the U.S. military, its high-technology forces are smaller and less capable. In this way, China hopes to use information warfare methods to both win and limit the scale of war in order to win with the least possible cost.

A major component for achieving a quick victory is the Chinese strategy of active defense. Active defense has been described by Mao Zedong as "offensive defense or defense through decisive engagements . . . for the purpose of counterattacking and taking the offensive."[12] There is little operational difference between China's active defense strategy and an offensive strategy, however. Within the context of protecting China's sovereignty, Chinese writers make clear that the full range of offensive actions, including preemptive strikes, are permissible.[13] As a result, active defense is best thought of as a politically defensive but operationally offensive strategy in which China will rhetorically maintain a defensive posture up until the time that war appears imminent. Thus, any U.S. military support or deployment that is deemed to be a precursor to U.S. action could be grounds for a preemptive strike.[14]

Central to the need to conduct offensive operations at the beginning of a campaign is the requirement to seize the initiative. Seizing the initiative at the outset of a campaign is made even more critical due to the propensity of modern conventional wars to be concluded after just one campaign.[15] The PLA, however, need not achieve absolute superiority for the entire campaign and can instead try to create windows of opportunity where it can achieve superiority for periods long enough to successfully strike key targets, paralyze the enemy, and potentially cause unacceptable casualties for the enemy.[16]

The focus on seizing the initiative at the beginning of a conflict has led to an emphasis in Chinese writings on the concept of "gaining mastery by striking first." This concept covers several types of strategies, including preemption, surprise attacks, and general aggressiveness. The targets of such a Chinese attack are those that are identified as an adversary's center of gravity. In attacking a center of gravity, the PLA's goal is not to achieve wholesale destruction of enemy forces but instead to attack a target or target set so critical that its destruction would gravely affect adversary operations and bring about victory.[17]

Aiding China in this effort is its ability to rely on its home territory for support and defense and the necessity of the U.S. military to fight thousands of miles away from its support system. This situation is thought to present opportunities for the PLA to exploit U.S. military vulnerabilities. Indeed, Chinese strategists encourage the PLA to fight asymmetrically against a superior force to compensate for PLA weaknesses.[18]

The Military Utility of Space

Since the late 1990s, Chinese military theorists and strategists have articulated views about the growing importance and priority of space and counter-space operations due to the role space assets play in collecting and transmitting information and the role ASAT weapons play in denying information. A frequent theme in Chinese writings on space is that "whoever controls space will control the Earth." These authors point to the use of space by the U.S. military for communications, intelligence collection, navigation and positioning, and meteorology and conclude that much of the success of recent U.S. operations was facilitated by space assets. Indeed, in their assessments of U.S. operations, Chinese analysts increasingly identify space as *the* source of U.S. information superiority. U.S. military performance in conflicts from the 1991 Gulf War to the present conflicts in Iraq and Afghanistan has demonstrated the force multiplying effect of space-enabled operations as well as the dependence of U.S. forces on space. Chinese writings often state that the U.S. military depends on satellites for 70–95 percent of its intelligence and 80 percent of its communications.[19] As a result, space will become the main battlefield that will determine success or defeat on the battlefield.[20]

This conclusion is based in part on the assumption that space power will develop as air power has. Air power developed from initially providing reconnaissance to performing counter-air and tactical ground support operations and eventually to conducting intercontinental strategic bombing missions. Chinese analysts believe that space power is in the initial stages of this development path as a provider of support to terrestrially based forces. Eventually the support that space provides to terrestrial forces will become so critical that space will inevitably become a battleground. This will result in the development of counter-space capabilities, defensive capabilities, and capabilities to strike the earth from space.[21]

Space and Its Antiaccess Roles

Chinese writings identify three separate uses for space in armed conflict. The first role involves force enhancement in which space provides critical support to terrestrially based forces. The second involves counter space in which space-based assets are attacked to deny the enemy the use of space. The third aspect, deterrence, involves the use of the first two aspects in an effort to prevent or contain conflict.

Force Enhancement

Space figures prominently in the PLA's conception of a modern C4ISR system, and a robust space-based C4ISR system is often described as a critical component of a future networked PLA. Space-based assets have global reach and are less susceptible to enemy countermeasures, if ASAT weapons are not used. Space-based information systems have been described as "possessing a unique dominance in integrating land, sea and air platforms, combining component operational networks, and creating a networked operational environment." It is also said that the increased employment of space-based information equipment will advance the formation of a network centric force.[22]

While space-based systems have their limitations, space-enabled operations conducted by the U.S. military have generated interest in the PLA to develop similar systems.[23] The necessity to develop space-based C4ISR systems appears to stem largely from the requirement to achieve antiaccess capabilities for use against the U.S. Navy. The development of long-range cruise missiles and antiship ballistic missiles for over-the-horizon attacks requires the ability to locate, track, and target enemy ships hundreds or thousands of kilometers from China's shores. In fact, Chinese analysts argue that development of this capability "cannot be separated from space power."[24]

Specifically, space-based C4ISR capabilities that could be used in an anti-ship role include navigation, imagery, synthetic aperture radar, and data relay satellites, all of which China possesses to some degree of quantity and sophistication.[25] While PLA analysts have ambitious plans, they also acknowledge that the PLA's current C4ISR structure is unable to meet its needs and is many years behind that of the U.S. military not only in satellite technology but also in the technologies that are required to fuse the information gathered from these technologies into a coherent, common battlefield picture.[26]

Counter-Space Missions

Because space holds such a preeminent position on the battlefield and because overall victory flows from space superiority, many authors advocate the development of ASAT weapons to achieve space superiority.[27] Because of the preeminence of the space battlefield, analysts argue that space will become *the* center of gravity in future wars, and one that must be seized and controlled. In fact, analysts argue that the first condition for seizing the initiative is to achieve space supremacy. Indeed, because space will become the center of gravity in future wars, the first shots of a war will take place in space as adversaries vie for its control.[28]

Chinese analysts have counseled that attacks on another country's space systems must not be taken lightly and must serve a country's political and diplomatic goals.[29] Analysts, however, also provide two reasons for achieving space control. The first is that armed force must be used to protect China's space assets from attack and to protect terrestrially based forces from attacks launched from space. Chinese analysts have designated space systems as the targets of key point strikes that must be defended. If China cannot defend its space systems, then it risks losing control of terrestrial battlefields and ultimate victory in the conflict.[30]

A second reason for achieving space control is to deny an adversary the use of space. In this context the PLA would plan to compensate for its lower level of informatization not by increasing the speed of its decision making through space-based force enhancement techniques but by slowing down an opponent's decision cycle through the denial of information derived from space.[31]

Indeed, Chinese analysts have noted that the U.S. military is inordinately dependent on space and that the loss of space for the U.S. military may result in its defeat.[32] Consequently, attacks against U.S. space systems offer an asymmetric means by which the PLA can strike at and debilitate U.S. forces, especially when compared to the relatively lower degree of dependence of the Chinese military on space.

Chinese writings discuss a range of attacks, including both "soft kill" and "hard kill" attacks. Soft kills involve to the use of electromagnetic radiation, infrared or laser interference, and jamming methods aimed at preventing information receipt, transmission, or processing that cause short-term or long-term losses of combat effectiveness. They can also include computer network operations to infiltrate space information systems in order to steal, tamper with, and delete computer code and information in an attempt to deceive or obstruct adversary operations.[33] Hard kills involve the employment of weapons systems to destroy space-based and terrestrially based space assets. Kill methods include nuclear weapons, kinetic weapons such as missiles and space kinetic weapons, and high-power directed energy weapons such as lasers, particle beams, and microwaves.[34]

Soft-kill measures are generally preferred over hard-kill measures because they do not produce debris and because their effects are, in some cases, temporary.[35] Hard kills are also more observable than other types of strikes and the adversary may be able to find out who conducted the attack.[36] Moreover, because directed-energy weapons are less observable than kinetic kill attacks they may be preferable in politically sensitive situations.[37] In this case, it appears that the authors may be suggesting that China could conduct covert attacks against adversary satellites.

A final reason for using soft-kill methods is to avoid permanently disabling or destroying third-party satellites. Permanently disabling or destroying third-party satellites can cause negative international reaction and escalate a conflict. Third-party satellites may also be concurrently used by China and its opponent, and their destruction could reduce China's space capabilities.[38] Hard kills can produce debris that can also interfere with, damage, or destroy Chinese satellites and uninvolved third-party satellites. Hard kills, however, are not discounted, and all analysts write that hard kills have their place in space warfare. Hard kills can complement soft kills when soft kills are ineffective or unsuitable for the mission.[39]

ASAT weapons can be placed upon a number of different platforms. These include basing on the ground or placing on aircraft, spacecraft, or satellites. Satellites of all sizes can play multiple roles in space warfare, both defensive and offensive. Constellations of satellites can provide a defensive screen of monitors and can carry a variety of weapons, including lasers, high-powered microwaves, and kinetic-energy weapons.[40]

A relatively large percentage of Chinese writings also include the utility of manned space platforms in space warfare. Manned platforms are described as being more responsive than unmanned platforms and able to employ a variety of weapons.[41] Manned space platforms include space capsules, space stations, and space planes. Space capsules and space planes can transport goods, carry out space rescue missions, and conduct reconnaissance and surveillance.[42] Space stations, conversely, can serve as command-and-control bases, communications nodes, surveillance and reconnaissance platforms, logistics and maintenance hubs, or platforms for weapons platform.[43]

Chinese analysts do not prioritize attacks against satellites and put equal weight on the value of all satellites. Chinese writings on information warfare, however, suggest that sensors may be a priority in any information warfare–based attacks. Sensors are seen as the eyes and ears of a military whose destruction may make it easier for the PLA to conduct stratagems. Chinese researchers, however, have identified attacking ground infrastructure, such as command-and-control nodes and launch facilities, as the most effective way to achieve space control.[44]

Space Blockade

A type of space war described by several researchers is space blockade. The definition of space blockade is "a space power independently or in support of other services within a certain period of time preventing the enemy from entering space or a special space area as well as severing the enemy's information chain. Space blockade operations ordinarily involve space power offensive operations to achieve space superiority. Their purpose is not to destroy enemy space power, rather they involve special enemy and space relationships."[45] The main purposes of space blockade operations are to conceal war preparations, to disrupt the economy, and to seize and maintain space control. Space blockades can be used to deny an adversary access to space-derived information prior to a conflict to conceal PLA preparations for war. As economies become more reliant on space, a space blockade can seriously affect a civilian economy and could lead to political instability and military imbalance. Space blockades can involve strikes against enemy space forces that enter the blockade area, thereby weakening enemy space power and limiting the freedom of operations for the enemy in those areas.[46]

Space blockade operations can be carried out using attacks against bases, orbital blockades, or information blockades. Operations against bases are designed to prevent the enemy from gaining access to space. These attacks can be carried out in conjunction with ground, air, and sea forces and can include strikes and jamming.[47] Orbital blockades prevent the enemy from entering a specific orbit. They can involve using spacecraft and ground, sea, and air forces to attack enemy forces entering the blockade area. They can also involve laying space mines or debris to deny the use of specific orbits. Information blockades control the electromagnetic spectrum and for a certain period in a certain area of space to cut off communication and information links between enemy spacecraft and ground stations.[48] This also involves using deception to distort enemy telemetry, tracking, and command-and-control information. Using an information blockade, it is possible to send information to spacecraft to make them self-destruct or lose control.[49]

Deterrence

The importance of space deterrence is gaining increasing attention in Chinese writings and appears to be viewed as an important component of a country's overall deterrence strategy as well as a country's counter-space strategy. Chinese researchers often refer to Sun Zi (Sun Tzu)'s precept that "to subdue the enemy without fighting is the acme of skill," and conclude that deterrence fits strongly with Chinese military strategy.[50] In fact, one book suggests that deterrence is an inherently Chinese concept due to the self-perceived Chinese predilection to avoid war at all costs.[51]

Chinese writers define deterrence as "countries or national groups displaying the will to use armed force or the will to prepare to use armed force to compel the other side not to rashly conduct hostile activities or conduct escalatory activities."[52] Its core ideology is, with a strong military force as a backup, to use various nonwar measures to form a complete deterrence posture to contain the enemy's war posture and to achieve the strategic goal of winning the war without fighting.[53] Ultimately, the goal of deterrence is to force the opponent to perform a cost–benefit analysis of entering into armed conflict with China by demonstrating that China's war-making potential will inflict unacceptable losses on the opponent.[54]

Chinese writers are unanimous in their judgment that for deterrence to be effective, China must not only possess real military capability but also display the will to use it.[55] Indeed, real power is deemed indispensible to deterrence; having a credible deterrent force with an "empty fortress" will be difficult.[56] In pursuit of this, Chinese writings on space deterrence advocate that China should build a comprehensive space program that can demonstrate China's overall space capability, and not just its ASAT weapons.

Space deterrence is compared to nuclear deterrence, which is likewise identified as being strategic in nature. However, space deterrence is considered more flexible and more believable.[57] Nuclear weapons will most likely not be used and threats to use them lose some of their credibility because of their immense destructive power.

Chinese writers identify three ways in which space deterrence can be conducted. These can be accomplished through ISR capabilities before a conflict begins, through force enhancement support to conventional forces, counterspace capabilities, and demonstrations of military space capabilities.

ISR Capabilities

Space enhances deterrent capabilities by detecting enemy movement and intentions before a conflict begins. These capabilities enable a country to potentially defuse a crisis before it escalates. The most common example provided by Chinese analysts of this type of deterrence is the Cuban missile crisis. Even though Soviet missiles were identified using air power, the principle remains the same. Space-based ISR capabilities remain the primary source of intelligence for the U.S. military, and their utility cannot be discounted.

Force Enhancement

Space-based capabilities also increase a country's deterrent potential by improving strike capabilities and overall mission performance. In this regard, space-based force enhancement capabilities increase the strength of a military to the extent that other militaries will not challenge it.

Counter Space

The final method in which space contributes to deterrence is more directly applied to operations in space. In this case, counter-space capabilities permit a country to threaten another country's space capabilities. In this way the ability to take out an adversary's satellites may deter the adversary from conducting its own counter-space operations.[58] Moreover, because a country's political, economic, military, and scientific activities are increasingly reliant on space, destroying space systems can lead to financial paralysis, a breakdown in communications, and transportation snarls as well as a reduction in military capabilities. In this way, counter-space operations may compel an adversary not to attack an opponent's satellites, and may compel an adversary to refrain from military conflict due to the impact the loss of space systems may have on its economy.

Demonstrations of Military Space Capabilities

Demonstrations of space and counter-space capabilities can play an important deterrent role by demonstrating capability and intent. These include ASAT tests, space war games, and using space in actual armed conflicts.

ASAT Tests

ASAT tests are the most aggressive form of deterrence due to their ability to display capability and intent to use. Chinese analysts state that even a failed test is beneficial for deterrence purposes because it still demonstrates an emerging capability and intent.

Space War Games

Space war games show the intent and preparations to conduct space war. The primary example of this type of deterrent measure is the series of Schriever war games. These war games are said to have had an "actual effect in faraway places."[59]

Use of Space

The use of space in operations also creates a deterrent effect. The primary examples of this type of deterrent method is the U.S. use of space in operations since the 1991 Gulf War. The Gulf War is referred to as the first "space war" for its use of space-based capabilities. Actual operations prove a country's space capabilities and their intent to use them.[60]

Legal Aspects

Chinese analysts recognize that there are legal aspects to the military use of space. Most prominent of these is the Outer Space Treaty, which prohibits the deployment of nuclear weapons and other weapons of mass destruction in space but does not prohibit the deployment of conventional weapons. Chinese analysts make clear that while international law can limit space war, international law should not be completely relied upon to guide China's conduct of space war. States can also interpret their obligations to suit their interests and can only ratify those parts of a treaty to which they agree.[61]

Finally, international public opinion may also be a limiting factor. There is a great amount of international public opinion against space weapons, and it is considered that the use of space weapons may negatively affect China's pursuit of its national security goals.[62]

Conclusion

Chinese writings on the use of space in military operations outline an ambitious plan to fully integrate space into Chinese warfighting. This includes integrating space into China's C4ISR systems as well as developing a comprehensive set of ASAT capabilities. If exploited fully, space will play a critical role in Chinese efforts to deny the U.S. military access to the region. This has particular importance for the U.S. Navy as well as the U.S. Air Force. Chinese writings on the use of space for force enhancement mainly chronicle its utility in relation to long-range precision strikes, most likely to be conducted against U.S. naval vessels. Chinese writings on space control and concomitant weapons programs seek to deny the U.S. military the use of space. If space is a center of gravity, and if the U.S. military is as critically reliant on space as has been reported, then the threat exists that the U.S. military could lose the critical sensor and communications capabilities that it has been able to use to achieve quick wars with minimal casualties. But Chinese writings also discuss space in a strategic context. The economic "force enhancement" aspects of space have been identified as an opportunity to hold a country's economy hostage and as a target to undermine an opponent's will. Attacks in space can increase the costs of a war to a populace and raise the risks of intervention for its leadership.

This places China's ASAT programs and their tests in a more comprehensive context. Since the January 2007 ASAT test, analysts have tried to pin the purpose of the test on one motive. In fact, the tests could have multiple motives. It is possible that the tests are meant to develop technologies to deny the U.S. military the use of space. These tests also have an inherent deterrent aspect. Chinese writings on space and deterrence possess a Strangelovian logic: not only must a capability exist, it must also be made known. To use space in a deterrence role, China must develop and publicize its possession of ASAT capabilities.

Previous studies on Chinese writings on space warfare have focused on its asymmetric aspects; this study is not intended to refute the logic of the asymmetric argument. This conclusion must be broadened, however. Chinese writings on space and its military applications are clear in stating that whatever asymmetric advantage China can gain from space control in the near to medium term, space will be a battlefield that must be seized comprehensively in the long term, especially if China becomes an advanced military power with interests in space. In doing so, if it operationalizes this vision, China will expose itself to the same vulnerabilities that it sees in the U.S. military. What is not debated in the literature is whether this approach is a sound one for China. Such a scenario may require the United States to consider the development of ASAT weapons. If China uses space as a primary means to locate, track, and target aircraft carriers, for example, debilitating those capabilities in defense of aircraft carriers may be a higher priority than keeping space weapons-free. Consequently, China's ambition to achieve space control must be considered not just in satellites potentially lost but in U.S. personnel put at risk.

Notes

1. Cai Fengzhen and Tian Anping, 空天战杨与中国空军 [*The Aerospace Battlefield and China's Air Force*] (Beijing: Liberation Army Press, 2004), 36.

2. Chang Xianqi, 军事航天学 [*Military Astronautics*] (Beijing: National Defense Industry Press, 2002), 213.

3. "Space Warfare," in *Chinese PLA Military Encyclopedia*, CD-ROM edition (Beijing: Academy of Military Science, 1997).

4. Hong Bing and Liang Xiaoqiu, "The Basics of Space Strategic Theory," 中国军事科学 [*China Military Science*] 1 (2002): 23.

5. Chang, *Military Astronautics*, 147–48.

6. Ibid., 282–83.

7. Ibid., vi.

8. Information Office of the State Council of the People's Republic of China, *China's National Defense*, December 2006.

9. Peng Guangqian and Yao Youzhi, 战略学 [*The Science of Military Strategy*] (Beijing: Military Science Press, 2001), 358.

10. Wang Wen and Huang Duanxin, "A Preliminary Discussion of Several Operational Command Requirements for Integrated Joint Operations," 战士报 [*Soldier News*], 7 April 2005, 3.

11. Chen Huan, "The Third Military Revolution," in *Chinese Views of Future Warfare*, ed., Michael Pillsbury (Washington, DC: National Defense University Press, 1998), 393.

12. Mao Zedong, *Selected Military Writings of Mao Zedong* (Beijing: Foreign Languages Press, 1967), 105.

13. Liu Zhenwu, "论国家安全与积极防御战略" ["National Security and the Active Defense Strategy"], 军事学术 [*Military Art Journal*], no. 4 (2004): 9.

14. Ibid.

15. Lu Linzhi, "Preemptive Strikes Are Crucial in Limited High-Tech Wars," *Liberation Army Daily*, 7 February 1996.

16. Wang Mingliang, "信息化战争特征简析" ["An Analysis of the Features of Information Warfare"], 中国军事科学 [*China Military Science*], no. 1 (2005): 25–26.

17. He Dingqing, 战役学教程 [*A Course on the Science of Campaigns*] (Beijing: Military Science Press, 2001), 244–45.

18. Zhang Xingye, "论联合战役指导的若干重要思想" ["Several Important Ideologies on Joint Campaign Guidance"], in 联合作战中的指挥自动化系统建设 [*Joint Operation's Command Automation System Building*] (Beijing: The Naval Equipment Demonstration Research Center Command Automation Research Institute, 2002), 141.

19. Chang, *Military Astronautics*, 257–58.

20. Xu Qing, "空间信息对抗能力与技术需求" ["Space Information Confrontation Capabilities and Technical Requirements"], 航天电子对抗 [*Aerospace Electronic Warfare*], no. 4 (2006).

21. Cai and Tian, *Aerospace Battlefield*, 201.

22. Chen Xuan and Wang Jiasheng, "美国天基信息系统发展与未来网络中心战" ["Development of Space-Based Information System in the U.S. and Network Centric Warfare in the Future"], 航天电子对抗 [*Aerospace Electronic Warfare*], no. 6 (2007): 20.

23. Zhu Bin and Chen Xuan, "基于天基信息系统的远程精确打击" ["Long-Range Precision Attack Based on Space-Based Information System"], 中国航天 [*Aerospace China*], no. 3 (2007): 27.

24. Wu Xiaopeng, Feng Shuxing, Zhang Yan, and He Zhonglong, "剖析一体化联合作战对空间力量的信息需求" ["Anatomizing the Integrative Joint Operations Information Requirement for the Space Force"], 装备指挥技术学院学报 [*Journal of the Academy of Equipment Command and Technology*], no. 6 (2006): 44.

25. Pan Changpeng, Gu Wenjin, and Chen Jie, "军事卫星对反船导弹攻防作战的职员能力分析" ["Analysis of the Capabilities of Military Satellite Support of Anti-Ship Missiles in Offensive and Defensive Operations"], 飞航导弹 [*Winged Missiles Journal*] (May 2006): 13.

26. Gao Qingjun, "高技术局部战争航天侦查的特点和局限性" ["Characteristics and Deficiencies of Space Reconnaissance in High-tech Local Wars"], 装备指挥技术学院学报 [*Journal of the Academy of Equipment Command and Technology*] (February 2006): 55.

27. Yan Liwei and Yang Jianjun, "反卫星武器装备发展探讨" ["An Exploration of Anti-Satellite Weapon Development"], 飞航导弹 [*Winged Missiles Journal*] (December 2004): 46.

28. Chang, *Military Astronautics*, 259–60.

29. Ibid., 226.

30. Ibid., 260.

31. Yan and Yang, "Exploration of Anti-Satellite Weapon Development," 46.

32. Zhao Shuang, Zhang Shexin, Fang Youpei, and Wang Liping, "Research on the Status and Development of the U.S. and Russia's Space Target Surveillance," 航天电子对抗 [*Aerospace Electronic Warfare*], no. 1 (2008): 27.

33. Chang, *Military Astronautics*, 295–96.

34. Qi Xianfeng, "空间信息系统防护探讨" ["Study on the Protection of Space Information System"], 装备指挥技术学院学报 [*Journal of the Academy of Equipment Command and Technology*], no. 5 (2007): 62.

35. Cai and Tian, *Aerospace Battlefield*, 28.

36. Ibid., 172.

37. Ibid., 173.

38. Chang, *Military Astronautics*, 273–74.

39. Ibid., 258.

40. Ibid., 48–49.

41. Ibid., 118–19.

42. Ibid., 123 and 145.

43. Cai and Tian, *Aerospace Battlefield*, 131 and 123.

44. Chang, *Military Astronautics*, 277.

45. Ibid., 292.

46. Ibid., 293.

47. Ibid., 294.

48. Ibid., 295.

49. Ibid.

50. Cai and Tian, *Aerospace Battlefield*, 146.

51. Zhao Xijun, ed., 导弹威慑纵横谈 [*A Comprehensive Review of Missile Deterrence*] (Beijing: National Defense University Press, 2003), 2.

52. Ibid., 1–2.

53. Ibid., 4.

54. Ibid., 12.

55. Ibid., 12–13.

56. Ibid., 6.

57. Yuan Zelu, 联合战役太空作战 [*Space Warfare of the Joint Campaign*] (Beijing: National Defense University Press, 2005), 43.

58. Ibid., 43.

59. 孙海洋 [Sun Haiyang] (Second Artillery Command College) and 常金安 [Chang Jin'an] (Second Artillery Command College), "军事威慑的新形势- 淘空威慑" ["A New Type of Military Deterrence—Space Deterrence"], 军事学术 [*Military Art Journal*] 10 (2003): 33.

60. Sun Haiyang and Chang Jin'an, "军事威慑的新形势—淘空威慑" ["A New Type of Military Deterrence—Space Deterrence"], 军事学术 [*Military Art Journal*], no. 10 (2003): 33.

61. Wang Kongyang, "国际外层空间法和国内外层空间法的关系" ["The Relationship between International Space Law and Domestic Space Law"], 中国航天 [*Aerospace China*], no. 11 (2006).

62. Yuan, *Space Warfare of the Joint Campaign*, 30.

.

PART II

Chinese ISR and Counter-ISR

Anthony J. Mastalir

The PRC Challenge to U.S. Space Assets

In a manner itself paradoxical, it is those who are materially weaker, and therefore have good reason to fear a straightforward clash of strength against strength, who can most benefit by self-weakening paradoxical conduct—if it obtains the advantage of surprise, which may yet offer victory.

—*Edward N. Luttwak*

FOLLOWING THE 11 JANUARY 2011 four-year anniversary of China's first successful antisatellite (ASAT) test and one-year anniversary of its first successful missile intercept test, it is not readily apparent whether U.S. civilian and military leaders are any closer to gleaning China's overall strategic intent vis-à-vis the acquisition of space weaponry. Four years after its first ASAT test, China still offers no answers to one of the most troubling strategic space questions of the twenty-first century: why is China building space weapons?

The United States, and the rest of the world, must accept that it may be a long time before the answer to this question becomes clear—if that ever happens at all. What is the best solution set for the United States to pursue? President George W. Bush wanted to know, as his successor, President Barack Obama, undoubtedly does. Bush reportedly issued a classified memo to various government agencies in the months following China's ASAT demonstration. The memo directed the State and Defense departments to form "a cohesive government-wide approach both to avoid future anti-satellite launches and formulate plans on how to deal with them if they occur."[1] The assignment is not an easy task, especially since China's intentions are unclear. Nonetheless, President Bush's choice of the word "cohesive" and his decision to include the State Department were most appropriate. In his manuscript on grand strategy, Edward Luttwak wrote of the importance of coherence, in both the horizontal and vertical dimensions. He argued that military efforts, even if well integrated vertically, will likely fail or become counterproductive if horizontal disharmony exists across, for example, other instruments of national power. Luttwak notes, "There are cases of weapons successful at all military levels but counterproductive at the level of grand strategy because they fail in the horizontal dimension. German pre-1914 battleships were wonderfully advanced and did well in combat, but all they ever gained for Germany was Britain's lethal hostilities . . . a wholly predictable result."[2]

Contextual Basis

The challenge for U.S. planners, therefore, is to assemble a U.S. response that not only addresses the strategic issue posed by an ASAT-armed China but also achieves both vertical and horizontal harmony. A forensic review of open-source Chinese literature—including the spoken and written words of China's military scholars, strategists, political leaders, and international diplomats—offers both keen insights regarding the issues upon which internal Chinese policy deliberations focus and the following contextual basis and attendant assumptions:[3]

- China's ascendance to regional superpower status is increasingly dependent on the preservation of its freedom of action throughout the global commons. China envisions a multipolar global security environment in which it exerts significant influence over international policy decisions. Its desire for national prestige and international relevance intensely shapes internal decision-making processes. Space power is perceived to be a key enabler of the attainment of China's long-term vision.

- China is making steady progress toward becoming a major space power. Its unprecedented economic growth has sustained a military modernization program making rapid advancements in nearly all aspects of warfare, most notably space-based effects. Its national leaders have embraced a revolution in military affairs, with space capabilities at the core, and they hope to further China's international prestige by implementing a robust space doctrine.

- China's emerging space doctrine is the driving force behind its efforts to develop antisatellite weapons. The People's Liberation Army (PLA) along with its closely associated research and development academies perceives a significant advantage in developing the capabilities to conduct space warfare.

- Strategically, China's military planners and strategist believe ASATs are a critical element of a robust space deterrent that can further protect China's nuclear and conventional deterrents against emerging threats such as U.S. ballistic missile defense (BMD) programs. Doctrinally, China places a premium on deterrence strategies and will relentlessly pursue the requisite capabilities to protect it from coercion or blackmail. The antisatellite test communicated unequivocally that China has a direct-ascent antisatellite capability and is willing to use it—thereby fulfilling all the criteria for a credible deterrent strategy.

Attendant Assumptions

From these conclusions about the overall context of China's ASAT test, it is possible to make three basic assumptions:

Assumption 1:
China appreciates the strategic deterrent value of antisatellite weapons.
Whether by design or not, China realizes that its ASAT test represents some measure of deterrent value. If Beijing meant to send a message, it aimed it at U.S. leaders supporting BMD and possible intervention in a Taiwan crisis. China's subsequent actions will indicate which model of strategic deterrence it has decided to follow.

Assumption 2:
China aspires for greater relevance within the international space community.
China believes it has attained a new level of status among the space-faring nations. The PRC is still looking for new ways to expand its cooperation and influence in international space politics.[4] Following on the heels of its successful manned-space program, its antisatellite demonstration places it among the three top space-faring nations that have successfully knocked a satellite out of orbit. The implication is that China must now be recognized as a major contributor toward any future discussions on the space environment.

Assumption 3:
*China believes space weapons are an obvious prerequisite to becoming
a major space power.*

China appears to have the political will, national resources, and technological elements necessary to become a major space power. China's emerging military space doctrine is informed by its time-honored precepts of asymmetric strategy, a pervasive sense of technonationalism, and a new revolution in military affairs aimed at propelling the PLA into the age of informatized warfare. With these assumptions in mind, it is time to explore Beijing's development of space weapons.

China's Space Weapons

> *During the Ming Dynasty, China once possessed the most formidable sea supremacy, which was capable of altering the history of the world, but gave it up through inattention, which led to China's decline in modern times. In the current space race, China will not easily allow its space power to lose its development direction, because history will not give a second-rate country which has lost in a military confrontation in space and which can only acknowledge allegiance to the space superiority of others another chance to stand up.*[5]
>
> —Gao Yan

Prior to the 2007 ASAT test, there was scant open-source evidence directly attributing an operational space weapons system to China. Nevertheless, numerous open-source publications support the notion that the direct-ascent ASAT is likely part of a larger Chinese space weapons program that includes ground-based lasers and electromagnetic jammers. Moreover, Chinese analysts, scientists, and strategists have written extensively about ASAT weapons as a potential means of countering U.S. military uses of space.

In China, preliminary research on antisatellite capabilities has been carried out since the 1980s, at least partly funded under the 863 Program for High Technology Development. Li Daguang's *Space Warfare* (2001) delineates a plan for China's space weapon development. Li suggests two stages of development, with the first extending to 2010 and the second extending to 2025. During the second phase, Li asserts, "we should build on the foundation of the first stage by further improving our offensive and defensive capability of space weapon systems. In particular, the offense capability in space should, if necessary, be capable of destroying or temporarily incapacitating all enemy space vehicles that fly in space above our sovereign territory. . . . In the short run, the key developments should be anti-satellites weapons including land-based anti-satellite weapons and anti-satellite satellites."[6]

In *Military Astronautics*, Luo Xiaoming outlines three approaches to ASAT warfare: the use of satellites against other satellites, the use of missiles against satellites, and the use of lasers against satellites. Numerous other articles have made similar contributions to the collective works advocating the development of ASAT weaponry. A 2004 manuscript proposes that China build orbital ballistic missiles, "a new-concept strategic ballistic missile that is a multi-task, multi-role attack weapon capable of implementing random orbit transfer from earth orbits and can serve the function of an intercontinental ballistic missile, an anti-satellite weapon, and an orbital bomber weapon."[7] In *Space Warfare of the Joint Campaign*, Colonel Yuan Zelu describes in detail the requirements to launch a space-based fire net once armed conflict becomes imminent. Yuan refers to ongoing research and developments efforts to build space-based kinetic-energy and directed-energy weapons, but he also warns that premature orbital deployment of such systems would expose future battle plans unnecessarily.[8] Furthermore, at least ten other recent studies regarding the development of kinetic-kill vehicles have been published by technical authors at some of China's most prominent technical institutions.[9]

The Chinese literature defining the research and development objectives associated with directed-energy weapons is impressive. Since 1995 more than twenty authors have detailed their research on directed energy or beam weapons as part of a larger class of weapons known to the Chinese as "new concept weapons" (*xin gainian wuqi*), which include high-power lasers, high-power microwaves, railguns, and particle beam weapons.[10] It is apparent that the PRC has not only shown high interest in developing directed-energy weapons, but more practically, it has invested heavily in the development of such weapons.[11] Chinese aerospace analysts view ground-based, high-powered lasers—able to degrade or destroy satellites at all altitudes, including medium and geosynchronous orbits—as an alternative to kinetic-kill vehicles. Directed-energy ASAT weapons are touted as the wave of the future.[12]

China's 11 January 2010 ground-based midcourse missile intercept test is likely an adaptation of its antisatellite program, as both use similar technologies. However, the exact relationship between China's space weaponry programs and its missile defense programs is unclear. Senior Chinese military officers have recently underscored the need for China to advance its missile defense technologies to field, as some analysts predict, a nation-wide missile defense system by the mid-2020s.[13] Interestingly, the international reaction following China's 2010 missile defense test has been relatively insignificant compared to the global condemnation that followed its 2007 antisatellite test, which suggests that China may face less international scrutiny if it simply identifies its programs accordingly.

The January 2007 ASAT test and the January 2010 missile defense test apparently represent milestones in what is likely a wide-ranging space weaponry development strategy. The evidence suggests that China is actively pursuing the research and development of the technologies necessary for advanced space weapons; however, only time will tell if Beijing plans to take the next step toward operational deployment.

U.S. Space Protection Strategy

The best U.S. response to China's antisatellite demonstration is one that properly aligns the U.S. instruments of national power to produce an enduring, coherent, multilateral approach toward space power. Fundamental changes in the way the United States approaches national security space are long overdue. China's test must serve to demarcate the end of failed American assumptions vis-à-vis the nation's future competitive edge in space. Diplomatically, the U.S. must extract the previously ignored kernels of soft power inherent in its dominant national security space enterprise. A new international security space alliance could enhance the security and influence of all like-minded space-faring nations. Finally, America's military forces must attend to the immediate crisis: critical lack of space situational awareness. In concert with the aforementioned policy changes, the U.S. military must take the lead in charting the international security space alliance. By implementing a shared space-surveillance strategy, military commanders can set standards for interoperability and shape the requirements process for all participating nations. As retired Air Force general Lance Lord often observed, "Space superiority is not America's birthright, but it can be its destiny."[14] However, it is no longer clear that America should pursue its destiny alone.

The Political/Diplomatic Dimension

The art of policy is to create a calculation of the risks and rewards that affect the adversary's calculation.[15]

—*Henry Kissinger*

U.S. diplomatic relations with China have long been bipolar, alternating between containment and engagement.[16] For instance, the Department of

Defense 2010 assessment of China's military warns that "the Department of Defense has a special responsibility to monitor China's military and to deter conflict" but quotes President Obama as stating that "the notion that we must be adversaries is not pre-destined."[17] Sir Lawrence Freedman maintains that throughout the Cold War, policy experts relied on containment strategies to counter the assumption that communism was naturally expansionist and so could only be held through the threat of force. "Containment as an objective lent itself to deterrence as a method," he wrote.[18] However, it was the policy of engagement, which peaked in the 1990s, that has propelled economic global-ization and has made China one of the United States' top trading partners. The result has been a hedging strategy that continues to expose a variety of incon-sistencies and vertical disharmony in America's foreign policy conduct.

Space as an Element of Soft Power

One aspect of America's foreign policy that is arguably undervalued is what Joseph Nye calls soft power. According to Nye, "Soft power is the ability to get what you want through attraction rather than coercion or payments. It arises from the attractiveness of a country's culture, political ideals, and policies."[19] The concept of soft power is readily apparent in the way China has managed its rise to power. For example, one of China's most influential modern lead-ers, Deng Xiaoping, instilled in his foreign policy apparatus the "24 charac-ter strategy": "observe calmly; secure our position; cope with affairs calmly; hide our capacities and bide our time; be good at maintaining a low profile; and never claim leadership."[20] However, Chinese officials deliberately exclude Deng's maxim from publicly circulated leadership speeches and documents to avoid stimulating additional concerns abroad that China will pose a threat once it becomes powerful. The same appreciation for soft power was evident in China's decision to reject the term "peaceful rise" in favor of the less threaten-ing term "peaceful development" in April 2004.[21]

The United States derives its soft power from many sources, yet foreign policy decisions seem all too often to generate counterproductive results. Furthermore, space has relevance to soft power that is often overlooked by policymakers. Simon Worden, director of the NASA Ames Research Center explains, "I recall when I worked for the national space council at the White House. They ignored us most of the time but whenever the President was going to talk with somebody, it could be Botswana, and they didn't have anything to talk about they could always talk about space. It's became a real positive entrée."[22] Worden argues that the most intensive and impressive application of space, as an element of soft power, is not supporting the warfighter but preventing wars. He concludes, "Until we figure out how to do that and how to work with other people we're going to have an increasing problem. Others are only going to take advantage of it."[23]

International Security Space Alliance

China's military modernization efforts in space, punctuated by its 2007 antisatellite demonstration, provide an opportunity for the United States to shape an international alliance of like-minded, space-faring nations. Given the universally negative reaction to China's actions, an opportunity exists to form an international security space alliance. The benefits of such an alliance are numerous. The United States could offer enticements, such as unprecedented access to its extensive space network, fewer restrictions on technology exports, and increased access to other space products. In return, the United States could negotiate standards for collectively acquired and shared space systems. Such systems could eventually include missile warning/defense, communication, navigation, remote sensing, and space surveillance capabilities.

As an instrument of policy, U.S. leaders must carefully consider the advantages and disadvantages of increasing partnership capacity in each national security space mission area. For example, a shared-source, multilateral space surveillance network distributed among alliance partners could achieve several objectives. Real-time data about the location of all space objects would decrease tensions about the purpose and activities of each nation's spacecraft. Future technologies will enable a robust space surveillance network to characterize attacks from within the space domain as well as terrestrial-based attacks. The real-time capability to detect and geolocate directed-energy attacks from the ground, for example, would be a powerful deterrent against any who might consider such hostile acts. One risk inherent in any U.S. response is what Robert Jervis calls the "security dilemma." Essentially, the security dilemma is a series of reactions whereby each adversary takes measures to counteract the other. In other words, if China builds ASATs, the United States must build counter-ASATs, and so forth. In offering suggestions to break out from a security dilemma, Jervis writes, "One way to do this is to procure the kinds and numbers of weapons that are useful for deterrence without simultaneously being as effective for aggression."[24] Since space surveillance alone does not pose the same threat as missile defense or offensive space control, it could serve as the nonaggressive form of deterrence that Jervis describes.

The only legitimate answer to the question of why this will work is increased security, and the North Atlantic Treaty Organization serves as an appropriate model.[25] In 2008 NATO celebrated its sixtieth anniversary, demonstrating an enduring capacity more impressive than the Outer Space Treaty of 1967. Encouraging nations to participate during the Cold War was relatively simple; the Soviets represented a common threat that unified the members of the alliance. Likewise, the modern-day proliferation of space weaponry, missile technology, and even nuclear weapons represents an increasing threat to all space systems. After the Cold War, many international security analysts believed NATO's future was uncertain, but NATO transformed to accept a broader scope of international engagement. Its continued involvement in Kosovo and Afghanistan demonstrate its enduring capacity to increase security for its member nations.

The continued relevance of the International Telecommunications Union (ITU) is another example of the enduring nature of organizations that effectively enhance security. The ITU traces its roots back to the nineteenth century, when international telegraph standards first became necessary. Today, the ITU is an office within the United Nations that governs orbital slot assignments in the geostationary belt and performs frequency deconfliction. The ITU has no formal mechanism to enforce its standards, but space-faring nations comply to protect against interference from other satellites. As attorney and author Lawrence Roberts notes,

> Legitimacy of a legal structure has a powerful impact on efficiency. Like most international legal regimes, the ITU does not have the authority to enforce its rulings directly; it is dependent upon its own legitimacy to influence the behavior of its Members. As a consequence, the ITU's effectiveness is bound up in the Member's perception of the process's efficacy. As perceptions of legitimacy decline, the tendency increases for individual Members to act in their own short-term best interest, rather than in accordance with a legal system that, under ideal conditions, maximizes community benefit over the long-term.[26]

The issue of legitimacy shapes the answer to the question of how this will work, which becomes more palatable when one accepts that an international space alliance is neither a dovish nor hawkish approach to national security space. The debates regarding the U.S. development of defensive and offensive space weapons must continue; after all, most NATO nations continue to build military capacity in excess of those forces each intends to contribute toward collective operations. Rather, the alliance would bring legitimacy and influence to the international dialogue that continues to shape responsible nations' activities in space. The very act of drafting an alliance charter and determining its conditions for entry provides member nations a platform to promulgate international norms for behavior. Would an international space alliance include a NATO-like Article 5 provision that states an attack on one member is an attack on all? Perhaps it should, if the members believe such a provision would enhance security. But more important than a unified response to a space attack is the deterrent value in the assurance that every member of the alliance will know immediately when an attack in space has occurred, and by whom, and against whom.

A truly cooperative approach to national security space will require policy endorsement from the highest level. Currently, too many policies prohibit the kind of information sharing that would be necessary to make an international space alliance a reality. Technology export laws and security classification guidelines remain significant hurdles. However, the United States has the most to lose; therefore, it must have the most to offer others in exchange for cooperation. The increased security derived from shared space surveillance data may be the catalyst for an international space alliance.

The Military Dimension

You can look at somebody's motives and say, "There's no real intent that I'm aware of that they want to do me harm." But if they've got the capability to do me harm, as a warfighter, that's what I've got to respect—because intent can change overnight. As the capability evolves on the part of the people who would want to do us harm in space, you've got to stay ahead of them.[27]

—*Air Force Major General William Shelton*

General Shelton's edict in the epigraph above reflects his warfighting pedigree. As a military strategist, he understands which capabilities the United States needs to defend against potential military adversaries. Of course, the salient question becomes, how? If indeed the U.S. military will one day conduct combat operations in space, as Shelton suggests, then what national security space strategy can successfully parlay America's limited resources into the proper force structure necessary to protect the nation?

The situation has all the makings of the classic security dilemma discussed previously. ASATs represent a relatively simple, cost-effective option to counter what Chinese military leaders describe as an expanding U.S. space hegemony—a perception pervasive throughout Chinese strategy circles. In response, U.S. military leaders interpret China's actions as overtly threatening, and implement measures to sustain America's hegemonic status. Within days of China's demonstration, Air Force Secretary Michael Wynne declared, "Space is no longer a sanctuary; that veil has now been pierced. . . . Freedom of space is crucial and the Chinese, wittingly or not, have sent a message that our guard must be stronger. . . . This change is seismic in nature. The recent Chinese test marks the turning point in the work our country must do to assure space dominance."[28]

Military leaders have suggested the "work" begins by developing a robust level of space situational awareness. In his 2007 written testimony to Congress, General James Cartwright explained, "Historically, space situational awareness (SSA) was focused on the cataloging, tracking, and monitoring of objects in space via the space surveillance network. Today it is clear we must have better space detection, characterization, and assessment tools. We require capabilities that enable rapid threat identification and attribution, facilitate a defensible architecture and provide fundamental shifts in space awareness."[29] Days earlier, Air Force general Kevin P. Chilton, commander of Air Force Space Command testified, "Today, our surveillance, analysis and data-sharing capabilities do not adequately support our future needs to rapidly identify and understand the threats to our space systems."[30] In truth, U.S. military leaders had long before identified the critical need for space situational awareness. As General Shelton describes it, "It's a work in progress . . . [but] the Chinese ASAT test put us on a much more rapid path than before."[31]

Shared Space Surveillance

The shared space surveillance (SSS) policy changes offer exciting options in the military dimension, and military leaders must consider teaming with other space-faring allies to form an international security space alliance. For the military's part, uniformed leaders must play an active role in beginning a dialogue with allied military leaders from around the world. Twenty-eight foreign militaries currently operate in space, and each one has a vested interest in protecting its assets on orbit.

The concept is not significantly different from one the U.S. Navy is considering. Faced with a dynamic operating environment and scarce resources, Admiral Michael Mullen, then chief of naval operations, envisioned in 2005 a "thousand ship navy"—an allied fleet of ships working collectively to police the world's blue waters and ensure viable sea lines of communication to every nation's benefit. A "thousand sensor SSS system" may produce the type of capability commanders will need to police space, even if fiscal limitations preclude the unilateral employment of such a system. A notional space surveillance architecture generated within the Pentagon suggests a need for sensors performing three distinct mission sets: routine surveillance, tactical surveillance, and tactical imaging. Through the employment of a variety of electro-optical and radar sensors, the SSA architecture must surveil both prograde and retrograde space objects launched from the world's major spaceports. Furthermore, a truly meaningful architecture must include a robust complement of space-based assets to surveil and image objects in both low-earth and geosynchronous orbits. The plan was labeled "Threshold Unconstrained Clean Sheet SSN," which suggests the Pentagon understands that current fiscal realities preclude such a plan from ever coming to fruition. The space-based component alone would bankrupt the Future Years Defense Program. For example, as depicted in figure 1, up to ten super synchronous-based, electro-optical satellites may be necessary to maintain law and order throughout the geosynchronous belt, with another seven traversing through geosynchronous and low-earth orbits.

When applied to the issue of space protection, the "thousand sensor architecture" means every allied ground and space-based SSA platform could potentially form an integrated system of systems designed to keep "space lines of communication" open to all who contribute. One construct worth considering is the existing Shared Early-Warning System (SEWS), because it may be a logical starting point for a multilateral acquisition program. The concept of shared early warning came about toward the end of the 1990s, when concerns over Russia's plummeting level of military readiness raised concerns about its ability to command and control its nuclear missile arsenal. The goal was increased transparency. The United States agreed to share the critical missile warning data it received via satellite remote sensing and radar to remove any ambiguity that might otherwise cloud the judgment of Russian command and control centers. Robert G. Bell, a senior aide on the National Security Council at the time, explained, "The agreement provides further protection against an inadvertent nuclear exchange triggered by misidentification of a launch."[32] As discussed previously, increased security remains the key to establishing an enduring architecture.

Top military officials admit such a plan has merit. General Chilton, commander of USSTRATCOM, testified that the United States "must continue to foster collaborative data-sharing with our allies to enhance global coverage. . . . The ability to leverage and expand space partnerships with our allies holds the potential to dramatically improve Space Situational Awareness."[33] Just weeks earlier at a conference in Washington, DC, General C. Robert Kehler sug-

Figure 1: Notional Space Surveillance Architecture

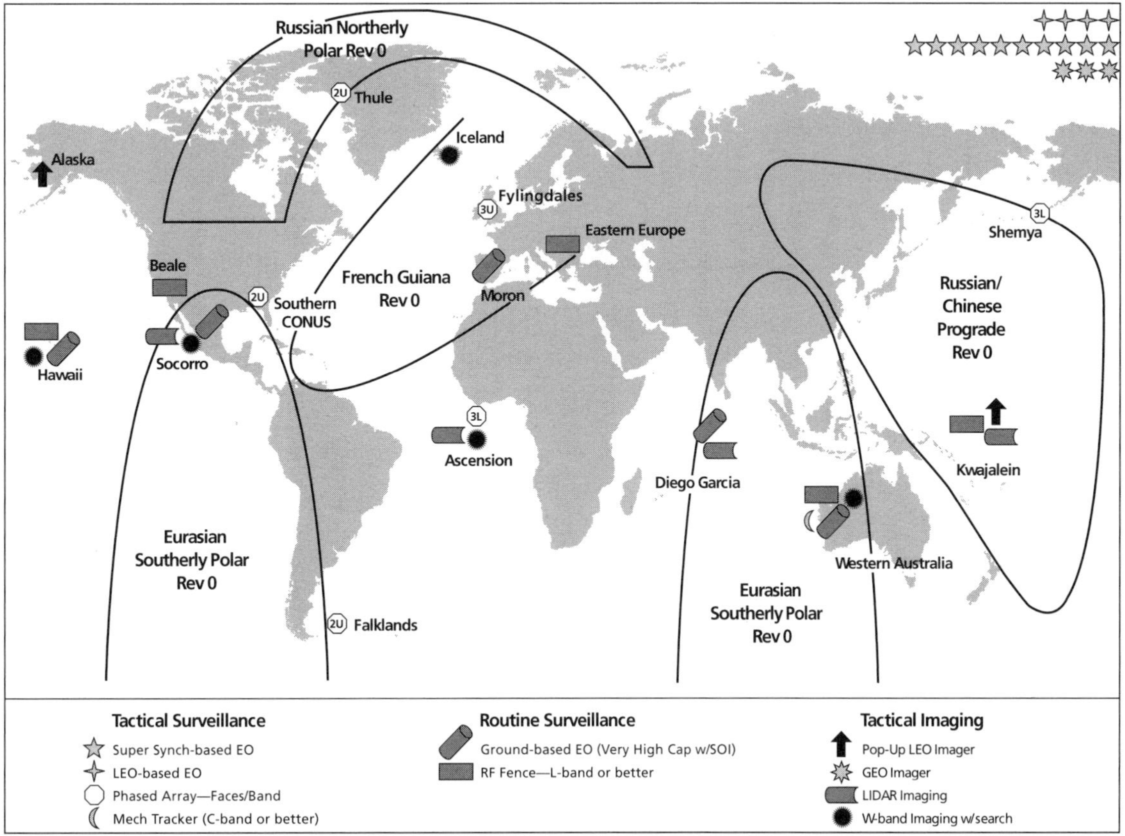

gested that it might be time to rethink America's approach to national security space and consider the role other space-faring partners might play in an integrated framework. He mused, "I don't think we've gone about this in the past with an underlying assumption that says we want to include allies and international partners as a core piece of how we conduct our national security business with space capabilities. I think that has to change. Much like we have had alliance and coalition agreements with all of our other elements of our national security power, I think that it's important for us to pursue as an objective when it comes to our space capabilities as well."[34] Kehler noted that Australia's decision to purchase a Wideband Global SATCOM satellite and become part of the U.S. military satellite communications architecture represents a very positive step toward an allied space force. "That one step that they have taken speaks volumes about a way for us to do business in the future," he observed.[35]

Leaders like General Kehler believe the old way of doing business is a poor strategy for future success. In other words, innovative ideas and new strategies and doctrine will be necessary to meet future requirements. Stephen Rosen suggests that military planners are "driven to consider the need for innovation by broad structural changes in the security environment in which their organizations would have to fight for the foreseeable future, not by specific capabilities or intentions of potential adversaries."[36] The implication is that senior leaders must recognize the Chinese ASAT test not as an isolated event, merely attributable to one nation, but as a structural shift toward space being a contested environment. In this context, a space alliance may prove to be the innovative strategy necessary to ensure national security.

Space leaders must also acknowledge the inherent deterrent value in sharing space surveillance with a global audience. General Shelton explains, "If our adversaries know that we know what's going on in orbit, then they're going to be constrained."[37] To this end, the United States ought to consider including China as a space surveillance partner. China's ambitious plans in space will continue to drive requirements for an increasingly sophisticated space surveillance network. Furthermore, China's overall economic growth continues to climb at an unprecedented rate, surpassed only by the rate at which China has increased defense spending. If major space-faring nations express interest in an international space alliance designed to ensure collectively the protection of global space assets through shared awareness, there is little doubt China will want to join. Beijing's desire for international prestige and relevance takes precedence over its desire to become a major space power, and from Beijing's perspective, the latter enables the former. As General Kehler notes, "When you get better situational awareness; when you have the capability to attribute; our view is that you are enhancing deterrence. It is becoming clearer to all that there's not a way to make an on orbit activity look like an anomaly or a technical problem. It informs what a whole range of response options might be."[38] Consequently, the United States' best option in response to China's space weapons program may be to join together to lift the veil of obscurity shadowing orbital operations.

Conclusion

Shortly after the Chinese ASAT demonstration, at a World Economy Forum dinner in Davos, Switzerland, Senior Colonel Yao Yunzhu of the PLA's Academy of Military Science issued a not-so-veiled warning when she stated that if there's going to be "a space superpower, it's not going to be alone. . . . It will have company."[39] This was a rather frank statement, considering the setting; nonetheless, it underscores China's determination to achieve parity among the world's elite space-faring nations.

To better appreciate China's pursuit of advanced space weaponry, one need only consider what these capabilities bring to China, as opposed to what they might take away from an adversary. First, China's growing potential toward realizing space elitism carries with it a tremendously high level of prestige for the largest "developing" country in the world. Toshi Yoshihara and William Martel argue that "China's obsession with national prestige, which forms the backdrop for its commercial and military interests, also animates the country's space policy. The PRC government has long boasted about its status as one of the few major space-faring nations."[40]

Second, it gives China sovereign options to control naval activity out to the Second Island Chain. A focus of Chinese concern has been on the security of the sea lines of communication upon which almost all of China's energy imports travel. China's strategists are aware that they do not exercise naval superiority through the seas linking their ports to the major oil producers in the Middle East, and that they remain dependent upon the willingness of other major powers not to disrupt their imports. One of their goals is to be able to use satellite reconnaissance systems and tracking and data exchange to have a Second Artillery antiship ballistic missile with a precision-guided maneuvering reentry vehicle strike a deployed U.S. carrier strike group.

Third, as China's burgeoning military space strategy begins to exert influence around the world, U.S. space hegemony begins to fade—as does its relative potency as a global superpower. Chinese writings suggest that the post–

Cold War balance of power has become "one superpower, many strong powers" (*yi chao duo qiang*) or "one pole, many powers" (*yi ji duo qiang*), with the latter able to check the former.[41] Beijing's vision for China is to attain regional superpower status in a global, multipolar (*duojihua*) security environment. As Su Enze, professor of the PLA Air Force Command Academy said, "We are not going to participate in a full-fledged space arms race . . . but we shall not avoid the choice of answering the challenges from others. . . . We should concentrate our resources, increase the investment and produce something with real deterrent as soon as possible in order to safeguard our national security and status as a great power in the 21st Century."[42]

The best possible U.S. response to China's military space strategy is one that energizes and harmonizes all U.S. instruments of national power. The disharmony in U.S. foreign policy toward China has been one source of the distrust that continues to handicap relations across the Pacific Ocean, and national security space is stalled in a paradigm no longer useful to adequately shape the global environment. A new, multilateral international security space alliance is one possible option for like-minded, space-faring nations to prepare for operations in the contested environment of space.

Shared space surveillance has the potential to underpin a space protection strategy for all alliance members. Significant change will require horizontal integration across the instruments of power, but the onus is on the U.S. military to begin the process by pursuing possible solutions with like-minded, space-faring nations and to present options to its civilian leaders. Space superiority can be America's destiny, but U.S. space forces must be prepared to achieve it with coalition partners, as do their air, land, sea, and undersea counterparts.

Notes

This chapter is adapted from Anthony Mastalir, *The U.S. Response to China's ASAT Test: An International Security Space Alliance for the Future* (Maxwell AFB, AL: Air University Press, 2009).

1. Amy Butler, "Bush Memo Orders Space Situational Awareness," *Aerospace Daily and Defense Report*, 12 October 2007.

2. Edward N. Luttwak, *Strategy: The Logic of War and Peace* (Cambridge, MA: Belknap Press of Harvard University Press, 2001), 259.

3. See Anthony J. Mastalir, "China's ASAT Test: Motivation with Chinese Characteristics" (Naval War College, 18 May 2007), 113–16.

4. Phillip C. Saunders and Charles Lutes, "China's ASAT Test: Motivations and Implications," National Defense University Institute for National Strategic Studies, Washington, DC, 7 March 2007. Published in *Joint Force Quarterly*, no. 46 (3rd quarter 2007): 39–45, http://www.dtic.mil/cgi-bin/GetTRDoc?AD=ADA517485&Location =U2&doc=GetTRDoc.pdf.

5. Gao Yan, "China Must Need to Become a Space Power May Lead to Confrontation with U.S.," *Kuang Chiao Ching*, no. 358 (16 July 2002): 10–13, OSC CPP20020719000040.

6. Li Daguang, 太空战 [*Space Warfare*] (Beijing: Military Science Press, 2001), 413–14.

7. Zhao Ruian, "The Concept of Orbital Ballistic Missiles," *Zhongguo Hangtian* [*Aerospace China*] (January 2004).

8. Yuan Zelu, *Space Warfare of the Joint Campaign* (Beijing: National Defense University Press, 2005), 41.

9. Michael P. Pillsbury, "An Assessment of China's Anti-Satellite and Space Warfare Programs, Policies and Doctrines," Report for the U.S.–China Economic and Security Review Commission, 19 January 2007, http://www.uscc.gov/researchpapers/2007/ FINAL_REPORT_1-19-2007_REVISED_BY_MPP.pdf.

10. Ibid.

11. Tseng Ming-yi, "An Investigation into the Status of the PRC in Developing Directed-energy Weapons," *Kuo-fang Tsa-chih* [*National Defense Magazine*] (January 2007).

12. Yang Chunfu and Liu Xiao'en, "Study on the Developmental Prospects for ASAT Weapons," *Aerospace Information Research*, HQ-93005, CASC 707 Institute, 77.

13. Bill Gertz, "Beijing Reports Successful 'Defensive' Missile Test," *Washington Times*, 12 January 2010, http://www.washingtontimes.com/news/2010/jan/12/beijing-reports -successful-missile-test/.

14. General Lance W. Lord (Commander, Air Force Space Command, Peterson AFB, CO), discussion with the author, 6 April 2006, Colorado Springs, CO.

15. Quoted in Frank C. Zagare and D. Marc Kilgour, *Perfect Deterrence* (Cambridge, MA: Cambridge University Press, 2000), 20.

16. John Feffer, "China: What's the Big Mystery?" *Foreign Policy in Focus*, 4 December 2006, http://www.fpif.org/articles/china_whats_the_big_mystery.

17. Office of the Secretary of Defense (DoD), *Military and Security Developments Involving the People's Republic of China 2010*, Annual Report to Congress (Washington, DC: Office of the Secretary of Defense, 16 August 2010), http://www .defense.gov/pubs/pdfs/2010_CMPR_Final.pdf, p. I.

18. Lawrence Freedman, *Deterrence* (Malden, MA: Polity Press, 2004), 11.

19. Joseph S. Nye Jr., *Soft Power: The Means to Succeed in World Politics* (New York: Public Affairs, 2004), x.

20. DoD, *Military and Security Developments*, 18.

21. Bonnie S. Glaser, "Ensuring the 'Go Ahead' Policy Serves China's Domestic Priorities," *China Brief*, 30 April 2007, http://www.asianresearch.org/articles/3010.html.

22. Brigadier General (Retired) Simon Worden, Address, National Space Forum, Washington DC, 7–8 February 2008, http://csis.org/event/national-space-forum-day-1.

23. Ibid.

24. Robert Jervis, *Perception and Misperception in International Relations* (Princeton, NJ: Princeton University Press, 1976), 111.

25. The ideas in this paragraph are attributed to Ambassador Claudio Bisogniero, NATO Deputy Secretary General (Address, National History Museum, Bucharest, Romania, 17 March 2007), http://www.nato.int/docu/speech/2008/s080317a.html.

26. Lawrence D. Roberts, "A Lost Connection: Geostationary Satellite Networks and the International Telecommunications Union," *Berkley Technology Law Journal* 15, no. 3 (Fall 2000), http://www.law.berkeley.edu/journals/btlj/articles/vol15/roberts/roberts.html.

27. "Shelton: Space Warfare Is Certain; DoD Must Get Ready," *Inside the Pentagon*, 1 March 2007.

28. "Cartwright: U.S. Needs Multifold Response to China's ASAT Test," *Inside the Pentagon*, 1 March 2007.

29. General James E. Cartwright, "Statement," U.S. Congress, Senate, Strategic Forces Subcommittee of the Armed Services Committee, 110th Cong, 1st sess., 28 March 2007, http://armed-services.senate.gov/statemnt/2007/March/Cartwright%2003-28-07.pdf.

30. General Kevin P. Chilton, "Statement," U.S. Congress, House, Strategic Forces Subcommittee of the Armed Services Committee, 110th Cong, 1st sess., 23 March 2007, http://armedservices.house.gov/pdfs/Strat032307/Chilton_Testimony032307.pdf.

31. Quoted in Vince Little, "Space Chief: Chinese ASAT Spurred Need for Space-Asset Protection," *Star and Stripes, Pacific edition*, 21 October 2007.

32. Quoted in Michael R. Gordon, "Summit in Moscow: The Accords; U.S. to Use Its Missile Warning System to Alert Russians to Launchings Worldwide," *New York Times*, 2 September 1998.

33. General Kevin P. Chilton, "Statement," U.S. Congress, House, Strategic Forces Subcommittee of the Armed Services Committee, 110th Congress, 2nd sess., 27 February 2008, http://armedservices.house.gov/pdfs/STRAT022708/Chilton_Testimony022708.pdf.

34. General C. Robert Kehler, Address, National Space Forum, Washington, DC, 7–8 February 2008.

35. Ibid.

36. Stephen Peter Rosen, *Winning the Next War: Innovation and the Modern Military* (Ithaca, NY: Cornell University Press, 1991), 75.

37. Quoted in Stew Magnuson, "Murky Picture of What's Happening in Space Worries Air Force Officials," *National Defense* (December 2007), http://www.nationaldefense magazine.org/archive/2007/December/Pages/Murky2405.aspx.

38. Kehler, Address, 7–8 February 2008.

39. Many sources originally quoted Yao as having stated "the weaponization of space is inevitable." Yao maintains that she was misquoted. The quote used here is purportedly a more accurate representation of her comments that evening. See Richard D. Fisher Jr., "Space to Manoeuvre—Satellite Attack Upsets U.S. Space Supremacy," *Jane's Intelligence Review* 19 (March 2007): 62–63; and James Mulveron, "Rogue Warriors? A Puzzled Look at the Chinese ASAT Test," *Chinese Leadership Monitor*, no. 20, 2007, http://media.hoover.org/documents/clm20jm.pdf.

40. Toshi Yoshihara and William C. Martel, "Averting a Sino-U.S. Space Race," *Washington Quarterly* (Autumn 2003): 23.

41. Pan Xiangting, ed., *Shijie Junshi Xingshi, 1997–98* [*The World Military Situation*] (Beijing: National Defense University Press, 1998), 1–7.

42. "Space Warfare: Challenge, Focus and Countermeasures," *World Outlook* 9 (May 2001).

Peter A. Dutton

China's Efforts to Assert Legal Control of Maritime Airspace

WITH CONTINUING TENSIONS on the Korean peninsula serving as a constant reminder that international security in East Asia is inherently fragile and the heightened concerns of all states about terrorist threats from the air since 11 September 2001, intercept of foreign military aircraft and national air defense identification zones (ADIZ) once again are topics that assume a prominence in national security discussions that they have not held in several decades. Nowhere have these concerns been more active than in East Asia. China, for instance, in advance of the 2008 Summer Olympic Games announced its intent to establish an ADIZ over the East China Sea and the Taiwan Strait to protect visitors from possible terrorist air attack.[1] Elsewhere in the region, Japan increased the number of air intercepts it performs each year.[2] Additionally in 2008, increased Chinese air exercises in the central East China Sea region, ownership of which is disputed by Japan and China, caused "emergency scrambling" by Japanese Self-Defense Force jets.[3] Most recently, in July 2010, Japan extended the southern portion of its ADIZ twenty-two kilometers closer to Taiwan to ensure air coverage over all portions of the southernmost island in the Ryukyu island chain, known as Yonaguni.[4] While this move was essentially administrative in that it adjusted Japan's ADIZ to cover the internationally recognized sovereign Japanese airspace over the airspace of Yonaguni

Island and the territorial sea surrounding it, the action nonetheless provoked a sharp response from the Taiwan authorities.

Air Defense and International Law

Clearly, air defense is of widespread concern among East Asian governments. One common misperception, however, is that ADIZ boundaries somehow denote a zone of coastal state sovereignty—a kind of international border in the air. This is simply not the case.[5] An ADIZ is a zone of airspace in which a state declares that it has a security interest and for which it publishes procedures on how it expects civil aircraft to behave in the region in order to avoid the misperception that the aircraft poses a threat to the security of the state. Military aircraft are sovereign immune from these requirements and only obey the ADIZ rules when operational circumstances permit, and even then only as a matter of courtesy and not of law.

There are two types of airspace—sovereign or national airspace, and non-sovereign or international airspace. International law recognizes the complete and exclusive sovereignty of the coastal state in the airspace above its territory and its surrounding twelve-mile territorial sea, allowing full state control of the air space in this region.[6] Because states have full sovereignty in this national airspace, they are free to create laws establishing various zones and areas in which limits are placed on aviation. This concept is included in Article 9 of the Chicago Convention; pursuant to this article, many states have prohibited or restricted air traffic in all or a portion of their national airspace, as the United States did around Washington, D.C., after 11 September 2001. These prohibited and restricted areas are clearly marked on air navigation charts and, at least in the United States, are broadcast to the public through the Notice to Airman, or NOTAM, system.

The stated justification for these restrictions is that they are essential to national security. However, such restrictions imposed on air traffic have as their foundation a solid base in the historical right of sovereign states to govern their own territory, including the airspace above it, and on positive treaty law recognizing the right of states to exclusive jurisdiction in the airspace above their territory and territorial waters. The calculus of rights shifts, however, when moving from national airspace to international airspace, which exists beyond the twelve-nautical-mile limit of coastal state sovereignty.

In response to heightened tensions between the United States and the Soviet Union caused by the outbreak of the Korean War, for instance, the

United States established in 1950 an ADIZ extending 300 nautical miles sea-ward of its own coastline.[7] The United States continues to maintain ADIZs off its Atlantic and Pacific coasts that extend well out into international air-space.[8] Additionally, the Alaska ADIZ has an irregular shape that extends from the Alaskan coastline hundreds of nautical miles into the airspace above the Bering Sea, and the ADIZ surrounding Guam extends a distance of 250 nauti-cal miles from the island.[9] All civilian aircraft entering the ADIZ are required to provide for identification prior to entry.

During the same period, similar ADIZ were established by the United States, as occupying power, in the airspace around Japan, and around South Korea and Taiwan pursuant to U.S. defense agreements.[10] The East Asian ADIZ system was created to suit the particular needs at the time of the nascent United States Air Force and the strategic circumstances it faced in stabilizing East Asia during the tense years of the early Cold War.

American planners, however, were either unaware of or insensitive to the ways that the ADIZ line drawing would in the future aggravate regional rivalry for islands and the national jurisdiction that attends them. As such, Japan's Yonaguni Island—the location of recent controversy—was for the convenience of the planners divided between the ADIZ of Taiwan and Japan, even though the island itself reverted to full Japanese sovereignty when the United States ended its occupation of Okinawa in 1972. A similar circumstance exists in the Sea of Japan.

Although both Japan and South Korea claim the islet of Dokdo/Takeshima, the fact that it was placed under the Korean ADIZ has added an additional aggravation in the friction between the two countries over the issue of sover-eignty. This fact aggravates Japan because aircraft operating within an ADIZ—even those merely transiting through—are generally required to check in with the appropriate air traffic control center, file and activate a flight plan for, at a minimum, the portion of the flight in which the aircraft will operate within the ADIZ, and in some cases provide regular position reports to air traffic control-lers. Japanese pilots occasionally grumble about being queried by controllers from the Korean ADIZ when approaching a "Japanese" island.

Likewise, pilots flying within a U.S. ADIZ are also required to operate with a transponder turned on and broadcasting an assigned identification code. Regulations require that they maintain a continuous listening watch on specified frequencies to readily hear and comply with instructions.[11] The U.S. government, like most governments that maintain an ADIZ, justifies these requirements based on the need to ensure national security, to control illicit drug activities, to minimize unnecessary intercept and search-and-rescue operations, and to decrease the risk of midair collisions and other public hazards.[12] As a matter of international law, these rules are not applicable to military and other foreign-state aircraft when these aircraft are merely transiting the U.S. ADIZ in international airspace and do not intend to fly into U.S. national airspace. Nonetheless, as a matter of comity and safety, nearly all international aircraft comply with the U.S. air traffic control requirements in the U.S. offshore ADIZ.

Chinese Views on Airspace and Security

Although the People's Republic of China (PRC) has never officially published an ADIZ of its own, Chinese government and civilian scholars have a well-developed perspective on the balance of coastal state and international rights in nonsovereign airspace that has informed official Chinese statements on the subject of ADIZ and air rights for more than a decade. One such perspective was articulated by two scholars from Ocean University of China (Qingdao). They correctly assess that "ADIZs do not constitute parts of the territorial airspace of coastal States, nor does their establishment alter the legal status of the affected areas as international airspace. However, as an international custom, ADIZs have gradually established their legitimacy. In practice ADIZs constitute part of the early warning system of a State, and they are established for the purpose of safeguarding national security."[13] However, in practice these scholars and the Chinese government apply international law differently than does the United States, especially in relation to American surveillance and reconnaissance flights, such as the one involving the 2001 EP-3 incident.

   On 1 April 2001 an American EP-3 naval reconnaissance aircraft and a Chinese F-8 fighter-interceptor collided over the South China Sea, approximately seventy nautical miles south of Hainan Island.[14] The U.S. government reported to the Chinese that the EP-3 was on a routine, overt reconnaissance mission in international airspace at the time of the collision, and stated that such flights by U.S. aircraft and Chinese interception of them were regular events.[15] The United States also acknowledged that Chinese intercepts became increasingly aggressive in the months preceding the collision.[16] Perhaps explaining the increasingly aggressive intercepts, a spokesman from the Chinese Foreign Ministry expressed the view that a foreign aircraft on a reconnaissance mission in the airspace above China's exclusive economic zone (EEZ) threatens the coastal state's national security.[17] The foreign minister demanded that the reconnaissance missions stop.[18] The spokesman stated that it was proper and in accordance with international law for Chinese military fighters to follow and monitor the U.S. military surveillance plane within airspace over China's exclusive economic waters. . . . The surveillance flight conducted by the U.S. aircraft overran the scope of "free over-flight" according to international law . . . [in that] any flight in airspace above another nation's exclusive economic zone should respect the rights of the country concerned . . . [and] the U.S. plane's actions posed a serious threat to the national security of China. . . . All countries enjoy the freedom of overflight in the exclusive economic waters of a nation, [but the EP-3's] reconnaissance acts were targeted at China in the airspace over China's coastal area . . . and thus abused the principle of overflight freedom.[19]

Additionally, the PRC official news agency Xinhua published an "in-depth analysis" of the international law aspects of the collision in which it claimed that reconnaissance flights over the EEZ of another country are threats to "national security and peaceful order of the coastal state" in violation of the United Nations Convention on the Law of the Sea (UNCLOS) and customary international law.[20]

Similar contemporaneous statements by Chinese military officials, however, indicated that they viewed the long-running U.S. reconnaissance program and Chinese intercepts of U.S. aircraft as routine, and Chinese military leaders called upon the United States only to take "effective measures to prevent similar incidents," rather than halting reconnaissance flights altogether.[21] This suggests that the statements of the Chinese Foreign Ministry that seemed to place limits on international reconnaissance flights may actually have reflected some other motivation or concern of the PRC government rather than an expression of actual Chinese policy, or at the very least that China intended to maintain some ambiguity about its official view concerning the rights of foreign military aircraft in the airspace above the EEZ. As such, the position of the government of China at the time was not clearly inconsistent with the general view that all aircraft have the right to freely navigate in the airspace above the EEZ for all purposes not specifically limited by positive international law, including the undertaking of open, nonthreatening military reconnaissance flights.

While acknowledging the routine nature of such flights—which reportedly occurred four to five times a week during the second half of 2000 and about two hundred times per year between 1997 and 1999—U.S. secretary of defense Donald Rumsfeld stated that between December 2000 and April 2001 there were forty-four People's Liberation Army (PLA) aerial interceptions of

U.S. reconnaissance flights off Chinese coasts.[22] Given the long-standing and frequent nature of the flights and China's routine acceptance of them, state practice between the United States and China rather strongly indicates that customary international law recognizes the right of the international community to fly nonthreatening military reconnaissance flights in the international airspace above the exclusive economic zone, with the concomitant right of the coastal state to safely intercept and observe such flights to ensure their non-threatening character.

Furthermore, there is some evidence that Chinese military aircraft also engage in similar military reconnaissance missions. The U.S. government asserted plainly in 2001 that China also engaged in reconnaissance flights in the international airspace above other Asian states' EEZs and that China possesses at least one platform specifically designed for that purpose, the Yun-8 reconnaissance aircraft.[23] The Yun-8 is a midrange, multipurpose, four-engine turboprop, the airframe of which is based on the Soviet An-12 tactical military transport. It is a multiuse platform with more than twenty variants, one of which is specifically designed for maritime surveillance and early-warning missions similar to those performed by the American EP-3.

Clearly, the PLA possesses the capability to perform surveillance and reconnaissance missions against its neighbors in East Asian airspace. The Chinese have also been active in developing and exercising nonmanned reconnaissance craft. With all of China's growing maritime surveillance capacity, it is perhaps surprising that a collective Chinese attitude against the legality of reconnaissance flights in the international airspace above the EEZ has hardened in recent years. In fact, two senior Chinese scholars—one a military officer and the other a civilian academic—have gone so far as to equate *any* foreign military operations in a coastal state's EEZ with a threat to use force. They state: "'freedoms of navigation and overflight' in the EEZ does not include the freedom to conduct military and reconnaissance activities in the EEZ and its superadjacent airspace. Such activities encroach or infringe on the national security interests of the coastal State, and can be considered a use of force or a threat to use force . . . inconsistent with the principles of international law embodied in the Charter of the United Nations."[24] Even so, perhaps as a reflection of the ambiguous nature of maritime boundaries in East Asia, the Chinese have undertaken surveillance and reconnaissance operations in much of the expansive airspace over which they claim some form of Chinese jurisdiction above the East and South China seas, disregarding the fact that the Chinese claims are disputed by Japan, Vietnam, the Philippines and other states. This fact highlights the challenges inherent in the relationship between East Asian security concerns and the many unresolved maritime disputes based on divergent historical claims and differing interpretations of the provisions of international law of the sea.

East Asian Air Defense and the Law of the Sea

After World War II, several countries, beginning with the United States, declared exclusive fishing zones and claimed authority to control the resources on and under the continental shelves off their coastlines. This was the outgrowth of long-standing legal recognition by many countries that certain coastal states should have exclusive rights to certain resources outside their territorial waters. Under this rationale, the United States and Tunisia claimed exclusive rights to coastal sponge beds in international waters. Bahrain, Sri Lanka, and Australia claimed similar rights to pearl beds as far as fifty miles off their coasts, and Ireland claimed the right to oyster beds more than twenty miles off its coast.[25] Even so, the American decision to assert jurisdiction and control over the resources of the entire continental shelf and the fish in the water column above it (out to two hundred nautical miles), announced in the 1945 Truman Proclamation, was a much wider departure from the general rule that states have no authority to claim jurisdiction or control outside the three-nautical-mile coastal band unless long-standing, widely accepted exclusive use can be demonstrated.[26]

Accordingly, the United States consulted with a number of other states in advance of the proclamations to determine whether there would be diplomatic objections to the assertion. There were none, which was in part based on the fact that the U.S. extension of authority was self-limited in that it specifically acknowledged and protected the long-standing international interests in these waters, such as freedom of navigation.

Commentators describe the international community's consent to the American declarations as having been granted in the nature of an easement by the international community in favor of the coastal state upon a zone in which the majority of rights continued to belong to the international community. This remains the case. As the United States made clear both before and after making its claims, "recognition of special property rights . . . outside the marginal belt . . . does not conflict in any way with the common enjoyment of all mankind of the right of navigation [in those waters]."[27] International consent to this legal development quickly resulted in similar declarations by other states and eventually to the 1958 Geneva Convention on the Continental Shelf, which recognized that coastal states are entitled to sovereignty over the natural resources on the continental shelf adjacent to their coastlines.[28]

In 1982 the right to exercise jurisdiction over all resources in and below the waters of a two-hundred-nautical-mile EEZ was established in the United Nations Convention on the Law of the Sea. Under UNCLOS the coastal states were granted "sovereign rights" to the resources in the waters, on the seabed, and under the seabed and sufficient jurisdiction in those areas to protect their sovereign rights.[29] However, the convention, like the customary and treaty law that went before it, remained silent concerning coastal state jurisdiction in the airspace over the EEZ because the international community never formed a consensus to relinquish to coastal states the right to control international airspace.

Although UNCLOS gives the coastal state certain specified rights and duties in the EEZ, the majority view, reflecting both customary international law and interpretation of treaty developments, is that these waters retain a predominantly international character, since all rights not specifically granted to the coastal state remain with the international community. UNCLOS specifically allocates to coastal states, for instance, sovereign rights to the nonliving and living resources in and below the EEZ's waters. Coastal states are also given sovereign rights to perform other activities for the economic exploitation and exploration of the zone (the convention specifically mentions production of energy from water currents or wind, for example); and they are given limited "jurisdiction"—rather than the more encompassing sovereign rights—over artificial islands and platforms, marine scientific research activities, and protection and preservation of the marine environment.[30] All other rights and activities remain with the international community but must be exercised in a manner that gives due regard for the interests of the coastal state.

From the inception of the negotiations and discussions that led to UNCLOS, however, the exact status of the EEZ was the subject of much dispute, with particular emphatic disagreement over the extent of a coastal state's right to "jurisdictionalize" or close the EEZ to international activities. Long after negotiations over the text of UNCLOS have been completed, there remain a minority of states that view the residual rights in the EEZ—that is, those remaining rights not specifically allocated by the convention to either the coastal state or the international community—as being held by the coastal state.[31] Ambassador Tommy T. B. Koh of Singapore, however, as president of the Third United Nations Conference on the Law of the Sea, has stated, "The question of military activities in the exclusive economic zone is a very difficult one. . . . Nowhere is it clearly stated [in the convention] whether [another] state may or may not conduct military activities in the exclusive economic zone of a coastal state. But it was the general understanding that the text we negotiated and agreed upon would permit such activities to be conducted."[32] Bernard Oxman, an American scholar who was a member of the U.S. delegation to the negotiating committee, has also emphasized that "the economic zone does not accommodate desires to exclude foreign military forces. Quite the contrary, the Convention text accomplished the reverse by holding back the territorial sea at 12 miles."[33]

But what of the airspace above the EEZ? The United Nations Convention on the Law of the Sea does very little to actually change the existing framework of air law. As airspace outside national control, it is still considered international airspace and therefore a zone of free navigation for military purposes. UNCLOS Article 58(1), for instance, enumerates the rights and duties of states appertaining to the EEZ but also refers to Article 87, "Freedom of the High Seas," to explicitly clarify that all states have in the airspace above the EEZ the same rights of overflight as above the high seas. Article 87 then reiterates the standard obligation for international aircraft operating in this airspace, which is that the one limitation on freedom of navigation is to operate with "due regard for the rights of other states in their exercise of the freedom of the high seas." That the airspace above the EEZ would remain international in character was therefore part of the "original package deal" put together during the UNCLOS negotiations.[34] This did not stop those whose coastal-state position was rejected during negotiations from making postnegotiation attempts to "clarify" the provisions of UNCLOS in their favor.

Specifically, according to some Chinese international law specialists, coastal states should have the authority in the airspace off their coasts to restrict the military activities of other states, especially surveillance and intelligence gathering.[35] This view fails in that articles 56 and 87 make clear that the international community retains all navigational rights—especially those accorded to sovereign immune aircraft—in and above the EEZ.[36] Additionally, a state's military activities are accorded special status in dispute resolution provisions and retain immunity from compulsory settlement procedures.[37] Finally, contrary to the Chinese perspective, such a major change in the international law landscape as the relinquishment of traditional rights in international airspace could not occur without the clear consent of sovereign states. The ambiguity of the language in UNCLOS dealing with airspace outside twelve nautical miles of a coastline is clear indication that there was no such clear consent to alter the rights of sovereign states in this zone.

The Chinese view is unenforceable against other states as a matter of customary international law. Customary international law is, generally speaking, the combination of state practice and the widespread belief that the practice is required or allowed. Evidence of state practice can be deduced in several ways, such as through scrutiny of the many different types of documents that governments produce, including domestic laws, judicial decisions, and diplomatic communiqués. It can also be seen in the activities undertaken by agents of the sovereign, such as military forces, police authorities, political leaders, and diplomats, to name a few. Evidence of state practice can even be based on the failure to object to certain practices or claims of other states. Likewise, evidence of a state's belief that it is legally bound can be observed in judicial opinions, political statements, and even scholarly writings.

Central to the development of customary law as binding upon a state is, of course, that state's manifestation of consent to be bound. Thus, much like a state's decision not to be party to a particular treaty or convention and therefore not to be bound by its provisions, even a generally accepted rule of customary international law cannot be held against a state that openly and steadfastly objects to the rule. This state becomes known as a "persistent objector" in relation to that rule and is excused from compliance with it.[38] That said, customary international law is often created as an extension of positive law; that is, customary rules of international law can grow out of the interpretation of ambiguous treaty provisions and can become binding on all states that do not specifically reject the application of the rules to them.[39]

Concerning the current state of the rules of international law governing the airspace above the EEZ, although individual states may have bound themselves to specific limitations in their activities in this airspace, they cannot alter the rights of those states that have not given such consent. The principle of freedom of navigation in international airspace is one of long usage. It flows out of the principle established for the high seas—"res communis omnium," which means "that which belongs to all"—and which allows no state the authority to subject any part of the high seas to its own sovereignty.[40] In more modern times, the principle of freedom of the air over the seas was recognized by the drafters of the 1919 Paris Convention for the Regulation of Aerial Navigation, the precursor to the Chicago Convention, which noted that "the airspace is also free above the sea, as the sea itself."[41] This was the perspective that informed the negotiations for the United Nations Convention on the Law of the Sea in the 1970s and 1980s, where a tally of the votes of the members of the UNCLOS drafting conference demonstrates that the principle of freedom of navigation on the high seas, including overflight, was well accepted as part of customary international law.[42]

In East Asia, of particular concern to the international community's interest in maritime airspace is that China and North Korea specifically claim some sovereign right to control the activities of the international community in the airspace above all or a portion of the EEZ.[43] They are part of a minority of 23 countries out of 163 coastal states and territories that continue to make excessive claims that could be construed as infringing on the rights of the international community in the airspace above the EEZ.[44]

Additionally, a collection of scholars and government representatives calling themselves "EEZ Group 21" met under the auspices of Japan's Ocean Policy Research Foundation to attempt to achieve an Asian consensus concerning guidelines for military activities in and above the EEZ. After four years of study and discussions, they concluded that there is little agreement between Asian states on the extent of authority belonging to coastal states to regulate the activities of the international community in the exclusive economic zone.[45] Nonetheless, the group published proposed "guidelines" for international conduct in the EEZ, some of which impose limitations that directly contradict the specific understanding of the majority of UNCLOS members.[46] One such guideline, for example, lends support for the handful of states that continue to claim the right to impede the military activities of the international community. It states, "Warships or aircraft of a State intending to carry out a major military exercise in the EEZ of another State should inform the coastal State and others through a timely navigational warning of the time, date and areas involved in the exercise, and if possible, invite observers from the coastal State to witness the exercise."[47] Other guidelines proposed by EEZ Group 21 included limitations on the international community's right to live fire exercises, a requirement to use adjacent high seas when available rather than to conduct exercises in an exclusive economic zone, and a prohibition on "sea bases" in the exclusive economic zone of another coastal state.[48]

Is there a developing Asian consensus on these points? From the record of coastal state laws governing EEZs, there clearly is not. Even so, should a regional consensus develop, it still cannot operate to remove existing rights from the remaining nonconsenting members of the international community. As customary law requires, such limits only apply to states that explicitly accept them, not to the international community generally, and certainly not to persistent objectors.[49]

The United States has persistently resisted attempts by coastal states to assert authority over non–resource-related international activities in and above the EEZ to prevent the development of any consensus that coastal states have such legal authority. The U.S. Department of State in conjunction with the Department of Defense, for instance, publishes the "Maritime Claims Reference Manual," which references each coastal state's maritime claims and any U.S. objections to them and conducts a Freedom of Navigation Program.[50] Accordingly, attempts by China, North Korea, and others to limit American military flights in the airspace above their EEZ have so far been met with legal and operational challenges.

Thus, under international law, an ADIZ can best be viewed as a zone of special interest tied to a coastal state's concern for respect for its sovereignty, safety of flight, prevention of criminal activities, national self-preservation, and the national right to self-defense. An ADIZ, however, does not confer to the coastal state additional jurisdiction or authority to control international activities of any kind. However, coastal states continue to have, as they have always had, the right to self-preservation, including the right to take military action to prevent imminent danger from invasion, bombardment, or similar action from the sea. This right pertains equally to coastal defense against invading fleets, military aircraft, or private vessels.

In the exercise of these rights to defense, states may establish conditions and procedures for entry into their national airspace. Military aircraft, of course, must always seek permission to enter another state's national airspace, except perhaps under circumstances of distress, in which case they should be entitled to such measures of assistance as are reasonable and necessary under the circumstances.[51] Thus, coastal states have the right to establish an ADIZ in the airspace over the EEZ in which they require civil and military aircraft to follow established identification procedures as a condition for entry into national airspace. If an aircraft appears to be following a flight path into a coastal state's national airspace but has failed to meet the established identification requirements, the coastal state can deny that aircraft entry into its national airspace. The coastal state can also direct its own aircraft to visually confirm that the inbound aircraft is not a hostile threat to the coastal state. Finally, if a military aircraft is merely passing through the ADIZ, then international law does not provide a basis for the coastal state to impose its identification regulations.[52] The coastal state must fully respect the international community's rights to use the international airspace in which the coastal state has established its ADIZ, and the international community retains the right to use international airspace for military activities, including intelligence gathering.[53] The armed forces of a coastal state may not use force against such military aircraft but must allow peaceful military activities, such as surveillance and reconnaissance, to take place.

In conclusion, a coastal state has the right to use international airspace, including the international airspace over the EEZ, to exercise its interests related to sovereignty and for identification of aircraft in national self-defense. The coastal state can protect these rights by establishing an ADIZ under customary international law, but the coastal state's authority is limited to imposing its identification requirements only when the aircraft intend to enter the coastal state's national airspace.[54]

Looking to the Future

In East Asia, China as a strong continental power exists in uneasy tension with its maritime neighbors and their American ally. China's security interests have led it to develop a defensive strategy based on control—military and legal—over the Yellow, East China, and South China seas, what China calls its "near seas." This runs directly counter to the security interests of Japan, South Korea, Taiwan, and others who rely in part on the ability of the United States to gain free access to the airspace in East Asia to meet their defense requirements.

Another dynamic is at play in this debate. On a global basis, the resurgence of concern about threats to national security from the air—stemming from the recent violent air attacks on the United States by international terrorists, among other reasons—mean that coastal states will continue to look for support from international law for measures to gain awareness of the presence of potential offshore threats and for the means to adequately defend their sovereignty from transnational terrorist threats when necessary. To enhance national security, the temptation will exist for some states to pursue changes to the historical balance of rights and obligations between the international community and the coastal state. Some coastal states are already seeking to generate legitimacy for the position that they should have enhanced authority over international waters and airspace by pursuing gradual acceptance of this perspective and attempting over time to establish a new principle of customary international law. Should this trend be discouraged? A number of factors suggest that the trend is not in the best long-term interests of East Asia or of the international community as a whole.

First, unfettered freedom of navigation and overflight promotes globalism, on which the economic future of the international community rests. In today's globally connected economy, all states have a keen interest in the maintenance of an efficient system of navigation that will keep the cost of shipping goods at a minimum. Thus, the freedom to move about in the global commons—in the waters and in the airspace—represents an important supporting, security-promoting activity for international commerce.

Roughly 38 percent of the world's oceans lie within two hundred nautical miles of a coastline, and the vast majority of international trade flows as a matter of right over the oceans and through the exclusive economic zones of coastal states.[55] Bernard Oxman refers to this as "the sovereign right of communication."[56] No sovereign may remove any other sovereign's freedoms. Thus, if a coastal state attempts to restrict the traditional right of international military flights in the airspace over the exclusive economic zone, it violates the sovereign right of communication.

Second, the current balance between coastal state rights to maritime resources and international rights to navigational freedoms is the most efficient balancing of interests and allocation of capabilities to prevent the global emergence of zones of instability. During the course of the twentieth century, more than one hundred new sovereign states emerged in the international system with equality of sovereignty and the full measure of territorial authority that sovereignty conveys but without, in many cases, the capacity to provide the security necessary for effective governance or sufficient security to foster stable economic development.[57] The trend toward increasing jurisdictionalization of the global commons, if not reversed, will likewise result in the emergence of zones in which weak coastal states have exclusive authority but do not possess the requisite capacity to provide the security and stability necessary to support international maritime communications. Access to airspace helps prevent the emergence of such zones of instability.

Third, if preventing instability is an international interest, then states with the capacity to provide security need the authority to provide it. In short, to be effective, naval and air power rely on access. Three decades ago Elliot Richardson stated presciently, "Clearly the classical uses of sea power have assumed fresh importance. . . . To back up friends, to warn potential enemies, to neutralize similar deployments by other naval powers, to exert influence in ambiguous situations, to demonstrate resolve through deployment of palpable force—all these are tasks that naval power is uniquely able to perform."[58] Additionally, Richardson noted that "since one of the great attributes of air power is speed, any factor that works to delay flight time, such as rerouting or the need to ask permission to overfly, would naturally downgrade its value."[59] Those countries that possess the capacity to provide security in the global commons need the accompanying authority to provide it.

Fourth, concerning reconnaissance and surveillance activities, information is inherently stabilizing. Access by states to information about other states, within limits prescribed by national airspace and territorial waters, is necessary to promote international stability. Just as routine interaction between citizens of states builds familiarity, trust, and confidence, so does the respectful gathering of information between sovereign states—as Russia has done openly off the coast of Norway and the United Kingdom. The existing framework of international law, which provides for full sovereignty within international airspace and extends that protective zone to twelve nautical miles off a coastal state's shore, strikes an acceptable balance between the right of coastal states to defend their interests and the interest of the international community to gain information.

Finally, there is something positive to be said for the routine interaction of members of the international community in the global commons under a framework of liberty subject only to the requirements of due regard for the safety and rights of other vessels and aircraft. It promotes the habit of respect. It builds trust. Given the ongoing disputes on the Korean peninsula, and in the East China Sea and the South China Sea, these are qualities that appear to be in dwindling supply in many regions of East Asia. Ships and aircraft operating near each other have a mutual interest in the personal safety that such trust and respect engender. This habit of trust builds bridges of goodwill within the international community that would be lost were states to wall themselves off behind legal edifices in zones of increasing separation.

Notes

1. Jamestown *China Brief* 8, no. 1 (4 January 2008): 2. Available at http://www.james town.org/programs/chinabrief/.

2. "Number of ASDF Scrambling Incidents Up in Response to PRC Military Planes," *Tokyo Sentaku*, 1 November 2007.

3. Tsuyoshi Nojima, "China's Sudden Show of Force Sent SDF Jets Scrambling," *Asahi Shimbun*, 2 January 2008.

4. Jens Kastner and Wang Jyh-Perng, "Japan Takes a Shot at China—via Taiwan," *Asia Times*, 7 July 2010, http://www.atimes.com/atimes/China/LG07Ad01.html.

5. Peter A. Dutton, "*Caelum liberum*: Air Defense Identification Zones Outside Sovereign Airspace," *American Journal of International Law* 103, no. 4 (October 2009): 691–709.

6. Oliver J. Lissitzyn, "The Treatment of Aerial Intruders in Recent Practice and International Law," *The American Journal of International Law* 47, no. 4 (October

1953): 559–89, at 559; and Convention on International Civil Aviation (Chicago Convention), International Civil Aviation Organization Document 7300/9 (9th ed., 2006), Articles 1 and 2.

7. David F. Winkler, *Searching the Skies: The Legacy of the United States Cold War Defense Radar Program* (Hampton, VA: Headquarters U.S. Air Force Air Combat Command, 1997), 22.

8. Federal Aviation Administration International Flight Information Manual, http://www.faa.gov/air_traffic/publications/ifim/.

9. 14 CFR § 99.45, Alaska ADIZ, and 14 CFR § 99.47, Guam ADIZ; GPO Access, http://ecfr.gpoaccess.gov/cgi/t/text/text-idx?c=ecfr&sid=aef1f41602310b2474727ee064e37710&rgn=div6&view=text&node=14:2.0.1.3.14.2&idno=14.

10. "Japan–U.S. Security Treaty after 50 years—In the Shadow of Peace," *Asahi Shimbun*, 11 August 2001.

11. 14 CFR § 99.7 through 99.17, http://ecfr.gpoaccess.gov/cgi/t/text/text-idx?c=ecfr&sid=aef1f41602310b2474727ee064e37710&rgn=div5&view=text&node=14:2.0.1.3.14&idno=14.

12. "Security Control of Air Traffic," 66 *Fed. Reg.* 49819 (2001), http://frwebgate.access.gpo.gov/cgi-bin/getdoc.cgi?dbname=2001_register&docid=01-24426-filed.pdf.

13. Xue Guifang and Xiong Xuyang, "A Legal Analysis of the Establishment of Air Defense Identification Zones," *Journal of Ocean University of China* (Social Sciences ed.), no. 6 (2007): 36, 38.

14. Shirley A. Kan et al., "China-U.S. Aircraft Collision Incident of April 2001: Assessments and Policy Implications," CRS Report for Congress, 10 October 2001, p. 1, http://www.fas.org/sgp/crs/row/RL30946.pdf.

15. Ibid., 7, 2.

16. Ibid., 2.

17. "Chinese Spokesman Gives Full Account on U.S.–China Air Collision," *Xinhua*, 3 April 2001.

18. "FM Tang Jiaxuan Receives U.S. Letter; PRC Decides to Allow Crew to leave," *Xinhua*, 11 April 2001.

19. "Chinese Spokesman Gives Full Account."

20. "U.S. Seriously Violates International Law: Signed Article," 15 April 2001, Embassy of the PRC in the U.S.A., http://www.china-embassy.org/eng/zt/zjsj/t36383.htm.

21. Kan et al., "China-U.S. Aircraft Collision," 11.

22. Thomas Ricks, "Anger over Flights Grew in Past Year," *Washington Post*, 7 April 2001; and Kan et al., "China-U.S. Aircraft Collision," 14.

23. Kan et al., "China-U.S. Aircraft Collision," 7; and John Keefe, "Anatomy of the EP-3 Incident, April 2001" (Alexandria, VA: Center for Naval Analysis-Project Asia, January 2002), 14.

24. Ren Xiaofeng and Senior Colonel Cheng Xizhong, "A Chinese Perspective," *Marine Policy* 29 (2005): 139, 142.

25. Green H. Hackworth, *Digest of International Law*, Vol. 2 (Washington, DC: Government Printing Office, 1941), 674–77.

26. See ibid., 651–58.

27. Ibid., 676.

28. Convention on the Continental Shelf (1958), United Nations Treaty Series, Vol. 499, Article 2, p. 311.

29. United Nations Convention on the Law of the Sea (UNCLOS), Article 56, http://www .un.org/Depts/los/convention_agreements/texts/unclos/unclos_e.pdf.

30. Ibid.; and R. R. Churchill and A. V. Lowe, *The Law of the Sea*, 3rd ed. (Manchester, U.K.: Manchester University Press), 166–69.

31. For a Chinese viewpoint, see Ren and Cheng, "A Chinese Perspective," 139.

32. Jon M. Van Dyke, ed., *Consensus and Confrontation: The United States and the Law of the Sea Convention* (Honolulu: Law of the Sea Institute, 1985), 303–4.

33. Bernard Oxman, "Customary International Law and the Exclusive Economic Zone," in *Consensus and Confrontation: The United States and the Law of the Sea Convention*, ed. Jon M. Van Dyke (Honolulu: Law of the Sea Institute, University of Hawaii, 1985), 153.

34. David A. Colson, "The United States, the Law of the Sea, and the Pacific," in *Consensus and Confrontation: The United States and the Law of the Sea Convention*, ed. Jon M. Van Dyke (Honolulu: Law of the Sea Institute, University of Hawaii, 1985), 39.

35. Ren and Cheng, "A Chinese Perspective," 139.

36. See UNCLOS Article 236 and 298(1)(B). Whereas UNCLOS specifies in Article 2 that the airspace above the territorial sea is a zone of coastal state sovereignty, Article 55, the corresponding article related to the EEZ, makes no mention of a change in the historical status of the airspace above that zone.

37. UNCLOS, Article 290.

38. Churchill and Lowe, *Law of the Sea*, 7–12.

39. R. P. Anand, "Odd Man Out: The United States and the UN Convention on the Law of the Sea," in *Consensus and Confrontation: The United States and the Law of the Sea Convention*, ed. Jon M. Van Dyke (Honolulu: Law of the Sea Institute, University of Hawaii, 1985), 110–13.

40. Churchill and Lowe, *Law of the Sea*, 166.

41. Nicholas Grief, *Public International Law in the Airspace of the High Seas* (Dordrecht, Netherlands: Martinus Nijhof Publishers, 1994), 53.

42. Ibid., 57n77.

43. "Maritime Claims Reference Manual," DOD 2005.1-M, June 2008.

44. Ibid. As of July 2009, 157 countries have both signed and ratified the convention. United Nations, "Oceans and Law of the Sea," http://www.un.org/Depts/los/index .htm.

45. "Guidelines for Navigation and Overflight in the Exclusive Economic Zone: A Commentary" (Tokyo: Ocean Policy Research Foundation, 2006), 3–8.

46. The twenty-three countries that currently claim some form of an EEZ-related right to regulate military activities are Bangladesh, Benin, Brazil, Burma, Cape Verde, China, Congo, Ecuador, Guyana, India, Iran, Kenya, Liberia, Malaysia, Maldives, Mauritius, Nicaragua, North Korea, Pakistan, Peru, Portugal, Somalia, and Uruguay. Of these, six—Congo, Ecuador, Iran, Liberia, North Korea, and Peru—are not UNCLOS members.

47. "Guidelines for Navigation and Overflight," 59.

48. Ibid., 63, 65, 55.

49. Churchill and Lowe, *Law of the Sea*, 8.

50. "Maritime Claims Reference Manual," Department of Defense Publication 2500-M (June 2005), http://www.dtic.mil/whs/directives/corres/html/20051m.htm; and "1995 Annual Defense Report," Appendix I, "Freedom of Navigation," http://www.dod.mil/execsec/adr95/appendix_i.html.

51. See, e.g., Convention on International Civil Aviation (Chicago Convention), Article 25, http://www.icao.int/icaonet/dcs/7300.html; and John Dugard, "Jurisdiction over Persons On Board Aircraft Landing in Distress," *The International and Comparative Law Quarterly* 30, no. 4, (October 1981): 902.

52. Chicago Convention.

53. Lissitzyn, "Treatment of Aerial Intruders," 141–42.

54. John Astley III and Michael Schmitt, "The Law of the Sea and Naval Operations," *Air Force Law Review*, 42 (1997): 119, 137.

55. See, e.g., "Primer on Ocean Jurisdictions: Drawing Lines in the Water," U.S. Commission on Ocean Policy, n.d., 70–73, http://www.oceancommission.gov/doc uments/full_color_rpt/03a_primer.pdf. See also, Robert B. Krueger and Myron H. Nordquist, "The Evolution of the 200-Mile Exclusive Economic Zone: State Practice in the Pacific Basin," *University of Virginia Journal of International Law* 19 (1978–79): 321.

56. "Statement of Professor Bernard H. Oxman before the Senate Committee on Foreign Relations," 4 October 2007, http://www.virginia.edu/colp/pdf/OxmanTestimony 071004.pdf.

57. *An Ocean Blueprint for the Twenty First Century*, "Primer on Ocean Jurisdictions, Drawing Lines in the Water" (United States Ocean Commission Publication, 2004), http://www.oceancommission.gov/documents/full_color_rpt/03a_primer.pdf. See also, e.g., the Failed State Index at www.fundforpeace.org.

58. Elliot Richardson, "Power, Mobility and the Law of the Sea," *Foreign Affairs* (Spring 1980): 906.

59. Ibid., 908 (quoting Geoffrey Kemp, "U.S. Naval Power and the Changing Maritime Environment," Paper presented at the 4th Annual Seminar of the Center for Oceans Law and Policy of the University of Virginia, January 1980, 4).

Richard D. Fisher Jr.

Maritime Employment of PLA Unmanned Aerial Vehicles

BEYOND ITS KNOWN use of small-target drones, the People's Liberation Army Navy (PLAN) appears to lag far behind its sister services in the use of unmanned aerial vehicles (UAVs). For that matter, after decades of being satisfied with a relatively small UAV research and development sector stressing target drones, and being largely tied to universities while absorbing foreign technology when possible, over the course of the 10th and 11th Five-Year Plans (2001–10) the PLA has apparently committed to investing in a world-class unmanned systems capability. As for UAVs, their use by all PLA services could increase dramatically over the next decade. While PLAN-specific programs are not apparent from open sources, Chinese military–technical literature suggests potential consideration of a number of naval missions for possible future PLA UAVs. Furthermore, the PLA appears to be reaching a critical mass in the broader development of large UAVs and unmanned combat aerial vehicles (UCAVs), which could be adopted for a range of PLAN missions in the future. In addition, the PLA is making advances in C4ISR (command, control, communications, computers, intelligence, surveillance, and reconnaissance), especially space- and ground-targeting systems, navigation satellites, and networked command-and-control systems, all essential for enabling the range of unmanned aerial combat capabilities similar to those being pursued by the United States and many of its friends and allies. Within the next decade it is possible that the PLA will be employing a range of land-based and sea-based surveillance and combat UAVs that could match many of the same systems now being employed by the U.S. military, and which the United States is developing in the hope of sustaining a degree of tactical and strategic superiority over the PLA. However, while it is possible to assess the PLA's accumulating UAV and other unmanned system talent in its universities and aerospace companies, it is more difficult to discern the PLA's plans to allocate and organize UAV capabilities or to integrate them into its doctrine and operations.

Zhuhai Aspirations

One useful barometer of the PLA's growing interest in UAVs and UCAVs has been the biannual airshows held in Zhuhai, China, starting in 1996. The 2008 show, held on 4–8 November, offered what was then the most expansive display of UAV and UCAV progress and visions by Chinese aerospace concerns in the history of these airshows. In the display hall of the Aviation Industry of China (AVIC) consortium, one could see three wall murals that depicted one level of aspiration for China's military use of UAVs and UCAVs. The most interesting mural was situated behind a display of UAV and UCAV models, which included new designs revealed for the first time. It showed what could be considered a current American or European goal for UAV/UCAV development over the next decade, to include high-altitude, long-endurance (HALE), medium-altitude, long-endurance (MALE), vertical takeoff UAVs (VTUAV), and airship UAVs, plus subsonic, supersonic, and even hypersonic UCAV platforms, all networked to ground sensor and control systems, satellites, and even to each other. A second nearby mural behind a model of the newly revealed CH-3 MALE UCAV showed this UCAV networked with an unarmed version, satellites, and ground control systems. A third wall mural highlighted the newly revealed Warrior Eagle, a subsonic turbojet- or turbofan-powered UCAV, flying in a group of three platforms, suggesting cooperative operations. Of the UAV models that China has revealed over the course of the 2004, 2006, and 2008 Zhuhai airshows, one could find analogues or close approximations to the U.S. Northrop Grumman Global Hawk UAV, X-47 UCAV demonstrator, the General Atomic Aeronautical Systems Predator and Reaper UAV/UCAV series, plus the Northrop Grumman Fire Scout and the U.S. Army Future Combat Systems ducted-fan VTUAVs. Whereas the 2008 show had roughly twelve UAV prototypes or models on display, the show held on 16–21

November 2010 boasted more than twenty-five. An appendix of known UAVs and UCAVs is given at the end of this chapter.

Tentative Background

While the Zhuhai shows at least project the impression that unmanned aerial surveillance and combat systems are an increasing priority for the PLA, these shows have shed little light on many other important questions pertaining to the PLA's overall unmanned system technology leadership, specific capability goals, allocation of UAV/UCAV missions to respective services, preparations for joint operations, or operational organization and training. While operational questions are more difficult to address, it is possible to review briefly the PLA's UAV history and to assess its gathering competence in UAVs and related technologies.

The PLA has been interested in unmanned aviation since the 1950s, but only since the late 1990s has it sought to pursue a world-class unmanned aircraft capability. Early research into unmanned aircraft took place at Northwestern Polytechnic University, which claims to have flown its first small UAV in 1958.[1] In the late 1950s or early 1960s the PLA obtained the Soviet Lavochkin La-17, originally a ramjet-powered target drone.

A second UAV technology windfall occurred during the Vietnam War in the form of downed U.S. Teledyne-Ryan Model 147 (later, Northrop BQM-34 Firebee) photoreconnaissance drones. More than five hundred were lost over Vietnam and China, some downed by People's Liberation Army Air Force (PLAAF) fighters over Chinese territory. The WZ-5 was first launched from a Chinese copy of the Tu-4 Bull, a copy of the Boeing B-29, and later launched by the Sha'anxi Y-8E. Chang Hong drones were reportedly used for photoreconnaissance during China's 1979 punitive war against Vietnam.[2]

By the 1980s the PLA's burgeoning military–technical relationship with Israel is reported to have included the transfer of UAV-related technologies. One unconfirmed report notes that the Xi'an ASN Technology Group Company, owned by the Northwest Polytechnic University, may have joined with Israel's Tadiran Spectralink Ltd. to produce the ASN-206 tactical UAV in 1994.[3] Having a broad resemblance to Israeli UAVs of the period, such as the Israeli Aircraft Industries' Scout, the ASN-206 represented a major advance for Chinese UAV technology in the early 1990s. In the early to mid-1990s China was reportedly trying to obtain the Israeli Aircraft Industries' turbojet-powered Delilah, and did purchase one hundred of the reciprocating engine-powered Harpy attack drones in 2001.[4] Both were designed to patrol target areas to detect hostile electronic emissions and then to destroy the source. While the alleged Delilah sale was linked to the PLA's cruise missile program, both systems would have potentially helped the PLA to obtain better guidance, flight control and command technology applicable for UAVs. Asian military sources indicate that China produces a version of the Harpy with the designation JWS01.[5]

During the 1970s the PLA apparently started a program to turn its J-5 (Ba-5, MiG-17), Shenyang J-6 (MiG-19), and Chengdu J-7 (MiG-21) fighters into unmanned target drones. These programs, as well as that of the Chang Kong, are associated with the career of Major General Zhao Xu, often called the "father" of China's UAVs.[6] Until at least 2002 Zhao served as the chief engineer at a PLAAF missile-testing base in the Badain Jaran Desert in Lanzhou Province, and at age seventy-two is apparently still at work on unmanned systems. In 1998 Zhao led the testing of China's first "supersonic" UAV, which was reportedly developed at the cost of less than $1 million.[7] This very likely was a modified J-7II fighter, photos of which have appeared in Chinese publications.

Russian technology has featured less in China's recent UAV developments, as opposed to other parts of China's aircraft sector, most likely because Russia has had less to offer. While the Soviets developed some single-purpose surveillance drones from the 1960s onward, they did not follow the U.S. and Israeli example of investing in modern UAVs during the 1980s, and thus could offer little for export during the 1990s. However, Russian sale of engines and general assistance with China's modern aircraft engine development may be of greater importance to China's UAV effort. But as Russia develops new unmanned systems, such as the MiG Skat (Skate) UCAV, it is likely that Russia will continue to push for codevelopment programs with China.

China's UAV Sector Today

As illustrated by the output on display at the most recent Zhuhai shows, it appears that the Chinese leadership has supported a decision by the PLA to invest in a far more capable and competitive UAV sector. Interest in unmanned systems has been occasionally demonstrated by China's top political leadership; in the early 1990s former paramount leader Jiang Zemin and Politburo member Li Peng attended a demonstration of an early surveillance UAV developed from a Xi'an ASN-105 target drone.[8] There is also evidence that the 1986 "863" strategic high-technology investment program has supported some UAV programs.[9] While it is difficult to find the "leader" of China's UAV effort today, one could speculate that leadership rests between respective offices or experts serving in the General Staff Department, General Armaments Department, and the logistics departments of the respective services.[10]

China's early efforts, starting in the 1960s, saw the PLAAF's target drone programs and supporting research and development conducted largely in the major aerospace universities. Today, unmanned aerial systems are big business in China. One measure of the size of this sector is indicated by a recent conference by the Chinese Society for Aeronautics and Astronautics (CSAA), "Vanguard of China: General Assembly on UAVs 2008," held in Beijing from 18–20 June 2008. This conference featured displays by 70 companies, was attended by 4,500 professionals and 530 experts, and gathered 287 academic papers.[11] This is likely only a fraction of the total number of professionals in China's UAV sector. From 9–11 June 2010, the third Vanguard conference was held at Northwest Polytechnic University in Xi'an and also featured more than 70 displays by UAV and UAV systems concerns.

UAV development is now conducted in most of China's major aircraft design bureaus and manufacturing companies, some cruise missile concerns, and in a growing number of smaller startup companies that seek to meet requirements for ever-better guidance, imaging, and control systems. The division of labor among the larger companies and universities appears to be as follows:

- Shenyang Aircraft Co: Supersonic and Subsonic UCAVs
- Chengdu Aircraft Co.: HALE and MALE UAVs
- Guizhou Aircraft Co.: HALE UAVs, MALE UAVs, and UCAVs
- China Aerospace Science and Industry Co.: VTUAVs, unmanned airships, and small UAVs

Personnel for company programs come in part from university aerospace programs, which have long been tasked with supporting basic research and directed research on UAV systems. The Northwest Polytechnic University, Beijing University of Aeronautics and Astronautics, and Nanjing University of Aeronautics and Astroanautics have all developed tactical UAVs, mainly for the army. For 2008 the Nanjing University of Aeronautics and Astronautics UAV design laboratory focused on waterborne UAVs.[12]

One important question is whether the UAV sector will be reorganized in a manner consistent with the early 2008 decision to remerge AVIC-1 and AVIC-2, with the intention to create "areas of excellence" in civil and military products. One 2008 reported noted there would be a "defense division" under AVIC control, but there are also suggestions that China seeks to build integrated defense system companies comparable to Lockheed Martin and BAE.[13] This move prompted questions: Will these newly integrated companies also have competing UAV sections? Or will there be a single unmanned systems entity? Although the Chinese UAV sector seems too diffuse to allow for the latter, this decision would likely influence the degree of competition and innovation. A subsequent March 2009 report indicated that only major aircraft companies would be gathered under the new AVIC "defense group."[14] While UAV development was said to be a goal of this new company, there was no additional reporting on consolidation among these companies that might affect UAV development or any indication this would affect other unmanned development centers at companies such as China Aerospace Science and Technology Corporation (CASC), China Aerospace Science and Industry Corporation (CASIC), China North Industries Corporation (NORINCO), or the universities. So there may not be a move to centralize unmanned system development in a way that might depress innovation.

Enabling Technology and Limitations

Critical to China's rapid advance in UAV design and manufacture has been its ability to master many other technologies that enable the development of modern UAVs. China has made steady progress in fabricating ever-better UAV control and guidance systems. The problems with digital controls for the J-7 target drone were overcome in the early 1980s when Chengdu and then Shenyang mastered digital fly-by-wire controls, which they tested on J-6 and J-8II fighters, respectively. China also quickly mastered the development of ever-smaller satellite navigation system. Today the Guilin Xinying Technology Co. can produce a matchbox-sized autopilot with a GPS system on a microchip.[15] Control systems have also progressed far from early radio-control, joystick-based affairs to current flight mission controls based on computer programs suitable for laptop computers, requiring minimal to no "manual" flying.

China's growing space- and land-based surveillance and information network will also better enable UAV operations on China's periphery and beyond its region. By 2016–20, China intends to loft its own 30+ Compass navigation satellite network. The PLA's surveillance satellite network now consists of the growing indigenous Yaogan and the Russian-aided Huanjing families of electro-optical and radar satellites.[16] One new development for the PLA that could have a great impact on distant UAV operations was the April 2008 launch of its first data relay satellite (Tianlian-1), which, when joined by others, can allow more rapid coordination of surveillance data with command decisions with less dependence on ground-station communications relay. New PLA land- and sea-based sensors could also assist UAV operations. Asian sources have noted that China may have up to five new long-range over-the-horizion (OTH) radar facilities, which would complement surveillance satellite and surveillance UAV coverage of target areas. These sources noted that the PLA's new OTH radars have given the PLA the ability to continually monitor U.S. naval activities in the Western Pacific for the first time. At the 2009 IDEX arms show in Abu Dhabi a Russian source confirmed Russia's sale of the 350-km-range Podsolnukh-E surface-wave OTH to China, while Russia also markets a 3,000-km-range sky-wave OTH system.[17] At the April 2010 CIDEX military electronics show, a Chinese company revealed a new movable "surface wave" OTH radar with a 300 km range. The PLA is also beginning to lay moored sonobuoy fields, at least near Taiwan. Close-in, and perhaps in the future more distant, deep-water sonobuoys could be used to help vector future antisubmarine warfare (ASW)–capable UCAVs. In 2010 Luoyang revealed a small sonobuoy that could be deployed by a UAV.

China's desire to increase UAV employment will also face limiting factors. In both the West and China, advanced UCAV development is limited by the lack of computers and programs that can fulfill combat requirements for reasoning, responsiveness, and intuition provided by the human mind. This limits the use of UAVs to narrow missions and during periods of least resistance, such as initial attacks. China will also face challenges in building and sustaining the electronic "tether" for its UAVs. As the United States has found, access to sufficient communication satellite bandwidth is a limiting factor, forcing greater use of commercial satellite links. The PLA may only have two dedicated communications satellites, although it is known to make great use of Chinese-controlled commercial comsats. Protecting this tether from random electronic interference, or from deliberate cyber attack, is another challenge. Recent U.S. Navy small-UAV operations in Iraq have been hampered by interference from communications and IED-jamming equipment.[18]

HALE and MALE UAVs

China is very likely developing several HALE and MALE UAVs that could be used to accomplish a range of maritime surveillance and combat-assistance missions. In early October 2008 there was rare confirmation of a Chengdu

Aircraft Co. HALE UAV program, a prototype of which had first been revealed just before the 2006 Zhuhai show. When the Tianyi HALE UAV first appeared at Zhuhai, Chinese officials said next to nothing about it, creating doubt about the existence of the program. However, in October 2008 confirming pictures were followed by an Internet-released short video showing the Tianyi taxiing a short distance. While the model of the Tianyi suggested a Global Hawk–size UAV, the vehicle seen in the October video was much smaller, perhaps a half- to third-scale test article, or perhaps a final design. Complicating analysis of the Tianyi's status was the appearance at the 2008 Zhuhai show of another HALE UAV, called the Long Haul Eagle, which bore an even closer resemblance to the Global Hawk. It is perhaps necessary to take this program more seriously given the recent confirmation of the Tianyi. Again, while data about the Long Haul Eagle was not made available, the clear suggestion is that Chengdu is most likely seeking to approach the capability of the famous U.S. UAV.

A second HALE UAV program revealed by China is the Soar Dragon concept of the Guizhou Aircraft Company revealed at the 2006 Zhuhai show. Employing a novel "box wing" design, the Soar Dragon was described on a placard as having a 7,500 kg weight, a mission payload of 650 kg, and a range of 7,000 km. The model featured a fuselage "tub" consistent with synthetic aperture radar. While a much smaller box-wing UAV appeared at the June 2008 CSAA convention, there is no public reporting on the status of the Soar Dragon program.

Both Chengdu and Guizhou have produced MALE designs. At the 2004 Zhuhai show, a Guizhou brochure contained a small image of what appeared to be a turboprop-powered UAV similar in size to the U.S. Predator or Reaper. A second MALE UAV program that has made progress is the Sunshine, very likely produced by Guizhou, which in the 2006 Zhuhai show was featured flying in an AVIC video. The model of this fifteen-hour endurance UAV was updated for the 2008 Zhuhai show, exhibiting sleeker lines and featuring a surveillance-targeting payload. An AVIC wall mural also showed the Sunshine digitally linked to other UAVs in an over-water flight.

The PLA has also demonstrated an increasing interest in airship UAVs. It appears that CASIC and NORINCO are developing unmanned airships. The 2008 Zhuhai show saw the revelation of FKC-1 airship UAV, which has a 30 kg payload and three-hour endurance. This unmanned airship was reported by a Chinese source to have flown on 11 January 2008.[19] A NORINCO-developed unmanned airship reportedly first flew at the end of November 2008.[20] However, Chinese Internet photo data gathered by the author indicates that China has undertaken experiments in the cooperative employment of up to four similarly sized airship UAVs.[21] Chinese academic engineering literature indicates the PLA is likely interested in larger higher-altitude capable airships for persistent surveillance missions, as are the U.S. armed forces.[22]

Crossing the line between UAV and UCAV is the CH-3, revealed for the first time at the 2008 Zhuhai show. This UAV is based on the design of the Burt Rutan Vari-Eze homebuilt aircraft and was noted by one Chinese source as having twelve-hour endurance. Of special interest, the CH-3 was featured as an armed UCAV, featuring the new AR-1, an air-to-surface missile that appears to have been designed for UCAVs. This canard design is noted for its stability and resistance to stalls. The appearance of photos of the CH-3 proto-type lends credibility to there being an active CH-3 UCAV program. At the 2010 Vanguard show, the similarly sized canard configuration Blue Eagle was revealed, also armed with unique attack missiles and a fixed machine gun. The Blue Eagle was being pitched to police organizations.

Large UCAVs

Visual evidence from the Zhuhai shows and Chinese military-engineering literature offer indications that China is seeking to develop UCAVs.[23] While a retargetable Harpy might almost qualify as a UAV, it is also reasonable to consider that the PLAAF has modified some Chang Hong drones to perform limited combat missions such as electronic jamming. The PLAAF has also converted a number of J-6 (MiG-19) fighters into UCAVs, up to two hundred to three hundred, according to some Asian military sources.[24] It is not known what ordnance these J-6 UCAVs employ, or whether their function may be closer to that of a drone for the purpose of forcing defenders to waste their SAMs. It is possible that China could consider converting a larger number of J-7 (MiG-21) into UCAVs inasmuch as they also serve as target drones. The J-7's advantage would be a higher dash speed during a final attack and with-drawal but would also have a higher landing speed.

The 2006 Zhuhai show was also significant in that the PLA appeared to be "announcing" that it would rely on the Shenyang Aircraft Company for future large, dedicated UCAV designs. At that show Shenyang created a minor sen-sation by unveiling its Anjian/Dark Sword supersonic UCAV concept. At the 2006 Zhuhai show it was displayed with a placard noting its main mission was air-to-air combat, but no other data was released then or at four subsequent displays of the Anjian model. Its very sharp delta configuration and under-slung air intake would support supersonic flight, perhaps even "supercruise"—

the ability to fly supersonically without engine afterburners—if the engine could provide sufficient unreheated thrust for the weight of the vehicle. The Anjian also appears to stress stealth inasmuch as it would likely use internal weapon carriage. Given his doubts that China has yet mastered the complexities of an air-to-air UCAV, one analyst speculates the Anjian may represent more of a future Chinese vision for unmanned strike UCAVs.[25] There may be a South African connection for the Anjian. A new company featured at the 2006 Zhuhai show (but not the 2008 show), Xinshidai, is an apparent partnership with South Africa's Denel Kentron Company.[26] Posters for this new company featured a sharply shaped supersonic drone and another supersonic UCAV firing a Denel antitank missile.

A more plausible UCAV concept was revealed at the 2008 Zhuhai show: the Warrior Eagle, a forward-swept-wing, tailless, single-engine vehicle apparently designed for subsonic speeds. Though not identified as such, this UCAV is very likely a product of Shenyang Aircraft Co. The Warrior Eagle's forward-swept wing is similar to a curious small forward-swept-wing fighter concept revealed by Shenyang at the 2006 Zhuhai show. A feature seen in the Russian Sukhoi S-37 fighter prototype and the U.S. X-29 of the early 1980s, forward-swept wings offer gains in lift-to-drag ratios and maneuverability. This feature is also better enabled by the advent of stronger composite materials that prevent wingtip bending and the lack of a human passenger to allow maneuvers at far higher than nine times the force of gravity.

While the Anjian design would have difficulty achieving the low speeds necessary for carrier recovery, this may not be very challenging for the Warrior Eagle design, which is comparable in potential to that of the Northrop Grumman X-47B. It is not clear whether the Warrior Eagle would require a catapult for launch, but the L-15 would clearly require such assistance. Of related interest, the 2008 Zhuhai show also saw the revelation of a model of a jet-powered, back-swept folding "morphing-wing" UAV. It remains unknown whether this is just a concept or represents an active development program. Lockheed Martin has reportedly tested a small folding morphing-wing UAV with the intention of enabling UAVs to achieve efficient low speeds for surveillance missions and then high speeds for attack missions.

An additional purpose-designed UCAV appeared first at the June 2008 CSAA "Vanguard" UAV conference, and then at the 2008 Zhuhai show. It appeared in model form without any descriptive information and, rather unusually, in conjunction with air-to-air missiles (AAM) and electro-optical system maker Luoyang Optoelectric Technology Company (LOEC). However, this model bore a resemblance to the Guizhou WZ-2000 turbofan-powered

UAV but had a thicker fuselage and less-swept wing. A rough estimate would put this UCAV in the same size category as the U.S. MQ-9 Reaper. At both shows, this model was armed with LOEC's TY-90 small AAM, originally designed for helicopters, and the new AR-1 ASM. The AR-1 is a 45 kg, semiac-tive laser-guided, 8-km-range ground-attack missile that appears to have been purpose-designed for UCAVs. The initial version carries a 10 kg warhead, likely shaped-charged, that can penetrate 1,000 mm of armor or 1,200 mm of concrete.[27] If this UCAV was a real design, it might then seek to fill the same long-endurance and light-attack mission profile of the Reaper.

At the 2010 Vanguard show, NORINCO displayed a model of its new UCAV ground-attack missile, the Blue Arrow-7 or BA-7. With a 46 kg weight and 7 km range, this missile is nearly identical to the HJ-10 air-launched antiarmor missile. Of some additional interest, the NORINCO and AVIC displays featured illustrations of a medium-sized delta-wing, turbofan-pow-ered UCAV. This illustration first appeared in the February 2005 issue of the Chinese magazine *World Outlook*. At that time, that illustration was assessed to have been yet another example of Chinese netizen "Fan Art" and perhaps not of a serious program. However, the use of the illustration by NORINCO and AVIC, plus the early revelation of the UCAV missile before the aircraft, as was done by Luoyang in 2008, raises the possibility it also is a distinct UCAV program. Asian military sources assess it to be a likely competitive program with the Luoyang UCAV, but it may rather represent a cooperative program, with the Luoyang UCAV performing higher-altitude target search and the "NORINCO" UCAV performing fast-killer missions.

VTUAVs

The PLA has long supported helicopter VTUAV programs. Following three years of development by Beijing University of Aeronautics and Astronautics (BUAA), the 300 kg coaxial rotor Seagull UAV was revealed in 1996. At the 2000 Zhuhai show, BUAA then revealed a much smaller M22 coaxial rotor VTUAV with an oval-shaped fuselage. BUAA's latest version of this format is the 60–70 kg FH-1, which has an endurance of 1.5 hours. BUAA illustra-tions from the 2004 Zhuhai show of the Seagull show it flying near a PLAN Type 730 close-in weapon system; however, it is not known from open sources whether these designs have been developed for PLAN service.

The PLA is also funding the development of conventional helicopter con-figuration VTUAVs. Nanjing University of Aeronautics and Astronautics

(NUAA) revealed its Soar Bird conventional helicopter format VTUAV at the 2000 Zhuhai show. This concept appears to have been taken up by a private company, perhaps associated with NUAA, and has produced a family of concepts. These include the 320 kg LE 110, the slightly more capable LE 200 and the 930 kg LE 300, which is closer to the 1,400 kg U.S. MQ-8 Fire Scout. With a 431 kg useful load and 3.8-hour endurance, the LE 300 would be able to carry useful surveillance or data link payloads, or might also carry a light rocket for limited attack missions. Again, it does not appear that the PLAN has yet adopted any of the "LE" family of VTUAVs. In the AVIC pavilion at the 2008 Zhuhai show, a prominent wall poster revealed the new U8E VTUAV. The manufacturer was not indicated, but the U8E has a maximum weight of 220 kg, a payload of 20–30 kg, an endurance of 4 hours, and a 100 km radius. While wall illustrations at the Zhuhai show clearly showed the U8E digitally linked to a combat ship, it is not known whether the PLAN has adopted this vehicle.

There are two types of Chinese VTUAVs in development that could prove useful from small ships and perhaps submarines. The June 2005 the Harbin Institute of Technology displayed a ducted-fan UAV with a camera, similar to those proposed for the U.S. Army Future Combat System.[28] These ducted-fan UAVs were then displayed at the 2006 Zhuhai show. Another interesting VTUAV revealed at the 2008 Zhuhai show was the D-1 ducted-fan VTUAV. Shaped like a flying saucer and colored garish yellow, it was located near the display area of CASIC, which has an interest in naval unmanned systems. The D-1 saucer shape would lend itself to greater utility from small boats or even submarines, should there be a storage area in the sail. Future larger saucer UAVs might be accommodated in large multipurpose submarine vertical silo tubes. In addition, at the June 2008 CSAA "Vanguard" conference NUAA revealed a tilt-rotor model VTUAV. The model was in sufficient condition for flight-testing, but performance data apparently was not available. It is not known whether the PLA may be considering more advanced tilt-rotor VTUAV projects.

Hypersonic and Space Unmanned Vehicles

The PLA may also be pursuing militarily useful unmanned space plane and hypersonic platforms.[29] It appears that a number of space-plane concepts were pursued during the 1980s, and a formal manned space plane was thought to be part of the 921 Program for manned space flight. In 1980s the 611 Institute also had access to early French efforts to develop its Hermes space plane, the first indication of which was the appearance of a wind-tunnel model of a similarly shaped space plane in a brochure obtained by the author at the 1996 Zhuhai show.[30]

In fact, the aforementioned photo appeared following the "declassification" of China's unmanned rocket-powered Shenlong space-plane program in December 2007.[31] The 611 Institute was apparently also involved in its design, and it also appeared to have been supported by 863 Program funding. An initial photo showed the space plane suspended from the fuselage of its Xi'an H-6 bomber airborne launcher, and there have been potentially official releases of computer-aided design images of Shenlong. The size of Shenlong indicates that its main purpose may be to test hypersonic control and reentry technologies. These technologies could be used for future manned space-plane programs or to develop unmanned platforms similar in size and function to the U.S. Air Force Boeing X-37B unmanned space plane. However, the Soviet experience with the Buran space plane indicates that much larger unmanned space planes are possible.

Like the United States, Russia, and others, China is seeking to develop hypersonic strike vehicles. They can also serve as low-earth orbit launch vehicles and be the successor to the strategic bomber and intercontinental ballistic missile (ICBM). The PLA has similar goals for this hypersonic research program, which has been ongoing for decades.[32] China has built a hypersonic propulsion test facility in Beijing, which includes a wind tunnel that can generate velocities up to Mach 5.6.[33] China has long been interested in Russian research on hypersonic vehicles. A French report in early 2007 suggested that China had tested a scramjet-powered hypersonic test vehicle in late 2006.[34] Then in December 2007 Chinese Internet imagery appeared to show a model of a possible hypersonic test vehicle, showing a missile shape with long tapered delta wings.[35] One of the wall murals of the AVIC pavilion at the 2008 Zhuhai show features a prominent illustration of a hypersonic UAV.

Operations and Missions

As mentioned earlier, despite China's impressive recent progress in developing a range of UAV technologies, as far as can be determined from open sources, the use of unmanned aerial systems is at a preliminary stage, especially for the PLAN. Beyond the use of small radio-control target drones for AAA practice, it is not known whether the PLAN has made use of many of the smaller tactical UAVs developed in China since the early 1990s, or whether it is making use of new cruise missile–like target drones. However, that does not mean there is inactivity concerning the PLA's maritime use of UAVs. There is a body of military engineering literature that suggests that the PLA may be considering a range of naval related missions for UAVs, to include short- and long-range surveillance, targeting of antiship missiles from ships and submarines, defense against and data relay to assist long-range cruise missile strikes, and communication relay.[36]

It is reasonable to expect that the PLAN will eventually make use of new HALE and MALE UAVs to provide additional depth to its intelligence, surveillance, and reconnaissance (ISR) systems being built as part of its "antiaccess" strategies intended to deter U.S. forces and thereby secure at least part of the Western Pacific from U.S. naval intervention in the event of conflict. As Global Hawk–class UAVs come into service, it is possible that the PLAN will be responsible for surveillance as far as they can fly, well into the Mid- and South Pacific, and down through the South China Sea. It should be considered that PLA controlled "maritime resource monitoring" HALE UAVs in the future might obtain refueling access to South Pacific states with which China may develop strong economic and military relations. Or the PLA may follow the U.S. example and develop UAV aerial refueling capabilities. China's next four-engine commercial airliner may be quickly developed into an aerial refueler.

Regarding potential combat missions, in addition to aiding and defending against cruise missile attacks, it should be expected that in the future PLA UCAVs may be performing attack missions against submarines, from future aircraft carriers and from low-earth orbit. The PLA appears to understand the limitations of current UCAV technologies and is designing initial UCAVs such as Warrior Eagle for initial attack and air-defense suppression missions. It could well be equipped to fulfill the same range of missions envisioned for the X-47B, to include long-range attack or surveillance, or both; air-defense suppression; and aerial refueling or even antisubmarine patrols. Potential hypersonic or transatmospheric UAVs could perform surveillance or attack missions. In 2005 three Chinese researchers from the Center for Precision Guidance Technology of the Beijing University of Aeronautics and Aeronautics indicated that China may have already been developing a space capability for attacking targets on earth. In one article they noted, "The greatest advantage of a space-based ground attack weapon system is its high speed and short reentry time. It is extremely difficult for the enemy to intercept such a weapon."[37] While this article does not identify Chinese space planes or space shuttles as a potential space-based "ground attack weapon," one cannot discount that China may be designing its unmanned or manned space plane for this purpose.

Conclusion

After a long history of focusing primarily on unmanned target drones, China has been investing in a world-class unmanned aerial systems sector during most of this decade. While its full dimensions are not known, China's UAV-development sector receives top-level attention from China's military and political leadership, it is likely directed from the PLA's General Staff Department, and it encompasses a large number of aircraft and cruise missile concerns supported by a growing research and development cadre in universities and in the private corporate sector. Nevertheless, the actual development and operational employment of this range of systems is at an early stage for the PLA and perhaps even at a more tentative stage for the PLAN. While the PLAAF and even the PLA ground forces have developed and put into some use a range of systems for target exercises, or for tactical surveillance, there are far less data on the PLAN's adaptation of these advanced unmanned systems. That said, there are suggestions in China's military engineering literature that the PLAN could be considering the next wave of sophisticated HALE, MALE, and VTUAVs to support a range of missions to include short- and long-range surveillance, targeting of antiship missiles from ships and submarines, data relay to assist long-range cruise missile strikes, and communication relay.

In the future is reasonable to expect that the PLAN will utilize HALE and MALE UAVs from land bases while VTUAVs will operate from many types of PLAN surface warships of varying size. Once the PLAN's amphibious assault ships and carriers enter service, it should be expected that a range of UAV platforms will operate from these ships. Subsonic UCAV designs possibly under development now may form the basis for carrier-based UCAVs performing the range of ISR and attack missions also envisioned for the platform to emerge from the X-47B program. In addition, the PLAN could also benefit from expected unmanned space and hypersonic platforms.

For the U.S. Navy as well as for the U.S. Air Force and the U.S. Army, China's broad investment in unmanned and robotic platforms, provided they meet with success, could shorten the period of strategic or tactical advantage that U.S. defense planners may have hoped to derive from these same systems. This example follows others in which China is seeking capabilities "symmetric" with those of the United States, such as aircraft carriers, amphibious projection forces, large transport aircraft, and fifth-generation combat aircraft. It has to be considered that China's future UAVs and UCAVs will enable future power projection capabilities and precision strike capabilities, and that China will sell these systems to its main partners. Furthermore, China could emerge in the next decade as a key innovator in unmanned technologies.

America's current advantages in unmanned technology, however, places two burdens on U.S. defense planners. First, the United States must make continued advances, such as developing the necessary computer-intelligence systems that enable truly useful autonomy and developing platform-sized energy-based weapons that offer significant combat flexibility. A second requirement is that U.S. resources must now be devoted to defending against China's new unmanned platforms, especially the detection of these stealthy platforms. This will affect requirements for future U.S. unmanned platforms and for future antiaircraft requirements as well as for requirements for space and cyber warfare.

Appendix: China's Emerging UAV/UCAVs Relevant to Naval Operations

	Type	Manufacturer	Range/Endurance	Comments
COMBAT/SURVEILLANCE				
J-6	UCAV	SAC	640 km radius with 2 drop tanks	Converted from J-6 fighters; about 200 said to be in service in 2008
Anjian/Dark Sword	UCAV	SAC	unknown	Concept revealed at 2006 Zhuhai Airshow; first described as a supersonic "fighter," but that descriptor was dropped in 2008; South African influence suspected
Warrior Eagle	UCAV	SAC (?)	unknown	Forward-swept-wing subsonic UCAV concept revealed in 2008; single engine, performance unknown; potential carrier-based UCAV
"L-15"	UCAV	Hongdu	550 km radius for trainer	Potential carrier-based UCAV derived from potential carrier training version of the supersonic L-15
"Luoyang UCAV"	UCAV	Guizhou	unknown	Likely based on WZ-2000; turbofan powered; revealed in 2008 to be armed with TY-90 AAM and AR-1 ASM; similar in size to U.S. Predator-2
"NORINCO UCAV"	UCAV	unknown	unknown	Medium-sized and turbofan powered, but with a delta wing indicating higher speeds; first seen in 2005 but possibly confirmed as a program in 2010
CH-3/PW-3	UCAV	unknown	12 hrs; 220 km max range	Revealed in 2008; reciprocating engine; armed with 2x AR-1; S-band data link

SURVEILLANCE

Chang Hong/ WZ-5	UAV/HALE	BUAA	2,400 km	Copy of U.S. Firebee; updated in late 1990s
Long Haul Eagle	UAV/HALE	CAC	unknown	Revealed in 2008; turbofan power; similar in size and shape to U.S. Global Hawk
Soar Dragon	UAV/HALE	Guizhou	7,000 km	Revealed in 2006; box-wing configuration; turbofan power; SAR; 650 kg payload
Xianglong/Tianyi	UAV/HALE	CAC	unknown	Revealed in 2006; shown being tested in 2008; may or may not be small test article; turbofan powered
WZ-2000	UAV/MALE	Guizhou	unknown	Updated version revealed in 2004; turbofan powered; reported sale to Pakistan
Unknown name	UAV/MALE	Guizhou	unknown	Revealed in 2004; reciprocating engine; V-tail; concept UAV similar in size and shape to U.S. Predator-1
Wing Long	UAV/MALE	?	20 hrs	Revealed in 2008; reciprocating engine; tested in 2008; 200 kg payload
Qianzhong-1	UAV/MALE	Guizhou	15 hrs	Revealed in 2008; 60 kg sensor payload

(continued)

China's Emerging UAV/UCAVs Relevant to Naval Operations *(continued)*

	Type	Manufacturer	Range/Endurance	Comments
VTUAV				
U8E	VTUAV	unknown	4 hrs	Revealed in 2008; likely tested; 20–30 kg mission load
LE 300	VTUAV	NUAA	3.8 hrs	NUAA concept; 930 kg takeoff weight; 431 kg useful load
LE 200	VTUAV	NUAA	2.5 hrs	NUAA project; tested; 320 kg takeoff weight; 67 kg useful load

Abbreviations: AAM: air-to-air missile; ASM: air-to-surface missile; BUAA: Beijing University of Aeronautics and Astronautics; CAC: Chengdu Aircraft Company; HALE: high-altitude, long-endurance; MALE: medium-altitude, long-endurance; NUAA: Nanjing University of Aeronautics and Astronautics; SAC: Shenyang Aircraft Company; UAV: unmanned aerial vehicle; UCAV: unmanned combat aerial vehicle; VTUAV: virtual takeoff unmanned aerial vehicle.

Sources: Author photo archives; company brochures; press reports.

Notes

1. "News," Northwestern Polytechnic University Web Page, no. 661, ver. 1-2 (15 October 2004), http://www.nwpu.edu.cn/web/view/news/xbgdb/33745.htm.

2. "Disclosed for the First Time: WZ-5 Reconnaissance Aircraft Combat Diagram," Military.China.com, 19 June 2006, http://military.china.com/zh_cn/dljl/uav/news/11047701/20060619/13411037.html.

3. "ASN-206 Unmanned Aerial Vehicle," *China's Defense Today*, 12 April 2008, http://www.sinodefence.com/airforce/uav/asn206.asp.

4. Douglas Barrie, "China Provides Cash for Israeli Cruise Missile," *Flight International*, 17 May 1995, 17; and Yitzhak Shichor, "The U.S. Factor in Israel's Military Relations with China," Jamestown *China Brief* 5, no. 12 (24 May 2005), available at http://www.jamestown.org/programs/chinabrief/.

5. Interview, Asian military source, June 2010.

6. Yang Jun, "Air Force Chief Expert: Our Military Has Been Developing Unmanned Bombers, Exclusive Interview with the Father of China's Unmanned Aerial Vehicles, Chinese Academy of Engineering Expert General Zhao Xu," 19 April 2007, http://military.china.com/zh_cn/top01/11053250/20070419/14051421.html.

7. Anil K. Joseph, "China Tests Indigenous Pilotless Plane," *Indian Express*, 12 May 1998, http://www.indianexpress.com/res/web/pIe/ie/daily/19980512/13250274.html.

8. "Performance: China's First Generation Unmanned Reconnaissance Aircraft on Display," Military.China.com, 28 June 2007, http://military.china.com/zh_cn/important/64/20070628/14187308.html.

9. While it is not known whether 863 Program funding for UAVs started with the inception of this program, it is possible that UAV program came to qualify for 863 funding during the late 1980s and 1990s. An oft-displayed Xi'an SE-1 twin-engine surveillance UAV carries a prominent "863" number on its fuselage, a possible indicator of 863 Program funding. Also, some Chinese sources noted that the Shenlong unmanned space plane test article may have had the 863 Program designator "863-706," an indication that it was also funded by the 863 Program.

10. Chinese Internet coverage of a June 2008 UAV conference organized by the Chinese Society of Aeronautics and Astronautics gave prominent attention to general officers from the PLA Air Force General Armaments Department.

11. This conference was hosted by the Institute of Air China, AVIC-1, AVIC-2, Northwestern Polytechnic University, Beijing University of Aeronautics and Astronautics, Nanjing University of Aeronautics and Astronautics, and the Air Force General Armaments Department; see "Vanguard of the Chinese UAV, General Assembly 2008," Chinese Society of Aeronautics and Astronautics Web Page, 25 June 2008, http://www.csaa.org.cn/New/ShowNew.aspx?placardid=2109&typeid=107; for photo coverage of this convention see, TSMX Web Page, http://www.tsmx.cn/bbs/viewthread.php?tid=4159&extra=page%3D1.

12. Nanjing University of Aeronautics and Astronautics, College of Aeronautics and Astronautics Aircraft Design Institute Web Page, http://aircraftdesign.nuaa.edu.cn/design_lab/.

13. "China Reorganizes Aerospace Industry," Forbes.com, 4 December 2008, http://www
.forbes.com/2008/12/03/china-aerospace-comac-cx_12040xford.html.

14. "China Aviation Sets Up a Defense Branch," *Xinhua*, 26 March 2009.

15. See the Guilin Xinying Technology Web Page, http://www.glxinying.com/cp/html/?81.
html.

16. Alexander Chebotarev, "Space Altitudes of the MEI Design Bureau," *Military Parade*,
April 2007, 4.

17. Author interview, IDEX arms show, Abu Dhabi, February 2009; and Vladimir
Ageikin, editor-in-chief, *Russia's Arms 2006–2007* (Moscow: Military Parade, 2006),
853–55.

18. "Radio Interference in Iraq Hampers USN's UAV Operations," *Jane's International
Defence Review*, May 2008, 8.

19. "FKC-1," *International Aviation* (affiliate of Aviation Week and Space Technology),
February 2008, 8.

20. "Successful Maiden Flight of Airship Developed by China Ordnance Group," 1
December 2008, http://xpb.hit.edu.cn/index.php?read-112.html.

21. Photo viewed on the Top81 website in June 2008. Photo is in author's collection.

22. Zheng Wei, Song Qi, Li Yong, Wu Zhihong, and Hu Linyun, "Computation and
Analysis of Power Generated by Solar Cell Array of Stratospheric Airship," *Journal of
Astronautics* (April 2010): 1224–30.

23. See, for example, Gong Xiying and Zhou Zhou, "Analysis of Combat Effectiveness of
an Unmanned Combat Air Vehicle," *Flight Mechanics*, no. 3 (2006).

24. Author interviews, April 2007 and June 2010.

25. Peter La Franchi, "China's Dark Sword Unmanned Aerial Combat Programme Raises
Questions," *Flight International*, 17 October 2007, http://www.flightglobal.com/
articles/2007/10/17/218683/chinas-dark-sword-unmanned-combat-air-vehicle
programme-raises.html.

26. Andrei Chang, "An Jian UCAV—PLA Air Force 4th Generation Fighter," *Kanwa
Defence Review*, 10 August 2007.

27. Poly Technologies brochure, "Short Range Air-to-ground Missile Type AR-1," obtained
at 2009 IDEX show in Abu Dhabi.

28. "HIT Shows Several New Unmanned Aerial Vehicles," Military.China.com, 22 June
2005, http://military.china.com/zh_cn/important/64/20050622/12423466_4.html.

29. See, for example, He Hetang, Zhou Bozhao and Chen Lei, "Aerodynamic
Configuration of Trans-atmospheric Vehicle Based on Waverider Research," *Journal
of National University of Defense Technology*, no. 4 (2007).

30. Mark Wade, "China," *Encyclopedia Astronautica*, http://www.astronautix.com/arti
cles/china.htm.

31. Richard Fischer Jr., "Shenlong Space Plane Advances China's Military Space Potential,"
International Assessment and Strategy Center Web Page, 17 December 2007, http://
www.strategycenter.net/research/pubID.174/pub_detail.asp.

32. Craig Covault, "China's Scramjet Ambitions," *Aviation Week and Space Technology*, 3 September 2007, 29.

33. Ibid., 30.

34. "Western Intelligence Seeks Proof of Chinese Hypersonic Test Flight," *Air and Cosmos*, 23 February 2007, 8, translated by Open Source Center.

35. See http://military.china.com/zh_cn/bbs2/11053806/20071216/14552048.html. This image is in the author's collection.

36. See, for example, Wang Ping, Du Yiping, and Song Zhiwei, "Carrier-Based Unmanned Aircraft and Early Warning Detection Research," *Cruise Missile* (November 2005).

37. Yuan Guoxiong, Bai Tao, and Ren Zhang "A Hybrid Reentry Guidance Method for Space-Based Ground Attack Weapon System," *Zhanshu Daodan Kongzhi Jishu* [*Tactical Missile Control Technology*] (September 2005) OSC CPP20060104424006.

Garth Hekler

Chinese Early-Warning Aircraft, Electronic Warfare, and Maritime C4ISR

THE FIRST GULF WAR (1990–91) demonstrated the power of precision weapons and integrated command, control, communications, computers, intelligence, surveillance, and reconnaissance (C4ISR). Following the allied victory, military leaders in China faced the question of whether they were able to counter such formidable capabilities. This eventually led China through a course of modernization aimed at "fighting local wars under informatized conditions." This effort to achieve "information supremacy" has meant developing both China's own C4ISR capabilities as well as effective means of disrupting a "strong enemy's" C4ISR advantage through electronic warfare. Aviation platforms have received a great deal of attention in this regard.

In keeping with the theme of this section, this chapter will examine China's efforts to develop both airborne C4ISR and counter-C4ISR capabilities. China has sought to acquire and develop airborne early warning and command (AEW&C or AWAC) aircraft, dedicated electronic warfare (EW) aircraft, and electronic countermeasures for its fighters and other aircraft. For example, starting in the early 1990s, China looked to acquire AEW&C capabilities from abroad through the KJ-2000 project, which sought to integrate Israeli radar technology with a Russian airframe. When China was unable to acquire Israeli radar systems, it was forced to develop domestic substitutes. Since then, China has been working to develop AEW&C and EW capabilities based on the Y-8 turboprop transport platform under the "Gaoxin Project."[1] Each of these projects is supported by other more general efforts to develop advanced radar systems as well as offensive and defensive EW capabilities. But what would the successful development of such technology mean in the context of China's military capabilities? More importantly, how would such developments affect the United States?

Any developments of this type must be considered within the context of the kinds of missions China is likely to undertake. In the near term, conflict over Taiwan remains the most likely flashpoint between China and the United States, with China's policy focusing mainly on preventing Taiwan from moving toward de jure independence. In terms of the United States, this has meant preventing U.S. intervention, which has translated into developing ways to counter a U.S. aircraft carrier strike group (CSG).

In a Taiwan scenario, AEW&C aircraft and EW assets would likely be most effective at enhancing China's air defenses, with AEW&C aircraft providing improved sensor coverage in conjunction with ground- and sea-based platforms, and EW assets providing cover, thereby making China's air defense systems harder to target. Indeed, with advanced surface-to-air missile systems and fighter aircraft equipped with their own advanced electronic countermeasures—such as digital radio frequency memory (DRFM)—China's air defenses would be formidable. Such air defense capabilities would in turn make China's shore-based antiship ballistic missile (ASBM) systems—the key platform, along with submarines, identified in most articles dealing with antiaircraft carrier operations—less vulnerable to attack.

Aside from enhancing China's air defenses, however, such aircraft are less likely to be used to support direct air assaults on a CSG without significant backing from other platforms. This assertion is based on a recurring refrain that appears in many articles asserting the inferiority of Chinese air power in the face of vastly superior U.S. air power, which would place such assets in severe jeopardy in all but the best-defended areas. Because of this, China will likely continue to rely on a wide array of ground- and sea-based platforms for both early warning and EW purposes, at least in the near term. Indeed, such airborne assets are less necessary in the near term given China's shortcomings in midair refueling, aircraft carriers, and overseas bases, which limit China's theater of operations to its coastal waters, where its forces can rely on its shore-based infrastructure.

However, Taiwan is not the only scenario where China may need AEW&C or EW aircraft. For example, during peacetime China could gain valuable intelligence by using electronic reconnaissance aircraft. China has also been showing signs of broadening its strategic focus into such areas as the South and East China seas, which contain points of contention with China's East Asian neighbors. At the same time, growing economic interests in distant parts of the world have made China increasingly dependent on countries far outside of its territorial waters. As China seeks to meet these challenges by extending its operational range through the acquisition and development of an aircraft carrier or midair refueling, its forces will no longer be able to rely on China's coastal C4ISR network. Under such circumstances, effective AEW&C and electronic support aircraft would be increasingly necessary. In this regard, China's investment in such aircraft could be an important enabler for China's future capabilities, even if not fully realized for decades to come.

It is also significant that many of the articles that were examined for this study, in addition to discussing the development of indigenous AEW&C capabilities, focused on ways in which China could nullify an opponent's C4ISR advantage through a host of counter-C4ISR measures. While beyond the scope of this chapter, certain themes are noted.

Methodology

This project relied heavily on the China National Knowledge Infrastructure (CNKI), an extensive database of academic journals, dissertations, and conference volumes. The process started with searches for articles with the subjects "AEW&C" and "EW aircraft," which produced 930 and 1,049 articles, respectively. Additional searches were then performed using more general keywords, including "electronic warfare," "radar and jamming" and "communications and jamming," which produced 6,805, 5,215, and 12,380 articles, respectively.

The articles were sorted first according to the number of times the article was cited in other papers in the database. This metric, while imperfect, provided an effective means of selecting articles with the greatest impact in terms of readership.

It was also possible to gain additional insight by tallying the most common keywords occurring across all articles. While the most common keywords were invariably synonyms of the search terms, after removing such terms from the analysis, overall publishing trends could be assessed. Before examining these findings in greater detail, some additional background is required on C4ISR, AEW&C, and EW.

C4ISR

As the modern battlefield has grown progressively larger, the electromagnetic spectrum has become the key medium through which military forces communicate and detect opposing forces. Over the years, different parts of the C4ISR suite have come to rely on different parts of the electromagnetic spectrum based on functionality.

For example, communications rely on several different frequency bands, including high frequency (HF: 3–30 MHz), very high frequency (VHF: 30–300 MHz), ultra high frequency (UHF: 300–3000 MHz), and extremely high frequency (EHF: 30–300 GHz) bands. Each enjoy certain advantages and suffer from certain disadvantages. For example, the HF band allows for communications over long distances but at the cost of limited information-carrying capacity. By contrast, VHF, UHF, and EHF each have progressively higher information-carrying capacity but have increasingly limited range, making it necessary to use satellites or other relays.

Similarly, radar comes in different varieties depending on its intended function. For example, surveillance radars are used to monitor wide areas to alert forces of the presence of potential enemies. Therefore, surveillance radars make use of relatively low frequencies that allow for longer-range tracking (200–150 MHz). Once a potential target has been identified, it is then tracked using radar that allows for more accurate monitoring, with shorter range requirements. Target-tracking radar therefore operates in higher frequency bands (3–20 GHz). Beyond tracking radar, fire control radars are used to aim weapons—e.g., surface-to-air missiles (SAM), antiaircraft artillery, and air-to-air missiles. Such radars typically function over relatively short ranges, allowing for precise measurement of position and velocity by using even higher frequency bands.

In addition, there are a number of special-purpose types of radar. For example, over-the-horizon radar allows for surveillance at ranges of more than 1,000 km using the HF frequency band. Synthetic aperture radar allows for all-weather imaging of targets. Finally, moving-target indication allows for simultaneous tracking of multiple moving targets.

Beyond active sensors, passive sensors are also important sensor assets. With different military forces using different communications and sensor systems, it is possible not only to locate enemy forces with infrared detection but also to identify them based on the unique characteristics of their sensors and communication systems. Taken together, these C4ISR capabilities are a significant force multiplier, which forms the basis of modern network centric warfare.

AEW&C

Aircraft have special advantages as C4ISR platforms due to their ability to operate at high altitudes. Whereas land- or sea-based platforms may be limited to detecting enemy forces at a distance of several nautical miles, an airborne platform can detect incoming aircraft from as far away as 250 nm. Airborne jamming platforms enjoy significant advantages for the same reason.

As a result, aircraft have become key platforms in the United States for early warning. Indeed, there have been a large number of Chinese articles addressing the subject of U.S. AEW&C platforms such as the E-3 Sentry, E-2 Hawkeye, and the E-8 JSTARS. A figure cited by two separate articles stated that a single airborne radar is as effective as eight to ten ground-based systems.[2] Indeed, such AEW&C aircraft allow U.S. fighter and attack aircraft to achieve situational awareness without using their own radar, making them less susceptible to passive detection by opposing forces. In conjunction with stealth, AEW&C aircraft give U.S. fighter and attack aircraft a significant advantage, particularly in beyond visual range (BVR) engagements. For this reason, in addition to many Chinese articles extolling the benefits of AEW&C, there were also several articles that discussed ways to degrade such capabilities through electronic warfare.[3]

EW

As military forces have come to rely on an increasingly varied array of communications and sensor equipment, EW has emerged as an equally important part of the modern battlefield. EW refers to measures used to exploit, deny, or manipulate the use of the electromagnetic spectrum by one's adversary while simultaneously preserving one's own use of the spectrum. EW is therefore generally divided into three main areas: electronic countermeasures (ECM, aka electronic attack—EA) aimed at denying the enemy's use of the electromagnetic signals; electronic countercountermeasures (ECCM, or electronic defense—ED) aimed at preserving the effectiveness of the electronic equipment under conditions of electronic warfare; and electronic support measures (ESM), which primarily deal with gaining valuable intelligence on enemy systems to enable ECM and ECCM.[4]

ECM techniques can serve both offensive (e.g., disruption of enemy communications, sensors, or navigation) and defensive (e.g., countermeasures against enemy fire control radar) purposes. Jamming works by filling different parts of the electromagnetic spectrum with noise. The most thorough approach to jamming would involve creating electromagnetic noise over entire portions of the electromagnetic spectrum (i.e., barrage jamming). However, such measures require a significant amount of power and can prevent one's own side from using the electromagnetic spectrum. A given military therefore benefits from knowing the frequency range of its enemy, which makes it possible to either jam specific frequencies (i.e., spot jamming) or to quickly alter the frequencies (i.e., sweep jamming) among those most likely to be used by the enemy.

In contrast to noise jamming, deception seeks to trick the radar or communications user into false conclusions rather than simply disrupting a system's function. This may be done by recording signals and then replaying them at a later time or transmitting altered signals to trick the radar operators into coming up with incorrect measurements. A particularly formidable deception device is digital radio frequency memory (DRFM), which functions by making digital recordings of radar signals. These digital recordings can then be manipulated to send altered position and velocity signals to enemy sensors, making it difficult to track platforms that are equipped with such devices. As will be discussed in greater detail, China is believed to be pursuing this technology for its next-generation fighter aircraft.

Still another category of attack that warrants mention is so-called hard-kill techniques, in contrast to the soft-kill techniques described earlier. These involve physically destroying enemy radar or communications facilities. Examples of this would include antiradiation missiles and electromagnetic pulse weapons. Electromagnetic pulse weapons work by emitting a powerful electromagnetic pulse that overloads integrated circuits to the point that they burn out. By contrast, antiradiation missiles work by homing in on sensor or communications signals. This latter item will be revisited later in the chapter.

For such techniques to work, one would need detailed knowledge of C4ISR being used by enemy forces, thus making it necessary to engage in a range of ESM. Given the range of possible frequencies available for different radar and communications systems, along with the number of different signal properties (e.g., pulse agility, pulse compression, and pulse Doppler), knowledge of an opposing force's signals is very important. As noted earlier, while it is possible to jam wide areas of the electromagnetic spectrum, jamming over wider bandwidths requires a great deal of power. Blanket jamming can also interfere with one's own efforts to use the electromagnetic spectrum. Electronic intelligence (ELINT) is therefore critical to designing both ECM and ECCM. For this reason, opposing forces work to develop a catalogue of signals connected with different platforms and functions by gathering signals intelligence (SIGINT), which is further subdivided into communications signals (i.e., communications intelligence—COMINT) and noncommunication electronic signals such as radar (i.e., ELINT). Indeed, intelligence gathering, which would be carried out during peacetime, may be one of the most important near-term missions for China's electronic warfare aircraft.

For this reason, both U.S. EW aircraft such as the EA-6 Prowler and electronic reconnaissance aircraft such as the EP-3 have gained a great deal of attention. With its combination of radar, radar detectors, tactical jammers, and the greatly feared AGM-88 high-speed antiradiation missiles (HARM), the Prowler is recognized by Chinese sources as a key element in the air defense systems in both Iraq and Kosovo.[5] Such findings were backed up by computer simulations demonstrating the potency of EW aircraft in degrading air defense capabilities.[6] For these reasons, China has been actively engaged in developing EW aircraft as well as AEW&C.

China's AEW&C and EW Aircraft

Given China's recognition of the capabilities of such U.S. platforms, it is not surprising that China is developing its own airborne EW and AEW&C capabilities. China's airborne EW program is seeking to adapt the Yun-8 (Y-8) airframe to several different missions under the Gaoxin Project, for which seven variants have been identified. The Y-8 EW/ELINT (Gaoxin 1) aircraft will likely be used to detect enemy radar signals. The Y-8 SIGINT (Gaoxin 2) variant would be used for detecting and monitoring communications signals. The Y-8 Communications Relay (Gaoxin 3) aircraft would likely be used to facilitate communications between the ground and air. The Y-8 EW/ECM aircraft (Gaoxin 4) aircraft appears to be designed for standoff electronic countermeasure missions along with another EW/ECM aircraft known designated as "Gaoxin 7." There is also a line of aircraft designated as "Gaoxin 6" for antisubmarine warfare purposes.[7] Detailed information on the electronic systems was not found in any publicly available sources, although some photos of the aircraft can be found online.

China also sought to acquire a series of AEW&C aircraft through the KJ-2000 program.[8] China had originally awarded the contract for a full early-warning aircraft system through a joint project with Russia's Rosoboronexport company, the Beriev Company for an A-50 airframe based on the Ilyushin-76. The plan originally called for an Israel Aerospace Industries EL/M-2075 Phalcon Radar System. By 1999 the aircraft had successfully completed its flight tests and was ready to be fitted with the Phalcon system; however, under heavy U.S. pressure, Israel backed out of the deal and removed the radar system from the aircraft. The aircraft were eventually delivered to China without radar systems in 2002. Since then, it is reported that China has been seeking to install indigenous radar systems.

In addition to the KJ-2000, China is also reportedly developing another early-warning aircraft based on the Y-8 airframe under the Gaoxin Project, which is referred to as the KJ-200, or as "Gaoxin 5" and appears to have a straight radar configuration similar to that of the Swedish Erieye AEW radar. The aircraft was featured in news reports after one crashed on 4 June 2006.[9]

While it is clear that China is developing such capabilities, a more important issue is how China might use such aircraft. To explore this in greater depth, additional background is needed on China's strategic means and objectives.

AEW&C and EW Aircraft in Chinese Strategy

The most likely flashpoint between the United States and China remains conflict over Taiwan. While Chinese rhetoric focuses on reunification, the U.S. Department of Defense (DoD) states that "an attempt to invade Taiwan would strain China's untested armed forces and invite international intervention."[10] Given such ongoing limitations, China has had to settle for more limited objectives. As DoD's 2010 report on China's military states, "Beijing argues that the credible threat to use force is essential to maintain the conditions for political progress, and to prevent Taiwan from making moves toward *de jure* independence."[11] The corollary to this objective is preventing the United States or any other country from intervening on Taiwan's behalf.[12]

A defining moment in China's thinking on this subject was the 1995–96 Taiwan Strait crisis, during which Beijing was forced to back down from a series of missile tests near the Taiwan Strait after the United States deployed a CSG to the area. Since then there have been a number of articles by Chinese analysts addressing the question of how to counter U.S. naval and air power.

As explained in a recent RAND presentation, U.S. air power revolves around four key issues: BVR combat capabilities, stealth, precision munitions, and maintenance of bases and platforms including aircraft carriers capable of supporting numerous sorties.[13] While China appears to be developing capabilities aimed at each of these areas, it is important to note that it has made particularly significant efforts to develop area denial capacity, which could enable China to deter a CSG from intervening outright, or at least force the CSG to operate at such distances that their ability to support multiple sorties would be degraded.

In examining Chinese writings on antiaircraft carrier operations, a recurring theme emerged based on the idea of a "saturation attack" in which China would essentially overcome U.S. quality with overwhelming Chinese quantity. To this end, a great deal of discussion was dedicated to the types of platforms that would be suited to such an attack in the face of the strike group's technological superiority. In general, most Chinese analysts concluded that China simply could not challenge the United States directly in terms of air power; indeed, without aircraft carriers or midair refueling capabilities, China's naval aircraft simply lack the range to threaten a CSG. Even if China could sufficiently extend the range of its aircraft, several Chinese authors expressed doubts that such aircraft could overcome the CSG's defenses. For these reasons, like the papers reviewed more generally, these same analysts argued that the most promising platforms would have to be a combination of antiship missiles—both ballistic and cruise missiles—and submarines.[14] Indeed, as the DoD report states, China has been developing both an ASBM variant of the DF-21 (CSS-5) and long-range land-attack cruise missiles.[15] China has also been working to expand its conventional submarine fleet, including through the acquisition of Russian conventional *Kilo*-class submarines and the development of the next-generation *Shang*-class (093) nuclear attack submarine.[16]

Although air power is not likely to be the mode of choice in deterring a CSG in the near to medium term, aircraft would nevertheless serve an important role in China's air defense system, which would defend China's missile assets from air attack. It is here that AEW&C and EW aircraft would make the most significant contribution. While an attack on the Chinese mainland would be extremely risky given the potential for nuclear escalation, U.S. forces may be tempted to remove the threat of missile attack by destroying the missile batteries, or possibly destroying China's command and control system. However, given the strength of China's air defense systems, such efforts would be extremely difficult.

China has advanced both the missile and aircraft components of its air defense system through the purchase of foreign technology. Since the first Gulf War, China has made efforts to acquire advanced SAM air systems from Russia, including the Almaz S-300PMU/SA-10 B/C Grumble, the Almaz S-300PMU-1/SA-20-A Gargoyle A, and the Almaz S-300PMU-2 Favorit/SA-20S Gargoyle B. These systems are used in addition to several domestic air defense systems, including the HQ-1/HQ-s Guideline, the HQ-12/KS-1A Kai Shan 1, and the CADT HQ-9/CPMIEC FT2000. According to the DoD, China's air defenses can now credibly intercept aircraft at ranges of up to 200 km off China's coast—enough to threaten parts of Taiwan.[17]

China also has a number of advanced Russian aircraft, most notably 300 Su-27/30 Flanker long-range fighters. China also has a number of indigenously built copies of the Su-27/30 (known as the J-11) and an indigenously designed fourth-generation aircraft, the J-10. The People's Liberation Army (PLA) also has numerous legacy fighter aircraft.[18] China's AEW&C and EW aircraft would significantly enhance these elements of China's air defense system.

As noted earlier, U.S. success against the PLA Air Force (PLAAF) and the PLA naval aviation forces would depend on U.S. superiority in BVR combat, stealth, and precision weapons. However, AEW&C and EW aircraft would likely hamper U.S. efforts. AEW&C aircraft would greatly improve the situational awareness of Chinese fighters and strike aircraft while simultaneously allowing the fighter aircraft to avoid using their own sensors, thus preventing passive detection. At the same time, EW aircraft would provide additional cover from U.S. sensors.

Engaging such aircraft would be made even more difficult if China were to deploy advanced defensive ECM-like DRFM on its fighter aircraft. Indeed, *Jane's* reports that the KG300G, a pod-mounted self-protection jammer developed by China Electronic Technology Corporation, incorporates DRFM technology.[19] (For a list of Chinese electronic warfare equipment, see the appendix to this chapter). Another report indicates that China is pursuing DRFM ECM for both the J-10 and the future stealth-equipped J-20.[20] As noted earlier, DRFM devices function by making digital recordings of radar signals. Using these digital recordings, an aircraft's ECM system is able not only to accurately reproduce radar signals over time—a key weakness of analog frequency memory devices with which the signal may be degraded—but also to alter these signals to produce credible false targets.

Indeed, more than two hundred documents were found covering various technical issues related to DRFM. Until 1999 most articles on DRFM concerned means of preventing spurious signal generation—that is, unwanted signals that could give away the false targets.[21] Articles from this period appeared to be geared toward basic digital signal processing issues, for example, the spurious signal performance of amplitude versus phase quantization schemes.[22] Since 2000, by contrast, subjects have turned toward more real-world applications such as deceiving pulse Doppler, pulse compression, and synthetic aperture radar.[23] However, the articles appearing in the open press generally only cover these issues in conceptual terms or through computer simulations rather than reporting actual laboratory or field tests, which on their own would indicate that the technology is in the early stages of development. Indeed, empirical research on DRFM applications—that is, lab and field tests—would almost certainly be classified, making it difficult to make a reliable assessment of current technology readiness levels based on available data.

Whatever the current state of China's technology development might be, if China can successfully deploy such technology in the near future, China could make it extremely difficult for U.S. fighter aircraft to engage in BVR combat. If U.S. aircraft were forced to engage in close combat, their advantage in terms of stealth would also diminish. Air combat would then come down to a numbers game. Given China's aircraft and SAM batteries, U.S. aircraft would face a serious challenge, to say the least.

However, with respect to fielding a functioning AEW&C capability, it is important to note that China still appears to be working out important details. For example, a 2005 article examined several key technologies needed for an airborne early-warning system. While using general terms, the author did point to several issues that need to be resolved to field an effective AEW&C capability. For example, the article addressed issues related to shaped phased-array radar and processing techniques for detecting low-altitude aircraft amidst ground clutter.[24] Indeed, ground-clutter and space-time adaptive processing were among the most popular topics related to AEW&C among the articles reviewed for this project.[25] Beyond this, the article also discussed issues related to data fusion, specifically the difficulties associated with fusing radar with passive location data. Data fusion received great deal of attention in several other articles as well, for which it was described as a key challenge.[26]

Yet one should not overstate the importance of AEW&C and EW aircraft to Chinese success in such a conflict. While China's AEW&C and EW aircraft would enhance China's air defense capabilities, there is evidence that China would continue to rely heavily on ground- and sea-based platforms to supplement such aircraft. In fact, in terms of communications, China already maintains a highly redundant array of shore-based fiber-optic networks with links to numerous HF, VHF, UHF, and EHF satellites and very low frequency (VLF) stations (for submarine communications) as well as air- and sea-based data links.[27] Another article discussing China's next-generation data link (i.e., the tactical information system, or TIS[28]) thoroughly explores measures to allow the system to function without air-based relays, the solution for which is a combination of shore-based cable communications and links to other networks.[29] All of these efforts are supported by developments in ECCM; that is, direct sequence spread spectrum technologies such as code division multiple access, frequency-hopping technologies, and other forms of spread spectrum technology—all of which would make Chinese wireless communications harder to jam.[30]

Similarly, China has accumulated a wide array of indigenous ground-based radar systems, including YLC-2/4/6 air-surveillance radars, CLC-1/2/3 short-range air-surveillance radars, and JY-14 "Great Wall" long-range three-dimensional radar as well as the full range of radar associated with the Russian PMU-300 SAM systems.[31]

Given that it would be fighting primarily in China's coastal waters, the PLA could continue to rely on such assets in the near term. However, as China becomes increasingly reliant on overseas oil and other resources, its leaders have shown greater support for missions far beyond China's immediate coastal waters. Under such circumstances, electronic support aircraft would be far more important.

AEW&C and EW Aircraft for Future Missions

While Taiwan continues to loom large in mainland China's strategic calculus, China's leadership has been facing a new set of challenges stemming from its integration into the world economy, a situation that led President and Central Military Commission Chairman Hu Jintao to announce a set of "New Historic Missions," which include a specific mandate for the PLA to safeguard China's interests in the maritime domain and the electromagnetic spectrum. While the global financial crisis has reduced trade for the time being, China remains heavily dependent on natural resources from abroad. A recent report from the Office of Naval Intelligence points to the growing importance of the Straits of Malacca, through which 90 percent of China's trade by value passes. An even more tangible example is the PLAN's recent deployments in the Gulf of Aden aimed at preventing piracy off the coast of Somalia.[32]

In addition to a growing interest in safeguarding distant sea lines of communication, China continues to have a number of territorial and maritime claim disputes in both the East and South China seas. While China has mainly sought to resolve such issues through diplomacy, the ability to engage operations outside of its coastal waters could have an important impact on the resolution of such disputes.

The need for such capabilities has led to renewed interest in developing aircraft carrier capabilities. Indeed in recent years, several senior Chinese military leaders, including the PLAN East Sea Fleet commander Admiral Xu Hongmeng, Major General Qian Qichen, and perhaps most importantly Defense Minister and Central Military Commission member Liang Guanglie, have publicly stated that China should develop its own aircraft carrier capabilities.[33]

Indeed, there have been recent signs that China is making the effort to develop this capability. For example, China has been refurbishing the Soviet-era *Kuznetsov*-class *Varyag* aircraft carrier, also reportedly known as *Shi Lang*

(施琅), which was originally purchased from Ukraine in 1998. There have also been reports that China will begin building two 50,000–60,000-ton aircraft carriers to be completed by 2015.[34]

While AEW&C and EW aircraft may be somewhat redundant in their air defense support role, if China does develop aircraft carriers, AEW&C and EW aircraft would be a necessary support function, as China would no longer be able to rely on its shore-based infrastructure to provide such capabilities. Indeed, several articles pointed directly to the role of the E-2 Hawkeye as the backbone of a U.S. carrier strike group's AEW&C capabilities.[35] Other articles discussed the power of EA-6B Prowler in disrupting enemy missile guidance and other functions.[36] In addition, at least two Chinese authors have argued that AEW&C and EW would be a necessary investment that would be essential to China's future aircraft carrier capabilities.[37]

However, it is also important to note that *Varyag* is not the kind of aircraft carrier that would support the kinds of AEW&C and EW aircraft that China is currently developing. As Nan Li and Christopher Weuve point out, *Varyag* is a type of aircraft carrier described as "short takeoff but arrested recovery" (STOBAR). Such aircraft carriers are generally not appropriate for larger aircraft, which need the much larger and more expensive "catapult-assisted takeoff but arrested recovery" (CATOBAR) aircraft carriers. China would therefore have to rely on lighter, less capable platforms that could take off from short runways or vertical takeoff platforms such as a helicopter.[38]

Based on this, China would have to make significant changes not only to its current AEW&C and EW aircraft programs but also to its aircraft carrier development programs. Taken together with the range of other issues associated with aircraft carriers—that is, support ships, fighter aircraft, antisubmarine warfare capabilities—China's aircraft carrier program will require many years to reach maturity. However, all new capabilities have to start somewhere, and China will not necessarily be facing a foe as formidable as the United States under conditions of an antipiracy campaign or in a territorial dispute over the South China Sea. In this regard, such efforts could therefore be an important step toward achieving a very long-term goal.

Other Electronic Warfare Issues

While this chapter by necessity focuses on AEW&C and EW aircraft, a number of other issues related to electronic warfare emerged in examining the literature. Given the importance of EW in general, this section presents several issues that warrant further attention.

In addition to searches related to AEW&C and EW aircraft, CNKI searches were also conducted for electronic warfare in general. After removing synonymous and trivial (e.g., "development trends") keywords from the terms found through EW searches, "antiship missile" emerged as one of the most popular keywords. The most cited articles dealt with means of improving the effectiveness of antiship missiles by overcoming a ship's protective ECM, such as chaff decoys and fire control radar jamming. In general, these measures focused on using multisensor infrared/radar seekers and data fusion.[39] This, of course, has great significance in improving the credibility of China's missile-based antiaccess capabilities.

Another keyword that appeared frequently was "antiradiation missiles." For example, one of the most-cited articles discussed means of developing antiradiation missile decoys.[40] Beyond this, numerous articles addressed the need to counter U.S. AGM-88 HARM missiles in order to maintain China's air defense capabilities. Indeed, such missiles have featured prominently in U.S. suppression of enemy air defense missions. If China could counter these weapons effectively, it would significantly improve the survivability of its air defense capabilities.

In addition, several keywords were found for counter low observable (CLO)—for example, antistealth—sensor technologies, including "passive location" and "bi-(multi)static radar" (for CLO applications, transmitters and receivers are placed in separate locations to better detect radar signals reflected off in different directions by stealth aircraft). For example, one article advocated using passive location to overcome stealth by tracking communications signals.[41] Another article discussed the CLO potential of using the background illumination of television and FM broadcast signals in conjunction with bi-(multi)static radar receivers.[42] Given the importance of stealth in U.S. air strategy, such technology could significantly reduce the U.S. advantage in this regard. For this reason, it is not surprising that "low observable" was also a prominent keyword, which covered areas ranging from shaping and radar absorbing substances to infrared and plasma stealth.[43]

It is also important to note that manned aircraft were not the only platform under consideration in China. For example, the most highly cited articles on EW aircraft argued that China should make use of a "distributed electronic jamming system" consisting of multiple UAVs.[44] Indeed, UAVs featured prominently as a key platform for EW because they can be made relatively cheaply and could be used in close contact with enemy forces without the risk of losing highly trained pilots and their crew.[45] Such platforms could serve an important role if China were to seek a more offensive posture vis-à-vis the CSG.

Conclusion

In the near term, China's AEW&C and EW aircraft will most directly affect China's air defense capabilities. In conjunction with fighter aircraft equipped with DRFM defensive ECM, they could greatly increase the survivability of China's aircraft and in the process increase the survivability of China's missile forces. They would also play an important role in collecting SIGINT and COMINT during peacetime operations.

While China's AEW&C and EW aircraft would enhance China's air defense capabilities, China will likely continue to operate for the most part in what Chinese strategists term the "Near Seas" (the Yellow, East, and South China seas). As a result, the PLA will continue to use redundant shore- and sea-based platforms as backup. In the near term, therefore, AEW&C and EW aircraft will represent an incremental improvement in China's air defense capabilities rather a "game changing" capability.

However, as China becomes increasingly integrated into the world economy, the country will have ever greater interests in safeguarding sea routes for oil and other resources, and this has led several Chinese military leaders to publicly advocate for the development of aircraft carrier capabilities. Under such circumstances, mobile AEW&C and EW will be an important part of the aircraft carrier's C4ISR capabilities. AEW&C and EW aircraft may be best viewed as an investment in China's future capabilities, which could be quite formidable if China is able to deploy aircraft with advanced ECM such as DRFM. However, China's current AEW&C and EW efforts are not compatible with the STOBAR aircraft carriers China appears to be developing, which indicates that China has a long way to go before such capabilities are able to support each other.

Beyond aircraft, China is working on a number of other EW-related issues that could have significant implications for the United States. Broadly speaking, there is a great deal of interest in developing ways to counter C4ISR capabilities that go well beyond manned aircraft. For example, UAVs have received a great deal of attention for close-support jamming purposes. China has clearly taken great interest in multisensor guidance systems that would allow antiship missiles to overcome defensive ECM. Researchers are also exploring decoys to counter the HARM missiles. Finally, several Chinese authors have been exploring CLO and stealth technologies. While some of these technologies are closer to fruition than others, it is important that the United States be prepared for the possibilities that these developments might bring.

Appendix: Chinese Electronic Warfare Equipment

EW Equipment	Platform	Specifications/Features
BM/KG300G Airborne Self-Defense Jammer Pod	Airborne	Pod-mounted, self-protection radar jammer; DRFM, a DF receiver, integral data-bus and a multitarget jamming capability.
BM/KJ 8602	Airborne	Radar warning receiver and airborne threat warning systems.
BM/KJ 8602A	Airborne	Miniaturized KJ 8602 radar warning receiver and airborne threat warning systems.
BM/KJ 8602B	Airborne	Augmented KJ 8602. A radar warning receiver and airborne threat warning systems with frequency measurement capability.
BM/KJ 8602BC	Airborne	Radar warning receiver and airborne threat warning systems that is integrated with KG300G jamming pod.
BM/KZ 800	Airborne	Airborne ELINT system designed to detect land- and ship-based radar transmitters.
GT-1E Aircraft Chaff/Flare Dispenser	Airborne	Airborne CMDS.
JN1102 Airborne Communications Jamming System	UAV-based system	Communications jamming system comprised of airborne intercept and jamming subsystems and a ground-based intercept and jamming control station. The system is specifically designed to jam ground-to-air command and control links.
DZ9001 Mobile Electronic intelligence System	Vehicle-based system	ELINT system capable of detection, interception, analysis, and recording of radar signals within the 1–18 GHz frequency range.
DZ9002 Mobile Electronic intelligence System	Fixed site and mobile	ELINT system capable of detection, interception, analysis, recording, and display of radar signals within the 100–1,000 MHz frequency range.

(continued)

EW Equipment	Platform	Specifications/Features
DZ9300 Man-Portable Radar Reconnaissance	Man-pack system; land-, sea-, and air-based applications	Man-pack radar reconnaissance system that covers the 50–250 MHz (DZ9300A subsystem) and 250–1,000 MHz (DZ9300B subsystem).
JN1105A Communications Jammer	Vehicle-based	Vehicle-mounted communications countermeasures system capable of detection, location, and jamming of hostile radio communications traffic.
JN1601 Communications Jammer	Land-based	Integrated high-frequency communications reconnaissance and jamming system capable of search, interception, monitoring, analysis, and jamming of conventional and nonconventional HF band signals.
Type 945PJ "Seawatch Shipborne" ECM System	Ship-based	Passive/electro-optic jamming system consisting of optical sensors for detection and identification of threats. The system includes an onboard decoy launcher system and ship movement calculation functions.
NRJ5 Ship-Based Electronic Warfare System	Ship-based	Naval EW suite capable of threat warning using radar and laser as well as active jamming geared toward antiship weapon systems.
BM/HZ 8610 (Bell Tap)	Ship-based	Combined electronic countermeasures/ESM system capable of direction-finding and analysis of threat radar equipment.
PK-2	Ship-based	Shipboard decoy system.
TM-53, TM-100, TM-442, and TM-542	Ship-based	Airborne laser warning receiver.
Type 923-1 (RW-23-1/ Jug Pair)	Ship-based	Electronic support and radar warning system.
Newton Beta Suite	Ship-based	Integrated EW system that consists of three systems: ELT 318–ECM/Noise Jamming; ELT 521–ECM/Deception Jamming; and ELT 211–ESM/Intercept.

Source: Jane's Radar and Electronic Warfare Systems, http://jrew.janes.com.

Notes

1. "Yun-8 Turboprop Transport Aircraft," *China's Defence Today*, 13 June 2008, http://www.sinodefence.com/airforce/airlift/y8.asp.

2. Zhu Lili, Feng Cunqian, and Zhang Yongshun, "Analysis of Key Technologies of Airborne Early Warning Systems," 情报指挥控制系统与仿真技术 [*Information Command Control System and Simulation Technology*] 27, no. 5 (October 2005).

3. Wang Zhibin, Zhu Yuanqing, and Du Kexin, "Analysis of Efficiency Assessment Based on Several Joint Airborne Radar Jamming Systems," 电子信息对抗技术 [*Electronic Information Countermeasures Technology*], no. 6 (2007).

4. Examples of ECCM include increasing transmission power to "burn through" the noise created by enemy jamming equipment. ECCM techniques commonly used for safeguarding communications include frequency hopping and direct sequence spread spectrum. Frequency hopping works by quickly altering transmission frequencies while direct sequence spread spectrum works by spreading the signal carrier wave over a wider bandwidth below background noise levels. Both measures force a would-be enemy jammer to jam over a wider bandwidth, which would require significantly greater power levels. ECCM techniques for radars include frequency agility, pulse compression, pulse-burst waveforms, and side-lobe suppression. Frequency agility is similar to frequency hopping in that it works by quickly altering frequencies, thereby forcing the jammer to use more power to jam the signal. Pulse compression, also known as frequency modulated chirping, works by altering the frequency from the beginning to the end of each radar pulse. Pulse-burst waveforms work by emitting a rapid series of pulses. At the most basic level, both techniques allow the processor to differentiate radar signals from the background noise. Side-lobe suppression works by reducing the radar antenna's side lobe sensitivity. Radar receivers often pick up signals outside of the area of their main beam, which can be exploited by a jammer to disrupt azimuth and position measurements, but side-lobe suppression cancels out these extra areas of sensitivity in the receiver to reduce the effectiveness of such jamming measures.

5. Sun Dehai, "An Overview of Overseas EW Development and Thoughts on Our Own Country's EW Development," 舰船电子对抗 [*Shipboard Electronic Countermeasures*] 26, no. 1 (2003).

6. Zhang Shunjian, "Combat Efficiency Calculation Method for Long-Distance Airborne Jamming Aircraft against Ground Early Warning Radar," 电子对抗技术 [*Electronic Warfare Technology*], no. 5 (2004).

7. "Yun-8 Turboprop Transport Aircraft," *China's Defence Today*, http://www.sinodefence.com/airforce/airlift/y8.asp.

8. "Shaanxi AEW Aircraft Crashed during Test," *China's Defence Today*, 8 June 2006, http://www.sinodefence.com/news/2006/news06-06-08.asp.

9. Joseph Kahn, "Blow to China's Military," *International Herald Tribune*, 7 June 2006, http://www.iht.com/articles/2006/06/07/news/crash.php.

10. Office of the Secretary of Defense [hereafter, DoD], *Military and Security Developments Involving the People's Republic of China 2010*, Annual Report to Congress (Washington, DC: Office of the Secretary of Defense, 16 August 2010), 52, http://www.defense.gov/pubs/pdfs/2010_CMPR_Final.pdf.

11. Ibid., 50.

12. Ibid., 51.

13. John Stillion and Scott Purdue, "Presentation: Air Combat Past, Present and Future," RAND, August 2008, http://www.defenseindustrydaily.com/files/2008_RAND_Pacific_View_Air_Combat_Briefing.pdf.

14. Wang Hui, "Weapons and Equipment for Attacking Aircraft Carriers," 当代海军 [*Modern Navy*], no. 10 (2004): 34–35.

15. DoD, *Military and Security Developments*, 2.

16. Ibid., 3.

17. Ibid., 50.

18. Carlo Kopp, "The Flanker Fleet—The PLA's 'Big Stick,'" *International Assessment and Strategy Center*, May 2006.

19. "CEIEC Active and Passive Airborne Electronic Warfare (EW) Systems," *Jane's Radar and Electronic Warfare (EW) Systems*, 16 February 2009, http://jrew.janes.com/public/jrew/index.shtml.

20. "China's Strategy to Achieve Military Technology Independence," *Aviation Week and Space Technology*, July 2008, 54.

21. Chen Ning, "DRFM Spurious Signal Spectrum Structure," 电子对抗技术 [*Electronic Warfare Technology*], no. 2 (1998).

22. Feng Cunqian, Zhang Yongshun, and Tian Bo, "Amplitude Quantized Digital Radio Frequency Memory Device Component Design," 无线电通信技 [*Wireless Communications Technology*], no. 2 (2003).

23. Wang Ru, Wu Zhihong, and Zhao Guoqing, "Synthetic Aperture Radar Jamming Based on DRFM," 电子信息对抗技术 [*Electronic Information Countermeasures Technology*], no. 2 (2006).

24. Phased-array radar is made up of numerous small transmitter-receiver units that are controlled to create a directed radar signal. The idea behind shaped phased-array radars is to create a radar system that would fit the shape of the aircraft. This would allow for better aerodynamic performance because the AEW&C aircraft could forgo the large radome seen on aircraft such as the E-3. Zhu Lili, Feng Cunqian, and Zhang Yongshun, "Key Technologies Analysis of Airborne Early Warning System" 情报指挥控制系统与仿真技术 [*Information Command Control System and Simulation Technology*] 27, no. 5 (October 2005).

25. Keywords found through searches for AEW&C were counted. After removing synonyms for AEW, "ground clutter" and "space time" adaptive processing were among the most common keywords. This pattern matched the subject of the most-cited article: Bao Zheng, Liao Guisheng, Wu Renbiao, and Wang Yongliang, "Phased Array

Airborne Radar Ground Clutter Suppression with Space-Time Adaptive Processing Filters," 电子学报 [*Electronics Bulletin*], no. 9 (1993).

26. Qu Dongcai, "Development of AWACS and Its Key Technologies," 航空科学技术 [*Aviation Science and Technology*], no. 2 (2003).

27. Sun Jingfang, "Technological Developments for Surface Ship Fleet Communications Networks under Conditions of Electronic Warfare," 舰船电子工程 [*Ship Electronic Engineering*], no. 4 (1999): 31.

28. Based on available descriptions, TIS appears to be closely modeled on the U.S. Link 16 tactical data-link system and its supporting joint tactical information distribution system hardware. Like Link 16, it is supposed to be a nodeless system with high anti-jamming capabilities based on a combination of direct sequence spread spectrum and frequency-hopping technologies.

29. Xu Lei, Wang Rong, and Yao Minli, "Windows NT-Based Research on Soft Real-Time Multi-Task Gateway of TIS," 电光与控制 [*Electronics Optics and Control*] 14, no. 4 (August 2007).

30. Hao Wei and Yang Lujing, "Development of Frequency Hopping Technology and Jamming Countermeasure," 舰船电子对抗 [*Shipboard Electronic Countermeasures*], no. 4 (2004).

31. *Jane's Radar and Electronic Warfare Systems*, http://jrew.janes.com.

32. "The People's Liberation Army Navy: A Modern Navy with Chinese Characteristics" (Suitland, MD: Office of Naval Intelligence, July 2009), http://www.fas.org/irp/agency/oni/pla-navy.pdf.

33. Nan Li and Christopher Weuve, "China's Aircraft Carrier Ambitions: An Update," *Naval War College Review* 63, no. 1 (Winter 2010).

34. Kenji Menmura, "China to Start Construction of 1st Aircraft Carriers Next Year," *Asahi Shinbun*, 31 December 2008, http://chinadigitaltimes.net/2008/12/china-to -start-construction-of-1st-aircraft-carriers-next-year/.

35. Meng Xianmin, Zhu Li, and Zhang Bo, "Study on Electronic Air Defense of Carrier Battle Group," 舰船电子对抗 [*Shipboard Electronic Countermeasures*] 29, no. 1 (2006).

36. Sun, "Overview of Overseas EW Development."

37. Jiang Yu, "A Unique Viewpoint on the Chinese Navy's Early Warning Aircraft," 舰载武器 [*Shipborne Weapons*], no. 5 (2008).

38. Li and Weuve, "China's Aircraft Carrier Ambitions."

39. Fang Youpei, Wang Liping, and Zhao Shuang, "Anti-Ship Missile Defense Penetration Technology Research," 航天电子对抗 [*Aerospace Electronic Warfare*], no. 12 (2004).

40. Gao Zhiguo, Cui Naigang, and Liu Wenye, "Anti-Radiation Missile Integrated Countermeasure Technology Research," 飞航导弹 [*Winged Missiles Journal*], no. 2 (2001).

41. Qu, "Development of AWACS."

42. Qu Changwen and He You, "Bistatic (Multistatic) Using Television of FM Broadcast," 现代雷达 [*Modern Radar*], no. 2 (2001).

43. Xia Xinren, "The Current State of Stealth Development and Trends," 中国航天 [*Aerospace China*], no. 1 (2002).

44. Qiao Fengwai, Lü Tao, Wang Guohong, and Liu Changxun, "Comparison of Several [Types of] Active Aviation Electronic Jamming Equipment," 电子对抗技术 [*Electronic Countermeasures*], no. 3 (2003).

45. Zhu Song and Wang Yan, "An Overview of Electronic Warfare UAV Development," 航天电子对抗 [*Aerospace Electronic Warfare*] 21, no. 1 (2005).

PART III

Contrasting Strategies

Protecting Bastions or Projecting Power?

Dennis J. Blasko

Chinese Helicopter Development
Missions, Roles, and Maritime Implications

HELICOPTERS ARE becoming an increasingly important element of the People's Liberation Army (PLA) arsenal. Missions are expanding; capabilities increasing. However, the ground forces (Army Aviation), PLA Navy (PLAN), and PLA Air Force (PLAAF) all suffer from a common shortfall: too few aircraft for their large forces. While numbers of helicopters are growing, rotary-wing aircraft are likely to remain a "high demand, low density" item for the near and mid-future (out to 2020).

This chapter first discusses the numbers and types of helicopters in the force and then briefly describes PLA helicopter pilots. It then examines the status of helicopter units in the PLA, PLAAF, and PLAN, including ships capable of conducting helicopter operations. Missions and training are addressed in each section. It concludes with observations of strengths and weaknesses and an estimate of future developments in the force.

Helicopters in the Force

The Chinese government has not provided a total number for rotary-wing aircraft in all services of the PLA. In July 2008 the chief of Army Aviation, Major

General Ma Xiangsheng, revealed that the army operated "nearly 500 attack and transport helicopters."[1] This number is higher than previous outside estimates (less than 400); however, most foreign observers work with only partial information that is not updated as frequently as necessary to be timely and accurate.[2] *The Military Balance 2010* estimates more than 80 helicopters each in the PLAN and PLAAF, but these numbers, too, probably understate to some degree the size of these forces. Chinese websites cite an unofficial number of 250 helicopters in the PLAAF, but this number likely is too large.[3] Based on the force structure described in the following, the total number of helicopters in all of the PLA may be in the range of 700–800 airframes (about 500 for the PLA, somewhere over 100 for the PLAN, and maybe close to 100 for the PLAAF).

While the total number of aircraft is not certain, the different types of helicopters in service in the PLA are fairly well known. Despite the relatively small size of the helicopter force compared to the overall size of the PLA, the PLA operates roughly twelve different types of helicopters (several of which have multiple variants). Nonetheless, there are very few heavy-lift helicopters in the force and the force currently lacks a dedicated attack helicopter, though one may be approaching deployment. The bulk of the new helicopters entering the inventory appear to be Mi-17-series aircraft imported from Russia, supplemented by Chinese-produced versions of multiple types of French aircraft. Smaller numbers (ranging from three to fewer than twenty) of several other types of helicopters from France, Russia, and the United States round out the force. Table 1 lists the types and estimated numbers of helicopters known to be in operation and in development.

France has granted the Chinese defense industry authorization to produce several French-designed helicopters.[4] The Zhi-8 is a copy of the SA-321 Super Frelon; the Zhi-9, a copy of the SA-365 Dauphin; and the Zhi-11, a copy of the SA-350 Ecureuil/Squirrel. All of these aircraft have been produced in China in militarily significant numbers, and production appears to be continuing. Only a few SA-316 Alouette III and SA-342 Gazelle were purchased roughly twenty years ago but still apparently are in operation and probably used mostly for training. The EC-120 Colibri Hummingbird is a joint project of China, France, and Singapore; the few EC-120s known to be in the PLA inventory are used for pilot training, and more may be purchased in the future.

Several decades ago the USSR provided China with Mi-4, Mi-6, and Mi-8 helicopters. Since the demise of the Soviet Union, Russia has sold the PLA some 250 or more Mi-17-series aircraft (upgraded Mi-8), which have become the workhorses of the force. In late 2007 the first local production (assembly) of a Mi-171 was reported with the eventual goal of an annual production of 80

Table 1: PLA Helicopters (all numbers are estimates)

Type*	Army	Navy	Air Force	Import from/Local Production
Zhi-8/SA-321 Super Frelon	7	40	10	France; license production
Zhi-9/SA-365 Dauphin (multiple variants)	206	25	20	France; license production
Zhi-10 (Attack)	In development			Indigenous production
Zhi-11/SA-350 Ecureuil/Squirrel	53			France; license production
Zhi-15/EC-175	In development			Cooperation with Eurocopter
EC-120 Colibri (Hummingbird)	8			Cooperation with Eurocopter and Singapore
SA-316 Alouette III	8			France
SA-342 Gazelle	8			France
AS-332 Super Puma			6 ?	France
Mi-6 Hook	3			Russia
Mi-17V5, Mi-17V7	200 ?	8 ?	50 ?	Russia; limited local production
Mi-26	4			
Ka-28 Helix/Ka-31		14 with 12 more to be delivered		Russia
S-70C Blackhawk	<20 operational			U.S.
Bell 214			4 ?	U.S.

Sources: International Institute for Strategic Studies, The Military Balance 2010 (London: Routledge, 2010), and China's Defense Today Web page, "Helicopters," http://www.sinodefence.com/airforce/helicopter/default.asp.

* Helicopters manufactured in China are identified by a "Z" or "Zhi" (for 直升机, zhishengji, helicopter) followed by a numerical designator. A "W" (for 武装, wuzhuang, armed) is inserted before the "Z" when weapons are added, such as the WZ-9. Foreign imports retain their native designations but are given Chinese characters to represent the initial foreign sound, that is, 米-17 (Mi-17) or 卡-28 (Ka-28).

aircraft, if a licensing agreement can be reached.[5] That production level will probably take several years to achieve, and not all aircraft will necessarily be sold to the PLA. As part of the PLAN's purchase of 4 *Sovremenny*-class missile destroyers, 8 Ka-28 Helix aircraft were also acquired from Russia. According to reports out of Russia, 6 more Ka-28 outfitted for antisubmarine warfare were delivered in 2009, with 3 more on order; another 9 reconnaissance and targeting Ka-31s are part of this package.[6] In the mid-1980s the PLA purchased 24 Sikorsky S-70C Blackhawks and a few Bell 214 (upgraded UH-1 Huey). Sanctions imposed by Washington after 1989 have halted the sale of spare parts for these platforms, but some Blackhawks are still apparently flying.

The Chinese defense industries are known to be developing the Zhi-10 attack helicopter. A prototype was reported to have flown in 2003, but the aircraft is not yet understood to be in the operational inventory. Apparently problems with obtaining production rights for the engines or developing alternative engines are delaying manufacture.[7]

China and Eurocopter are working together on a follow-on medium helicopter, the Zhi-15, to replace the existing Zhi-8, Zhi-9, and Mi-17 fleets as well as to supply the growing Chinese civilian market. The aircraft, also known as EC-175, is expected to make its first flight in 2009 with certification in 2012. It is reported "likely to enter PLA service in 2015–2020."[8] Based on past performance of the Chinese aviation industry, this time frame may well be optimistic.

Finally, there is also a report of Chinese cooperation with Poland to purchase 150 helicopters over a ten-year period.[9] It is unclear if this deal is aimed at the Chinese civilian or military market, but at that rate of production, the impact on the PLA would appear to be marginal in the near term. In March 2009 the Chinese press revealed that a memorandum of understanding on developing heavy helicopters (with maximum takeoff weight of twenty to thirty tons) was signed in October 2008 by China's Premier Wen Jiabao and Russia's Premier Vladimir Putin. A contract "is expected to be signed soon" with production to begin in "five to six years."[10] If this project comes to fruition, it will help solve a major shortfall in both the Chinese military and civilian helicopter sectors.

In general, the PLA uses each type of its helicopters in a variety of missions. All helicopters in the PLA inventory can be used for transport and supply missions, observation and reconnaissance, command and control (including radio relay), search and rescue (SAR), and medical evacuation. Once assigned to units, some helicopters are dedicated to specific missions while others perform multiple roles. For example, Zhi-8, Zhi-9, Mi-17-series, and S-70C are commonly used in transport missions, and the Zhi-8 specifically for SAR.

Mi-17-series aircraft are also used for paradrop. Zhi-9, Zhi-11, Mi-17-series, Ka-28, and SA-342 can be armed with machine guns, rockets, torpedoes, air-to-surface missiles, or air-to-air missiles. A few aircraft have reportedly been equipped for electronic warfare missions. Zhi-11, SA-316, and EC-120 are used as basic training aircraft.

PLA Helicopter Pilots

PLA helicopter pilots follow generally the same education and training path as do PLA fixed-wing pilots. Unlike in some other militaries, where warrant officers may fly helicopters, all PLA helicopter pilots are officers. Pilots first attend a PLA academy to receive a bachelor's-level college education and learn to fly training aircraft. Since its establishment in 1999, the Army Aviation Corps Academy educates and trains Army Aviation cadets.[11] Yearly classes number roughly 100 cadets. In December 2005 the academy set up a flight simulation center to help shorten training time.[12] PLAN helicopter pilots attend the Naval Aviation Academy. Initial helicopter training appears to include about 130 hours of flight time.[13] For a decade, PLAAF cadet helicopter pilots attended the Army Aviation Corps Academy. However, that mission was turned over to the PLAAF Second Flight Academy in 2009 when "the first [Air Force] organic helicopter training regiment" was formed there.[14]

Upon arrival in operational units, pilots receive training in the aircraft assigned to that unit. All PLA pilots appear to follow the same progression through a series of grades (or classes) from third-grade to second-grade to first-grade and finally special-grade:

> Following two to three years of technical training and basic tactics training, the pilots can be awarded wings as a third-grade pilot. As their training continues, they have the opportunity to become a second-grade pilot by flying in day and night using instrument flight rules (IFR), maintaining flight safety, and reaching a certain proficiency level. Next, if they have conducted combat and training missions under day and night IFR conditions, flown a certain number of hours, reached the level of instructor pilot and flight controller, and maintained flight safety, they can become a first-grade pilot. Finally, they can become a special-grade pilot if they have made special achievements in combat, training, and test flights, and maintained flight safety.[15]

From this description as well as from reports of unit flight training, it is likely that most PLA helicopter pilots learn fewer advanced skills, such as night vision qualification, IFR, nap-of-the-earth flight, and so forth, during their initial training than do pilots in other militaries, especially the United States.

However, unlike U.S. pilots, PLA pilots probably spend much more time on flight status because they stay in operational units for most of their careers and are not subject to frequent reassignments that remove them from flight duty. As a result, units will have a relatively high percentage of special-grade pilots who are in their forties and perhaps even early fifties. This level of experience may add to pilots' ability to make judgments in the air, but at those ages, reflexes, eyesight, strength, and stamina may decrease in many senior pilots. Older pilots (in their late forties and fifties) may be quite effective in many missions but perhaps are less than optimum in low-level, fast, night operations, which are increasingly prevalent in modern combat where younger pilots thrive.

The one PLA helicopter lost during the earthquake relief operations in Sichuan in the spring of 2008 was flown by a 51-year old special-grade pilot who was scheduled to retire in 10 months.[16] Bad weather and difficult terrain are believed to have caused the crash. At the time of the accident, Senior Colonel Qiu Guanghua had about 5,800 flight hours in a 34-year career.

While the specific number of hours flown by PLA helicopter pilots is not known exactly, the flight history of lost pilot Senior Colonel Qiu provides some insight. Qiu began flight training in 1974 and would have averaged about 170 hours per year to accumulate 5,800 hours at the time of his death. Another article describing a PLAN helicopter regiment that provided Olympic security revealed that the unit had 13 special-grade pilots, each a senior captain with more than 3,600 hours (four of them were approaching 50 years old).[17] Assuming this group each had at least 22 years of flight time, they then would have averaged up to 160 hours annually.[18] A few years earlier, a special-grade naval helicopter pilot with 26 years of service was reported to have only about 2,500 hours, averaging a little less than 100 hours per year.[19] Thus, average flight hours probably vary among pilots and units and are influenced by training and real-world missions beyond the control of the pilots themselves.

These numbers suggest that some PLA helicopter pilots may fly more hours than many PLA fixed-wing fighter pilots. One estimate from 2005 noted, "Three articles between 2002 and 2005 provide information on three non-Sukhoi fighter pilots, who have averaged 115 to 125 hours of flight time per year."[20] In any case, because of the relatively small numbers of helicopters in the PLA, helicopter pilots in any service are likely kept fairly busy due to training and emergency requirements.

Army Aviation

The Army Aviation Corps was established in 1986 and first manned by personnel and fewer than one hundred aircraft transferred from the PLAAF.[21] In more than twenty years of its existence, its growth rate can be called modest at best. Although gradually expanding in size and capabilities, the number of helicopters in the ground force (approximately five hundred) is by any calculation small for a total force level of around 1.5 million active-duty personnel.

Army Aviation units are subordinate to the General Staff Department (apparently one operational and one or two training regiments), some Military Region headquarters, and several group armies. At least six of eighteen group armies are known to have organic helicopter regiments, including the 26th, 31st, 38th, 39th, 42nd, and 54th group armies. Many helicopter units that are now subordinate to group armies originally were subordinated to the General Staff Department, then to Military Region headquarters, before finally being assigned to group army level. This decentralization of command reflects both the expansion of the force in size and its maturity. As helicopter units go further down the chain of command, they can train more frequently with conventional units with less bureaucracy than when they are assigned to higher-level headquarters.

Army Aviation units now work fairly routinely with many ground force organizations in combined arms operations. They also frequently support special operations units, which have been established over the past fifteen to twenty years and are now, too, increasingly being pushed down to group army command. Most helicopter support to special operations forces, however, appears to be transport of small units to tactical or operational objectives located not too far beyond friendly lines. While armed helicopters may provide escort, PLA special operations forces do not appear to have developed mission-specific helicopters for long-range transport, SAR, or continuous close-in fire support.

This list has proven fairly accurate from analysis of reporting and photographs that have appeared in the Chinese media, especially during the earthquake relief efforts in Sichuan, but it does not reflect the expansion of the army aviation regiment in the Lanzhou Military Region to a brigade. It is obvious from table 2 that most (and probably all) regiments are composed of a combination of helicopter types. While the exact number of aircraft per regiment is not known, based on the information, an average of about forty airframes per regiment appears to be the norm. It would not be surprising if training regiments had more aircraft while some operational units had fewer. Each

Table 2: Army Aviation Regiments

Military Region (MR)	Regiment	Location	Equipment	Serial No.
Army Aviation Department	Training	Tongzhou, Beijing	Zhi-11, SA-316	LH90XXX
	Training	Linfen, Shanxi	Zhi-11, HC120	LH90XXX
	4th	Tongzhou, Beijing	S-70C, SA-342, Mi-17	LH94XXX
Beijing MR	8th	Baoding, Hebei	Zhi-9, Mi-17	LH98XXX
Shenyang MR	9th	Shenyang, Liaoning	Zhi-9, Mi-17	LH99XXX
Jinan MR	1st	Xinxiang, Henan	Zhi-9, Mi-17, Mi-6	LH91XXX
	7th	Liaocheng, Shandong	Zhi-8	LH97XXX
Nanjing MR	5th	Xuzhou, Jiangsu	Zhi-9, Mi-17	LH95XXX
	10th	Xiamen, Fujian	Zhi-9	LH910XXX
Guangzhou MR	6th	Foshan, Guangdong	Zhi-9, Mi-17	LH96XXX
Chengdu MR	2nd	Chongqing	S-70C, Mi-17	LH92XXX
Lanzhou MR	3rd	Hetian, Xinjiang	S-70C, Mi-8, Mi-17	LH93XXX

Source: This chart appeared on the *China's Defense Today* website (accessed in May 2007) at http://www.sinodefence.com. It is no longer available at this website.

Notes: Some units may be changing the system of aircraft tail numbers. Sufficient information is not yet available to confirm the extent of tail number changes. This chart does not reflect the 2009 report of an Army Aviation Brigade, vice regiment, in Lanzhou Military Region.

regiment would then require at least eighty pilots and copilots, but probably more would be needed to conduct continuous operations. Many helicopters (such as the Mi-17-series) also require flight engineers and enlisted crew members. The helicopters themselves are supported by ground maintenance and supply personnel. Operations and support are planned and controlled by regimental and battalion-level headquarters staffs.

Chinese media reports show Army Aviation training exercises becoming increasing larger and complex. News reports frequently mention the transition of the force from a purely transport role to also include attack missions.[22] Photographs of helicopter operations from the 1990s usually showed six or fewer aircraft in training. Recent reports frequently include twelve to eighteen helicopters in the air at the same time.[23] Armed helicopters often accompany troop transport aircraft, but most ground-attack missions appear to be directed against preplanned targets. In addition to landing on the ground, units experiment with various methods for personnel to exit the aircraft while hovering, including rappelling, "fast-rope," and climbing down ladders. Army Aviation units are also reportedly training at night, at low-level, and in missions conducted over water, although the percentage of training in these conditions is not known.[24] Significantly, the use of forward arming and refueling points has not been observed in the PLA literature, which suggests most Army Aviation operations are conducted on a single tank of gas.

The earthquake relief effort in Sichuan undertaken in the spring of 2008 was the largest-ever extended deployment of PLA helicopter assets. Six Army Aviation regiments dispatched approximately 100 aircraft to the disaster zone. Army assets operating out of 3 airfields were augmented by a considerably smaller number of Air Force helicopters and approximately 30 civilian helicopters.[25] Early in the operation 62 aircraft were reported flying 106 sorties in complex weather conditions and in difficult terrain in what was called the "largest number of helicopters operating at once in a single day."[26] General Ma told foreign military attachés, "Many young pilots gathered significant experience, which could not have been possible in day-to-day training. . . . In the first 10 days after the quake, many pilots also had to fly for more than 10 hours a day."[27]

As mentioned earlier, bad weather and harsh terrain caused the loss of one Mi-17-series helicopter with all its crew and passengers. However, in general PLA helicopter units performed admirably during this crisis, conducting an array of missions including reconnaissance, transport, resupply, medevac, and SAR. Nonetheless, the overall inventory of aircraft available was insufficient for the urgent requirements. *People's Daily* commented, "With this earthquake, we mustered as many helicopters as possible, but overall they were still too few, and their capabilities not yet improved."[28] General Ma agreed about the inadequate size of the force and further acknowledged that no heavy-lift military helicopters were available.[29] This situation forced the use of a Russian-made Mi-26 from the civilian company China Flying-Dragon Special Aviation Corporation to transport earth-moving equipment.[30]

The earthquake relief effort was a prime example of the PLA's participation in nontraditional security missions. It seems reasonable for the military leadership to cite the performance of helicopter units in this effort to further justify the expansion of the overall force, perhaps at a faster pace than in past decades. Larger numbers of helicopters will provide PLA leaders with increased capabilities and greater flexibility in planning and executing both warfighting and nontraditional security missions.

Air Force Helicopter Units

The PLA's first helicopter unit was established in the PLAAF in May 1959. Currently PLAAF helicopter units have been identified in the Beijing, Chengdu, Guangzhou, and Nanjing military region air forces but not confirmed in the Shenyang, Lanzhou, and Jinan military region air forces. According to Chinese Central Television, in 2007 a transport unit (the 13th Division) in the Beijing Military Region Air Force was issued at least six WZ-9 helicopters and ordered to prepare for Olympic security duty. The unit selected 19 pilots for the new helicopter unit and within a few months had reached operational status. During the Olympics, 5 aircraft teams flew more than 370 sorties for a total of 570 hours.[31]

Operating out of the Guangzhou Military Region, the 15th Airborne Army established a helicopter *dadui* (大队; group, considered smaller than a regiment) by mid-2005.[32] This development parallels the assignment of helicopter regiments to group army command in the ground force and provides the airborne with a dedicated helicopter support force. The exact number of aircraft in the unit is not known but both Zhi-8 and Zhi-9 helicopters have been seen in photos of the unit. The unit deployed Zhi-8s to the Sichuan earthquake zone and both Zhi-8 and Zhi-9 to provide aerial support to the Qingdao venue during the Olympics.[33] Another PLAAF helicopter unit operating in the Guangzhou Military Region is the Hong Kong Garrison Aviation unit composed of Zhi-9 helicopters.

In the Nanjing Military Region Air Force, the 26th Air Division has a SAR Regiment that includes a number of Zhi-8 helicopters. This unit dispatched approximately six aircraft to the Sichuan operations. Likewise, the 12th Transport Regiment of the 4th Transport Division of the Chengdu Military Region Air Force, stationed in Sichuan, also provided helicopter support to the earthquake relief operations.[34] In the case of both of these units, the exact number of helicopters per regiment is not known.

Naval Aviation Helicopter Units

The PLAN's first "shipborne" helicopter regiment was established in 1975 in the North Sea Fleet. Over the following decades two more helicopter regiments were added—one each in the East Sea Fleet and South Sea Fleet—although the precise history of their formation is unclear. Currently, the PLAN helicopter force is comprised mainly of Zhi-8, Zhi-9, and Ka-28 helicopters, with perhaps a few Mi-8/Mi-17-series in the inventory (mostly seen in support of amphibious operations). In total, the PLAN is estimated to operate roughly one hundred helicopters of all types. Analysis of photographs available on the Internet suggest that each of the three naval helicopter regiments is composed of a combination of three types of aircraft, Zhi-8, Zhi-9, and Ka-28 (perhaps assigned only temporarily), even though the Ka-28 is generally associated with the *Sovremenny*-class destroyer purchased from Russia, all of which are assigned to the East Sea Fleet. These numbers imply that the average number of helicopters per regiment may be slightly smaller than Army Aviation regiments—approximately thirty to thirty-five aircraft.

PLAN helicopters are home-based at airfields on land and assigned to ships when they are at sea. (No insights into this assignment process have been ascertained, but it is likely that ships and aircraft are matched for temporary duty as required by missions and training and availability.) The ship list found in the appendix following this chapter provides information about thirteen destroyers (out of a total of approximately twenty-seven destroyers in the PLAN), twenty frigates (out of a total of approximately forty-eight frigates[35]), twenty amphibious warfare vessels, and twelve auxiliaries capable of helicopter operations divided among the three fleets. In recent years the PLAN has taken significant steps to upgrade the education of the officers who command aircraft operations in the naval aviation departments on all of these vessels.

Like Army Aviation, PLAN helicopter units are expanding their mission task list from primarily SAR, medevac, transport, and resupply roles to combat roles. Navy helicopters are increasingly taking on antisubmarine warfare (ASW) and antisurface warfare missions, including reconnaissance and surveillance as well as attack. In August 2008 *Jane's* reported the roll-out of a Zhi-9D helicopter capable of firing a radar-guided TL-10B (KJ-10B) antiship missile with a range of 18 km. The missile was developed in cooperation with Iran and is the first instance of an antiship missile appearing on a PLAN helicopter.[36] The helicopter was reported to be a prototype and is not yet confirmed to be in service in the fleet.

Training is becoming increasingly complex as multiple aircraft practice operations with multiple ships on a routine basis. Navy helicopters also reportedly perform low-level flights over water and conduct night takeoffs and landings on ships under way in all weather. Nonetheless, the PLAN helicopter force has taken a considerably longer time to achieve some operational standards that other navies have maintained for decades and apparently still does not undertake some important missions. For example, although the SA-321/Zhi-8 may be equipped with mine countermeasures equipment, research found no examples of PLAN helicopters performing countermine operations. Likewise, no PLA helicopters have in-flight refueling capability and few, if any, PLAN helicopters or ships are equipped with recovery, assist, secure, and traverse (RAST) systems to aid in takeoff and landing operations at sea in adverse conditions.[37]

PLAN helicopter training apparently has taken a very conservative approach to expanding its missions over the three decades the force has been in existence. Although the first PLAN helicopter regiment was established in 1975, it took until 1980 for it to conduct its first landing on a ship at sea.[38] Nighttime takeoff and landing on ships at sea in all-weather conditions, which is the basis for conducting twenty-four-hour air operations, was not successfully conducted during the first two decades of the PLAN helicopter fleet's history. PLAN helicopter pilots made their first night landing in good weather on a moving ship at sea in November 2004 after having successfully landed on stationary ships beginning in 2002.[39] "High-risk night landings" (presumably in poor weather) were achieved in October 2006.[40]

Once these initial achievements were made, however, units worked to acquire proficiency, such as making 180 takeoffs and landings in twenty-four hours. In 2007 PLAN helicopter pilots reportedly had not had an accident for twenty-four years.[41] This safety record was continued through November 2008, when a new Chinese-made North Sea Fleet helicopter flying over land as it returned to its base suffered a power failure that caused loss of altitude, speed, and course indicators. The crew took emergency procedures and landed safely. As a result of their actions, the crew was awarded a second-class collective merit citation.[42] The fact that this emergency warranted both a news report and citation for the crew reflects command emphasis on training safety consistent with an overall trend throughout the PLA as exercises become more complex and realistic.

In the summer of 2008 *Liberation Army Daily* carried a series of articles about a multiday East Sea Fleet ASW training exercise in which PLAN helicopters operated in conjunction with surface vessels and a submarine. At least one Ka-28 ASW helicopter was pictured landing on Frigate 526, the *Wenzhou*, a Type 054 *Jiangkai*, which was said to be working with a destroyer. Moreover, the helicopter navigator and submarine sonar operator were reportedly communicating with each during the operation, which lasted from 6:00 in the morning until 4:30 in the afternoon. On another day of training, after a surface vessel detected an underwater acoustic target, the ASW helicopter performed a live-ammunition attack run. In an interesting twist, the subsurface target "black box," which allegedly can track the movements of the ASW helicopter, was operated by Ship 862, the *Chongmingdao*, a Type 925 *Dajiang*-class ocean salvage and rescue ship. Thus, this exercise included at least three surface ships, a submarine, and helicopters. Signifying the importance of the exercise, senior PLAN officers were present. Sun Laishen, a deputy commander of the East Sea Fleet was identified as the "aviation force commander" and Zhu Ruiyun, a deputy political commissar of the East Sea Fleet, was identified as "a seaborne commander of the fleet."[43]

Chinese media reports contain many examples of naval helicopter training, including nighttime low-level flights, multihelicopter ASW operations, helicopter–surface ship coordinated ASW exercises, and over-the-horizon reconnaissance missions in support of surface ship antisurface missile operations. Over at least the past two years, operations in a complex electromagnetic environment have been highlighted. Objective evaluation by foreign analysts of the degree of difficulty or realism in these exercises is not possible from the amount of open-source information available, however.

In September 2008 one report from *Liberation Army Daily* received widespread foreign attention. The report read, in its entirety:

> The Dalian Naval Academy held an orientation course for the first batch of 50 newly recruited pilot cadets yesterday. The first pilot program of recruiting pilot cadets is an important decision made by the PLA Navy to realize a strategic transformation in the new period.
>
> The first batch of pilot cadets will receive a four-year education in the ship-borne aircraft flight field of study by relying on the automation

field of study of the Dalian Naval Academy. During the four years, they will focus on the basic theories of surface ship and flight apart from the basic theories and skills required in the automation field of study.[44]

This report was interpreted frequently in the foreign (and some Chinese) press that China had begun to train its first batch of fixed-wing fighter pilots for aircraft carrier operations.[45] However, the 2008 report is better understood if read in light of a similar report from 2003 about training naval aviation pilots to work in the naval aviation departments assigned to PLAN vessels. In addition to helicopter pilots to fly the aircraft, each of the more than sixty PLAN vessels capable of operating helicopters currently needs qualified officers to man the ships' aviation departments to control helicopter flight operations and integrate airborne activities with other tasks undertaken by the ships themselves. The 2003 report reads as follows:

> After 5 years of united cross-discipline and cross-specialty education, the first group of chief officer *candidates for various aviation departments of naval ships* has successfully finished their study at 3 different colleges and was assigned to naval ships on July 18. This has put an end to the history in which the Chinese naval aviation department has no "regular graduates."
>
> *In recent years, as the shipboard aircraft's role in naval ship's antisubmarine operation, operations against hostile land forces and naval forces becoming more and more important, it is high time for us to cultivate a group of highly qualified chief officers for aviation departments of naval ship who are well versed in the knowledge of naval ship as well as aviation.*
>
> The chief officer candidates for aviation departments this time entered the Dalian Naval Academy last March. Before that, they had studied three years and a half in the Naval Aeronautical Engineering Academy and the Naval Aviation Academy, where they finished study of general knowledge courses and aviation courses. Each student, having piloted airplanes for over 130 hours or above, has got some practical experience of aviation.
>
> In the Dalian Naval Academy, they studied systematically 30 specialty courses, including *organization, management, navigation, operation and tactics of surface ships*, and the theory, performance, operational skill and operational command of armaments, *which the chief officer of aviation departments should grasp.*

Through one year and a half's cultivation, they have acquired the basic quality for a junior commanding officer on a surface ship.[46] (Emphasis added.)

As reported in the 2008 article, the officers being trained at the Dalian Naval Academy are studying in the "Shipborne Helicopter Command" course, one of the nine disciplines for bachelor's degrees offered at the academy.[47] Now they will study for four years in Dalian instead of eighteen months in the previous program. The 2008 report appears likely to be a variation or refinement to the program established earlier in the decade to prepare officers to perform duties in naval aviation departments to command helicopter operations; the report is not about a program to train carrier pilots.

Finally, two PLAN Ka-28 helicopters were deployed on the destroyers *Wuhan* and *Haikou*, along with supply ship *Weishanhu*, which conducted the PLAN's first long-range, extended, nontraditional security mission to protect commercial shipping from pirate attacks off the coast of Somalia beginning in December 2008. The helicopters appeared to conduct three main types of missions: (1) patrol and, when necessary, pursuit of pirate vessels to drive them away from merchant ships, as occurred on 29 January 2009 to protect a Greek ship; (2) transport of special operations forces, including inserting and extracting SOF troops onto and off of Chinese merchants in convoys; and (3) ship-to-ship supply operations. It is probable that, like the earthquake relief mission, the helicopter pilots assigned to this effort flew more hours in more complex situations than they otherwise would in routine training. By all accounts, the two Ka-28s and crews performed well, setting new records for "sortie and flight time of ship-based helicopters."[48] Two Zhi-9 helicopters were also deployed with the PLAN's second rotation of ships to the mission, the destroyer *Shenzhen* and the frigate *Huangshan*, which arrived on station in mid-April 2009.[49] On 27 April they were used to thwart an attempt to capture a Philippine-flagged chemical tanker.[50] Subsequent deployments of PLAN vessels to the mission in the Gulf of Aden all have included shipborne helicopters, which have continued to perform successfully the missions described earlier.

Conclusions and Potential Developments

The evidence is clear that the PLA's helicopter force is expanding in size and scope of its missions. Helicopter units in all three services are without doubt more capable than they were a decade ago. Recent real-world experience in performing disaster relief operations in Sichuan, security operations at the

Olympics, and antipiracy operations off of Somalia provided essential planning, operational, and logistics experience in stressful conditions. These operations also highlighted the shortfalls of the force.

The size of the helicopter force remains too small for the requirements of such a large standing army, navy, and air force. Despite the decision over two decades ago to create the Army Aviation Corps, the force has grown at what can only be called a slow and deliberate pace over the past twenty years. By now, however, an education, training, and support infrastructure appears to have been built, and perhaps in future years the number of aircraft and units in all services can expand efficiently.

Nearly every mission the PLA faces in the future could be better accomplished with a larger helicopter force providing a wider array of capabilities than currently exist. In this regard, today's PLA helicopter force defies the conventional wisdom about the "rapid" and "massive" modernization of the PLA. Instead, as demonstrated by the report of training pilots for jobs in shipboard naval aviation departments, the PLA understands that command and control and support infrastructures must be built before the force can be modernized fully. The modest growth of the helicopter force reflects a professional approach to PLA army-building moderated by limited funding.

While missions have expanded, the helicopter force appears still to be in the rudimentary phase of execution for most tasks. For example, in the PLAN, helicopter units and surface and subsurface forces appear to be in the learning stages of combined arms operations. Nonetheless, in all cases, training reportedly is being conducted at larger scale in more complex environments than in previous decades.

Some shortfalls are exacerbated by lack of specific equipment to fulfill specific tasks. Lack of large-deck ships suitable for rotary-wing or fixed-wing operations also limits the number of PLA helicopters that can be deployed outside of China over great distances. This situation has been ameliorated to some degree with the commissioning of the Type 071 landing platform dock *Kunlunshan* (which was deployed as part of China's sixth counterpiracy task force in the Gulf of Aden in June 2010), and potentially the introduction of PLAN aircraft carriers in the future. In that regard, the PLAN helicopter force is already prepared to provide aircraft, pilots, and crews for a small-deck carrier capable of supporting multiple vertical takeoff and landing aircraft. The expansion of the program to train personnel for naval aviation departments to control helicopter operations may be an indicator of the PLAN's movement toward a small-deck, rather than large-deck, carrier in the future. PLAN helicopter pilots could perform those tasks now if a carrier were to be deployed, whereas training fixed-wing carrier aircraft pilots will take a considerably longer period to reach operational proficiency.

Continued expansion of the helicopter fleets in all services appears likely. If the Chinese aviation industry can produce kit-assembled Mi-17-series aircraft, fleet growth may be more rapid than if helicopters must be purchased from Russia or other countries. Similarly, increased domestic production of Zhi-8 and Zhi-9 helicopters could add to the numbers of aircraft in the inventory, but it is uncertain that the recently reformed China Aviation Industry Corporation is up to the task. If possible, reducing the number of different types (and countries of origin) of helicopters in the inventory while increasing overall numbers would greatly simplify the logistics and training challenges of a force composed of twelve different types of aircraft, many with multiple variants.

Expansion of the helicopter fleet will be expensive, both in acquisition and operational and training costs, but not as expensive as adding new fixed-wing aircraft. For example, several years ago rumors abounded concerning the creation of a new 16th Airborne Army, which would have necessitated the addition of many additional large, fixed-wing transport aircraft to deliver the paratroopers to their operation areas. A more cost-effective and flexible option might now be to develop a dedicated airmobile (helicopter-borne) infantry unit instead.

A larger, but still moderately sized, helicopter fleet (perhaps twice to three times as large as today's inventory) would provide the PLA with increased operational flexibility that can be applied to both warfighting and nontraditional security missions. A larger helicopter fleet seems to be within the scope of existing technology and support infrastructure. A larger fleet would not be too great a challenge to be managed within the general current force structure with slightly increased budgets. However, that same reasoning could have been applied in 1986 when the Army Aviation Corps was founded. At this time, however, helicopters seem to represent the right mix of "mechanization and informatization" for the present stage of PLA development. Perhaps that logic will prevail in the future in a way it did not two decades ago.

Appendix: PLA Navy Ships Capable of Helicopter Operations

	North Sea Fleet	East Sea Fleet	South Sea Fleet
DESTROYERS (13)			
Type 051C *Luzhou* (landing pad, no hangar)	115 *Shenyang* 116 *Shijiazhuang*		
Type 052C *Luyang-II*, (landing pad, hangar for one Ka-28 or Zhi-9)			170 *Lanzhou* 171 *Haikou*
Type 052B *Luyang* (landing pad, hangar for one Ka-28 or Zhi-9)			168 *Guangzhou* 169 *Wuhan*
Project 956/956EM *Sovremenny* (landing pad, hangar for one Ka-28)		136 *Hangzhou* 137 *Fuzhou* 138 *Taizhou* 139 *Ningbo*	
Type 051B *Luhai* (landing pad, two hangars for Ka-28 or Zhi-9)			167 *Shenzhen*
Type 52 *Luhu* (landing pad, two hangars for Ka-28 or Zhi-9)	112 *Harbin* 113 *Qingdao*		
Type 051 *Luda* (one ship modified with landing pad and hangar)	105 *Jinan* (decommissioned)		
FRIGATES (20)			
Type 054A *Jiangkai-II* (landing pad, hangar for one Ka-28 or Zhi-9)		529 *Zhoushan* 530 *Xuzhou*	568 *Chaohu* 570 *Huangshan*

Type			
Type 054 *Jiangkai* (landing pad, hangar for one Ka-28 or Zhi-9)		525 *Maanshan* 526 *Wenzhou*	
Type 053H2G *Jiangwei* (landing pad, hangar for one Zhi-9)		539 *Anqing* 540 *Huainan* 541 *Huaibei* 542 *Tongling*	
Type 053H3 *Jiangwei-II* (landing pad, hangar for one Zhi-9)	527 *Luoyang* 528 *Mianyang*	521 *Jiaxing* 522 *Lianyungang* 523 *Putian* 524 *Sanming*	564 *Yichang* 565 *Yulin* 566 *Yuxi* 567 *Xiangfan*
Type 053HTH *Jianghu-IV* (landing pad, hangar for one Zhi-9)	544 *Siping* (decommissioned, now at Dalian Naval Academy)		
AMPHIBIOUS WARFARE (20)			
Type 071 Landing Platform Dock (large flight deck, two–four Zhi-8, two hangars)			998 *Kunlunshan*
Type 072-III *Yuting-II* (large landing pad, hangar for one Zhi-8)	911 *Tianzhushan* 912 *Daqingshan*	913 *Baxianshan*	992 *Huadingshan* 993 *Luoxiaoshan* 994 *Daiyunshan* 995 *Wanyangshan* 996 *Laotieshan* 997 *Yunwushan*
Type 072-II *Yuting* (large landing pad, capable of Zhi-8)		908 *Yandanshang* 909 *Jiahuashan* 910 *Huanggangshan* 939 *Putuoshan* 940 *Tiantaishan*	934 *Danxiashan* 935 *Xuefengshan* 936 *Haiyangshan* 937 *Qingchengshan* 991 *Emeishan*

(continued)

PLA Navy Ships Capable of Helicopter Operations *(continued)*

	North Sea Fleet	East Sea Fleet	South Sea Fleet
AUXILIARIES (13)			
Qiandaohu/*Fuchi* class (large landing pad, hangar for one Zhi-8)		886 *Qiandaohu*	887 *Weishanhu*
Fuqing class (landing pad, no hangar)	882 *Poyanghu* (former *Taicang*)	881 *Hongzehu* (former *Fengcang*)	
Fuxianhu class (landing pad, no hangar)			888 *Fuxianhu*
Type 904 *Dayun* class (landing pad, no hangar)			883 *Nanyun* (decommissioned) 884 *Jingpohu*
Auxiliary Oiler Replenishment Ship (from Russia) (landing pad, hangar for one Zhi-8)			885 *Qinghaihu* (former *Nancang*)
Type 925 *Dajiang* class Ocean Salvage and Rescue Ship (landing pad, hangar for two Zhi-8)	861 *Changxingdao*	862 *Chongmingdao*	863 *Yongxingdao*
Type 920 Hospital Ship (landing pad, hangar for one Zhi-8)		866 (*Peace Ark-Daishandao*)	
Training Ships	81 *Zhenghe* (landing pad, no hangar) 82 *Shichang* (two landing pads)		

Source: This table is derived from ship lists found at *China's Defense Today,* http://www.sinodefence.com/navy/default.asp.
Note: Two additional *Jiangkai-II* frigates may have been launched in 2009, but no pennant numbers or names are available.

Notes

1. Jiao Xiaoyang, "Helicopter Corps Aims to Build on Quake Experience," *China Daily*, 5 July 2008, http://www.chinadaily.com.cn/china/2008-07/05/content_6821846.htm.

2. *The Military Balance 2010* counts about 489 helicopters in the army, very close to the Chinese numbers. International Institute for Strategic Studies, *The Military Balance 2010* (London: Routledge; 2010), 400.

3. See "International Institute for Strategic Studies—China," http://news.chinaiiss.org/content/2008-10-13/13155712.shtml, accessed December 2008.

4. "Register of Transfers of Major Conventional Weapons, 2008," Stockholm International Peace Research Institute, available at http://armstrade.sipri.org/armstrade/page/trade_register.php.

5. "Mi-171 Helicopter Succeeded in Test-fly, Helicopter Made in Wuhou Can Be Expected Soon," http://english.cdwh.gov.cn/newsall.asp?pid=8&cid=94&id=447.

6. "Kamov Is Counting on the 'Small One," *Vremya Novostey*, 8 February 2010, OSC CEP20100211358054.

7. "Z-10 Attack Helicopter," *China's Defence Today*, http://www.sinodefence.com/airforce/helicopter/z10.asp.

8. "Zhi-15 (EC 175) Medium Helicopter," Sinodefence.com, http://www.sinodefence.com/airforce/helicopter/z15.asp.

9. "China Buys 150 Polish Helicopters," http://www.upi.com/International_Security/Industry/Analysis/2008/03/03/analysis_european_defense_contracts/9656/.

10. Yuan Fang, "China, Russia Deal on Heavy Helicopters Expected Soon," 12 March 2009, http://www.china.org.cn/government/NPC_CPPCC_2009/2009-03/12/content_17431315.htm.

11. 中国人民解放军陆军航空兵学院 [PLA Army Aviation Corps Academy] Web page, http://www.edu10.com/web/888/ljhk/.

12. Tian Qiang and Zhou Jiawang, "Army Aviation's Simulated Training Shortens Pilot's Training Cycle," *Liberation Army Daily*, 21 December 2005, http://english.pladaily.com.cn/site2/militarydatabase/2005-12/21/content_368104.htm.

13. "Graduate Officers Go to Their Posts," *China Daily*, 22 July 2003, http://chinadaily.com.cn/en/doc/2003-07/22/content_247537.htm. Flight engineers probably attend the Naval Aeronautical Engineering Academy.

14. Tang Shenglong, "First Helicopter Training Regiment of PLA Air Force Boasts Teaching Capability," *Liberation Army Daily*, 16 March 2010, http://eng.chinamil.com.cn/news-channels/china-military-news/2010-03/16/content_4154772.htm.

15. Office of Naval Intelligence, *China's Navy 2007*, 48, www.fas.org/irp/agency/oni/chinanavy2007.pdf.

16. Hu Yinan, "No Trace of Crashed Relief Copter Yet," *China Daily*, 3 June 2008, http://www.chinadaily.com.cn/china/2008-06/03/content_6730283.htm.

17. Qian Xiaohu, Li Binfu, and Tan Jingchun, "Sea-Air Security Leader Tian Jinhe," 19 August 2008, *Liberation Army Daily*, http://english.pladaily.com.cn/site2/special -reports/2008-08/19/content_1431507.htm.

18. Assuming average promotion times, a senior colonel or senior captain should achieve that rank after about twenty-two years in service.

19. "Falcon of the Ocean—A Record of Zhao Zhumin, Director for Antisubmarine Warfare Tactics and a Special Class Pilot in an Unidentified Shipborne Aircraft Unit in the Navy," *Modern Navy* (November 2005): 20–21, OSC CPP20051107325002.

20. Kenneth Allen, "Reforms in the PLA Air Force," Jamestown *China Brief*, 5 July 2005, http://www.jamestown.org/single/?no_cache=1&tx_ttnews[tt_news]=30613.

21. Li Chuanxin and Zhou Jingbo, "1986: Giving Wings to the Army," *Liberation Army Daily*, 22 October 2008, http://english.chinamil.com.cn/site2/special -reports/2008-11/27/content_1563529.htm.

22. Li Chuanxin and Zhou Jingbo, "Army Aviation Force Seeks Breakthroughs in Key and Difficult Training Subjects," *Liberation Army Daily*, 1 March 2006, http://english .chinamil.com.cn/site2/news-channels/2006-03/01/content_421308.htm.

23. *People's Daily* reported that eighteen helicopters were used to transport a special operations unit across the beach during the Sino-Russian joint exercise "Peace Mission 2005." See "Chinese, Russian Forces Practice Amphibious Landings," *People's Daily*, 25 August 2005, http://english.peopledaily.com.cn/200508/25/eng20050825_204452.html.

24. Li Chuanxin and Zhou Jingbo, "PLA Army Aviation Units Have Acquired Initial Fighting Capability over the Sea," *Liberation Army Daily*, 8 December 2006, http:// english.chinamil.com.cn/site2/news-channels/2006-12/08/content_670994.htm.

25. "此次参加抗震救灾的直升机隶属关系（最新更正）" ["Helicopters Participating in Earthquake Disaster Subordination Relationships (Updated)"], 18 May 2008, http:// www.fyjs.cn/viewarticle.php?COLLCC=2434880113&id=141946. Lanzhou Military Region sent helicopters to Gansu to assist in emergency operations there.

26. "救人! 全军陆航部队群鹰奋飞" ["Rescue! Army Aviation Group from the Entire Army Soars"], *Liberation Army Daily*, 18 May 2008, http://www.chinamil.com.cn/ site1/zbxl/2008-05/18/content_1255338.htm.

27. Jiao Xiaoyang, "Helicopter Corps Aims to Build on Quake Experience," *China Daily*, 5 July 2008, http://www.chinadaily.com.cn/china/2008-07/05/content_6821846.htm.

28. "PRC: Military Commentator Praises PLA's Involvement in Quake-Relief Efforts," *Renmin Wang [People's Net]*, 22 May 2008, OSC CPP20080523436001.

29. "Helicopter Corps Aims to Build on Quake Experience."

30. "Mi-26 Helicopter Flew Earth-Moving Machines to Tangjiashan Lake," 28 May 2008, http://www.avbuyer.com.cn/e/2008/24654.html.

31. "Beijing MR Transport Aircraft Group Undertakes Olympic Security Mission," *CCTV-7*, 3 October 2008, OSC CPM20081103051005.

32. "空降兵某直升机大队小漫画展示安全观" ["Airborne Force Helicopter Group Cartoon Shows Safety"], 13 September 2005, http://www.chinamil.com.cn/site1/ zbxl/2005-09/13/content_293370.htm.

33. "空降兵某部緊急出動兩架直升機趕赴汶川救災" ["Airborne Unit Urgently Dispatches Two Helicopters to Wenchuan Earthquake Disaster Relief Effort"], 14 May 2008, http://www.cns.hk:89/tp/jsxw/news/2008/05-14/1250207.shtml.

34. "Helicopters Participating in Earthquake Disaster."

35. Office of the Secretary of Defense, *Military Power of the People's Republic of China* (Washington, DC: Department of Defense, 2009), 64.

36. Robert Hewson, "China Rolls out Naval Variant of Z-9 Helo Armed with New Anti-Ship Missile," 4 August 2008, http://www.janes.com/news/defence/air/jdw/jdw080804_1_n.shtml.

37. Two observers have stated that one or two PLAN frigates may have been equipped with a RAST or RAST-like system for experimental purposes. In additional to telltale equipment on the landing pad for RAST operations, the helicopters themselves must have special equipment installed. During research for this chapter, the author could find no definitive photographs of such a system on PLAN vessels or helicopters. Sales to China are not mentioned on the Curtiss Wright Web page, "RAST Recovery Assist, Secure and Traverse System," http://indaltech.cwfc.com/products/spokes/01a_RAST.htm.

38. "Backgrounder: Brief History of China's People's Liberation Army Navy," *Liberation Army Daily*, 16 April 2009, http://english.chinamil.com.cn/site2/news-channels/2009-04/16/content_1728330.htm.

39. Hu Baoliang and Qian Xiaohu, "Night Landing of Shipboard Copters on Moving Naval Ship Successful," *Liberation Army Daily*, 9 November 2004, http://www.chinamil.com.cn/site1/xwpdxw/2004-11/09/content_62844.htm.

40. "PLA Expanding Combat Capabilities of Shipboard Air Troop," *Xinhua*, 30 July 2007, http://news.xinhuanet.com/english/2007-07/30/content_6452642.htm.

41. Ibid.

42. Hu Baoliang and Si Yanwen, "Failed Helicopter Lands Successfully," *Liberation Army Daily*, 27 November 2008, http://english.chinamil.com.cn/site2/news-channels/2008-11/27/content_1563737.htm.

43. "市政协举行拥军书画笔会活动" ["City Political Consultative Conference Holds Support-the-Military Painting and Calligraphy Activity"], http://www.nbzx.gov.cn/article.jsp?aid=4326. This exercise was reported in both the English language and Chinese language editions of *Liberation Army Daily*; see Sun Yang, Wang Luxun, and Wang Chaowu, "East China Sea Fleet Conducts Three-Dimensional Anti-Submarine Training," 1 July 2007, http://english.pladaily.com.cn/site2/news-channels/2008-07/01/content_1343186.htm.

44. Deng Youbiao, "Dalian Naval Academy Recruits Pilot Cadets for the First Time," *Liberation Army Daily*, 5 September 2008, http://english.chinamil.com.cn/site2/news-channels/2008-09/05/content_1462801.htm.

45. For example, see Manu Pubby, "China Begins Training First Batch of Aircraft Carrier Fighter Pilots," 20 September 2008, http://www.indianexpress.com/news/China-begins-training-first-batch-of-aircraft-carrier-fighter-pilots/363638.

46. "Graduate Officers Go to Their Posts," *Liberation Army Daily*, 22 July 2003, http://chinadaily.com.cn/en/doc/2003-07/22/content_247537.htm.

47. Dalian Naval Academy Web Page, http://english.chinamil.com.cn/site2/special-reports/2007-06/19/content_851587.htm.

48. "'Firsts' Created by First Chinese Naval Escort Taskforce," *Liberation Army Daily*, 29 April 2009, http://english.chinamil.com.cn/site2/news-channels/2009-04/29/content_1745045.htm.

49. "Military Report," *CCTV-7*, 1130 GMT 31 March 2009, OSC CPM20090427017010.

50. "Chinese Navy Foils Attempt to Recapture Filipino Ship," *Liberation Army Daily*, 28 April 2009, http://english.chinamil.com.cn/site2/news-channels/2009-04/28/content_1743776.htm.

Lyle J. Goldstein, Miguel Martinez,
and William S. Murray

China's Future Airborne Antisubmarine Capabilities

Light at the End of the Tunnel?

THIS CHAPTER ANALYZES Chinese airborne antisubmarine warfare (ASW) capabilities and prospects by examining closely Chinese strategic and technical writings. These writings largely confirm conventional wisdom on Chinese airborne ASW: it remains an area of fundamental weakness. Nevertheless, they reveal a clear and open consciousness regarding this weakness—a vital step in rectifying the problem. In tracing Chinese submarine force development and air defense capabilities, the pitfalls of straight-line projections have been revealed. Given the apparently high level of research now ongoing in this area in China, similar caution is also in order with respect to Chinese airborne ASW twenty years hence.

China's Airborne ASW Today—What Is Known

The first edition of Bernard Cole's classic treatise *The Great Wall at Sea: China's Navy Enters the Twenty-First Century*, published a decade ago, offers a baseline understanding of Chinese airborne ASW. Cole concludes: "The PLAN is not taking advantage of available ASW technology, some of it forty years old. . . . China's Navy also lacks . . . airborne . . . ASW resources. There are only a dozen old aircraft assigned to the ASW mission."[1] Some updating is certainly advisable, particularly in continuing circumstances of limited information, but even today, Cole's conclusions with respect to Chinese airborne ASW remain largely intact.

Rotary-Wing ASW Platforms

The five primary platforms that conduct airborne ASW in the PLAN are described in Cole's book and remain the same today, including the Z-8, Z-9, and Ka-28 ASW helicopters, the Y-8X maritime patrol craft, and the SH-5 seaplane. Before producing the Z-8, China may have previously built up to 545 Z-5 helicopters, of which 54 served in the navy, according to a recent detailed history of Chinese naval helicopter aviation published in the PRC journal *Modern Ships* in early 2008.[2] This information contradicts claims that the Z-8 was China's first naval helicopter, although the Z-8 was most certainly China's first helicopter capable of deploying from ships (albeit too large for China's force of destroyers and frigates).[3] While adaptation for the new ASW mission occurred during the 1980s, it was not until 1994 that China's indigenous copy of the French helicopter entered service with the PLAN as the Z-8.[4] Currently, Chinese naval Super Frelons and Z-8s have search radars and are capable of carrying two Yu-7 lightweight torpedoes.[5] The number of Z-8s (including Super Frelons) operating in the Chinese navy is uncertain, ranging from a low estimate of 18 aircraft to a higher one of 35 helicopters of this type—although still higher numbers are also possible.[6] One Chinese source suggests that engine problems have caused the PLAN to limit production of this helicopter.[7]

For the future of the Chinese navy, an even more critical airborne ASW platform is the Z-9C shipboard helicopter, which (unlike the much larger Z-8) is capable of operating from most PLAN surface combatants. Starting in 1980 Beijing began importing several Dauphin II French-made naval helicopters— a sale that apparently included the delivery of parts for an additional fifty kits that were assembled in China during the 1980s.[8] The Z-9C ASW helicopter flew for the first time in late 1994, and the final design was approved in 1999.[9] The Z-9C, unlike the French imported Dauphin II, appears to have lacked a dipping sonar until relatively recently.[10] Another problem with the Z-9C may be that it is only capable of carrying one Yu-7 torpedo.[11]

Recent upgrades to the Z-9C, in addition to the dipping sonar, include a search radar mounted in the nose and a likely data link to provide targeting information for antiship cruise missiles. A recent appraisal of Chinese airborne

ASW from *Shipborne Weapons* reflects evident frustration with the Z-9C: "This helicopter, whether with respect to carrying capacity or range, suffered from congenital defects. Its basis, the *Dauphin* series, was originally designed to be a non-combat multi-use helicopter."[12] The Office of Naval Intelligence (ONI) in 2009 estimated "there are now approximately ten active Z-9Cs in the PLANAF inventory."[13] However, as with the Z-8, higher numbers are possible, if unlikely.

China has simultaneously opted to import moderate numbers of Russian Ka-28 ASW helicopters. Chinese sources consistently rate the Ka-28 over the Z-9C: "The *Ka*-28 helicopter is wholly superior to the Z9C in terms of equipment and weaponry for searching out and attacking submarines."[14] In addition to surface-search radars, it is reported that the Ka-28 has a dipping sonar, a magnetic anomaly detector, carries sixteen to twenty-four sonobuoys, and can attack a target submarine with torpedoes, rockets and depth, charges. The Ka-28's range is also said to outperform China's own Z-9C, but Chinese analysts are also critical of the Ka-28, reporting that "in comparison to the equipment of the world's leading navies . . . the *Ka*-28 is rather backward in terms of electronics."[15] ONI estimated in 2009 an inventory of only eight.[16]

Fixed-Wing ASW Platforms

The Chinese navy's underdeveloped shipborne aviation is mirrored by the anemic state of large, fixed-wing maritime patrol aircraft—the ASW workhorse among most of the world's leading navies. The PLAN's two extant platforms were introduced in the mid-1980s: the Y-8X maritime patrol aircraft and the SH-5 amphibious (seaplane) ASW aircraft.[17] The former is possibly equipped with a search radar, foreign avionics, and infrared sensors, and can carry sea mines, torpedoes, depth charges, and sonobuoys. Despite this claim, no dispensers for sonobuoys are visible in pictures of the Y-8X. One report, however, suggests an expedient: "the rear cargo door [on the transport version] was removed and replaced by a large mission [compartment] for sonobouy racks and cameras."[18]

The SH-5 seaplane is said to have a surface-search radar and to be capable of carrying up to twenty-four depth charges, but apparently it cannot deploy ASW torpedoes—a major flaw.[19] Unlike the Y-8, it does have a visible magnetic anomaly detector (MAD). Though still operated from a seaplane base near Qingdao, at least one SH-5 has been modified for use as a firefighting aircraft.[20] Conventional estimates are consistent in stating that the PLAN's inventory of fixed-wing ASW aircraft is very low; with just four Y-8X and four SH-5, according to the International Institute for Strategic Studies.[21] These low numbers of fixed-wing ASW aircraft suggest considerable angst, or disinterest, within the PLAN aviation community concerning both these platforms—with both aircraft described as obsolete and inappropriate to the ASW challenge.[22] The Y-7, a two-engine turboprop copy of the Antonov 24 could potentially be converted into an ASW platform, though there is little hard evidence in support of this actually being undertaken.[23]

A 2006 Chinese analysis examines all options, including the Y-7 and Russian possibilities, and concludes that Y-8 is the most logical choice. Not only does it have reasonably good range, payload, and internal space, but, perhaps most important, it is 100 percent indigenously built, and so vastly simplifies maintenance and logistics.[24] This analysis proposes an improved ASW design for the Y-8, designated Y-8AF, for "岸基反潜" (land-based antisubmarine). This design is estimated to be capable of a 7,000 km range or 14 hours on patrol, and would be equipped to a maximum of 200 sonobuoys and up to 12 ASW torpedoes. Some interesting features of this potential design are that it would be capable of aerial refueling, that it would have MAD, and that it could also deploy antiship or land-attack cruise missiles.[25] Outside of this single, detailed analysis and diagram, no hard evidence for this design is available.

Airborne ASW Exercises

The trajectory of Chinese airborne ASW is not solely dependent on hardware, such as platforms, sensors, and ASW weaponry. The importance of the human factor is, if anything, increased in the context of highly complex ASW operations in wartime. A major challenge confronting Chinese ASW is a paucity of real world experience. As Captain Sun Mintai, an airborne ASW expert and professor at the Qingdao Naval Aeronautical Engineering Academy, notes in an interview, "Our navy has never had the experience of submarine warfare or anti-submarine warfare, and thus our airborne ASW forces and development got a relatively late start."[26] This lack of experience may be decisive for any overall assessment of Chinese airborne ASW capabilities. It is worth noting, for example, that China's first-ever night landing of a helicopter on a ship may have occurred as recently as 2004.[27] Conversely, there is also evidence that China has sought to redress the experience gap in airborne ASW from an early point. Thus, one report from *Modern Navy* emphasizes the importance of PLAN officer training in airborne ASW that took place in both France and Italy during the mid-1980s.[28]

Nonetheless, there seems to have been an up-tick in airborne ASW exercises in 2007–8. For instance, one source reports a September 2007 North Sea Fleet (NFS) shipborne helicopter ASW exercise.[29] Another NSF shipborne helicopter exercise, reported in December 2007, practiced multihelicopter prose-cution of a submarine.[30] In February 2008 a Z-9C from the Luda destroyer 112 flew in a red–blue exercise against multiple submarines.[31] In May 2008 the East Sea Fleet (ESF) exercised one or more Ka-28s against a *Song*-class subma-rine—some portion of this exercise took place at night.[32] Later, in June 2008, the East Sea Fleet conducted another ASW exercise that apparently involved aircraft, submarines, and surface ships in an effort to move in the direction of combined operations for ASW.[33] July 2008 saw a North Sea Fleet red-versus-blue ASW exercise that involved a "new model" helicopter deploying a dipping sonar.[34] Chinese analysts are also considering the difficult problem of how to prevent "friendly fire" casualties by Chinese airborne ASW forces.[35] Suggesting that the PLAN may understand and be redressing this training weakness, Captain Sun, the aforementioned PLAN airborne ASW instructor, indicates that the human factor is understood within the Chinese navy: "It is appar-ent that ASW involves a complex interactive process between people and air-craft. We want to be unequivocal about this fact: having the equipment does not mean that one has attained combat capability, especially in the domain of airborne ASW. Having ASW equipment only establishes the material basis for ASW, and is still relatively far from forming genuine ASW combat capability, which requires a long and arduous period of exercises and drills."[36]

China's Future Airborne ASW—Light at the End of the Tunnel?

This chapter seeks to not only evaluate the present state of Chinese airborne ASW but also to probe its future potential, especially a decade or two in the future. Any future estimate must be made in light of past and present trends, of course, and so the foregoing summary establishes a baseline understanding of current Chinese airborne ASW capabilities. If China's future airborne ASW is to improve radically, China must satisfy a variety of conditions, elaborated in turn below.

Strategic Significance of Airborne ASW

There appears to be a strong conviction among Chinese observers that air-borne ASW has a high strategic value. Back in 1996 an analysis from *Naval and Merchant Ships* concluded: "Combined remote-sensing, signal-processing and digital computer technologies spell a bright future for airborne submarine detection equipment. . . . Air units will clearly be the most effective antisubma-rine elements for naval operations in the future."[37] A decade later, this thinking had become conventional wisdom among Chinese naval strategists: "It is common knowledge that airborne ASW is the most effective method."[38] A 2008 Chinese analysis explains: "Among the many types of ASW methods, airborne ASW has rapid reaction times, strong mobility, high combat effectiveness, and survivability . . . among many obvious advantages are that it is the most essential combat method."[39] Nevertheless, these balanced analyses also note that airborne ASW assets have limitations as well, since their self-defense capability is weak.[40]

Debate is evident among Chinese naval authors on whether to prioritize fixed-wing maritime patrol craft or shipborne helicopters. One article in *Contemporary Military Affairs*, for instance, notes that fixed-wing aircraft have a more extended range as well as a much larger payload than helicopters for sensors and weapons.[41] Other Chinese analysts stress the major advantages of helicopters possessing potent dipping sonars.[42] Another analysis prioritizes helicopters explicitly over fixed-wing ASW platforms: "We must build an aerial ASW force taking helicopters as the main force, with fixed-wing aircraft in a supporting role."[43]

Historically Informed

Analyses of the Allied ASW campaigns in both world wars are common in Chinese naval writings. For example, one recent article observes that Allied ASW aircraft were responsible for 37 percent of U-boat sinkings in World War II.[44] Nor are ASW operations in the Pacific ignored: one analysis, for instance, concludes that U.S. ASW operations were much more successful than Japanese ASW efforts because the latter lacked patience in prosecuting enemy submarines.[45] Cold War airborne ASW, naturally, is also of great interest to Chinese naval analysts.[46]

The Falklands War (1982) has been thoroughly analyzed by Chinese strategists. A history of Chinese shipborne helicopters goes so far as to suggest that the vital importance of shipborne helicopters in that conflict gave a powerful boost to China's own Z-9 program, which did indeed gain momentum in the mid-1980s.[47] Another analysis notes that ASW capabilities formed a critical asymmetry between the Argentine and U.K. fleets—and that British surface forces, thanks to escort by long-range ASW patrol aircraft, were able to contain the Argentine submarine threat.[48] Chinese analysts have taken special note of ASW weaponry lessons from the conflict.[49] They have also explored the emerging concept of low-cost ASW weapons (e.g., Seapike) that have been developed in a partial response to the lessons from the Royal Navy's experience with ASW in the Falklands War.[50]

Awareness of Global Airborne ASW Trends

Analyses of U.S. Navy airborne ASW capabilities are very common in a wide variety of Chinese sources. This no doubt reflects a high degree of respect for the U.S. Navy, including the judgment that "in becoming today's dominant navy, the USN during the Cold War devoted immense human and material resources to ASW in order to deal with the huge submarine fleet of the USSR. In the course of this rivalry over several decades . . . the U.S. Navy developed and maintained from beginning to end comprehensive, advanced and precise tactics and equipment."[51] Chinese analysts have also devoted considerable effort to understanding the platforms that will conduct airborne ASW for the U.S. Navy in the future, especially the P8 program.[52] There is a strong interest in the history of U.S. Navy airborne ASW and an understanding of the roles that key platforms played, that is, an awareness that the S-3 Viking was capable of hefting a single nuclear depth charge if necessary.[53] It is also not surprising that Chinese naval analysts take a keen interest in U.S. Navy airborne ASW weaponry, especially in lightweight torpedoes. One such analysis described the late 2006 test of a "longshot wing adapter" for a P-3C–launched ASW torpedo— concluding that such technology could increase the survivability of long-range ASW aircraft in contested airspace.[54] Other U.S. Navy ASW capabilities of interest to Chinese analysts include space ASW surveillance, development of USN shipborne unmanned aerial vehicles, and development of critical battery technologies to support sonobuoys and other distributed ASW sensors.[55] As noted in the first section of this chapter, Beijing has significant numbers of Russian shipborne ASW helicopters. There appears to be a consensus in the PLAN that even the newest Z-9C cannot measure up to the performance of the Russian Ka-27/28 since the latter is described as a smaller helicopter that can lift twice the weight of the Chinese-made helicopter.[56] While concluding that China must continue to rely on Russia's Kamov Company in the short and medium term, this analysis also notes that this imported helicopter is not a perfect match for China's navy, observing that the U.S. Navy's SH-60F Seahawk is "obviously" far superior in capabilities.[57] According to another Chinese analysis, these Russian airborne ASW platforms have good flight performance but do not meet China's future ASW requirements because of backward electronics, limited functionality, and problems with associated weaponry.[58] Multiple Chinese articles note that all Russian aerial ASW platforms were capable of carrying tactical nuclear ASW weaponry. Chinese analysts also scrutinize European and Japanese airborne ASW developments.[59] Indeed, Captain Sun says the Japanese airborne ASW capabilities may exceed those of the U.S. Navy in some aspects.[60]

Threat Perception and Accurate Self-Assessment

Chinese strategists are quite conscious of a perceived threat that has been emerging from foreign submarine forces. Thus, one detailed 2008 analysis in *Shipborne Weapons* concludes: "From Northeast Asia to Southeast Asia . . . this large area has developed one of the world's most concentrated grouping of submarines, and since included among these [submarine] forces these forces are both world-class equipment and crews, this [issue] has emerged as one of the most acute problems confronting China's maritime security."[61] The article surveys impressive submarine developments in Japan, South Korea, India, Malaysia, Singapore, Indonesia, and even Vietnam. The U.S. Navy submarine force is singled out as representing a major threat to China: "When in 2006 the U.S. published its *Quadrennial Defense Review* and said that in the future six submarines deployed to the East Asian region would be ready to enter combat at any time, [American] intentions were abundantly clear."[62]

Despite much evident progress in developing shipborne helicopters, one detailed analysis concludes that "compared to advanced foreign systems, there is still a relatively large gap, especially in the area of the capabilities of shipborne [helicopter] types; there is no possibility that [those belonging to China] can fulfill the [Chinese] navy's requirements for ASW."[63] Attempting to explain the current problems with airborne ASW, one Chinese analyst observes: "For the Chinese Navy in the era of offshore defense, the submarine threat was not acutely felt. However, in the development of combat abilities for distant sea operations, and the increasing, long-range attack capabilities of submarines, the lack of long-range, blue water ASW capability has become a major blemish on the Chinese navy's combat capabilities."[64]

Advanced Airborne ASW Research

Examples of ongoing indigenous research related to airborne ASW weaponry include a team from the Naval Aeronautical Engineering Institute in Yantai working on modeling the hit probability of an air-dropped torpedo that includes looking at different "drop heights and speeds."[65] Chinese researchers also study how to improve lightweight torpedo effectiveness in noisy environments.[66] In a potential "leap-frog" strategy for Chinese efforts, authors from the Chinese Naval Command College in Nanjing examine the possible use of unmanned combat aerial vehicles for "cooperation and sharing of weapons" in airborne ASW.[67]

Basic research on optimal searching patterns includes "Quasi-Optimal Search for ASW Helicopter in Some Special Cases" by a team from the Dalian Naval Academy, and "Target Movement Analysis on a Passive Sonar Buoy," by researchers at the Naval Armaments Department in Beijing.[68] Slightly more advanced studies include one from Yantai on using a dipping sonar in tandem with sonobuoys.[69] Another from Harbin Engineering University and Wuhan Naval Engineering University researches how "propeller shaft frequency . . . can be applied to underwater target identification."[70] Chinese researchers are interested in shallow water ASW, examining the performance of active sonars, and other means of detection such as airborne synthetic aperture radars.[71] Other ASW research in Chinese journals includes analyses of multistatic buoy arrays and employing explosive echo ranging in combination with buoys. It is worth noting that China did begin testing its first dipping sonar in 1976, giving it more than three decades to refine the technology, according to a Chinese dipping sonar expert interviewed in 2007.[72]

Chinese research into airborne ASW can also naturally benefit the effective operations of the Chinese submarine force in avoiding or countering airborne operations directed against it. For instance, research undertaken at Yantai Naval Aeronautical Engineering Institute shows that "under certain conditions the combat effectiveness of active sonobuoys against submarines can be reduced by proper evasion strategies."[73]

Several other characteristics of this voluminous research are noteworthy. First, an article on developing an "Integrated Simulation Environment for Anti-Submarine Warfare" shows at least some understanding that modern ASW forces are not simply reliant on advanced sensors and the latest software but require a vital human element as well.[74] Also, in recognition of the importance of airborne ASW, a specialized institute, the Naval Airborne Anti-Submarine Research Center (海军航空兵反潜研究中心), has been established in Qingdao.[75] Finally, it is not unusual to see airborne ASW articles in PLAAF publications.[76]

Scenarios for China's Future Airborne ASW

Observers should remember that China cannot develop effective airborne ASW in isolation from other naval missions. Airborne ASW is not an independent prerequisite for blue water naval operations but rather a synergistic operational capability that must be conducted with a variety of other related capabilities. Three possible scenarios for Chinese airborne ASW are discussed below.

Continuation of the Status Quo

China might well determine that it is unnecessary to develop airborne ASW forces that would operate much beyond its exclusive economic zone. In such a scenario, observers would see few dramatic changes to the status quo. Indeed, China has apparently elected to live with this weakness for some time.

This apparent warfighting deficiency could be explained by the PLA's focus on preventing Taiwan's independence and deterring or delaying the intervention of outside powers if military coercion becomes necessary. One could theorize that Beijing has developed a concept of operations for coping with a Taiwan contingency that does not depend on defeating large numbers of adversary submarines operating in its exclusive economic zone. This hypothetical Taiwan-focused strategy of deterrence of intervention by outside powers would obviate the need for expensive ASW capabilities. Chinese naval analysts may have concluded that the Taiwan Strait's shallow waters preclude or limit the effectiveness of submarines to such a degree that it is not worthwhile to challenge them directly.

Effective Airborne ASW to the First Island Chain

In contrast to essentially disregarding the threat posed by adversary submarines, a second approach would be to develop the ability to detect and prosecute submarines by air in water up to, and even slightly beyond, the first island chain. To achieve this objective, China would have to achieve air superiority in the areas where it expects to operate airborne ASW assets. In such a scenario, the PLAN (working in concert with the PLAAF and possibly the Second Artillery) would need to acquire and master the operations of area air defense surface combatants, the ability to successfully attack regional air bases, and the ability to defeat opposing aircraft carriers and area air defense surface combatants.

To the extent that China's airborne ASW strategy has favored helicopter development over long-range patrol aircraft, it may comport with this "green water" approach to ASW operations. The notion may hold that there is little logic to developing long-range aircraft that cannot possibly be defended. In this context China might accelerate development of helicopter capabilities, emphasizing superior Russian imports in the near term while continuing to defer investment in a long-range MPA. In undertaking to overhaul its ASW capabilities in the near seas, the PLAN would also likely pursue an integrated ASW architecture including surface combatants with low-frequency sonars and quiet attack submarines with sophisticated torpedoes, complemented perhaps by a network of undersea sensors. To date, there is little evidence of such an ambitious upgrade in Chinese ASW capabilities, even within the first island chain.

Blue Water ASW

In its present form, the PLAN is a very long way from being able to successfully conduct open ocean ASW. To rectify this, the airborne ASW force would have to be rebalanced from favoring helicopters toward more fixed-wing assets. Long-range maritime patrol craft would protect large, high-value ships from the extant submarine threat and could support other distant missions. Nuclear submarines and even aircraft carriers might prove to be essential adjuncts for Chinese long-range airborne ASW. Development of either capability will take years and perhaps even decades, and would require a major psychological shift for China's national security elite. An equally significant shift might also be required with respect to foreign basing.

Another major change that could result from this ambitious goal would be a move toward the deployment of tactical nuclear ASW weapons, like those the Soviets relied upon. However, such effort, if undertaken by Beijing, will be quite visible, allowing various states to take measures to counter China's growing capabilities.

Conclusion

This survey of Chinese airborne ASW capabilities confirms the conventional wisdom on this matter: this is a glaring weakness of the contemporary PLAN. Even if PLAN helicopters were effective, the available numbers are still extremely low relative to other navy force structures. However, an even more glaring shortfall is evident in the vital domain of maritime patrol aircraft. This paucity does not bode well for the future of Chinese airborne ASW.

Nevertheless, it would be premature to conclude that Chinese airborne ASW shows no prospects for significant improvement. This survey of Chinese writing on airborne ASW, to the contrary, has demonstrated that Chinese naval analysts grasp the strategic significance of airborne ASW. The literature, moreover, suggests that Chinese naval thinkers feel an acute sense of threat regarding the submarine buildup in East Asia. Of vital significance is that they also objectively analyze the poor state of current Chinese capabilities in airborne ASW. Finally, this research reveals a very broad Chinese ASW effort including studies of respectable sophistication.

To summarize, the overall conclusion is that Chinese airborne ASW will remain weak for the near future. Over the long term (i.e., two decades hence) there is the potential for substantial improvement, however. One policy option for the United States is rather obvious. If Washington must hedge against China's rise (even as it simultaneously pursues engagement), the U.S. Navy submarine force is a very logical place to invest. Nevertheless, change is always difficult to predict because it is simple to extrapolate trend lines but always difficult to find inflection points. This chapter shows that significant potential for improvement in Chinese airborne ASW does exist.

Notes

1. Bernard D. Cole, *The Great Wall at Sea: China's Navy Enters the Twenty-First Century* (Annapolis, MD: Naval Institute Press, 2001), 111.

2. 老毕 [Lao Bi], "中国海军航空兵族谱之八: 直升机简史" ["An Abbreviated History of the Helicopters of the Chinese Naval Aviation Forces"], 现代舰船 [*Modern Ships*] (February 2008): 20.

3. Cole, *Great Wall at Sea*, 107.

4. Ibid., 23.

5. "Z-8," *China Defense Today*, www.sinodefense.com. Although this source credits the Z-8 with possessing a dipping sonar, the authors are not aware of any photos to confirm the existence of such a system on the Z-8.

6. The low estimate is by *China's Defence Today*, www.sinodefence.com, while the high estimate is by the International Institute for Strategic Studies.

7. 巡抚 [Xun Fu], "中国海军反潜武器的发展" ["The Development of the Chinese Navy's ASW Weaponry"], 舰载武器 [*Shipborne Weapons* (August 2005): 30.

8. Lao, "Abbreviated History," 24.

9. Ibid., 26.

10. Lao, "Abbreviated History," 26. A similar claim is made on *China's Defence Today* website.

11. Lao, "Abbreviated History," 26. Other sources claim that the Z-9C is capable of carrying two Yu-7 torpedoes. See 天鹰 [Tian Ying], "航空反潜对当前中国海军的重要意义" ["The Vital Significance of Airborne Anti-Submarine Capabilities for Today's Chinese Navy"], 舰载武器 [*Shipborne Weapons*] (March 2008): 52.

12. Tian, "Vital Significance," 52.

13. ONI, *The People's Liberation Army Navy: A Modern Navy with Chinese Characteristics* (Suitland, MD: Office of Naval Intelligence, July 2009), 24.

14. Tian, "Vital Significance," 52.

15. Ibid., 52.

16. ONI, *People's Liberation Army Navy*, 24.

17. There are many Y-8 variants. In this case, the "X" likely stands for 巡/xun (patrol).

18. "Y8," *China's Defence Today*, www.sinodefense.com.

19. 天一 [Tian Yi], "对-8改中国岸基巡逻机的探讨" ["Prospects for an Upgraded Y-8 Land-Based Patrol Aircraft"], 舰载武器 [*Shipborne Weapons*] (January 2006): 25.

20. "SH5," *China's Defence Today*, www.sinodefense.com.

21. James Hacket, ed., *The Military Balance 2008* (London: Routledge, 2008), 379.

22. 离子鱼 [Li Ziyu], "轰-6改装海上反潜机的用途和价值" ["The Significance and Value of Refitting the H-6 into a Naval Anti-Submarine Aircraft"], 舰载武器 [*Shipborne Weapons*] (July 2008): 36–37.

23. On the Y-7, see Tian, "Vital Significance," 48.

24. Tian, "Prospects for an Upgraded Y-8," 27–28.

25. Ibid., 30–31.

26. 谢京 [Xie Jing], "目标: 水下潜艇, 开火! 采访人: 航空反潜专家, 海军航空工程学院青岛分院教授孙明太" ["Target: Submerged Submarine, Open Fire! An Interview with Airborne Anti-Submarine Expert, Qingdao Naval Aeronautical Engineering University Professor Sun Mingtai"], 航空知识 [*Aerospace Knowledge*] (February 2008): 15.

27. "Night Landing of Shipboard Helicopters on Moving Naval Ship Successful," *Liberation Army Daily*, 9 November 2004, available at http://www.chinamil.com.cn.

28. 胡宝良, 俞振英, 于海波 [Hu Baoliang, Yu Zhenying, and Yu Haibo], "大洋猎鹰: 记海军某舰载机部队反潜战术主任, 特级飞行员赵树民" ["Ocean Falcon: Record of a Director of a Certain Shipborne Antisubmarine Helicopter Unit, Specialist Pilot Zhao Shumin"], 当代海军 [*Modern Navy*] (November 2005): 20–21.

29. 中国国防报 [*China Defense News*], 18 September 2007.

30. Ibid., 11 December 2007.

31. 姜祥杰 [Jiang Xiangjie], "春潮深处 '猎鲨' 忙" ["A 'Shark Hunt' in the Depths of the Spring Tide"], 现代军事 [*Conmilit*] (April 2008): 8–9.

32. 王朝武 [Wang Chaowu], "雄鹰猎鲨" ["Heroic Eagle Hunting for Sharks"], 解放军画报 [*PLA Pictorial*] (May 2008): 34–35.

33. 孙阳 [Sun Yang], "东海舰队立体反潜: 织网布阵海天间" ["The East Sea Fleet's Three-Dimensional Anti-Submarine Warfare: Weaving a Net for the Battle Front Between Sea and Sky"], 解放军报 [*Liberation Army Daily*], 20 June 2008, 2.

34. Sun Yinfu, "The Dragon Fights with the Falcon—an Account of a North Sea Fleet Submarine Flotilla in Going up against Modern Anti-Submarine Aircraft with Old Submarines," 人民海军 [*People's Navy*], 2 July 2008.

35. Xie, "Target," 14.

36. Ibid., 15.

37. Li Chenye, "Brief Discussion on Airborne ASW," 舰船知识 [*Naval and Merchant Ships*], December 1996, OSC FTS19970728002413.

38. 蓝杰斌 [Lan Jiebin], "中国反潜装备的发展" ["China's ASW Equipment Development"], 舰载武器 [*Shipborne Weapons*] (February 2004): 29.

39. Tian, "Vital Significance," 44.

40. Xie, "Target," 12–13.

41. 倪卫星，马明昭 [Ni Weixing and Ma Mingzhao], "海上巡逻机:从潜艇猎手到海战全能勇士" ["Maritime Patrol Aircraft: From Submarine Hunting Tool to All-Round Sea Combat Warrior"], 现代军事 [*Conmilit*] (August 2005): 33.

42. 司古 [Si Gu], "鹈鹕本纪—管窥反潜机" ["Origin of the Pelican: A Close Examination of Anti-Submarine Aircraft"], 航空知识 [*Aerospace Knowledge*] (February 2008): 37–38.

43. Lan, "China's ASW Equipment Development," 29.

44. Ni and Ma, "Maritime Patrol Aircraft," 33.

45. "耐心的胜利" ["Patient Victory"], 中国国防报 [*China Defense News*], 9 October 2007, 7.

46. 杨温利 [Yang Wenli], "深海争霸: 冷战时代美国海军的反潜作战" ["Struggle for Supremacy under the Sea: U.S. Navy Anti-Submarine Warfare During the Cold War"], 国际展望 [*World Outlook*] (June 2006): 57.

47. Lao, "An Abbreviated History," 25.

48. Ni and Ma, "Maritime Patrol Aircraft," 33.

49. 徐锦城 [Xu Jincheng], "鹈鹕之喙—航空反潜武器" ["The Pelican's Beak—Airborne Antisubmarine Weaponry"], 航空知识 [*Aerospace Knowledge*] (February 2008): 39.

50. 钱东, 高军保 [Qian Dong and Gao Junbao], "低成本反潜器 '海矛'" ["'Seapike,' a Low Cost Anti-Submarine Warfare Weapon"], 鱼雷技术 [*Torpedo Technology*] (March 2005): 49–51.

51. Yang, "Struggle for Supremacy under the Sea," 54.

52. See, for example, Si, "Origin of the Pelican" 36.

53. Ibid., 37.

54. 马玲 [Ma Ling], "浅海作战的轻鱼雷新秀" ["A New Crop of Lightweight Torpedoes for Littoral Warfare"], 现代舰船 [*Modern Ships*, (June 2008): 34–36.

55. 李坤, 荣海洋 [Li Kun and Rong Haiyang], "浅析美军航天反潜侦察能力" ["Brief Discussion of U.S. Space Capabilities for Anti-Submarine Surveillance"], 飞航导弹 [*Winged Missiles Journal*] (September 2006): 12–14; 任伟, 马海涛, 李勇, 霍磊 [Ren Wei, Ma Haitao, Li Yong, and Huo Lei], "美国A-160蜂鸟新概念无人机" ["The U.S. A-160 Humming Bird New Concept Unmanned Aerial Vehicle"], 飞航导弹 [*Winged Missiles Journal*] (April 2008): 32–33; and 张毫娟 [Zhang Haojuan], "美国海军对电池的需求及研制" ["U.S. Navy Battery Requirements and Development Efforts"], 电池工业 [*Battery Industry*] (April 1999): 71–74.

56. 离子鱼 [Li Ziyu], "非典型性经验: 苏武舰载直升机的发展与应用" ["Atypical Experience: The Soviet Experience in Developing and Employing Shipborne Helicopters"], 现代舰船 [*Modern Ships*] (August 2008): 23.

57. Ibid.

58. Tian, "Prospects for an Upgraded Y-8," 26.

59. See, for example, 唐劲松, 张春华, 李淑秋, 尹力, 何国健, 李启虎 [Tang Jingsong, Zhang Chunhua, Li Shuqiu, Yin Li, He Guojian, and Li Qihu], "水声工程的新进展—欧洲UDT'99观感" ["Development in Underwater Acoustic Engineering—A Survey of Underwater Defense Technology Europe 1999"], 应用声学 [*Applied Acoustics*] (May 1999): 5–10; and 阿波 [A Bo], "空中浪人: 日本海上自卫队P-X反潜机," ["Air Surfer: The Japanese Maritime Self Defense Force's P-X Anti-Submarine Aircraft"], 现代舰船 [*Modern Ships*] (August 2008): 31–33.

60. Xie, "Target," 14.

61. Tian, "Vital Significance," 44.

62. Ibid., 48.

63. Lao, "Abbreviated History," 26.

64. Li, "Significance and Value of Refitting the H-6," 37.

65. 赵绪明, 样跟, 黄暄, 姜前卫 [Zhao Xuming, Yang Genyuan, Huang Xuan, and Jiang Qianwei], "一种计算航空反潜鱼雷发现概率的新方法" ["A New Method to Calculate Detection Probability of Aerial Antisubmarine Torpedo"], 鱼雷技术 [*Torpedo Technology*] (December 2006): 54.

66. 李钊, 郑援 [Li Zhao and Zheng Yuan], "空投主动声自导鱼雷反潜仿真与分析" ["Simulation and Analysis of Airdrop Active Homing Torpedo for Anti-Submarine Warfare"], 计算机仿真 [*Computer Simulation*] (June 2007): 9–12.

67. Abstract for 许腾, 章华平, 徐杰 [Xu Teng, Zhang Huaping, and Xu Jie], "基于武器协同共用的无人机反潜作战效能研究" ["Research on the Effectiveness of Anti-Submarine Warfare Using UCAV Based on the Cooperation and Sharing of Weapons"], 指挥控制与仿真 [*Command, Control and Simulation*] (January 2008).

68. 李长明, 董朝峰, 杨健 [Li Changming, Dong Chaofeng, and Yang Jian], "反潜直升机在几种特殊情况下的准最优搜索初探" ["Research on Quasi-Optimum Search by Anti-Submarine Helicopter in Some Special Cases"], 海军航空工程学院学报 [*Journal of the Naval Aeronautical Engineering Institute*] (September 2007): 569–72.

69. 张晓利, 陈建勇 [Zhang Xiaoli and Chen Jianyong], "吊放声纳与声纳浮标在应召搜潜中的联合运用" ["Employing Dipping Sonar and Sono-Buoys Together to Search for Submarines"], 海军航空工程学院学报 [*Journal of the Naval Aeronautical Engineering Institute*] (November 2006): 669–71.

70. 殷敬伟, 惠俊英, 姚直象, 杨春 [Yin Jingwei, Hui Junying, Yao Zhixiang, and Yang Chun], "基于DEMON线谱的轴频提取方法研究" ["Extraction of Shaft Frequency Based on the DEMON Line Spectrum"], 应用声学 [*Applied Acoustics*] (November 2005): 369–74.

71. 潘翔 [Pan Xiang], "基于时间反转处理的水声信号增强研究" ["Research on Underwater Acoustic Signal Enhancement Based on Time Reversal Processing"], 传感技术学报 [*Chinese Journal of Sensors and Actuators*] (June 2006): 847–48; 姜可宇, 蔡志明, 丁云高 [Jiang Keyu, Cai Zhiming, and Ding Yungao], "主动声纳中目标回波的一种非线性提取方法" ["A Non-linear Method for Echo Extraction from Targets in Active Sonar"], 声学技术 [*Technical Acoustics*] (June 2006): 192–96;

and 朱振波, 汤子跃, 蒋兴舟 [Zhu Zhenbo, Tang Ziyue, and Zhang Xingzhou], "机载双站SAR频率同步与误差补偿" ["The Frequency Synchronization and Synchronization Error Compensation of Airborne Bistatic SAR"], 电子学报 [*Acta Electronica*] (December 2006): 2417–20.

72. 蒋辉 [Jiang Hui], "翱翔浪尖猎铁鲸: 马远良院士谈航空吊放声呐" ["Soaring over the Wave Tops and Hunting the Whales: Director Ma Yuanliang Discusses Dipping Sonars"], 舰船知识 [*Naval and Merchant Ships*] (September 2007): 9.

73. 高学强, 样日杰, 杨春英 [Gao Xueqiang, Yang Rijie, and Yang Qunying], "潜艇规避对主动声纳浮标作战效能影响研究" ["Research on the Effects of Submarine Evasion on the Combat Effectiveness of Active Sonobuoys"], 系统工程与电子技术 [*Systems Engineering and Electronics*] (February 2008): 300–304.

74. Abstract for 韩瑞新, 张宏军, 祝笑舟, 卢厚清, 李春洪 [Han Ruixin, Zhang Hongjun, Zhu Xiaozhou, Lu Houqing, and Li Chunhong], "反潜作战一体化仿真环境" ["Integrated Simulation Environment for Anti-Submarine Warfare"], 解放军理工大学学报 [*Journal of PLA University of Science and Technology*] (January 2008).

75. 杨日杰, 何友, 孙明太 [Yang Rijie, He You, and Sun Mingtai], "主被动联合多基地航空艘潜范围分析" ["Scope Analysis for Active/Passive Combined Multi-base Anti-Submarine Warfare"], 航空学报 [*Acta aeronautica et astronautica sinica*] (July 2004): 381–84.

76. 杨利平, 吴值民 [Yang Liping and Wu Zhimin], "主成分分析法在航空反潜机性能评估中的应用" ["Application of Principal Components Analysis in Evaluating the Maneuverability of Typical Anti-Submarine Aircraft"], 航空工程大学学报 [*Journal of the Air Force Engineering University*] (April 2007): 14–17.

Gabriel Collins, Michael McGauvran,
and Timothy White

Trends in Chinese Aerial Refueling Capacity for Maritime Purposes

CHINA'S AIR REFUELING (AR) program today appears primarily geared toward enhancing Beijing's ability to project power into the South China Sea, although it also is useful in other regional contingencies.[1] AR can boost China's offensive and defensive air capabilities by providing Chinese aircraft greater range (flight distance), increased load (weapons, bombs, cargo, fuel) capacity, greater time on station (loiter time at a specific point), and greater operational flexibility. Although a robust AR program can enhance its regional air power projection capacity, China faces significant cost and technical and operational challenges.

Advantages, History, and Challenges

China's AR development is a matter of both military modernization and intense national pride. A September 2005 article published by the state-controlled Xinhua News Agency extols the strategic benefits that will flow from the People's Liberation Army Air Force (PLAAF)'s new overwater AR capability and calls China's new AR abilities "a major technological breakthrough" that brings PRC air warfare capabilities in line with those of the United States,

United Kingdom, France, and Russia.[2] An August 2009 article in *People's Daily*, which discusses an exercise in the Guangzhou Military Region (MR) in which J-10 fighters practiced AR, states that AR can give Chinese aerial forces an important strategic capability with both offensive and defensive applications.[3]

Creating a force that can employ AR credibly in combat would be a very expensive and time-consuming venture for the People's Liberation Army (PLA). Figure 1 illustrates the steps needed to achieve combat-capable AR ability and estimates China's current position with regard to these metrics of progress. An AR-capable force needs a comprehensive support infrastructure; basing, force protection, training, maintenance, and logistics are but a few considerations. Bases capable of maintaining and supporting tankers must be established near potential conflict zones. Then planners must decide if tanker-supported strike or combat air patrol operations might require airborne early warning and control aircraft support as well as fighter protection for the strike aircraft and tankers themselves.[4] Even well-protected tankers would face challenges against capable adversaries of the type that China could face in a Taiwan scenario (e.g., U.S. F-15, F-16, F-22, F-35, or FA-18 fighter aircraft) or a South China Sea contingency (Vietnam, Malaysia, and others are now acquiring Russian Flanker-series fighters).

Figure 1: Chinese Progress Regarding Key AR Capability Benchmarks

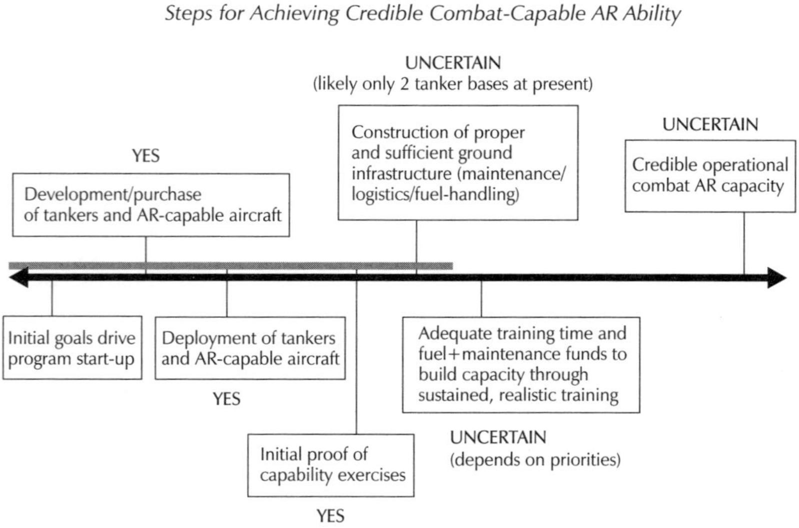

Steps for Achieving Credible Combat-Capable AR Ability

Additional challenges arise in the training of crews to fly the tankers. U.S. aircrews have the advantage of fifty years of training experience in AR. One could estimate that following basic flight training, China could realistically train a tanker aviator to be proficient in AR within three to five months. Moreover, Chinese pilots could then be upgraded to aircraft commanders after two years of experience, and to instructor status a year later. Training the fighter pilots in AR is also a consideration. Based on the U.S. Navy receiver training, it is probable that Chinese fighter pilots could acquire the skills required to conduct AR during their standard fighter training and need few additional flights to qualify in drogue AR. Arguably, the United States places much more training emphasis on its AR program in total, but this training is focused on training crews to refuel large aircraft, e.g., bombers and transports.

Although the cost of training may be minor, the cost to retrofit aircraft with AR capability and the acquisition of large AR-capable aircraft is not. These costs are by no means insurmountable, but justifying such a large investment necessitates a careful examination of what missions, in what areas, and against which potential adversaries might require an AR capability. Later sections will examine scenarios in which AR might be useful to the Chinese military.

While China's strategic goals influence AR acquisition plans, past experience also plays a part. During the 1979 Sino-Vietnam border war, Chinese F-6 [J-6] strike aircraft were unable to offer sustained air support inside Vietnam. The aircraft's short combat range, lack of AR capability, and operation from rear area bases in China meant that the F-6 had little loiter time, or "time on station," when it arrived in the combat area.[5]

In a March 1988 clash between China and Vietnam in the Spratly Islands, top Chinese military leaders again realized that their aircraft lacked the combat range, or "legs," necessary to reach distant combat zones and still have acceptable amounts of time on station. In response to the lessons derived from these experiences, China sought longer-range strike aircraft (such as the JH-7) and also launched its tanker aircraft project in January 1989. It completed the first H-6U (modified Badger) tanker in November 1994.[6]

China first publicly displayed its new AR platforms on National Day in 1999, when an H-6U, accompanied by two J-8II fighter-bombers and trailing two hoses and drogues, overflew Tiananmen Square. Chinese sources note early problems with AR training, including near collisions, pilots refusing to fly AR training missions due to lack of proper preparation, and outdated equipment. Despite these challenges, the PLA has persevered in solving technical and safety problems through training and multiple exercises as well as the use of AR training simulators.[7]

China's AR program, though advancing, is likely to remain limited as China's current priority appears to be enhancing air combat capability in the South China Sea region. The Guangzhou Military Region forces are responsible for conducting operations tasks revolving around the South Sea. To resolve air refueling shortcomings, these troops innovate and improving training methods to ensure that fighters can air refuel successfully, increasing the open seas operations capabilities of this unit. Air refueling exercises have increased in frequency; photos from a July 2009 exercise appeared to show professional operations.[8]

Chinese analysts take great pains to note that they have no need for an American- or Soviet-style AR program aimed at refueling strategic bombers. They instead liken China to European countries that use AR to support tactical aircraft operations.[9] Chinese analysts also frame China's need for AR in defensive terms, stating that it "will give a new boost to the PLA in its duties of maritime security and safeguarding national unity."[10] The maps show the range gains and increased aerial force projection capabilities that could arise from enhanced Chinese AR capability. The range bars on these maps assume that: (1) fighters will return to launch location; (2) aerial refueling is fixed-orbit, out-

Map 1: Notional Potential Range Gains from AR with J-10 Aircraft

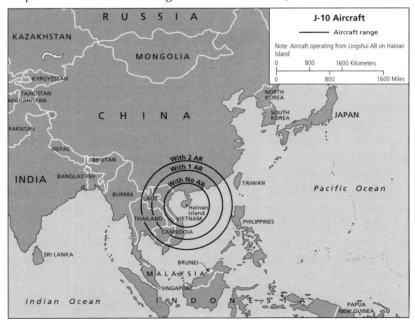

Map 2: Notional Potential Range Gains from AR with J-8II Aircraft

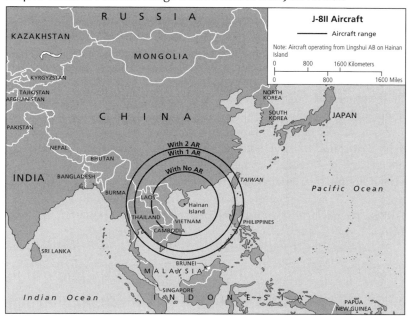

Map 3: Notional Potential Range Gains from AR with Su-30 Aircraft

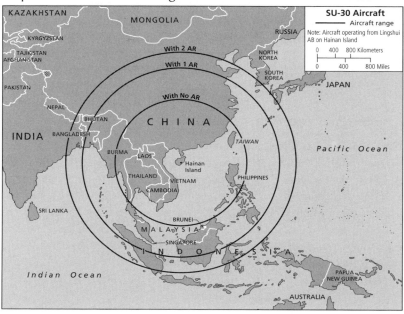

bound leg only (unrefueled return); and (3) Chinese forces would be able to maintain sufficient air control to send their tankers several hundred kilometers into the South China Sea.

Chinese analysts' claims of a defensive AR or "tactical" capability are in part supported by China's exclusive use of the "probe and drogue" AR system, for the probe and drogue (or "basket") is more suited for fighter and small aircraft. The basket is more difficult to use with large aircraft because it has a limited fuel transfer rate and it is much harder for the pilot of a larger aircraft to "poke," or connect to, the basket in order to refuel. As a pilot maneuvers his aircraft into position behind the drogue, the basket has a tendency to move away from the receiver aircraft as the aircraft approaches the basket due to a pressure or "bow" wave created in front of the receiver aircraft. The larger the aircraft, the larger the bow wave, and the harder it is to position the aircraft behind the drogue and to connect with it successfully.

Conversely, the "boom" system used by the U.S. Air Force is a maneuverable metal tube controlled from within the tanker. For boom AR, the receiver pilot flies the aircraft into the "contact position" below and behind the tanker aircraft. The boom operator on the tanker then "flies," or directs, the boom into the receptacle of the receiver aircraft. The boom's maneuverability compensates for a larger, less maneuverable receiver aircraft. Moreover, the boom system can off-load fuel at a substantially higher rate: 6,000 lbs of fuel per minute versus 2,000 lbs per minute for the probe and drogue. Although the U.S. Air Force uses the boom to refuel its fighters, it is more for reasons of single system efficiency (one AR system for all Air Force aircraft). Current fighters cannot on-load fuel at a high enough rate or quantity to require the higher off-load capability of the boom system.[11]

Chinese AR Capabilities: Aircraft

China's primary in-flight refueling platform is the Hong-6U (H-6U), based on the Xi'an H-6 bomber, which itself is a copy of the Russian TU-16 Badger. The H-6U first entered Naval Aviation and Air Force service in the mid-1990s (Chinese sources mention 1996 as the primary date) and serves the J-8II strike fighter flown by both services. The new J-10 strike fighter can also refuel from the H-6U and video clips are available from CCTV (via YouTube) showing J-10s tanking from an H-6U. Knowledgeable sources state that one H-6U can refuel 6 J-8IIs.[12] Table 1 shows an estimated inventory of Chinese AR capable aircraft.

Table 1: Estimated Air Force/Naval Aviation AR Capable Aircraft Inventory

Aircraft*	Type	Number†	AR Capable
J-8II	Fighter	~50	Yes
J-10	Strike fighter	~100	Yes
SU-30MK	Strike fighter	~100	Yes
J-11	Strike fighter	~115	Uncertain

Sources: *China Defense Today, Jane's*, authors' estimates.
* The JH-7, early J-8s, IL-76, Y-7, Y-8, and the SU-27 are not AR capable.
† Total at least 250, possibly up to 365 AR capable aircraft.

The PLA's larger SU-30 strike fighters cannot refuel from the H-6U. Reasons for this incompatibility include different probe and drogue equipment as well as the fact that the H-6U carries too little fuel and cannot transfer it quickly enough to effectively serve the SU-30, which is a much larger fighter aircraft than the J-8II and J-10.[13] The H-6 itself apparently cannot be refueled in the air, although later versions of the Russian TU-16 Badger (of which the H-6 is simply a "Sinicized" version) can AR using the probe and drogue.[14]

The H-6 is limited in the fuel it can offload; it carries only 37,000 pounds of transferable fuel. Recent Chinese analyses claim that the Air Force and Naval Aviation need a 300,000–380,000-pound gross takeoff weight tanker that carries 80,000–100,000 pounds of fuel (or 13,000–17,000 gallons).[15] The PLAN's aviation forces have already moved to address this issue, ordering 30 IL-76 transports and 8 IL-78 MIDAS tankers (modified IL 76s) from Russia in 2005. These tankers have a three-point probe and drogue system (one on each wing and one on the fuselage) and can carry (with additional internal tanks) more than 200,000 pounds of transferable fuel; thus, they are suitable to refuel the SU-30s.[16]

No delivery of these aircraft has yet been made. The original plan was to build the China-bound IL-78s at a plant in Uzbekistan. However, production delays caused by lack of specialists and key manufacturing equipment forced the company to shift the order to a Russian plant that has also proven unable to quickly fulfill the order.[17] A Russian news report in May 2007 quoted the director general of Ilyushin (IL-78 manufacturer) as stating that the IL-76/78 contract with China was stalled.[18] The delay is apparently rooted in a dispute between the Tashkent plant management and Rosoboronexport, as well as unexpected cost increases triggered by changes in the U.S. dollar's value relative to that of the yuan, and especially the ruble.[19] Talks between Chinese and Russian delegations, held in December 2009, demonstrated that the Chinese remain interested in acquiring larger and more capable AR aircraft.[20]

Table 2: Sample Global Tanker Comparison

Aircraft	IL-78 MIDAS	H-6U	KC-135	KC-10
Length (m)	46.59	34.8	41.53	54.4
Height (m)	14.76	10.36	12.7	17.4
Wingspan (m)	50.5	33	39.88	50
Maximum takeoff weight (kg)	210,000	79,000	146,285	265,500
Maximum range (km)	6,700	7,200	17,766	18,503
Transferrable fuel (kg)	96,000	16,800	90,719	160,000
Cargo capacity (kg)	40,000	N/A	37,648	76,560
Crew	7	4	3	4
User countries	Russia, China, India, Algeria	China	USA, Turkey, France, Singapore	USA, Netherlands

Sources: Global Security, www.globalsecurity.org; Federation of American Scientists, www.fas.org.

Table 2 compares the H-6U and IL-78 to the U.S. KC-135 and KC-10 tankers. Perhaps due to the delivery delays, in November of 2009, Hu Xiaofeng, the president of Aviation Industries of China, announced that China was in the process of developing a large military-transport aircraft similar to Russia's IL-76.[21] If China succeeds in manufacturing a large military-transport aircraft, the PLA will no longer have to rely on outside vendors. Additionally, the PLA could adapt this aircraft to become an air refueling platform, much as Russia did with the IL-78. In coming years, the PLA will likely look to China's large airliner programs as one possible place to derive a large air tanker airframe. An article in the April 2009 issue of *Shipborne Weapons* points out that just as the KC-135 is closely related to the Boeing 767 commercial airframe, so the PLA should also consider basing its large tankers off of large civilian aircraft.

The authors note that while China's ability to manufacture aircraft is improving, their ability to produce an engine for the large transport domestically has yet to be developed.[22]

Chinese AR Capabilities: Hose and Drogue Equipment

At present, PLAAF and PLAN aviation appear to be focusing on the probe and drogue system. Most nations' air forces use the probe and drogue, which consists of a hose drum unit (HDU) from which a flexible hose with a shuttlecock-like drogue is trailed behind the tanker aircraft. The receiver aircraft is equipped with a receiving probe that is "flown" into the drogue, after which fuel is transferred. It is cheaper than a boom, allows tankers to refuel multiple aircraft at once by adding HDU pods, and allows ground-attack and other aircraft not originally designed as tankers to carry HDUs and external fuel pods known as in "buddy tanks."

China's indigenous refueling pod is the RDC-1, which was developed by the China Research Institute of Aero Accessories and apparently is derived from the Mk. 32 AR pod built by the United Kingdom's FRL Ltd.[23] The pod is primarily powered by a "fueldraulic" system (a hydraulic system that uses the supplied fuel instead of hydraulic fluid). The system generates fueldraulic pressure through the small propeller affixed to the front of the pod. These fueldraulics are the primary force used to extend and retract the basket as well as take up slack in the hose when a receiver is in contact and closes on the tanker while refueling. Although the pods are the most efficient option for modification of current aircraft to tankers, they have several drawbacks. First, the pods' size and, in small part, weight reduce the fuel efficiency of the tanker, further reducing the tanker's range or off-load capability to the receiver. Second, without the addition of winglets on the tips of the tanker, wingtip vortices generated by the heavy tanker can cause problems for the lighter fighters as they reach the AR position. The vortices strike the outboard wing of the fighter, causing the pilot a considerable challenge in maintaining smooth control and "contact" with the basket. Use of an integrated centerline basket or drogue system from the underside of the aircraft fuselage, rather than the wings, could reduce the destabilizing aerodynamic factors, be more fuel efficient, and perhaps garner a greater offload rate than the wingtip pods.

Chinese AR Platforms: Control, Exercises, and Basing

According to Chinese sources and *Jane's* data, the PLAAF currently controls the majority of tanker assets. The PLAAF controls at least ten H-6U tankers while PLAN aviation controls at least four.[24] If the eight IL-78 MIDAS tankers on order from Russia are delivered, it is unclear who will control them. Many of China's AR-capable aircraft are operated by PLAN aviation, which could pose problems since PLAAF (which operates most of the tankers) and PLAN aviation rarely train together.

Information on the frequency of PLAAF and PLAN aviation AR exercises remains sparse. However, one source states that simulator training has become an important tool for improving Chinese pilots' AR proficiency.[25] The article does not provide details on locations or amounts of time spent in the simulator; it merely states that such training is increasingly important.

The PLA's H-6Us appear to be based primarily in the Guangzhou Military Region at Leiyang Airbase (AB).[26] One key reason the H-6Us are based at Leiyang is because it is an existing bomber base for the H-6 and already has the maintenance and logistics infrastructure for handling and working on the H-6 airframe.

Because the IL-76 and IL-78 are based on a common airframe, IL-78s acquired by China would likely be colocated with the PLAAF's IL-76 transports, which are based primarily at Dangyang AB in Hunan Province.[27] Dangyang AB is roughly 2,200 km from the Spratlys, and Leiyang is more than 1,500 km from the Spratly area, but both tankers have sufficient range that they could reach the combat area and still be able to support receivers.[28]

Based on available photographic sources, China has practiced AR in large international exercises such as Peace Mission (held with Russia in 2005 and 2007). Photos show a Russian IL-78 possibly preparing to refuel two Chinese SU-30s during Peace Mission 2005. It is not conclusively known whether Chinese aircraft have actually "tanked up" in earnest, as opposed to simply producing photo ops during high-profile exercises.[29]

AR: Possible Military Applications for China

AR offers a number of operational advantages. AR increases aircraft range and weapons load out because an aircraft can trade fuel weight for ordnance on initial takeoff and then refuel in the air. Additionally, AR provides mission flexibility; it can extend both fighter range and loiter time, thus allowing China to mass fighter aircraft from many airfields and overwhelm an adversary's defense. In China's case, the tanker's "force multiplier" effect will also increase maritime power projection capability in the South China Sea by boosting both the range and loiter time of PLAN aviation's tactical aircraft. The South China Sea is a primary responsibility area of PLAN aviation and as such, PLAN avi-

ation may be called on to conduct long-range strike missions in support of
PLAN surface operations.

Table 3 sets forth a range of scenarios where Chinese forces might use AR.
It also gauges the feasibility of employing AR supported forces against a range
of potential adversaries.

Table 3: Possible China In-Flight Refueling Use Scenarios

Mission	Possible Adversaries	Timeframe	Challenges	Difficulty
South China Sea sovereignty showdown—long-range strike, CAP, air coverage for surface combatants	Vietnam, Philippines	2010+	Coordination, self-defense, acquisition of heavy tanker to support SU-30s	Medium
Long-range air and maritime strike	USA, Japan, India	2015+	AWACS, OTH targeting, self-defense	Very high
Taiwan contingency	Taiwan, USA, Japan	2012+	AWACS, OTH targeting, self-defense, high op-tempo	High
Shipping protection/ counter blockade (likely linked with Taiwan contingency)	India, Japan, USA	2012+	AWACS, OTH targeting, self-defense	Very high

Key: AWACS = airborne early warning and control; OTH = over the horizon; CAP = combat air patrol.

Taiwan Scenario: Access Denial Benefits

Reports from the U.S. Department of Defense and other sources note that
China has more than four hundred land-based fighters and strike aircraft that
could be used against Taiwan without aerial refueling.[30] One should not discount, however, the value of AR to the Chinese military as it gives substantive
combat advantages even in a close-in fight such as combat over Taiwan.

Air refueling could allow Chinese forces to push their air defense perimeter further offshore, thereby denying opposing strike aircraft easy access to
China's target-rich Southeast Coast. Each 100 km that China can extend its
fighter patrols or strike flights potentially pushes maximum forward deploy-

ment of the opponent's naval forces back by a similar distance. It also shaves 100 km off air-launched enemy precision-guided munitions penetration range by pushing enemy strike aircraft further offshore. AR-capable Chinese fighters could also make it more difficult for enemy aircraft to attack PLAN warships operating near Taiwan during a blockade or invasion. Additionally, long-range fighter aircraft could be used as scouts to locate an adversary's fleet for targeting by other long-range assets.

Between 2010 and 2015, an effective AR capability could increase the range and loiter capability of Chinese air defense fighters, thereby allowing the J-10 and other AR-capable fighters to spend more time on station and engage threats further from the area the fighters are protecting. These fighters could also respond more rapidly to incoming threats if on-station and supported by tankers. In this scenario, the fighters would be already airborne and at altitude, and could spend considerably more time at full-combat (afterburner) power knowing they have dedicated air refueling assets. Combined with new surface to air missile (S-300 series) acquisitions and deployment of AWACS aircraft, AR-supported interceptors could substantially bolster, even double, the Chinese air defense network effectiveness.

South China Sea Contingency

Between 2015 and 2020, AR could enhance China's ability to quickly and effectively enforce sovereignty claims in the South China Sea by bolstering the PLA's long-range strike and long-distance combat air patrol capacity.[31] China has no known overseas basing rights, and establishing overseas bases would violate a central precept of PRC foreign policy. It might also seriously antagonize regional stakeholders, including the United States. China might also have trouble securing overflight rights from regional countries, which could face severe diplomatic and military pressure to deny Chinese forces access.[32] Chinese forces likely could, with some attrition, prevail over Vietnam and other South China Sea littoral states in an aerial conflict. However, if U.S. forces arrived, this could change the equation completely, since even the mere presence of highly capable U.S. carrier-borne fighters and ship-based air defenses could seriously hamper Chinese air operations in the region.

China's best base for aerial power projection into the South China Sea would be Hainan Island, but the Spratly Islands are 1,100 km from China's main airbase at Lingshui, Hainan. This is beyond the unrefueled combat radius of all Chinese tactical aircraft except for the SU-27 and SU-30. Even these long-legged platforms would be operating near their maximum range and would have little ability to loiter.[33] An airstrip on Woody Island in the Paracels could conceivably handle tactical aircraft, including the SU-27. However, Chinese planners might not depend on it during a conflict because of its limited space and vulnerability to attack. AR could substantially increase China's ability to project military power in the South China Sea region by allowing Chinese forces to conduct long-range air operations without relying on foreign airfields or airspace to fulfill their objectives.

Future Directions

China's air power is in the midst of change. China's 2008 Defense White Paper states that the "Air Force is working to accelerate its transition from territorial air defense to both offensive and defensive operations, and increase its capabilities for carrying out reconnaissance and early warning, air strikes, air and missile defense, and strategic projection, in an effort to build itself into a modernized strategic air force."[34] However, even major AR improvements over the next ten to fifteen years will not give the PLA a capability resembling the global power projection capability the United States has with its more than four hundred tankers. China's AR progress will not come in a quantum leap but rather in measured steps that can come only through significant financial and training investments. In the short term, China will focus the majority of its aviation effort on the acquisition of fighters rather than a significant investment in tankers for a simple reason: to fully use a "force multiplier" such as the tanker, one must first possess the forces (fighters) to multiply. However, one should not ignore developing tanker capacity, as China already possesses the world's sixth largest AR fleet.

Due to the high costs and complexity of fielding a combat-capable force, as well as Chinese foreign policy objectives, Chinese AR development will focus on enhancing the PLA's ability to project air power over the South China Sea and the Taiwan Strait. Additionally, it remains to be seen to what extent China's military leadership will promote AR. Another uncertainty is whether (and, if so, how) China will promote smooth interservice tanker operations, since tanker assets are currently divided between the PLAAF and PLAN aviation.

Long-range AR-supported operations would pose challenges that the current generation of Chinese pilots have not faced during wartime. These include air intercept control, combat identification, early warning, joint coordination, and rules of engagement. The PLAAF is developing the KJ-2000 airborne early-warning aircraft, while Naval Aviation is pursuing an airborne early-warning platform based on the Y-8 airframe. It is currently unclear whether these aircraft will also have command and control functions, or whether they are early-warning platforms only. The PLAAF and PLAN aviation can likely overcome current barriers posed by inexperience and lack of a joint operations mindset, but doing so will exact significant costs in money, training time, and command structure refinements geared toward allowing smooth joint operations.

China has maintained its practice of using probe and drogue AR to multiply the combat power of its tactical air forces. For the near future, China does not seem interested in conducting large-scale strategic AR missions. However, a shift toward a different AR system, that is, the more capable USAF boom AR system, might signal a change toward a growing strategic air power projection mindset.

Finally, one cannot consider China limited in its capability to rapidly procure a modern tanker fleet. There are numerous options available to China in the near future, including the aforementioned ongoing negotiations with Russia, modifying domestically produced passenger and cargo aircraft, and the possibility of purchasing existing tanker platforms from international aircraft corporations. This last option, though unlikely, could gain China a modern fleet in a relatively short period of time. In addition, as budget cuts begin to more deeply affect military procurement in the United States and Europe, sales of tankers and subcomponents to other parties will become increasingly attractive. As these tanker aircraft could also be delivered with a boom, it could conceivably mask Chinese intentions to pursue a strategic aircraft capability. One would then need to focus on receiver modifications to China's bombers and transport aircraft as an indicator of China's strategic AR intent.

With at least 14 H-6U tankers and up to 350 AR-capable tactical aircraft, the PLAAF and PLAN aviation now have an operational "first-generation" AR capability. Assuming, conservatively, that one tanker can service four tactical aircraft, the PLAN aviation and PLAAF have the ability to assemble and support a formidable strike package for the South China Sea region if they could protect their tankers from enemy fighter attacks, develop strong electronic countermeasures capabilities, and create an AWACS-like capability based on the KJ-2000 or other platforms now being developed. If China is willing to bear the costs and develop key supporting infrastructure, AR could significantly enhance Chinese regional air power projection options by 2015.

Notes

1. *The People's Liberation Army Navy: A Modern Navy with Chinese Characteristics* (Suitland, MD: Office of Naval Intelligence, July 2009).

2. "The Chinese Air Force's Aerial Refueling Technology Achieves a Breakthrough," *Xinhua*, 14 September 2005, http://news.xinhuanet.com/mil/2005-09/14/content_3488708.htm.

3. "中国歼-10空中加油剑指南海 准备应对最复杂局面" ["Aerial Refueling Will Help China's J-10 Handle the Most Complex Situations in the South China Sea"], *People's Daily*, 5 August 2009, http://military.people.com.cn/GB/42969/58519/9789315.html.

4. U.S. airborne warning and control system (AWACS) aircraft cost roughly $270 million apiece to produce, and there would also be substantial research and development costs to develop the system. See "E-3 AWACS," *Federation of American Scientists*, http://www.fas.org/man/dod-101/sys/ac/e-3.htm.

5. Kenneth W. Allen, Glenn Krumel, and Jonathan D. Pollack, *China's Air Force Enters the 21st Century* (Santa Monica, CA: RAND, 1995), 96, http://rand.org/pubs/monograph_reports/MR580/.

6. 刘华清 [Liu Huaqing], 刘华清回忆录 ["The Memoirs of Liu Huaqing"] (Beijing: People's Liberation Army Press, 2004), 104.

7. "China's Aerial Forces Complete Long Range Aerial Refueling Training and Raise Their Combat Capability," 中国新闻网 [*China News Network*], 25 April 2007.

8. "Guangzhou Military Region Air Force Aviation Unit Conducts Mid-Air Refueling Exercise with New-Type Fighters," *Xiandai Junshi* [*Conmilit*] (September 2009), OSC CPP20100222090001.

9. Jiang Yu, "Development of In-flight Refueling Techniques and the PLA Air Fighting Power," *Shipborne Weapons* (December 2006): 51.

10. Guang Zi, "Aerial Refueling: Extending the Long Arm to Hit the Enemy," *Modern Navy* (April 2000): 34.

11. KC-135 Aerial Refueling Manual T.O. 1-1C-1-3.

12. "Hong-6U Tanker," *China's Defence Today*, 17 January 2009, http://www.sinodefence.com/airforce/airlift/h6tanker.asp.

13. Jiang, "Development of In-flight Refueling Techniques."

14. "TU-16 Badger (Tupolev)," *Federation of American Scientists*, http://www.fas.org/nuke/guide/russia/bomber/tu-16.htm.

15. Jiang, "Development of In-flight Refueling Techniques."

16. "Ilyushin IL-78MKI MIDAS," *Indian Military*, http://www.indian-military.org/air-force/support/mid-air-refuellers/9-ilyushin-il-78mki-midas.html.

17. "Moscow Said to Be 'Seriously Alarmed' by Loss of PRC Arms Export Market," *Nezavisimaya Gazeta*, 29 January 2008, OSC CEP20080129021011.

18. "Contract for the Delivery of IL-76MD and IL-78s to China Is Effectively Stalled," *Interfax*, 11 May 2007.

19. International arms contracts are often denominated in dollars. Interview with knowledgeable specialist, March 2008.

20. "Latest Round of Russia-China Military Technology Cooperation Conference Ends on a Sour Note," *Kanwa Asian Defense*, no. 66 (April 2010): 22–24, OSC CPP20100422702023.

21. "East Asian Strategic Review 2010," *National Institute for Defense Studies*, 25 March 2010, OSC JPP20100526134001.

22. Ma Shiqiang, "The Development of the PLA's Air-to-Air Refuelling Technology," *Shipborne Weapons* (April 2009): 44.

23. Carlo Kopp, "The PLA-AF's Aerial Refueling Programs," *Airpower Australia*, July 2007, http://www.ausairpower.net/APA-PLA-Tanker-Programs.html.

24. "Air Force, China," *Jane's Sentinel Security Assessment—China and Northeast Asia*, 7 January 2008, available at http://www8.janes.com.

25. "China's Aerial Forces Complete."

26. "Air Force, China," *Jane's Sentinel Security Assessment*.

27. Ibid.

28. Distances obtained via Google Earth.

29. Kopp, "PLA-AF's Aerial Refueling Programs."

30. See, for example, *Military Power of the People's Republic of China: 2008* (Washington, DC: Department of Defense, March 2008), 52, http://www.defenselink.mil/pubs/china.html.

31. The PLAAF and PLAN aviation would need to enhance cooperation, acquire AWACS systems, and then train to achieve operational proficiency. This would be expensive in terms of increased funding, higher maintenance costs, greater fuel use, higher flight-time quotas, and heightened bureaucratic energy spent on enhancing interservice cooperation.

32. Daniel Kostecka, "The Chinese Navy's Emerging Support Network in the Indian Ocean," Jamestown *China Brief* 10, no. 15 (22 July 2010), http://www.jamestown.org/programs/chinabrief/single/?tx_ttnews%5Btt_news%5D=36659&tx_ttnews%5Bback Pid%5D=25&cHash=010590e601.

33. Chinese analysts have also studied the 1982 Falklands War and note that lack of AR and range restrictions seriously weakened the Argentine Air Force's combat effectiveness. Argentine A-4 Skyhawks, Mirages, and Super Etendards did manage to hit several British ships but were operating at their maximum range and had little ability to loiter or provide close air support for Argentine troops on the islands.

34. Information Office of State Council of People's Republic of China, *China's National Defense in 2008*, 37, http://merln.ndu.edu/whitepapers/China_English2008.pdf.

Nan Li and Christopher Weuve

Chinese Aircraft Carrier Development
The Next Phase

THIS CHAPTER ADDRESSES two principal analytical questions: First, what are the necessary and sufficient conditions for China to acquire aircraft carriers? Second, what are the major implications if China acquires aircraft carriers?

Existing analyses on China's aircraft carrier ambitions are quite insightful but also somewhat inadequate, and must therefore be updated. Some, for instance, argue that with the advent of the Taiwan issue as China's top threat priority by late 1996 and the retirement of Liu Huaqing as vice chair of China's Central Military Commission (CMC) in 1997, aircraft carriers are no longer considered vital. This is because China does not require aircraft carriers to capture sea and air superiority in a war over Taiwan, and China's most powerful carrier proponent (Liu) could no longer influence relevant decision making. Other scholars suggest that China may well acquire small-deck aviation platforms such as helicopter carriers to fulfill secondary security missions. These missions include naval diplomacy, humanitarian assistance, disaster relief, and antisubmarine warfare. The present authors conclude, however, that China's aircraft carrier ambitions may be larger than the current literature has predicted. Moreover, the major implications of China acquiring aircraft carriers may need to be explored more carefully in order to inform appropriate reactions on the part of the United States and other Asia-Pacific naval powers.

This chapter is organized around documenting major changes in the four major conditions that are necessary and largely sufficient for China to acquire aircraft carriers: leadership endorsement, financial affordability, a relatively concise naval strategy that defines the missions of carrier operations, and availability of requisite technologies. This chapter shows that in spite of some unresolved issues, these changes suggest that China is likely to acquire medium-sized aircraft carriers in the medium term for "near-seas" missions and for gaining operational experience, so that it can acquire large-sized carriers for "far-seas" operations in the long term.

These four major conditions or variables can be both dependent and independent, depending on circumstances. Generally speaking, central leadership endorsement of the idea of acquiring aircraft carriers may depend on whether the required money and technologies are available and whether an appropriate naval strategy is formulated. There are some circumstances, however, in which central leadership endorsement may determine whether money and technologies are more readily available and whether the appropriate strategy is more forthcoming. Because of such a variation in the relationship among these four major conditions or variables, each is addressed separately, followed by a concluding section discussing the major implications if China acquires aircraft carriers.

Leadership Endorsement

Even though Liu Huaqing (the People's Liberation Army Navy [PLAN] commander during 1982–88 and a CMC member and vice chair during 1988–97) strongly advocated carrier operations, his idea was not endorsed by the central civilian leadership such as Jiang Zemin.[1] Lack of funding and requisite technologies may have played a role, and China's rapid economic growth had not yet caused a dependence on external sources of energy and raw materials shipped over vulnerable sea-lanes. More importantly, however, this contradicted the "new security concept" Jiang endorsed in 1997, which highlights "soft" approaches when dealing with China's maritime as well as land neighbors. This concept contributed significantly to China's signing of a Declaration of Conduct in South China Sea in 2002 and the Treaty of Amity and Cooperation in 2003 with ASEAN countries as well as the founding of the Shanghai Cooperation Organization in 2001. Because of these political and diplomatic initiatives, the primary missions Jiang assigned to the People's Liberation Army (PLA) during his rule were rather narrow and limited, and confined primarily to defending

China's national sovereignty and territorial land, air, and waters and to deterring Taiwan from declaring former independence.

Hu Jintao succeeded Jiang as the Chinese Communist Party general secretary in 2002, and he has served as the CMC chair since 2004. He has required the PLA to fulfill more expansive and externally oriented missions that were absent in Jiang's era: to secure China's newly emerging interests in maritime, outer, and electromagnetic space; and to contribute to world peace through international peacekeeping and humanitarian relief. Hu has also endorsed a far-seas operations (远海作战) concept for the PLAN that implies some new level of power projection capabilities.[2]

Such a change is understandable for two reasons, both due to years of rapid economic growth. First, China has begun to develop a stronger sense of vulnerability stemming from its growing dependence on external energy and raw materials, and has become more interested in sea-lanes used to ship these resources as well as traded goods. Second, both China's investment overseas and the number of its citizens working there are growing. These factors suggest that the idea of expanding China's naval power, and hence of acquiring aircraft carriers, has become more acceptable to the central civilian leadership since Jiang's era.

There are several indictors that this idea has been endorsed by the central civilian leadership. On 6 March 2007 a PLA lieutenant general revealed to the media at the convened annual National People's Congress that the project to develop aircraft carriers was proceeding smoothly. Ten days later minister of China's Commission of Science, Technology and Industry for National Defense, Zhang Yunchuan, stated that China would build its own aircraft carriers, and preparation was well under way.[3] More recently, in 2010 the spokesperson of China's Ministry of National Defense, Major General Qian Lihua, claimed that China has every right to acquire an aircraft carrier.[4] But more importantly, China's defense minister, General Liang Guanglie, told visiting Japanese defense minister Yasukazu Hamada in 2008 that China would not remain the only major power without an aircraft carrier forever.[5] All of these statements indicate that China has the intention to acquire aircraft carriers. These positive comments on a politically sensitive issue such as aircraft carriers would have been impossible had they not been endorsed by the central party leadership.

Financial Affordability

One major reason for China's past hesitation to acquire aircraft carriers was a lack of funding. While Mao proposed at a CMC meeting held on 21 June 1958 to build "railways on the high seas" consisting of oceangoing fleets of merchant ships escorted by aircraft carriers, China's defense budget that year was a mere 5 billion yuan. Of that, only 1.5 billion yuan could be allocated to weapons acquisition, and out of this share the PLAN received less than 200 million. A 1,600-ton *Gordy*-class destroyer cost 30 million yuan, and the PLAN could only afford to acquire four of them.[6]

The carrier project was again placed on the policy agenda in the early 1970s, but financial constraints still prevented the initiation of a serious program. From 1971 to 1982, China's annual defense budget averaged about 17 billion yuan. Out of less than 6 billion yuan allocated for weapons acquisition each year, the PLAN could only receive several hundred million yuan, while one Type 051 destroyer cost 100 million. Endorsed by party leader Hua Guofeng in the late 1970s, China had planned to acquire an 18,000-ton light aircraft carrier either through import or coproduction, and it was to be armed with the British Harrier vertical/short takeoff and landing (V/STOL) aircraft. The project had to be scrapped because the price asked by British suppliers was too high. Furthermore, Deng Xiaoping, after succeeding Hua as the paramount leader, decided to cut defense spending to free up more resources for developing the civilian economy.[7]

From the middle to late 1980s, Liu Huaqing lobbied feverishly for carrier operations. He proposed feasibility studies in the 7th Five-Year Plan (1991–95), research and development on key aspects of platform and aircraft in the 8th Five-Year Plan, and production in the early 2000s. His plan was shelved partly because of insufficient funding.[8] While the defense budget had been increasing since the early 1990s, the rate of increase could not catch up with the rising cost of acquiring aircraft carriers as they integrated more advanced aircraft, air-defense systems and electronics. Funding priority was instead given to developing submarines.

By 2007, however, China's finances had improved remarkably, with government revenue reaching $750 billion, lower than the U.S. $2.6 trillion but higher than Japan's $500 billion. China's foreign exchange reserve also ranked first in the world, reaching $1.4 trillion. As a result, China's annual formal defense budget had grown to $46 billion (350.9 billion yuan). According to official estimate, about one-third of China's formal defense budget, or $15.3 billion that year, was used for weapons acquisition. Given that naval modernization currently is a high priority, the PLAN is likely to receive several billion dollars a year just for weapons acquisition, and this figure is likely to grow in coming years.

Aircraft carriers come in a wide variety of sizes, costs, and capabilities, from small vessels capable of operating a handful of vertical takeoff and landing (VTOL) aircraft to supercarriers with complements approaching a hundred large conventional aircraft. In the middle of that range, more or less, is the Russian *Kuznetsov* class, an example of which, the *Varyag*, was purchased by China in the late 1990s. Taking into consideration the lower labor and material costs in China, the cost to build a medium-sized, conventional-powered 60,000-ton carrier similar to the Russian *Kuznetsov* class is likely to be above $2 billion. But the cost to acquire a carrier itself is just the start because a carrier needs aircraft and escorts. A Russian Su-33 carrier-based combat aircraft costs $50 million, so a notional carrier air wing of about fifty Su-33s, several airborne early warning (AEW) aircraft, and several antisubmarine warfare (ASW) and search-and-rescue helicopters may cost more than $3 billion. A Russian *Sovremenny*-class guided missile destroyer costs about $600 million, so an escort force consisting of a number of guided missile destroyers, frigates, and supply ships may cost more than $4 billion. With the total cost of one carrier group likely to be about $10 billion, two carrier groups, which is the number that China is likely to acquire, would cost around $20 billion. Spreading the cost over a development period of ten years, it would constitute only a moderate proportion of the projected naval weapons acquisition budget during that time. The annual cost for regular training, maintenance, repairs, and fueling of two carrier groups is estimated to be about 10 percent of the construction cost, or $200 million for each of the two groups. Such an extra cost can be well covered by another one-third of the annual naval budget, which is specifically allocated for such a purpose. This proportion, like the weapons acquisition proportion, is also likely to grow over the years as the defense budget grows because of rapid economic growth.

Naval Strategy

Leadership endorsement and financial affordability are necessary but not sufficient for China to acquire aircraft carriers. For this to take place, a relatively concise naval strategy that defines the missions of the carrier groups is also needed. Compared to the two previous conditions, however, this is more problematic.

Near-coast defense (近岸防御) defined China's naval strategy from the 1950s until the early 1980s. It highlights counteramphibious landing operations earlier against the Taiwan Guomindang government's attempt to recapture the mainland and later against a possible Soviet invasion from the seas; as a result, this strategy did not require aircraft carriers. Since the late 1980s, a near-seas active defense (近海积极防御) strategy, largely operationalized by Liu Huaqing, was endorsed to replace near-coast defense. This strategy requires the PLAN to develop credible operational capabilities against potential opponents in China's three "near seas": the South China Sea, East China Sea, and Yellow Sea, or the space within and slightly beyond the first island chain, which extends from the Kurile Islands, through the main islands of Japan, Ryukyu Archipelago, Taiwan, and the Philippines to Borneo Island.

According to Liu, there are at least two major issues within this expanded operational space that require aircraft carriers: "to solve the need for struggle against Taiwan [independence] (解决对台斗争需要) and to resolve the dispute over the Nansha [Spratlys] Archipelago (解决南沙群岛争端)." In operational terms, Liu believed that "whether the attack type or the V/STOL type, they (aircraft carriers) are for the purpose of resolving issues of (fleet) air defense and sea attack (防空和对海攻击问题)." Liu particularly stressed that "the objective for us to acquire aircraft carriers is not to compete against the U.S. and the Soviet Union."[9] This implies that what Liu considered to acquire was a medium-sized, conventional-powered platform for limited, air-defense–dominant missions, but not a large, nuclear-powered one for expansive, sea/land attack–dominant missions.

Of the two major issues, Liu was more concerned about lack of air cover for more distant naval operations over the Spratlys. As a result, he highlighted the need to compare the cost-effectiveness of employing carrier and carrier-based combat aircraft with that of employing land-based aircraft supported by air refueling tankers. Naval operations over Taiwan, conversely, could be covered by land-based combat aircraft, even though Liu did mention that without carriers, air operations over Taiwan could be more costly because more airfields and land-based aircraft are needed due to reduced loitering time in the air.[10] The 1996 Taiwan Strait crisis and the 1997 retirement of Liu, which helped to further consolidate Jiang Zemin's position as the CMC chair, had clearly contributed to the shelving of the PLAN's carrier project.

While Liu Huaqing articulated the near-seas active defense strategy in the 1980s, he stated that the PLAN would operate within and around the first island chain, or in China's "near seas" for a long time to come. But he also suggested that the growth of the economy and strengthening of science and technology would translate into expansion of Chinese naval power in the long run. This in turn would allow the PLAN to extend its operational range from the "near seas" to the "middle and far seas" ("中远海"), or the space between the first island chain and the second island chain, which stretches from northern Japan to Northern Mariana Islands, Guam and further southward, and beyond. This would also allow the PLAN to "strike the enemy's rear" through exterior-line operations if China's coastline, or interior line, were attacked by an opponent. Liu, however, placed emphasis on the "primacy of near-seas operations" (近海作战为主) and regarded "middle- and far-seas operations as [only] supportive and auxiliary" (中远海作战为辅).[11]

By 2004, however, such an emphasis seemed to have shifted somewhat. China's naval analysts, for instance, argue that China's naval strategy should shift from "near-seas" to "far-seas" operations.[12] They argue that such operations are necessary because of China's increasing vulnerability stemming from its growing dependence on more distant sea-lanes and "chokepoints" for shipping imported oil and traded goods. China's ever-expanding oceangoing fleets of merchant ships and oil tankers also need to be protected, as does China's growing overseas investment and number of Chinese citizens living and working overseas. Moreover, China's prosperous coastline and resource-rich exclusive economic zones and territories in dispute need to be secured. These areas, however, are difficult to secure because they are too long and wide and their flanks are too exposed. This problem extends into the close forward positions such as the "near seas," which are partially blocked by the first island chain, and the few strait- and channel-based exits are mostly narrow and controlled by others, making it difficult to gain initiative by maneuvering out of the blocked near seas. Many of the navies operating in these near seas are quite formidable, including the U.S., Japanese, Russian, Taiwanese, and Indian navies as well as various Southeast Asian navies. They render the PLAN more vulnerable, and they limit and reduce the effectiveness of the near-seas active defense strategy for both deterrence and warfighting.[13]

According to China's naval analysts, to alleviate vulnerability and enhance effectiveness, the PLAN needs to break out of the interior-line constraints, or those associated with the narrow and near seas within and around the first island chain. Acquiring capabilities to operate in the far seas, or the vast space beyond the first island chain, would allow the PLAN to regain initiative and momentum. While "interior-line operations require near-seas capabilities, exterior-line operations are based on far-seas capabilities. . . . Far-seas capabilities make it possible to carry out offensive operations and ambush and sabotage operations in the far and vast naval battle-space beyond the First Island

Chain, and would have the effect of shock and awe on the enemy."[14] Forward operations and offense are central to naval combat because oceans have few invulnerable physical objects on which to base the defense, and naval platforms, once crippled, are hard to restore. An emphasis on offense also helps to optimize naval force structure and is more cost-effective. This is because as strikes are more long-range, precise, and powerful, and therefore more lethal, defense becomes more expensive to maintain. History also shows that a strategy of close and static defense led to the decisive defeat of the Qing Navy in the first Sino-Japanese War of 1894.

Far-seas operations strategy suggests that the PLAN needs to develop power projection capabilities that can operate effectively in the more distant West Pacific and the East Indian Ocean. It also implies that the PLAN may come in direct confrontation with the U.S. Navy in the Western Pacific, for instance, in a competition for sea access and denial in a crisis over Taiwan. Moreover, in the worst-case analysis, the PLAN may come into direct contact with the U.S. and Indian navies in competition to secure vital sea-lanes in the South China Sea and East Indian Ocean, and in "chokepoints" such as the Malacca Strait. These scenarios may require the PLAN to acquire large, nuclear-powered aircraft carriers, the kind of platforms that are very different from the medium, conventional-powered ones for limited missions as envisioned by Liu Huaqing. A key variable that may determine whether China would acquire medium, conventional-powered carriers or the large, nuclear-powered ones is whether requisite technologies are available.

Availability of Requisite Technologies

Before discussing the specific carrier development route that the PLAN might follow, it is useful to consider briefly general principles of aircraft carrier development and operations. There are four main types of aircraft carriers operating worldwide today, as defined by their method of launching and recovering aircraft. The first and most capable (but also most expensive) is the catapult assisted takeoff but arrested recovery (CATOBAR) design. Originally created by the United Kingdom but perfected by the United States, this design philosophy is currently employed by the United States and France. CATOBAR-type carriers use powerful catapults to launch their aircraft, and they facilitate aircraft recovery through the use of arresting gear, a complicated series of cables the aircraft snags with a hook upon landing. Catapults and arresting gear are large, sophisticated, and expensive installations. Because catapults (which currently use steam although electromagnetic versions have been proposed) are necessary for heavy aircraft capable of long range or heavy payloads (which in turn can perform a wider variety of missions at greater range), CATOBAR carriers are generally considered a prerequisite for a significant carrier-borne power projection capability.

The second carrier design is the short takeoff but arrested recovery (STOBAR) type. This design uses a rolling takeoff—often assisted by a ski-jump ramp—but returns are via arrested recovery. Most current non-U.S. aircraft carriers are of this type, including the Russian *Kuznetsov* class. A STOBAR design is generally less capable and much simpler to build and maintain than a CATOBAR design but may still be a large, fast ship. STOBAR is less appropriate for the strike role, so a decision to forgo catapults may indicate intent to not perform the strike mission.

The third design, the short takeoff, vertical landing (STOVL) design, uses a rolling takeoff—often assisted by a ski-jump ramp—with a vertical landing recovery. This is the system Spain and the United Kingdom have used on their most recent designs. As a general rule, aircraft capable of vertical landing can theoretically also take off vertically, but the performance penalty for doing so is high; the rolling, ski-jump-assisted takeoff maximizes load and range. A STOVL design will likely be smaller than a CATOBAR or STOBAR design, but it still requires relatively high speed to generate wind over the deck. The STOVL design severely limits strike and long-range missions, but is easier to build and maintain. STOVL is generally the minimum capability needed to provide for fighter-based air defense.

The fourth and final carrier type is the vertical takeoff and landing (VTOL) design. Compared to STOVL, a VTOL design foregoes even more aircraft operational capability and allows for a slower ship. Selecting VTOL over STOVL generally means the ship is only intended to operate helicopters, is also designed for another function (e.g., amphibious assault) that constrains performance (such as limiting the size of the propulsion plant), or is only really envisioned for noncombat or general support missions. For fixed-wing aircraft, the difference between STOVL and VTOL is generally the presence of a ski-jump ramp at the front of the flight deck, and the ability of the ship to generate wind over the deck.

Thinking about Aircraft Carriers

There are several general rules of thumb that are useful when considering aircraft carrier size and capabilities:

Any increase in capability drives toward a larger ship.

There are two ways that a larger carrier facilitates the operation of larger, heavier aircraft in greater numbers. First, a larger carrier has more space to devote to propulsion, allowing for more wind over the deck for launching and landing aircraft. Second, a larger carrier has a larger flight deck, which allows more airplanes on deck at the same time and facilitates simultaneous launch and recovery operations.

The longer the range or heavier the payload of the aircraft, the more likely the carrier will need catapults and arrested recovery. Catapults and arrestor gear are large installations, which also drive toward a larger ship.

Vertical takeoff and landing costs!

Even assuming that the design of the aircraft does not involve performance compromises, which is a big assumption, it is still true that it takes extra fuel to takeoff vertically ("there's no such thing as a free launch") and there will be much more restrictive weight limits on what one can "bring back" on landing, forcing unused ordnance to be jettisoned. This is at best inefficient and at worst affects overall combat capability.

A large multipurpose aircraft carrier is more efficient than a small carrier.

A large carrier carries more aircraft per ton of displacement. In addition, the large deck allows better plane handling than a small carrier.

Taken together, these considerations are powerful tools in analyzing what a PLAN carrier might look like, based on discussions of design features on the one hand (i.e., "what can they do with what they intend to buy?") and missions on the other (i.e., "what do they need to buy to do what they say they want to do?"). For example, the Russian-built *Varyag* is a ski-jump–equipped STOBAR design of 60,000–65,000 tons displacement with a long (1,000 feet) flight deck. This makes it a large carrier, smaller than an American *Nimitz* but larger than the French *Charles de Gaulle*, and roughly comparable to both the American *Kitty Hawk* class and the planned British *Queen Elizabeth* class. Note that one must be careful comparing displacements—with large, voluminous ships like carriers, the difference between empty, full, and standard load can be tens of thousands of tons.

Due to the lack of catapults, fixed-wing aircraft on *Varyag* are essentially limited to air superiority—fleet air defense or offensive air superiority—operations, or relatively short-range strike missions. *Varyag* was intended to operate with a steam propulsion plant capable of 32 knots, but as sold to China it reportedly has no engines.

Russia officially categorizes the *Kuznetsov* class as a "heavy aircraft-carrying cruiser"; the limited ability of its embarked aircraft and its Russian-style heavy missile load are consistent with this description. Its usual suggested role was to support and defend strategic missile-carrying submarines, surface ships, and maritime missile-carrying aircraft. In other words, while it may have some antiship capability both in its aircraft and its missiles, it is not really designed to support long-range strike missions.

Medium Carrier Options

Major General Qian Lihua stated in 2010 that if China acquires an aircraft carrier, it will serve mainly the purpose of near-seas active defense. If we accept this statement at face value (and it does appear consistent with other statements and the external evidence), then it appears that in the short run China is likely to acquire a medium-sized carrier for limited, air-defense–dominant missions. For a medium, conventional-powered carrier intended for these missions, requisite technologies are relatively available. China has been analyzing the Russian-built *Varyag* since 2002. The Chinese design and construction of super container ships and of oil tankers and liquified natural gas carriers should also help to gain experience for building the hull of aircraft carriers, although it must be noted that aircraft carriers are much more complex ships. China also has the necessary simulation and testing facilities for research and development such as large-scale ship model basins and wind tunnels, and it has been gaining engineering and technical assistance from Russia and Ukraine, countries that have experience in designing and building medium-sized STOBAR-type aircraft carriers. Furthermore, specialized construction materials such as high-grade steel can either be indigenously developed or acquired through import. Moreover, China has made substantial progress in information, automation, new materials, and maritime and space technologies, many of which can be integrated in carrier construction. Finally, while major technical bottlenecks exist and need to be resolved, China has experience in producing heavy steam and gas turbines, and several units can be grouped together to provide sufficient speed and range.

For takeoff and landing, China is likely to choose a STOBAR design. China's naval analysts have identified several benefits of a no-catapult STOBAR design over steam catapult-equipped CATOBAR designs, including minimizing space for water and fuel storage, maximizing energy available for ship's propulsion, simpler production and maintenance requirements, and less vulnerability to mechanical breakdowns.[15]

Because medium carriers are better suited for providing air cover for naval operations and less well suited for more distant sea and land attack, air superiority fighters with some sea/land attack capabilities are sufficient. China has several options based on the Russian Su-27 Flanker. China already has purchased Su-27s and Su-30MK2s and has been negotiating the purchase of the STOBAR-capable Su-33 combat aircraft, which can carry eight air-to-air missiles and one or two antiship cruise missiles (ASCM). In the meantime, we have photographic evidence that China is attempting to upgrade the design of its land-based indigenous J-11B (an upgraded Chinese variant of the Su-27) into a carrier-based aircraft, the J-15.[16] At a minimum, such an attempt would involve reinforcing the landing gears, wings, and fuselage of the aircraft for arrested recovery, which puts heavier stress on these components than standard runway landings. The indigenous land-based J-10 has also been suggested as possible carrier aircraft conversion prospect, but certain elements of the design (such as the height and placement of the landing gear) make it a less likely option.

One important mission that would not be covered by the aircraft discussed earlier is airborne early warning. China is reportedly acquiring carrier-based KA-31 AEW helicopters from Russia.[17] The KA-31 can patrol for two to three hours consecutively, with a detection range of 150 km for sea targets and 100–150 km for low-altitude aircraft and ASCMs, and it can direct engagement against fifteen targets at one time. Assisted by shipborne phased array radars, these ranges and capacity are sufficient for limited missions in the near seas. It is also likely that China may upgrade its shipborne Z-8 (Chinese variant of the French Super Frelon) to carrier-based AEW platform. Note, though, that AEW helicopters are inherently less capable than fixed-wing AEW platforms due to limitations on altitude, endurance, and the size of the radar antenna that can be carried. Possibly as a response to these limitations, China is also interested in developing carrier-based unmanned aerial vehicles (UAV) with electro-optical, infrared, and radar sensors for sea intelligence, surveillance, and reconnaissance. This is because UAVs can patrol for a long time at high altitude and are difficult to detect.

It is likely to be a long and difficult process for China to develop a carrier air capability; therefore, one might expect its aircraft acquisition program to start slowly. The Chinese approach to carrier development is likely to be incremental as well. China may attempt to gain engineering and operational experiences by moving from smaller and simpler platforms to larger and more complex ones.

This means that the option of building small V/STOL carriers should not be completely excluded. Conversely, many Chinese naval analysts argue that small carriers are inadequate because the number and types of aircraft they carry and their operational radius are too limited. To secure China's 18,000 km-long coastline, the so-called three million square km of maritime territories and the expanding maritime and overseas interests as well as for learning and adaptation, these analysts believe that building medium-sized carriers is more appropriate as the first step in realizing China's aircraft carrier ambitions.[18]

Large Carrier Options

For "far-seas" operations, a medium-sized carrier may not be adequate. A STOBAR design, for instance, limits aircraft takeoff weight while simultaneously shifting the full burden of takeoff propulsion onto the aircraft, thus increasing the amount of fuel consumed during takeoff. This restricts and reduces the fuel and weapons payload that an aircraft can carry, thereby reducing its range, loitering time, and strike capabilities. STOBAR is also more affected by wind, tide, rolling, and pitching. Furthermore, it needs more flight deck space for takeoff and landing, thus limiting the parking space and affecting the takeoff frequency-based crisis reaction. In comparison, the CATOBAR design, which is mostly associated with large carriers, minimizes aircraft fuel consumption on takeoff, thus enabling better payload, range, loitering time, and strike capabilities. Its runway requirement, while greater than a V/STOL design, is also minimal, thus allowing more flight deck parking and simultaneous launch and recovery operations, resulting in quicker crisis response. CATOBAR designs can also launch aircraft much faster and launch heavier fixed-wing AEW and ASW aircraft.

For far-seas operations, heavier fixed-wing AEW platforms are particularly indispensible. Chinese military analysts, for instance, are particularly impressed by the U.S. E-2C, which can patrol for up to 6 hours, monitor a sea area of 12.50 million square km, track 2,000 targets, and direct engagement against 40 targets simultaneously. They believe that with a detection range of 741 km for surface targets, 556 km for aircraft, and 270 km for missiles and patrolling 180–200 km away from the carrier strike group, the E-2C together with the patrolling combat aircraft has established a 300-km-range outer air-defense perimeter, which is more than the range of most ASCMs. Without a similar air-defense perimeter, China's carrier group would be reduced to a vulnerable "sitting duck," particularly if it engages the highly stealthy U.S. combat aircraft.

Similarly, far-seas operations require far more capable carrier-based combat aircraft than near-seas active defense. Such an aircraft should be capable of high speed, large combat radius, long-range sea/land attack, and stealth. Finally, the tremendous thermal energy that a large carrier consumes, particularly for propulsion and catapult steam generation, suggests that a nuclear power plant is more desirable than a conventional one.

Because China has had no experience in building and operating an aircraft carrier, acquiring a working medium-sized carrier may be a necessary stage to gain such experience in the near future. Nevertheless, China's naval analysts are particularly impressed by the large U.S. carriers, including the most advanced *Gerald Ford* class and related technologies.[19] There are indicators that research has been done on resolving some major technical issues for constructing large carriers.[20] The process of acquiring such carriers, however, is likely to be more costly and protracted.[21]

Conclusion

In spite of some unresolved issues, China is getting closer to realizing its aircraft carrier ambitions in terms of leadership endorsement, financial affordability, appropriate naval strategy, and requisite technologies. China is likely to develop medium-sized aircraft carriers in the medium term for near-seas missions and for gaining operational experience, so that it can develop large-sized carriers for far-seas operations in the long term.

What are the major implications for the rest of the world if China acquires aircraft carriers? In the short to medium term, China's acquisition of aircraft carriers offers more opportunities than challenges. Medium-sized carriers are for limited, air-defense–dominant missions in local conflicts within the first island chain. They can be easily contained because these platforms are more exposed and vulnerable due to their large profile in such a limited operational space. Constructing such carriers also diverts funding from building advanced submarines and missiles, which pose a more serious threat to China's potential opponents. Also, these platforms can perform nontraditional, nonthreatening security missions that are compatible with the goals of other navies in the Asia-Pacific region, thus contributing to regional maritime security cooperation.

In the long term, however, if China can overcome technological obstacles and gain operational experience to the point of being capable to build large, nuclear-powered carriers in substantial numbers, the PLAN may pose more challenges than opportunities. This is because several such carrier-based strike groups can project Chinese power to the more distant and vast far seas, and even to the still more distant and vast "far oceans" (远洋). With much improved sensors, sustainability, stealth, networking, range, strike capabilities, and self-protection, the cost of containing and fighting these highly integrated groups could become much higher.

Notes

1. Liu Huaqing, *Liu Huaqing huiyilu* [*Liu Huaqing's Memoirs*] (Beijing: Liberation Army Press, 2004), 477–81.

2. Hu Jintao, as cited in Tang Fuquan and Wu Yi, "A Study of China's Sea Defense Strategy," *Zhongguo junshi kexue* (*China Military Science*), no. 5 (2007): 93.

3. *Wen Wei Po* (Hong Kong), 7 March 2007; *China Review News*, 17 March 2007, available at http://chinareviewnews.com.

4. "Experts Defend Naval Rights," *China Daily*, 19 November 2008.

5. "China Confirms Intent to Build Aircraft Carrier," *Agence France-Press*, 23 March 2009.

6. Lu Ting, "China's Finance Is Sufficient to fulfill the 'Aircraft Carrier Dream,'" *Junshi wenzai* (*Military Digest*), no. 5 (2008): 12–13.

7. Ibid., 13.

8. See Liu, *Liu Huaqing's Memoirs*, 480; and *Selected Military Works of Liu Huaqing* (Beijing: Liberation Army Press, 2008), 269–70, 473, 477, 522–23.

9. Liu, *Liu Huaqing's Memoirs*, 479.

10. Ibid., 480.

11. See ibid., 437.

12. Ye Xinrong and Zuo Liping, "Strategic Reflections Regarding the March of the Navy from Near Seas to Far Seas," *Junshi xueshu* [*Military Art Journal*], no. 10 (2004).

13. Ibid., 31.

14. Ibid.

15. See Li Jie, "Aircraft Carrier-based Aircraft: Catapult or Skip-Jump Takeoff?" *Xiandai junshi* (*Contemporary Military*), no. 6 (2006); and Liu Jiangping, Jiang Yongjun and Yang Zhen, "Medium-sized Aircraft Carrier Has Prominent Advantages," *Dangdai haijun* [*Modern Navy*] (November 2006).

16. Huitong, *Chinese Military Aviation*, http://cnair.top81.cn/J-10_J-11_FC-1.htm

17. "A Follow-up Batch of 9 More KAs Ordered by the PLAN," *Interfax-AVN*, 26 July 2010.

18. Anonymous naval specialists cited in "Is China's Aircraft Carrier Journey Still Very Long?" *Zhongguo guofang bao* (*China National Defense News*), 7 April 2009; CCTV

Jinri guanzhu (Today's Concerns) Program Interview with Zhang Zhaozhong and Li Jie, 20 April 2009.

19. Li Jie, "Future Aircraft Carriers Are More Powerful," *Jiefangjun bao* [*Liberation Army Daily*], 16 March 2009, 8.

20. Li Meiwu, Cui Ying, and Xue Fei (713 Institute of China Ship Building Heavy Industry Group), "Electromagnetic Catapult System—the Optimal Takeoff Method for Aircraft Carrier-based Aircraft," *Jianchuan kexue jisu* [*Ship Science and Technology*], no. 2 (2008).

21. Upgrading the J-11B to a STOBAR-design carrier aircraft may indicate that catapult design is not yet a near-term option for China's carrier program.

Daniel J. Kostecka

From the Sea

PLA Doctrine and the Employment of
Sea-Based Airpower

DESPITE AN IMPRESSIVE naval modernization over the past two decades, the People's Liberation Army Navy (PLAN) currently possesses no sea-based airpower beyond a small number of shipborne helicopters. As China's navy modernizes and matures, the development of force projection capability through the acquisition of aircraft carriers is essential if PLAN forces are to develop the capacity to engage in the full spectrum of traditional and nontraditional operations to protect Chinese interests regionally and abroad. At this time the most visible manifestation of the PLAN's desire to possess this type of force projection capability is the ongoing refurbishment of an incomplete former Soviet *Kuznetsov*-class aircraft carrier at Dalian Shipyard in northern China. Along with follow-on indigenous platforms, aircraft carriers will enable the PLAN to employ sea-based airpower beyond the range of land-based air cover. However, China's desire to possess and employ aircraft carriers is the source of widespread misunderstanding. Speculation runs from forward-leaning predictions that by the early 2020s China could have as many as five aircraft carriers, including two nuclear-powered hulls, to a recent prediction from an Australian policy research think tank that claims despite evidence to the contrary, the Chinese are not serious about building aircraft carriers because it would be "dumb for them to do so."[1]

Modern force projection capability embodied in aircraft carriers is essential for China to maintain a sustained naval presence away from China's immediate waters (e.g., in the South China Sea and the Indian Ocean). Additionally, authoritative publications from the PLAN as well as the PLA's National Defense University and Academy of Military Sciences provide clues regarding how the PLAN intends to employ aircraft carriers in both traditional and nontraditional security missions. Understanding China's future force projection capabilities and PLA doctrine is necessary to make predictions regarding the types of missions PLAN aircraft carriers could be tasked to execute.

China's Aircraft Carrier Program

Probably the most commonly cited example of China's desire to expand its naval power beyond Chinese coastal waters is Beijing's pursuit of aircraft carriers capable of operating conventional fixed-wing fighter aircraft. The PLAN has been interested in acquiring aircraft carriers for decades, but financial, technological, political, and strategic constraints have prevented serious pursuit of this capability. Outside of China, discussion of this issue is highly polarized. To some, China's pursuit of aircraft carriers represents a direct challenge to the United States and is a clear indication that China seeks to project naval power into the Indian Ocean and Western Pacific. To others, China's aircraft carrier program is nothing more than a quixotic exercise in national vanity and any Chinese carrier will be nothing more than a nationalistic showpiece with very little operational value.

Further confusing the situation is Beijing's obfuscation. Despite years of interest in aircraft carriers and evidence indicating experimentation with aircraft carrier technology, as late as 2004 Chinese officials including then–deputy chief of the General Staff General Xiong Guangkai stated that China did not have plans to build aircraft carriers.[2] One year after General Xiong's statements, the unfinished Soviet *Kuznetsov*-class aircraft carrier *Varyag* (which China purchased from the Ukraine in 1998) went into dry dock at Dalian Shipyard in northern China for an extensive refitting that continues today. Anyone with Internet access can track the extensive modifications to the ship by viewing photographs posted on a number of blogs and websites. Six years after the ship was first put in dry dock, it is clear to even the most skeptical observers that China intends to put the ship into operation soon.

Roughly coincident with work on *Varyag*, Chinese rhetoric on this issue has softened considerably, with Chinese officials and the media discussing China's interest in aircraft carriers with increasing candor.[3] These include positive statements in April 2009 regarding aircraft carriers by Chinese defense minister General Liang Guanglie and PLAN commander Admiral Wu Shengli as well as a March 2010 editorial in the English-language version of the *Global Times* stating that it is time for the world to prepare for China's aircraft carrier.[4] Earlier, in November 2008, Major General Qian Lihua (PLA) asserted China's right to possess an aircraft carrier stating, "The question is not whether you have an aircraft carrier, but what you do with your aircraft carrier. . . . Even if one day we have an aircraft carrier, unlike another country, we will not use it to pursue global deployment or global reach."[5]

In addition to ongoing work on *Varyag*, China is also developing the aircraft that will compose its carrier air units. Press and Internet reports claim China is producing an indigenous carrier fighter (J-15) based on the Russian Su-33 Flanker D, with one website claiming the first prototype made its maiden flight on 31 August 2009 and its first takeoff from a land-based ski-jump on 6 May 2010.[6] While the exact dates of these flights cannot be confirmed, recent Internet pictures show a Chinese Flanker variant prototype that has the same canards and shortened tail stinger as the Russian carrier-capable Su-33 in flight; a video of the prototype flying is also available on the Internet. While externally the J-15 appears to be a near copy of the Su-33, internally it likely possesses the same radar and avionics as China's domestically produced land-based Flanker, the J-11B. It will probably be capable of employing a full suite of China's most advanced air-to-air and air-to-ground munitions, including the PL-12 active radar homing medium-range air-to-air missile.[7] For an airborne early warning (AEW) platform, according to Russian press, China will acquire nine Ka-31 AEW helicopters, while Internet photographs indicate China has fielded a prototype of an AEW variant of the Z-8 medium lift helicopter.[8] It is presently unknown which one will be chosen as the primary AEW helicopter for the PLAN's aircraft carrier force; perhaps the PLAN views an indigenous platform based on the Z-8 as a long-term solution, with Ka-31s acquired from Russia serving as a near-term gap-filler. The Z-8 prototype could also be serving as test aircraft for an AEW variant of a more modern helicopter such as the developmental Z-15.[9] Regardless of whether the PLAN chooses the Z-8, Ka-31, or a more modern airframe for its carrier-based AEW aircraft, it should be noted that a rotary-wing AEW platform is much less capable than fixed-wing AEW platform (e.g., the U.S. E-2C Hawkeye).

PLA Theory and Aircraft Carrier Employment

How the PLAN would employ an aircraft carrier is open to speculation as aircraft carriers are versatile platforms. The development of a theoretical construct for how the PLAN would employ aircraft carriers dates back to at least the early 1970s, when Liu Huaqing (who would command the PLAN from 1982–88) led a feasibility study on the construction of aircraft carriers. As PLAN commander, Liu pushed for the serious study of aircraft carrier design, stating that given China's more than three million kilometers of sea territory, aircraft carriers were necessary to safeguard its sea rights and interests, enhance national prestige, and add to its peacetime deterrent posture.[10] In 1987 Admiral Liu directed the establishment at the Guangzhou Naval Vessel Academy a course of study to train PLAN pilots to command surface combatants with the first class of nine officers graduating with bachelor's degrees in Ship Command in 1991.[11] Apparently, the PLAN chose to follow the American model of selecting its aircraft carrier captains from its naval aviation community. After commanding the PLAN, Liu served as vice chairman of the Central Military Commission from 1989 until retirement in 1997, when he continued to argue the case for aircraft carriers.[12] More recent works include authoritative PLA publications such as 战役学 (*Science of Campaigns*) and 战役理论学习指南 (*Campaign Theory Study Guide*). These handbooks provide clues into Chinese thinking on this issue. Based on these and other publications, it is possible to glean insights into how the PLAN would employ aircraft carriers operationally.

It is in the South China Sea that one should first look as to where and how the PLAN might employ aircraft carriers. While China's military modernization is primarily geared to deterring independence-minded forces on Taiwan, it is worth noting that over the past forty years, the only actual combat that the PLAN has engaged in has been in the South China Sea. These clashes occurred in 1974, when Chinese forces captured the Paracel Islands from South Vietnam; in 1988, when PLAN forces captured Johnson Reef in the Spratly Islands and sank three Vietnamese supply vessels; and in 1995, when PLAN forces occupied Philippine-claimed Mischief Reef.[13] Recent statements from Beijing regarding China's sovereignty over islands in the South China Sea and their surrounding waters in response to statements from Washington expressing concern over competing maritime claims in the area and the potential threat to navigation have brought new and increased international attention to this area of key Chinese national interest. With China claiming a substantial portion of the South China Sea as its territorial waters along with increased competition over fishing waters and potential oil and natural gas deposits between the nations of the region, the PLAN has a need for modern force projection capabilities and the ability to employ sea-based airpower in operations against enemy held islands and reefs. PLA doctrine clearly indicates that providing air cover to landing operations is one of the primary wartime missions the Chinese envision for PLAN aircraft carriers. Both the 2000 and 2006 editions of *Science of Campaigns* discuss the importance of aircraft carriers in providing air cover to amphibious invasions against islands and reefs that are beyond the range of land-based aircraft, a clear reference to the potential use of aircraft carriers in a conflict in the South China Sea. The 2000 edition of *Science of Campaigns* points to the employment of the USS *Independence* in this role during Operation Urgent Fury, the 1983 invasion of Grenada.[14]

Science of Campaigns is also clear in stating that three-dimensional attacks are essential to executing the PLA's Coral Island Assault Campaign (对珊瑚岛礁进攻战役) against islands and reefs in the South China Sea during a regional conflict. This campaign, first detailed in the 2006 edition of *Science of Campaigns*, discusses requirements for effective seaborne command and control, three-dimensional encirclement of enemy-held islands, and complex logistics support in assault operations against coral island reefs far from the mainland.[15] An aircraft carrier with its fighter and rotary-wing aviation capabilities and command-and-control facilities is tailor-made for this sort of campaign. Additionally, given the small size of the islands and reefs in the South China Sea, even a modest force of one or two carriers would be sufficient for enforcing China's territorial claims against regional competitors such as Vietnam, the Philippines, or Malaysia, should tensions during a crisis cause Beijing to attempt to claim territory as it did in 1974, 1988, and 1995.

Reinforcing statements in *Science of Campaigns* is similar analysis in a book published in 1998 titled *Winning High-Tech Local Wars—Must Reading for Military Officers*. This book states that there should be one to two aircraft carrier groups protecting amphibious forces engaged in long-distance landing operations and that carrier groups should be stationed 100–150 nautical miles (nm) from the shore to provide air support to landing forces and escort for helicopter assault forces. That *Winning High-Tech Local Wars* discusses "long-distance" landing operations and provides a requirement for stationing aircraft carriers 100–150 nm from the shore indicates the authors were considering the conduct of non-Taiwan landing operations since the Taiwan Strait is only about 100 nm wide.[16] The important role the Royal Navy's aircraft carriers played in the Falklands War in 1982 (despite their small sized and limited air groups), along with the role of British and French carriers operating air groups less capable than contemporary U.S. carriers in the 1957 Suez Crisis, are indicative of how crucial even a limited amount of carrier-based airpower can be in regional conflicts beyond the range of effective land-based air cover.

Campaign Theory Study Guide discusses the employment of aircraft carriers to protect sea lines of communication (SLOCs) in the Sea Traffic Protection Campaign. As evidenced by the ongoing deployment of PLAN warships to the Gulf of Aden, this campaign is increasing in importance for China. In support of this campaign, *Campaign Theory Study Guide* states that the PLA should develop a mixed fleet with an aircraft carrier as its core and missile destroyers and nuclear-powered attack submarines as the backbone. *Campaign Theory Study Guide* describes a number of missions to be executed in the Sea Traffic Protection Campaign including air defense, antisubmarine warfare, and antishipping, all capabilities an aircraft carrier could bring to the campaign. In this campaign, a carrier group could also be employed as a zone cover force to control a designated sea area to ensure the safe passage of merchant ships. air forces are designated as a key component of this force.[17] Additionally, while the Sea Traffic Protection Campaign is described as defensive, all PLA defensive campaigns have an offensive component. In this case PLA doctrine describes the importance of organizing sea and air forces to attack enemy forces that pose a threat to sea transport operations.[18] While carrier-based aviation would not carry sole responsibility for offensive operations in a Sea Traffic Protection Campaign, carrier aircraft could provide a valuable supplement to surface ships, submarines, and land-based aircraft depending on the type of threat and the proximity of operating areas to Chinese bases.

Beyond specific references to aircraft carriers in PLA doctrine, books such as *Science of Campaigns* and *Campaign Theory Study Guide* are replete with references for the employment of air forces for air defense and offensive strike, including in a Taiwan contingency. In such a scenario, the missions discussed for both the PLA Air Force (PLAAF) and PLAN aviation can likely be met with land-based aircraft. However, in non-Taiwan contingencies fought in the maritime domain farther from the Chinese mainland, it is possible that the requirements of the campaign air forces will need to be met at least in part with sea-based aviation. *Science of Campaigns* discusses the employment of naval air forces for both strike and air superiority missions in the antiship and countersea traffic campaigns. Additionally, the book *Air Raid and Anti-Air Raid in the 21st Century*, published by the PLA Press, discusses the importance of long-range naval fleet bomber and fighter forces in counterstrike operations in the Joint Anti–Air Raid Campaign, specifically in attacking sea-based targets and in providing air defense for warships.[19] While none of these references refer specifically to sea-based aviation, the stated requirement for the employ-ment of naval aviation in these campaigns can be seen as an implicit reference to aircraft carriers due to the limitations of land-based airpower in long-range maritime operations.

Overall, it is likely that China views the primary role of its future carriers to be regional in nature: defending China's maritime claims in East Asia. This is consistent with PLA doctrine that discusses the use of carriers in providing air cover to long-distance landing operations with scenarios in the South China Sea serving as the primary underpinnings for these writings. Discussion of the employment of aircraft carriers in the Sea Traffic Protection Campaign can be applied to a wider set of scenarios. However, PLAN aircraft carriers would most likely be employed to protect China's SLOCs in the South China Sea, where disputed maritime claims and even the potential for Chinese shipping to be threatened in a regional conflict between other rival claimants (in which China is a neutral party). A primarily regional role for PLAN aircraft carri-ers is also consistent with the preponderance of discussion within official and unofficial Chinese media, where there is a relatively consistent theme regard-ing the need for aircraft carriers to protect China's extensive maritime terri-tory in the East and South China seas. As one Shanghai-based military expert states, "Our carrier will definitely not engage with powerful U.S. aircraft car-rier fighting groups. But it is enough to be a symbolic threat among neighbor-ing countries like Vietnam, Indonesia, and the Philippines who have territorial disputes with China."[20] This line of discussion is also consistent with Admiral Liu Huaqing's primary argument for aircraft carriers.[21] Rear Admiral Zhang Zhaozhang elaborated in April 2009:

> The Chinese navy does not need to fight in the Atlantic Ocean, the Indian Ocean or at the center of the Pacific Ocean. The Chinese navy follows a proactively defense strategy. However, in order to defend the security of the national territory, marine territories and the waters within the First Island Chain, this proactive defense strategy does not mean that our navy only stays within the First Island Chain. Only when the Chinese navy goes beyond the First Island Chain, will China be able to expend its strategic depth of security for its marine territories.[22]

It is highly unlikely for several reasons that China will seek to use its car-riers to assert U.S.-style sea dominance in the Indian Ocean or elsewhere in what Chinese sources term far-seas operations.[23] First, it is currently estimated that China will build three to four aircraft carriers. Because it is highly unlikely that all of them will be combat-ready at the same time, PLAN carriers would find themselves outnumbered and outgunned by the Indian Navy, which is looking to field a force of three aircraft carriers. In the Indian Ocean, India's carriers would be supported by land-based airpower, including AEW and intelligence, surveillance, and reconnaissance platforms. They could call on India's fleet of submarines for additional support. China's carriers, by contrast, would be operating beyond the support of land-based airpower with minimal support, at best, from China's small force of nuclear-powered attack submarines.[24] This does not even address the possibility of U.S. involvement, which would only make the situation more untenable for PLAN carrier groups operating in the Indian Ocean during wartime. Additionally, even if all of China's carriers were combat-ready, regional security concerns would likely preclude the PLAN from surging all of its carriers and their attendant escorts into the Indian Ocean because this would leave the PLAN significantly weakened in home waters vis-à-vis powerful regional competitors.

There is also the question of just how much combat capability PLAN carriers will bring to the fight in a traditional force-on-force conflict. It can be safely assumed that at the very least the PLAN's first two carriers (including *Varyag*) and potentially additional carriers will employ a short takeoff but arrested recovery (STOBAR) launch and recovery or ski-jump system. This represents a significant capability limitation because ski-jump–equipped carriers are far less capable than U.S. Navy–style catapult assisted takeoff but arrested recovery–equipped ships, which employ powerful steam catapults to launch heavily laden fighter and strike aircraft. STOBAR-equipped carriers are forced to employ a rotary-wing AEW platform, which is far less capable than a fixed-wing AEW aircraft in terms of range, operating altitude, and the size of the radar it can carry, thereby severely inhibiting the situational awareness of a battle group. For regional operations (e.g., in the South China Sea) this would not be as much of a problem because PLAN carriers could count on support from land-based AEW aircraft such as the KJ-2000 and KJ-200, now in service in the PLAAF. In the Indian Ocean, this would likely not be the case. Recent Internet reporting claims that China has fielded a prototype fixed-wing AEW platform based on the twin engine Y-7 transport that is at least superficially similar to the U.S. E-2C, which indicates the potential for future carrier use.[25] This raises the possibility that China is looking to field CATOBAR carriers in the future and that its carrier force will ultimately include a mix of CATOBAR and STOBAR ships. However, the Y-7 is considerably larger than the E-2C, a challenging aircraft to operate off the U.S. Navy's large supercarriers. This means that if China is going to field a carrier capable AEW platform based on the Y-7, the airframe will likely require significant modifications before it is ready for employment at sea.[26]

Second, although the J-15 may be able to employ a wide variety of air-to-air and air-to-surface munitions, fighters operating off of STOBAR-equipped carriers are limited in the amount of fuel and weapons they can carry and are primarily relegated to providing air defense to a carrier group as opposed to acting as offensive weapon systems. Again, in a regional conflict where land-based strike aircraft can be called upon for offensive strikes this is not so problematic. Outside of East Asia, however, China could not call on land-based strike aircraft without the development of air bases in foreign nations.[27] STOBAR-equipped carriers also cannot generate as many sorties as U.S. flattops because they cannot simultaneously launch multiple aircraft, and aircraft carriers based on the *Kuznetsov* class or a similar design cannot carry air groups as large as those of U.S. aircraft carriers, thereby further limiting overall combat capability.[28] For regional force projection missions, all of these disadvantages are not as crucial because PLAN carriers could be supported by land-based airpower. They would likely be operating against opponents such as Vietnam in a supporting role for antishipping, island seizure, and sea traffic protection operations—as opposed to serving as the centerpiece of an offensive fleet deployed thousands of miles beyond Chinese waters.

Aircraft Carriers and Vertical Assault Operations

In addition to employing aircraft carriers as platforms to provide defensive and offensive airpower for the fleet, China could also employ aircraft carriers as platforms to launch expeditionary assault operations. China's intent to address the gap in the PLAN's modern long-range expeditionary capability was first made public on 22 December 2006 with the launching of the Type 071 LPD-998 *Kunlunshan*.[29] The Type 071 class of LPD offers significant increases in lift capacity not possessed by other amphibious assault ships in the PLAN and, just as important, the capability to employ small-but-flexible air group helicopters in assault and attack roles. However, with only one ship in the class and a second reportedly in the early stages of construction, the PLAN's long-range assault capability is still quite limited, and it is unknown at this time how many LPDs the PLAN intends to build, with estimates ranging from a total build of two ships to eight ships. In addition to the Type 071 LPD, press reports claim China plans to build the Type 081 LHD helicopter assault ship, similar in size and capability to the French *Mistral*-class LHD or approximately half the size of a U.S. Navy *Wasp*-class LHD.[30] A three-part series of articles in the Chinese journal *Modern Navy* calls for balanced force of LPD- and LHD-type amphibious assault ships. given their complementary capabilities, citing the U.S. Navy's force of LPD-, LSD-, and LHA/LHD-class vessels as an appropriate example.[31] Chinese authorities, including former PLAN commander Admiral Liu Huaqing, have also speculated on the utility of dedicated helicopter carriers, either in their own right as versatile platforms or as stepping-stones to dedicated aircraft carriers.[32] Beyond press speculation, very little is known about the Type 081 program in terms of how many (if any) platforms the PLAN will acquire or what capabilities it will possess because China has yet to begin construction on such a platform, much less integrate it into is force structure.

While it is unlikely the PLAN views vertical assault as a primary mission for aircraft carriers, this type of operation does represent a legitimate and proven use of aircraft carriers. The U.S. Navy has employed carriers in this role numerous times in the past. Notable examples include the launching of helicopters from the USS *Nimitz* in 1980 for Operation Eagle Claw, the failed mission to rescue American hostages in Iran; during Operation Restore Democracy in Haiti in 1994 when the USS *Eisenhower* embarked soldiers and helicopters from the 10th Mountain Division; and in 2001 during the early stages of Operation Enduring Freedom, when the USS *Kitty Hawk* served as the afloat forward staging base for U.S. Army and Air Force special operations troops and helicopters.[33] In a two-part series of articles published in the January and February 2009 editions of *Modern Navy* titled "How Big a Role Do Aircraft Carriers Play in Non-Combat Operations," the authors discuss the role of the *Eisenhower* off of Haiti in 1994, pointing out that sometimes it is necessary to reorganize a carrier's air group for nontraditional security missions, to include removing some or all of its fixed-wing aircraft to make room for additional helicopters.[34]

Nontraditional Security Missions for Aircraft Carriers

In addition to traditional missions in regional conflicts in areas such as the South China Sea, it is likely that China views aircraft carriers as important platforms in executing nontraditional security missions such as maritime antiterrorism, prevention of maritime transportation of weapons of massive destruction, maritime peacekeeping, humanitarian assistance and disaster relief (HA/DR), and noncombatant evacuation operations (NEO). While it is unlikely that the PLAN views nontraditional security missions as the primary role for its aircraft carriers, these are the types of missions that navies often find themselves engaged in on a day-to-day basis. Nontraditional security missions also provide a useful means for the PLAN to engage in operations in East Asian waters and beyond in a manner that does not inflame China threat rhetoric and uphold an image of China as responsible nation state that takes international security issues seriously and is willing to engage in operations that promote cooperation and stability.[35] These missions also provide useful on-the-job training for the PLAN; Captain Xu Ping writes in the influential journal *China Military Science* that nonwar military actions are increasingly becoming one of the best forms of training for testing and enhancing the core military functions that are necessary for winning local wars under informatized conditions.[36]

HA/DR is a significant nontraditional security mission. China was embarrassed in the aftermath of the 26 December 2004 Indian Ocean tsunami, when several countries, including the United States, Japan, India, and Thailand, deployed naval forces to provide humanitarian relief while the PLAN stood on the sidelines due to a lack of suitable platforms. As China continues to develop its force of amphibious assault ships and eventually aircraft carriers, it is likely that these platforms will be employed in HA/DR operations in East Asia. These platforms also represent a mission set in which these ships could be employed outside of China's regional seas in areas such as the Indian Ocean. One Chinese article discussing the role of naval forces in disaster relief specifically names Cyclone Nargis (which struck Burma on 27 April 2008). Another article, in discussing the deployment of naval forces to assist in the aftermath of the 2004 tsunami that struck Indonesia primarily, notes that tidal waves from the earthquake also hit India and Sri Lanka.[37] As stated earlier, while it is unlikely that the PLAN views HA/DR operations as the primary mission for its aircraft carriers, the deployment of a task group built around a carrier to provide disaster relief could go a long way in quieting fears regarding China's military modernization. Participation in HA/DR operations in East Asia or the Indian Ocean would also allow the PLAN to establish an increased presence in the region in a nonintrusive and even friendly manner that would likely find approval from the international community. Additionally, similar to the ongoing counterpiracy deployments, such missions would provide PLAN forces with valuable experience operating in close proximity to other major naval forces.[38]

While aircraft carriers lack some of the specialized support and logistics capabilities of amphibious assault ships and hospital ships, China will still likely employ its carriers to execute this mission in East Asia and possibly further abroad. Chinese commentators have noted the important role that USS

Abraham Lincoln played in relief operations after the Indonesian tsunami in 2004. The participation of the USS *Saipan* in disaster relief in the Caribbean and Mexico in 1954 and 1955 has also been discussed.[39] While the launching of even a single refurbished Soviet-era aircraft carrier will cause some to label it as evidence of a growing China threat, the diplomatic counterweight of the positive news the deployment of a PLAN aircraft carrier to a coastal disaster area in East Asia will help offset all but the most extreme trepidations. As U.S. Naval War College professors Andrew Erickson and Andrew Wilson state, "the aftermath of the 2004 tsunami has convinced many Chinese that good carriers make good neighbors and they are a necessity if China's force structure available for deployment to Southeast Asia is to match and complement its diplomatic initiatives."[40]

PLAN forces could be called upon to execute another task beyond HA/DR missions: protecting Chinese citizens living abroad in nations bordering the Indian Ocean. It is estimated that more than 5 million Chinese citizens live and work overseas; including forty-five thousand in Nigeria; twenty-four thousand in Sudan; ten thousand in Congo; and ten thousand in Pakistan. Chinese citizens living in such unstable countries are increasingly at risk. In April 2007 seven Chinese oil workers were killed in Ethiopia with another five abducted and murdered in Sudan in 2008. In 2004 three Chinese engineers were murdered in Gwadar, while in 2007 a busload of Chinese engineers was bombed in southwestern Baluchistan, killing several policemen.[41] Most recently, in July 2010, Chinese oil workers staying at a hotel in Gwadar were subjected to rocket attack.[42] In addition to Chinese workers, about half of the approximately 2,000 Chinese soldiers currently deployed on U.N. peacekeeping missions are in Sudan and the Congo, nations where future instability could lead to a mission requirement to provide sea-based support.[43] It is not difficult to imagine a scenario in any of these nations where the PLAN is called upon to support and even evacuate Chinese citizens in danger. While diplomatic channels have successfully secured the release of Chinese citizens including nine people kidnapped in Nigeria in 2007 and the twenty-five Chinese sailors on the pirated coal carrier *Dexinhai*, growing nationalism and confidence in China's military could put pressure on Beijing to take more muscular action in the future.[44]

In missions such as NEO and support to peacekeepers, PLAN carriers could be employed to provide air support with fixed- and rotary-wing aircraft to Chinese forces. The deployment of a carrier group near a nation where Chinese citizens were threatened could also serve as a powerful instrument of diplomacy. Furthermore, depending on how forces are committed elsewhere and the readiness of other ships, a carrier (while not as versatile as an amphibious assault ship) could even serve as the launch platform for assault forces going ashore to conduct a mission such as an attack against pirate lairs in support of U.N. Security Council resolutions. The use of USS *Kitty Hawk* as an afloat forward-staging base in 2001 for special operations forces is instructive in this regard. China could also deploy carrier groups to the Indian Ocean on a semiregular basis for goodwill cruises and participation in bilateral and multilateral exercises as a means of establishing some level of peacetime presence to support nations such as Pakistan and Sudan and to ensure other regional actors that China's interests and concerns are not ignored.

Conclusion

The PLAN currently possesses little in the way of sea-based airpower. However, between now and 2020, the acquisition of aircraft carriers will afford the PLAN the capacity to conduct force projection operations in East Asia. It will also give the PLAN the ability to engage in smaller force projection missions beyond East Asia—particularly in support of nontraditional security missions such as counterpiracy, support to peacekeeping forces, NEO, HA/DR, and peacetime presence patrols. While the PLAN's overall aircraft carrier capability will likely be closer to that of the British and French navies as opposed to that of the U.S. Navy, its aircraft carrier force will still likely be the most powerful of any East Asian navy. A force of this size will not be sufficient to provide robust force projection capability beyond East Asian waters but should be enough to protect China's regional maritime interests and serve as a significant element of Chinese diplomacy outside of East Asia when called upon to do so. This force will also likely be able to conduct a variety of nontraditional security missions both regionally and beyond.

While it cannot be predicted with certainty how China will seek to employ its aircraft carriers, authoritative publications such as *Science of Campaigns, Campaign Theory Study Guide, Modern Navy,* and *China Military Science* do provide significant insight into the operational role of these platforms in both wartime and peacetime. Most importantly, these publications clearly show that the PLA is aware of the flexibility of aircraft carriers, likely views them as more than simply one-mission platforms, and will instead seek to employ them in a variety of traditional and nontraditional security missions to accomplish "diversified military tasks."[45]

Notes

1. Richard Fisher Jr., "Update—China's Aircraft Carriers," *International Assessment and Strategy Center*, 10 March 2009, http://www.strategycenter.net/research/pubID.193/pub_detail.asp.

2. Quote in Zhu Lin, "The PLA Has No Plans to Build Aircraft Carriers for the Time Being," *Wen Wei Po*, 11 March 2004.

3. Feng Changhong, "Developing an Aircraft Carrier to Uphold China's Ocean Rights and Interests," *Tzu Ching*, 1 April 2006.

4. "Time to Prepare for China's Aircraft Carrier," *Global Times*, 11 March 2010, http://opinion.globaltimes.cn/editorial/2010-03/511703.html.

5. Quoted in Mure Dickie and Martin Dickson, "China Hints at an Aircraft Carrier," *Financial Times*, 16 November 2008, http://us.ft.com/ftgateway/superpage.ft?news_id=fto111620081845232520&page=2.

6. "J-15 Flying Shark," *Chinese Military Aviation*, 7 July 2010, http://cnair.top81.cn/J-10_J-11_FC-1.htm.

7. Ibid.

8. Mikahil Kukushkin, "Kamov Is Counting on the Small One," *Vremya Novostey*, 8 February 2010.

9. "Zhi-15 (EC 175) Medium Helicopter," *China's Defence Today*, 15 March 2008, http://www.sinodefence.com/airforce/helicopter/z15.asp.

10. Liu Huaqing, *Memoirs of Liu Huaqing* (Beijing: PLA Press, August 2004).

11. Wang Yucheng, "The Making of a Chinese Captain," 当代海军 [*Modern Navy*] (March 2005).

12. Ian Storey and You Ji, "China's Aircraft Ambitions," *Naval War College Review* 57, no. 1 (Winter 2004).

13. Michael Studeman, "Calculating China's Advances in the South China Sea," *Naval War College Review* 51, no. 2 (Spring 1998).

14. Wang Houqing, 战役学 [*Science of Campaigns—2000 Edition*] (Beijing: National Defense University Press, May 2000); and Zhang Yulang, 战役学 [*Science of Campaigns—2006 Edition*] (Beijing: National Defense University Press, May 2006).

15. Zhang, *Science of Campaigns*.

16. Wang Qiming and Cheng Feng, *Winning High-Tech Local Wars—Must Reading for Military Officers* (Beijing: Military Translation Press, August 1998).

17. Zhang Xingye, 战役理论学习指南 [*Campaign Theory Study Guide*] (Beijing: National Defense University Press, May 2002).

18. Zhang, *Campaign Theory Study Guide*; Wang, *Science of Campaigns*; and Zhang, *Science of Campaigns*.

19. Ibid.; and Cui Changqi, ed., *Air Raid and Anti-Air Raid in the 21st Century* (Beijing: PLA Press, May 2002).

20. Minnie Chan, "Challenge Will Be Training Pilots, Ex-General Says," *South China Morning Post*, 1 April 2010.

21. Liu, *Memoirs of Liu Huaqing*, ch. 17.

22. Quoted in Cai Wei, "Dream of the Military for Aircraft Carriers," *Sanlian Shenghuo Zhoukan* [*Sanlian Life Weekly*], 27 April 2009.

23. Nan Li and Christopher Weuve, "China's Aircraft Carrier Ambitions—an Update," *Naval War College Review* 63, no. 1 (Winter 2010).

24. Arun Prakash, "India's Quest for an Indigenous Aircraft Carrier," *Rusi Defense Systems* (Summer 2006).

25. "Y-7 AWACS," *Chinese Military Aviation,* 18 September 2010, http://www.cnair.top81 .cn/

26. I would like to thank Lieutenant Commander Cory Gassaway, USN, for his valuable insights into operating the E-2C off aircraft carriers.

27. Li and Weuve, "China's Aircraft Carrier Ambitions."

28. *Jane's Fighting Ships 2009–2010* (Cambridge: Cambridge University Press, 2009).

29. "Type 071 Landing Platform Dock," *Chinese Defence Today*, 5 June 2008, http://www .sinodefence.com/navy/amphibious/type071.asp.

30. "Shanghai, LCAC, and a New LPD under Construction?" *China Defense Blog*, 11 May 2010, http://china-defense.blogspot.com/2010/05/shanghai-lcal-and-new-lpd-under .html.

31. Li Jie, "On What Should the Development of Amphibious Assault Ship Focus—Part 3," 当代海军 [*Modern Navy*] (November 2008).

32. Liu, *Memoirs of Liu Huaqing*.

33. "Afloat Forward Staging Base (AFSB)," GlobalSecurity.org, 18 June 2006, http://www .globalsecurity.org/military/systems/ship/afsb.htm.

34. Li Jie, "How Big a Role Do Aircraft Carriers Play in Non-Combat Operations—Part 1," 当代海军 [*Modern Navy*] (January 2009); Li, "How Big a Role, Part 2," (February 2009).

35. Bai Yanlin, "The Use of the Navy in Disaster Rescue and Relief Operations," 当代海军 [*Modern Navy*] (August 2008).

36. Xu Ping, "Tentative Analysis of Hu Jintao's Strategic Thinking on Accomplishing Diversified Military Tasks," 中国军事科学 [*China Military Science*] (March 2010).

37. Bai, "Use of the Navy."

38. Xu, "Tentative Analysis."

39. Li, "How Big a Role—Part 2."

40. Andrew S. Erickson and Andrew R. Wilson, "China's Aircraft Carrier Dilemma," *Naval War College Review* 59, no. 4 (Autumn 2006).

41. "Why Are Chinese Engineers Being Targeted," *Daily Times*, 20 July 2007, http://www .dailytimes.com.pk/default.asp?page=2007%5C07%5C20%5Cstory_20-7-2007_pg3_1.

42. B. Raman, "Chinese Engineers Escape Rocket Attack," *Sri Lanka Guardian*, 10 July 2010, http://www.srilankaguardian.org/2010/07/chinese-engineers-in-gwadar-escape .html.

43. "Chinese Blue Helmets Renowned as Devoted Peace Keepers," *Liberation Army Daily*, 26 April 2010, http://eng.chinamil.com.cn/news-channels/pla-daily-commen tary/2010-04/26/content_4194309.htm.

44. "Chinese Oil Workers Set Free in Nigeria," *China Daily*, 5 February 2007, http://www .chinadaily.com.cn/cndy/2007-02/05/content_800742.htm.

45. Xu, "Tentative Analysis."

PART IV

Maritime Strike
Air-Launched Cruise Missiles

Roger Cliff

Chinese Military Aviation Capabilities, Doctrine, and Missions

CHINA'S AIR FORCES have made substantial strides over the past decade and are well on their way to becoming fully modern. Coupled with the geographic advantage China would enjoy in the most likely military conflict between China and the United States—a war over Taiwan—the capabilities of China's air forces have the potential to present a significant obstacle to U.S. success in such a conflict. Understanding these capabilities, therefore, is critical to understanding the nature of the military challenge that China is presenting to the United States.

As is true in many country's militaries, China's air forces are distributed across more than one service. The U.S. Army, for example, likes to say that it operates more aircraft than the U.S. Air Force, a reference to its helicopter force. Likewise, the People's Liberation Army's (PLA) ground forces also operate a substantial helicopter force, and the PLA Navy (PLAN) operates both fixed-wing aircraft and helicopters. This chapter will not cover the PLA Army or PLAN helicopter forces but will cover the PLAN's fixed-wing aviation forces.

China's air force, the People's Liberation Army Air Force (PLAAF), operates not only fixed-wing aircraft and helicopters, its combat forces also include long-range surface-to-air missiles (SAMs), large-caliber antiaircraft artillery, and paratroops. In addressing China's "air forces," therefore, this chapter will include not only the fixed-wing aviation forces of the PLAN and PLAAF but also the PLAAF's land-based air-defense forces and airborne forces.

It should be noted that, although the term is commonly used, there is not actually an organization in China called the People's Liberation Army Navy Air Force. The PLAN has aviation forces, but they are not collected into a single, unified organization. Rather, each of China's three fleets (the North Sea Fleet, East Sea Fleet, and South Sea Fleet) has its own aviation organization subordinate to it. (Interestingly, this is similar to the U.S. Navy, which also does not collect its aviation forces into a single organization separate from the rest of the Navy but rather divides its aviation forces into two entities: Naval Air Forces U.S. Pacific Fleet and Naval Air Forces U.S. Atlantic Fleet.)

A Decade of Progress

China's air forces have improved significantly over the past ten years. In 2000, of the estimated thirty-two hundred fighter aircraft operated by the PLAAF and PLAN, for example, all but approximately seventy-five "fourth-generation" Su-27s ("Flankers") imported from Russia and 20 domestically designed and built third-generation JH-7s were based on the 1950s-era second-generation MiG-19 and MiG-21. China's fighters, moreover, were dependent on ground-based radar or their largely outdated onboard sensors to locate and identify enemy aircraft because China had only one operational airborne early warning aircraft. In addition, except for the Flankers, they were limited to within-visual-range engagements because China's domestically produced aircraft were not equipped with beyond-visual-range (BVR) missiles. China's electronic warfare capabilities were minimal as well. By comparison, the U.S. air forces of 2000 were equipped entirely with fourth-generation fighters, all of which carried BVR missiles and operated numerous airborne early warning and control (AEW&C) and electronic warfare aircraft. In an air-to-air engagement between Chinese and U.S. air forces in that year, the United States would likely have enjoyed an advantage at least as great as it did in the 1991 Gulf War against Iraq, when thirty-three Iraqi aircraft were shot down by U.S. air forces while only one U.S. aircraft was lost in air-to-air combat.

Except for a few bombers equipped with antiship cruise missiles or torpedoes, China's strike aircraft in 2000 carried only unguided gravity bombs and rockets, and certainly none of them had the low-observable capabilities of the U.S. F-117 and B-2. Thus, the ability of China's air force to conduct effective attacks against surface targets or even survive the attempt against a modern adversary was highly questionable.

The training of China's air forces was considered poor. Pilots of all aircraft types were believed to average fewer than one hundred hours of flight training a year, and exercises appeared highly scripted, with predetermined outcomes. Virtually all officers in China's air forces were either graduates of PLA-run military academies, the quality of whose education was questionable, or had been directly promoted from the enlisted ranks without receiving a higher education. Finally, the PLAAF and PLAN were in the process of absorbing an entirely new set of doctrinal guidelines that had just been issued in 1999, in many cases replacing doctrine that had not changed for twenty years.

The Situation Today

Today the picture is very different. China has reduced the overall size of its air forces, with the PLAAF alone cutting approximately one hundred thousand personnel—roughly a quarter of the force—and halving the size of its fighter force. Its top-heavy organizational structure has also been streamlined, with the PLAAF eliminating one entire organizational level—the corps-level—and all of its associated general officer billets. The remaining forces are considerably more capable than those in 2000. The number of second-generation fighters in China's inventory has been reduced by two-thirds, and the number of fourth-generation fighters has more than quadrupled.

There have been improvements in other dimensions as well. Many of China's fighters are now capable of carrying BVR missiles, China operates at least a dozen AEW&C aircraft, many strike aircraft are now equipped with precision-guided munitions (PGMs), and China's electronic warfare capabilities have improved substantially as well. Many Chinese fighter pilots are now believed to receive roughly the same number of training hours as their U.S. counterparts, and the quality and realism of training has also improved. Roughly half of all new officers in China's air forces are now graduates of China's increasingly rigorous civilian universities. Finally, China has had an additional ten years to absorb the modern doctrinal guidelines issued in 1999.

Ongoing Limitations

Nonetheless, China's air forces are still only partly modernized. Two-thirds of the roughly sixteen hundred fighter aircraft operated by China's air forces, for example, are still based on the MiG-19 and MiG-21, and less than a quarter of China's fighter force consists of fourth-generation aircraft. Many of China's aircraft are still not capable of carrying BVR missiles or PGMs, and none are stealthy. In addition, China lacks long-range heavy bombers and has only limited aerial refueling and strategic airlift capabilities. Finally, while the quality of training in China's air forces has improved markedly in the last ten years, it still falls well short of U.S. standards.

Old Missions, New Emphases

The fundamental missions of the PLAAF and PLAN aviation have not changed in recent years. The primary missions of the PLAAF are to seize and hold air superiority, thereby defending China against enemy airstrikes, and to conduct airstrikes on enemy forces. The PLAAF also has missions of conducting airborne operations (the PLAAF controls not only the transport aircraft for China's airborne forces but also the paratroops that they carry), performing surveillance and reconnaissance and providing early warning of enemy attack, conducting airlift operations, providing disaster relief, and performing search-and-rescue operations. The PLAAF does not appear to have a nuclear strike mission. The missions of fixed-wing PLAN aviation are to conduct naval strike operations and defend naval bases against enemy air attack.

Offense Prioritized Equally with Defense

Although the fundamental missions of the PLAAF and PLAN aviation have not changed in recent years, emphases among and within some of the missions have. In 2000, for example, the PLAAF was largely a defensive force. Its bomber force was small, most of its fighter aircraft were capable only of air-to-air combat, and it had no precision ground-attack aircraft. Its primary mission, therefore, was to defend China against enemy air attack. Conducting attacks on enemy ground forces and targets was a secondary priority. Today, the PLAAF's bomber force is expanded even as the size of the fighter force has shrunk, a greater proportion of fighter aircraft are capable of ground-attack missions, and the PLAAF possesses a wide range of PGMs. This has both improved the PLAAF's capability to achieve air superiority by enabling it to more effectively attack enemy air forces on the ground and has significantly increased its ability to support ground and naval operations through air-to-surface operations. Thus, the missions of defending China from enemy airstrikes and conducting airstrikes on enemy forces are now accorded equal importance. The doctrinal shift to equal emphasis on offensive and defensive operations probably actually occurred in 1999, with the issuance of the PLAAF's new doctrinal guidelines but was not officially acknowledged in the PLA's overall strategy until 2004, when the PLAAF's component of the PLA's National Military Strategic Guidelines was identified as including "preparing for both the offense and the defense" (攻防兼备). This, in turn, was alluded to in China's 2004 national defense white paper, the English version of which stated that "the Air Force has gradually shifted from one of territorial air defense to one of both offensive and defensive operations." The capabilities for conducting offensive operations are still developing, however, because the PLAAF's inventory of PGMs is probably still small, it does not have stealth aircraft, and it does not appear to practice true close air support operations.

SAM Force Strengthened

The doctrinal shift to the offense, moreover, does not mean that the PLAAF's air-defense capabilities have been neglected. Indeed, an argument can be made that the greatest improvements in PLAAF capabilities over the last ten years have occurred in its SAM forces. In 2000, other than four battalions of Russian-made S-300 (SA-10B) systems, the bulk of the PLAAF's SAMs consisted of modernized versions of the 1950s-era SA-2 supplemented by a domestically produced version of the short-range French Crotale system. Today the total number of missiles in the PLAAF's SAM inventory has more than doubled, and the majority of them are now modern ("double-digit") systems. The four battalions of S-300s (100 km range) have been supplemented by at least sixteen battalions of the more-capable S-300PMU1 (150 km range) and comparable domestically produced HQ-9 along with at least eight battalions of the even more capable S-300PMU2 (200 km range). This improvement in SAM capability, moreover, has been accompanied by improvements in the coverage and integration of China's national air-defense network. The Xinhua News Agency announced in 2007 that an "air intelligence radar network" covering the entire country had been completed.

Contribution to Disaster Relief

Another shift in PLAAF mission emphasis in recent years has been toward disaster relief. Disaster relief has always been a mission of China's armed forces. China's first national defense white paper, issued in 1998, listed "participating in emergency rescues and disaster relief work" as one of the principal tasks of the PLA and touted the PLA's contributions in this area over the previous two decades. Since Chinese president and Central Military Commission chairman Hu Jintao's pronouncement of "new historical missions" for the PLA in 2004, however, and particularly since the Sichuan earthquake of 2008, disaster relief has been accorded a new priority. The intention seems to be that the PLA will not simply perform this task on an ad hoc basis when directed to do so by the national leadership but will actually organize, train, and equip for performing it.

That said, the extent to which the PLA actually is organizing, training, and equipping for this mission is not clear. The PLAAF's primary contribution to disaster relief, for example, would probably come in the form of using its tactical airlift capabilities to deliver personnel and supplies to small airports near the site of the disaster and to evacuate the sick and injured. The PLAAF could also provide visual and imagery reconnaissance to survey damage, locate survivors, and so on. The PLAAF's inventory of tactical airlift aircraft (e.g., the Y-7 and Y-8 turboprops), medium-lift helicopters, and reconnaissance aircraft, however, appears to have actually shrunk since 2004. It is possible that the eliminated airframes were old and nonfunctional anyway, and to some degree the roles of manned reconnaissance aircraft may be in the process of being replaced by unmanned aerial vehicles (UAVs), so the reduction in inventory may not represent a reduction in capability. Nonetheless, there is no clear evidence to support a conclusion that the PLAAF is acquiring aircraft for the specific purpose of supporting disaster relief operations. Likewise, it remains unclear whether the PLAAF has been conducting significant training devoted to disaster relief operations, although this is possible, or if any dedicated disaster relief units have been created, though this seems doubtful.

Other Missions—Incremental Improvements

The relative importance of the other PLAAF missions—conducting airborne operations, performing (wartime) surveillance and reconnaissance and providing early warning of enemy attack, conducting airlift operations, and performing search-and-rescue operations—does not appear to have changed significantly, although in some cases capabilities have. As noted earlier, the size of the PLAAF's tactical airlift inventory has actually shrunk since 2004 (this is even more true when it is compared to 2000), and the size of its strategic airlift inventory (e.g., Il-76s) has increased only slightly from quite modest levels. Thus, the priority accorded to airlift does not appear to have increased and may actually have decreased somewhat.

Also as noted earlier, the size of the PLAAF's inventory of manned reconnaissance aircraft has also shrunk since 2000. This does not necessarily mean that the importance of the mission of performing (wartime) surveillance and reconnaissance and providing early warning of enemy attack has been reduced, however. The sensors on the PLAAF's remaining reconnaissance aircraft may have been upgraded, many of their roles are probably being played by UAVs, and China's reconnaissance satellites can now perform many of the functions formerly performed by aircraft. Moreover, China's ability to conduct surveillance (of airspace) and provide early warning of airborne attack has actually increased with the acquisition of airborne early-warning aircraft and completion of an air-intelligence radar network covering the entire country. Thus, although there is no evidence that the PLAAF's mission of performing surveillance and reconnaissance and providing early warning of enemy attack has increased in priority relative to its other missions, its capability to conduct this mission has on the whole improved, just as its capability to perform its other missions has improved.

Similarly, there is no evidence that the PLAAF's mission of conducting search-and-rescue operations has increased in priority, but its capability to do so appears to have improved somewhat over the past decade with the acquisition of dedicated search-and-rescue helicopters (based on the Aerospatiale Super Frelon design) and, presumably, associated training and procedures.

The importance accorded to the PLAAF's one other current mission—conducting airborne operations—is unclear. There is some evidence that suggests that its priority has increased somewhat in recent years. The overall size of the airborne forces has remained the same and, as noted, the PLAAF's airlift capacity has not expanded significantly over the past decade. China's defense industries, however, have been developing a range of air-transportable and air-droppable vehicles, suggesting a desire to increase the ground combat capabilities of the airborne forces. The potential utility of increased airborne capabilities in an invasion of Taiwan is clear because the greatest challenge in such an operation would be transporting ground forces across the water that separates Taiwan from mainland China. However, there does not appear to be a large-scale push to develop an improved airborne capability. This may reflect skepticism about the military viability and effectiveness of airborne operations against Taiwan or the low priority accorded to airborne operations in a PLAAF for which aviation is the dominant branch.

An Emerging Space Mission

A final PLAAF mission area that must be addressed is space operations. The PLAAF's component of the PLA's 2004 National Military Strategic Guidelines reportedly included not just "preparing for both the offense and the defense" but also "integrated air and space" (空天一体) operations. Unlike references to preparing for both the offense and the defense, however, this element has never been alluded to in any of China's official national defense white papers. In fact, a struggle is currently under way within the PLA over the control of space operations. Today, China's space assets are controlled by the headquarters-level General Staff and General Armaments Departments. Both the PLAAF and the Second Artillery Force, however, are contending that they should be in control of space operations. The PLAAF's argument is based in part on the assertion that air and space are a single integrated medium. The ultimate outcome of this bureaucratic contest is difficult to predict, but if the PLAAF is successful, conducting space operations will become one of its missions.

Strategic Projection

China's 2008 national defense white paper suggests that the PLAAF may now have an additional mission: strategic projection. The official English-language version of the white paper states that the PLAAF has "certain capabilities to execute long-range precision strikes and strategic projection operations" and that it is working to increase its capabilities for carrying out a number of operations, including strategic projection. At first glance, this language sounds close to "strategic power projection," something the Chinese government would be unlikely to admit to in a public document. Examining the Chinese version of the white paper clarifies Beijing's intended meaning: a better translation of the term would be "strategic force delivery" (the Chinese word translated as "projection" is 投送), which, for an air force, means strategic airlift. So the "strategic projection" capabilities that the PLAAF claims to be working to increase are its strategic airlift capabilities. And, as noted earlier, the PLAAF's progress in this area over the past decade has been modest.

PLAN Aviation

As with the PLAAF, the missions of PLAN aviation have not fundamentally changed in recent years, but its capabilities to conduct them have improved. The primary mission for PLA aviation is naval strike operations. In 2000, however, the PLAN's most effective strike aviation assets were twenty JH-7 fighter-bombers armed with the Exocet-like C-801K antiship cruise missile (ASCM), and a comparable number of subsonic H-6D bombers (based on the Soviet 1950s-era Tu-16) armed with an improved version of a 1950s-era ASCM. Today the number of JH-7s has quadrupled and they are now capable of carrying the improved, 180-km-range C-803K ASCM, and the number of H-6Ds has nearly doubled. Most significantly, the PLA has acquired a squadron (i.e., twenty-four) of Su-30 MK2s armed with the supersonic Kh-31A (AS-17A) air-to-surface missile.

At one time PLAN aviation played an important role in defending China's airspace from attack, with the PLAN responsible for the air defense of certain sectors of China's coastal boundary. As the capabilities and ranges of the PLAAF's fighters and SAMs have improved, however, it appears that the air-defense role of PLAN aviation has shrunk to simply defending naval bases from air attack.

Hardware and Software

Virtually all of the improvements discussed earlier are based on newer and more capable platforms and hardware. New platforms and hardware alone, of course, do not necessarily translate into improved capabilities. The platforms and hardware also require organization, doctrine, and training to effectively employ them, as well as the logistics to maintain and supply them. As noted earlier, however, China has been making progress in many of these dimensions. Conversely, without newer and more capable platforms and hardware, improvements in combat effectiveness would be difficult to achieve because there is a limit to how much performance can be squeezed out of 1950s-era designs.

During the 1990s and the first half of the 2000s, most of the PLAAF and PLAN aviation's new platforms and hardware were imported, largely from Russia but with some technologies and equipment acquired from Israel and other countries. In recent years, however, this equipment has increasingly been domestically produced. In the area of fighter aircraft, for example, China now produces a single-engine fighter, the J-10, which is comparable in performance to the U.S. F-16; and a heavy fighter, the J-11B, an improved version of the Russian Su-27, which is regarded as superior in performance to the U.S. F-15. China now also produces AEW&C aircraft comparable to the U.S. E-2 Hawkeye and E-3 AWACS. And China is now in the process of developing a heavy-airlift aircraft, which may explain why the PLAAF has not moved more aggressively to expand its airlift capacity by purchasing imported airlifters. Finally, China is developing long-endurance UAVs that are comparable in range and endurance to the U.S. Predator and Global Hawk.

In the area of munitions, China now produces a BVR-active, radar-guided, air-to-air missile, the PL-12, that is comparable to the U.S. advanced, medium-range, air-to-air missile or the Russian R-77 (AA-12), and a variety of laser-,

TV-, and satellite-guided PGMs. In the area of SAMs, as noted earlier, China now produces the HQ-9, a system that is believed to be comparable in performance to the Russian S-300PMU1 (SA-20).

Possible Near-Term Developments

Future developments we can expect to see in China's aviation capabilities certainly include a fifth-generation fighter. Rumors of such a program and even photos of an alleged full-scale mockup have long circulated; last year, He Weirong, a PLAAF deputy commander, stated that such an aircraft was scheduled to enter service in the 2017–19 time frame. The specific capabilities of this "J-20/project 718" aircraft, however, are unclear, despite widely available photos and Internet speculations surrounding the initial flight test of a prototype on 11 January 2011. The full-scale mockup photo and subsequent Internet photos suggest that the J-20 has a reduced radar cross section, although perhaps not in the class of the U.S. F-22 and F-35. At the rate at which China's electronics capabilities are progressing, an active electronically scanned array radar and advanced data links for this aircraft seem plausible. Whether it will have the F-22's thrust-vectoring and supercruise capabilities, however, is less certain.

Other than a fifth-generation fighter, what other aviation capabilities China will develop is much less clear. The commercial jetliner and jet airlifter that China is developing could also form the bases for aerial refueling aircraft. The technologies that China will acquire in the course of these two programs would also support the development of a long-range, heavy bomber, but no reliable information has yet appeared to suggest the existence of either a tanker or a heavy bomber program. Models of unmanned combat aerial vehicles have been displayed at air shows, but these may merely represent conceptual projects produced purely for the purpose of showing off an enterprise's design capabilities at air shows as opposed to actual development programs. Determining what future air force capabilities China is likely to acquire will require further research and analysis.

Missiles versus Aircraft

A related question is whether China's Second Artillery Force, especially its conventional short-range and medium-range ballistic missile forces, obviates the need for traditional air platforms. The short answer is "no"—traditional air platforms are still needed. However, China's conventional short-range and medium-range ballistic missile forces do provide unique capabilities that enhance the effectiveness of traditional air platforms rather than obviating the

need for them. The most important of these capabilities are speed and penetration. Ballistic missiles reach their targets within minutes of being launched.
This minimizes the amount of warning time that the subjects of the attack have
to respond. If the target is an airbase, for example, only a few of the aircraft
on the ground at that base will be able to take off before the missiles arrive.
Any aircraft that are in the air at the time the missiles arrive will not be able
to actually help defend the airbase against the attack, and those that remain
on the ground may be destroyed, if unprotected, or trapped there, if the effect
of the attack is to damage the base's runways. Ballistic missiles, moreover, are
very difficult to intercept. The actual combat effectiveness of current ballistic
missile defense systems is questionable, and even the best missile defense systems could be overwhelmed by the sheer numbers of missiles that China could
launch simultaneously against them. In the U.S. military, reduced warning
time and assured penetration capability are provided by stealth aircraft. For a
country that lacks stealth aircraft, however, conventional ballistic missiles are
a logical way of achieving the same effects, at least against targets on its immediate periphery.

The single-use nature of ballistic missiles means that they have important disadvantages relative to aircraft. China's entire inventory of conventional
ballistic missiles, for example, could deliver about a thousand tons of high
explosives on their targets. The U.S. Air Force's aircraft, by comparison, could
deliver several times that amount of high explosives every day for an indef-
inite period. Moreover, although the accuracy of China's conventional ballistic missiles is reportedly very good, they are still not as accurate as PGMs.
The speed and penetration capabilities of conventional ballistic missiles, however, can significantly enhance the effectiveness of traditional air platforms by
enabling the neutralization of enemy air forces. For example, conventional ballistic missiles can be used to attack enemy air bases, destroying aircraft on the
ground before they can be scrambled into the air and damaging the runways
so that any aircraft not in the air at the time of the missile attack are trapped
on the ground where they are vulnerable to more precise follow-on attacks by
either the Second Artillery's ground-launched cruise missiles or aircraft with
PGMs. Similarly, if China succeeds in developing a ballistic missile capable
of hitting a moving ship at sea, as they are reportedly attempting to do, then
an adversary's carrier-borne air forces could also be neutralized. Thus, China's
Second Artillery forces should be seen not as a substitute for, but rather as an
effectiveness-multiplier for, China's air forces.

Conclusion

China's air forces are no longer those of a third world country. Improvements in China's air force capabilities, coupled with improvements in the conventional missile capabilities of its Second Artillery Force, mean that prevailing in an air war with China will be increasingly challenging. Continuing to carefully follow the development of China's air forces is vital to the security interests of the United States.

Note

The opinions and conclusions expressed in this chapter are the author's alone and should not be interpreted as representing those of RAND or any of the sponsors of its research. The RAND Corporation is a nonprofit research organization that provides objective analysis and effective solutions to address the challenges facing the public and private sectors around the world. RAND's publications do not necessarily reflect the opinions of its research clients and sponsors.

This chapter is based on Roger Cliff, "The Development of China's Air Force Capabilities," Hearing on "China's Emergent Military Aerospace and Commercial Aviation Capabilities," U.S.-China Economic and Security Review Commission, Washington, DC, 20 May 2010. This testimony is available for free download at http://www.rand.org/pubs/tes timonies/CT346/. This product is part of the RAND Corporation testimony series. RAND testimonies record testimony presented by RAND associates to federal, state, or local legislative committees; government-appointed commissions and panels; and private review and oversight bodies. For related publications and research by the author, please see Roger Cliff, John Fei, Jeff Hagen, Elizabeth Hague, Eric Heginbotham, and John Stillion, *Shaking the Heavens and Splitting the Earth: Chinese Air Force Employment Concepts in the 21st Century*, MG-915-AF (Santa Monica, CA: RAND Corporation, 2011); Roger Cliff, "The PLA in the Asia-Pacific Region: Implications for the Evolving Regional Security Order," in *Assessing the Threat: The Chinese Military and Taiwan's Security*, eds. Michael D. Swaine, Andrew N. D. Yang, and Evan S. Medeiros (Washington, DC: Carnegie Endowment for International Peace, 2007); Roger Cliff, Mark Burles, Michael S. Chase, Derek Eaton, and Kevin L. Pollpeter, *Entering the Dragon's Lair: Chinese Antiaccess Strategies and Their Implications for the United States* (Arlington, VA: RAND Corporation, 2007); Roger Cliff, Evan Medeiros, and Keith Crane, "Keeping the Pacific: An American Response to China's Growing Military Might," *RAND Review* 31, no. 1 (2007); and Roger Cliff, *The Military Potential of China's Commercial Technology*, RAND Corporation, 2001. Additional publications may be found at http://www.rand.org/pubs/authors/c/cliff_roger.html.

Kevin Lanzit and David Chen

Integrating Aerial Platforms for Maritime Strike

*The Navy has been striving to improve in an all-round way its capabil-
ities of integrated offshore operations, strategic deterrence and strategic
counterattacks, and to gradually develop its capabilities of conducting
cooperation in distant waters. . . .*

*[The Air Force] now has relatively strong capabilities to conduct
air defensive and offensive operations, and certain capabilities to execute
long-range precision strikes and strategic projection operations.*[1]

—China's National Defense in 2008

WITH GROWING INVENTORIES of fourth-generation multirole fighters and
an expanding arsenal of stand-off precision-guided munitions needed to confront a modern naval adversary, the aviation forces of the People's Liberation
Army Air Force (PLAAF) and People's Liberation Army Navy (PLAN)
together stand poised to play a major role in any potential conflict off China's
coast. The emerging capacity to conduct maritime strike embodies the realization of a long-held PLA goal to develop forces capable of executing operations
in support of the country's active defense (*jiji fangyu*) strategy, the essence of
which is to "take the initiative and to annihilate the enemy."[2] Ongoing and pro-
jected force enhancements will add further to the combat effectiveness and

lethality of China's air forces. New command, control, communications, computers, intelligence, surveillance, and reconnaissance (C4ISR) systems that already have entered service, or will soon, will greatly improve China's capability to find and fix maritime targets. Advancements are likewise anticipated in electronic countermeasures and stealth, and air refueling, which will provide combat air forces with added range, increased weapons loads, and enhanced endurance. Collectively, these and other developments are contributing to the maturation of China's air power.

Yet to fully harness the potential of its new arsenal—including aircraft, sensors, munitions, and C4ISR systems—China's air and naval air forces must resolve long-term deficiencies in doctrine, training, and command and control that lie at the heart of the PLA's current drive toward building a modern force capable of winning a local war under informatized conditions. Chinese military leaders recognize the need for reforms and have instituted PLA-wide programs for developing new operational capabilities through training for integrated joint operations. This chapter examines the current doctrine of the PLA for employing air power in maritime strike and the current training methods of the PLAAF and PLAN aviation forces to carry out maritime strike missions.

Strategic Underpinnings of Maritime Strike

China's pursuit of maritime strike capabilities stems from decisions made in 1979 to transition toward a strategy that emphasized confronting enemies at or beyond the periphery of the country rather than in the interior.[3] During the past thirty years, this adjustment has led to a series of modifications in the PLA's doctrine, training, equipment, and organization as the military has attempted to adapt to meet the requirements of the new "active defense" strategy. In 1985 the Central Military Commission (CMC) approved a naval component of the modified active defense strategy known as "Offshore Defense," thus launching the PLAN's transition from a coastal defense force to a seagoing navy.[4] A decade later the PLAAF began its own transition "from territorial air defense to both offensive and defensive operations."[5] The PLAAF component of the modified active defense emerged in 1997 in the form of a four-character slogan "simultaneous offense and defense" (*gongfang jianbei*).

PLA strategists currently envision a number of potential scenarios that might bring the offshore defense strategy into play. Although the near-term focus remains fixed on the Taiwan Strait, Beijing harbors other concerns about seabed resources, disputed territories and maritime claims in the South and East China seas, and "longer-range capabilities," such as protecting sea lines of communication.[6] In response to these issues and worries over the possibility of intervention by foreign air and naval forces, the PLA has concentrated its efforts on building its capacity for force projection and antiaccess/area denial.[7] This has been reflected in PLA weapons modernization programs as well as in the military's development of doctrine and training.

The PLA's Maritime Air Strike Forces

Over the past twenty years, the PLAAF and PLAN aviation have sharply reduced inventories by retiring obsolete aircraft while gradually introducing new platforms. The Department of Defense currently estimates China's combined air fleet at 2,300 operational combat aircraft, including 1,680 air defense and multirole fighters, 620 bombers and attack aircraft, and more than 100 surveillance and reconnaissance aircraft with intelligence, surface search, and airborne early-warning capabilities.[8] Of these, perhaps as many as one-quarter could contribute substantially to a direct assault against modern naval forces. The remaining aircraft lack the range, avionics, or weapons to directly threaten an advanced naval adversary but could potentially be employed to fly deception missions that complicate the operational environment.

By a ratio of nearly 5:1, China's combat air power is concentrated in the PLAAF (see table 1). Submarine and surface forces constitute the bulk of PLAN force structure; just 10 percent of PLAN personnel are assigned to naval aviation. In contrast, an estimated 35 percent of the PLAAF's manpower is assigned to the aviation branch. Despite differences in size, China's two air arms share a number of similarities in their general mix of combat and support aircraft and with their concentrated basing within the five military regions on China's eastern seaboard. As figure 1 indicates, naval aviation has assigned two fighter divisions—with roughly sixty aircraft per division—to the East Sea Fleet and South Sea Fleet areas of operation while deploying a mix of fighter, fighter-bomber, and bomber divisions to the North Sea Fleet (NSF) area of operations. PLAAF forces assigned to coastal military regions (MR) include ten fighter divisions, two fighter-bomber divisions, and two bomber divisions.

Table 1: PLA Aviation Forces

Category	PLAAF	PLAN
Total force	400,000 personnel	255,000 personnel
Aviation forces	140,000 personnel	26,000 personnel
Fighter (J-7, J-8, J-10, J-11, SU-30)	1,350 aircraft	300 aircraft
Bomber/attack (Q-5, JH-7A, H-6)	520 aircraft	120 aircraft
Transport	375 aircraft	75 aircraft

Sources: Office of the Secretary of Defense (DoD), *Military Power of the People's Republic of China 2009* (Washington, DC: DoD, March 2009), http://www.defenselink.mil/pubs/pdfs/China_Military_Power_Report_2009.pdf; and "Naval Forces," *China's Defence Today,* http://www.sinodefence.com/navy/default .asp. The PLA does not publicly disclose end strength and weapons inventory. This chart was compiled based on a review of the tables published in the DoD report and order of battle information maintained by *China's Defence Today.*

Figure 1: Fleet Naval Aviation Forces

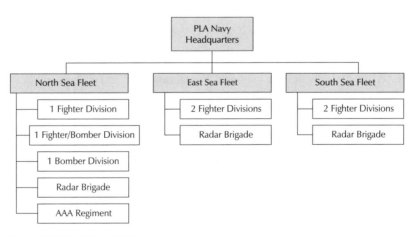

Source: ONI, *China's Navy 2007,* 47.

PLA doctrine emphasizes the "employment of crack forces (*shiyong jin-grui liliang*)—especially in the initial attack phase of an offensive strike or air assault.[9] This advice is repeated in discussions on both strikes against maritime forces and in the air offensive campaign. China's most lethal combat aircraft include approximately 440 third- and fourth-generation fighters, 120 JH-7A fighter-bombers, and 20 late-production H-6H bombers configured to carry antiship cruise missiles or antiradiation missiles.[10] The advanced fighter fleet is comprised of 280 Flanker variants and approximately 150 domestically developed J-10A aircraft. Within the Flanker fleet, there is a combined total of approximately 100 multirole SU-30MKK and MK2 fighters. They may be configured to support maritime strike with precision-guided munitions, including the Russian Kh-59MK Kazoo and other standoff weapons.[11] China's other 180 Flankers, including the single- and tandem-seat models of Russian-built SU-27SK and the J-11A produced in Shenyang from 1999 to 2004, provide decent beyond-visual-range air intercept capabilities but are not equipped for stand-off strikes against surface targets. J-10A fighters and JH-7A fighter-bombers are both assessed to be capable of mixed loads of subsonic radar-guided, antiradiation, TV-guided missiles, or laser-guided bombs.[12] For protection against air and surface threats PLAAF and naval aviation fighters are equipped with a variety of state-of-the-art air-to-air missiles, onboard jammers, and chaff and flare dispensers.[13]

Even before factoring in the potential for air refueling, the range and endurance of China's newest fighters are three to four times greater than those of legacy aircraft. Strike missions in older J-7 and J-8 fighters and Q-5 fighter-bombers were generally restricted to a combat radius of 200 to 300 nautical miles (nm). Improved aerodynamics and increased fuel loads permit the SU-30, J-10A, and JH-7A to conduct strikes out to ranges of 800 nm.[14] Air refueling could extend strike ranges even further, although this operational advantage might be complicated by the limited numbers of PLA tankers, a lack of standardization between domestic and foreign-built air refueling systems, and the PLA's lack of experience in the conduct of long-range operations.[15]

Emerging new air surveillance, airborne early warning (AEW), and command-and-control platforms entering the PLA's inventory contribute to a growing capability to project air power offshore. PLAN aviation has operated Y-8J maritime surveillance aircraft equipped with Racal Searchwater radars since the late 1990s.[16] New Y-8 variants entering service provide the aviation forces with electronic and signals intelligence, communications relay, electronic warfare, antisubmarine warfare, and AEW. Collectively these systems are intended to provide the PLA with the ability to "strengthen reconnaissance and intelligence support, and grasp the battlefield situation in real time" (*jiaqiang zhencha qingbao baozhang, shishi jiangwo zhanchang qingkuang*) as called for in antisurface warfare campaigns.[17] It remains to be seen what these new systems can collectively contribute to offensive strike capabilities; these platforms have only been produced and deployed in small numbers and none have been tested in combat operations.

A majority of China's combat aircraft are based in the eastern half of the country, where they stand poised to support a variety of operational missions along the length of China's coastline.[18] Additionally, an abundance of auxiliary wartime airfields and dozens of modern civil airfields provide the capacity to forward deploy additional combat aircraft during an emerging national security crisis. Main operating bases employ dispersed parking, hardened aircraft shelters, and deep tunnels to withstand attack. The coastal regions are further protected by 10 surface-to-air missile regiments operating 160 SA-10 launchers that extend air-defense protection out to 150 to 200 km.[19] Collectively, these factors favor the forward deployment of additional aircraft into the region to support "feint and deception plans" advocated in PLA operational doctrine. This doctrine includes specific guidance to use such measures as "large scale forces, electronic feints, and use of the news and media to deceive, blunt, and confuse the enemy in order to create 'time gaps' and 'space gaps' in enemy decision making, so as to achieve the purpose of concealed surprise."[20] The abundance of forward bases in the coastal provinces means that there is a large reservoir of capacity to host and field such forces for deception.

Evolving Joint and Naval Campaign Doctrine

The role of shore-based air power in maritime strike operations is largely absent from contemporary PLA discussions about operational-level doctrine.[21] *Science of Campaigns*, published by the PLA National Defense University, provides operational guidance for seventeen categories of campaigns. Seven campaigns among these—five naval and two joint—are oriented around maritime scenarios in which air power could potentially play a pivotal role in the overall success or failure of operations. Yet, as table 2 notes, they give little indication that PLA theorists envisage a key role for either of the aviation forces in maritime strike operations.

For example, in a chapter titled "Campaigns to Eliminate Naval Combatant Groups," maritime campaign forces are described as chiefly comprised of "medium and large surface combatants, submarines, and on-board aviation forces" without giving due consideration to the potential contribution of land-based, fixed-wing air.[22] And, while the chapter warns against the threat of enemy "fixed-wing aircraft," it fails to indicate whether or how shore-based air power might be employed in either attacking or supporting roles during the prosecution of this campaign.

Table 2: PLA Campaigns with Potential for Maritime Strike Operations

Campaign Title	Comments
Eliminate naval combatant groups	No mention of air force or joint
Attacking SLOCs	No mention of air force; one reference to joint
Coral Island Reef offensive	No mention of air force or joint
SLOC defense	Recommends organizing operational coordination when supported by air force or Second Artillery
Naval base defense	No mention of air force; acknowledges that the campaign could be a subcampaign of a larger joint campaign
Joint landing	Emphasizes joint assault to achieve sea superiority, but focus is on attacking "enemy bases and ports" first, then "enemy naval formations at sea."
Joint blockade	Air superiority strike actions emphasize taking out "enemy air bases, command elements, and SAMs." Sea superiority discussion emphasizes joint attacks on ports and bases, if attack is authorized. Assaults on blockade violators employ "submarines, aviation troops and guided missile ships."*

Source: Derived from review and analysis of Zhang, *Science of Campaigns.*

* Zhang, *Science of Campaigns*, 306–7. In implementing maritime inspections, boarding, seizure, and attacks, aviation forces "often employ multi-ship early warning, assault, screening and blockade formations for concealed intercepts and multi-axis, multi-wave attacks."

Even in discussions on joint operations, it is unclear what specific role fixed-wing air will play in conducting strikes at sea. For example, while joint assault (*lianhe tuji*) is stressed as the means to achieve sea superiority during the joint landing campaign, the guidance remains vague as to the extent to which air and missile forces should be integrated: "First, use fierce electronic attack to harass the enemy; afterwards, carry out assaults with firepower and forces. . . . The assault on the enemy naval formations at sea should adopt all effective measures to strive for concealed surprise and decisive timing to control the enemy. Concentrate forces and firepower to form total superiority; strive for rapid war, rapid resolution."[23] The guidance on naval "ambush" also reflects an antiquated approach devoid of specific guidance for air power: "Ambush is the stationing of naval forces in the enemy's sea lanes, transportation routes or their vicinity, to await the passing of enemy naval formations before suddenly initiating attack and rapidly decimating the enemy's operational capacity in the sea lanes."[24]

Yet a 2006 article in *Shipborne Weapons* notes that during the Falklands War, the technologically inferior Argentine Air Force, at the limits of its operational range with minimal targeting information and intelligence, destroyed five Royal Navy ships and seriously damaged five others by using surprise and deception, very low-altitude ingress, and varied weapons and attack profiles. The article notes that modern warfare pits system against system and advocates for opening with "an all-aspect attack [on] the enemy's primary nodes and critical targets using organically integrated multi-service, multi-style joint operations."[25] This suggests that there may be a gap between the practitioners' discussion on employment of air power in naval campaigns and the orthodoxy of approved doctrine.

Impediments to Integrated Operations

As U.S. military planners discovered in the run up to Operation Desert Storm, Cold War operational assumptions put land-based and naval air forces on divergent development paths. U.S. Air Force planners prepared forces for high-density air operations over the European continent while naval planners prepared to fight independently over the open seas. U.S. Navy investments in precision munitions, avionics, and air-battle management systems were insufficient to facilitate the fullest integration of its carrier air wings into the dense operational environment of a land-based air campaign.[26] It would take another ten years and sustained participation of naval air alongside the U.S. Air Force in operations Southern Watch and Northern Watch to fully bridge the operational and technical gaps that had developed between the two services.

Although China has not yet acquired aircraft carriers, it still faces certain operational and bureaucratic obstacles that must be overcome to integrate its two aviation forces in support of maritime strike operations.[27] Over the years divergent mission responsibilities, operating environments, and resource priorities have pushed the PLAAF and PLAN aviation down different paths. Only within the past few years has the PLAAF begun its transition from a territorial air-defense force to an "informationized air fighting force with both offensive and defensive capabilities," including operations offshore.[28] Historically, the PLAAF has placed primacy on continental air defense while giving secondary priority to supporting the ground forces. Through the mid-1990s, the

PLAAF maintained a large fleet of point defense fighters to guard the skies over China's major population and industrial centers while keeping relatively modest numbers of attack and bomber aircraft on hand for strike and interdiction missions. Moreover, during this period the PLAAF was largely prohibited from flying beyond the coastline, thus precluding the opportunity to even contemplate maritime strike.[29]

By contrast, the primary responsibilities for PLAN aviation rest with supporting naval missions, including projecting power seaward and defending naval ports and coastal maritime areas. With only seven air divisions, in comparison to the thirty in the PLAAF, PLAN aviation is about one-fifth the size of its sister service branch.[30] Yet this small force encompasses a diverse cross section of mission-optimized aircraft that includes fighter, fighter-bomber, attack, medium bomber, antisubmarine and aerial reconnaissance, electronic countermeasures, transport, rescue, and air refueling. Prior to the 1990s, PLAN aviation focused on repelling attacks from the sea and defense of naval ports and installations; since then PLAN aviation has expanded its efforts toward maritime strike by adding to its inventory new air surveillance platforms and antiship missile capabilities. With the more recent introduction of upgrades to offboard and onboard navigational aids, improved communications, and weapons, PLAN aviation has begun to project a more forward posture.

The weapons system development and acquisition programs of Chinese aviation forces reflect the mission priorities of the individual services. China's 2004 Defense White Paper describes PLAN aviation development needs vaguely as "various kinds of special-purpose aircraft and relevant equipment," while PLAAF needs are identified as "new fighters, air defense and anti-missile weapons, means of information operations and Air Force automated command systems."[31] Importantly, while flight operations are at the core of the PLAAF mission, aviation occupies a lower status within the PLAN, falling behind submarine and surface forces in the navy's protocol order and in priority for resources. This helps explain why force modernization for PLAN aviation lagged behind the PLAAF as well as other branches within the PLAN. The refit of PLAN aviation with an advanced Russian fighter bomber did not take place until early 2004 when the East Sea Fleet began receiving initial deliveries of SU-30MK2 at Feidong Air Base in Zhejiang Province.[32] This was nearly twelve years after the PLAAF began operating the SU-27 and long after the PLAN's procurement of *Kilo*-class submarines and *Sovremenny*-class destroyers.[33]

Development of Joint Training Mechanisms

Prior to the 1990s, the PLAAF and PLAN had no history of cooperative train-ing or integrated operations. By the mid-1990s, the PLA had altered its war-fighting concept to "local wars under high-tech conditions" and began to stress the importance of joint operations (*lianhe zuozhan*).[34] By 2004 the PLA's warfighting concept had advanced to "local wars under informatized condi-tions" and with it the PLA raised the requirement for integrated joint opera-tions (*yitihua lianhe zuozhan*).

Since 2004 the PLA has taken a number of steps to foster the develop-ment of both joint operations and integrated joint operations. One important measure has been the CMC's establishment of military training coordination zones (MTCZ; *junshi xunlian xiezuo qu*) in each of the military regions (MR) in 2004, which are based on an experimentation zone in Jinan MR, later chris-tened the Weifang MTCZ. Jinan MR has held a series of joint exercises con-ducted since 1999, dubbed "Lianhe," or "Joint," which has helped field-test joint operational methods. First reported activities occured in April 1999, when the North China Sea Fleet and the Jinan MR Air Force "jointly held a coordina-tion meeting on training at sea . . . setting up a joint operations training coor-dination mechanism."[35] In July 1999 Jinan MR hosted the first reported Lianhe exercise. Since then, at least four additional Lianhe exercises have been con-ducted with growing complexity. Lianhe-2007 and Lianhe-2008, in particu-lar, included maritime strike elements and detailed the MTCZ organizational structure, including direct oversight by the MR commander and political com-missar and responsibilities of joint tactical commanders at division- and bri-gade-level units of each service.

In 2003 the theory behind MTCZs was crystallized by Major General Ai Husheng, then-commander of the 39th Group Army, writing in *Military Art* (*Junshi Xueshu*). He suggested the establishment of a "joint training zone" as a mechanism for joint training experimentation. He envisioned "using units sta-tioned near each other . . . in joint operations training organized by joint train-ing zones."[36] General Ai's primary goal was to establish a focal point around which operational-level commanders could plan and organize triservice joint training activities. To coordinate multiservice training, he recommended the establishment of a "leading small group" (*lingdao xiaozu*) within the MR head-quarters to provide direction. Lianhe-related reporting suggests that the orga-nizational structure outlined by Ai has been implemented within Jinan MR, and within other MRs as MTCZs have proliferated.[37]

Training Events Analysis

The maritime-strike training activities of the PLAN aviation and PLAAF demonstrate how each aviation force is focused on particular subsets of the maritime strike mission. Fixed-wing naval aviation units, which are subordinate to one of the PLAN's three fleets, focus their maritime strike training on reconnaissance and ship-air combined assaults on surface ships. Certain naval aviation units, such as the "Sea and Air Heroic Eagle Regiment" of the 4th Naval Aviation Division, East Sea Fleet (ESF), conduct long-range maritime-strike training. More often, however, PLAAF units are the ones reported to be conducting long-range maritime strikes against both mobile and fixed targets. PLAAF units also tend to be the ones that participate in coordination with naval flotillas in large-scale joint exercises, though similar combined arms exercises between PLAN aviation and surface ships also take place.

Maritime Reconnaissance

Among other responsibilities, PLAN aviation units are tasked to patrol and protect areas surrounding naval bases and ports. Reporting indicates that PLAN aviation units also conduct reconnaissance of enemy naval assets at sea. For example, during an opposing forces training event on 24 August 2007, a naval formation of the 1st Destroyer Flotilla was in harbor when warning came of approaching enemy warships. As the ships set sail to intercept the opposing blue force, "a warplane took off from an airfield in Jiaodong." The PLAN aviation plane provided reconnaissance information to the naval formation of approaching missile boats, allowing the ships to launch an "over-the-horizon missile attack" against the formation.[38] The PLAN aviation aircraft and PLAN ships were in communication with one another directly and were able to reestablish communications after encountering jamming. This stands in contrast to reports from 1999 that indicated training between PLAN aviation and other PLAN units was "carried out separately without any communication between aircraft and warship" and indicates the progressive development of capabilities.[39] This Shandong-based PLAN aviation division held its first direct "joint" exercise with PLAN warships in 2006, sending encrypted transmissions "to a surface ship a long distance away."[40]

Combined Air Assault

PLAAF and PLAN single-type or multitype air formations have regularly conducted maritime strike training for several years. In recent years, however, the training emphasis has been placed on extending the range of operations and of operating in increasingly complex weather and light conditions. Yet little suggests that PLAN aviation and PLAAF units cooperate or train together for such missions. One report indicated that in 2001 PLAAF units may have taken on the role of air superiority fighters while PLAN aviation units constituted a strike element, "under the cover of several Air Force fighters, Naval Air Force fighters of a certain new type reached the battle zone . . . and launched zoom-bombing and torpedo attacks on the 'enemy' from different altitudes."[41] In our survey of subsequent years, there has been no further reporting of similar PLAAF–PLAN aviation cooperation in maritime strike training. Rather, maritime air assaults have largely been single-service training activities involving mixed packages of air assets.

The apparent preference for single-service training in maritime strike suggests that it may be more effective than attempting to combine the services. For instance, the "Sea and Air Heroic Eagle Regiment" of the 4th Naval Aviation Division, ESF, has consistently trained for long-distance maritime strikes in single-service mixed formations. In June 2007 the formation "launched surprise attacks against an enemy ship formation at sea after maneuvering a long distance and by employing the method of low altitude and multi-directional penetration."[42] These tactics may reflect lessons the PLA adopted from its review of the Falklands War, using low-altitude and multiple attacks to overwhelm a technically superior foe. The regiment again conducted a "long distance maneuver to launch surprise attacks against the enemy at sea" two months later.[43] This regiment would appear to have an assigned training focus of conducting maritime strikes. Notably, the 4th Naval Aviation Division is equipped with SU-30MK2s and J7-Es. NSF PLAN aviation has also trained for maritime strike using multiple types of aircraft. In August 2006 "a patrol aircraft under the escort of several fighters" took station over a sea area, and "guided a bomber formation to launch precision strikes at a formation of 'enemy' ships with bombs and torpedoes."[44] While such reporting is far from comprehensive, there is a pattern of regular training by PLAN aviation units in maritime strike operations.

Particular PLAAF units also focus on maritime strike mission training, including units based far from China's coastal regions. For example, a Lanzhou air regiment regularly conducts long-range bombing training in the South China Sea, as it did in November 2007, when "several new-model warplanes took off . . . to launch unexpected long-range precision attacks against targets at sea."[45] Again in March 2008 an unidentified Lanzhou MRAF regiment conducted long-range maritime strikes by "evading powerful enemy electromagnetic jamming" and carrying out bomb attacks on a "large ship."[46] Air units in other military regions also conduct maritime strike training under increasingly complex conditions. In a Nanjing MRAF division, "bombing groups adopted methods of ultra-low altitude, multi-directional entry to launch another round of attacks against 'enemy' targets at sea," and the division "made over-the-sea training a regular technical and tactical activity."[47] Such training activities indicate the growing repertoire of PLAAF training scenarios over water but with a focus on long-range strikes. In another example of increasing PLAAF maritime strike complexity, a combined arms PLAAF formation of fighters and bombers from Guangzhou MRAF conducted a bombing exercise at sea in July 2007. According to *Air Force News*, "coordinating with fighter groups for long distance bombing against moving targets is a regular training subject of the division, but it was the first time the division carried heavy bombs to attack moving targets deep in the ocean."[48] The "joint warplane group" was effective in coordinating the fighter formation's fire suppression to allow the bomber formation to accomplish the strike mission. These reports indicate that certain PLAAF units train regularly for "long-range maritime strike missions," suggesting that they have been designated for these missions.

Air-Naval Opposition and Coordination Training

Tactical training against naval surface units by fixed-wing aircraft is an increasingly important training scenario practiced by both PLAN aviation and PLAAF forces. Often, opposing forces training appears to be an accessible starting point for air-naval units to begin multibranch or multiservice maritime strike training before progressing to coordinated joint training. In Jinan MR, for instance, the Lianhe series of exercises evolved from air-sea identification exercises to opposing forces exercises over the course of several years. In 1999 the 1st Destroyer Flotilla and an unidentified PLAAF attack division established a joint training relationship that evolved into the more complex triservice joint operations exercises. The two units established a "coordination mechanism" during an air-naval opposing forces exercise in 2000. In 2003 opposition continued to be the model, when two destroyers played the blue force against a PLAAF air regiment.[49] Lianhe-2006 included coordinated air-naval antisurface ship scenarios with air units both providing over-the-horizon targeting information for the ship formation and directly conducting attacks against enemy ships.[50] This pattern of introducing units to joint training by beginning with opposition between service units and then advancing to interservice coordination has been observed in the reporting of joint training activities in other MRs as well.

A similar pattern was observed in Nanjing MR and Guangzhou MR "joint" air-naval training. In September 2007 a Nanjing MRAF division established "coordination relationships" with other units, including PLAN units, playing the "role of adversaries in air-sea coordinated defense" and in "air-to-ship defense penetration and assault" scenarios.[51] If opposing force training is part of the evolution of joint training in PLAN–PLAAF coordination, the 2007 ESF and Nanjing MRAF activities would be considered an intermediate pattern of joint training. In contrast, South Sea Fleet (SSF)–Guangzhou MRAF joint training for maritime strike was at a more advanced level of joint training in 2007. Also in September 2007 units of the SSF and Guangzhou MRAF conducted a "joint defense operations exercise."[52] The units conducted "ship-aircraft coordinated attacks," where a PLAAF fighter formation "coordinated with ships and boats to implement attacks against sea targets."[53] The difference in the nature of the joint training would suggest that the SSF had a more mature training relationship with the Guangzhou MRAF in 2007. From these examples of maritime strike training, a pattern of beginning with opposing forces scenario seems to presage more advanced coordinated joint training between PLAN and PLAAF units. The opposing or coordinated nature of the training may thus be useful to gauge the overall developmental maturity in maritime strike training of a particular joint grouping.

PLAN aviation units appear to conduct air-naval training in maritime strike missions under a separate training mechanism from PLAAF–PLAN joint training. For instance, in 2006 the ESF established a "joint training mechanism" composed of "its aviation, surface combatant, submarine, coastal defense, observation and communications, radar, electromagnetic countermeasures, and technical reconnaissance units."[54] The ESF joint training mechanism included the establishment of common command-and-control systems, such as the "warship-aircraft combined arms tactical training data link system" and "warship-aircraft integrated support system."[55] The following year, in April 2007, a destroyer flotilla of the ESF trained with PLAN aviation, submarine, and other naval branch units in an exercise in which the focus of the training scenario was a "destroyer and frigate formation and aviation force joint assault on enemy formations under the guidance of reconnaissance elements."[56] Compared with the Nanjing MR PLAN–PLAAF oppositional training in September 2007, this nominally "combined arms" exercise would appear to be at the more advanced stage of coordinated air-naval maritime strike. This is one example of the uneven development, even within a fleet or MR, of air-naval integration. Notably, after the ESF established its multiple-arms training platform, the 6th Destroyer Flotilla conducted opposing forces exercise against

PLAN aviation Flying Leopard fighters and again later in the year in "ship-to-aircraft joint opposing forces exercises" before conducting the April coordination exercises.[57] Therefore, from these reports it would appear that the ESF and subordinate arms moved from opposing forces to coordinated training in the span of about a year.

Coordinated maritime strike is only a subset of the airborne maritime strike mission. Single-branch training of PLAN aviation units against surface targets continues to evolve and improve. For instance, examples of nighttime or low-altitude maritime strike training have increased, as have examples of such training combined into more complex scenarios, such as those practiced by a PLAN aviation regiment in the North Sea Fleet, led by "problem solving teams" [*gongguan xiaozu*] made up of pilots and experienced trainers.[58] Similar focused training has occurred in other PLAN aviation regiments, which indicates that solving these "bottlenecks" in maritime strike operations has become a priority for the force.[59] Next steps would involve practicing these new capabilities in opposing or coordinated exercises with other surface naval or PLAAF assets.

Concluding Thoughts

Although maritime strike operations have historically been a low priority for the PLA, in recent years it has begun to assign greater importance to developing the capacity to perform this mission. New air platforms, weapons, and targeting systems indicate a growing capacity for PLA air forces to support and conduct maritime strike. Yet PLA campaign doctrine does not appear to have kept pace with the PLA's evolving operational capabilities and employment concepts. In the years ahead, as the PLA gains additional experience with new platforms and weapons technologies, one should expect the PLA to better articulate its plans for integrating air power in support of the full range of maritime missions. Today wide gaps exist in the PLA's doctrine for offshore operations.

The PLA's introduction of new air weapons and platforms with significant maritime strike capability initially spawned the development of single-branch and single-service employment tactics. More recently, as the PLA has shifted its training focus to joint and integrated operations, it has developed and institutionalized specific training mechanisms designed to foster combined arms and joint operations training. These initiatives are leading to an incremental but steady progression in joint maritime strike training. An example of this has been the relatively recent transition from air-naval opposition training to air-naval coordination training.

A central organizing mechanism of the PLA's joint training activities has been the MTCZ, and Chinese military literature indicates that these zones have played an important role in integrating PLAAF and PLAN forces, especially in Jinan and Guangzhou MRs. Originating from discussions that began as early as 1999, the MTCZ concept was tested, proven, and eventually popularized throughout the PLA in 2004. Since then the MTCZs have played a vital role in the overall expansion of PLA joint training activities. Currently, each of the PLA's seven military regions has established at least one MTCZ, and Guangzhou MR is known to have four MTCZs. Within each MTCZ, specified units are encouraged to experiment with command models and training methods according to their operational missions, operating environment, and available training resources. Other MRs may also have multiple MTCZ, creating the possibility of ten or more of these special zones scattered across the country. Thus, the MTCZ system constitutes a series of regional battle labs for joint experimentation and innovation as the PLA fields new equipment and establishes new operational concepts.

While the PLAAF and PLAN aviation are making important gains in their ability to conduct joint operations, dissimilarities in missions and equipment requirements could present obstacles to interservice collaboration and coordination going forward. Historically, relations between China's two air services have been strained as a result of bureaucratic clashes over resource and program issues. That relationship could be further tested if the PLAN pursues, as is widely expected, costly and resource-intensive programs to field a fleet of conventional aircraft carriers and the required aviation forces to fly from their decks. If PLAN aviation evolves toward carrier-based air operations, its operational role will become decidedly more specialized and increase the complexity of integrating naval and land-based air forces. At the same time, the introduction of an aircraft carrier into the PLA arsenal would likely be preceded by efforts to ramp up PLA joint maritime strike capacity. In either event, the integration of PLAAF and PLAN aviation air operations into the maritime strike is likely to be an increasingly important priority for the PLA as long as "active defense" remains a guiding strategic doctrine in its military modernization.

Notes

The views and opinions expressed in this paper are those of the authors and do not necessarily reflect the views of CENTRA Technology Inc. or any organization of the U.S. government.

1. *China's National Defense in 2008* (Beijing: State Council Information Office, January 2009), http://merln.ndu.edu/whitepapers/China_English2008.pdf.

2. Office of the Secretary of Defense (DoD), *Military Power of the People's Republic of China 2009* (Washington, DC: DoD, March 2009), 1, http://www.defenselink.mil/pubs/pdfs/China_Military_Power_Report_2009.pdf.

3. Nan Li, "New Developments in PLA's Operational Doctrine and Strategies," Jamestown *China Brief* 6, no. 20 (9 May 2007), http://www.jamestown.org/programs/chinabrief/single/?tx_ttnews[tt_news]=3996&tx_ttnews[backPid]=196&no_cache=1.

4. Office of Naval Intelligence (ONI), *China's Navy 2007* (Washington, DC: ONI), 26, http://www.fas.org/nuke/guide/china/oni2007.pdf.

5. DoD, *Military Power*, 26.

6. Ibid., I.

7. Ibid.

8. Office of the Secretary of Defense (DoD), *Military and Security Developments Involving the People's Republic of China 2010*, Annual Report to Congress (Washington, DC: DoD, 16 August 2010), 62, http://www.defense.gov/pubs/pdfs/2010_CMPR_Final.pdf.

9. Zhang Yuliang, ed., *Science of Campaigns* (*Zhanyi Xue*) (Beijing: National Defense University Press, May 2006), 529, 579.

10. Richard Fisher, *China's Military Modernization: Building for Regional and Global Reach* (Westport, CT: Praeger Security International, 2008), 136–48. These figures are estimated total aircraft inventory and do not reflect that aircraft may be under maintenance or assigned to training units.

11. Ibid., 138–44.

12. "Jian-10 Multirole Fighter Aircraft," *China's Defence Today*, 21 March 2009, http://www.sinodefence.com/airforce/fighter/j10.asp; and "JianHong-7 Fighter-Bomber," *China's Defence Today*, 24 October 2008, http://www.sinodefence.com/airforce/groundattack/jh7.asp. See *China's Defence Today* for a review of PLAAF and PLAN aviation aircraft and weapons systems.

13. "Aircraft Systems," *China's Defence Today*, 24 October 2008, http://www.sinodefence.com/airforce/groundattack/jh7.asp. See website for a review of PLAAF and PLAN aviation aircraft weapons specifications.

14. "Military Aircraft," *China's Defence Today*, 21 March 2009, http://www.sinodefence.com/airforce/fighter/j10.asp.

15. Reporting on China's various air refueling systems and capabilities remains sketchy. Some experts believe that the probe on the Russian-built SU-30 aircraft is not com-

patible with the drogue system on China's domestically developed H-6U tankers, thus creating a requirement for IL-78 Midas tankers to support the SU-30s.

16. "Yun-8J Maritime Patrol Aircraft," *China's Defence Today*, 3 September 2007, http://www.sinodefence.com/airforce/specialaircraft/y8j.asp.

17. Zhang, *Science of Campaigns*, 524.

18. DoD, *Military and Security Developments*, 62. DoD estimates that 490 combat aircraft operating from home airfields could conduct combat operations against Taiwan without air refueling.

19. DoD, *Military Power*, 66.

20. Zhang, *Science of Campaigns*, 577.

21. James C. Mulvenon and Richard H. Yang, eds., *The People's Liberation Army in the Information Age* (Santa Monica, CA: RAND, 1999), 99–145.

22. Zhang, *Science of Campaigns*, 523.

23. Ibid., 321.

24. Ibid.

25. Tian Ying, "Qiantan xiandai haijun hangkongbing de tufang zuozhan" ["Discussion on Modern Naval Aviation Defense Operations"], *Shipborne Weapons* (August 2006): 20–27.

26. Benjamin S. Lambeth, "Air Force–Navy Integration in Strike Warfare: A Role Model for Seamless Joint Service Operations," *Naval War College Review* 61, no. 1 (Winter 2008): 27–48.

27. ONI, *The People's Liberation Army Navy: A Modern Navy with Chinese Characteristics* (Suitland, MD: ONI, July 2009), http://www.fas.org/irp/agency/oni/pla-navy.pdf.

28. *China's National Defense in 2006* (Beijing: State Council Information Office, 29 December 2006), http://www.china.org.cn/english/features/book/194421.htm.

29. Kenneth Allen, "Reforms in the PLA Air Force," Jamestown *China Brief* 5, no. 15 (5 July 2005), http://www.jamestown.org/single/?no_cache=1&tx_ttnews[swords]=8fd58 93941d69d0be3f378576261ae3e&tx_ttnews[exact_search]=Reforms%20in%20the%20 PLA%20Air%20Force&tx_ttnews[categories_1]=8&tx_ttnews[tt_news]=30613&tx_ ttnews[backPid]=7&cHash=c5cb2e1644.

30. ONI, *China's Navy 2007*, 47.

31. *China's National Defense in 2004* (Beijing: State Council Information Office, 27 December 2004), http://www.china.org.cn/e-white/20041227/index.htm.

32. See "Su-30MKK Multirole Fighter Aircraft," *China's Defence Today*, 20 February 2009, http://www.sinodefence.com/airforce/fighter/su30.asp.

33. Ronald O'Rourke, "China Naval Modernization: Implications for U.S. Navy Capabilities—Background and Issues for Congress" (Washington, DC: Congressional Research Service, 19 November 2008).

34. Considerable confusion surrounds the Chinese meaning of "joint" (*lianhe*). Chinese media often use "joint" when referring to single-service, combined arms, and oppo-

sition training. Recent Chinese media appear to clarify the term "joint," by specifying "tri-service joint" (*sanjun lianhe*) or "integrated joint" (*yitihua lianhe*).

35. Yao Yan and Si Yanwen, "PRC, Navy, Air Force Stage Combined Training Exercises at Sea," *Jiefangjun Bao* [*Liberation Army Daily*], 19 July 2000, 2.

36. 艾虎生 [Ai Husheng], "Zuzhi lianxunqu junbingzhong "yitihua" lianhe xunlian de ji dian yijian" ["A Few Ideas about Organizing Joint Training Zone Service-Arms 'Integrated' Joint Training"], *Military Art*, no. 6 (2003): 57–59. *Military Art* is the military-only theoretical journal published by the Academy of Military Science.

37. "JFJB Cites Weifang Training Area's Role in Promoting Changes in PLA Joint Operation," *Jiefangjun Bao*, 2 November 2007.

38. Zhang Jian, Jiang Xiangjie, Zhang Gang, "Jiang laixi daodan dajin haili—muji Beihai Jiandui fuza dianzi huanjing xia shidan duikang yanlian" ["Incoming Attack Missile Hit into Ocean—Witness North Sea Fleet Live Missile Confrontation Exercise under Complex Electromagnetic Conditions"], *China National Defense News*, 4 September 2007, http://www.chinamil.com.cn/site1/zbxl/2007-09/04/content_939288.htm.

39. "Jian feiji zhijie 'duihua'" ["Warship Aircraft Direct 'Dialogue'"], *Jiefangjun Bao*, 20 October 1999, 2.

40. Zhang Qingbao, "Beihai jiandui hangkongbingshi miaozhun xinxihua zuozhan xuyao zhuoli tigao zhihuiyuan xinxi chuli nengli" ["North Sea Fleet Aviation Division Aims at Information Operations Requirements, Strives to Raise Commanders' Information Management Capabilities"], *Jiefangjun Bao* , 18 March 2006, 2.

41. Lu Hairong, "Tiejin shizhan zuzhi duo jizhong xietong yanlian" ["Approaching Real Combat, Multi-type Coordinated Exercise"], *Renmin Haijun* [*People's Navy*], 9 August 2001, 2.

42. Zhu Lisu, "Zouchu 'hongjun' bisheng 'lanjun' bibai moshi donghai jiandui mou shui-jingqu duikang xunlian gao yixiangqingyuan" ["Leaving the 'Red Force' Must Win, 'Blue Force' Must Lose Model: ESF Coastal Defense District No Longer Conducts Opposition Training as Wishful Thinking"], *Renmin Haijun*, 24 July 2007, 1.

43. Yang Yuansong, Fang Lihua, and Wang Chaowu, "Zhanying, kaixuan zai ziye—haijun hangkongbing mou xinxing zhanji shenye feixing xunlian muji ji" ["Fighting Eagle, Triumphant Return from Midnight: Personal Observations of Night Training of Naval Aviation Troops with New Model Aircraft"], *Jiefangjun Bao*, 30 August 2007, 2.

44. Li Ruixiang and Kang Zhijun, "Mou feixingtuan lian jiu zhenchan yinggong: gong-guan xiaozu qude yipi zhanfa yanjiu chengguo" ["Flying Regiment Trains on Difficult Reconnaissance Hard Work: Problem Tackling Group Achieves a Batch of Results in Methods of Operations Research"], *Renmin Haijun*, 1 September 2006.

45. Yan Guoyou, "Nankong hangkongbing mou shi jiaqiang zonghe zhandou keti xun-lian" ["Nanjing Air Force Aviation Division Strengthens Comprehensive Tactical Subject Training"], *Kongjun Bao* [*Air Force News*], 15 November 2007, 1.

46. Cao Zhuanbiao, Zhang Junjie, and Fu Zhidong, "Tuji xiangzhe dahai" ["Assault Toward the Open Sea"], *Zhongguo guofang Bao* [*China Defense News*], 18 March 2008, 19.

47. "Shenanzhixian haixunlianyi, nankong hangkongbing mou shi cong gaonan kemu ladong xunlian xiaoyi tisheng" ["Set up Difficult, Place Risk, Naval Training Wing: Nanjing Air Force Aviation Division Pulls Increase in Training Benefits through Highly Difficult Topics"], *Kongjun Bao*, 13 September 2007, 2.

48. Yu Caishan, Yin Bangshi, "Fei yueyuan haichuang 'di' hou guangkong hangkongbing mou shi hongzha yanlian ceji" ["Distant Sea Flight Assault on Enemy Rear: Guangzhou Air Force Division Bombing Exercise News"], *Kongjun Bao*, 14 July 2007, 4.

49. Yao Yan, "Jiaolong xiongying lianyan haikong yiti huoju" ["Dragon and Eagle Jointly Perform Air-Sea Integrated Live Performance"], *Jiefangjun Bao*, 19 July 2000; and *Kongjun Bao*, 4 November 2003.

50. "Sanjun xietong lianyan quanmian jianyan lieanhe zuozhan shuiping" ["Tri-service Coordinated Joint Drill Comprehensively Examines Joint Operations Level"], *Qianwei Bao*, 20 October 2006, 1.

51. Chen Hanzhong and Wu Yi, "Nankong hangkongbing moushi chuilian xinxihua tiaojianxia zhozhan benling" ["Nanjing Air Force Air Division Hammers Out Operational Skills under Informatized Conditions"], *Jiefangjun Bao*, 16 September 2007, 1.

52. Si Yanwen, "Mou shuijingqu zuzhi quyu lianhe fangwei zuozhan yanlian" ["Regional Coastal Defense District Organizes Regional Joint Defense Operations Drill"], *Jiefangjun Bao*, 22 September 2007, 2.

53. Ibid.

54. Li Yibao, "Donghai jiandui queli yitihua xunlian linian zhuajin zongjie jicheng jianshe" ["East Sea Fleet Firmly Establishes Integrated Training Concept, Tightly Grasps Comprehensive Integration Construction"], *Renmin Haijun*, 5 July 2006, 1.

55. Ibid.

56. Yang Guangzhai, "Donghai jiandui mou qujujian zhidui jianjiqian'an lianhe yanlian liti gongfang keti" ["East Sea Fleet Destroyer Flotilla, Three-Dimensional Offense-Defense Ship-Aircraft-Submarine-Shore Joint Training Drill"], *Renmin Haijun*, 3 April 2007, 1.

57. "Laizi sanjun budui shouzhang jiguan nianzong xunlian kaohe de xinwen" ["News from Three Armed Services Command Organs Year-end Training Evaluation"], *Jiefangjun Bao*, 18 November 2006, http://www.chinamil.com.cn/site1/xwpdxw/2006-11/18/content_649943.htm.

58. Liu Weiquan and Chou Yujun, "Chaodikong tuxi chulou fengmang," ["Minimum Altitude Air Raid Displays One's Talents"], *Renmin Haijun*, 15 December 2009.

59. Lu Hong, "Yehang xunlian chuilian zhanying shizhan benling," ["Night Flight Training Forges War Eagles' Live Combat Capability"], *Renmin Haijun*, 19 July 2009.

Andrew S. Erickson and Jingdong Yuan

Antiaccess and China's Air-Launched Cruise Missiles

FOR THE PEOPLE'S LIBERATION ARMY (PLA) to confront a stronger opponent in local conflicts under modern, informatized conditions, the only path to victory—or at least to avoid defeat—would be to disrupt and deny access to U.S. forces and exploit their points of vulnerability with so-called assassin's mace weapons as necessary. This chapter examines the role of one such "silver bullet"—air-launched cruise missiles (ALCMs)—in the PLA's antiaccess strategy, and seeks to address the following questions:

- What has been China's development path with respect to ALCMs?

- What are the advantages of ALCMs vis-à-vis other means of delivery (e.g., surface ships and submarines) for various relevant scenarios?

- How are Chinese cruise missiles related to their Soviet/Russian counterparts?

- What are Chinese ALCM trends with respect to range, speed, and electronic warfare capabilities?

The chapter will analyze the role of ALCMs in support of the PLA objectives of dissuading and deterring U.S. intervention by disrupting and denying it access to the vicinity of the Taiwan Strait.

Cruise Missiles' Advantages and PLA Antiaccess Strategies

Chinese analysts increasingly recognize the potential for cruise missiles to serve as decisive long-range precision weapons in modern warfare. Cruise missiles are easy to maintain for extended periods in harsh environments because (unlike some missiles) they may be placed in canisters if desired. Like many other weapons, modern cruise missiles offer multiple launch options (land, sea, and air). This affords a "two-stage" form of delivery that extends the missiles' already substantial range. Cruise missiles need only rudimentary launch-pad stability, thus enabling shoot-and-scoot tactics. Because cruise missiles do not produce large infrared launch signatures, they are not detectable by space-warning systems, which makes postlaunch counterforce attacks problematic. Cruise missiles are also cheaper than airplanes—in effect, they allow the force employing them to avoid having to buy an aircraft that has to penetrate air defenses in order to deliver ordnance. Finally, because of their supersonic speed, small radar signature, and earth-hugging flight profile, cruise missiles greatly tax ground-based and airborne surveillance and tracking radars, thereby increasing the likelihood that they will successfully penetrate defenses.

Cruise missiles have potential advantages over ballistic missiles for a country such as China. Indeed, cruise missiles, together with ballistic missiles, will likely play a prominent role in what is described as the PLA's missile-centric strategies, especially in the Taiwan Strait war theater, where the Chinese military could put at risk U.S. targets in Guam, Okinawa, and at sea. Employed in salvoes (e.g., in a stream raid, a form of salvo on a single axis), perhaps in tandem with ballistic missiles, cruise missiles potentially could saturate or overcome defenses. A saturation attack would consist of a large number of cruise missiles arriving at a specific target in a short period in hopes of overwhelming defenses. Saturation could take a variety of forms, including the dispatch of more missiles than enemy radar systems or interceptors could handle.

There are two major varieties of cruise missiles, both of which may be air launched. Antiship cruise missiles (ASCMs), which can be launched from PLA Navy (PLAN) submarines, surface vessels, and aircraft, employ alternative targeting methods that often eliminate reliance on satellite surveillance capabilities. These include inertial navigation systems and radar and electro-optical sensors. Land-attack cruise missiles (LACMs), currently ground-launched by the Second Artillery and air-launched by the PLA Air Force (PLAAF), are long-range strategic strike weapons not currently deployed on PLAN surface ships, perhaps because they are redundant in regional scenarios and hence suggestive of extraregional offensive strike capability. LACMs, typically used against fixed targets, may also rely on similar targeting methods to ASCMs as well as terrain contour mapping and digital scene-matching area correlation technology.

Key Chinese ALCM Trends

China is working to deploy large numbers of highly accurate air-launched antiship and land-attack cruise missiles, the latter of which has figured prominently in regional military campaigns around the world since 1991. Cruise missiles are seen as a key to a short-duration, high-intensity military campaign against Taiwan as well as to inhibit U.S. intervention in such a contingency. According to the U.S. Department of Defense (DoD), "The PLA Navy has or is acquiring nearly a dozen ASCM variants. . . . The pace of ASCM research, development and production within China and procurement from abroad—primarily Russia—has accelerated over the past decade."[1]

China has developed its own advanced, highly capable ASCMs, the Yingji (Eagle Strike), or YJ-series, while also importing supersonic ASCMs from Russia for which there is no operational Western equivalent. China is capable of launching its ASCMs from a growing variety of land, air, ship, and undersea platforms, thus providing redundant multiaxis means of massing offensive firepower against targets at sea, or at least against their predicted locations. China has furnished its ASCMs with improved guidance and satellite navigation capabilities. A variety of platforms, including unmanned aerial vehicles (UAVs), may be increasing the already respectable accuracy and targeting capability of these weapons via data link. Still, over-the-horizon targeting remains a difficult challenge at present. Chinese researchers are studying how to best overcome (i.e., by saturating) Aegis defenses and target vulnerabilities. Chinese aviation training has become more diverse and realistic in recent years, with increasing focus on cruise missile operations.

China's most potent air-launched cruise missiles are LACMs. Operating in tandem with China's huge inventory of conventionally armed ballistic missiles, LACMs offer the PLA the ability to threaten Taiwan's capacity to use its previously superior air force to thwart Chinese attack options. Chinese planners emphasize the shock and paralytic effects of combined ballistic and LACM attacks—in large volumes or salvos—which could overwhelm enemy missile defenses and enable follow-on aircraft strikes. They view LACMs as particularly effective against targets that require precision accuracy (e.g., airfield hangars and command-and-control sites). As Mark Stokes (assistant U.S. air attaché in Beijing, 1992–95), has reported, some Chinese believe that, due to the low cost of developing, deploying, and maintaining LACMs, cruise missiles possess a 9:1 cost advantage over the expense of defending against them.[2]

China still lags in its capacity to realize the full potential of precision delivery systems such as cruise missiles. Shortcomings remain in intelligence support, command and control, platform stealth and survivability, and post-attack assessment, all of which are critical to mission effectiveness. Time and dedicated effort will increase China's ability to employ LACMs even in challenging combined arms military campaigns.

Chinese ALCM Capabilities

Chinese military dictionaries categorize cruise missiles based on their launch platform, although most (or at least their variants) may be launched from multiple launch platforms. Many of China's cruise missiles may be launched by aircraft; several types, including some LACMs, may only be launched from that platform. This is a distinction with a difference: with the exception of some newer LACMs, a cruise missile's limited range typically necessitates that its launch platform approach within 100–200 km of a target, thereby tying the missile's effectiveness to that platform's performance parameters (particularly stealth). In this sense, ALCMs have trailed their submarine and even surface vessel–launched counterparts, both of which boast far greater range unrefueled, while China's conventionally powered submarines are potentially far more survivable as well.

Nevertheless, this volume demonstrates that while China's missile systems remain far superior to its aviation counterparts and that this disparity seems unlikely to narrow soon in many respects, Chinese military aviation is gradually improving. Moreover, some LACMs, including the indigenous DH-10, promise to have ranges in excess of 2,000 km, thereby enabling significant strike reach even if launch platforms remain within a protected "bastion" far closer to China's shores. For all these reasons, it is time to revisit the evolution, role, and potential of Chinese ALCMs. For the attributes of China's major air-launched cruise missiles, see table 1.

Antiship Cruise Missiles

China has perhaps made the greatest progress to date regarding ASCMs. Here Beijing has truly developed comprehensive indigenous capabilities that approach world-class levels in many areas. PLAN ASCM programs include a variety of surface-, subsurface-, and air-launched weapons. This mixture of

Table 1: Performance Parameters of Major Chinese Air-Launched Cruise Missiles (ALCMs)

Name	Launch Platform/Type	Range (km)	Payload (kg)	Speed (sub/super)	Guidance (inertial/terminal)
LAND-ATTACK CRUISE MISSILES (LACMs)					
YJ-63/KD-63[1]	Air	200–500	500	Sub	INS/Sat/Active/Passive; electro-optical terminal guidance
DH-10/CJ-10[2]	Ground, air (?)	1,500–2,500	500	Sub	INS/TERCOM/Probable DSMAC for terminal guidance
YJ-100[3]	Air	1,500–2,000	500	Sub	INS/TERCOM
YJ-91[4]	Air, ship	120	90	Super	Passive/Antiradiation
KD-88[5]	Air	180–200	165	Sub	Inertial; active terminal guidance
ANTISHIP CRUISE MISSILES (ASCMs)					
Name	Launch Platform/Type	Range (km)	Payload (kg)	Speed (sub/super)	Guidance (inertial/terminal)
YJ-83[6]	Ground, ship, air, sub	160	165–250	Sub	INS, data link, active/passive radar

Sources:

1. Office of the Secretary of Defense (DoD), *Military and Security Developments Involving the People's Republic of China 2010*, Annual Report to Congress (Washington, DC: Office of the Secretary of Defense, 16 August 2010), 31; *Ballistic and Cruise Missile Threat* (Wright-Patterson Air Force Base, OH: National Air and Space Intelligence Center, April 2009); and "KongDi-63 Air-Launched Land-Attack Cruise Missile," *China's Defence Today*, 20 October 2008, http://www.sinodefence.com/airforce/weapon/kd63.asp.

2. DoD, *Military and Security Developments*, 31.

3. Chen Wen-cheng, 國防, 问答斷 ["Defense Turning Back"] (Taipei: Taiwan Defense Policy and Strategy, 2009), http://www.taiwanncf.org.tw/ttforum/46/46-04.pdf.

4. The YJ-91 is based on the Russian Kh-31P. See DoD, *Military and Security Developments*, 31; "YingJi-91 (Kh-31P) Anti-Radiation Missile," *China's Defence Today*, 20 October 2008, http://www.sinodefence.com/airforce/weapon/kh31.asp.

5. The KD-88 is a derivative of the YJ-83, roughly comparable to the U.S. land-attack variant of Harpoon. See DoD, *Military and Security Developments*, 31; "KD-88," *China's Defence Today*, 26 October 2008, http://www.sinodefence.com/airforce/weapon/kd88.asp.

6. The YJ-83 is a third variant of the basic YJ-8 ASCM (export designation of C-803). See DoD, *Military and Security Developments*, 3; Bill Gertz, "Chinese Missile Has Twice the Range U.S. Anticipated," *Washington Times*, 20 November 2002; and "YJ-83," *Missile Threat.Com*, http://www.missilethreat.com/cruise/id.67/cruise_detail.asp. The air-launched version is sometimes referred to as the YJ-83K.

ASCMs gives the PLAN flexibility and tactical depth, utilizing sub- and super-sonic speeds, short and extended ranges, and various warhead packages. The precise total of ASCMs in China's inventory is unavailable in open-source documents; however, estimates from available data and specifications indicate an arsenal in the several thousands.

The C-801 (YJ-8/HY-5)/802 (YJ-83) and C-802 (YJ-82) series is currently the backbone of China's ASCM inventory. It has a flight speed of Mach 0.9 and an operational range of 8 to 42 km. Strongly resembling and influenced by (though, according to one source, not reverse engineered from) France's MM38/MM39 Exocet, the C-801 is employed by the PLAAF JH-7 fighter. According to Chinese sources, one C-801 can immobilize a 3,000-ton destroyer and thereby render it a mission kill. This is a reasonable assessment: a C-801 carries a 165 kg semi-armor-piercing warhead, which is the same size as the Exocet, and there are ample examples of that size warhead disabling destroyers or frigate-sized warships.[3]

Developed by China Haiying [Sea Eagle] Electro-Mechanical Technology Academy (CHETA, alternatively known as the 3rd Space Academy), the C-802 is based on the C-801 but employs a different rocket motor, a turbojet with paraffin-based fuel. It was flight-tested in 1990 and, according to Western media sources, entered the PLAN inventory in 1994. Its launch weight has been reduced by 100 kg (warhead mass remains 165 kg) and its range has been increased to 15–120 km. Its speed is Mach 0.9, and it skims the sea at an altitude of 20–30 m. The major difference from France's Exocet, on which it is closely modeled, is the "installation of a rudder flight control system on the bottom."[4]

According to its manufacturer, the China National Precision Machinery Import and Export Corporation, the C-802A export variant has "strong defense penetrating capability, high hitting accuracy, [a] powerful warhead, [and] easy operation and maintenance." It is designed to attack a 5,000-ton-class destroyer with a radar cross section of at least 3,000 square meters. The C-802A can be launched from air-, ship- and land-based platforms. It features "multiple flight path[s] and waypoints, sea skimming flight altitude, multiple anti-jamming capabilities . . . fire and forget . . . and over-the-horizon attack [capabilities]." The C-802A's range is 15–180 km. It has up to four attacking paths with up to three points per path. A booster and turbojet propels it at Mach 0.8–0.9. Its flight altitude is 20 m when cruising and 5 or 7 m in terminal phase. For guidance, it uses strapdown intertial navigation system, a frequency agility radar, and digital control to achieve a single-shot kill probability of 90 percent. Its response time is 9 minutes cold, 30 seconds hot. The C-802A is 6.383 m long and 0.360 m in diameter, with a wingspan of 1.220 meters and a weight of 800 kg. Its 190 kg semi-armor-piercing blast warhead employs an electromechanical contact delay fuse.[5]

Chinese air-launched ASCMs also include the third-generation YJ-83K (C-803), which features a new high-frequency agile radar seeker and employs sea-skimming (20–30 m) during the terminal phase, delivering a 165 kg warhead to ranges up to 180 km. In September 2005 China unveiled a new ASCM known as the YJ-62, exported as the C-602. Propped alongside a much smaller YJ-82 (C-802) ASCM, the YJ-62 display model claimed subsonic speeds, striking ships at ranges of up to 280 km, against sea targets moving at speeds of less than 30 kn. The Office of Naval Intelligence (ONI) states that the "subsonic, sea-skimming" YJ-62 has a range of approximately 278 km and is "designed to sink or disable medium to large size ships."[6] According to Scott Bray, senior intelligence officer-China, ONI, "The YJ-62 is China's most capable indigenously produced ASCM. However, unlike the SS-N-27 *Sizzler*, the YJ-62 is a sub-sonic missile that does not have a super-sonic sprint vehicle."[7]

China has also reportedly acquired both variants of Russia's greater than Mach 2 Zvezda-Strela Kh-31 (AS-17 "Krypton") 70–200 km-range ramjet-powered sea-skimming missile. Following a joint program with Russia, China apparently has produced them indigenously (perhaps initially under license) as the YJ-91 and -93 variants.[8] China is also believed to have introduced the antiship radiation missile (ARM) variant, Kh-31A, capable of targeting a variety of maritime targets. The Kh-31A is expected to reach speeds of Mach 3.5 with an extended target range of 130 km, depending on cruise altitudes.[9] The PLAN's Sukhoi Su-30MK2 Flanker fighters, as well as perhaps its JH-7As, are reportedly fitted with the Kh-31. Russia specifically designed the Kh-31P passive high-speed anti-radiation (as opposed to Kh-31A active radar) version to assault Western radar systems (e.g., the U.S. Navy's SPY-1 and the U.S. Army's Patriot radar).

LACMs of the YJ Series

Other than building an LACM from scratch, the most direct route to developing one is to convert a simpler ASCM into a more complex land-attack system. China has explored precisely this route to developing cruise missiles for attack over land. China has turned to its own HY-2 (Haiying-2) ASCM, named Silkworm by Western intelligence, which has a range of about 100 km, as a test bed for a much more potent and capable LACM, the YJ-63, an air-launched LACM developed by CHETA and carried by the H-6D bomber. This missile possesses two to five times the range of its progenitor, the Silkworm, and, of course, true land-attack capability.[10]

The YJ-63.

At present, China's principal long-range air-launched weapons system is the YJ-63 (C-603) air-launched LACM. It was designed to provide standoff air-launched precision strike capabilities for PLAAF's H-6H bomber.[11] Some sources claim that the YJ-63 was developed from the HY-2 ship-to-ship or coast-to-ship cruise missile, which was subsequently replaced by a more advanced version, the YJ-6 (C-601). The latter antiship missile was employed on the naval variant of H-6 medium bomber, designated the H-6D. Both the H-6D naval variant and the H-6H PLAAF variant carry two cruise missiles launched from wing pylons. Reportedly deployed in 2004–5, it was apparently displayed during the 2005 Sino-Russian Peace Mission joint exercises. The YJ-63 is said to use a combined inertial and GPS/GLONASS mid-course guidance system and an electro-optical television system for the terminal attack phase, achieving a circular error probable (CEP) of 10–15 m while carrying a payload of 500 kg.[12] A later or perhaps slightly different version of the YJ-63, called KD-63, appears to have a solid rather than a glass window, implying that the KD-63 may employ a terminal guidance system other than an electro-optical television one, or that it may simply depend exclusively on satellite guidance updates of its inertial reference system.

The YJ-63's reported range varies from 200–500 km. This variance is not surprising for an ALCM: the actual range capability of aircraft-launched LACMs can be significantly longer than what manufacturers typically advertise publicly. Nothing is publicly known about the YJ-63's turbojet engine (called the FW41-B by one source), but it should propel the missile at a speed of roughly Mach 0.7. The YJ-63's lineage from the Silkworm missile is evident in available photographs of the missile. Looking very much like the HY-2 or its air-to-ground cousin, the YJ-6 (C-601), and the turbojet-equipped HY-4, the YJ-63 has a large round body with a correspondingly round nose. Its turbojet engine inlet, like the HY-4's, is located under the missile's body just behind the large delta wings. Like the HY-4, the YJ-63's tail control surfaces are arranged in an X-shape pattern. Open sources furnish little of value with regard to the dimensions of the YJ-63, but given its lineage, one might expect the missile's length to be just under 7.5 m, its diameter about 0.75 m, and its wingspan, 2.4 m. The overall weight is estimated to be in the range of 2,500 kg. Conceivably, the YJ-63 could be stretched to accommodate additional fuel plugs that would permit it to achieve a range of roughly 700 km without reducing the existing conventional payload of 500 kg. But what would really improve the range performance of first-generation Chinese LACMs would be a highly fuel-efficient turbofan engine.

The Dong Hai-10 (DH-10).

The challenge of monitoring LACM development programs is no more apparent than with the sudden emergence of China's DH-10, which was reported to have been tested for the first time in fall 2004. As described by a *Jane's* writer in 2004, the DH-10 is a ground-launched second-generation LACM with a range of 1,500 km. Conversely, DoD reports that the DH-10's range is 1,500+ km, and 200–500 missiles are already available for use on 45–55 ground-based launchers.[13] The missile is likely guided to its target by an integrated inertial/GPS reference system supported by a terrain contour mapping and digital scene matching for terminal homing, the combination of which should provide a 10 m CEP.[14] From the general appearance of the DH-10 in Internet pictures, the missile's lineage seems related to the Russian Kh-55, although its range is only half that of the Kh-55's.

While DoD's 2010 report refers to the DH-10 as "ground-launched," an air-launched variant may be developed as well.[15] DoD also states that "China is upgrading its B-6 bomber fleet . . . with a new variant which, when operational, will be armed with a new long-range cruise missile."[16] The report indicates that the B-6 variant armed with this air-launched LACM will extend the reach of China's regional precision strike capabilities out to 3,300 km, which is sufficient to reach Guam.[17]

Conclusion

Chinese air-launched ASCM and LACM development, like that of cruise missiles overall, has progressed rapidly. These efforts have yielded a significant increase in PLA capabilities. ASCMs and LACMs, along with other systems, are key components in Chinese efforts to develop antiaccess/area denial capabilities that will increase the costs/risks of U.S. forces operating along China's sensitive maritime periphery, including in a Taiwan contingency. LACMs offer China new options for conventional strike. These apply most to Taiwan scenarios, where ground-, sea-, and air-based systems could be employed, but are also of concern to Japan and the U.S. territory of Guam and provide a limited capability wherever PLAN aircraft can deploy. As their launch platforms improve steadily, ASCMs are increasingly poised to challenge U.S. surface vessels, particularly in situations in which the quantity of their fires is sufficient to overwhelm Aegis air-defense systems through saturation tactics. China plans to employ cruise missiles in ways that exploit synergies with other strike systems and that can allow cruise missiles to degrade air defenses and command and control to enable air strikes. Defenses and other responses to the People's Republic of China's cruise missile capabilities exist but will require greater attention and a focused effort to develop countermeasures and other responses.

While ALCMs have many advantages for China, their optimal employment requires accurate and timely intelligence; suitable and ideally stealthy delivery platforms; mission planning technology; command, control, and communications systems; and damage assessment. China has incorporated antiship and land-attack cruise missiles into its force structure, employing ground, air, surface, and subsurface means of delivery for particular missions. But to realize fully the potential benefits of such precision delivery systems, China will likely have to invest further in all the relevant enabling technologies and systems required to optimize cruise missile performance.

For now, however, China still lags in its capacity to orchestrate the delicate timing involved in coordinating combined missile and air strikes. China will also require time and dedicated effort to develop the confidence to rely on its ASCMs and LACMs to perform as imagined, particularly in challenging combined arms military campaigns. This is particularly true of air-launched variants, which are tethered to the performance parameters of their launch platforms.

Two caveats are particularly important to keep in mind. Force modernization depends not just on relentlessly building up missile inventories. Even more important is developing the capacity to extract as much value from these weapons as the order of battle suggests they might provide in principle. That depends on a multitude of additional factors, two of which bear mentioning here. First is the challenge of carefully orchestrating what is a complex multifaceted air and missile campaign over many days of execution. This depends critically on both human and technical factors—extremely well-trained military personnel who have practiced these routines in diverse ways over many years and the command and control architecture needed to deal with complex combined arms operations. Chinese planners envision creating a Firepower Coordination Center within the Joint Theater Command, which would manage the application of air and missile firepower. Separate coordination cells would be created to deal with missile strikes, air strikes, special operations, and ground and naval forces. Absolutely critical to achieving the delicate timing between waves of missile strikes designed to leverage the effectiveness of subsequent aircraft attacks is developing the skill to coordinate and deconflict large salvoes of missiles and waves of aircraft operating in multiple sectors. That China could be confident in successfully orchestrating such a complex joint campaign at present seems doubtful.

The second factor is a less obvious but nonetheless essential element to successful use of cruise missiles in warfare: the optimization of missiles to achieve their desired mission objective. Conventional wisdom has it that the revolution in information technology easily enables the precision delivery of conventional payloads over great distances in the form of LACMs aided by advances in global positioning technologies. To be sure, the advent of global positioning technology has eased the process somewhat, and sheer volume of fires can compensate for accuracy limitations to some extent. But the process of becoming truly proficient requires more than simple access to technology. To learn from their successes and errors requires that missile developers have not only the kind of sophisticated diagnostic equipment that provides hints about system performance but also highly skilled systems integration specialists who possess specialized know-how accumulated over years of interaction with other skilled missile developers.

Notes

Portions of this chapter draw on Dennis M. Gormley, Andrew S. Erickson, and Jingdong Yuan, *Chinese Cruise Missiles: A Quiet Force-Multiplier*, *China Security Perspective*, vol. 10 (Washington, DC: National Defense University, Institute for National Strategic Studies, 2011). The authors thank Jasper Liao for his research assistance, Dennis Gormley for reviewing the manuscript, and Phillip Saunders for numerous useful insights.

1. Office of the Secretary of Defense (DoD), *Military and Security Developments Involving the People's Republic of China 2010*, Annual Report to Congress (Washington, DC: DoD, 16 August 2010), 31, http://www.defense.gov/pubs/pdfs/2010_CMPR_Final.pdf.

2. Mark A. Stokes, *China's Strategic Modernization: Implications for the United States* (Honolulu: University Press of the Pacific), 81.

3. Unless otherwise specified, data in this paragraph derived from "CSS-N-4 'Sardine' (YJ-8/C-801); CSS-N-6 (YJ-83/C-802/Noor); YJ-62/C-602; YJ-82; CY-1," *Jane's Naval Weapon Systems*, 25 November 2009.

4. 姚绍福, 刘庆楣 [Yao Shaofu and Liu Qingmei], "中国的C-802岸舰导弹武器系统" ["China's C-802 Land Anti-Ship Missile System"], 中国航天 [*Aerospace China*] (July 1991): 39–42.

5. "C802A Anti-Ship Missile Weapon System," China National Precision Machinery Import and Export Corporation, 2008, trade brochure.

6. Office of Naval Intelligence (ONI), *The People's Liberation Army Navy: A Modern Navy with Chinese Characteristics* (Suitland, MD: ONI, July 2009), 27.

7. Scott Bray, senior intelligence officer-China, ONI, November 2009, statement obtained through ONI Public Affairs Office.

8. "Kh-31 (AS-17 'Krypton')," *Jane's Strategic Weapon Systems*, 4 September 2009.

9. Li Ziyu, "On the Development of China's Air-to-Ship Missiles," *Shipborne Weapons* (July 2006): 24–25. See also Chinese Military Aviation, "Air-Launched Weapons," June 2005, http://mil.jschina.com.cn/huitong/missile.htm.

10. Richard Fisher Jr., "China's New Strategic Cruise Missiles: From the Land, Sea and Air," International Assessment and Strategy Center, 3 June 2005; and "YJ-63 (KD-63) Land-Attack Cruise Missile," available at http://www.sinodefence.com.

11. The source for the YJ-63 manufacturer is "KongDi-63 Air-Launched Land-Attack Cruise Missile," *China's Defence Today*, http://www.sinodefence.com/airforce/weapon/kd63.asp.

12. Evan S. Medeiros, Roger Cliff, Keith Crane, and James C. Mulvenon, *A New Direction for China's Defense Industry* (Santa Monica, CA: RAND, 2005), 94. The deployment date comes from www.sinodefence.com.

13. DoD, *Military and Security Developments*, 66.

14. Wendell Minnick, "China Tests New Land-Attack Cruise Missile," *Jane's Missiles and Rockets*, 1 October 2004. Minnick cited a "U.S. defense source" as furnishing this information, which certainly sounds speculative.

15. DoD, *Military and Security Developments*, 2.

16. Ibid., 4.

17. Ibid., 32.

Michael S. Chase

Strategic Implications of Chinese Land-Attack Cruise Missile Development

MUCH SCHOLARLY ATTENTION has been devoted to China's rapidly growing ballistic missile force in recent years, but relatively little has been written
on China's development of its land-attack cruise missile (LACM) capabilities.[1] Considering the rapid increase in the number and sophistication of
Chinese short-range ballistic missiles (SRBMs), the deployment of China's
DF-31 and DF-31A road-mobile intercontinental ballistic missiles (ICBMs),
and the development of conventionally armed medium-range ballistic missiles
(MRBMs), including one intended to target aircraft carriers, it is understandable that Chinese LACM developments have been overshadowed to some
extent by these impressive ballistic missile force modernization efforts. The
development of Chinese LACM capabilities is clearly worthy of greater analytical attention, however, especially given its potential strategic implications
for the United States and its friends and allies in the region. Indeed, China's
public display of DH-10 LACMs during the 1 October 2009 military parade
that marked the sixtieth anniversary of the founding of the People's Republic
of China (PRC) appeared to demonstrate the People's Liberation Army's (PLA)
growing confidence in its LACM capabilities. As if to underscore the message sent by the appearance of the DH-10 LACM launchers in the parade, an
official Chinese media report carried comments by Lieutenant Colonel Gou

Yi, the Second Artillery officer in charge of the cruise missile formation, who described China's LACMs as "sharp swords" for precision attacks against regional targets. The same report also highlighted remarks by deputy commander of the Second Artillery Yu Jixun, who emphasized several key characteristics of the LACMs that were on display during the parade, including their long-range precision targeting, concealed deployment, and rapid response capabilities.[2]

This chapter attempts to fill some of the many large gaps in the unclassified literature on China's development of LACMs. Drawing on a variety of open sources, including Chinese scientific and technical journal articles, PLA newspapers, and unclassified U.S. government reports on Chinese military modernization, the chapter examines China's evolving LACM capabilities and assesses their likely implications for U.S. planners and policymakers. The key findings of the chapter are as follows:

- Chinese writings on the employment of Tomahawk cruise missiles by the United States in the Gulf War, Kosovo, Afghanistan, and Iraq not only reflect a deep interest in drawing on the "lessons learned" from these conflicts to improve the PLA's ability to defend against cruise missile attacks but also reveal that Chinese analysts have devoted considerable attention to analyzing the strengths and weaknesses of cruise missiles for conducting long-range precision strikes.

- China is developing and deploying air- and ground-launched LACMs in order to contribute to the enhancement of the PLA's conventional long-range precision-strike capabilities.

- Official Chinese media reports indicate that LACMs were first delivered to Second Artillery troops in 2006.[3] The U.S. Department of Defense (DoD) estimates that China had deployed about two hundred to five hundred DH-10 LACMs and forty-five to fifty-five launchers by December 2009.[4]

- The deployment of these LACMs is giving the PLA a number of options against potential targets in Taiwan, Japan, and the Philippines; China's LACMs will represent an especially potent threat if successfully integrated with China's growing air power, ballistic missile, intelligence, surveillance, and reconnaissance, and information and electronic warfare capabilities.

- China's development of a new long-range air-launched LACM and an upgraded variant of the B-6 bomber is likely intended to enable the PLA to conduct conventional attacks on regional targets it historically has been unable to reach with conventional weapons. Specifically, this development is probably motivated primarily by the desire to deny the U.S. military the opportunity to use Guam as a sanctuary during a regional conflict.

- China presumably could also develop conventionally armed intermediate-range ballistic missiles (IRBMs) capable of reaching Guam, but because such missiles could potentially be mistaken for nuclear-armed IRBMs, this would probably complicate escalation control dynamics more than the deployment of manned bombers armed with LACMs.

- The PLA's emerging LACM capabilities could also augment China's strategic forces if some of the cruise missiles were to be armed with nuclear warheads, but if China deploys both conventional and nuclear variants of its LACMs, this could increase the possibility of inadvertent escalation in a regional conflict, especially if an adversary were to accidentally strike nuclear-armed LACMs or their supporting command-and-control systems in the course of operations intended to target conventionally armed systems.

- Even if China does not deploy any nuclear-armed LACMs, employment of its conventionally armed LACMs could result in horizontal escalation by widening the geographic boundaries of a conflict to include Japan and the Philippines; bombers carrying long-range air-launched LACMs could broaden the geographic scope of a conflict to even more distant locations, including U.S. territory if they were used to strike targets on Guam.

- Looking further into the future, it is also possible that China could eventually attempt to develop conventional strategic strike capabilities to at least partially address the asymmetry in conventional strategic warfare capabilities that currently prevents the PLA from retaliating in kind if the United States launches conventional attacks against targets on the Chinese mainland. If so, the interaction between U.S. development of "conventional prompt global strike" weapons and China's potential interest in developing highly advanced long-range conventional strike capabilities of its own may further complicate efforts to maintain strategic stability in the U.S.–China relationship.

The remainder of the chapter explores Chinese views on the employment of LACMs in recent U.S. military operations, with particular attention to what Chinese analysts have written about the use of Tomahawk cruise missiles in the conflicts in Kosovo, Afghanistan, and Iraq; presents a brief overview of China's LACM capabilities; considers possible strategies and targets; and assesses the implications for the United States and its friends and allies in the region.

Chinese Writings on the Employment of LACMs in Recent Conflicts

Chinese analysts have studied recent U.S. military operations very closely, and quite a few authors have published their views on the employment of land-attack cruise missiles in recent conflicts. The employment of Tomahawk cruise missiles in Kosovo, Iraq, and Afghanistan has been of particular interest to Chinese writers, and they have noted what they see as both the advantages and the weaknesses of U.S. cruise missile capabilities. Many Chinese articles emphasize the importance of enhancing China's ability to defend itself against cruise missile attacks, but some also discuss the use of cruise missiles more broadly, perhaps providing some hints as to how China would plan to employ its own cruise missiles in a regional conflict. Indeed, Chinese writings on the employment of Tomahawk cruise missiles by the United States in the Gulf War, Kosovo, Afghanistan, and Iraq not only reflect a deep interest in drawing on the lessons learned from these conflicts to improve the PLA's ability to defend against cruise missile strikes but also reveal that Chinese analysts have devoted considerable attention to analyzing the strengths and weaknesses of cruise missiles as precision-strike weapons.

Chinese analysts highlight the long range, accuracy, multidirectional attack capabilities, and ability to launch from a variety of platforms as some of the key advantages of LACMs. Cruise missiles can be used to penetrate enemy air defense networks at low altitudes. They are highly accurate, highly maneuverable, and can be used to attack a target from any direction.[5] According to one recently published technical journal article,

> Cruise missiles can be launched in the air, at sea and on land, and they are usually long range, the maximum range being up to 1,000 km to 4,000 km. Cruise missiles mostly use inertial, terrain matching and image matching guidance systems, and with predetermined track flight they can attack from any direction. Current cruise missiles usually have Ma = 0.7 high subsonic flight (the development trend is toward supersonic speed), and they can execute ultra-low altitude defense penetration at altitudes of 50 to 100 meters. They are small, highly accurate and highly maneuverable.[6]

Among the other advantages of cruise missiles are that they are often difficult to detect and track. According to a Chinese military media report, "the cruise missile flies at a low altitude, can fly close to the ground in radar blind spots, and can maneuver to detour anti-air fire positions of the defensive side. It has weak radar and infrared signatures and can exploit surface-clutter cover and favorable terrain at minimum altitude for stealthy flight, making it hard for the defensive side to detect and track and even harder to down."[7] Similarly, analysts from the PLA Air Force Engineering University highlight detection of enemy cruise missiles as one of the main challenges of cruise missile defense. In their words, "detection by land-based radar is difficult because cruise missiles use low-altitude defense measures and stealth technology, and detection is affected by the curvature of the earth. The effect of land and sea clutter is also an important factor in reducing the probability of detection and identification."[8] In addition, Chinese analysts have also pointed out that cruise missiles (and ballistic missiles, for that matter) are relatively inexpensive, especially when compared to manned strike aircraft.[9]

Chinese analysts conclude that these advantages make cruise missiles an ideal weapon for long-range precision strikes and that this is why the U.S. military has employed cruise missiles extensively to conduct such strikes in a number of recent conflicts, including the Gulf War, Desert Fox, and Kosovo. According to a Chinese military media report,

> Cruise missiles are becoming main air attack weapons. After the Gulf War, having electronic warfare lead an operation, using cruise missiles first, and providing support with electronic reconnaissance have become the basic method of operation regarding modern air attacks. In the 38-day Desert Storm Operation, the multilateral force launched 323 cruise missiles. In the Desert Fox air attack operation against Iraq, the United States and Britain did not use warplanes to conduct air attacks, but, instead, achieved their operational objective by launching 415 cruise missiles in four days. In the first day of the Kosovo War, NATO lobbed 100 cruise missiles into the territory of Yugoslavia; NATO launched a total of 1,800 cruise missiles in the first 30 days of air attacks. With the continual development of technical performance of cruise missiles, cruise missiles are becoming the main "killers" in air attack operations under high-tech conditions.[10]

Chinese writers have also noted that cruise missile strikes are often among the opening shots of a conflict. According to one Chinese assessment of U.S. employment of cruise missiles in Operation Allied Force,

At 19:00 on the evening of 24 March [1999], the U.S. Navy "Philippines Sea" missile cruiser in the Adriatic Sea fired the first sea-based BGM-109D "Tomahawk" cruise missile at the FRY [Federal Republic of Yugoslavia], which was the "first shot" in the "Allied Force" air raids against the FRY. In the following two-month-plus large-scale air raids, the U.S.-led NATO forces fired over 2,600 air- and sea-launched cruise missiles such as the AGM-86B/C and BGM-109C/D at the FRY, for the largest missile strike since the Gulf War, which struck and destroyed many military and civilian FRY targets. We have seen clearly from this that cruise missile strikes have become the first killer in modern high-tech air raids.[11]

Another assessment that discusses the first-strike role of cruise missiles points out that they are often employed to enable follow-on strikes by manned aircraft but may also be used on their own. "With development in modern air defense weapons," according to the authors, "the traditional method of using aircraft to breach defense has been replaced by using cruise missiles to 'clear the way' first and then using aircraft and cruise missiles jointly to attack targets; sometimes, only cruise missiles are used to achieve air attack objectives."[12]

Chinese writers have also highlighted the employment of cruise missiles in Operation Desert Fox as a form of "non-contact warfare." According to a 1999 *Liberation Army Daily* article,

It should be noted that the use of a large number of tactical and cruise missiles in a war is nothing new. However, [Desert Fox] was perhaps the first time that a belligerent had used nothing but naval base-launched or air-to-surface missiles at the initial stage of an air strike. In the past, hundreds of planes would launch a surprise air strike at the same time. However, this time, the U.S.-British forces employed a new no-personnel and no-contact combat mode marked by "missiles carrying out and pilots watching the air strike."[13]

Overall, therefore, it is fair to say that the Tomahawk cruise missile generally receives high marks from Chinese writers. In the words of one Chinese analyst, for example, "The 'Tomahawk' cruise missiles on which the U.S. relied from the Gulf War and the war in Kosovo in the '90s to the recently concluded war in Afghanistan can be said to have performed in a dazzling manner."[14]

Despite the attention devoted to the Tomahawk's advantages and the favorable evaluations of its use in recent conflicts, however, Chinese authors also highlight some perceived weaknesses of cruise missiles. According to one source, "Developed in the 1970s, the U.S. 'Tomahawk' cruise missiles have displayed some vital weak points, including a low cruise speed, a small combat body, a large size, and so on. In all previous battles, the U.S. 'Tomahawk' cruise missiles had been shot down by the enemy."[15] Similarly, other Chinese authors highlight the vulnerability of Tomahawk cruise missiles to "hard kill," "soft kill," and deception.[16]

According to the authors of one article, "a 'hard kill' means using weapons such as SAM, air, and air-to-air missiles, or antiaircraft artillery [AAA] and machine guns, for a fire intercept of a cruise missile."[17] A number of Chinese military analysts have stated that Tomahawk cruise missiles are vulnerable to antiaircraft fire. For example, according to one Chinese author, "During the Gulf War in 1991, U.S. troops fired a total of 288 ship-launched Tomahawk missiles, and eight were hit by Iraqi antiaircraft artillery. They fired 24 Tomahawks at the Iraqi intelligence headquarters in June 1993, and one was hit by antiaircraft artillery. During 'Operation Desert Fox' by British and U.S. troops in December 1998, six Tomahawks were intercepted by Iraqi antiaircraft artillery. During NATO's air strike against Yugoslavia, over 100 cruise missiles were 'downed' by artillery."[18] Furthermore, according to the same author,

> The electromagnetic interference that accompanies their attack can easily paralyze radar early warning systems and missile guidance systems, which [operate based] on electromagnetism. Antiaircraft guns, however, mainly use optical devices and visual control. The shells are fired directly at the targets and are therefore not affected by electromagnetic interference. Antiaircraft guns also do not have blind spots. Restricted by their field of fire, they are usually deployed around protected targets. No matter how concealed their flight path is, cruise missiles have to pass through the air space covered by antiaircraft guns before reaching their targets. Thus, antiaircraft guns can engage cruise missiles in close quarters. They have a fast firing rate and have a large ammunition reserve. They form a thick artillery shield in the defense area when they are fired. Cruise missiles run the risk of being hit by missiles running through the gauntlet of this shield.[19]

Chinese analysts also discuss "soft kill" methods, such as electronic jamming. According to one article, electronic jamming "keeps the cruise missile from receiving the GPS navigation signal, keeps it from exchanging guidance signals between launch platforms, and makes the missile radar guidance head and altimeter malfunction, making the Tomahawk 'deaf' and 'blind,' finally leaving it 'deranged.'"[20] Denial and deception are also seen as potentially effective countermeasures. According to a military media report, "To 'guide into a trap,' one can place many fake AAA and SAM missile launch positions along its likely course, deliberately leaking 'secrets,' while tightly camouflaging the real launch positions, to lead the Tomahawk astray, so that it will bypass the real target and throw itself into the net. To 'practice deception,' one can issue phony battle reports on the types, numbers, locations, and means of downing cruise missiles, making it hard for the enemy to investigate battle damage."[21]

Similarly, another Chinese analyst writes: "Before launching cruise missiles, enemy forces need to input data on attack targets, and the data are based on analyses of various terrain reconnaissance and information analysis. In this regard, we can exploit our advantages in manpower and materials. Deploy large numbers of dummy targets and rapidly change terrain features around targets, so as to make cruise missiles attack the wrong targets or self-destruct because of having got lost."[22] Other Chinese writers have noted some additional weaknesses. For example, another Chinese writer argues that the Tomahawk missile has four serious shortcomings: limited maneuverability, subsonic speed, problems in environmental and weather conditions, and high per unit cost (about $1.45 million).[23]

Chinese analysts have noted that simply having deployed some cruise missiles is insufficient to carry out long-range precision strikes effectively. They point out that there are many requirements beyond possessing the missiles themselves. The strikes must be supported by effective intelligence collection and analysis, and battle damage assessment capabilities. Indeed, Chinese analysts have highlighted the importance of timely and accurate intelligence information to effective targeting of cruise missile strikes. According to one article about Operation Desert Fox, "It is no easy matter to launch an air strike on some hard-to-identify targets in a densely populated metropolis with hundreds of cruise missiles. The latest air strike showed that the U.S.-British forces had accurately reconnoitered, identified, and located targets; accurately transmitted information; and carried out accurate calculations."[24]

This level of attention to the shortcomings and vulnerabilities of cruise missiles may be largely a function of China's strong interest in improving its own cruise missile defense capabilities. This is a high priority for the PLA given the threat of cruise missile attack against high-value targets by the United States or perhaps Taiwan in the event of a cross-strait conflict. As the authors of one article published in *Liberation Army Daily* put it, "Cruise missiles pose a serious threat to our important targets," and cruise missile defense "is a critical issue with bearings on the overall operation."[25] Furthermore, according to the same article:

By effectively combating cruise missiles, we will be able to disrupt enemy air attack plans and make enemy forces not dare to throw their other air attack weapons into combat without inhibition, thereby protecting a substantial number of important targets and the main force of the air defense system and stabilizing the battlefield situation. In view of all this, we must be tilted in favor of combating cruise missiles in such areas as intelligence and early warning, electronic countermeasures, air- and ground-based air defense forces, and command and support and must center on combating missiles in operational deployment.[26]

Nonetheless, Chinese writings that address the limitations of the Tomahawk and other cruise missiles suggest that these assessments of cruise missile vulnerabilities may also influence China's plans for the employment of its own land-attack cruise missiles in future conflicts. For example, Chinese writers have clearly concluded that cruise missiles are much easier to intercept than ballistic missiles, suggesting that this would be taken into account in their planning for future military operations.[27]

Chinese Land-Attack Cruise Missiles

Not surprisingly, given that Chinese analysts view cruise missiles as very effective weapons, China is developing and deploying air- and ground-launched LACMs to contribute to the enhancement of the PLA's conventional long-range precision-strike capabilities. Indeed, the 2009 edition of DoD's annual report states that China is supplementing its SRBM forces with a variety of other conventional strike capabilities, including "at least two land attack cruise missile (LACM) variants capable of ground or air launch."[28] This section provides a brief review of some of China's current and emerging land-attack cruise missile capabilities. The first part covers ground-launched land-attack cruise missiles. The second covers air-launched land-attack cruise missiles. The third discusses potential types of warheads for China's LACMs, including conventional warhead options as well as possible nuclear-armed land-attack cruise missile developments.

Ground-Launched Cruise Missile Capabilities

Ground-launched cruise missiles (GLCMs) appear to form the cornerstone of China's emerging LACM deployments. According to the 2010 DoD report to Congress on Chinese military power, "The PLA is acquiring large numbers of highly accurate cruise missiles, such as the domestically-produced ground-launched DH-10 land attack cruise missile (LACM)."[29] The 2010 DoD report to Congress estimates that by December 2009 China had deployed about 200–500 DH-10 LACMs and 45–55 launchers, a dramatic increase from the estimate of 50–250 DH-10 LACMs and 20–30 launchers provided in the 2008 edition of the report.[30]

The 2010 edition of the DoD report states that the DH-10 has a range of about 2,000 km, allowing it to reach potential targets throughout Japan and the Philippines as part of China's emerging antiaccess strategy.[31] In a recent analysis of China's cruise missiles, Dennis Gormley, Andrew Erickson, and Jingdong Yuan assess that the DH-10 "may use not only a GPS/inertial guidance system but also terrain contour mapping for redundant mid-course guidance complemented by a digital scene-matching sensor to permit an accuracy of 10 m."[32] This level of accuracy could allow the DH-10 to be used against targets that must be struck with a high degree of precision, such as aircraft shelters and command-and-control facilities.

Air-Launched LACM Capabilities

China's land-attack cruise missile capabilities also include air-launched land-attack cruise missiles such as the YJ-63 and a new long-range air-launched LACM. The YJ-63 reportedly has a range of about 200 km and is carried by the PLAAF's B-6 bombers.[33] According to Gormley, Erickson, and Yuan, the YJ-63 employs "combined GPS/inertial navigation systems complemented by an electro-optical terminal sensor to achieve 10-15 m accuracy."[34] The range of the YJ-63 is relatively limited, but China is currently enhancing the PLAAF's air-launched LACM capability with an upgraded bomber and new long-range air-launched cruise missile (ALCM). According to the 2010 DoD report, "China is upgrading its B-6 bomber fleet (originally adapted from the Russian Tu-16) with a new variant which, when operational, will be armed with a new long-range cruise missile."[35] The same report indicates that this new variant of the B-6, when armed with this long-range LACM, will extend the reach of China's regional precision-strike capabilities out to about 3,000 km, bringing Guam within range of China's conventional antiaccess capabilities and for the first time enabling the Chinese military to strike targets on U.S. territory with conventional weapons.[36]

Types of Warheads

Cruise missiles are capable of carrying a variety of types of warheads, including conventional and nuclear weapons. Varieties of the U.S. Tomahawk cruise missile, for example, include the TLAM-N, which carries a W-80 nuclear warhead; the TLAM-C, which carries a 1,000-pound unitary conventional warhead; and the TLAM-D, a submunitions dispenser variant that carries 166 combined-effects bomblets.[37] Similarly, the U.S. AGM-86C/D conventional ALCM can carry a conventional high explosive warhead, blast fragmentation warhead, or advanced unitary penetrator warhead.[38]

Not surprisingly, therefore, China appears to be interested in a variety of types of warheads for its own LACMs. Indeed, Chinese researchers have written about several types of conventional warheads. For example, Chinese researchers have published articles that discuss arming cruise missiles with ground-penetrating warheads. The authors of one such article state that warheads with ground-penetrating submunitions can be used to attack targets such as airbase runways, and that other types of ground-penetrating munitions may be used against hardened shelters and underground facilities. The authors note that ground-penetrating submunition warheads are capable of "destroying airfield runways, tarmacs and hangars to paralyze enemy aircraft on the ground and prevent them from taking off for engagement, thereby gaining air supremacy."[39] Other types of missions indentified for ground-penetrating warheads include destroying hardened command, control, and communications facilities; power facilities; underground storage sites; and hardened shelters, and attacking enemy logistics facilities, such as ports, ordnance factories, and oil storage facilities.[40] Some observers have speculated that China may be interested in developing electromagnetic pulse or high-power microwave warheads for its cruise missiles.[41] In addition, according to an article recently published in *Jane's Missiles and Rockets*, China reportedly has developed a carbon filament warhead "designed to attack and disable a nation's electrical power grid."[42]

Chinese air- and ground-launched cruise missiles may also be capable of carrying nuclear warheads. The U.S. National Air and Space Intelligence Center's 2009 *Ballistic and Cruise Missile Threat* report indicates that the YJ-63 carries a conventional warhead only but lists the DH-10's warhead type as "conventional or nuclear."[43] Similarly, according to the 2009 DoD report, "New air- and ground-launched cruise missiles that could potentially perform nuclear missions would similarly improve the survivability, flexibility, and effectiveness of China's nuclear forces."[44] If armed with nuclear warheads, the PLA's emerging LACM capabilities could supplement China's strategic ballistic missile forces, which are currently being modernized to enhance their survivability and striking power. Whether China will ultimately choose to deploy nuclear-armed GLCMs or ALCMs, however, appears to remain an open question. Indeed, as Jeffrey Lewis has noted, the DoD report does not state that China has deployed nuclear-armed LACMs; it simply indicates that some Chinese cruise missiles may be capable of carrying nuclear warheads.[45] Whether China ultimately deploys an exclusively conventional LACM force or some conventional and some nuclear systems, however, China's development of LACM capabilities will have strategic implications for the United States and its allies and friends in the Asia-Pacific region.

Strategy and Potential Targets

According to the 2009 DoD report, "China is developing air- and ground-launched LACMs, such as the YJ-63 and DH-10 systems for stand-off, precision strikes."[46] Indeed, the deployment of highly capable LACMs will give the PLA a number of options to conduct strikes against targets in Taiwan, Japan, and the Philippines. According to Gormley, Erickson, and Yuan, "Employed in salvoes, perhaps in tandem with ballistic missiles, cruise missiles potentially could saturate, or overwhelm, defenses. A saturation attack would consist of a large number of cruise missiles arriving at a specific target in a short period of time in hopes of overwhelming defenses. Saturation could take a variety of forms, including the dispatch of more missiles than enemy radar systems, or interceptors, could handle."[47] Yet successfully executing such attacks requires much more than the cruise missiles themselves. As Gormley, Erickson, and Yuan note, "optimal employment of cruise missiles requires accurate and timely intelligence, suitable and ideally stealthy delivery platforms, mission planning technology, command, control, and communications systems, and damage assessment."[48] Indeed, some of these areas present technological and organizational challenges, but China's LACMs will pose an especially potent threat if the PLA is able to successfully integrate its emerging LACM forces with its manned aircraft, ballistic missile, intelligence, surveillance, reconnaissance, and information and electronic warfare capabilities. Land-attack cruise missiles thus represent an important aspect of China's growing antiaccess/area denial approach.

As part of a Taiwan campaign incorporating the PLA's antiaccess/area denial capabilities to blunt U.S. intervention, Chinese LACMs could threaten regional air and naval bases as well as transportation, communications, and logistics targets. In particular, ground- and air-launched LACMs could pose a serious threat to air bases when employed as part of an antiaccess approach that also incorporates large numbers of ballistic missiles. According to a recent study by the RAND Corporation, "China's ability to suppress Taiwan and local

U.S. air bases with ballistic and cruise missiles seriously threatens the defense's ability to maintain control of the air over the strait."[49] For example, LACMs could be used in a Taiwan scenario to conduct precision strikes against targets such as command-and-control nodes and hardened aircraft shelters. The latter could be an especially important target for LACMs. According to the RAND study, "Low-flying, accurate cruise missiles can be effective against aircraft shelters because, absent deliberate precautions on the part of the defense, they can be targeted on the shelter's doors. The doors must, of course, move and are therefore lighter and more vulnerable than the shelter's thick concrete walls and roof. Even if the missile cannot penetrate the door, it can achieve a 'functional kill' on the shelter by jamming it closed, preventing the aircraft inside from getting out."[50]

Chinese sources confirm that these cruise missile strikes would be part of a broader campaign of combined firepower and information warfare attacks. Specifically, the Second Artillery plans to conduct "missile firepower strikes" (导弹火力打击) that combine ballistic and cruise missile attacks and to integrate these operations with "information attacks" (信息攻击) involving computer network and electronic warfare capabilities.[51] Indeed, DoD also assesses that Chinese attacks against regional bases and logistics facilities would incorporate LACMs, short-range ballistic missiles, medium-range ballistic missiles, special operations forces, manned aircraft, and computer network and electronic warfare attacks.[52]

Perhaps most importantly, the PLAAF's long-range air-launched LACMs could be employed to deny the United States the opportunity to use more distant bases as sanctuaries in a U.S.–China conflict over Taiwan or another potential regional flashpoint. Specifically, manned bombers carrying air-launched LACMs could pose a serious threat to targets as far away as Guam. As the 2008 DoD report on Chinese military power notes, "Strike aircraft, when enabled by aerial refueling, could engage distant targets using ALCMs equipped with a variety of terminal-homing warheads."[53] Even a relatively small number of bombers could carry enough cruise missiles to conduct a potentially serious attack against a target such as Andersen Air Force Base, which is located on the northern end of Guam.

Conclusion and Implications

Although much greater attention has been devoted to China's rapidly increasing ballistic missile capabilities, the PLA's development of LACMs will also have strategic implications for the United States in a number of areas. First, cruise missiles will contribute to a growing threat to facilities in Taiwan as well as Japan and other countries, including U.S. military bases. Indeed, Chinese cruise missiles will pose a serious threat to a number of critical bases and other facilities that could potentially be used by U.S. forces in the event of a regional crisis or conflict. This threat will become especially serious if China is able to successfully integrate cruise missile strikes into plans that also incorporate manned aircraft strikes, ballistic missile attacks, and information and electronic warfare operations.

Second, China's development of long-range ALCM capabilities will transform Guam from a possible sanctuary into a potential target for long-range precision strikes.[54] Indeed, China's interest in developing such a capability is presumably intended to enable the PLA to conduct long-range conventional attacks on regional targets that it historically has been unable to reach with conventional weapons. This option is probably motivated primarily by the desire to deny the U.S. military the opportunity to use Guam as a sanctuary during a regional conflict with China.

Third, there is a possible risk of inadvertent escalation if China deploys both conventionally and nuclear-armed LACMs. The PLA's emerging LACM capabilities could also augment China's strategic forces if some of the cruise missiles were to be armed with nuclear warheads, but if China deploys both conventional and nuclear variants of its LACMs, this could increase the possibility of inadvertent escalation in a regional conflict, especially if an adversary were to accidentally strike nuclear-armed LACMs or their supporting command-and-control systems in the course of operations intended to target conventionally armed systems.

Fourth, even if China chooses not to deploy any nuclear-armed LACMs, the deployment of conventional LACMs could increase the possibility of horizontal escalation. Ground- and air-launched LACMs could expand the geographic boundaries of a regional conflict, and further escalation control complications could arise if Chinese bombers carrying long-range LACMs were used to attack Guam.

Fifth, there is at least some possibility of facing even more difficult escalation control issues related to future conventional strategic warfare capabilities. China is almost certainly uncomfortable with its inability to retaliate in kind if the United States launches conventional attacks on the mainland. China presumably would like to address this imbalance and thus may be expected to at least consider pursuing capabilities that would allow it to do so. For example, China could eventually develop conventional strategic weapons that would allow the PLA to address, at least partially, the asymmetry in conventional strategic warfare capabilities that currently prevents China from retaliating in kind if the United States launches conventional attacks against targets on the mainland. In the longer-term, the interaction between the possible U.S. development of "prompt global strike" weapons and China's potential interest in developing highly advanced long-range conventional strike capabilities of its own may further complicate the U.S.–China strategic security relationship. U.S. development and deployment of revolutionary "prompt global strike" capabilities would likely increase Beijing's incentives to respond with similar conventional strategic attack capabilities of its own, potentially raising unprecedented escalation control issues in the event of a U.S.–China crisis or conflict.

Notes

1. One notable exception is Dennis M. Gormley, Andrew S. Erickson, and Jingdong Yuan, *Chinese Cruise Missiles: A Stealthy Force-Multiplier*, China Strategic Perspectives (Washington, D.C.: National Defense University, Institute for National Strategic Studies, 2011).

2. "China's Cruise Missiles 'Sharp Swords' for Precision Attacks," *Xinhua*, 1 October 2009, http://news.xinhuanet.com/english/2009-10/01/content_12146104.htm.

3. Ibid.

4. Office of the Secretary of Defense (DoD), *Military and Security Developments Involving the People's Republic of China 2010*, Annual Report to Congress (Washington, DC: DoD, 16 August 2010), 31–66, http://www.defense.gov/pubs/pdfs/2010_CMPR_Final.pdf.

5. Zhao Jiandong and Zhao Yingjun, "Analysis of U.S. Military Precision-Guided Weapons and Counterattack Technologies," 飞航导弹 [*Winged Missiles Journal*] (June 2007): 12–16.

6. Ibid.

7. Liu Jiangping, Zhu Weitao, and Hu Ziwei, "Three Ways to Counter Cruise Missiles: Soft Kill, Hard Destruction, and Clever Inducement," 解放军报 [*Liberation Army Daily*], 15 September 1999, 7, OSC FTS19990927001872.

8. Zhao and Zhao, "Analysis of U.S. Military."

9. Ibid.

10. Li Jie and Gong Zhiming, "Where Should the Focus of Air Defense Be Located?" 解放军报 [*Liberation Army Daily*], 7 March 2000, 6, OSC CPP20000308000046.

11. Liu et al., "Three Ways to Counter Cruise Missiles."

12. Li and Gong, "Where Should the Focus of Air Defense Be Located?"

13. Zhang Zhaozhong, "'Desert Fox' in Perspective," 解放军报 [*Liberation Army Daily*], 12 January 1999, 6.

14. Tang Baodong, "U.S. Intensifies Weaving of New 'Space Net'—From TMD and NMD to CMD," 解放军报 [*Liberation Army Daily*], 25 December 2002, 12.

15. Zhang, "'Desert Fox' in Perspective."

16. Liu, Zhu, and Hu, "Three Ways to Counter Cruise Missiles."

17. Ibid.

18. Yang Yulin, "Antiaircraft Artillery—Magic Weapon against Tomahawk," 解放军报 [*Liberation Army Daily*], 20 July 1999, 6, OSC FTS19990810000893.

19. Ibid.

20. Liu et al., "Three Ways to Counter Cruise Missiles."

21. Ibid.

22. Jia Fengshan, "Will It Be Possible to Fight 'Quality' With 'Quantity'?" 解放军报 [*Liberation Army Daily*], 7 March 2000, 6.

23. Yang, "Antiaircraft Artillery."

24. Zhang, "'Desert Fox' in Perspective."

25. Li and Gong, "Where Should the Focus of Air Defense Be Located?"

26. Ibid.

27. Tang, "U.S. Intensifies Weaving of New 'Space Net.'"

28. Office of the Secretary of Defense (DoD), *Military Power of the People's Republic of China 2009* (Washington, DC: DoD, March 2009), viii, http://www.defenselink.mil/pubs/pdfs/China_Military_Power_Report_2009.pdf.

29. DoD, *Military and Security Developments*, 2.

30. Ibid., 66. For the 2008 estimates, see DoD, *Military Power of the People's Republic of China 2008* (Washington, DC: Department of Defense, March 2008), 56, http://www.defenselink.mil/pubs/china.html.

31. DoD, *Military and Security Developments*, 32.

32. Gormley et al., *Chinese Cruise Missiles*.

33. See "KongDi-63 Air-Launched Land-Attack Cruise Missile," *China's Defense Today*, 20 October 2008, http://www.sinodefence.com/airforce/weapon/kd63.asp.

34. Gormley et al., *Chinese Cruise Missiles*.

35. DoD, *Military and Security Developments*, 4.

36. Ibid., 23.

37. "United States Navy Fact File: Tomahawk Cruise Missile," 20 February 2009, http://www.navy.mil/navydata/fact_display.asp?cid=2200&tid=1300&ct=2.

38. Boeing, "AGM-86C/D Conventional Air-Launched Cruise Missile (CALCM)," http://www.boeing.com/defense-space/missiles/calcm/docs/CALCM_overview.pdf.

39. Liu Yongyuan, Jiang Zhengping, and Zhang Jin, "Ground Penetration Munitions and Their Development Trends," 飞航导弹 [*Winged Missiles Journal*] (March 2006): 34–37.

40. Ibid.

41. See Richard Fisher Jr., "China's New Strategic Cruise Missiles: From the Land, Sea, and Air," 3 June 2005, http://www.strategycenter.net/research/pubID.71/pub_detail.asp.

42. Robert Hewson, "China Develops Cluster Bomb to Target Power Supplies," *Jane's Missiles and Rockets*, 18 March 2009, http://www4.janes.com/subscribe/jmr/doc_view.jsp?K2DocKey=/content1/janesdata/mags/jmr/history/jmr2009/jmr71372.htm@current&Prod_Name=JMR&QueryText=.

43. National Air and Space Intelligence Center, *Ballistic and Cruise Missile Threat*, April 2009, 29, http://www.fas.org/programs/ssp/nukes/NASIC2009.pdf.

44. DoD, *Military Power of the PRC* (2009), 24.

45. See Jeffrey Lewis, "DH-10," *Arms Control Wonk*, 14 July 2008, http://www.armscontrolwonk.com/1945/dh-10. As Lewis points out, "the language is *could* and *would*, not *do* and *will*."

46. DoD, *Military Power of the PRC* (2009), 22.

47. Gormley et al., *Chinese Cruise Missiles*.

48. Ibid.

49. David A. Shlapak, David T. Orletsky, Toy I. Reid, Murray Scot Tanner, and Barry Wilson, *A Question of Balance: Political Context and Military Aspects of the China-Taiwan Dispute* (Santa Monica, CA: RAND, 2009), 139, http://www.rand.org/pubs/monographs/MG888/.

50. Ibid., 61.

51. Second Artillery Corps, 弟二炮兵战役学 [*The Science of Second Artillery Campaigns*] (Beijing, PLA Press, 2004), 78.

52. DoD, *Military Power of the PRC* (2008), 23.

53. Ibid., 21.

54. Ibid.

PART V

Maritime Strike

Ballistic Missiles

Ron Christman

Conventional Missions for China's Second Artillery Corps
Doctrine, Training, and Escalation Control Issues

OVER THE LAST SEVENTEEN YEARS, China's land-based offensive missile force has developed a conventional missile component, and its inventory is now seven times as large as the Second Artillery Corps' nuclear arsenal. Key drivers of this inventory of more than one thousand short-range ballistic missiles and an emerging class of theater ballistic and ground-launched cruise missiles have been a need for firepower support to combat operations in potential conflict scenarios involving Taiwan, China's assessment of the role of missiles in modern warfare, and requirements for missiles at other points on its periphery than Taiwan.

Potential missions for China's conventional missile force in crisis situations would be to perform military deterrence operations, including shows-of-force and "surgical strikes" against crucial enemy assets as a form of "strategic deterrence." In wartime, conventional missile force units would serve missions related to providing preparatory or direct fire support to combat operations by People's Liberation Army (PLA) services to seize air, sea, ground, and information superiority or to conduct follow-on operations. Wartime operations would usually be directed by a joint command, especially firepower strike or anti–air raid campaigns; however, conventional missile units might also be organized into an "independent" missile strike campaign formation.

Data and access limitations make it difficult to discern if there are cultural frictions between the majority of Second Artillery officers with predominantly nuclear backgrounds and the growing number of officials with conventional missile credentials. The emergence of a conventional missile force in the PLA has created new opportunities for PLA ground, navy, and air force campaigns to receive conventional firepower support from the Second Artillery Corps. In return, the PLA services are likely to provide operational and defensive support to conventional missile force operations, given deficiencies in the Second Artillery Corps' organic reconnaissance, early warning, information operations, and air, ground, or electronic defense capabilities.

The Second Artillery Corps' growing conventional missile force provides an operational-tactical and strategic capability in-theater without the political and practical constraints associated with nuclear-armed missiles. The Corps' emerging inventory of conventional antiship ballistic missiles (ASBMs) also affords the PLA an extra employment option that enhances its layered defense posture against potential offshore threats beyond Taiwan. This conventional ASBM inventory extends the outer edge of this layered defense beyond the current operating range of most of its PLA Navy (PLAN) and PLA Air Force (PLAAF) components.

The Second Artillery Corps' conventional missile force provides the PLAN with a nonorganic means of fire support to potential PLAN campaigns, including operations to seize local sea superiority, conduct a naval blockade, or support an amphibious landing. Over time, conventional Second Artillery Corps units and PLAN antiship cruise missile units might explore coordinated structured attack options, especially in a missile defense environment.

Finally, the Second Artillery Corps' conventional missile capability, operational doctrine, and threat perceptions create conditions for China's escalation to conventional missile attacks against U.S. or allied forces and bases in the Asia-Pacific region, including potential ASBM strikes against U.S. Navy aircraft carriers in any hypothetical mainland China–Taiwan conflict. China's senior leaders would be more likely to authorize such strikes if they endorse Second Artillery Corps perceptions of a severe threat to missile operations from potential U.S. electronic warfare–based information operations and joint firepower attacks.

Modernizing and Expanding Conventional Missile Force

For most of its forty-five-year history, China's land-based offensive missile force, the Second Artillery Corps of the PLA, has served noncombat and combat missions involving the use of nuclear weapons: nuclear deterrence, counternuclear deterrence intimidation, and nuclear counterattack operations. Since 1994 the Second Artillery Corps has added a conventional missile component to its existing offensive missile force.[1]

This conventional component is only seventeen years old, and it comprises roughly one-quarter of the Second Artillery Corps' composition of deployed operational units. Nonetheless, its inventory of conventional weapons and equipment is about seven times as large as the Second Artillery Corps' relatively small nuclear-capable weapons arsenal. Moreover, the conventional inventory of the Second Artillery Corps continues to modernize and expand, as outlined below:

- According to the Department of Defense (DoD) 2010 annual China report, as of early 2010, China's Second Artillery Corps maintains at least five operational short-range ballistic missile (SRBM) brigades.[2] Another SRBM brigade is deployed with the PLA ground forces in Nanjing Military Region (MR), and a second one is deployed in the Guangzhou MR.[3]

- These units are garrisoned opposite Taiwan, based on official U.S. DoD and Republic of China documents as well as other sources.[4] DoD's 2010 report indicates that, as of December 2009, the major weapons and equipment inventory of these deployed units totals between approximately 1,050 and 1,150 SRBMs (350–400 CSS-6 and 700–750 CSS-7 SRBMs) and 210–250 associated mobile launchers.[5] In the past few years this inventory of deployed missile systems has increased at a rate of more than 100 missiles per year, although the rate has recently slowed.[6]

- China is reportedly upgrading the quality of these short-range missiles systems—including methods to counter ballistic missile defenses. China reportedly has developed a new version of the CSS-6 SRBM, the DF-15C, with a terminally guided warhead, maneuvering fins, and the capability to penetrate underground bunkers.[7] An improved version of China's original CSS-7 missile has an extended range of 500–700 km, an accuracy of 500–600 m, and fuel-air explosive and submunitions warheads.[8]

- These SRBMs are accurate enough and possess enough variety of warheads to pose a serious threat to a wide range of targets on Taiwan. A recent RAND Corporation assessment used Monte Carlo techniques to model an SRBM attack on Taiwan. According to this simulation, depending on accuracy, between 90 and 240 SRBMs could, with proper warheads, crater every runway at Taiwan's half-dozen main fighter bases and destroy essentially all of the aircraft parked on ramps in the open at these installations.[9]

In recent years the Second Artillery Corps has moved to enhance the capability and range of its conventional missile force component by developing and fielding theater ballistic and cruise missile capabilities that would enable Beijing to threaten Taiwan or other potential adversaries at deeper ranges (along or beyond its periphery) with weapons systems that project force beyond the 1,000-km-range limit of SRBMs.

The Second Artillery Corps reportedly has formed at least three cruise missile brigades, two based in southern China and one in northwestern China, presumably equipped with DH-10 ground-launched, land-attack cruise missiles (LACMs).[10] China reportedly tested a DH-10 in 2004, which could rely on multiple navigation systems and achieve a circular error probable of 10 meters.[11] DoD's 2010 report reveals the Second Artillery Corps is equipped with 200–500 DH-10s and 45–55 associated launchers as of December 2009.[12] A recent nongovernmental study asserts China has the world's largest inventory of ground-launched LACMs.[13] Combined with air-launched YJ-63 or DH-10 cruise missile systems, the ground-launch DH-10 and these air-launched systems provide China with different options for standoff precision attacks.[14]

The Second Artillery Corps is also reportedly acquiring land-based conventional medium-range ballistic missiles (MRBMs) with ranges extending beyond 1,500 km to increase the range to which it can conduct precision strikes, including any possible use in targeting naval ships operating far from China's shore—including counter-carrier operations.[15] According to nongovernmental sources, the Second Artillery Corps fielded a new-type conventionally armed, solid-propellant, mobile MRBM in 2004–5 with a maximum range of 1,700 km.[16] A conventional version of the nuclear DF-21 MRBM has been deployed, according to media commentary by Chinese officials during the 1 October 2009 National Day Parade. DoD's 2010 report indicates PLA defense planners are investing in a combination of conventionally armed ASBMs based on the CSS-5 (DF-21) airframe, C4ISR (command, control, communications, computers, intelligence, surveillance, and reconnaissance) for geolocation and tracking of targets, and onboard guidance systems for terminal homing to strike surface ships on the high sea or their onshore support infrastructure.[17]

The total number of conventional-theater ballistic missiles China is developing or intends to deploy is unclear. DoD's 2008 report describes a new ASBM "based on a variant" of the DF-21. Some nongovernmental experts speculate that the variant would be a DF-21C, and they contend this would make the ASBM system a DF-21D.[18] One Chinese shipbuilding industry source also posits that by 2010 the Second Artillery Corps would control one ASBM brigade armed with DF-21E ASBMs.[19] Another expert opines that up to five Second Artillery Corps brigades are candidates to be equipped with DF-21C MRBMs.[20]

China continues to enhance and diversify its existing nuclear arsenal of an estimated 130–160 nuclear-capable delivery systems, which is capable of ranging most of the world, including the continental United States.[21] Key trends include integrating solid propellant road-mobile intercontinental-range ballistic missiles, building up to 5 *Jin*-class nuclear-powered ballistic missile submarines—each capable of carrying 10–12 submarine-launched ballistic missiles (SLBMs), and researching ballistic missile defense (BMD) countermeasures—including maneuvering reentry vehicle warheads, multiple independently targeted reentry vehicles, technical BMD countermeasures, and antisatellite weapons.[22] Nonetheless, these nuclear force trends and developments are taking place in a context in which land-based conventional missile systems and associated operational units are assuming a greater proportion of the Second Artillery Corps' order of battle.

The emergence of this conventional missile force raises important issues regarding the origins, drivers, missions, doctrine, training activities, and institutional dimensions of this relatively new component. This chapter will establish a baseline understanding of these issues. It will conclude by assessing the implications for escalation control in any possible future war between China and Taiwan, the PLA's development of long-range strikes at sea, and PLAN development.

Origins of the Conventional Missile Force

Over the last fifteen years, various observers have periodically opined that China's original motive in developing conventional missiles was to acquire weapons for export abroad to generate foreign capital in support of military and other modernization efforts.[23] This line of reasoning alleges that China's equipping the PLA with conventional missiles was a response to domestic and international support for the independence movement in Taiwan, tensions in relations between China and Taiwan, and China's analysis of global military trends—including the increased role of high technology weapons during the first Persian Gulf War in 1991 and several conflicts since then.

The author does not doubt China has sold conventional missiles abroad to generate currency, including the earlier sale of M-11 (CSS-7 Mod 1) missiles to Pakistan and the more recent codevelopment of B611 short-range surface-to-surface missiles by the China Academy of Defense Technology and the Turkish weapon manufacturer MKEK.[24] However, careful analysis of Chinese military decision-making and strategic assessments in the mid-1980s suggests that the Chinese Communist Party's (CCP's) Central Military Commission (CMC) directed China's space and missile industry in late 1984 to shift its emphasis from liquid- to solid-fueled ballistic missiles, and from strategic to "tactical" ballistic missiles. This new emphasis on tactical (presumably conventional) missiles was driven by a requirement to provide the PLA an effective means of countering the former Soviet Union's limited war fighting style of "deep operations" by land, air, and naval forces.[25]

By the mid-1980s, the PLA faced a fundamental threat to the three northern MRs from the Soviet Union's style of "limited war" fighting that involved more than the Soviet Union's deployment of highly accurate SS-20 nuclear intermediate-range ballistic missiles (IRBMs), modern Backfire bombers, and an expanded Pacific Fleet in the Soviet Far East. From the PLA's perspective, the Soviet Union was in fact preparing to conduct a multidirection, air/land, deep-penetration operation against China that emphasized ground forces as the operational keystone of combined operations; a deep, swift offensive battle exploiting nuclear and conventional firepower; and the use of tanks and armor for land advance with rocket troops, aviation, and airborne landings to seize or strike key targets in the deep rear of the Chinese front, with a goal of rapidly achieving the most immediate operational objectives.[26] The PLA assessed that the Soviets would seek to rapidly pierce the front lines of any PLA defense, drive deep into the PLA's rear area, sever lines of communication, destroy key targets, and seize key operational objectives within the northern three MRs.

After contrasting the operational agendas, combat potentials, and doctrinal tenets of the Soviet Red Army and the PLA, Chinese planners concluded that the PLA's best choice was to develop the ability to delay Soviet invasion forces and their heavy weapons and deliver a devastating blow against the Soviet deep rear while strengthening the PLA's frontal defensive line against frontal attacks.[27] They assessed that China's traditional center of gravity was a frontal land battle; however, they doubted that the PLAAF or PLAN would be able to provide any real-time, accurate fire support to ground force operations along the front, which would force the PLA to employ force mobility to compensate for inadequate firepower. PLA infantry forces would never be able to compete with the mobility of Soviet firepower and advancing mechanized forces. Nonetheless, these planners identified weaknesses in Soviet combat potential, including its unfamiliarity with the terrain, undefended space between its offensive and defensive combat formations, and vulnerable combat systems that could be paralyzed by striking weapons—command, control, communications, and intelligence (C3I) assets; logistical systems; and a relatively undefended rear area.[28]

The PLA intended to develop the capability to initiate asymmetric strikes—including the employment of tactical conventional missiles—against limited, high-value targets located in the Soviet deep rear. In part, this intent was based on an assumption that new conventional weapons and more revolutionary technologies could generate the same effects in future limited war as do nuclear weapons, but with more precision and less collateral damage.[29] It was also based on an assumption that the employment of precision-guided munitions in asymmetric strikes would offer some force protection in the face of a mechanized second echelon of Soviet forces. The PLA judged there were weak and susceptible nodes in the Soviet operational system—including command posts, C3I, weapon control systems, and electronic warfare troops. Because these "soft targets" were complicated structures based on unified systems, the PLA speculated that damaging one part could lead to the collapse of entire systems and significantly degrade the effectiveness of advancing Soviet forces.[30]

Key Drivers of the Conventional Missile Force

The origin of China's interest in conventional missiles is rooted in the PLA's response to a bygone threat from the former Soviet Union along its northern land frontier. Since the demise of the former Soviet Union, key trends in China's approach to conventional missile warfare—the development of a diverse portfolio of conventional systems, the equipment of deployed Second Artillery Corps (SAC) units with conventional SRBMs, and the more recent emergence of new theater ballistic and cruise missile capabilities in the Corps' inventory—have been driven by potential conflict scenarios for the PLA involving Taiwan, China's assessment of global warfare trends, and the need for the PLA to prepare for conflict scenarios at other points along its strategic periphery than the Taiwan Strait area.

As former deputy undersecretary of defense Richard P. Lawless described it in 2004, Beijing's growing conventional missile force provides a strategic capability without the political and practical constraints associated with nuclear-armed missiles. The PLA's SRBMs (and theater missiles) provide a survivable and effective conventional strike force and represent a real-time coercive option.[31] China's conventional theater missiles provide conducting a means of large-scale theater air raids which, when combined with other force enablers, would position China to gain decisive advantage in seizing control of the skies in any conflict along its periphery due to inherent difficulties in defending against these missiles.[32] The deterrent and coercive value of these SRBMS, for instance, was widely recognized in the run up to Taiwan's first presidential election in March 1995. In two separate episodes, China launched CSS-6 SRBMs near Taiwan in June 1995 to demonstrate its displeasure with the visit of former Taiwan president Lee Teng-hui to Cornell University, and later, in March 1996, in an effort to intimidate support of independence for Taiwan and to influence the outcome of Taiwan's first direct presidential election.[33] These demonstrations failed to deter Taiwan's populace from electing Lee Teng-hui as president. However, PLA books and journals point to these shows of force as demonstrating "powerful deterrence" against the "swollen arrogance" of the influence of Taiwan independence, as "displaying" China's "determination and capability" to maintain the unity of the homeland, as "demonstrating" China's serious and justified stand" on the Taiwan issue to the entire world, and as serving to "check the conspiracy to split the motherland."[34] The use of missile launches near Taiwan in 1995–96 is credited by Second Artillery Corps strategists with generating multiple studies that have "filled a blank in conventional guided missile theories of the Second Artillery Corps."[35]

China's emphasis on conventional ballistic and cruise missiles is also driven by its perception that the lethality and destructiveness of such firepower has resulted in it becoming the "primary method of annihilating enemies in modern warfare" which "permeates through offensive combat so that it has become an independent form of combat to achieve offensive goals.[36] The role of missiles in high technology warfare has created circumstances in which the position and role of the fire component in combat operations has been elevated to the point where "fire is no longer merely a support power, but a means of attack with equal value to maneuver. It can even play a decisive role in certain specific phases of a war" and "missile weapons can achieve the strategic objective of deterring and restraining the enemy."[37]

In emphasizing the development of conventional offensive missiles, the PLA and the SAC systematically studied and derived lessons from every major recent war or limited conflict since Israel's attack on Iraq's Osirak nuclear reactor in 1981 in which offensive missile firepower has played an important role.[38]

For example, the PLA's National Defense University completed case studies on eight conflicts between 1986 and 2003.[39] China's military and its civilian leadership have drawn some important lessons from these recent cases of firepower warfare.

One of the main lessons derived from these case studies is that the massive employment of air-power weapons with high information content, precision-guided weapons, and cruise missiles make it possible to accomplish campaign objectives directly through the combined firepower attack of multiple services.[40] The joint firepower strike campaign has emerged as a new PLA campaign form in recent years. In most scenarios where a joint firepower strike campaign would be organized and implemented, commentary by PLA authors indicate the Second Artillery would be the "primary assault force."[41]

A second lesson learned is that deep strikes within a theater of war are an important new operational pattern in modern warfare. According to the Second Artillery's seminal document on missile campaigns, former CCP general secretary and CMC chairman Jiang Zemin indicated the use of "middle-distance strikes" by allied forces in the 1991 Gulf War, the 1998 Desert Fox operation, and NATO air operations in Kosovo in 1999 revealed that the use of missiles with "tactical" and "campaign" ranges was a new operational pattern in warfare.[42] The precise meaning of Jiang's reference to "middle-distance strikes" or "campaign ranges" is unknown. In the context of current PLA weapons system developments, Jiang is probably referencing conventional MRBMs and possibly IRBMs—including various MRBMs current being developed and deployed to field units.

A third lesson learned is that conventional missile firepower would be a useful tool for deterrent, coercive, or war-fighting purposes in various non-Taiwan contingencies for which the PLA must plan and prepare. According to DoD, new SAC units outfitted with conventional theater-range missiles at various locations in China could be used in a variety of non-Taiwan contingencies.[43] A quick scan of Corps literature reveals that the offensive missile force contemplates the use of conventional missiles in several non-Taiwan scenarios, mostly "joint border counterattack campaigns" and "joint anti-air raid campaigns."[44] Presumably, these border or anti–air raid campaigns would involve potential contingencies with India, North Korea, Russia, Vietnam, and the Central Asian states.

Conventional Second Artillery Corps Missions

Based on analysis of PLA and SAC documents and on commentary by SAC officials, the Second Artillery has specific conventional missions in peace, crisis, or wartime. Peacetime missions include conducting training launches for new conventional SRBMs, participating in joint triservice operational exercises, and demonstrating for senior CCP Politburo CMC leaders.[45] Depending on the circumstances, these specific missions can be executed by Second Artillery Corps units independent of other PLA service operations, or these units can serve as one force component of a joint PLA operation. In general, the conventional SAC force is responsible for the core missions of deterring threats to national unity, sovereignty, and territorial integrity and of military deterrence of any foreign intervention in dispute resolution between China and third parties over sovereignty and territorial integrity.

Some PLA sources characterize the conventional missile force as serving solely "defensive" missions of containing the outbreak of war, preventing a war from escalating, protecting Chinese targets, and reducing damage from an adversary's attack.[46] However, the missions of the Corps' conventional missile force also require the initiation of preemptive or coercive offensive missile attacks against adversaries at or beyond China's periphery. The current emphasis on initiating missile attack operations contrasts with the original Chinese impetus for developing conventional missiles for defensive counterattacks against deep-strike operations into northern China by the former Soviet Union.

Crisis-Related "Deterrent" or "Surgical Strike" Operations

Conventional missile forces are responsible for implementing two types of missile operations to employ in crisis situations to meet the force's core missions of defending Chinese sovereignty and territorial integrity and exercising "military deterrence" of a foreign force. While these operations are characterized as a form of military deterrence, some of these operations would involve limited conventional missile strikes against an adversary's high-value assets to meet "strategic deterrence" missions.

The Corps' concept for missile deterrent operations has been articulated in the 2001 and 2006 versions of the PLA's *Science of Campaigns* publication as well as in the Second Artillery Corps' 2004 *Science of Second Artillery Campaigns* document.[47] In 2005 a former deputy commander of the Second Artillery Corps published a comprehensive book on "coercive deterrence warfare," which provides a more detailed explanation of these concepts.[48] The PLA defines "deterrence fire support" as the use of firepower assets, including conventional ballistic missiles, in activities designed to "instill fear in our adversary by a show of force or by demonstrating our resolve and readiness to use our fire support forces" in a "war of nerves between the enemy and us."[49] The goal of instilling fear is to "coerce our adversary either to refrain from taking hostile actions or to abandon its military objectives completely." Actions that the PLA has contemplated taking to exercise deterrence firepower support include using the "physical existence of fire support" to coerce the enemy to "yield psychologically" by "displaying our colors" in a show of force, or to "dominate the initiative" in the balance with the enemy by "executing a small portion" of our fire support.[50]

As this last reference implies, the PLA's concept of so-called conventional deterrence includes threatening to use or using conventional ballistic missiles or other firepower assets during local wars in a "surgical strike," according to seminal PLA Academy of Military Science and National Defense University writings.[51] The academy's *Science of Strategy* document explicitly identifies these surgical strikes as the employment of "strategic deterrence" rather than the coercive use of force.[52] According to a definitive PLA writing on modern firepower warfare, firepower assets—including conventional ballistic missiles—can be employed in "psychological fire support" operations involving "selective strikes" against crucial enemy assets to coerce the enemy into yielding to Chinese interests.[53] More specifically, selective strikes against Taiwan have been referenced in these writings as a potential response to "provocative activities" or "threats" by Taiwan or as a form of firepower support of Chinese combat operations designed to seize the offshore islands.[54] The PLA's concept of a surgical strike appears to be a by-product of its case study of what it refers to as the joint "surgical war" on Libya by the United States on 15 April 1986 in the name of antiterrorism. During Operation El Dorado Canyon, China has concluded, the United States employed advanced electronic warfare aircraft, bombers, carrier-borne attack aircraft, antiradiation missiles, laser-guided missiles, and other Navy and Air Force weapons to paralyze the Libyan armed forces' air defense system and to accurately destroy five high-value targets covered by these air defenses.[55]

Potential Wartime Missions

Multiple sources indicate conventional missile forces are assigned wartime missions involving either conducting independent firepower strikes or supporting PLA combat operations designed to achieve air, ground, naval, and information superiority.[56] According to the PLA's authoritative definition of a conventional missile strike campaign, combat operations by conventional missile units are "usually conducted as one component of a joint PLA campaign."[57] The Chinese conceive of the missions of these units as either preparatory or direct fire support to surface maneuver operations. Most wartime missions involve supporting maneuver operations by other PLA services or otherwise contributing to a joint PLA operation. However, the PLA and the Second Artillery see the potential for conventional missile units to meet missions involving an "independent" conventional missile strike campaign geared to seize strategic objectives without any significant coordination with other PLA services.

PLA doctrine has identified specific fire support missions for the Second Artillery Corps. These missions support combat operations by PLA ground, air force, and navy surface offensive forces and information operations units at the direction of a joint command authority.[58] Initial operations are usually intended to seize air, sea, ground, and information superiority on the battlefield as a necessary precondition for follow-on operations against specific operational objectives. These fire support missions can be characterized as follows:

- Assisting PLA ground force, amphibious landing, and counter-landing campaigns. Preparatory fire support to ground operations is likely to involve the following potential enemy targets: artillery and missile launch positions, command posts and communications hubs, radar stations, air defense systems, transportation hubs, rear base and supply systems, and deep enemy force concentrations.

- Supporting PLAAF and PLAN aviation air assault and air defense operations designed to counter enemy air raids, seize control of the skies, or conduct long-range firepower assaults. Potential enemy targets include airfields, radar stations, air defense systems, and communications and command centers as well as missile launch positions.

- Supporting PLAN operations, especially amphibious landing operations and naval blockades of key control points. Conventional missile units could create a firepower blockade line by launching missiles. Potential enemy targets would include maritime operations support infrastructure (harbors and naval bases), warship formations, and aircraft carrier strike groups.

- Participating in operations to gain control of the information spectrum by assaulting enemy command centers and electronic warfare systems. Potential enemy targets would include operational command centers, electronic warfare systems (reconnaissance, early warning, and air defense radars). High-value targets would include destroying important enemy ground and sea-based reconnaissance and surveillance platforms.

Conventional missile units are mostly likely to be assigned a wartime mission to support joint PLA operations under the direction of a joint command authority. However, a so-called firepower campaign large formation could also be organized to command and coordinate an "independent conventional missile strike campaign" by SAC units. An independent conventional missile campaign might be implemented to provide "preparatory fire assault" to create conditions for maneuver forces to achieve offensive combat objectives.[59] If so, while Corps unit activities would be conducted under the rubric of an "independent" campaign, the mission would involve applying firepower to support maneuvers by other PLA services.

In contrast, an independent conventional missile campaign could also be organized during wartime to conduct a selective "warning strike" against some sensitive target. The goals of such a warning strike would be to display China's military strength and determination to prevent an ongoing war from escalating, to protect Chinese targets, to limit damage from an adversary's attack, or to coerce the enemy into yielding to Chinese interests.[60] Potential targets would include important civilian industrial and nuclear power bases as well as urban targets such as political, war-supporting industry and economic centers. Were this the case, the Corps would be positioned, relative to other PLA services, as a separate service tasked with meeting a specific strategic-type mission assigned by higher authorities independent of missions and activities being performed by PLA ground, naval, and air forces.

Operational Doctrine

The Second Artillery Corps' concepts for deploying and employing conventional missile units are heavily influenced by perceptions of a severe threat environment that these units are likely to operate in during any future conflict scenario—especially a mainland China–Taiwan war involving direct foreign military intervention to help Taiwan defend itself. Hence, this section will first summarize these perceptions and characterize how they impact operational missile force concepts.

Threat Environment

The SAC assumes, in any hypothetical wartime scenario including U.S. military intervention, that its conventional missile forces would face a severe, multidimensional, in-depth threat from electronic warfare–based information operations and destructive joint firepower attacks involving long-range precision-strike capabilities and a potential surprise attack. The battlespace would include six spectrums (land, air, maritime, space, electromagnetic, and cyberspace) and all-weather day or night operations.[61] The Corps also assumes that its units would operate in conditions of nuclear threats, at a minimum, because of the perceived unwillingness of the United States to declare a "no first use of nuclear weapons" policy and because of Chinese views of the evolution of the U.S. nuclear posture.[62]

Strategists anticipate Chinese offensive missile operations would face specific "hard" and "soft" threats from U.S. and allied operations, as outlined below.

- *Satellites and airborne reconnaissance.* The battlefield would be transparent for the United States because of its possession of multiple and "incessant," high-resolution, space-based reconnaissance satellites and airborne reconnaissance means. The prospect for missile exposure would be high, especially at fixed support installations, because missile units mobilize large quantities of equipment, and these units are active on a regular basis in operational areas.[63] As one document described it, "under a situation when the enemy's military reconnaissance technology and missile aiming precision is continually increasing, their appearance is equivalent to destruction."[64]

- *Electronic- and information-based warfare.* The enemy will conduct electronic, computer network, and communications "confrontation activity" against missile units—especially prior to the initiation of firepower attack. This activity would include electronic jamming and interference, computer network penetration, and software virus attacks against the SAC's "nervous system" for communications and coordination.[65]

- *Air raids and precision strikes.* The enemy would massively employ aviation Corps weapons, precision-guided weapons, and cruise missiles from air-, sea-, and land-based platforms—including long-range precision-strike assets. The SAC assesses sea- and land-based weapons using precision guidance to have a direct hit ratio of greater than 50 percent.[66]

- *Ground attack.* Missile force operations would face a ground threat from enemy airborne landings, special operations forces, and "agents" operating in China.[67] Although the SAC anticipates a threat from enemy airborne landings of ground troops, it views this threat as a secondary air threat compared to air raids with precision-guided weapons.

- *Missile defense.* The Corps assumes its conventional ballistic missile attack on any potential enemy targets would have to penetrate midcourse and terminal-phase ballistic missile defenses deployed in the Asia-Pacific region, based on its assessment of the trends in the U.S. nuclear or strategic posture and of U.S. missile defense deployments and bilateral missile defense cooperation and arrangements with Japan, South Korea, and Taiwan.[68] The Chinese recognize that any future missile attack by the Corps might have to penetrate boost-phase ballistic missile defenses. However, they view the prospects of this capability emerging as less likely than improvements in midcourse or terminal defenses due to political and technical challenges. This point of view has probably been reinforced by recent political developments associated with the U.S. airborne laser program.[69]

Based on these threat perceptions, the Corps anticipates that its missile forces would be one of the first PLA assets attacked during any conventional PLA campaign, to include a surprise attack by the enemy. The missile force has identified the following components of its operational system as being high on the enemy's target list, in descending order of importance: command, communication, and intelligence processing centers; missile bases; engineering and logistics support systems, including storage sites; wartime operational deployment positions, including technical, readiness, transit, and launch positions; and movement infrastructure, including highways, railway lines, tunnels, bridges, and traffic hubs.[70]

Concept of Operations

The Second Artillery Corps' approach to campaigns prioritizes gaining "information superiority" to create conditions enabling an effective first strike. Because the Corps assumes its enemy (i.e., the United States) would have absolute superiority in conventional missile firepower, its strategists believe that the only way China can gain the initiative in missile warfare is to first gain information superiority.

The Second Artillery Corps' basic operating concept is to implement electronic warfare–based information operations prior to initiating a first strike.[71]

In most circumstances, this first strike would be executed as a component of a joint firepower strike campaign. The intent is to "control the enemy in advance" by executing before the enemy expects China to do so.[72] From the Corps' perspective, several elements would be critical to enabling the success of such operations:

- "Strong maneuverability" and "defensive" attributes would be critical to forestalling the enemy's effort to use initiative and firepower to counter China's attempt to control the enemy by seizing information superiority.[73]

- Operating in darkness or poor weather, exploiting gaps in the enemy's reconnaissance coverage, or otherwise concealing deployment activities would be central to the survival of deployed forces as they move from garrison or storage locations to original launch positions, concealed areas, or follow-up launch positions.[74]

- To minimize exposure to enemy reconnaissance and attack, operations would also emphasize quick operating tempos by crews as they prepare for field operations and as they relocate to hide or reload sites.[75] During rapid maneuver drills at a missile base in the summer of 2010, information on enemy "satellite passes" was transmitted through the command network at an operational site when orders were sent to different units.[76]

While most operational activities would seek to enable a "preemptive" or "initial" launch, the Corps anticipates the need to conduct "follow-up" and "supplemental" strikes against a second list of targets or against targets that have not received sufficient damage to cause functional or physical defeat.[77] The Second Artillery Corps' operating concept emphasizes "integrated and unified" operations as the key to victory. Conventional missile firepower strike and conventional deterrence activities as well as offensive, defensive, or support activities should all be integrated.[78] Indeed, strategists have expressed concern that necessary reconnaissance intelligence, air defense, and communications support from other services constitute an "out-of-control" factor in missile force campaign plans.[79]

Based on its perception that missile force operations will be conducted under conditions of nuclear deterrence or threat, conventional missile strike operations "will necessarily involve the Second Artillery Corps nuclear missile unit's deterrence activities."[80] The Corps intends to apply the "law of steadily increasing the strength of nuclear deterrence to prepare for the transition" to unlikely but possible nuclear counter-attack operations. Nuclear missile and warhead units should be the "basic deterrence forces" used to deter nuclear threats or attacks and contribute to political and diplomatic struggles during a conventional missile campaign.[81]

Notes

The viewpoints and opinions expressed in this chapter reflect solely the author's personal views and do not represent the views of the Defense Intelligence Agency, the Department of Defense, or any other U.S. government agency.

1. See Richard D. Fisher, "China's Missiles over the Taiwan Strait: A Political and Military Assessment," in *Crisis in the Taiwan Strait*, ed. James R. Lilley and Chuck Downs (Washington, DC: National Defense University with American Enterprise Institute, 1997), 169.

2. Office of the Secretary of Defense (DoD), *Military and Security Developments Involving the People's Republic of China 2010*, Annual Report to Congress (Washington, DC: DoD, 16 August 2010), http://www.defense.gov/pubs/pdfs/2010_CMPR_Final.pdf, 66.

3. See Mark Stokes and Ian Easton, *Evolving Aerospace Trends in the Asia-Pacific Region: Implications for Stability in the Taiwan Strait and Beyond* (Arlington, VA: Project 2049 Institute, 27 May 2010), 15.

4. DoD, *Military and Security Developments*.

5. Ibid., 2, 66.

6. Office of the Secretary of Defense (DoD), *Military Power of the People's Republic of China 2008*, Annual Report to Congress (Washington, DC: Department of Defense, March 2008) http://www.defenselink.mil/pubs/china.html, 2; and DoD, *Military and Security Developments*, 31.

7. See Richard Fisher Jr., "New Chinese Missiles Target the Greater Asian Region," *International Assessment and Strategy Center*, 24 July 2007, available at http://strategy.center.net.

8. See "DF-11/M-1 (CSS-7) Short Range Ballistic Missile" data sheet, *China's Defence Today*, available at www.sinodefense.com.

9. David A. Shlapak, David T. Orletsky, Toy J. Reid, Murray Scot Tanner, and Barry Wilson, *A Question of Balance: Political Context and Military Aspects of the China-Taiwan Dispute* (Arlington, VA: RAND Corporation, MG888, 2009), xv.

10. See the data sheet for "Land-Attack Cruise Missile (LACM)," last updated on 7 May 2007, available at www.sinodefence.com.

11. Wendell Minnick, "China Tests New Land-Attack Cruise Missile," *Defense News*, 21 September 2004.

12. DoD, *Military and Security Developments*, 31, 66.

13. Stokes and Easton, *Evolving Aerospace Trends*, 14–15.

14. See DoD, *Military Power of the PRC 2008*, 24, 56.

15. DoD, *Military and Security Developments*, 2.

16. See "DF-21C/DF-25 Conventional Medium Range Ballistic Missile" data sheet, *China's Defence Today*, November 2008, available at www.sinodefence.com.

17. DoD, *Military and Security Developments*, 2.

18. See Jeffrey Lewis, "DF-21 Delta aka CSS-5 Mod 4," *Arms Control Wonk*, 14 October 2008, available at www.armscontrolwonk.com.

19. See Qiu Weizhen and Long Haiyan, "A Discussion about the Development of Chinese Anti-Ship Ballistic Missiles (Combat Scenario)," *Modern Ships* (January 2007).

20. See Stokes and Easton, *Evolving Aerospace Trends*, 13.

21. Admiral Robert Willard, Commander, Pacific Command, March 2010 Testimony to Congress, available as appendix B, in Ronald O'Rourke, *Chinese Naval Modernization: Implications for the U.S. Navy, Background and Issues for Congress*, Congressional Research Service, RL33153, 9 April 2010.

22. See DoD, *Military and Security Developments*, 34–35, and table, p. 66.

23. Meredith Lauren Blank, "Hugging with Tactical Arms: What Motivates China to Export Weapons?" Thesis, Department of Political Science, University of Michigan, May 2009, http://deepblue.lib.umich.edu/bitstream/2027.42/63929/1/blank_meredith_2009.pdf.

24. See "B611 Tactical Short-Range Ballistic Missile" data sheet, *China's Defence Today*, available at www.sinodefense.com.

25. For more on this shift in ballistic missile development priorities, see Mark A. Stokes, "The People's Liberation Army and China's Space and Missile Development: Lessons from the Past and Prospects for the Future," in *The Lessons of History: The Chinese People's Liberation Army at 75*, eds. Laurie Burkitt, Andrew Scobell, and Larry M. Wortzel (Carlisle, PA: Army War College, 2003), 211–12.

26. See Li Jijun, *Military Theory and War Practice* (Beijing: Military Studies Dictionary, 1994), 149–57.

27. See Bi Jianxiang, "Unlimited Means and Limited Targets: PLA Operations 1985–2000," unpublished manuscript, Carleton University.

28. Huang Xuejun, ed., "Opinions on the Tactics Development of our Army in 2000," in *New Explorations of Tactics Development*, vol. 1, Hao (first name unknown), ed., 89–94 (Beijing: Military Science Press, 1988).

29. Gao Rui, "View on Tactics Development and Research," in *New Explorations of Tactics Development*, vol. 1, ed. Hao (first name unknown), 5–10 (Beijing: Military Science Press, 1988).

30. See Huang Hanbiao, "Explorations of Total Deep, Three-Dimensional Offensive Tactics," in *New Explorations of Tactics Development*, vol. 1, ed. Hao (first name unknown), 251–53 (Beijing: Military Science Press, 1988).

31. "Statement by Richard P. Lawless," Deputy Under Secretary of Defense, International Security Affairs, Asia-Pacific, Senate Foreign Relations Committee, Subcommittee on

East Asian and Pacific Affairs, 23 April 2004. The text of this statement is included in the following article: "Defense Official Says China Transforming Its Military Establishment," 23 April 2004, *The Information Warfare Site*, http://www.iwar.org.uk/news-archive/2004/04-23-3.htm.

32. See Stokes and Easton, *Evolving Aerospace Trends*, 11–12.

33. See Fisher, "China's Missiles over the Taiwan Strait," 167.

34. "Second Artillery Force," section 4 in *Fundamental Artillery Tactics* (Changsha: National Defense Technology University, February 2001), 295; see also Zhang Wannian, *Contemporary World Military Affairs and China's National Defense* (Beijing: Liberation Army Press, December 1999), ch. 4, sec. III.

35. See Toshi Yoshihara, "Chinese Missile Strategy and the U.S. Naval Presence in Japan: An Operational View from Beijing," *Naval War College Review* 63, no. 3 (Summer 2010): 57n64.

36. Yao Gangning, *Teaching Materials on Tactics for Combined Armed Offensive Attacks* (Beijing: Academy of Military Science, May 2000).

37. Li Yuankai, chief editor, *High Technology and Modern Warfare*, 1st ed. (Beijing: Military Art and Literature Press, 1998), OSC CPP20061220320004.

38. Academy of Military Science, Strategic Research Department, *Science of Strategy* (Beijing: Military Science Press, 2000), 347.

39. Hu Limin and Ying Fucheng, *Study on Joint Firepower Warfare Theory* (Beijing: National Defense University Press, 2004).

40. Yu Jixun, ed., *The Science of Second Artillery Campaigns* (Beijing: Liberation Army Press, March 2004), 29.

41. Zhou Xin and Zou Hanbing, "Issues of Second Artillery Coordination in Joint Operations," *Military Art Journal* (July 2004): 71–74.

42. Yu, *Science of Second Artillery Campaigns*, 69.

43. See DoD, *Military Power of the PRC 2008*, 29.

44. See ch. 12 in Yu, *Science of Second Artillery Campaigns*.

45. Liu Xiaodu and Wang Xuezhong, "Reporter's Interview with Missile Brigade Commander Xie: Charging to Control the High Ground of Training," *Huojianbing bao* [*Rocket Forces News*], 6 October 2001.

46. Li, *High Technology and Modern Warfare*.

47. Huang Bin, *Science of Campaigns* (Beijing: National Defense University Press, 1999), ch 14; Wang Houqing and Zhang Xingye, editors, Huang Bin, associate editor, et al., *On Military Campaigns* (Beiijing: National Defense University Press, May 2000); Yu, *Science of Second Artillery Campaigns*; Part 6, Chapter 31, "Campaigns of the Second Artillery," in Zhang Yulang, Chief Editor, *The Science of Campaigns* (Beijing: National Defense University Press, May 2006), 616–28.

48. Zhao Xijun, ed., *Coercive Deterrence Warfare: A Comprehensive Discussion of Missile Deterrence* (Beijing: National Defense University Press, May 2005).

49. *Modern Firepower Warfare* (Changsha: National Defense Science and Technology University, 2000), ch. 12, "Special Fire Support," sec. 1, "Psychological Fire Support."

50. Ibid.

51. Hu and Ying, *Study on Joint Firepower Warfare Theory*; and Peng Guangqian and Yao Youzhi, *Science of Military Strategy* (Beijing: Strategic Research Department, Military Science Press, 2005), 182, 187, 347, and 407.

52. Peng and Yao, *Science of Military Strategy*, 182.

53. *Modern Firepower Warfare*, in particular, ch. 12, sec. 1, "Psychological Fire Support."

54. *Modern Firepower Warfare*.

55. Hu and Ying, *Study on Joint Firepower Warfare Theory*, ch. 7, sec. 1, "U.S. Military's 'Surgical'-Style Joint Firepower Strikes Against Libya," 289–94.

56. See Yu, *Science of Second Artillery Campaigns*, ch. 12; *Science of Campaigns*, 1999, 2001, and 2006 editions; *Fundamentals of Artillery Tactics* (Changsha: National Defense Technology University, February 2001); *Modern Firepower Warfare*; "Operational Command of Conventional Missile Forces," and "Conventional Missile Strike Campaign," in Fu Quanyou, Chief Editor, *Chinese Military Encyclopedia*, suppl. vol. (Beijing: Military Science Press, 2002), 25; National Defense University (NDU), *Campaign Theory Study Guide* (Beijing: National Defense University Press, 2003); and Wang Xiadong and Sun Shihong, "Operational Employment of Second Artillery in Joint Firepower Strikes," *Military Art Journal* (July 2004).

57. Lu Xiangdong and Huang Wei, "Conventional Missile Strike Campaign," in Fu, *Chinese Military Encyclopedia*, 26.

58. See NDU, *Campaign Theory Study Guide*, question 52.

59. See Yao, *Teaching Materials on Tactics*. See also Liu Xinli, "Missile Strike Groups Should Be the Basis for Coordinating the Organization of Initial Comprehensive Fire Power Strike," *Military Art Journal*, no. 4 (April 2003).

60. See *High Technology and Modern Warfare*; and *Fundamentals of Artillery Tactics*.

61. The elements of the SAC's perceived threat environment have have been extracted, for the most part, from various sections of Yu, *Science of Second Artillery Campaigns*. These threat perceptions are corroborated in other documents or statements authored by the Second Artillery Headquarters or its subordinate organizations as well as individual SAC officials.

62. Yu, *Science of Second Artillery Campaigns*, 27, 50, 73, 104, 126, 127, 168, 220, and 227.

63. Ibid., 52–58, 63, 70, 78, 242, 260, and 285.

64. Ibid., 242. For an additional source that identifies enemy reconnaissance operations as the Corps' primary threat, see Wang Xueping and Huang Hei, "The Main Forms of Diversified Security Threat," *Xuexi Shibao* [*Study Times*], 31 March 2008, OSC CPP20080409622003.

65. Yu, *Science of Second Artillery Campaigns*, 64. For an additional source identifying the electromagnetic threat as the second-most important threat to Corps operations, including the use of nonnuclear electromagnetic pulse bombs, see Wang and Huang, "Main Forms," n57.

66. Yu, *Science of Second Artillery Campagins*, 287.

67. References to a ground-based threat can be found in Yu, *Science of Second Artillery Campaigns*, 92, 264, 113, 188, and 193–95.

68. See "CCTV-7 Defense Review Week Discusses Purpose of Japan's Missile Defense System," CCTV-7, 29 November 2008, OSC CPP20081201338002.

69. See "U.S. House Panel Adds Missile Defense Funds, *Defense News*, 12 May 2010. Available in the "Missile Defense Headline Update, May 7, 2010 to May 13, 2010," at http://www.missiledefenseadvocacy.org.

70. References to the enemy's target sets and the relative ranking of these sets can be found in Yu, *Science of Second Artillery Campaigns*, 42, 47, 49, 70, 77–79, 93, 103, 124–26, 153–54, 161, 187, 238, 241, 260, 279, 287, and 297.

71. For a detailed argument that SAC conventional missile doctrine "is in a nascent stage and thus potentially incomplete, see Evan S. Medeiros, "Minding the Gap: Assessing the Trajectory of the PLA's Second Artillery," in *Right Sizing the People's Liberation Army: Exploring the Contours of China's Military*, ed. Roy Kamphausen and Andrew Scobell, 165–69 (Carlisle, PA: Army War College, 2007). In contrast, the findings in this chapter suggest that the Corps has a well-developed and thought through operational doctrine directly related to an in-depth capability-based understanding of the threat posed to these operations.

72. Yu, *Science of Second Artillery Campaigns*, 91.

73. Ibid., 76. For additional information on the SAC's emphasis on maneuvering operations, see Sun Xianfu, Xia Hongqing, and Xu Yeqing, "Make the Main Artery to the Battlefield Smoother—On the Spot Report on Improvement of Diversified Support Capability of the Military Traffic System of the PLA SAC," *Liberation Army Daily*, 15 August 2008, OSC CPP20080815710010.

74. Yu, *Science of Second Artillery Campaigns*, 182, 196, 265, 303, 309, and 311.

75. Ibid.

76. Yang Yonggang, Xu Ruibin and Feng Jinyuan, "Thick Smoke on the Drill Ground . . ", Notes from the Rapid Maneuver Operation Drills of a Base in the Second Artillery," *Jiefangjun Bao* [*Liberation Army Daily*], 4 July 2010, OSC CPP20100705708006.

77. Yu, *Science of Second Artillery Campaigns*, ch. 12, sec. 3, 263–70.

78. See ibid., 48–49, 73, 99, and 168.

79. Ibid., 170.

80. Ibid., 127.

81. The quotations in this sentence and the one before refer to ibid., 232.

Andrew S. Erickson and David D. Yang

Chinese Analysts Assess the Potential for Antiship Ballistic Missiles

CHINA'S ANTISHIP BALLISTIC MISSILE (ASBM) system of systems, which reached the equivalent of initial operational capability by December 2010, is the world's first weapons system potentially capable of targeting a moving aircraft carrier strike group (CSG) from long-range, land-based mobile launchers. Achieving an ASBM capability offers China the prospect of limiting the ability of other nations, particularly the United States, to exert military influence on China's maritime periphery, which contains several disputed areas of core strategic importance to Beijing (e.g., Taiwan). ASBMs are regarded as a means by which technologically limited developing countries can overcome by asymmetric means their qualitative inferiority in conventional combat platforms because the gap between offense and defense is the greatest here.

China's open-source literature does not establish conclusively the extent to which its land-based ASBMs or operational tactical ballistic missiles (TBMs) are capable of effective attacks on surface ships. But while China has not been truly transparent with respect to ASBM development, the different open-source voices do cohere in their own way. This shift in tone suggests that China is conducting advanced flight tests on, and may even be in the process of fielding, an ASBM. In the view of most Chinese and some Western analysts, even the mere perception that China might have achieved an ASBM could represent a paradigm shift with profound consequences for deterrence, military operations, arms control, and the balance of power in the Western Pacific. In light of these developments, it is useful to survey relevant Chinese writings for possible insights into the challenges that People's Liberation Army (PLA) faces in developing a successful ASBM system, and to explore how the PLA might ultimately seek to use an ASBM system for deterrence purposes—and, in a worst-case scenario, operationally.

Historical Background

For more than three decades, with a slow and uncertain beginning, Chinese leaders and strategists have been thinking of using land-based missiles to hit threatening targets at sea. Figure 1 offers a timeline of these efforts.

The U.S. MaRVed Pershing II (潘兴-2) TBM—deployed in 1983—was studied intensively by Chinese analysts beginning in the late 1970s, resulting in more than fifty related articles. The Pershing II has been cited in Chinese sources as influencing the development of China's DF-15C and -21 ballistic missiles. Following the Pershing II's deployment, similar initial "research work" was reportedly completed in 1991, published in 1994, and incorporated into China's Dongfeng missiles in the form of a "warhead that possesses terminal homing guidance and maneuvering control capability" in 1999.[1]

The end of the Cold War removed the Soviet threat, eliminating what had been a potent rationale for U.S.–China cooperation; Beijing's 1989 Tiananmen crackdown and Taiwan's concomitant democratization further ruptured what had been a robust strategic understanding. Following these two historic events, Beijing sought to credibly threaten U.S. military access to strategically vital areas along China's maritime periphery. Despite progress toward this end, however, Chinese naval and maritime analysts have written consistently that their nation's naval capabilities remain insufficient to address critical operational threats. For all these reasons, the concept of ASBM development has assumed new urgency as part of a larger effort to deter U.S. CSGs from intervening in a potential conflict. This notion emerged rapidly in later years in Chinese writings and even conversations with Chinese interlocutors.

Taiwan: A Central Catalyst

Chinese ASBM development dates at least to the 1995–96 Taiwan Strait crisis, which underscored Chinese feelings of helplessness against U.S. naval power. In July–August 1995 and March 1996, concerns about President Lee

Figure 1: Chinese (Antiship) Ballistic Missile Development Timeline

1955	Qian Xuesen returns to China, subsequently founds missile and space programs with Chairman Mao Zedong's support.
1955–56	USSR provides China with R-1 and R-2 missiles, engineering documentation, equipment, and specialists.
May 1956	CCP Central Committee prioritizes development of strategic missiles and atomic bomb. Ministry of National Defense 5th Research Academy (China's first missile organization) established; Qian appointed head.
1960: 12 August	Soviet specialists leave 5th Research Academy as part of Sino-Soviet split. September: first launch of Chinese-made R-2.
1965: August	Premier Zhou Enlai orders development of solid-propellant rocket technology. Design team formed within 4th Space Academy, single-stage ballistic missile design Dongfeng-61 (DF-61) proposed.
1966: 1 July	Second Artillery Corps founded.
1967	PLA decides to build its first nuclear-powered missile submarine, requires medium-range ballistic missile to be carried onboard; decides to abandon DF-61 design and instead develop submarine-based, two-stage, solid-propellant ballistic missile (JL-1).
1970	Design of JL-1 airframe reassigned to 1st Space Academy while 4th Space Academy concentrates on the development of the solid-propellant rocket technology.
1972	Vice Premier Zhang Chunqiao advocates use of "guided missiles" to hit maritime targets.
Early 1970s	PRC makes several major breakthroughs in developing solid-propellant rocket technology. Begins to explore developing land-based version of JL-1.
1975	Two parallel development programs under way based on same airframe and engine design: submarine-based JL-1 and land-based DF-21.
1976	JL-1/DF-21 program is reassigned to the 2nd Space Academy (previously responsible for missile defense program). Huang Weilu appointed chief designer. 2nd Space Academy also assigned DF-21 support systems, e.g., development of transporter-erector-launcher vehicle, missile canister, and missile testing and guidance.
1983–88	U.S. deploys Pershing II MRBM.
1985: May	First successful DF-21 flight from Base 25 (Wuzhai).
1987: May	Second successful DF-21 flight from Base 25.
1987	DF-21A development program initiated. Missile features 60 percent range increase.
1988	DF-21 MRBM certified for design finalization. U.S. retires Pershing II MRBMs per INF Treaty.
1993	Second Artillery assumes conventional mission.
1995	First successful DF-21A flight test from Base 25. July–August: Second Artillery fires DF-15 SRBMs into sea near Taiwan.
1996	DF-21A achieves initial operational capability. March: Second Artillery fires DF-15 SRBMs into sea near Taiwan. Senior General Staff Department officer warns U.S. attaché that CSGs face future ballistic missile threat.

Timeline *(continued)*

1997–2002	Major Chinese ASBM conceptual studies published.
1999	First *Shenzhou* spacecraft launch; orbital maneuvering technologies demonstrated. PLA National Defense University publishes ASBM concept chapters.
2002–06	Limited number of Chinese ASBM studies published openly.
2003	Second Artillery publishes ASBM feasibility study.
2004	Second Artillery publishes doctrinal handbook; two pages devoted to ASBM use. U.S. Office of Naval Intelligence first mentions Chinese ASBM interest publicly.
2005	First mention of Chinese ASBM exploration/research in U.S. Department of Defense annual PLA report.
2006–Present	Major increase in Chinese ASBM publications.
2007	Chinese ASBM development mentioned in testimony before U.S.-China Economic and Security Review Commission.
2009	August: DF-21D rocket motor factory completed. November: ASBM program broadcast on CCTV-7. ONI's Scott Bray states ASBM "nearing an operational capability." ASBM begins to receive widespread attention in United States.
2010	5 March: three Yaogan surveillance satellites placed in similar orbits. 20 May: CASIC 4th Dept. Deputy Director quoted stating DF-21D can hit "slow-moving targets" with a CEP of dozens of meters. July: Second Artillery may be constructing ASBM missile brigade facilities in the northern Guangdong Province municipality of Shaoguan. 24 August: Admiral Robert Willard, Commander, U.S. Pacific Command, tells Japanese media in Tokyo: "To our knowledge, [China's ASBM] has undergone repeated tests and it is probably very close to being operational." December: Admiral Willard tells *Asahi Shimbun*'s Yoichi Kato that China's ASBM has reached equivalent of "Initial Operational Capability" (IOC).

Sources:

Andrew S. Erickson, "China's Anti-Ship Ballistic Missile (ASBM) Reaches Equivalent of 'Initial Operational Capability' (IOC)—Where It's Going and What it Means," *China Analysis from Original Sources*, 30 December 2010, http://www.andrewerickson.com/2010/12/china%E2%80%99s-anti-ship-ballistic-missile-asbm -reaches-equivalent-of-%E2%80%9Cinitial-operational-capability%E2%80%9D-ioc%E2%80%94where -it%E2%80%99s-going-and-what-it-means/; Yoichi Kato, "U.S. Commander Says China Aims to be a 'Global Military' Power," *Asahi Shimbun*, 28 December 2010, http://www.asahi.com/english/TKY201012270241.html; Andrew S. Erickson and Gabriel B. Collins, "China Deploys World's First Long-Range, Land-Based 'Carrier Killer': DF-21D Anti-Ship Ballistic Missile (ASBM) Reaches 'Initial Operational Capability' (IOC)," *China SignPost* (洞察中国), No. 14 (26 December 2010), http://www.chinasignpost.com/2010/12/china-deploys -world%E2%80%99s-first-long-range-land-based-%E2%80%98carrier-killer%E2%80%99-df-21d-anti-ship -ballistic-missile-asbm-reaches-%E2%80%9Cinitial-operational-capability%E2%80%9D-ioc/; Andrew S. Erickson, "China Testing Anti-Ship Ballistic Missile (ASBM); U.S. Preparing Accordingly—Updated With Latest Analysis & Sources," *China Analysis from Original Sources*, 25 December 2010, http://www .andrewerickson.com/2010/12/china-testing-anti-ship-ballistic-missile-asbm/; Yoichi Kato, "China's Anti-Ship Missile is Nearly Operational," *Asahi Shimbun*, 26 August 2010; 王根彬 (中国航天科工集团四部副总指挥) [Wang Genbin, Deputy Director of the 4th Department under CASIC], as quoted in "审时度势, 大打固体之 仗物—回顾与思考" [Sizing Up the Situation, Solid-Fuel Is Required for Battle—Review and Reflections], 两 弹一星 [*Two Bombs and One Satellite*], 20 May 2010, http://gongxue.cn/guofangshichuang/ShowArticle.asp ?ArticleID=81143; John Wilson Lewis and Xue Litai, *China Builds the Bomb* (Stanford, CA: Stanford University Press, 1988); and DongFeng 21 (CSS-5) Medium-Range Ballistic Missile," *China's Defence Today*, http://www.sinodefence.com/strategic/missile/df21.asp.

Teng-hui furthering measures that it associated with Taiwan independence led Beijing to order missile tests and other military exercises near the strait. The resulting U.S. dispatch of the *Nimitz* CSG through the strait in December 1995 and of the *Independence* (CV 62) and *Nimitz* (CVN 68) CSGs toward the region in March 1996 was a move that China could not counter. The PLA Navy (PLAN) "felt pain keenly."[2] It is reasonable to assume that Beijing vowed such an action, which it perceived as a violation of China's sovereignty, should never be repeated. Leaders such as president and CMC chairman Jiang Zemin reportedly instructed key defense industrial institutions to spare no expense in solving the problem.

Consequently, PLA development in general, and PLAN development in particular, was marked by the emergence of many new platforms and weapons systems beginning in the early 2000s. Asymmetric in nature and anti-access in focus, they are difficult to counter, in our view, because they target specific characteristics and limitations based on immutable laws of physics and thus potentially place the United States on the "wrong end of physics" in terms of the difficulty and expense in attempting to do so. The ASBM differs markedly from the quiet submarines, lethal antiship cruise missiles (ASCMs), and copious sea mines that China has been adding to its inventory. China's ASBM draws on more than a half century of Chinese experience with ballistic missiles; is fired from mobile, highly concealable platforms; and has the range to strike targets hundreds of kilometers from China's shores.

In fact, there is specific evidence that the 1996 debacle gave a new impetus to ASBM-related research and development. Dr. Xin Wanqing at China Aerospace Science and Technology Corporation began ASBM feasibility studies and concept demonstration work in 1996, particularly in the areas of guidance and control. A sudden profusion of relevant technical papers by Xin and others starting in 1996 would seem to support these assertions. A 2006 article, published originally on the online portal of the official *China Youth Daily* and subsequently removed, claims that Xin "completed proof of concept work on anti-aircraft carrier ballistic missiles."[3] Additionally, in 2003 the Second Artillery published what appears to be a conceptual feasibility study.[4] Collectively, these factors suggest that related concepts have been under development at the highest levels of the PLA for well over five years, and perhaps for over a decade.

Official Statements

Chinese officials have yet to address their nation's ASBM development directly in an open public forum. They have made a variety of more general statements, however, that would appear to be compatible with ASBM development. General Xu Caihou, CMC vice chairman, has stated that ballistic and cruise missile development is necessary for mainland China to safeguard its interests vis-à-vis Taiwan.[5] China's military has publicly provided significant hints of its own ASBM progress. PLAN armament expert Qiu Zhiming states that targeting specific ships in a CSG is the greatest problem in ASBM development but that ASBMs have the potential to damage an aircraft carrier significantly.[6]

Discussions of ASBMs in the Chinese Literature

There are numerous Chinese writings on ASBMs in open-source literature that can be divided into three broad categories in descending level of demonstrable authoritativeness:

- PLA doctrinal publications that describe how ASBMs might be used in operational scenarios; official military doctrinal publications serve as sources of directive guidance for PLA personnel.

- Specialized and narrowly focused technical analyses of specific aspects of such weapons and their supporting infrastructure that involve computer simulations, mathematical calculations, and other technical endeavors regarding specific systems and operations.

- Generalist deliberations and didactic discussions on the technical and operational feasibility of such weapons designed to appeal to a broad audience, typically concerning the feasibility of ASBMs.

Areas of Agreement

While there are clearly differences among Chinese ASBM writings, it is important to examine the issues on with which there is no disagreement regardless of forum, institutional affiliation, or individual viewpoint. Chinese commentators agree that an ASBM would be based on an upgraded version of an existing Chinese MRBM, such as the DF-21/CSS-5. Interestingly, some Chinese sources state that the Pershing II ground-to-ground TBM deployed from 1984–88 inspired Chinese research and development relevant to an ASBM. While the United States does not have an ASBM, the Pershing II did have an emerging if distantly related capability in this area. Washington relinquished this capability when it ratified the Intermediate-Range Nuclear Forces (INF) Treaty with Moscow on 27 May 1988, preventing both the United States and Russia from possessing conventional (and nuclear) ground-launched ballistic (and cruise) missiles. Chinese assessments generally concur that ASBMs, if realized in practice, would offer a variety of operational effects and value for Chinese maritime strategy—particularly vis-à-vis Taiwan. Finally, there is also general agreement over the identification of the key technical challenges, including target acquisition and terminal guidance.

Doctrinal Sources

Three volumes—largely ignored by Western scholarship—deserve special scrutiny as the most authoritative writings available on the use of ballistic missiles in operational and tactical scenarios. The headquarters of the PLA General Staff declares that two of them, *The Science of Campaigns* and *The Science of Second Artillery Campaigns*, have been "printed and distributed to all military forces, colleges, and universities as a training and learning reference."[7] A third book, *Intimidation Warfare*, edited by Lieutenant General Zhao Xijun, Second Artillery deputy commander from 1996 to 2003, echoes many of the statements on strategic signaling outlined in *Science of Second Artillery Campaigns*.

The Science of Campaigns was written by researchers at China's National Defense University. The 2006 edition offers a basic overview of conditions under which conventional ballistic missiles might be used to "implement sea blockades" and "capture localized campaign sea dominance" by "implementing missile firepower assault or firepower harassment attacks against important targets on which the enemy depends for . . . sea-based maneuvering," which aims to "apply great psychological pressure on the enemy" and make him think "that no rules apply, thereby achieving the maximum effectiveness."[8]

Even more relevant and sophisticated is *Science of Second Artillery Campaigns* (2004). It likely serves as a high-level professional military education handbook for campaign-level command personnel in the Second Artillery and the PLA in general. The document represents the best theoretical work by the PLA's foremost thinkers on the use of ASBMs in operational scenarios with no indication that their approaches are aspirational or beset with insurmountable difficulties. In introducing the section describing ASBMs' potential employment, it states that "conventional missile strike groups" should be used as an "assassin's mace" (or silver bullet)—a term commonly used to describe weapons that match Chinese strengths with an enemy's weaknesses to achieve disproportionately powerful effects.[9] Additionally, a two-page section describes five ways to use ASBMs against CSGs, a centerpiece of "military intervention by a powerful enemy," including firing intimidation salvos, destroying shipborne aircraft with submunitions, or disabling Aegis destroyers' sensor systems with electromagnetic pulses designed to make CSGs retreat or render them inoperable.[10]

Intimidation Warfare sheds additional light on China's possible calculus and tactics in various scenarios, emphasizing the value of demonstration training and tests, among other measures to influence the enemy.[11] Zhao's team also suggests four methods to deter enemy ships without hitting them directly: conducting test launches that impact near a sea-based target; launching two or more missiles to bracket or encircle a target; exploiting the psychological impact of missiles overflying "strategic targets" when fighting an enemy controlling an island (e.g., Taiwan?); and "launching missiles toward the flanks or the front of the aircraft carrier strike groups that have entered one's territorial waters."[12] Particularly noteworthy of the wide variety of uses suggested for ASBMs against carriers in this publication and in *Science of Second Artillery Campaigns* is that they place less of a premium on high warhead accuracy. Rather, missile range and defense penetration capability seem to be the key factors.

Science of Second Artillery Campaigns states that TBMs extend the Second Artillery's strike range, and it seems to assume that the Second Artillery would have an ASBM inventory sufficient to permit numerous warning shots. Horizontal escalation in the short run, it argues implicitly, can achieve de-escalation in the long run. One section of *Science of Second Artillery Campaigns* also emphasizes the need for "no-fly" and "restricted navigation zones," and calls for the use of "very precise missiles in order to prevent errors in precision or losing control of the missile when it is in flight such that it enters enemy territory (or an enemy-occupied island), or such that it directly strikes an enemy aircraft carrier." Otherwise, such errors "could cause the nature of deterrence to change, giving the enemy an excuse to use force or make follow-up deterrence in a passive situation."[13]

Technical Sources

The Second Artillery dominates available technical ASBM assessments, which implies that it largely, if not completely, controls Chinese ASBM programs. The vast majority of available technical articles devoted explicitly to ASBM issues are authored in full or in part by individuals associated with the Second Artillery Engineering College in Xi'an and the Second Artillery Equipment Department in Beijing. Such involvement may suggest that some degree of procurement, or at least active consideration thereof, is under way.

Generalist Literature

The available doctrinal literature should clearly be seen as the most demonstrably authoritative category of open-source writings, with endorsements by identifiable individuals associated with the Second Artillery, the National Defense University, or the PLA. Nevertheless, care must be taken in extrapolating actual capabilities from these sources. Available Second Artillery technical articles and mathematical feasibility studies devoted explicitly to ASBM issues do not detail concrete Chinese capabilities. In fact, Chinese doctrinal publications often discuss theoretical capabilities as if they existed, which U.S. joint publications typically do not.

Therefore, it is useful to examine the diverse and detailed generalist literature for indications of challenges and dilemmas that China might face in ASBM development and employment. These opinions matter because deploying and perfecting such a weapon would entail resolving a wide variety of complex challenges and policy considerations and the transcending of many industrial and bureaucratic boundaries.

Strategic Rationale and Scenarios.

There is broad (though not complete) consistency in the generalist literature concerning the operational effects of ASBMs and their potential value for Chinese maritime strategy writ large. ASBMs are promoted as a means to overcome conventional inferiority (by exploiting technological asymmetry), deter intervention, give China more maneuvering space, and offer both escalation control and an "assassin's mace" for victory if deterrence fails.

Of supreme importance to Beijing is Taiwan's political status. At the strategic level, Beijing seeks to deter Taipei from declaring independence while progressively constraining its political space and encouraging eventual reunification with a wide variety of hard- and soft-power tools. In addition to their psychological and deterrent effects, ASBMs are believed to offer China a way to exert hard-power pressure and convey strategic signals in scenarios that do not rise to the level of war. This would seem in concert with Chinese strategic writings, although we have not located any Chinese sources that directly mention any scenarios beyond Taiwan.

At the same time, ASBMs are recognized to have significant limitations, even potential dangers. According to one analyst, they "cannot replace aircraft carriers, submarines, and other traditional naval weapons"; they "can be used to destroy enemy forces at sea but not to achieve absolute sea control, let alone to project maritime power."[14] Two writers in the China Shipbuilding Industry Corporation (CSIC) publication *Modern Ships* go much farther, declaring that while ASBMs are technically feasible, their employment in practice is fraught with difficulties: they offer limited power projection capabilities, are highly escalatory if employed, and might in fact trigger nuclear retaliation.[15] These can be overcome, in their view, if one is dealing with a minor power but not with a superpower like the United States.

Even if ASBMs were indeed developed successfully, the *Modern Ships* authors contend, a critical problem would remain: whether anyone would dare to use such weapons in an actual conflict scenario. In their view, ASBM employment against U.S. carriers would immediately create a nuclear conflict: "All the major nuclear powers have developed ballistic missile warning systems against possible nuclear attacks, and there has not been a single precedent of a major nuclear power attacking another with ballistic missiles." It must be emphasized that sinking or disabling a ship that is a symbol of American power and has a crew of thousands could provoke a very serious response.

Technological Feasibility: Convergence and Divergence of Views.

Chinese generalist debates about the utility of ASBMs are closely related to widespread disagreements over their technical feasibility. Analysts generally concur that five major technical challenges must be surmounted to achieve a functioning ASBM:

- *Detection.* There is disagreement on whether carriers would be too small relative to the potential search area to be detected easily by satellite images, and too difficult to detect electromagnetically.

- *Tracking.* There exists skepticism about whether requisite satellite coverage and other tracking methods are attainable past China's immediate shores.

- *Target defense penetration.* There is debate on how best to penetrate defenses of an enemy, whether it is slowing the warhead for terminal guidance or via multiaxis saturation attacks.

- *Hitting a moving target.* There is disagreement on whether a ballistic missile's trajectory can make appropriate homing corrections on a moving CSG.

- *Causing sufficient damage.* The conventional wisdom seems to be that the use of a multiaxis saturation attack (to defeat defenses) or submunitions (to distribute damage), delivered accurately, can achieve a mission kill by targeting critical exposed areas, such as the carrier's aircraft, island, and C4ISR equipment.

Assessments

Available Chinese literature follows a logical pattern of ever-widening concentric circles of awareness and, to a lesser extent, involvement. At the center, authoritative PLA publications assume an (eventual) ASBM capability. Further out, a variety of institutes are working to validate specific concepts and perhaps also technologies to support such a capability. Beyond these inner circles, a wide range of individuals weigh in, revealing diverse opinions and institutional interests. There exists a general climate of institutional biases and competition, with individuals favoring precisely the outcomes that would benefit their organizations most. Overall, literature suggests that organizations, analysts, and policy entrepreneurs may be jockeying for position in an attempt to influence the course of decision making on the part of at least two of China's armed services, its military leadership, and ultimately its civilian authorities.

Particularly noteworthy is that direct claims of existing Chinese capabilities in ASBM development are extremely limited; the focus of the discussion is typically on theoretical feasibility. Discussion of terminal guidance technology, for instance, is illustrated largely by examples drawn from the Pershing II missile. It is likely that some Chinese authors do not know what the Chinese capabilities actually are, while others know but cannot say.

Several other issues, though not directly addressed by the Chinese authors surveyed, may merit further attention and are highlighted below.

Possible Interservice Rivalry

The tone of ASBM analyses may be interpreted as signs of Second Artillery–PLAN bureaucratic competition. Momentum, direction, and contention about programs may reflect diverse institutional interests. Articles written by analysts associated with the Second Artillery tend to take the feasibility of ASBM development for granted, perhaps because an ASBM program would be (or now is) controlled by the Second Artillery, furthering its institutional interests.

It is not surprising, then, that the PLAN publication *Modern Navy* and the CSIC-affiliated *Modern Ships* have published by far the most skeptical assessment of ASBM technology. The vast majority of analyses affiliated with the PLAN suggest that ASBM development is technically problematic, or that actual use would have dangerous unintended consequences. Perhaps the Second Artillery's involvement in antiship warfare might compete with the navy's own programs for resources. The PLAN might well prefer to develop more conventional antiship capabilities (e.g., ASCMs, attack aircraft, and attack submarines) and may worry that Second Artillery monopoly of ASBM stewardship could undermine funding for these more traditional priorities.

A Coercive Quarantine?

Synthesizing the considerations above, it is possible that to the extent that tactical ballistic missiles are employed as antiship weapons, they would most likely be used as part of a multiservice combined arms operation as an added component of a saturation attack to overwhelm a carrier's defensive systems. For this purpose, targeting precision would be less important, and the more general Chinese tradition of numbers over accuracy could be employed to good effect. This tactic could divert carrier defense systems from other threats, such as other ASBMs or simultaneous cruise missile volleys, and perhaps exhaust scarce interceptors. To escape this problem, CSGs might simply opt to stay out of the range of the TBMs.

Messages for the U.S. Military?

Given the sensitivity of the topic, it is possible that the current Chinese literature on ASBM development is a discussion whose parameters are controlled. Information manipulation should certainly be expected, especially considering that most technical analyses reviewed were published in journals fairly accessible to foreigners, complete with English titles and abstracts. Discussion is likely regulated to send a desired signal, rendering different explanations for Chinese writings on ASBMs possible. To the extent that they are manipulated, they could represent a "placeholder" partial deterrent, a reflection of ongoing ambivalence and debate, a targeted effort to obscure actual capabilities, or a statement of conditional intent.

While plenty of discussion surrounding China's ASBM program exists, there has been no official Chinese indication that any weapon of this kind will be tested comprehensively at sea under fully realistic conditions in the foreseeable future. From a signaling perspective, this may be a highly cost-effective way to achieve partial deterrent effect until the capability is fully realized, which may be sometime in the future.

Second, it is possible that the confusion and contradictions among Chinese writings instead signify a larger debate and ongoing ambivalence within China concerning the actual efficacy of ASBMs regardless of their technological feasibility—as appears to have been the case with Chinese aircraft carrier development in recent years.

A third possibility is that strategic articles could be manipulated to obscure or divert attention from an extant capability or one in rapid development.

Manipulating a few strategic articles in journals known to be read outside China might be a particularly effective instrument in an information campaign. A somewhat peculiar two-part series in *Modern Navy* could be a prime example of this, especially as it appears to contain many misused technical concepts and even outright errors.

Finally, the significant and growing amount of Chinese ASBM literature could be part of a larger pattern in which Beijing is becoming increasingly "translucent" (if still not fully transparent) regarding selected capabilities to enhance deterrence. It might regard the ASBM as a weapon whose very evidence of development could alter U.S. military behavior, thereby enhancing China's strategic leverage. It is even possible that there is an effort to send a measured signal—that China may be preparing certain capabilities but has not yet made definitive plans for their large-scale deployment, the actual realization of which will be calibrated in response to American strategic actions (e.g., vis-à-vis Taiwan and China's "near seas").

Testing?

In any case, if and when the DF-21D is developed sufficiently, Beijing might reveal a dramatic weapon test to the world—with or without advance warning—in some way geared to influencing official and public opinion in the United States, Taiwan, Japan, and elsewhere in the Asia-Pacific. Alternatively, unpublicized flight tests could be conducted to deter foreign militaries without alarming foreign publics (though classified information might ultimately be leaked to them). In any case, some sort of integrated over-water flight tests would be necessary to generate Chinese confidence in ASBM capabilities. As figure 1 indicates, China's ASBM has undergone repeated tests that are probably advanced and include flight tests. The fact of a hit on a maritime target, however manipulated and revealed, could change the strategic equation regarding Chinese leverage in the Western Pacific.

Implications

While there is ongoing disagreement as to their feasibility and efficacy, a successful Chinese deployment of ASBMs would probably have the following impact on PLA thinking:

- Reinforcement of continental approaches to maritime security—"using the land to control the sea"
- Reinforcement of centralized approaches to command

- Further emphasis on multiaxis saturation attacks
- Greater confidence in China's ability to restrict U.S. Navy operations and to control escalation

China's ASBM is thus part of a much larger pattern in which the development and proliferation of various antiaccess/area denial weapons systems—such as ballistic and cruise missiles, submarines, and naval mines—threatens to hold U.S. platforms at risk in vital areas of the global maritime commons.

Notes

The views expressed in this article are solely those of the authors and in no way represent the policies or estimates of the RAND Corporation, the U.S. Navy, or any other element of the U.S. government. The authors thank Dennis Blasko, Michael Chase, Peter Dombrowski, Ian Easton, David Finkelstein, Joseph Gavin Jr., Lyle Goldstein, Kristen Gunness, Scott Harold, Craig Koerner, Carnes Lord, William Murray, Jonathan Pollack, Kevin Pollpeter, Robert Rubel, Mark Stokes, Christopher Weuve, Christopher Yeaw, and Toshi Yoshihara for their incisive comments. This chapter draws on several previously published articles, including Erickson and Yang, "Using the Land to Control the Sea? Chinese Analysts Consider the Anti-Ship Ballistic Missile," *Naval War College Review* 62, no. 4 (Autumn 2009); and Erickson and Yang, "On the Verge of a Game-Changer: A Chinese Antiship Ballistic Missile Could Alter the Rules in the Pacific and Place U.S. Navy Carrier Strike Groups in Jeopardy," U.S. Naval Institute *Proceedings* 135, no. 3 (May 2009): 26–32; as well as Erickson, "China's Anti-Ship Ballistic Missile (ASBM) Reaches Equivalent of 'Initial Operational Capability' (IOC)—Where It's Going and What It Means," *China Analysis from Original Sources*, 4 January 2011, http://www.andrewerickson .com/2011/01/china%E2%80%99s-anti-ship-ballistic-missile-asbm-reaches-equivalent-of-%E2%80%9Cinitial-operational-capability%E2%80%9D-ioc%E2%80%94where-it%E2%80%99s-going-and-what-it-means/.

1. 邱贞玮 [Qiu Zhenwei], "中国反船弹道导弹发展研讨" ["A Discussion of China's Development of an Anti-Ship Ballistic Missile"], http://blog.huanqiu.com/?uid -6885-action-viewspace-itemid-2009.

2. Ibid.

3. "China Aerospace Science and Technology Corporation First Academy Completes Proof of Concept Work on Anti-Aircraft Carrier Ballistic Missile," 中国在线 [*China Online*], 30 April 2006, available at www.cyol.com, OSC CPP20070110318001.

4. 黄洪福 [Huang Hongfu], "常规弹道导弹打击航母编队的设想" ["Conceptualizing the Use of Conventional Ballistic Missiles to Strike Aircraft Carrier Battle Groups"], 科技研究 [*Scientific and Technological Research*], (第二炮兵科学技术委员会 [Scientific and Technological Committee of the Second Artillery Corps]) 1 (2003): 6–8.

5. Gen. Xu Caihou, Vice Chairman of the Communist Party of China Central Military Commission, People's Republic of China, "Statesmen's Forum: General Xu Caihou," Center for Strategic and International Studies, Washington, D.C., 26 October 2009, http://csis.org/event/statesmens-forum-general-xu-caihou.

6. See "中国中央电视台防务新观察　2009.11.29—反舰弹道导弹—航母的天敌?" Part 1 ["China Central Television New Observations on Defense: ASBM—The Aircraft Carrier's Natural Enemy?"], http://www.youtube.com/watch?v=Ofe1SYkLJgk; "Part 2," http://www.youtube.com/watch?v=R-nNVvtacXU (especially cartoon sequence starting at minute 7:18); Part 3, http://www.youtube.com/watch?v=LaDXzCC5aCU&NR=1; all available at http://space.tv.cctv.com/video/VIDE1259487727975889.

7. Statement by the headquarters of the PLA General Staff. 于际训 [Yu Jixun], 中国人民解放军第二炮兵 [People's Liberation Army Second Artillery Corps], 第二炮兵战役学 [*The Science of Second Artillery Campaigns*] (Beijing: 解放军出版社 [Liberation Army Press], 2004), 3.

8. Zhang Yulang, chief ed., et al., 战役学 [*The Science of Campaigns*] (Beijing: National Defense University Press, May 2006), ch. 31, 616–28, and ch. 32, 629–36.

9. Yu, *Science of Second Artillery Campaigns*, 395.

10. Ibid., 401.

11. Zhao Xijun, ed., 慑战—导弹威慑纵横谈 [*Intimidation Warfare: A Comprehensive Discussion on Missile Deterrence*] (Beijing: National Defense University Press, May 2005), 188.

12. Ibid., 190–91.

13. Yu, *Science of Second Artillery Campaigns*, 293.

14. 王伟 [Wang Wei], "战术弹道导弹对中国海洋战略体系的影响" ["The Effect of Tactical Ballistic Missiles," on the Maritime Strategy System of China"], 舰载武器 [*Shipborne Weapons*], no. 84 (August 2006): 12–15.

15. Unless otherwise specified, all data in this and the following paragraph are derived from 火飞, 罗世伟 [Huo Fei and Luo Shiwei], "无弓之箭—反航母弹道导弹效能及实用化评估" ["Arrows without Bows—An Evaluation of the Effectiveness and Employment of Anti-Aircraft-Carrier Ballistic Missiles"], 现代舰船 [*Modern Ships*], no. 325 (April 2008): 27–28.

Toshi Yoshihara

Chinese Views of Sea-Based Ballistic Missile Defense

THE PROSPECT OF CHINA acquiring the technical capacity to field and employ antiship ballistic missiles (ASBMs) has fired imaginations among Chinese and American analysts alike, conjuring up apocalyptic visions of a crippled or sunk U.S. aircraft carrier in the Pacific. While the temptation to entertain nightmare scenarios is entirely understandable, the ASBM—if or when it reaches operational status—would likely endanger all surface vessels of a carrier strike group (CSG). Particularly worrisome is the ballistic missile threat to Aegis-equipped destroyers and cruisers. Given that a CSG typically relies on a few Aegis vessels to perform a wide array of counterforce measures against enemy firepower, the loss of even one of these picket ships could impair the task force's overall ability to assert sea control, project power ashore, or maintain forward presence. Defeating Aegis—densely packed as it is with weaponry to ensure that nothing gets through—is thus tantamount to undermining the survivability of the carrier itself.

As respected theorist on naval tactics Wayne Hughes observes, "Modern American firepower tends to be clumped together, striking power in a few aircraft carriers, defensive firepower in AAW [anti–air warfare] missile cruisers and in the fighter aircraft aboard carriers."[1] By implication, severe harm to surface units that provide the protective umbrella over the fleet could radically tip the tactical balance in favor of the adversary. It is conceivable that a significant loss of ship-borne AAW capabilities could either keep at bay or even turn back a strike group from a particular theater of operations without ever directly threatening the carrier itself. The sobering reality is that attacking secondary targets, such as the Aegis, could pay operational and strategic dividends to enemy forces, making them as lucrative as the aircraft carrier.

Intriguingly, a substantial body of Chinese sources concurs. The literature suggests an intensifying interest in striking the Aegis at sea as a part of a broader anticarrier strategy. Moreover, some of the writings identify the new anti–ballistic missile roles assigned to the Aegis as an added impetus for Beijing to take aim at these escort ships. It is notable that the debut of the Aegis technology in the mid-1980s dramatically restored mobility to U.S. naval plans against the Soviet Union.[2] If Beijing perfects the techniques for effectively using ASBMs against the Aegis, then China could very well reverse the maneuverability that the United States has enjoyed and taken granted for decades. As Ronald O'Rourke observes, "The U.S. Navy has not previously faced a threat from highly accurate ballistic missiles capable of hitting moving ships at sea."[3] In short, Chinese views of the Aegis merit close analytical scrutiny. This chapter specifically examines how China's analysts assess the introduction of sea-based ballistic missile defense (BMD) systems to the Aegis warships as a window into evolving Chinese strategic thought about maritime strike missions.

Threat Assessment

Chinese analysts have expressed alarm at the numbers of Aegis-equipped ships operating in the Asia-Pacific region. In an article provocatively titled "Aegis Ships Encircle China" (宙斯盾舰合围中国) the author observes that Aegis deployments in the Asian littorals virtually surround China.[4] According to Ren Dexin, a disproportionate percentage of the U.S. Aegis fleet is being devoted to the Pacific theater. One commentary observes that the acquisition programs of the Aegis combat system among the Asian navies are likely to set the stage for "Aegis inundation" (宙斯盾泛滥) along China's nautical periphery.[5] For Chen Lihao, the substantial presence of such ships reflects an American determination to establish an "anti-ballistic missile net" (导弹防御网) across the Pacific.[6] Given that the recipients of Aegis technologies are either treaty allies or friendly to the United States, such a conclusion is entirely understandable.

Some Chinese commentators frame their suspicions of a U.S.-led seaborne encirclement in stark geopolitical terms. They see concentrations of sea-based BMD capabilities falling roughly along three lines of defense across the Pacific. One analyst describes Yokosuka as the frontline while Pearl Harbor and San Diego provide additional layers of defense against ballistic missiles.[7] Yokosuka, for example, is evocatively described as the "forward battlefield position" (前沿 阵地), representing an indispensible component of the sea-based BMD architecture.[8] To some Chinese eyes, these concentric rings or picket lines of sea power are tailored specifically to target the flight path of ballistic missiles fired across the Pacific from locations as diverse as the Korean peninsula, mainland China, India, and even Iran.[9] Aegis ships in Yokosuka, Pearl Harbor, and San Diego would be positioned to shoot down a missile in its boost, mid-course, and terminal phases, respectively.[10]

Chinese observers pay particular attention to the Aegis deployments along the first island chain, which roughly encompasses the bodies of water bounded by the Japanese home islands, Taiwan, and the Philippine archipelago. Some believe that several Aegis ships operating in the Yellow, East, and South China seas would have the capacity to monitor the launching of all long-range ballistic missiles deployed in China's interior and perhaps intercept them in their boost phases. Dai Yanli asserts, "Clearly, if Aegis systems are successfully deployed around China's periphery, then there is the possibility that China's ballistic missiles would be destroyed over their launch points."[11] Concurring, Qi Yanli from the Beijing Aerospace Long March Scientific and Technical Information Institute declares, "If such [sea-based BMD] systems begin deployment in areas such as Japan or Taiwan, the effectiveness of China's strategic power and theater ballistic missile capabilities would weaken tremendously, severely threatening national security."[12] Somewhat problematically, the authors' assessments assume that Beijing would risk its strategic forces by deploying them closer to shore, and forecasts a far more capable Aegis fleet than what is technically possible in the near term.

Aegis presence in the Asian littoral is not the only threat that worries Chinese analysts. In its October 2007 issue, *Modern Navy* published a special feature on global naval power premised on the island chain concept that similarly depicts the U.S. BMD system in geostrategic terms. Bai Yanlin describes the second and third island chains, centered on the Mariana Islands and Pearl Harbor, respectively, as America's "sea wall" (防波堤) in the Pacific.[13] According to Bai, Aegis ships operating between the two island chains have become strategic weapons because they provide multilayered defenses on the open seas. Consequently, he believes that such capabilities promise to undermine the strategic leverage of all states possessing ballistic missiles in the Asia Pacific region. Similar to the other analyses recounted earlier, Bai appears to believe that the sea-based BMD will soon acquire the capacity to intercept long-range strategic missiles, which at the moment remains a major technical hurdle for the United States.

Chinese analysts also monitor closely the testing of the Aegis system and display acute sensitivity to apparent technical breakthroughs. The destruction of a U.S. spy satellite by an interceptor launched from an Aegis ship in February 2008 provoked a storm of speculation in China, yielding several dire conclusions. For some, the incident confirmed the extension of conflict to space.[14]

The Japan Factor

Chinese perceptions of a more competitive sea-based antimissile environment along the littorals of the mainland have stimulated debate over Japan's potential role in the U.S. BMD system. Many Chinese analysts assume the worst of Japanese intentions. Some believe that Japanese participation in the joint research and development of ballistic missile defense with the United States reflects Japan's underlying great power ambitions.[15] Wang Baofu, deputy director of the Institute of Strategic Studies at the PLA National Defense University, asserts that the deployment of missile defense parallels a broader Japanese effort "to break its pacifist constitution and expand military might in an attempt to become a world political heavyweight."[16] American and Japanese assurances that the missile shield is designed to be used against rogue states are clearly unconvincing to some Chinese.

In addition to questionable motives, the Chinese view with alarm the potential strategic consequence of Japan's missile defense ambitions. Luo Shanai observes that as U.S.-Japan BMD cooperation deepens allied interoperability, Tokyo will be tied increasingly to the U.S. regional strategy in Asia.[17] Others go even further, asserting that Pyongyang's missile threat serves as a convenient pretext for Japan to develop BMD against China.[18] For Shi Jiangyue, the primary American motive for deploying the newest Aegis ship, USS *Halsey*, to the Pacific in 2006 was unequivocal: "to contain China" (遏制中国).[19] Two analysts argue that the prospective BMD system would undermine China's limited and defensive nuclear deterrent.[20]

In terms of the operational and technical aspects of missile defense, the Chinese fully appreciate the value of sea-based BMD. Aegis ships offer a wide range of strategic options to the theater commander—including mobility, rapid response, flexibility, and the ability to function independently of other missile defense systems—that the ground-based counterparts generally do not.[21] Not surprisingly, analysts have watched Japan's naval modernization very closely. Analysts pay particular attention to the upgrade programs of the Japanese Maritime Self-Defense Force's (JMSDF) Aegis fleet. Most concur that two of these very capable Aegis vessels would be sufficient to "bolster warning and interception of Chinese and North Korean ballistic missiles."[22] Armed with the more advanced Standard Missile-3 Block II interceptor that promises greater range and speed, a single *Atago*-class destroyer would be able, in the judgment of some Chinese analysts, to provide full coverage over the entire Japanese archipelago.[23]

Chinese speculation on how the Japanese might employ the Aegis fleet is perhaps the most interesting dimension of the existing literature. The Chinese are deeply skeptical of U.S. and Japanese claims that the sea-based component of missile defense is exclusively defensive in nature. Indeed, they foresee the operational lines that divide defensive and offensive platforms blurring in the coming years. One commentator asserts that Japan's sea-based BMD fleet would "extend the 'defense' spearhead ('防卫'矛头) several hundred, even several thousand, kilometers from Japan's homeland to the Taiwan Strait and the South China Sea."[24] This analysis is consistent with prevailing Chinese suspicions that Japan's BMD capability is directed at China rather than North Korea. Wen Deyi argues that the missile shield would open up "strategic space" (战略空间) for Japan's development of more offensively oriented weapons, including its own aircraft carriers and ballistic missiles.[25] Consequently, this defensive umbrella supplies a foundation for Japan's willingness and capacity to intervene militarily on the Korean peninsula and in the Taiwan Strait.

Yuan Lin offers perhaps the most complete treatment of the offense–defense balance. He argues that the defensive armaments of Aegis ships enable them to operate in coastal waters, thus extending the reach of their offensive weapons deep into the enemy's interior.[26] Yuan cites the shoot down of Iran Flight 655 by USS *Vincennes* as an example of the air threat that an Aegis-equipped ship can pose in littoral waters. Yuan further asserts that BMD technologies provide the basis for developing offensive capabilities. For example, he observes that SM-2 antiair missiles onboard the Aegis have been converted into antisurface weapons. Yuan concludes, "Obviously, in the future, the U.S. Navy's Aegis ships will not only serve as shields against air and ballistic missile threats, but they will also become platforms for offensive guided missiles, while Japan's Aegis ships will naturally possess the potential capacity to conduct guided missile attacks."[27] Whether the author is referring to Japan's potential for developing long-range land-attack missiles is unclear. Given that Japan already possesses abundant supplies of very capable Harpoon antiship missiles and boasts a world-class space launch vehicle industry, the value of the potential technological spin offs may be more marginal than the author ascribes to the BMD system.

Not surprisingly, Chinese analysts worry most about U.S.–Japanese intervention in a Taiwan Strait scenario.[28] A long-standing fear that mainland Chinese observers have expressed for many years is Taiwan's direct participation in the U.S.–Japan missile defense architecture. Most of the analyses thus far have been couched in rather abstract terms. But there is evidence that some have ventured into more concrete territory. For example, Wang Pengfei and Sun Zhihong believe that Japan will rely on BMD-related intelligence assets to gather information about the PLA's ballistic missile and air forces, which could be transferred directly to Taiwanese authorities or indirectly through the U.S. military. Enhanced strategic and battlefield awareness may even tempt Japan to join in air- and missile-defense operations should the United States intervene in a Taiwan contingency.[29]

Another fascinating dimension of the Chinese discourse on sea-based BMD is the prospect of a multinational coalition centered on the joint employment of Aegis ships. Some analysts argue that the United States cannot rely exclusively on Japan to offer complete protection against the ballistic missile threat. Thus, they speculate, Washington is seeking to entice other powers, such as South Korea and Australia, to join a regional architecture that maximizes the maritime geography of Asia along the first and second island chains.[30] Others are particularly concerned with Australia's apparent interest in developing its own Aegis fleet, which they believe could provide an operational basis for joining the U.S.–Japan missile shield.[31]

Consequently, Ren Dexin postulates that China may soon be confronted with a "U.S.-Japan-Australia anti-ballistic missile coalition" (美日澳反导联盟).[32] Given the vast distances involved in defending Australia against long-range missile threats, Japan and the United States would provide early warning of missile launches from mainland Asia and from submerged launches in the Pacific. Ren concludes that the sea-based BMD alliance would effectively erect a "protective shield" (屏障) reaching fifty kilometers above the earth's atmosphere along the entire first island chain. Another observer depicts a division of labor in which Japan would furnish forward defense against land-based missile threats while Australia would monitor launches by submarines operating in the Pacific.[33] It is notable, however, that these authors envision a far more capable missile defense system, including the detection of SSBN launches, than currently planned by the United States. Nevertheless, the Chinese are clearly contemplating creative configurations of sea-based missile defense beyond the U.S.–Japan alliance.

Operational and Tactical Assessments

Given the central role that Aegis ships play in bolstering the U.S. missile defense architecture and in protecting American CSGs, China's naval community has devoted substantial attention to the combat capabilities of the *Ticonderoga*-class cruiser and the *Arleigh Burke*–class destroyer.[34] Chinese observers have produced in-depth comparative analyses of Aegis-equipped ships with other capable vessels to highlight both the operational strengths and weaknesses of the U.S. surface fleet. A major conclusion from these assessments is the relative inferiority of the Aegis in prosecuting antiship missions. A study that pits the *Ticonderoga* against Russia's *Kirov*-class nuclear-powered cruiser gives the latter a decisive edge. The author notes that the *Kirov* is designed almost exclusively for striking the enemy's carrier while the *Ticonderoga* is saddled with multiple tasks, including fleet air defense, thus diluting its ability to contest sea control.[35] Another article provocatively titled "Carrier Killer vs. Carrier Bodyguard" examines the potential asymmetries between the *Ticonderoga* and Ukraine's *Slava*-class cruiser. The analyst reaches roughly the same conclusion, implying that the Aegis ship would be unable to cope with the sea-skimming cruise missiles launched from the *Slava* in a ship-to-ship engagement.[36]

Other commentators compare U.S. ships with similar platforms deployed by other Asian navies. One Chinese reporter records his personal observations of USS *Lassen*, an *Arleigh Burke*–class destroyer that made a port call to Shanghai in April 2008. He was apparently struck by the conspicuous absence of Harpoon antiship missiles onboard the *Lassen*. The analyst attributes this apparent departure from the customary configuration of armaments to the U.S. Navy's belief that (1) naval aviation would be sufficient to conduct sea control missions; (2) the probability of fleet engagements on the high seas is extremely low; and (3) Aegis ships should focus on its comparative advantages, namely air and missile defense. In contrast, he notes, the Aegis equivalents in the Japanese, South Korean, and Chinese navies are being "armed to the teeth" (武装到牙齿) with antiship missiles.[37] Although the article does not elaborate on the operational implications of this apparent divergence among the regional navies, it represents a broader analytical attention to potential vulnerabilities of the U.S. Aegis.

Chinese analysts similarly examine the weaknesses of the Japanese Aegis. They note that the *Kongou-* and *Atago*-class destroyers are relatively feeble in antiship missions due to the multiple roles assigned to them. One analyst observes that as the centerpiece of Japan's theater missile defense system *Atago's* other combat capabilities, including ship-to-ship engagements, will likely be compromised.[38] Another far more critical assessment argues that the Japanese destroyers are unable to fully maximize the operational potential of the Aegis combat system due to U.S. concerns over the military balance in Asia and the associated restrictions on technology transfers to Japan. Such limits have given birth to a class of surface combatants that the author evocatively describes as a "deformed child" (畸形儿).[39] An unusually revealing study pits China's *Sovremenny*-class destroyer against the *Kongou*, echoing the comparisons between the *Ticonderoga* and the *Slava* noted earlier. In a ship-to-ship match, Tian Ying concludes that the *Kongou* would have difficulties defending against the *Sovremenny's* Sunburn cruise missiles.[40]

Intriguingly, these assessments of the U.S. and Japanese surface fleets conform to Mahanian precepts of sea power that extol aggressive offensive action at sea. Indeed, some strategists conceive of operational plans against the JMSDF in terms that would have been instantly recognizable to Alfred Thayer Mahan himself. Since Japanese planners consider the *Kongou* their capital ship, they contend offensive operations must focus on defeating this center of gravity.[41] This line of reasoning parallels Chinese explorations of anticarrier strategies against a potential U.S. intervention in the Asian littorals. Moreover, such a conclusion has operational implications for a potential U.S.–Japan intervention in a Taiwan-related contingency. For some Chinese, attacking the capital ships of the weaker ally might accrue strategic benefits by undermining coalition cohesion, demonstrating China's resolve, shoring up deterrence, and precluding the prospects of escalation with the more powerful alliance partner.[42]

In addition to ship-to-ship engagements, some of the literature examines options to defeat the Aegis from the air. One article criticizing Taiwan's apparent interest in purchasing the decommissioned *Ticonderoga*-class cruiser dismisses the value of the ship to Taipei's overall defense strategy. In wartime, Guan Dai argues, the Taiwanese navy would likely be confronted with air-launched saturation attacks and super saturation attacks (超饱和攻击) from the mainland, instantly rendering the *Ticonderoga's* air defenses useless.[43] In one of *Modern Navy's* nine-part series on the JMSDF, Zhao Yu asserts that in the absence of organic naval aviation units, Japan's Aegis air defense remains highly vulnerable to penetration.[44] Another article from *Naval and Merchant Ships* make a rough estimate of the numbers of fighters armed with antiship missiles that would be required to put eight Aegis ships out of action. Using reasonable figures on likely loss and failure rates, the author concludes that 150–200 SU-30s or equivalent aircraft would be needed to complete such a mission.[45] That Chinese analysts are thinking in such concrete terms about penetrating Aegis missile defenses is a rather remarkable analytical phenomenon.

Although mentioned far less frequently, it is still notable that the Chinese have begun to assess in a preliminary way the use of ASBMs against Aegis-equipped platforms. Observers have taken note of recent U.S. research and development efforts over the SM-6, the next-generation interceptor that is reportedly a direct response to China's potential ASBM threat.[46] Wang Xiangsui, the director of the Strategic Studies Center at the Beijing University of Aeronautics and Astronautics, explains the utility of ASBMs against the JMSDF.[47] He argues that while Japanese naval planners exhibit confidence in their ability to defeat the Chinese fleet in a force-on-force naval engagement, reports that China plans to employ ASBMs have introduced significant uncertainty in their calculus. Wang evinces the belief that Japan's interest in joint BMD development with the United States is partly animated by the perceived requirement to defend against Chinese antiship ballistic missiles. His candid analysis reveals that some Chinese believe that ASBM capabilities are likely to shore up deterrence against superior naval forces.

China's Hierarchy of Anti-Aegis Tactics

The range of options identified by Chinese analysts suggests that the threats to the Aegis could originate from multiple vectors. None of the anti-Aegis alternatives are necessarily mutually exclusive. Provided that Beijing devotes the necessary resources and possesses the capacity for joint coordination, the combined employment of fleet-on-fleet engagements, air-launched saturation attacks, and ASBMs would more likely overwhelm sea-based air and missiles defenses than if used singularly. Given the varying degrees of risk and costs involved among the three anti-Aegis tactics, prioritizing them in relation to each other and in relation to geospatial and temporal considerations would be prudent. In other words, China would likely hold in reserve its antiship options that are more likely to fail or more difficult to carry out while prosecuting those enjoying higher probabilities of success in the early phases of a campaign. It is therefore possible to envision PLA planners applying each capability in sequential terms—in proportion to the escalating costs of each tactic—thereby erecting a layered defense against approaching U.S. naval forces.

Ship-to-ship engagements are perhaps one of the riskiest options available to Beijing. Finding, tracking, and targeting ships on the open seas are difficult undertakings, requiring a range of intelligence, surveillance, and reconnaissance assets. Moreover, confrontation at sea plays to the U.S. Navy's comparative advantage. It is unlikely that China's surface combatants on their own would survive the U.S. Navy's offensive strikes intact while attempting to close in sufficiently for antiship missiles to reach the American surface fleet. Air-launched saturation attacks using over-the-horizon "fire and forget" missiles against the U.S. fleet may be a less costly approach than a fleet-on-fleet engagement. However, not only do Chinese bombers and fighters need sufficient ranges and targeting capabilities to hit ships at sea, they also need to contend with U.S. and allied air forces based across the first island chain in order to fire their first salvo.

It is in this context that the potential value of antiship ballistic missiles becomes more apparent. Launched from the Chinese mainland, an ASBM requires neither expensive ships nor aircraft to carry it to the target. In other words, the employment of such missiles does not entail the potentially high levels of human and material costs that fleet engagements or air attacks would likely incur. Moreover, Chinese strategists are acutely aware of the physical vulnerabilities of U.S. warships.[48] Analysts in China thus believe that successful attacks against key subcomponents of a ship would be sufficient to inflict disabling blows without sinking the vessel. According to the Office of Naval Intelligence, "Researchers considered that aircraft carrier sub-systems, such as catapults, arresting wires, topside electronics, and elevators, would be vulnerable to 'mission kill' strikes by sub-munitions deployed from an ASBM."[49] For Chinese strategists, the logic of such fragility applies with equal force to Aegis ships.

Chinese planners foresee the use of warheads armed with submunitions that could be scattered across a wide geographic area to compensate for potential missile imprecision. For example, ASBM warheads could release antiradiation submunitions designed to home in on the radar emissions of the Aegis combat system. Similarly, electromagnetic pulse submunitions detonated far above the U.S. surface fleet could produce devastating electrical surges that shut down the Aegis sensors onboard the carrier escorts. According to *The Science of Second Artillery Campaigns*, an authoritative doctrinal guide for China's strategic rocket forces, such ASBMs would be used to blind and confuse the CSG.[50] Senior PLA officers are clearly thinking in astonishingly specific and imaginative ways about defeating the Aegis system with the ASBM.

Equally troubling, ASBMs may not need to produce mission kills against the surface fleet to complicate U.S. plans. They only need to reach the fleet's defensive envelope for the Aegis to engage the incoming threats, thus forcing the defender to expend valuable ammunition that cannot be easily resupplied at sea under combat conditions. Even inaccurate ASBMs, then, could compel the Aegis to exhaust its weapons inventory, leaving it defenseless against further PLA actions. Used in conjunction with conventional ballistic missile strikes against U.S. bases and other land targets across Asia—strikes that would elicit more interception attempts—ASBM raids could deprive the United States and its allies of their staying power in a sea fight. Beijing could then multiply the U.S. Navy's problems by launching successive waves of attacks from the air and at sea. The PLA could unleash air-launched saturation attacks followed by undersea and seaborne cruise missile salvos to wear down the fleet's defenses as it approached the first island chain. If planned and executed properly, such a layered sequence of offensives could set the stage for some type of a breakthrough. Advanced guidance systems onboard these missiles would further stress U.S. defenses.[51] In other words, a Chinese missile could very well reach its intended target. The strategic and politico-psychological impact of a direct hit on the U.S. theater commander and the national command authority are unknowable. But it is possible to imagine that the very possibility of a breach in the U.S. fleet's defenses would give Washington pause when deliberating a decision to intervene in a crisis. This admittedly dark scenario suggests that the ASBM, if or when it becomes operational, could become Beijing's weapon of first resort when contemplating options to defeat the Aegis.

Implications

As the Chinese direct their attention to sea-based BMD and consider plans for defeating Aegis defenses, U.S. planners must similarly grapple with Beijing's potential responses to this emerging nautical dimension of Sino-American strategic ties. What follows are the distillation of the Chinese discourse reviewed earlier and the types of missile defense–related challenges that Washington could confront in the future.

- At the strategic level, analysts who tend to exude a greater sense of confidence about China's invulnerability to the seaborne missile shield stand on firm ground. Their conclusion that BMD-capable Aegis ships patrolling the Asian littorals will not fundamentally undermine the deterrent value of the Chinese intercontinental ballistic missile (ICBM) arsenal is fully consistent with geographic and technological realities. In addition to China's strategic depth, the next-generation road mobile ICBMs and the emerging undersea deterrent virtually secures Beijing's retaliatory capabilities.

- At the theater level, Chinese alarm at seaborne missile defense is not necessarily misplaced. An effective sea-based BMD could very well erode Beijing's ability to threaten regional targets with selective, limited ballistic missile strikes for demonstration purposes during a crisis. But this does not guarantee that China would be deterred from exercising its coercive option altogether.

- If Beijing concludes that it must overcome the BMD system either by launching more missiles or by targeting the Aegis ships themselves, then the potential for crisis instability and escalation will likely increase. In other words, the more missiles fired and the more targets acquired by China, the greater the likelihood that Beijing would trigger punishing retaliation by its adversaries.

- In terms of alliance politics, some Chinese seem to assume that Japan will inevitably join U.S. intervention in a Taiwan-related contingency. If Beijing does in fact view Japan as the weak coalition partner that can be picked off through an early or preemptive strike against the JMSDF's Aegis destroyers, then escalation control could become an even more complex undertaking.

- At the operational level, long-standing U.S. naval doctrine assumes that naval forces can shoot the archer before the archer shoots his arrow. This deeply embedded American operational preference for the offense will likely come under severe strain given that the Chinese are thinking about ways to preclude the United States from ever reaching the archer.

The voluminous writings on sea-based BMD and the Aegis suggest that China's interest in these topics is not an ephemeral analytical anomaly that will fade away anytime soon. Indeed, the competitive intellectual environment within which this discourse on missile defense is occurring provides outside observers with an invaluable opportunity to monitor the progress and maturation of Chinese thinking on missile and antimissile interactions. In particular, China watchers should expect analysts to revisit these subjects in the coming years as new options, such as the prospective ASBM capability, become technically viable and more widely available.

Notes

1. Wayne P. Hughes, *Fleet Tactics and Coastal Combat* (Annapolis, MD: Naval Institute Press, 2000), 305.

2. Lisle A. Rose, *Power at Sea: A Violent Peace* (Columbia: University of Missouri Press, 2007), 216–18.

3. Ronald O'Rourke, *China's Naval Modernization: Implications for U.S. Navy Capabilities—Background and Issues for Congress*, Congressional Research Service, RL33153, 9 April 2010, 5.

4. 任德新 [Ren Dexin], "宙斯盾舰合围中国" ["Aegis Ships Encircle China"], 舰船知识 [*Naval and Merchant Ships*] (September 2007): 12.

5. "17 艘宙斯盾围绕中国" ["Seventeen Aegis Vessels Surround China"], 晚霞 [*Sunset*] (July 2007): 18.

6. 陈位昊 [Chen Lihao], "宙斯盾舰成功拦截中程导弹" ["Aegis Ship Successfully Intercepts Medium-Range Ballistic Missile"], 国际展望 [*World Outlook*], no. 531 (January 2006): 9.

7. 任德新 [Ren Dexin], "太平洋的宙斯盾反导系统" ["Aegis Anti-Ballistic Missile System in the Pacific"], 当代军事文摘 [*Modern Military Digest*] (October 2007): 18–19.

8. 海研 [Hai Yan], "军事重镇—横须贺军港" ["Strategic Military Site—Yokosuka Naval Base"], 当代海军 [*Modern Navy*] (September 2006): 59.

9. 刘江平 [Liu Jiangping], "太平洋上的宙斯盾反导战舰群" ["Aegis Anti-Ballistic Missile Fleet in the Pacific"], 当代海军 [*Modern Navy*] (June 2008): 29.

10. 任德新, 程健良 [Ren Dexin and Cheng Jianliang], "宙斯盾反导系统在太平洋的部署及使用" ["The Deployment and Use of Aegis Anti-Ballistic Missile System in the Pacific"], 舰船知识 [*Naval and Merchant Ships*] (July 2007): 17.

11. 戴艳丽 [Dai Yanli], "我周边宙斯盾舰的运行及威胁" ["The Functioning and Threat of Aegis Ships on Our Periphery"], 舰船知识 [*Naval and Merchant Ships*] (September 2007): 18.

12. 齐艳丽 [Qi Yanli], "美国海基中段防御系统" ["The U.S. Sea-Based Midcourse Defense System"], 导弹与航天运载技术 [*Missiles and Space Vehicles*], no. 3 (2005): 61.

13. 白炎林 [Bai Yanlin], "岛连上的世界海军" ["World Navies along the Island Chains"], 当代海军 [*Modern Navy*] (October 2007): 14.

14. 吴勤 [Wu Qin], "美国太空战的矛与盾" ["The Spear and the Shield of U.S. Space Warfare"], 现代军事 [*Conmilit*] (May 2005): 47.

15. 彭灏, 张素梅 [Peng Hao and Zhang Sumei], "日本导弹防御系统面观" ["A View of Japan's Ballistic Missile System"], 飞航导弹 [*Winged Missiles Journal*], no. 1 (2007): 22.

16. Wang Baofu, "Why U.S., Japan Speed Up Missile Shield Deployment?" *Renmin Ribao* [*People's Daily*], 17 July 2006, OSC CPP20060717701001.

17. 罗山爱 [Luo Shanai], "日本用啥保卫东京?" ["What Does Japan Use to Protect Tokyo?"], 环球军事 [*Global Military*], no. 118 (January 2006): 17. For similar commentary, see 林炎 [Lin Yan], "日本首次海基弹道导弹拦截分析" ["An Analysis of Japan's First Sea-Based Ballistic Missile Interception"], 当代海军 [*Modern Navy*] (February 2008): 17.

18. 周晓光, 陈永红 [Zhou Xiaoguang and Chen Yonghong], "日本海军战略的新动向" ["New Trends in Japan's Naval Strategy"], 当代海军 [*Modern Navy*] (July 2006): 64.

19. 石江月 [Shi Jiangyue], "美国加速提升太平洋军力瞄准谁?" ["At Whom Are America's Accelerated Increases in Pacific Military Power Directed?"], 现代舰船 [*Modern Ships*], no. 10A (2006): 11.

20. 王鹏飞, 孙志宏 [Wang Pengfei and Sun Zhihong], "联合美台, BMD即将建成日本反导系统介入台湾" ["Joining U.S. and Taiwan, BMD Will Soon Enable Japan's Antiballistic Missile System to Intervene over Taiwan"], 国际展望 [*World Outlook*], no. 18 (2007): 55.

21. For Chinese descriptions of the operational advantages of sea-based BMD, see 孟昭香 [Meng Shaoxiang], "21世纪的宙斯盾" ["Aegis of the Twenty-First Century"], 情报指挥控制系统与仿真技术 [*Information Command Control System and Simulation Technology*], no. 6 (December 2005): 3; and 钟建业 [Zhong Jianya], "日本的导弹防御系统" ["Japan's Ballistic Missile Defense System"], 中国航天 [*Aerospace China*], no. 10 (October 2005): 38.

22. 候健军 [Hou Jianjun], "日本海上自卫队的新战略与新装备" ["The New Strategy and New Equipment of Japan's Maritime Self-Defense Forces"], 当代海军 [*Modern Navy*] (February 2006): 20; and 吕修顺 [Lu Xiushun], "点评日韩最新型宙斯盾驱逐舰" ["Comments on Japan's and South Korea's Newest Aegis Destroyers"], 舰载武器 [*Shipborne Weapons*] (July 2007): 64.

23. 高山 [Gao Shan], "对付中国—日本未来主力舰艇发展构想" ["Coping with China—The Conceptual Development of Japan's Future Capital Ships"], 现代舰船 [*Modern Ships*], no. 2A (2006): 31; 李杰 [Li Jie], "日韩新一代宙斯盾驱逐舰" ["Japan's and South Korea's New Generation Aegis Destroyers"], 当代海军 [*Modern Navy*] (May 2007): 33; and "雷锡恩公司将进行标准-3 Block 2A 的开发" ["Raytheon Corporation Will Soon Develop Standard Missile-3 Block 2A"], 飞航导弹 [*Winged Missiles Journal*], no. 9 (2006): 9.

24. 博慧军 [Bo Huijun], "日本: 加速向军事强国迈进" ["Japan: Forging Ahead Rapidly to Become a Great Military Power"], 环球军事 [*Global Military*], no. 120 (February 2006).

25. 温德义 [Wen Deyi], "盾与刀—日本加速建立弹道导弹防御系统及影响" ["The Shield and the Sword—The Influence of Japan's Accelerating Development of Ballistic Missile Defense System"], 现代兵器 [*Modern Weaponry*] (January 2006): 12.

26. 远林, 金琳 [Yuan Lin and Jin Lin], "防御导弹的奥秘在攻" ["The Subtlety of Ballistic Missile Defense Is in the Offense"], 当代军事文摘 [*Contemporary Military Digest*] (June 2006): 64.

27. 远林 [Yuan Lin], "导弹防御系统以攻为守" ["Ballistic Missile Defense System Relies on Offense for Defense"], 中国新闻周刊 [*China Newsweek*], 23 January 2006, 87.

28. 李瑞 [Li Rui], "美日加快军事一体化对台海安全态势的影响" ["The Influence of Rapid U.S.-Japan Military Integration on Taiwan Strait Security"], 科教文汇 [*The Science Education Article Collection*], December 2007, 124–25.

29. Wang and Sun, "Joining U.S. and Taiwan" 55.

30. 李杰 [Li Jie], "宙斯盾为啥齐聚亚太?" ["Why Are Aegis Ships Gathering in the Asia Pacific?"], 当代海军 [*Modern Navy*] (November 2007): 26.

31. Cao Zhigang, "U.S., Japan Suffer from 'Missile Allergy,'" *Jiefangjun bao* [*Liberation Army Daily*], 19 July 2007, 5, OSC CPP20070719710015.

32. Ren, "Aegis Ships Encircle China," 15.

33. 杜朝平 [Du Chaoping], "东经135°的网—日本和澳大利亚军事合作走向" ["The Net at East Longitude 135 Degrees—The Direction of Japanese-Australian Military Cooperation"], 现代舰船 [*Modern Ships*] (May 2007): 10–11.

34. For an overview of the evolution of the Aegis system, see 施征 [Shi Zheng], "美国海军的保护伞—宙斯盾系统" ["The U.S. Navy's Protective Umbrella—The Aegis System"], 海洋世界 [*Ocean World*], no. 8 (2006): 40–46.

35. 肖鹏 [Xiao Peng], "近看两种现代巡洋舰龙虎斗—提康德罗加 VS 基洛夫" ["A Close Look at Competition between Two Types of Modern Cruisers—Ticonderoga vs. Kirov"], 当代世界 [*Contemporary World*], no. 4 (2007): 58.

36. 王逸峰 [Wang Yifeng], "航母杀手 VS 航母守护神—简评光荣级与提康德罗加级" ["Carrier Killer vs. Carrier Guardian—A Review of the Slava Class and the Ticonderoga Class"], 舰载武器 [*Shipborne Weapons*] (May 2005): 17.

37. 一翔 [Yi Xiang], "细品宙斯盾" ["A Close Look at Aegis"], 现代兵器 [*Modern Weaponry*] (August 2008): 7.

38. 闻舞 [Wen Wu], "爱拓级 VS KDX-3—东北亚宙斯盾大比拼" ["Atago Class vs. KDX-3—Aegis Competition in Southeast Asia"], 当代海军 [*Modern Navy*] (July 2007): 73.

39. 陈安刚 [Chen Angang], "点击日本宙斯盾战舰" ["Opening up Japan's Aegis Warship"], 现代舰船 [*Modern Ships*], no. 10A (2006): 22.

40. 天鹰 [Tian Ying], "剑与盾—东亚水域的现代与金刚" ["The Sword and Shield—The Sovremenny and the Kongou in East Asian Waters"], 舰载武器 [*Shipborne Weapons*] (March 2007): 44.

41. 海潮 [Hai Chao], "日本铸造海上防空盾牌—日本金刚级宙斯盾驱逐舰的性能演变" ["Japan Forges an Air Defense Shield at Sea—The Evolution of the Performance of Japan's Kongou-Class Aegis Destroyer"], 舰载武器 [*Shipborne Weapons*] (August 2005): 56.

42. 吴红民 [Wu Hongmin], "目标—金刚 虚拟战场" ["Target—Kongou Fictitious Battlefield"], 舰载武器 [*Shipborne Weapons*] (June 2004): 87.

43. 管带 [Guan Dai], "提康德罗加巡洋舰对台湾的影响" ["The Influence of the Ticonderoga Cruise On Taiwan"], 现代舰船 [*Modern Ships*], no. 2A (2005): 22.

44. 赵宇 [Zhao Yu], "全景扫描日本海上军事力量—海军海上作战力量" ["Comprehensive Assessment of Japan's Naval Power—The Navy's Combat Power"], 当代海军 [*Modern Navy*] (September 2005): 58.

45. "中国航空兵如何突破宙斯盾合围" ["How China's Air Arm Can Penetrate Aegis Encirclement"], 舰船知识 [*Naval and Merchant Ships*] (October 2007): 18.

46. 陈娜 [Chen Na], "无限打击之刃—盘点美国未来舰载作战系统" ["Unlimited Striking Power of the Sword—Taking Stock of America's Future Shipborne Combat Systems"], 国际展望 [*World Outlook*], no. 24 (2007): 53.

47. 杨承军, 王湘穗 [Wu Guifu, Yang Chengjun, and Wang Xiangsui], "21世纪初的航天科技与新军事变革" ["Aerospace Technology and the Transformation of New Military Affairs in the Early Twenty-First Century"], 太平洋学报 [*Pacific Journal*], no. 3 (2006): 14.

48. For an assessment of the frailties of modern warships, see David A. Shlapak, David T. Orletsky, Toy I. Reid, Murray Scot Tanner, and Barry Wilson, *A Question of Balance: Political Context and Military Aspects of the China-Taiwan Dispute* (Santa Monica, CA: RAND, 2009), 102.

49. Office of Naval Intelligence, *The People's Liberation Army Navy: A Modern Navy with Chinese Characteristics* (Washington, DC: ONI, August 2009), 27.

50. 中国人民解放军第二炮兵 [China's People's Liberation Army Second Artillery Corps], 第二炮兵战役学 [*The Science of Second Artillery Campaigns*] (Beijing: Liberation Army Press, 2004), 402.

51. ONI, *People's Liberation Army Navy*, 28.

Paul S. Giarra

A Chinese Antiship Ballistic Missile
Implications for the U.S. Navy

CHINA IS PURSUING the testing and deployment of very long-range, land-mobile, maneuverable reentry vehicle-equipped (MaRVed) antiship ballistic missiles (ASBMs), apparently the "D" variant of the DF-21 medium-range ballistic missile (MRBM). Like the Chinese development program itself, public awareness of the potential regional "keep out" capability of Chinese ASBMs is gaining steam in the West, as evidenced by the May 2009 issue of the U.S. Naval Institute *Proceedings*.[1] The sobering cover illustration depicts a U.S. Navy *Nimitz*-class aircraft carrier and its AEGIS escort in flames after being struck by a Chinese ASBM. In December 2010, Admiral Robert Willard, Commander, U.S. Pacific Command, revealed that China's ASBM had reached the "equivalent" of "initial operational capability."

This chapter's approach is to parse the implications of ASBMs for the United States, consider how to organize for the coming challenge, and, more fundamentally, how to "think about thinking about" Chinese ASBMs. After all, confronting China's ASBM capability is not that different from thinking through and responding with all sources of defense and national power to, for instance, the Soviet submarine threat during the Cold War. Perhaps the biggest challenge will be to suspend disbelief regarding having, yet again, to go through the travails and danger of a grand challenge of this magnitude.

China is playing to win, and ASBMs are emblematic of Beijing's serious-ness. As part of a broad front of military developments since the mid-1990s, such an unprecedented antiaccess capability—to hit a ship under way with a ballistic missile—has numerous implications for the U.S. Navy, the U.S. mil-itary, and American strategic mobility both in the Asia-Pacific and globally. China's successful deployment of an ASBM would give it an antiaccess weapon that could hold U.S. carrier strike groups (CSGs) at bay. Experts believe such a missile would be a DF-21 variant, a member of the Dongfeng family of mis-siles. Imagine very long-range artillery with great accuracy that was land mobile, making counterbattery fire virtually impossible. Then imagine that someone had the idea to turn it seaward and make it capable of hitting a ship under way by adding a "shell" that could actively seek and home in on its tar-get. This is what China's ASBM amounts to: extraordinarily long-range mobile coastal artillery.

Chinese ASBMs are a "keep out" capability designed to attack naval sur-face platforms, which are the centerpiece of American naval power and the basis for U.S. deterrence strategy. In any reasonable future scenario, American security depends on unimpeded naval power. China's development of ASBMs makes moving to and remaining in near-ashore sea areas problematic for the United States.

If left unchecked, Chinese ASBMs will have dramatic implications for the other U.S. services as well as for friends and allies. No other American military operations, whether air, ground, or amphibious, are feasible in a region where the Navy cannot operate. China's strategic intent is to put at severe risk the "eyes, ears, and fists" of American power projection systems built for short-range, persistent operations in the Asian littoral and China's maritime approaches. Conversely, ballistic missiles ranging American bases and en route facilities make naval operations very problematic. Thus, Chinese ASBMs represent a remarkably important asymmetric attempt to control the sea from the shore. The capability is not yet fully operational but has been tested in some fashion.[2]

The Chinese capability will depend upon—and represents the real advent of—network warfare. Their missiles have to be aimed at the general area of a network-detected naval target, where their internal guidance systems can take over. Like the Soviets before them, the Chinese are now trying to solve this dif-ficult reconnaissance-strike problem. But unlike the Soviets, and armed with technology Moscow never had, the Chinese appear to believe that they can make this complex capability work.

For persistent long-term operations, the U.S. Navy relies primarily on air-craft carriers and their embarked air wings. Without extraordinary efforts to provide for air-to-air refueling, naval aircraft have an effective tactical radius of less than 1,000 nm. The DF-21, a relatively short-range option for ASBM capability, has a similar range, "in excess of 1,500 kilometers" according to the 2010 Defense of Department report on China's military.[3]

The numbers are going to be in China's favor. In a wartime situation, even if every U.S. interceptor hit and destroyed an inbound ASBM, naval missile magazines are very limited and cannot be reloaded at sea. This is a glaring deficiency for the U.S. Navy. It severely limits the attributes of mobile and flexible striking power and turns high-tech network warfare into a simple battle of attrition favoring the offense. Furthermore, a salvo-by-salvo contest between the shore and the sea holds huge advantages for the shore-based opponent including, in this case, magazine capacity and the far lower cost of offensive shore-based missiles versus ship-based interceptors.

Bad news does not improve with age. Once the Chinese deploy a successful ASBM capability, it is bound to escalate in sophistication and effectiveness and proliferate widely over time—"the gift that keeps on giving"—further complicating America's military posture.

Fair Warning

The publication in the *Naval War College Review* of a translation of the Chinese *Shipborne Weapons* journal article "The Effect of Tactical Ballistic Missiles on the Maritime Strategy System of China" has permitted an early unclassified analysis of the threat.[4] In what amounted to fair warning to U.S. Navy commanders and strategic planners, the *Shipborne Weapons* article raised a series of important and timely questions for American strategic planners and introduces a set of challenges that will stretch the capabilities, resources, and imaginations of American analysts. Several years on, the *Shipborne Weapons* article now is only one of many unclassified Chinese resources addressing ASBMs and available for analysis.

Not since the fifteenth century has China's navy come to sea in a meaningful way. Ultimately it will be up to Beijing to answer the question of whether the People's Liberation Army Navy (PLAN) is "coming out" in a determined challenge to U.S. naval dominance. The question often posed by American naval officers and maritime strategists has been whether the Chinese would mirror American naval capabilities as reflected by the perennial interest in whether a PLAN aircraft carrier was looming on the horizon. However, the PLAN's more or less symmetric "coming out" is not the same as asymmetric

Chinese measures designed to hold the U.S. surface fleet at long range on the maritime approaches to China. The prospect of Chinese land-mobile MaRVed ASBMs able to range U.S. and allied surface units at extremely long-range (thousands of miles) is sufficiently different in kind from conventional maritime antiaccess capabilities to merit very serious due diligence in Washington, Canberra, and Tokyo. Such an asymmetric land-based Chinese system aspires to achieve nothing less than a stifling effect on American strategic mobility as the U.S. Navy has come to understand and exploit it.

It is increasingly apparent from unclassified sources that the PLA is preparing to field land-mobile MaRVed ASBMs. The *Shipborne Weapons* article suggests that there is more than one channel to the sea buoy for China, and there are alternatives to Western doctrine and practice for Chinese maritime strategy and naval capabilities. Even at the time of its translation in 2008, the *Shipborne Weapons* article on Chinese ASBMs was not "new news." Since then, Chinese writers have been publishing prolifically on the subject for some time.[5]

Chinese ASBMs have the potential to be a genuine manifestation of asymmetric power. For very little investment relative to the capacity of the Chinese economy, the Chinese seem to be acquiring an effective answer to forward U.S. deployment against them.

Chinese ASBMs will be "visible" during their development, given that such an inherent technically demanding system-of-systems capability is going to be so intrinsically part of a large reconnaissance-strike complex. While not a "surprise" per se, like any other "trump card" or "silver bullet" that the PLA might attempt to leverage for disproportionate effect, ASBMs are nevertheless a perfect example of China's propensity to pursue an asymmetric "assassin's mace"—that is, post-nuclear-weapon super weapon—approach to sea control and maritime security. The PLA's Second Artillery even refers to the ASBM as an "assassin's mace."

Chinese Commentary and American Caveats

As with other significant defense programs and strategies, the Chinese are saying quite a bit publicly regarding speculation, rationale, and plans for a new ASBM capability in open-source academic, military, and media writing. This springs from the literary nature of China, similar to that in the United States, where writing and the keeping of records serves an important cultural purpose—a process now more widespread than ever with the advent of a modern publishing industry. As a result, media reporting and speculation plays a particularly significant role in publicizing potential new capabilities such as Chinese ASBMs and, as elsewhere, the wonders of the Internet enable sharing and distribution of relevant information. While the prospect of Chinese ASBMs to challenge the American Navy in the Asia-Pacific may not be exactly new news, the issue is reaching critical analytical mass in the unclassified realm of open-source materials and unclassified analysis.

Caveats Regarding Chinese Writings

Strategic Signaling.

With these caveats in mind, strategic signaling by Beijing regarding this new ASBM capability appears to be authentic. This presents an ineluctable challenge to the United States and to the U.S. Navy in particular: no nation that depends upon strategic mobility and maritime power can afford to be wrong about such a capability.

"The Effect of Tactical Ballistic Missiles on the Maritime Strategy System of China."

The *Shipborne Weapons* article calls for a certain analytical perspective from the outset. The present analysis stipulates that comments by the author of the *Shipborne Weapons* article regarding Taiwan-related geopolitics, strategic space, escalation control, and so on, apply equally to both theater-wide operations against the U.S. Navy absent considerations of Taiwan—that is, in the broader context of Sino-American relations. Likewise, the *Shipborne Weapons* author's comments apply more generally at the strategic level in the Asia-Pacific in the Sino-American state relationship, again with its own fundamental dynamic separate and distinct from considerations of Taiwan.

Parsing the Article

The observations contained in the *Shipborne Weapons* article may be summarized as follows. ASBMs

- Resolve China's operational inferiority at sea
- Enable China to penetrate defensive systems
- Provide an asymmetric antinaval capability that would enable China to control the sea from the shore
- Are technically achievable
- Increase China's strategic-military space on its maritime approaches
- Provide China strategic-political room for maneuver

- Enable China to avoid strategic complications of land attacks
- Facilitate for China the establishing of escalation control/dominance
- Require extensive operational and intelligence preparation of the battlefield
- Justify a necessary and appropriate national-level Chinese "public investment"

Initial Analytical Conclusions

The *Shipborne Weapons* article suggests an analytical decalogue for American strategic planners, military commanders, defense officials, and political leaders.

1. ASBMs are an extremely attractive, self-reinforcing option for China. They reinforce the Chinese propensity for centralized control of military operations and the preponderance of land power.

2. Chinese ASBMs would provide the PLA a potential significant operational-level capability with strategic ramifications. This may be one instance of a technical advance with inherent strategic importance.

3. At least some Chinese analysts think that ASBMs are technically feasible for China to deploy successfully and significantly in the foreseeable future. American technical experts will have to draw their own conclusions as a first analytical priority.

4. Chinese ASBMs would be part of a Chinese system of systems reconnaissance-strike complex. This has distinct implications for the necessity to consider the growing significance of network warfare.

5. Chinese ASBMs would be potentially destabilizing, to considerable U.S. strategic disadvantage. As "if" China fields ASBMs becomes "when" China fields ASBMs, the military-strategic balance of power will change in the Asia-Pacific.

6. Although they aim explicitly at controlling the seaward approaches to China, thereby reorienting the balance of power in the Asia-Pacific, the military-strategic effects of ASBMs will be global.

7. More than ever before, the U.S. Navy cannot afford to forego the advantages of joint approaches to data collection, analysis, planning, or operations. If ever there was a rationale for "jointness" in American military art, this is it.

8. Conversely, the U.S. Air Force has a significant strategic stake in this ostensibly maritime issue because the Asia-Pacific is an aerospace theater as well as a maritime one: when the U.S. Navy catches cold, the U.S. Air Force sneezes.

9. Obviously, this is the time to muster significant analytical resources to verify or disprove the prospect of an effective future Chinese ASBM capability. The United States cannot afford to be wrong about this potentially destabilizing Chinese development.

10. The significance of this military-technical and military-operational challenge by China for the geostrategic balance of power is profound. It suggests a thought experiment in which this challenge and the responses to it are compared to the breadth and scale of the American response to the Soviet submarine challenge during the Cold War.

Chinese Actions Speak Louder than Words

Early analytical speculation regarding ASBM developments largely has been proved correct. Constant updates to technical analysis regarding Chinese ASBM developments, especially those published by Mark Stokes and his colleagues at the Project 2049 Institute, provide definitive unclassified reporting and exhaustive analysis of Chinese ASBM developments. Most significantly, Stokes and Ian Easton provide thoroughly researched information and analysis from unclassified and publicly available Chinese-language sources of overall Chinese aerospace developments.[6]

According to press accounts in August 2010, China is setting up the first operational DF-21D units, which will conduct lengthy prototype testing. On July 28 China's state-run Xinhua News Agency reported the visit of local government officials to a new Second Artillery Corps missile base in the northern Guangdong municipality of Shaoguan in southeastern China and thereby became the first to acknowledge its existence. China's new ASBM may be deployed here first.[7]

Sino-American Competition: Antiaccess versus Strategic Mobility

Broader considerations related to China's stake in the maritime domain point to Chinese motivations deeper than concerns regarding a conflict over Taiwan and suggest a more fundamental bilateral competition with the United States, which, inter alia, pits a Chinese antiaccess strategy against the U.S. dependence on strategic mobility in the Asia-Pacific and globally. In their all-important context, Chinese interests in these areas do not lead to conflict with the United States: in their broad-front challenge, they presuppose bilateral conflict. It is only necessary to read Chinese writings. They speak of disabling America's "eyes, ears, and fists" in an explicitly confrontational context of consistent strategic logic.[8]

In the context of a military net assessment, such a conflict can be seen as a competition that takes place over time between rival powers striving for military advantage with strategic implications. The Battle of Britain is an example of one campaign in a strategic aerial bombardment versus air defense competition between the Allies and the Axis powers during World War II. The outcome of a competition depends upon myriad intuitive but less obvious factors in addition to capabilities, systems, platforms, tactics, and operations, such as

- Doctrine
- Personnel
- Governance
- Command and control
- Decision processes
- Organizations
- Industrial base
- Scientific base
- Technology
- Strategic choices and proclivities
- Defense economics
- Sustainability

These factors suggest the beginnings of the broadest outline for an analytical schema regarding Chinese capabilities, applicable to each of the above Chinese challenge areas, and to the issue of Chinese ASBMs in particular.

Defining the nature of the competition is the first salvo in anticipating, equipping for, and deterring or fighting the battle envisioned in it, and this includes "winning without fighting," one of the ideals of Chinese military doctrine. Competitions can take place without a shot being fired but result in strategic outcomes nevertheless, such as the Soviet-U.S. submarine versus anti-submarine warfare competition of the Cold War.

Implications for Competitive Strategies

This competition raises all sorts of implications for competitive strategies, both American and Chinese. Because it takes two sides to compete, American planners should consider ways to strengthen aspects of the competition that favor the United States, and alternatives and work-arounds to those factors favoring China.

Internal to the Sino-American antiaccess versus strategic mobility competition, many options for doctrinal, strategic, and operational tactics, techniques, and procedures are available as well as those technological and asymmetric responses the United States might consider to defeat Chinese capabilities in detail. Once the competition has been parsed, possibilities such as command and control warfare and ways to deconstruct the necessary integrity of a Chinese over-the-horizon targeting (OTHT) system of systems will begin to make themselves evident. External to the competition and defined by it are numerous opportunities for competitive strategies that in concept would prompt desired responses or preclude negative actions by Beijing at the strategic level.

This competition is much more sophisticated and complex than simply considering whatever missile the PLA might develop, just as a complex OTHT capability envisioned here is about more than simply the land-mobile, MaRVed ASBM. Both competitions and systems of systems generally amount to more than the sum of their parts. Considering each part in turn is a prerequisite to understanding how to derail the competition by diverting it, or how to defeat the system in detail by disconnecting it. Therefore, thinking about the array of technical, doctrinal, and operational components that embody such a capability and its attendant collection and analysis challenge is the necessary first step in managing effective organizational, resource, analytical, and political responses at both the strategic and operational levels.

Interservice Dependence: The U.S. Air Force Stake in Countering Chinese ASBMs.

Interservice dependence is an old subject worth reviewing in the Asia-Pacific context. Americans remember with thanks that it was Japan that wrote the book during World War II on exposing its own strategic flanks. The woeful lack of coordination between the Imperial Japanese Army and Navy prior to and during World War II dealt a mortal blow to Tokyo's aspirations in the region, just as the disastrous broader lack of strategic and operational coordination between Japan, Germany, and Italy dealt a fatal blow to the Axis. The U.S. military cannot afford this sort of disjunction in any theater of operations, least of all at this time in the Pacific.

Range and Risk in Naval Warfare: The Potential Operational Effect of Chinese ASBMs.

At the operational level, maritime commanders try to range their adversaries at sea through stealth or weapons range because the offense—firing first from the greatest range—has the advantage. When Chinese analysts write that modern naval vessels are "highly integrated physical platforms," they mean that naval weapons have a high probability of at least mission kill if they can hit the target.[9] If opponents can be ranged routinely, then the operational effect becomes strategic, hence the importance of aircraft carriers—optimized for long-range strike—to American strategic maritime dominance.

The inherent range advantage of Chinese MaRVed ASBMs able to range surface ships at sea—at thousands of miles versus ranges of less than thirty miles of the most advanced coastal artillery—will affect the range and risk calculations of surface unit commanders and could shift the maritime balance for the U.S. strategic commander in the Pacific.

Numbers Count.

Numbers matter when the range advantage monopoly is broken, especially to a force structure that has so much capability concentrated in so few hulls. Consider that there are only about two dozen capital ships in the U.S. surface fleet: eleven or twelve heavy aircraft carriers operating in CSGs, and twelve aviation capable "straight deck" amphibious assault ships operating in expeditionary strike groups. Even adding to these numbers the other high-value units of the U.S. and potential coalition fleets—major combatants, command ships, replenishment ships, hospital ships, and transports—there are relatively few capital ship targets.

The capital ships—the big deck carriers—are robust, but they are by no means unsinkable. With so few high-value assets, commanders and planners have to consider whether a successful attack against even one of these ships, let alone a loss, would be psychologically devastating at home and operationally debilitating at sea. The potential result of such effects would be a significant decrease in overall U.S. naval power—real and perceived—in the region.

U.S. Navy and regional and functional combatant commanders would have to give high priority to active fleet defense against Chinese MaRVed ASBMs, against which even "minimal" operational and technical options would be difficult and expensive. While too early for definitive comparisons, much less conclusions, planners will have to consider the level of effort in the Navy's Cold War response to the Soviet anticarrier threat as well as that period's strategic investment in significant collection, analysis, war planning, decision making, and procurement. Over the course of the competition with the Soviets, for example, the heavy opportunity costs of defensive systems in navy hulls detracted considerably from battle group strike power.

Implications of the Loss of Air Dominance in the Asia-Pacific.

In essence, the emergence of a viable Chinese ASBM capability equates to the potential loss of American naval air dominance. If this loss comes to pass, it will be excruciatingly unpleasant for the U.S. Navy. The possibility of such a development mandates thinking now about its consequences and the requirement, together with the U.S. Air Force and allied air and naval commanders, of considering the full range of strategic, operational, and tactical responses, including enhanced network warfare capabilities; strategic and tactical dispersal afloat and ashore; and new modes of air defense at sea at the operational level of war.

Caution Will Dictate the Quest for Understanding.

In the context of the developing bilateral antiaccess versus strategic mobility competition—currently referred to as "antiaccess/area denial"—and in the event of specific ASBM developments, prudence will dictate great political and operational caution on both sides. It will be incumbent upon U.S. leaders to understand Chinese calculations from a Chinese perspective regarding decision making on the part of the PRC leadership that might lead in the future to ASBM attacks at extremely long ranges on American CSGs and expeditionary strike groups. Among other scenarios, Americans will have to consider Chinese reactions to American naval deployments as well as surprise attacks when these U.S. naval formations have not yet made any overtly aggressive moves against China.

Can the Chinese Succeed Where the Soviets Failed?

In fielding its ASBM capability, China is in a position to leverage the myriad technical advantages that were not available to the Soviets. While the full catalogue of its technical characteristics should be the basis for a serious technical review of China's ASBM program—that is, the technical structure of the program; the character of the technologies applied to it; its technical efficacy; the origin of the technologies involved; and its technical vulnerabilities— a number of obvious advancements suggest many clear advantages over Soviet programs. In many cases these relative Chinese technical advantages are based upon but by no means limited to fielded and unfielded American, Western, Soviet, and Russian technologies. They include the proliferation of dramatically advanced computing power, the availability of advanced sensors, much enhanced propulsion technology, great leaps in miniaturization, the synergistic emphasis upon ballistic missiles as a key pillar of the Chinese arsenal, deadly improvements in warhead capabilities, and a robust Chinese on-orbit capability. These technical achievements and aspirations should be seen against the backdrop of China's military modernization in general and its naval modernization in particular. Equally significant are reinforcing Chinese military doctrinal advancements that emphasize technology, speed, reach, and area denial.

A Chinese ASBM capability would be the realization of what once were the Soviet navy's aspirations for a reconnaissance-strike complex of sea- and space-borne sensors and regiment-sized attacks by antiship bombers armed with long-range antiship cruise missiles coordinated with submarine and surface vessel attacks. Cold War historians might consider whether the Soviets actually did fail, or whether their reconnaissance-strike achievements were masked by the inconclusive way the Cold War ended. At the least, perhaps the Soviet Union left as its legacy a reconnaissance-strike complex poison pill. Furthermore, metrics of success differ. It will be up to savvy American China analysts to determine, from the Chinese perspective, how Beijing would measure reconnaissance-strike success given its deterrent and political as well as operational implications.

From an American perspective, the offense at sea has an inherent advantage. For the U.S. Navy, technical breakthroughs that would make MaRVed ASBMs a viable option for China would be particularly dramatic for three reasons. First, the reconnaissance-strike complex as a whole is not cheap, but it is much less expensive than defensive systems. Second, for that reason, large numbers of penetrating systems can be fielded that are able to overwhelm defenses in coordinated attacks. Third, in a naval context, interceptor missile at-sea magazine capacity is severely limited, and defensive load-outs would be exhausted rapidly in a saturation-attack scenario, given current U.S. Navy force structures and ship designs. This third point plays out time after time in various analytical venues.

Obviously, fleet ballistic missile interceptors would not be the only countermeasure fielded against a Chinese ASBM threat. The U.S. Navy learned during the Cold War not to concentrate on the arrow if the archer could be targeted. This is one area in which U.S. and allied interservice cooperation could be a significant point of leverage because offensive counterair (i.e., penetrating stealthy missile, unmanned combat aerial vehicles, and aircraft counter-ASBM attacks against launchers, bases, and command, control, communications, computers, intelligence, surveillance, and reconnaissance facilities) is a possible capability that the Air Force can bring to bear to support and reinforce naval access to the region. Since China's integrated intelligence, surveillance, and reconnaissance system may be especially vulnerable, this is an obvious potential topic for joint, regional combatant commander, and combined allied planning.

Clearly, difficult technical and system integration hurdles will have to be overcome before China can field a viable MaRVed ASBM force. However, in addition to significant Chinese investments and coordinated domestic development, Beijing has exploited American developments that the Chinese freely admit to having analyzed exhaustively (including the Pershing II missile and its MaRVed warhead).

Implications for the U.S. Navy

Chinese OTHT reconnaissance-strike success where the Soviets failed would stimulate a strong technical and operational response from the U.S. Navy. For the U.S. Navy, successful Chinese OTHT capability would raise the prospect of Chinese antisurface unit warfare being waged at extreme ranges from homeland-based, distributed, and on-orbit platforms that would be component parts of a PLA over-the-horizon reconnaissance-strike complex. American force structures and platforms optimized for offense at the expense of defensive capabilities, and assuming relatively insignificant maritime opposition, would find themselves unexpectedly in harm's way. Without an effective counter, the surface fleet's power projection capabilities effectively would be held beyond operational range, and potentially at very long ranges.

This means, among other things, that strategic and operational power projection calculations based on the ranges of U.S. Navy carrier aircraft would be upended. Short-range aircraft in the Navy's current and future air wings, and even offensive land-attack cruise missiles, would not be relevant to peer competitions. Likewise, Marine Corps assumptions of near-shore over-the-horizon ship-to-objective maneuver would not appear to be realistic in the face of an effective Chinese ASBM capability because the naval platforms from which the Marines would stage would be held out of the peer and proliferated peer client conflict. The limiting factor of U.S. Navy shipboard BMD interceptor magazine capacity would be one factor in prompting development of shipborne and off-board distant early warning defenses against ASBMs. In sum, the U.S. fleet on the defensive would be at the strategic disadvantage vis-à-vis China, marking a drastic shift in the correlation of forces for the United States in the Asia-Pacific for the first time since 1942. This, of course, is exactly what China appears to be trying to achieve.

Would the U.S. Navy Change Its Force Structure in Response to Chinese Mobile MaRVed ASBMs?

Senior observers have opined that the U.S. Navy would not or could not change its force structure and that the fleet is being built as much for "soft" operations as for "hard" ops (witness the littoral combat ship's 2-inch main gun, and the proliferation of joint high-speed vessels [essentially long-range ferries] in the Navy's ship count).

Considerations of significant force structure changes necessarily come hard to a service built around platforms with a fifty-year service life. When external factors intrude on program objective memoranda and shipbuilding plans, might the Navy change course? There are a number of historical examples from the last century that illustrate possible alternatives to doing nothing: whether the models of reformers such as Arleigh Burke or Hyman Rickover or programmatic "revolutions" such as occurred after Pearl Harbor (as in the Manhattan Project), all furnish examples of radical institutional change within the U.S. Navy.

National Strategic Considerations

Apart from the potentially drastic consequences that an effective Chinese ASBM capability would have for the United States at the military operational and military strategic level, American political leaders would have to consider national level geostrategic effects varying in degree based on the success of professed Chinese aims.

Diminished Escalation Control.

If one may apply the first law of thermodynamics to preliminary Chinese calculations of increased escalation control through ASBMs, then in such a Sino-American competition the total control over available escalation remains constant; in other words, in a zero sum game, the United States would lose some ability to dominate escalation. This is especially true in a future proliferated world of more than the current four nuclear players in the Asia-Pacific (the United States, China, Russia, and North Korea).

Diminished Political Dominance.

In the global political system as presently configured, American political dominance has been enabled by military dominance, as reflected in its virtually unchallenged strategic mobility. This dominance manifests itself through a strategic doctrine of forward deployment that emerged at the end of World War II and was defended and pressed home against the Soviet Union during the Cold War. Chinese ASBMs would be intended to challenge the idea of that political and military dominance by physically threatening its basis in fact.

Limited Effects-Based Options.

In the military vernacular, effects-based options are those alternatives made available to political leaders through the effects of military action. Effective Chinese ASBM capabilities and strategies would preclude many military effects heretofore available to American commanders in support of desired political goals.

Unintended Consequences, Multiplayer Scenarios, and Cascading Drivers

China already casts a large shadow in the Asia-Pacific. Given this discussion of military hard-power potential, it is ironic that until the summer of 2010 it had been China's soft-power "charm offensive" that appeared to be making significant inroads into American spheres of influence. The prospect of a near-peer military competitor as exemplified by China's potential challenge areas, in combination with this charm offensive and China's growing economic clout, seemed to be forcing a reconsideration throughout the region of loyalties and commitments vis-à-vis the United States. Ironically, that charm offensive seems to have run aground—at least for now—on China's aggressive legal, political, and military maritime assertions in the South China Sea.

However Chinese military diplomacy proceeds, it might force choices by regional actors leading to unintended and unforeseen consequences, new regional security drivers, new multiplayer alignments, unprecedented escalation scenarios, and cascading geostrategic and operational effects. This has the potential for very different geostrategic outcomes and places a very high premium on careful surveillance, data and intelligence collection, extensive wargaming, and thoughtful technical and political analysis.

What Next?

Countering China's ASBM challenge will require early and astute collection and analysis. Analytically, this will require the United States to connect the dots, by getting the right warfighters talking to intelligence analysts and strategic planners in order to assess collection requirements, judge analysis, and recommend actions based on conclusions produced. This will necessitate all-source information gathering, including from allies and from China's rich trove of open-source material as well as an across-the-board analysis of

Chinese capabilities: from universities and research institutes to the factory floor, and to the barracks and the waterfront. There will be potentially very significant force structure implications for the Navy, including, inter alia, far less reliance upon surface vessels.

Not since the early days of the Cold War has there been such an analogous requirement for penetrating intelligence collection and analysis, and effective military-technical responses. The emergence of a Chinese OTHT system of systems antiaccess capability described earlier and the fielding of ASBMs has many implications for analysis organization, processes, and resources. This is the time for a fundamental review of strategic reconnaissance, surveillance, and analysis approaches, procedures, organization, and resources. Delaying consequential analysis that otherwise could lead to effective action would only transform an operational and strategic challenge into a moral one.

Notes

1. See Andrew S. Erickson and David D. Yang, "On the Verge of a Game-Changer," U.S. Naval Institute *Proceedings*, 135, no. 5 (May 2009); and Paul S. Giarra, "Now Hear This: Watching the Chinese," U.S. Naval Institute *Proceedings* 135, no. 5 (May 2009).

2. Defense Writers Group, "Vice Admiral David J. Dorsett, Deputy CNO for Information Dominance, Transcript of Q and A," *Air Force Magazine* website, 5 January 2011, http://airforce-magazine.com/DWG/Documents/2011/January%2011/010511dorsett.pdf.

3. Office of the Secretary of Defense (DoD), *Military and Security Developments Involving the People's Republic of China 2010*, Annual Report to Congress (Washington, DC: Office of the Secretary of Defense, 16 August 2010), 2.

4. Wang Wei, "The Effect of Tactical Ballistic Missiles on the Maritime Strategy System of China," *Shipborne Weapons*, no. 84 (August 2006): 12–15.

5. Jason E. Bruzdzinski, *Military Operations Research in the People's Republic of China: The Influences of Culture, "Speculative Philosophy" and Quantitative Analysis on Chinese Military Assessments* (McLean, VA: MITRE, June 2007).

6. In particular, see Mark A. Stokes and Ian Easton, *Evolving Aerospace Trends in the Asia-Pacific Region* (Arlington, VA: Project 2049 Institute, 27 May 2010), http://project2049.net/documents/aerospace_trends_asia_pacific_region_stokes_easton.pdf.

7. See Wendell Minnick, "China Builds First Anti-Ship Ballistic Missile Base?" *Defense News*, 5 August 2010, http://www.defensenews.com/story.php?i=4735654.

8. See, for example, Ashley J. Tellis, "China's Military Space Strategy," *Survival* 49, no. 3 (September 2007): 41–72.

9. Wang, "Effect of Tactical Ballistic Missiles," 10–11.

PART VI

Maritime Implications of Chinese Aerospace Power

Eric Hagt

Integrating China's New Aerospace Power in the Maritime Realm

HOW CAN CHINA apply its aerospace (air and space) power to the maritime environment, and what does this mean in practice? Collectively, the conceptual battle space includes outer space, the electromagnetic realm, the earth's atmosphere, the littoral regions, and the near seas. As such, the People's Liberation Army's (PLA) war-fighting capability in these combined realms entails forces from the air force, the navy, the Second Artillery (ballistic missiles), and substantial portions of the space program run by the noncombat General Armaments Department (GAD). All of these entities have traditionally held exclusive command and control over their respective domains, and a high degree of stovepiping between services is widely acknowledged in the PLA. Thus, from an organizational and technical point of view, the PLA's ability to facilitate joint operations across these services and their array of weapon platforms will be a critical issue in assessing China's aerospace power in the maritime realm.

But there is an additional demand for the PLA to overcome in order to achieve real operational effectiveness. As Chinese military strategists fully grasp, combat in a distant maritime theater by definition requires a degree of power projection because aerospace (fighter jets, early warning, and air defense), naval (surface and submarine), and missile (cruise and ballistic) forces must all operate over a potentially vast area and away from fixed, land-based nodes of command and control, communication, logistics, and supply lines.[1] A long-range theater of operations will require a high level of connectivity, and space and other command, control, communications, computers, intelligence, surveillance, and reconnaissance (C4ISR) infrastructure will be critical to linking these systems together. Reflecting this reality, integration and joint operations have been a primary focus of the PLA as it seeks to enhance an antiaccess/area denial (A2/AD) capability. Other chapters have detailed many of the specific weapon platforms related to aerospace and maritime power capabilities; therefore, this chapter will focus on two issues that are particularly relevant to aerospace power in the maritime realm. First, it will survey the PLA's progress in developing an overall concept for integration and joint operations, and will then assess the strategy for China's aerospace and maritime development. Second, it will focus on the space program's contribution to the goal of integration, which plays a critical role but also presents a unique challenge for the PLA at a number of levels. The example of China's antiship ballistic missile (ASBM) system is explored in depth because this provides an important benchmark in judging China's antiaccess capabilities. The chapter will conclude with some implications for the United States and coexistence with China in this domain.

The PLA Embarks on Integration

The focal lesson drawn by the PLA since the first Iraq War is that a revolution in military affairs is the central driving element in global military modernization, and that China must also adapt to this new trend or risk falling dangerously behind. Mastering information technologies and digitizing systems will provide the seamless connectivity across the full spectrum of military operations that will allow the PLA to reach its full combat effectiveness, currently defined as the ability to fight local wars of high intensity under conditions of informatization. The cornerstone to this strategy was introduced by the PLA under the conceptual rubric of "revolution in military affairs with Chinese characteristics." These ideas were further consolidated in 2004 when the Central Military Commission formally defined "integration and joint operations." Integration was formally incorporated with its inclusion in the 2006 Defense White Paper and the 17th Party Congress in 2007, marking it as the new direction for PLA military development. The concept was further operationalized when it became the focal point for PLA training guidelines in 2008—published by the General Staff Department (GSD).[2]

While integration was instituted as a central component of overall PLA doctrine, the PLA Air Force (PLAAF) has been its most vocal proponent, adapting it for its own purposes in the form of "integrated air and space, using both offense and defense" (空天一体, 攻防兼备). This may suggest that the PLAAF has been a key driver behind the new PLA strategy, which in turn intimates its growing clout. Membership in the powerful Central Military Commission (beginning in 2004) certainly gives the PLAAF a stronger voice within the PLA on resource allocation matters, and the call for air–space integration is an important means to compete for more control over space assets and applications. Air–space integration has now become a central tenet of PLAAF strategy, as was illustrated in a major air force symposium in 2005 and updated by the speech by Xu Qiliang at the ceremony for the service's sixtieth anniversary celebrated in November 2009.[3]

How is the PLAAF developing the concept of air–space integration, and how can we assess its progress? First, if we examine the definition, it is highly reflective of the expansive doctrines offered by both the United States and Russia.[4] However, there is a subtle but important divergence from the U.S. and Russian approaches, which becomes clearer as the PLAAF developmental phases and their timelines are laid out. In abbreviated form they include: (1) to engage in information fusion using aerospace-based systems to integrate information, intelligence, command and control, and weapons platforms for the support of PLAAF missions; and (2) to develop air and space into one unified combat domain, which would translate into the ability to battle in, from, and through both space and air interchangeably and seamlessly. With reference to U.S. Air Force doctrine for space, the first phase roughly equates to space support and force enhancement, and the second to space control and force application. However, the PLAAF estimates consistently that China will remain in the first stage until 2030–50.[5] Whether this is accurate or not is debatable, but by pushing back a more independent and substantial combat role for space so far into the future, it effectively calls for space to be a subordinate "integration" mechanism for existing PLAAF systems and traditional missions.

The differences between the PLAAF and other services and departments in the PLA over the call for space forces illustrate the previous points. In the PLAAF schematic, space forces would be independent though still remaining within its command and control structure.[6] The principle alternative version (championed primarily by GAD and generally supported by other services) shows space forces integrated with other services but directly subordinate to and under the command of the four general departments (though principally GAD and GSD).[7]

Recent developments illustrate that the PLAAF position has shifted from talk to action. First of all, much of the theorizing on the subject of integrated air and space that marked the period from 2005–7 has been replaced with specific applications in operations and weapon systems. For instance, one popular discussion is the integration of aerospace information technologies into aerial offensive attacks and air defense/missile defense operations.[8] This is a specific stage that the PLAAF has termed "航天支援, 空地作战" (aerospace support for aerial-ground combat). This trend is supported by a number of military exercises that took place in 2009.[9] The application of other systems to air–space integration, such as theater missile defense and near-space hypersonic weapon defense systems, is increasingly the subject of PLAAF-authored papers. The PLAAF has also published the most material on using space resources. In fact, it was an early proponent of China's data relay satellite program (Tianlian), an asset that is critical to building an aerospace data-link system.

Military exercises also reveal a growing emphasis on joint and combined operations, particularly following the latest update of the "Outline of Military Training and Evaluation," published in 2008, which put these concepts at the forefront for future training. Examination of military exercises in 2009 reveals that six of the nine major openly reported events concentrated on joint combat and integration of forces.[10] However, the particular emphasis of these exercises appears to be less on weapons systems integration and more on establishing mechanisms to coordinate war planning, communication and intelligence, and leadership across services, military regions, and operational units, thereby indicating ongoing difficulties in command and control. Moreover, the thrust of these exercises appears to be on joint operations between land and air forces—with a subsidiary role for the Second Artillery and naval forces—and makes little mention of space. Nevertheless, the PLA has clearly begun to undertake more sophisticated training that incorporates a range of weapon and information technologies and their command units. This in turn requires increasingly higher levels of integration. China's first red team/blue team war game occurred in 2009, which reportedly allowed greater "independent command and control without department interference"—a feature that suggests these exercises are also becoming less scripted.

Lessons from Military Operations Other Than War

Another useful window into the PLA comes by way of its performance during military operations other than war, including responses to domestic crises—particularly natural disasters, since there has been substantial coverage of these events in recent years. Due to the magnitude and devastation of the 2008 Wenchuan earthquake, the PLA deployed thousands of soldiers and equipment from a wide range of services and regions to the area, providing valuable clues as to how joint command and control and integration have progressed. Some evidence can also be gleaned from the Yushu earthquake of 2010, although both its scale of destruction and the level of PLA assistance were considerably less than in Wenchuan. Moreover, since these earthquakes occurred in remote regions, air and space resources were especially critical to support rescue efforts involving helicopters, airborne and satellite imagery, and communication and navigation-positioning (nav/pos) equipment.

The PLA's contribution to Wenchuan earthquake relief was one of the largest mobilizations of the PLA for a national disaster in China's recent history, with roughly 130,000 troops deployed. While the brute strength of the PLA was brought to bear quickly and massively, various problems arose in the coordination, communication, and use of information.

A variety of communication problems within the military was clearly an issue during the relief efforts. The People's Armed Police forward command reportedly used direct satellite video communication links.[11] However, many deployed units had no mobile satellite or even radio communication access at all.[12] This kind of "mobile communication" (动中通) has also been a popular topic of discussion in recent PLA literature as part of an increasing C4ISR ability. Still, as was seen both from the Wenchuan relief effort and military exercises, China does not yet have a truly versatile system that may be used by lower level units and individuals.[13] A highly mobile communication system would need to be supported by a network of tactical communication satellites (in low earth orbit), something the PLA does not yet possess.[14]

During the earthquake, China's remote-sensing imaging abilities were also poorly utilized. Although China for years has been employing sophisticated airborne and space-based synthetic aperture radar (SAR) for all-weather day and night imaging to aid in such relief efforts, numerous obstacles have impeded their effective application. The images for the disaster site were available with up to 0.2-meter resolution and three-dimensional terrain imagery, yet problems with software processing systems and lack of experience reading the results often rendered them unusable. Ground stations for receiving data were also reported to be ineffective as well as lacking sufficient experienced personnel. In addition, the SAR imaging platforms were not properly outfitted to transfer data quickly to areas where it was needed.[15] Translating this experience directly to a battlefield capability is a dubious enterprise; yet while China obviously possesses advanced technologies for imaging and reconnaissance, it does not seem to have surmounted numerous hurdles in applying these in the field (such as would be needed for real-time target identification).

Route mapping and planning has also been an area of deficiency. The PLA has begun employing modern Geospatial Information Systems software using remote sensing data for its surveying and mapping activities, yet it was not able to apply them to many of the flight paths of aviation units during the disaster relief.[16] Other reports on the problems regarding the handling and sharing of mapping and surveying data suggest the lack of an efficient and common platform to access information within the PLA. Reporting on previous military exercises supports this conclusion. The lack of a unified mechanism to share valuable remote sensing data is echoed in the civilian sector as well. Various relevant agencies are reluctant to "give it away" for communal use across military-civilian sectors. As a result, the rate of utilization of this data may be as low as 5 percent.[17]

Although the April 2010 earthquake at Yushu was smaller in magnitude and the extent of its devastation was less, a comparison of the PLA response to Yushu with that of Wenchuan points to several developments. First, the newly established PLA Emergency Management Small Leading Group coordinated an effort that included more than twelve thousand PLA personnel from several military regional commands and services.[18] Moreover, real-time command and control was aided by effective fixed and mobile satellite-supported communication systems for both commanders and PLA rescue workers.[19] In this instance the PLA appeared to coordinate well with the State Council's Emergency Management Office.[20] In comparison with the Wenchuan earthquake, for which the PLA was criticized for its poor performance in terms of command coordination, equipment supply, and speed of response, the military's response to Yushu showed substantive improvements, particularly in establishing effective ad hoc command and control.[21]

The PLA employed unmanned aerial vehicles (UAV) and other aircraft (the B-4101 remote sensing airplane) with SAR and high-resolution electro-optical technology to provide imagery within twenty-four hours of the earthquake.[22] These images were sent to the Chinese Academy of Science's recently established Earth Observation and Digital Earth Remote Sensing Center, where it was processed and placed on an open-access data-sharing system for all relief units to use. Although these examples of assistance provided through aerospace resources are vast improvements over the effort following the Wenchuan earthquake, the coverage from China's own Huanjing-1 and Beijing-1 small satellites and a SAR-capable satellite, in addition to SPOT-5 imagery, was reportedly incomplete and had insufficient refresh rates.[23]

Assessing Integration

The PLA appears to be making headway in enhancing its overall joint combat effectiveness. This appears particularly true for improvements in supporting technologies in space, air, and land. However, judging from available sources, the scale of integration remains limited in several ways. First, while the PLA's performance at Yushu was mostly seen as positive, the demands were dramatically less than in the far larger undertaking at Wenchuan, where performance was poor. The standard for integration in even a limited conflict would surely far outstrip that of a natural disaster. Thus integration on a larger scale still appears problematic. As one extensive article in *Shipborne Weapons* states, "even though Jinan Military Region has made some progress in conducting joint operations, similar mechanisms have not been put in place in other military regions and across services."[24] Another fundamental issue is the apparently limited progress the PLA has made with command and control. Namely, it is not just a lack of technology, platforms, and C4ISR infrastructure but also organizational barriers and the ability to institute effective integrated command systems. According to *Liberation Army Daily*, "In many instances, it is impossible to escape the departmental and service 'interest groups,' even though the awareness for the necessity of joint training and operations is widely recognized."[25] Second Artillery officers have put it the most pointedly, claiming that the most urgent task of the military is to establish a scientific, unified, and authoritative joint operations command structure.[26]

Prospects for integrated air and space are even more amorphous. While the PLAAF has been the most vocal proponent of incorporating space into its operations, much of this appears to be part of the campaign to win control over space resources. The PLAAF's claim that space is a natural domain for the air force is boosted by the U.S. system as a successful model in comparison to the Soviet system.[27] Also, as bureaucratic levels represent power in China's military system (more so than ranks), higher positional appointments can be a way of distributing influence over resources. It is notable, therefore, that the PLAAF has made significant gains in this regard, particularly with respect to space.

The former head of the GSD's 2nd Department, General Chen Xiaogong, is currently deputy commander of the PLAAF. It is rumored that General Ma Xiaotian, current director of the same department, may be promoted to commander of the PLAAF following the upcoming 18th Party Congress in autumn 2012. This suggests that the PLAAF could gain more influence over space operations in the years ahead. Conversely, there is little evidence to indicate an integrated air–space strategy has been embraced by the PLA outside of the PLAAF. The 2006 and 2008 defense white papers mention only "攻防兼备" (offense and defense), not "空天一体" (air–space integration), implying that the strategy has not yet been accepted. Regardless of the outcome of this debate, the PLAAF is providing substantial impetus to an integration strategy.

In assessing aerospace power in the maritime environment, there is even less discussion on the PLAN's role in the debate over how integration should proceed. This is not for lack of recognition among naval officers that space will be vital to the PLAN's effective combat ability. From writings on this subject, it is clear that the PLAN sees space as highly important to its own mission in two ways. The first is that the navy will be critically dependent on C4ISR and "informatization" to integrate its array of platforms, including early-warning, electronic defense, long-range precision munitions, reconnaissance, communications, battlefield awareness, and nav/pos. Given the distance the PLAN will potentially have to venture out (as far as the second island chain), space could become the mainstay in sustaining this architecture.[28] Second, space will one day itself be a theater of conflict even as space power contributes to combat operation in other theaters.

Space and Antiaccess

Even under the limited definition of an integrated air and space command that the PLAAF has vocally promoted, space resources will play a critical role in achieving this integration, particularly as aerospace power is applied to a maritime environment. Communications, real-time battle-space management, targeting and tracking, and precision guidance will all be central to the PLAAF and PLAN utilizing high-tech weapon platforms and achieving a larger strategy that emphasizes mobility, speed, and long-range attack under joint operations and integrated command and control. As this section will detail, China's space program is growing rapidly and will fundamentally transform the PLA's overall combat effectiveness. Yet the unique features of the space program could prove resistant to a fully integrated role as envisioned by the PLAAF.

First, China's distinctive space organization, both in terms of its authority structure as well as the infrastructure for real-time data exchange across a large interservice information network, appears unwieldy. Effective military utilization of space will require a high level of coordination between the various agencies with authority over China's space assets and their applications. This will be a complex undertaking for China's decentralized, dual-use space program. Although the PLA unquestionably plays the most prominent role in overseeing China's dual-use space infrastructure, as figure 1 demonstrates, many satellites and their applications are owned or operated apart from the military by a dozen agencies spread across the government, universities, and the quasi-private sector.

The primary authority over launch facilities and on-orbit command and control is the General Armaments Department (GAD), while the overall military operation of satellites and their applications is the purview of various departments within the General Staff Department (GSD). Furthermore, approximately 75 percent of China's space-based assets are ostensibly run under nonmilitary entities such as the China Meteorological Administration, the State Oceanic Administration (SOA) and a number of state-owned enterprises. The transfer of authority and expertise to the PLA during a time of conflict is cited as a concern among some in the military.[29] Achieving a common platform with a highly coordinated organization would require linking relatively equal military bureaucracies (GAD and GSD), different levels of military bodies (GAD and 2nd Artillery, PLAAF, PLAN, and the seven military regions) as well as military and nonmilitary agencies (e.g., PLAN and SOA). In short, integration of the command and application of on-orbit assets would entail coordination horizontally and vertically both within the military as well as across military and civilian organizations.

This points to a larger concern in the PLA regarding whether China has a sufficient legal structure to mobilize disparate dual-use and civilian space assets in a time of war.[30] The authority structure spelled out in the newly promulgated National Defense Mobilization Law does not address space assets specifically; however, its contents make clear that these resources would be made available to the military in a time of conflict. Various chapters of this law call for civilian technical operators trained for combat situations and the design of certain national projects to incorporate military needs.[31] It also states that civilian assets can be used to supplement military demands.[32] Also, given the overall control that the military has over the space program, allocation of its resources to the military during a conflict seems likely. Thus, diverting space-based resources during a conflict would be possible, at least in theory.

Figure 1: China's Space Organization

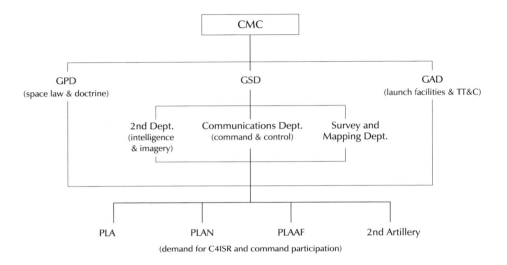

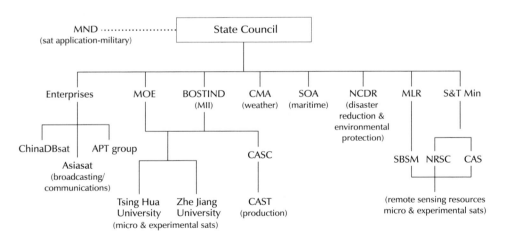

CMC: Central Military Commission
GPD: General Politics Department
GSD: General Staff Department
PLAN: PLA Navy
PLAAF: PLA Air Force
MND: Ministry of National Defense
MOE: Ministry of Education
BOSTIND: Bureau of Science & Technology
 Industry for National Defense
MII: Ministry of Industry & Information

CASC: China Aerospace Science & Technology Corporation
CAST: China Academy of Space Technology
CMA: China Meteorological Administration
SOA: State Oceanic Administration
NCDR: National Committee for Disaster Reduction
MLR: Ministry for Land and Resources
SBSM: State Bureau for Surveying & Mapping
NRSC: National Remote Sensing Center
CAS: China Academy of Sciences

Nevertheless, aside from a few examples of imagery sharing during natural disasters, the PLA has little experience in a full-scale commandeering of space resources. The transaction costs in working with so many agencies could be critical during the time-sensitive demands under wartime conditions. The vociferous calls for more coherent space leadership and lawful guarantees of its effectiveness in a time of conflict signal a lack of integration at present.[33] Requests for more dedicated satellites for the military reinforce this concern.[34] The initial confusion over organizing remote sensing data from domestic and foreign sources during the Wenchuan earthquake was, if nothing else, a testament to the difficulties inherent in such a system.[35]

Compounding the problem is the absence of a space command structure even within the military itself. To take an operational example, the use of space in a conflict would require a coordinated effort between counter-space ballistic missiles and satellite space support and force enhancement capabilities. No such PLA organization currently exists to accomplish this, although several of the services are vying vehemently for organizational leadership of the military space program. The struggle—at least publically—is mainly between the PLAAF on one side and GAD and GSD on the other, with the Second Artillery and the PLAN playing a less visible role. With no space assets currently under the PLAAF's remit and with no official changes to incorporate a space force under the PLAAF, however, it does not seem likely that GAD will relinquish its hold over space.[36]

China's direct-ascent kinetic energy antisatellite program exemplifies these bureaucratic challenges. It currently falls under GAD's authority, along with all deep-space launch facilities and the control of all on-orbit satellite operations. This would make GAD a natural candidate for a counter-space command authority. Yet while GAD is a military organization, it is principally responsible for procurement, research and development, and command and technical training. GAD does not have a combat role in the PLA. And there are no signs that the antisatellite program is being transferred to the Second Artillery, for instance, where it might be readied for operational use in combat.[37]

Another fundamental problem of integration stressed in the PLA is that of information and data dissemination, particularly regarding command and control both vertically, within a command structure, as well as horizontally, across services and units under different command. This is central to real-time battlefield command and control and is embodied in the Qu Dian (区电) integrated command, control, communications, computer, and intelligence (C4I) system. China appears to have established a number of building blocks for a robust command-and-control system, with support from land lines, direct broadcasting, data relay, and wideband data satellite transmission, all giving the potential for real-time or near-real-time communication. Yet, the degree of overall connectivity remains constrained. Noted deficiencies include incompatible platforms, lack of equipment, skills and training, poor mobility, and insufficient networking. Furthermore, the architecture of those lines still does not provide a common platform among the various services, or among lower echelons within a service, let alone among the units at the operational and combat levels across services—the kinds of connectedness required for deeper integration and jointness. The communication networks have multiplied but still principally move in a vertical direction, passing through hubs at upper levels within the same vertical command structure, decreasing speed and mobility of coordination.

These challenges do not invalidate the headway the PLA has certainly made in terms of using space for higher speed, mobility, and accuracy in command and control, battlefield awareness, communications, and precision-guided munitions. As has been widely noted by U.S. observers, there are numerous indications of significant progress. Nevertheless, the range of problems suggests that the PLA is far from finished in realizing a seamless and robust communication infrastructure across the battlefield.

The ASBM: Aerospace Power and the Maritime Realm

In addition to the qualitative dimensions of "integrated joint operations," as measured by the coherence of China's military organizational, command, and communication systems, the ability to integrate weapons systems and combat operations is also critical to the application of aerospace power in the maritime realm. In short, the PLA is acquiring many of the components to execute specific long-distance, anti–naval access missions (best embodied by China's evolving ASBM system). However, several elements remain underdeveloped, including continuous space and airborne assisted battlefield awareness, target acquisition, and more demanding C4I capabilities for broader, flexible maritime antiaccess and control missions.

Of a range of possible scenarios, a western Pacific naval engagement with the United States (and possibly Japan) is one of the most plausible and applicable for an analysis of China's capabilities. The recent stir in Western military circles over China's development of an ASBM is accompanied by the implication that it could be used to fatally strike a U.S. carrier en route to an engagement surrounding the Taiwan Strait. But what capabilities are needed to execute such a strike, and does China have them? The Department of Defense's 2009 report on *The Military Power of the People's Republic of China* states that a feasible ASBM would use the DF-21 airframe with a range of 1,500+ kilometers, C4ISR for target location and tracking, and a warhead equipped with terminal guidance and terminal stage maneuvering capabilities (MaRV). China probably has the ability to accomplish this in principle, albeit only under optimal conditions. In terms of the ballistic missile, warhead terminal guidance, and MaRV technologies, the evidence, though not conclusive, strongly suggests these will be operational soon.

However, the ability to operationalize what is described as a "system of systems" will involve a series of capabilities that go far beyond the core missile components. The most uncertainty lies in China's battlefield awareness, its C4ISR system, a real-time sensor-to-shooter network, and other capabilities required to support such a mission—in other words, the "kill chain." This would involve key components of China's air and space power applied to a sea-based conflict at great distance. Broadly, the aerospace systems needed for this capability require the ability to identify the carrier group; locate its precise position; uplink current target information to missile launch site; and, optionally, perform midcourse or terminal-phase course correction based on live updates of target information.

Early Warning

To strike any target with an ASBM, China would have to first form an accurate idea of its recent location. In the kill-chain formulation, this would comprise detecting, identifying, tracking, targeting, and engaging the threat. Detecting a carrier at great distances would depend on early-warning systems such as over-the-horizon (OTH) radar or electronic signals intelligence to give China a general idea of the target's coordinates.[38] China likely has at least one OTH system up and running and may have up to three.[39] This radar capability could be used to identify targets at long range, although at a resolution of 20–40 km (substantially lower than the U.S. OTH accuracy of roughly 8–30 km) it would be unable to perform target location independently.[40] Long-distance early warning could also come from electronic and signal intelligence (ELINT/SIGINT), whether airborne, shipborne, or space-based. China's ability to use airborne and shipborne electronic surveillance would be limited, however, since both would require a closer approach to the carrier group (a high-risk strategy). The recent launch of Yaogan-9 A, B, and C suggests China may now have this capability. This system consists of three small satellites flying in formation in a configuration strikingly similar to the U.S. NOSS/

Whitecloud system, which is also used as an ELINT system.[41] No matter what China's precise OTH and ELINT/SIGINT assets are, neither system would be used to derive targeting information; rather, they would be used to cue other more accurate sensors.

Once the carrier is identified, its position needs to be pinpointed accurately. This will require real-time target recognition and geolocation systems sent to the launch pad for uploading to the missile guidance systems prior to launch. The various technical discussions suggest that although China may have the capability for continuous in-flight sensor-to-shooter data links, the DF-21's inertial guidance system and the MaRV's terminal guidance capabilities are likely sufficient to hit a distant and slowly moving target without real-time data feeds. The ASBM would be, in effect, a ballistic–cruise missile hybrid. China's MaRV and passive/active radar or IR terminal homing technology would allow for a 20 km radius course correction upon reentry at an altitude of roughly 30 km. According to calculations made in the cited articles, within a twelve-minute flight time for the missile, the carrier strike group (CSG) would at most be able to change course by roughly 11 km in any direction—a distance that remains within the window of the assumed terminal guidance for China's ASBM.

Thus, recent and accurate imagery is key to plotting a missile's path pre-launch, and this remains the weakest link in China's targeting capabilities. Long-range UAVs could in theory gather such information. China is apparently committed to investing in such programs and has several operational and planned high- and medium-altitude long-endurance UAVs capable of carrying out reconnaissance far out at sea. However, support systems such as communication links are still lacking. The critical data link to the UAV would be prone to both random signal interference and deliberate electronic attack by a CSG's formidable air defenses. Overall, China's current UAV capabilities and the risks involved in obtaining targeting information from surface vessels, submarines, and air forces near the carrier suggest the PLA would not depend solely upon these platforms to determine the exact location of the target. The task, therefore, would fall to China's imaging satellites and nav/pos satellites.

Target Imaging

Chinese writings reveal a consensus that a space-based reconnaissance system, though critical to the effective operations of conventional missiles, remains the weakest link in China's targeting capabilities.[42] China currently has roughly fifteen imaging satellites useful for reconnaissance missions. They include a variety of electro-optical (visible), multi- and hyper-spectral and radar—particularly synthetic aperture radar (SAR)—remote sensing technologies (see appendix 1). Using Analytic Graphic Institute's Satellite Toolkit modeling software, I have approximated China's ability to view given targets. For imaging a carrier somewhere between the first and second island chains (a reasonable distance for an ASBM attack), China's suite of satellites gets an average of twenty-two looks per day (eighteen to twenty-five minutes per pass). This translates into coverage for a given object of roughly 7–10 percent of the day. However, the key to understanding China's ability to view a target is only partly dependent on the number of satellites. It also depends on their distribution. Thus, if evenly distributed, viewing could average almost once per hour. However, due to the current orbital configurations, gaps between revisit rates are often longer, averaging roughly every two hours and less frequently, extending up to every four hours. The gaps between satellite flyovers could provide a window for evasive and defense-related maneuvers for the CSG. Although China currently does not possess continuous coverage capability, it looks to be on track to meet these fairly stringent requirements in the next five to ten years.

Most significantly, with the recent launch of Yaogan 7, 8, 9 A/B/C, 10, and 11 China has already increased its reconnaissance coverage by 75 percent in most areas within second island chain. As a result, China's constellation of satellites appears to be crossing a threshold, transitioning from a limited general strategic picture to providing near real-time imagery supporting tactical operations. Over the next few years a steady rate of launches in the Yaogan series alone could achieve near continuous coverage of this region. Moreover, other initiatives, including the Haiyang and Huangjing programs, may see launches of between eight and twelve new-generation satellites within the next five years (see appendix 2). The steady progress in the satellite sensor technology and the emphasis placed on remote sensing technology overall in the last two Five-Year Plans and the space white papers augur a likely continuation of these efforts.

Data Links and Communication

China would also need fairly robust communications satellite (comsat) links to network this system from command and control to information exchange between early warning, target acquisition, and possibly sensor-to-shooter course correction data feeds. For this relatively specific mission, China's current suite of comsats would probably meet minimal requirements. China possesses a number of civilian, dual-use, and military dedicated comsats of fairly sophisticated technology, and it also plans to launch four to five more new-generation comsats (mainly based on the new Dongfanghong-4 bus) by 2011 (see appendix 2). However, China's tactical communications satellites (requiring LEO orbiting satellites) are notably absent. Since the imagery collected for a target up to 2,000 km offshore would be too distant to down-link directly to a ground station, China's recently launched data relay satel-lite (Tianlian-1) is key to an effective ASBM system and would significantly extend the reach of linking imaging satellites with ground stations. The cur-rent Tianlian-1 provides roughly 50 percent coverage of the earth's surface; China's plans to launch a second one, which could provide a combined cov-erage exceeding 75 percent. The launch dates in this series are not known, but some evidence suggests China plans to complete a series of three second-generation data-relay satellites by 2020.

Beidou/Compass

China has stated emphatically that an effective positioning and navigation satellite system is vital to the security of China's national territory and its econ-omy. Such a system is central to the C4ISR capabilities needed for China to engage in any maritime conflict. While it may not be essential to the ASBM system per se, it could augment it.

Details of China's second-generation satellite navigational system are becoming increasingly clear. Beidou-2/Compass will be operational at the regional level by 2011, with twelve satellites on orbit. The entire constella-tion of thirty-two to thirty-five satellites, to be completed by 2020, will pro-vide global coverage. Five Beidou-2 satellites will be geostationary and the rest in a medium earth orbit. The system will be unique in that it will combine a passive, differential nav/pos system (comparable to GPS) along with an active regional communication function.[43] Accuracy varies with different reports, but ranges from 5–10 m in the early phase to centimeter (and even millimeter) pre-cision upon its completion around 2020.[44] All of these features are improve-ments on Beidou-1 and will be far more flexible for both civilian and military applications.

Beidou-2 has been in the planning stages for a number of years but was formally established as a program in 2004. It is being designed not only to upgrade the Beidou-1 system but also with an eye to improving on other nav/pos systems (GPS, Galileo, and Glonass).[45] Beidou-2 will primarily inte-grate navigation with communication functions. While other systems provide a user with the "where" and "when" information regarding location, there is no ability to share positional data among different users. To accomplish this, Beidou-2 will employ both the radio-navigation satellite service (passive) at the global level, as used by GPS, and Beidou-1's radio-determination satellite service (active) at the regional level, offering the ability to use the system for communication as well as in stealthier passive mode. China's earlier plans for a global navigation satellite system (GNSS) included making it fully compatible with other GNSS systems. Although there is a sense of increasing competition both militarily and commercially in the GNSS market, compatibility remains an important goal for China.[46] As such, any country that would provide nav/pos data to China in a time of conflict would constitute an invaluable backup system to China's own.

Beidou-2 will also be designed with a number of strategically significant attributes in mind.[47] The system's high "refresh rate" for positioning would augment inertial guidance to increase the accuracy of China's full arsenal of ballistic and cruise missiles.[48] Most practically, it will greatly improve the precision guidance of conventional strike weapons. Positioning at the meter level will be sufficient for precision guidance of munitions while centimeter-level accuracy would be highly effective for detailed mapping and surveying. The ability to communicate and share information on positioning with others would yield a particularly important service for the integration of fighting forces. Measures to guarantee reliability and seamless coverage, including a full range of risk and accident management systems, have also been carefully considered.[49] For instance, the program calls for two or more satellite tracking systems to ensure continuous coverage and reduce the system's vulnerability at various levels. Such measures include satellite laser tracking, which would be immune to electronic jamming measures; a space-based tracking augmentation system, which would achieve greater automation of the network; and integrated multisatellite data receiving and processing equipment.

While China's overall plan for a "regional navigation system under a global framework" is well developed, critical obstacles to full implementation remain.[50] From a technical point of view, China's ability to undertake its first large-scale satellite constellation is still untested. With military, civilian and commercial organizations (such as Beidou Star) all participating in the system's development and its applications, there is still internal debate over how the system should be constructed and operated. The military obviously has a strong hand in these discussions, a fact that could hamper the openness required for commercial success. In addition, a primary uncertainty about the future success of China's indigenous navigation system is whether it will be economically viable. Beidou-2 could be constructed to service China's own civilian, commercial, and military needs, but the cost would be enormous and something that even the PLA would not likely entertain. The key to a truly successful system is to access the global market for positioning and navigation.

Implications for the United States: Escalation Risk

The strategies of joint operations and integration across services, domains, and weapon platforms have become principal drivers in China's broader military modernization efforts and are a central goal for its space program. To date, these initiatives have met with limited success with respect to overcoming organizational barriers, as outlined earlier. Nevertheless, significant progress has been made in combining key operations and technologies in aerospace, naval, and missile sectors to constitute a growing A2/AD capability, from submarine and surface vessels, to long-range cruise and ballistic missiles, to an expanding space infrastructure for tracking and targeting.

These developments have already triggered a debate in the U.S. military (and in regional countries) about how to address this rising challenge to America's traditional dominance in the maritime realm. In the first place, this evolving strategic dynamic could deeply impact U.S. military planning, perhaps in terms of doctrine as well as the direction of defense acquisition and spending. In fact, this has already taken place with the "AirSea Battle" concept, initiated by the U.S. Air Force and Navy in 2009. This concept is billed as "an offsetting strategy" that reaffirms a U.S. commitment to maintaining presence, coalitions, and influence in the Western Pacific, a strategically vital area. It has the potential to significantly shift American military posture in that it is a "point of departure" operational concept and in that it would call for a new focus on procurement that emphasizes "stealth, long-range and prompt strike, redundancy and Air Force and Navy interoperability."[51]

Adapting war planning and the capabilities to meet changing threats wherever they emerge (including growing Chinese A2/AD capability) is a natural response, even if the prospects for conventional war with China remain slim. More worrying, however, could be the impact of these developments on peacetime routine and standard operating procedures, such as patrols, port calls, search and rescue missions, surveillance activities (sea and aerial), and military exercises (individual and joint). China has shown a growing determination to protect what it perceives as its core interests and has challenged the United States and other nations in the region. With regard to the United States, this has been especially acute for issues concerning China's exclusive economic zone, but the PLA's actions have recently extended beyond this region to the South China Sea and increasingly cover a wider area in the Western Pacific. This indicates that China is growing more confident to press its interests. It appears that the U.S. Navy could increasingly face the unsavory choice of holding its position (e.g., over surveillance missions in China's exclusive economic zone), and therefore risk escalation, or stand down. If the latter results in modifying U.S. behavior over time, the perception of U.S. maritime staying power in the Western Pacific and concomitant reassurance to allies in the region could shift accordingly.

This strategy raises other potential risks for escalation crisis management, since China's A2/AD capabilities are heavily dependent on land-based systems (air defense, long-range early warning, ballistic and cruise missiles, and their infrastructure). One of the initial phases in the AirSea Battle concept calls for a "blinding campaign" that would hit cyber, ISR, sensor, counter space, and air-defense targets on the mainland from coastal regions to Xinjiang. A campaign based largely on striking military assets on Chinese territory, whatever the rationale, would likely carry significantly greater escalatory risks than a conflict largely confined to a maritime domain. The political cost (acute public anger over U.S. aggression), collateral loss of life and nonmilitary infrastructure, and a perceived increased threat to sovereignty are a few of the possible increased risks to such a strategy. While a land-based campaign may be the only effective way to suppress China's A2/AD capabilities, the question of proportionality nevertheless arises and should be factored in. AirSea Battle is "designed" to "maintain crisis stability" and "prevent war"—paradoxically—by demonstrating to China it could not prevail in a conflict. The merits of this are debatable, however, as China would be unlikely to back down over deep-seated interests.

This is particularly true as time (and money) appears to be on China's side. Although the United States will remain the dominant military power on a global scale for decades to come, in the regional context of Taiwan, China's near seas, or even within the second island chain, the demands for power projection are far less onerous for China. Moreover, as this chapter illustrates, integration and joint operation capabilities and the critical force enabler of space are focal points for the PLA and look set to grow steadily with time and increased spending, both of which look promising for China's military.

Appendix 1: China's Satellite Program

Function	Program[1]	Launch Date	Capability/Characteristics
REMOTE SENSING			
Weather	Fengyun 1d–2d	2002–6	
Civ/gov	Fy-3a	2008	FY-3: 3-axis stab, 4.4x2x2 m size; visible, infrared, and microwave for global mapping; color (day), thermal infrared imaging (night) scanning
Civ/gov	Fy-2e	2008	Geostationary orbit[2]
Civ/gov	Fy-2c	2004	On orbit, but not operational since 2008[3]
Civ/gov	Huanjing-1a, 1b*	2008	Real-time imaging of emergency areas, 30m spatial res, optical, IR sensors
Earth Monitoring	Cbers 2[4], 2b (Ziyuan-1, 1b)	2003–7	ZY-1 (20m res optical imager, 80, 160 res. sensors), digital transmission
Mil	Zy-2a and 2b (Jb-3a and 3b)	2000–2004	Precursors to Zy-2c (3 sats, global coverage)
Mil	Zy-2c (Jb-3c)*		Zy-2c: ~2m res, CCD, digital imaging recon, infrared/ multispectral scanner
Mil	Yaogan-2*	2006	Electro-optical-2m res, multispectral sensors
Mil	Yaogan 3*	2007	SAR (high res: < 5 x 5 m)
Mil	Yaogan 4 *	2008	Electro-optical (0.5m res)
Mil	Yaogan 5*	2008	SAR
Mil	Yaogan 6*	2009	SAR (estimated ground res, 0.6–1m)

Mil	Yaogan 8*	2009	SAR? (similar orbit to Yaogan 9)
Mil	Yaogan 9a,b,c*	2010	3 sat formation, SAR/electro-optical/ELINT (orbital inclination), 63.4, similar to U.S. NOSS[5]
Mil	Yaogan 10*	2010	
Mil	Yaogan 11*	2010	
Mapping	Tianhui-1*	2010	Stereo-topographic mapping
Ocean-monitoring Gov	Haiyang-1b	2007	Imager 250 m res. Infrared/visible light sensors; scan 1.1 km, real-time survey of Yellow, East China, South China seas (1-C may have SAR capability)
COMMUNICATIONS			
Mil	Zx20 (Chinasat 20)	2003	Milsat com. secured uplink voice/data for ground users; steerable spot beam antenna, on the move; powerful onboard data processing
Mil	Zx-22, 22A (Fh-1-1, 1-2)	2000–2006	Fenghuo-1 first dedicated military communications satellite-secured digital comm of video/voice for theater (C4I) network
Gov	Zx-9 (Chinasat 9)	2008	Spacebus-4000C2 platform, 22 active Ku-band transponders for broadcast satellite services (BSS), 18 36-MHz and 4 54-MHz channels. 4500 kg, 11 kW power
Com	Apstar 1, 1a, 2r, 6[6]	1994–2005	C and Ku-band transponders
Com	Asiasat 2, 3s, 4, and 5[7]	1995–2009	C and Ku-band transponders
Gov/com	Chinasat 6, 6b, 10[8]	1997–2007	C and Ku-band transponders
Com	Sinosat-1, 3	1998–2007	C and Ku-band transponders; services financial and air transport
Gov	Tianlian-1	2008	Data-relay, (12%–50% global coverage) 2 sats: 85% global coverage

(continued)

China's Satellite Program *(continued)*

Function	Program[1]	Launch Date	Capability/Characteristics
NAVIGATION			
Mil/com	Beidou 1b and 1c	2000–2007	RDSS system, 2 in GEO min for 20 m, 2-way comm, regional coverage
Mil/com	Compass M-1	2007	10m res, 30 sats MEO, 5 in GEO, global, same system as GPS, not 2-way
Mil/com	Beidou 2/M (unoperational)	2009	
Mil/com	Compass-G1	2010	GEO 144.5 E
Mil/com	Compass-G3	2010	GEO 84.7 E
Mil/com	Compass-IGSO-1	2010	Unclear
SMALL/MICROSATS			
Gov	Chuangxin-1	2003	LEO comm sat; 100 kg
Civ	Beijing-1 (Tsinghua-2)	2005	4 m res imaging; 166 kg, panchrom cam, 600 km swath, multispectral
Gov	Shiyan-1 (Tansuo-1)	2004	High-res. electro-optical; near infrared; CCD survey cameras (10 m res; 120 km wide image swath), 200–300 kg
Gov	Shiyan-2 (Tansuo-2)	2004	Electro-optical
Civ	Zheda Pixing 1	2007	Scientific research, made by Zhejiang University
Civ	Xiwang 1	2009	China's first amateur satellite

Scientific

Gov/mil	Shiyan 3*	2008	Experiments on new technologies in atmospheric exploration
Gov	Shijian 6c–6h*	2004–8	Scientific experiments, possible SIGINT mission
Gov	Doublestar 2 (ESA)	2004	Earth's magnetosphere
Gov	Shijian 11	2009	Space environment exploring
Gov	Shijian 12*	2010	Space environment exploring

1. An asterisk (*) indicates China's likely reconnaissance satellites. Criteria for selection include (1) sufficient resolution, < 30 meters (excludes Fengyun series); (2) three-axis stabilization (excludes Beijing-1); (3) currently operational (possibly excludes CBERS-2, 2b. Ziyuan-2a, 2b [Jianbing 3a, 3b] possibly still active but orbital life listed as only two years).
2. China Meteorological Administration, "FY-2E," http://fengyunuds.cma.gov.cn/FYCV_EN/Sensors/SateliteInfo.aspx?SateliteID=10035.
3. National Satellite Meteorological Center, "Satellite Operation State Diagram," http://fengyunuds.cma.gov.cn/FYCV/index.aspx.
4. Perhaps no longer functioning.
5. Global Network Forum, http://bbs.huanqiu.com/tushuoshijie/thread-343181-1-1.html.
6. Apstar 1, 1a, on orbit but not operational.
7. Asiasat 2, on orbit, not operational.
8. Chinasat 6, on orbit, not operational.

Appendix 2: China's Satellite Program Plans

Program	Designation	# in Plan	Planned Launch Time	Operator/Owner	Users	Purpose
Ocean Observation Satellites[1]	HY-1	8	HY-1C/D, E/F; G/H, I/J (2010–19)	State Oceanic Administration (SOA)	Government	Ocean Monitoring
	HY-2	4	HY-2A-D (2010–19)			Sea Surface Ocean Monitoring (microwave sensors sea-surface features and temperature, including altimeter, Ku and C-bands, scatterometer, microwave imager)
	HY-3	3	HY-3A-C (2012–22)			Marine Monitoring Satellite (maritime surveillance and protection and resource management)
Environmental and Disaster Monitoring Satellite System[2]	HJ-1C	1	2011 (launch postponed from 2009 to 2011)	SEPA and the National Committee for Disaster Reduction	Government	Remote Sensing (1 SAR satellite)
	HJ-2	8	Unknown			Remote Sensing (4 optical satellites and 4 SAR satellites)
Beidou/Compass Navigation System[3]	Beidou-2/M	9	Regional: 2009–12	Chinese Defense Ministry (Survey & Mapping Bureau under GSD)[4]	Military/Commercial	Navigation/Global Positioning
		20	Global system: by 2020			
Earth Resource Satellites[5]	CBERS-03	1	2010	Chinese Academy of Space Tech & Institution Nacional de Pesquisas Espaciais (Brazil)	Government/Commercial	Remote Sensing. Panchromic multispectral camera, multispectral camera, infrared multispectral camera, wide field imager
	CBERS-04	1	2013			

Category	Satellite	Number	Production/launch date	Organization	Type	Description
Fengyun Meteorological Satellites[6]	FY-2F/G	2	FY-2F (2011) FY-2G (2012)	China Meteorological Administration	Government	Earth Science. FY-3 series is an improved generation of polar orbiting heliosynchronous weather satellites
	FY-3	10	FY-3 (2011–19)			
	FY-4	7	FY-4 (2013–20)			Optical and microwave satellites, advanced generation of geosynchronous meteorological satellites
Remote Sensing[7]	Yaogan-11, 12	2	Yaogan-12 (2011)	Military	Military	LEO, electro-optical and SAR
Telecom Satellites[8]	SinoSat-4	1	Production date 2009, launch time unknown			DFH-4 platform, 18 x 36 MHz and 4 x 54 MHz Ku BSS transponders
	SinoSat-5	1	2011	ChinaDBSat	Commercial	DFH-4 platform. Will feature a 15-year design lifetime and a 5,000-kg launch
	SinoSat-6	1	2011			DFH-4 bus, hybrid communications payload made up of 24 C-band, 8 Ku-band and 1 S-band active transponders
	ChinaStar-2	1	Unknown			
	Chinasat-10	1	2011?		Commercial	
Data Relay	Tianlian-2	3	Before 2015–16[9]	Chinese Academy of Space Technology	Government	Larger antennas, faster tracking and acquisition, wider transponder band, coverage expanded to GTO/GEO orbits and deep space[10]

(continued)

China's Satellite Program Plans (continued)

Program	Designation	# in Plan	Planned Launch Time	Operator/Owner	Users	Purpose
Surveying & Mapping Satellites[11]	Ziyuan-3	1	2011	State Bureau of Surveying and Mapping	Government	Producing detailed national geo-graphic data and investigation and monitoring of land and resources
Micro-satellite	Environmental monitoring[12]	4–6	By 2030	Shanghai's administration	Local government	2 water monitoring satellites, 1 urban heat island satellite, 1 small SAR satellite

Sources:

1. Jiang Xingwei, Lin Mingsen, and Tang Junwu, National Satellite Ocean Application Service, SOA, "China's Satellite Ocean Observation and Application Program," in "Working Group on Calibration and Validation," February 2008, http://www.ceos.org/images/wgcv/wgcv28/2_OceanObservations_of_China_Jiang_b.pdf; and 国家海洋局 [State Oceanic Administration of China], "中国海洋卫星应用报告" ["The Report of China's Oceanic Application"], http://www.soa.gov.cn/hyjww/ml/wx/A025007/index_1.htm.

2. Jiang Jingshan, "Earth Observations in China: Present Status and Future Developments," in "Working Group on Calibration and Validation," February 2008, http://www.ceos.org/images/wgcv/wgcv28/1_China's_EOS_Jiang_b.pdf.

3. "中国第一代卫星导航系统专项管理办公室" ["China 2nd Generation Satellite Navigation System Project Office"], Beidou Satellite Navigation System, available at http://www.beidou.gov.cn/.

4. "总参测绘局赵康宁副主任一行在临航天基地" ["General Staff Survey and Mapping Bureau Deputy Director Zhao Kangning Leads Visit to Space Base"], Space Base Information Center, 26 July 2010, http://www.xcaib.com.cn/content.jsp?urltype=news.NewsContentUrl&wbnewsid=67224&wbtreeid=10460; and "中国标准时间, 北斗导航系统: 守护中国时间" ["Beidou System Safeguards China's Time Accuracy"], Beijing Capital House, 29 June 2010, http://www.renwenguancha/1120.html.

5. China Center for Resources Satellite Data and Application, The Introduction of Satellites, http://www.cresda.com/n16/n1130/index.html.

6. Peng Zhang, "Chinese Meteorological Satellite and Calibration Activities," in "Working Group on Calibration and Validation," February 2008, http://www.ceos.org/images/wgcv/wgcv28/CMA_ZHANG_b.pdf; and National Satellite Meteorology Center, "Fengyun Satellites," available at http://www.nsmc.cma.gov.cn/.

7. These are unconfirmed estimates taken from NasaSpaceflight.com, http://forum.nasaspaceflight.com/index.php?board=40.0.

8. "China DBSAT" Satellite Resources, http://www.chinadbsat.com.cn/satellite.asp?theName=%D6%D0%CE%C01%BA%C58&id=1.

9. 王家胜 [Wang Jiasheng], China Space Technology Research Institute, "数据中继卫星系统的研制与分析" ["Development and Analysis of Data Relay Satellite System"], 航天器工程 [Spacecraft Engineering] 17, no. 5 (September 2008); and "Tianlian-1—China's First Data Relay Satellite," Sina blog, http://blog.sina.com.cn/s/blog_5a53af350100c614.html.

10. 王家胜 [Wang Jiasheng], China Space Technology Research Institute, "数据中继卫星系统的研制与分析" ["Development and Analysis of Data Relay Satellite System"], 航天器工程 [Spacecraft Engineering] 17, no. 5 (September 2008).

11. 周音 [Zhou Yin], "中国首颗民用 '资源三号' 测绘卫星将于明年发射" ["China Plans to Launch the first Civilian Surveying and Mapping Satellite, Ziyuan 3, in 2011"], 中新社 [China News Agency], 29 July 2010.

12. 陈抒怡 [Chen Shuyi], "上海拟发射 '东方号' 小卫星监测水源" ["Shanghai Plans to Launch Small Satellite Named 'East' to Monitor Water Resources"], 东方网 [EastDay.com], 5 January 2010, http://news.qq.com/a/20100105/000886.htm.

Notes

1. 王凌 [Wang Ling], "海军舰载卫星应用知识" ["Naval Shipborne Satellite Application Knowledge"], 科技资讯 [*Science and Technology Information*], no. 36 (2009).

2. 中国人民解放军总参谋部 [General Staff Department of PLA], "军事训练与考核大纲" ["Outline of Military Training and Evaluation"], published in 2008. See also "全方位解读新一代军事训练与考核大纲" ["Comprehensive Interpretation New Outline of Military Training and Evaluation"], 解放军报 [*Liberation Army Daily*], 1 August 2008.

3. Compilation of eighty-two articles on air–space integration as conceived by the PLAAF in 空军指挥学院科研部编辑 [Air Force Command College Research Department], ed., 空天一体与空军建设征文选集 [*Collected Works of Aerospace Integration and Air Force Construction*], 2005; and "China's PLA Eyes Future in Space and Air: Air Force Commander," *People's Daily Online*, http://english.peopledaily.com.cn/90001/90776/90786/6799960.html .

4. See 向际阶 [Xiang Jijie], "对空天一体作战的认识与思考" ["Understanding of Air-space Integration Combat"], in *Collected Works*.

5. 纪荣仁 [Ji Rongren], "适应信息化战争需要加强我军空天一体化力量建设" ["Construction of Air-Space Integration Is Needed to Adapt to Information Warfare"], in *Collected Works*, 301.

6. See 苏荣, 满广志, 奚丹, 车万方, 金光 [Su Rong, Man Guangzhi, Xi Dan, Che Wanfang, and Jin Guang.], "空天一体作战初级阶段的典型作战运用" ["Study on Typical Operational Mode of Space-Aeronautics Incorporate Battle in Junior Stage Applying Primary Stage Air-Space Integration Combat"], 导弹与航天运载技术 [*Missiles and Space Vehicles*], no. 2 (2009).

7. 母仕民, 李勇翔, 常显奇 [Mu Shimin, Li Yongxiang, and Chang Xianqi], "关于确立军事航天指挥体制的探讨与思考" ["Thoughts on Establishing a Military Space Command System"], 装备指挥技术学院学报 [*Journal of the Academy of Equipment Command and Technology*], no. 4 (2003); and 秦大国, 周威 [Qin Daguo and Zhou Wei], "空天信息系统一体化指挥控制系统体系结构研究" ["Architecture Research on Integrated Command and Control System of Air and Space Information System"], 装备指挥技术学院学报 [*Journal of Academy of Equipment Command and Technology*], no. 1 (2009).

8. See Su et al., "Study on Typical Operational Mode."

9. "Vanguard-2009," *Chinamilitary.com.cn*, http://chn.chinamil.com.cn/zt/2009qfjy/; "Vanguard-2009A," *Peopleonline.com.cn*, http://military.people.com.cn/GB/8221/69693/171424/171425/; "Victory-2009," *Peopleonline.com.cn*, http://military.people.com.cn/GB/8221/69693/173612/; and "First Theater-Level Joint Campaign Exercise Involving the Whole PLA," *Xinhuanet.com*, http://www.chinanews.com.cn/gn/news/2009/06-28/1752291.shtml.

10. "2009年中国军队重大演习全扫描" ["Comprehensive Scan to Important Military Exercises of PLA in 2009"], 新华网 [*Xinhuanet.com*], http://news.xinhuanet.com/mil/2009-12/18/content_12660674.htm.

11. 李文明, 吕福玉 [Li Wenming and Lu Fuyu], "论突发事件的电视传播—以汶川特大地震前期电视报道为例TV" ["Reporting of Crises: A Case Study of the Wenchuan Earthquake"], 国际新闻界 [*Journal of International Communication*], no. 5 (2008).

12. "'乌蒙铁军'失联系30小时　海军陆战队进山搜寻" ["'Wumeng (Mountain) Iron Army' Loses Contact for Thirty Hours, Marines Advance in a Mountain Search"], 华西都市报 [*Huaxi City News*], 19 May 2008.

13. 樊厚东, 何勇民 [Fan Houdong and He Yongmin], "青藏线汽车兵装备'动中通'" ["Auto Soldiers along Qinghai-Tibet Line All Equipped with System of Vehicle Satellite 'Communication in Motion'"], 光明日报 [*Guangming Daily*], 6 July 2005.

14. 周越, 初大庆 [Zhou Yue and Chu Daqing], "建立我军低轨道卫星移动通信构想" ["Concepts on PLA's Low Earth Orbit Mobile Communication Satellite System"], 海军工程大学电子工程学院学报 [*Journal of Naval Engineering University Institute of Electronic Engineering*], no. 4 (2002).

15. 张祖勋, 郭大海, 柯涛, 王建超 [Zhang Zhuxun, Guo Dahai, Ke Tao, and Wang Jianchao] "抗震救灾中航空摄影测量的应急响应" ["Contingency Response of Aviation Camera Measurement in Earthquake and Disaster Relief"], 遥感学报 [*Journal of Remote Sensing*], no.8 (2008).

16. 张强 [Zhang Qiang], "抗震救灾科技在行动" ["Earthquake Relief Science and Technology in Action"], 科技日报 [*Science and Technology Daily*], 17 June 2008.

17. Interviews with staff at the Beijing University Remote Sensing Center.

18. 国务院新闻办公室 [State Council Information Office of China], "解放军和武警参加青海玉树抗震救援工作情况" ["The Qinghai Yushu Earthquake Aid by the PLA and People's Armed Police"], 20 April 2010, http://www.scio.gov.cn/xwfbh/xwbfbh/wqfbh/2010/0420/.

19. 李秦卫 [Li Qinwei], "解放军中将称玉树救灾72小时黄金时段突出快速时" ["A PLA Lieutenant General Praises the Speedy Assistance to Yushu that Occurred within the Critical Period of 72 hours"], 解放军报 [*Liberation Army Daily*], 23 April 2010.

20. James Mulvenon, "Party-Military Coordination of the Yushu Earthquake Response," *China Leadership Monitor*, no. 33 (2010).

21. Minnie Chan, "Forearmed by Sichuan, Military Response Swift," *South China Morning Post*, 16 April 2010.

22. 科技部 [Ministry of Science and Technology of China], "863计划成果在青海玉树地震灾情监测中发挥重要作用" ["The 863 Plan Plays Important Role in Monitoring Qinghai Yushu Earthquake"], *www.gov.cn*, 28 April 2010, http://www.gov.cn/gzdt/2010-04/28/content_1594559.htm.

23. "玉树地震灾情遥感监测报告" ["Yushu Earthquake Remote Sensing Monitoring Report"], *China Water Conservancy and Hydropower Research*, 18 April 2010, http://www.iwhr.com/special/yushu/News_View.asp?NewsID=22925.

24. Dou Chao, "On Joint Operations and Combined Services Training of Our Army," *Shipborne Weapons* (March 2010).

25. 董贵山 [Dong Guishan], "我军联合训练思想观念滞后存在4大问题" ["Four Lagging Areas for the Military's Joint Training Concepts"], *Liberation Army Daily*, 27 November 2009.

26. 张训立, 高桂清,张欧亚 [Zhang Xunli, Gao Guiqing, and Zhang Ouya], "积极应对新军事变革大力提升我军联合作战指挥能力" ["Actively Deal with the New Revolution in Military Affairs by Vigorously Promoting Joint Operations Command"], 四川兵工学报 [*Sichuan Ordinance Technology Journal*], February 2010.

27. 窦超 [Dou Chao], "联合就是力量: 透过国外实践看我国军联合作战与训练" ["Unity is Power: PLA's Joint Operations and Combined Service Training from Experiences by Foreign Countries"], *Shipborne Weapons*, no. 3 (2010).

28. Wang, "Naval Shipborne Satellite Application Knowledge."

29. 刘江, 李青 [Liu Jiang and Li Qing], "关于空军 '空天一体, 攻防兼备' 转型建设的几点思考" ["Thoughts on Air Force Transition toward 'Integration of Aerospace, Combination of Defense and Attack'"], in *Collected Works*.

30. 孟祥春, 蔡杰超 [Meng Xiangchun and Cai Jiechao], "促进空间系统一体化建设对策研究" ["Studies of Countermeasures of Enhancing Integration of Space Systems"], in *Collected Works*, 329–37.

31. The 11th National Congress of China, "National Defense Mobilization Law," 26 February 2010, chs. 5 and 9, http://news.xinhuanet.com/politics/2010-02/26/content_13057688.htm.

32. Ibid., ch. 10.

33. 沈世禄, 冯书兴, 王佳, 李亚东 [Shen Shilu, Feng Shuxing, Wang Jia, and Li Yadong], "浅析军事航天任务指挥决策" ["Research on the Command Decision-Making for Military Space Mission"], 装备指挥技术学院学报 [*Journal of the Academy of Equipment Command and Technology*] 18, no. 1 (February 2007).

34. 李杰, 郭建平, 鞠百成 [Li Jie, Guo Jianping, and Ju Baicheng], "太空力量对海上作战的影响及发展对策" ["Impacts of Space Forces on Maritime War-Fighting and Countermeasures"], in *Collected Works*.

35. Eric Hagt interview with 焦维新 [Jiao Weixin], 北京大学地球与空间科学学院教授 [professor of Earth and Space, Science Institute, Beijing University].

36. Qin and Zhou, "Architecture Research."

37. Eric Hagt interview with former GAD officer.

38. See "OTH Radar and the ASBM Threat," *IMINT and Analysis* blog, 11 November 2008, http://geimint.blogspot.com/2008/11/oth-radar-and-asbm-threat.html.

39. See "厦门地基电离层观测站开始建设" ["Construction Begins on Xiamen Ground-Based Ionosphere Observation Station"], 13 April 2007, http://www.xmnn.cn/xwzx/xmyw/zhxw/200701/t20070123_117540.htm. See also 海上网络战 [*Network Warfare at Sea*] (Beijing: 国防工业出版社 [National Defense Industry Press], November 2006), 179; "反舰导弹信息汇总" [The Information about ASBM], *CJDBY.net*, September 2006, http://lt.cjdby.net/thread-286369-1-1.html; and 中国航天科工集团 [CASIC], 第十届全国雷达学术年会" 录用论文 [Collected articles by the 10th China

Radar Academic Anniversary Conference], September 2010, http://www.casic23.com .cn/newEbiz1/EbizPortalFG/portal/html/InfoContent.html?InfoPublish_InfoID=c373 e91f9404488a8f7ea9fc6c0631ce.

40. 包养浩, 王军 [Bao Yanghao and Wang Jun], "超视距雷达系统设计考虑" ["Design Consideration for Beyond Visual Range (BVR) Radar Systems"], 现代雷达 [*Modern Radar*], no. 1 (1991).

41. See A. Andronov, "The U.S. Navy's 'White Cloud' Spacebourne ELINT System," trans. Allen Thomson, *Foreign Military Review*, no. 7 (1993): 57–60, http://www.fas.org/spp/ military/program/surveill/noss_andronov.htm.

42. Ibid.

43. 陈超 [Chen Chao], "星光引路—访著名卫星导航专家樊春明" ["The Road Guided by Stars, Interview with Satellite Navigation Scholar Fan Chunming"], 科技日报 [*Science and Technology Daily*], 23 July 2007.

44. 邓丽 [Deng Li], "北斗与GPS兼容或成商用方向" ["Compatibility between Beidou and GPS May Be Direction of Commercial Usage"], 21世纪经济报道 [*21st Century Business Herald*], 13 November 2008.

45. "'北斗' ≠ 'GPS'" ["'Beidou' Does Not Equal 'GPS'"], 科学时报 [*Science Times*], 1 July 2003.

46. 金一南 [Jin Yinan], "中国北斗战略意义远超神舟嫦娥工程" ["The Strategic Implications of China's Beidou Program are More Important Than Chang'e and Shenzhou"], 大军事网讯 [*Great Military Net Dispatch*], 21 April 2009, http://www .dajunshi.com/Mil/China/200904/30593.htm.

47. 谭述森 [Tan Susen], "北斗卫星导航系统的发展与思考" ["Development and Thought of Beidou Navigation Satellite System"], 宇航学报 [*Journal of Astronautics*] 29, no. 2 (2008).

48. "航天二炮及新概念武器" ["Spaceflight, Second Artillery, and New Concept Weapons"], 超级大本营论坛 [Super Base Camp Forum BBS], 16 April 2008, http:// bbs.cjdby.net/archiver/?tid-607038.html.

49. "我国民用全球定位系统发展战略" ["China's Civilian Global Positioning System Development Strategy"], 国家测绘局测绘发展研究中心 [Surveying and Mapping Development Center of State of Surveying and Mapping Bureau], 18 May 2008, http:// drcsm.sbsm.gov.cn/article/wxzy/200805/20080500035479.shtml.

50. Tan, "Development and Thought of Beidou."

51. Jan van Tol with Mark Gunzinger, Andrew Krepinevich, and Jim Thomas, *AirSea Battle: A Point-of-Departure Operational Concept* (Washington, DC: Center for Strategic and Budgetary Assessments, 2010).

James R. Holmes

Integrated Chinese Saturation Attacks
Mahan's Logic, Mao's Grammar

CAPTAIN WAYNE HUGHES supplies with U.S. Navy mariners a primer for missile warfare at sea. His *Fleet Tactics and Coastal Combat* constitutes a baseline for any consideration of the challenges posed by Chinese antiship cruise missiles. However useful Captain Hughes' treatise, though, it cannot stand alone. This is no indictment. The book aspires to school tacticians. Hughes describes his purpose as "to illustrate the processes—the dynamics—of naval combat" rather than to foresee how particular contingencies might turn out.[1] The abstract approach is entirely appropriate.

Fleet Tactics is largely silent on operational matters and completely silent on political, cultural, and strategic context. It implies that technology, not fighting men and women, decides the outcome of martial encounters at sea. Enemy forces slug it out with volleys of precision-guided arms, and the side that lands the first blow is the most likely victor.

Such accounts constitute the norm in U.S. Navy technical training institutions. Hughes describes the arbiters of high-tech naval combat as (a) "scouting effectiveness," meaning the proficient use of shipboard and offboard sensors, combat systems, and computer data links; (b) "weapon range," or the ability to inflict damage at a distance; and (c) tactics shaped by scouting effectiveness and the range of a fleet's weaponry.[2]

Yet outdistancing an opponent's sensors and weaponry is far from the only challenge any U.S. naval offensive will face. *Fleet Tactics* shares this deficit of vision with net assessments that tally up numbers of platforms and their technical characteristics—slighting the human dimension. To cope with an increasingly formidable China, U.S. forces must school themselves in how Chinese warfighters may use platforms and weapon systems in times of strife. I maintain that

- Alfred Thayer Mahan's geopolitical logic helps impel Chinese maritime strategy and could help bring about a trial of arms involving the United States.

- The South China Sea is the most likely maritime theater for Beijing to deploy armed force to achieve its geopolitical and strategic goals.

- Mao Zedong's writings will inform Chinese tactics and operational practices should an armed clash come to pass.

- Chinese forces will integrate cruise missiles into "orthodox" and "unorthodox" attacks rather than simply battering away at U.S. task forces with cruise missiles.

My central insight comes from Prussian strategic theorist Carl von Clausewitz, who observes that that war's "grammar . . . may be its own, but not its logic."[3] By this Clausewitz means that war, the pursuit of national policy with the admixture of martial means, differs from other international interactions by virtue of its coercive nature, the impassioned environment, and a host of other factors. If so, the logic and grammar of Chinese sea power hint at how the People's Liberation Army Navy (PLAN) may use antiship cruise missiles in an armed clash.

Tactical Scenarios: Near Shore and on the High Seas

Hughes considers two very broad sets of wartime contingencies. First, U.S. forces might close in on the coasts of an adversary boasting considerable land-based defenses but without a fleet able to fight the U.S. Navy in open waters. Second, prospective opponents might possess fleets able to meet the U.S. Navy in high-seas combat, operating more or less independently of land support. Skillful though weaker adversaries enjoy certain advantages when operating on their home turf, including nearby shore-based assets and manpower, short lines of communication, and familiarity with the tactical environment. Such factors can translate into a distinct strategic advantage over the United States, imposing costs that might be politically unacceptable for Washington. U.S. decision makers might hesitate in times of crisis or even withdraw U.S. forces following a traumatic event such as the crippling or sinking of an aircraft carrier. China holds marked advantages in these terms.

Hughes sets forth three representative scenarios for missile engagements on the high seas: an attack by massed forces on massed forces, a dispersed attack, and a sequential attack (figure 1).[4] These crude indicators suggest a range of possibilities for how Chinese forces may respond to a U.S. naval offensive. The attacking force—"Force B" in Hughes's nomenclature—could represent a mix of shore- and sea-based missile shooters. The important question is whether Chinese strategic preferences would incline Chinese defenders toward a massed, dispersed, or sequential response. A related question: would the Chinese prefer to keep the PLAN closer to home, in keeping with a "fortress fleet" approach, or would they dispatch the fleet beyond shore-based cover?

Figure 1: Closing on Enemy Shores, Facing Land-Based Defenses and Submarine Pickets

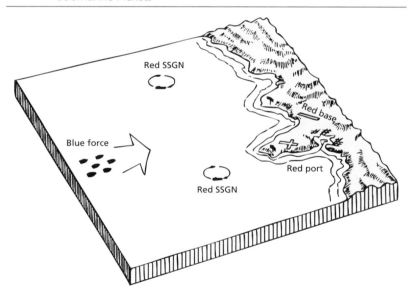

Some composite of land and sea defenses will constitute China's offshore defense posture. As the Chinese military extends its reach seaward, China will push the Clausewitzian "culminating point of the attack" outward from

Chinese coasts. As it does so, the People's Liberation Army (PLA) will amass military superiority farther and farther from China's near seas.

Mahanian Logic

If politics imparts the logic to warfare and determines the ends for which statesmen and soldiers strive, grammar refers to the ways and means for realizing these ends. Unlike most strategic theorists, Mahan prescribed both a logic of sea power and a grammar of naval warfare. The latter has fallen into disuse verging on irrelevance in U.S. naval circles, but his logic continues to beguile— as Chinese naval development attests. While Chinese officials, mariners, and scholars take their inspiration in part from the American theorist, however, they will consult indigenous sources of guidance such as Mao Zedong's military writings for help with the grammar of marine combat.

China is turning its attention to the seas in large part because it can. The collapse of the Soviet Union rendered the overland threat that preoccupied Chinese strategists for centuries largely moot. This frees up resources formerly needed to guard land frontiers. Beijing has used diplomacy to consolidate hospitable surroundings, settling lingering border disputes with its neighbors. It can contemplate accumulating sea power without undue fear of forfeiting its interests ashore.

Beijing also perceives a pressing need to turn its gaze seaward. With the ideological appeal of communism in freefall, Chinese leaders have staked their legitimacy on improving the standard of living for the Chinese populace. Beijing has sought out supplies of oil and gas as far away as the Persian Gulf and the Horn of Africa, casting anxious eyes on the sea lines of communication (SLOCs) conveying raw materials into Chinese seaports. For top Chinese leaders, ensuring free navigation in the Yellow, East China, and South China seas has become a matter of surpassing importance.

They understandably hesitate to entrust this vital interest to Washington's uncertain goodwill. To China, the first island chain, which roughly parallels the Chinese coastline, looks suspiciously like an American barrier to Chinese maritime aspirations. Chinese commentators recall that Secretary of State Dean Acheson once inscribed a U.S. "defense perimeter of the Pacific" on the map of Asia, more or less coincident with the first island chain.[5] Sea-power advocates, then, will tend to regard the island chain as an impediment to Chinese maritime operations, and thus to China's economic vitality, so long as it remains in unfriendly hands. Once PLA forces can operate at will among the islands,

China will in effect have pushed its own defense perimeter offshore—giving pause to foreign naval powers contemplating hostile entry into nearby waters.

The islands also possess offensive value as Beijing gazes eastward into the Pacific and southward toward the South China Sea and the Indian Ocean. General Douglas MacArthur once portrayed Taiwan as "an unsinkable aircraft carrier and submarine tender" off China's coasts, an implement of U.S. containment.[6] Admiral Ernest King believed seizing Formosa would let the U.S. Navy "put the cork in the bottle" of the South China Sea during World War II, severing Japanese SLOCs and thus Japan's supply of oil and raw materials.[7] Beijing, likewise, appears acutely sensitive to the geopolitical value of offshore islands, both as a defensive and an offensive asset.

Alfred Thayer Mahan's logic of sea power rested on the "three pillars" of overseas commerce, naval stations along the sea lines of communication, and merchant and naval fleets.[8] The sea was a "wide common, over which men may pass in all directions."[9] "Communications," meaning secure passage through this watery medium, was "the most important single element in strategy, political or military."[10] The "eminence of sea power" thus lay in its ability to control the sea-lanes, along with critical geographical nodes that facilitated or impeded the flow of commercial and naval shipping. The ability to ensure communications "to one's self, and to interrupt them for an adversary, affects the very root of a nation's vigor," concluded Mahan.[11]

Maoist Grammar

While Mahan vehemently denied that he craved battle on the high seas, he defined "command of the sea" as "that overbearing power on the sea which drives the enemy's flag from it, or allows it to appear only as a fugitive; and which, by controlling the great common, closes the highways by which commerce moves to and fro from the enemy's shores."[12] His grammar was offensive-minded in the extreme: "The offensive element in warfare is the superstructure, the end and the aim for which the defensive exists, and apart from which it is to all purposes of war worse than useless. When war has been accepted as necessary, success means nothing short of victory; and victory must be sought by offensive measures, and by them only can be insured."[13] Beyond that, Mahan's writings about the grammar of naval war have an antiquarian feel about them. If Beijing looks to Mahan for inspiration on grand-strategic matters, consequently, it seeks out operational and tactical guidance from China's own rich martial heritage.

Mao Zedong is one source of such guidance. Indeed, China's "offshore active defense" strategy takes both its name and its guiding precepts from Mao's doctrine of "active defense," an approach to warfighting distilled from his experiences waging land war against Japanese and Chinese Nationalist armies. What was active defense? The Red Army replied to Nationalist ground offensives not through passive means but through highly offensive operations and tactics placed at the service of defensive strategic aims.

U.S. mastery of East Asian waters looks like a maritime variant of the Nationalists' strategy of "encirclement and suppression."[14] Suitably adapted, the strategy Mao's Red Army deployed against the Nationalist encirclement-and-suppression campaigns can apply to naval combat. It appears that many Chinese strategists do transpose his land-warfare strategy to the near seas. If so, Chinese strategists will look to the doctrines of Mao for strategies and tactics needed to execute a Mahanian grand strategy—applying concepts distinctive to land combat to naval combat.

The defensive was a temporary expedient for Mao, then, not a permanent or still less a desirable state of affairs. If Beijing heeds his advice, Washington must consider seriously the prospect that Beijing will adopt an offensive strategy inspired by Mahan and Mao.

Applying Mahan's Logic to Chinese Strategic Thought

Mahan, then, furnishes both a logic and a vocabulary of assertive sea power. In many cases Chinese Mahanians explicitly cite his works to justify an ambitious maritime strategy. The notion of "overbearing power" pervades these thinkers' discourse on maritime affairs. Should they win out among the cacophony of voices clamoring for senior policymakers' attention, Chinese strategy will take on distinctly offensive overtones.

Consider the words of Professor Ni Lexiong of the Shanghai Institute of Political Science and Law. Ni uses sea-power theory to evaluate competing claims from sea-power advocates and globalization enthusiasts. Globalization theorists, he writes, beseech Beijing not to embark on a naval arms buildup because it would alert "today's naval hegemon," the United States. This would render Chinese naval development "a self-destructive play with fire" reminiscent of Imperial Germany's quixotic bid for sea power.[15]

Ni postulates that the world is entering a Kantian era of perpetual peace, as many globalization proponents prophesy, but he points out that the most pacific international system ultimately rests on force. China must build up a muscular PLAN to play its part in the "world Navy," should one emerge. Until then "it is China's necessary choice to build up a strong sea power," warding off "threats to our 'outward-leaning economy' by some strong nations"—code for the United States—in today's lingering "Hobbesian era."[16]

Ni reminds readers that a powerful Japanese fleet crushed the Qing Dynasty's Beiyang Fleet in 1894–95, and that the "key to winning that war was to gain the command of the sea." Mahan "believed that whoever could control the sea would win the war and change history; that command of the sea is achieved through decisive naval battles on the seas; that the outcome of decisive naval battles is determined by the strength of fire power on each side of the engagement."[17] If Ni's brand of thinking comes to prevail in Chinese policy circles, Washington and its Asian partners must gird themselves for a newly assertive Beijing.

The South China Sea and Mao's Grammar of Active Defense

Chinese and Western strategists commonly assume the Pacific is the most likely theater of twenty-first century maritime competition between the United States and China. And indeed, Admiral Liu Huaqing, "China's Mahan" and the father of the modern PLAN, espoused such a strategy. But the South China Sea is a more probable locus for contingencies involving the rival fleets. At least four strategic challenges direct the attention of Chinese strategists to this expanse:

- Taiwan, along the sea's northern edge, preoccupies Beijing. China has gained the confidence to start looking past Taiwan to other pursuits in Southeast and South Asia. Still, settling affairs in the Taiwan Strait will free up resources and energies, bring about national unification, breach Acheson's island-chain perimeter, and give the PLA its own offshore (and unsinkable, if also immovable) aircraft carrier and submarine tender. By occupying the island, moreover, Beijing can ensure that the bottle of the South China Sea remains uncorked for Chinese shipping.

- China's "Malacca dilemma" or "Malacca predicament" persists. Ensuring free passage through the SLOCs connecting the Persian Gulf region and the Horn of Africa with Chinese harbors—in particular through the Strait of Malacca—remains a matter of overriding importance. If anything, guaranteeing an uninterrupted flow of oil, natural gas, and other raw materials will assume an even greater place in China's maritime calculus.

- China has staked maritime-territorial claims to most of the South China Sea, making Southeast Asia a natural theater for nautical endeavor. National sentiment fuels Beijing's policy toward the region, as does its value for maritime communications and the undersea resources reportedly found in the seabed. Chinese officials' redefinition of the sea as a "core national interest" equal to Taiwan and Tibet testifies to the value they attach to their objectives there.

- Undersea warfare imparts momentum to China's southward maritime turn. The PLA has constructed an impressive naval base complete with underground pens for fleet ballistic missile submarines, or SSBNs, on Hainan Island, in the northern reaches of the South China Sea. The Sanya base gives Beijing the second of China's "two eyes" at sea (Taiwan being the other), to borrow the metaphor Chinese officials use. Basing SSBNs in the South China Sea would bypass U.S. and Japanese anti-submarine-warfare forces in Northeast Asia, extend the PLAN's reach toward the Malacca Strait, and expedite access to the Pacific Ocean via the Luzon Strait, which separates Taiwan from the Philippines.

However useful his geopolitical theorizing and his advocacy in general terms for sea power—one historian called him America's "evangelist of sea power"—Mahan's vision of battles between big-gun battleships holds little relevance for today's age of high-tech naval combat. Beyond his injunction to mass combat power for decisive fleet engagements, few Chinese analysts pay his grammar much attention.

Mao evinced little interest in sea power, but he shared Chinese Mahanians' scorn for the notion of passive defense—even during the grim years when his Red Army barely clung to life. Mao insisted that passive defense represented "a spurious kind of defense," and that "the only real defense is active defense." By this he meant "offensive defense," or "defense for the purpose of counter-attacking and taking the offensive."[18] For him even defensive aims were best attained by offensive means. Passive measures represented a transient measure dictated by an unfavorable balance of forces—not the core of China's national strategy, let alone its strategic preference. The weaker party deliberately protracted a conflict to sap the will of the stronger to fight. Resort to the strategic defensive did not limit military strategy or tactics to the purely defensive or passive.

Mao foresaw that his theory of protracted war might be misconstrued and took pains to distance himself from the passive approach. "Only a complete fool or a madman," he proclaimed, "would cherish passive defense as a talisman." Active defense referred to the art of preparing conditions for a strategic counteroffensive culminating in a decisive engagement: "there is no military manual of value nor any sensible military expert, ancient or modern, Chinese or foreign, that does not oppose passive defense, whether in strategy or tactics. . . . That is an error in war, a manifestation of conservatism in military matters, which we must resolutely oppose."[19] Mao was writing of Chiang Kai-shek's encirclement-and-suppression campaigns during the Chinese Civil War. Despite the Nationalists' material superiority, the Red Army artfully combined direct and indirect attack (cheng and ch'i) in the tradition of Sun Tzu, one of Mao's favorite strategists. After biding their time on the strategic defensive, the communists shifted the balance of forces in their favor, seized the strategic offensive, and prevailed. Dexterity was at a premium. "Militarily speaking," declared Mao, "our warfare consists of the alternate use of the defensive and the offensive." A period of strategic retreat was permissible at the outset of a defensive campaign, but only to allow Chinese forces to ready a devastating counterblow: "defensive warfare, which is passive in form, can be active in content, and can be switched from the stage in which it is passive in form to the stage in which it is active both in form and in content. In appearance a fully planned strategic retreat is made under compulsion, but in reality it is effected in order to conserve our strength and bide our time in order to defeat the enemy, to lure him in deep and prepare for our counter-offensive."[20] For Mao, Chinese forces were like a "clever boxer" who "gives a little ground at first, while the foolish one rushes in furiously and uses up all his resources at the very start, and in the end he is often beaten by the man who has given ground." He quoted Sun Tzu, who urged, "Avoid the enemy when he is full of vigor, strike when he is fatigued and withdraws."[21] After falling back on predesignated bases to weary their opponents and to concentrate force, the defenders would unleash an overwhelming counteroffensive.

There was a pronounced geospatial component to this theorizing. Stronger enemies typically operated along "exterior lines" in an effort to envelop the defenders, who operated on "interior lines." Then as now, the prospect of encirclement fueled anxieties among Chinese leaders, stimulating thought about countermeasures. According to Milan Vego, "A force moves along interior lines when it runs between those of the enemy's lines of operations. Interior lines always originate from a central position. They are formed from a central position prolonged in one or more directions or they can also be understood as a series of central positions linked with one another. Interior lines in general allow concentration of one's forces against one part of the enemy force, while holding the other in check with a force distinctly inferior in strength."[22]

Even when forced onto the interior lines, granted Mao, it was both "possible and necessary to use tactical offensives within the strategic defensive, to fight campaigns and battles of quick decision within a strategically protracted war and to fight campaigns and battles on exterior lines within strategically interior lines." This maxim held "both for regular and for guerrilla warfare."[23] To wage microlevel offensives within a macrolevel defensive campaign, commanders should stage forces to deplete enemy forces. "Concentrate a big force to strike at a small section of the enemy force" and annihilate it, he advised. Better to cut off one of an enemy's fingers entirely than to injure them all.[24] Interior lines had their advantages.

Mao's strategic wisdom applies to sea as well as land combat, and on the level of grand strategy. Indeed, the Chinese Communist Party chairman was given to musing about operating on diplomatic exterior lines against Japanese imperialism. Although Chinese forces were strategically encircled, an "anti-Japanese front in the Pacific area" constituted a sort of counterencirclement.[25] Maoist theory, then, informed the logic of Chinese statecraft as well as its operational and tactical grammar.

Prompted by Mahan and Mao, Chinese naval strategists such as Ni Lexiong now talk routinely of prying control of the waters within the first island chain from the U.S. Navy's grasp. Indeed, it is increasingly commonplace for Chinese strategists to urge Beijing to seize "absolute control" of the seas within the island chain.[26]

Applying Mao's Active Defense to Offshore Operations

The concept of sea denial furnishes perhaps the best indicator of how China will put its Mao-inspired naval strategy into practice. A navy intent on sea denial seeks to impose conditions that deter or prevent an adversary from operating within a given nautical expanse for an extended period. Sea denial is a strategically defensive stance generally taken by inferior naval powers—the PLAN's plight for the foreseeable future—but the operations and tactics used to execute the strategy are offensive in orientation. Such an approach conforms philosophically both to Mao's concept of active defense, which yoked offensive means to defensive ends, and to Mahan's injunction for even inferior navies to strive for command of vital sea areas.

The Chinese military already possesses or plans to acquire capabilities useful for sea denial in littoral waters and airspace. China has purchased arms from Russia lavishly while pressing ahead with an array of indigenous programs. The result: a leap in offensive combat power suitable for sea denial. Sophisticated warships armed with antiship missiles and next-generation air-defense radars and missiles—designed to increase their survivability against long-range air strikes—increasingly form the backbone of the Chinese surface fleet. Modern diesel submarines, difficult to detect and track in the littoral environment, are entering service in significant numbers. Construction of indigenous nuclear-powered boats proceeds apace. More accurate and longer-range ballistic and cruise missiles, advanced ground-based air-defense systems, and capable naval fighter/attack aircraft are some of the other key features of China's military modernization effort. If the Chinese package these assets wisely and develop the requisite tactical proficiency, they will gain confidence in their ability to deter or defeat any foreign power that contemplates hostile entry into nearby waters.

Interestingly, many of China's emerging military capabilities, including antiship missiles, air-defense systems, and attack aircraft, are designed to launch strikes against targets along the littoral from bases on the mainland. This approach would exploit China's deep continental interior, which in effect furnishes a safe haven from which to punish forces operating along the coastline. Beijing could dare adversaries to launch strikes against the mainland and risk seeing a limited conflict at sea escalate to full-blown war, with repercussions disproportionate to their presumably modest strategic goals.

In other words, a PLA that exploited the mainland's vast strategic depth would have the luxury of waiting for enemy forces to enter weapons range, accepting battle on China's geographic and military terms. Dispersed attacks on exterior lines would become thinkable. This recalls Mao's savvy boxer who gave ground while preparing a counterpunch. Using Wayne Hughes' three models of fleet tactics (again, in the casual sense I am employing them here), Maoist preferences would incline Chinese defenders to

- Let U.S. forces close on Chinese shores before mounting dispersed attacks from a variety of shore- and sea-based missile shooters, complemented by submarine attack, minefields, and the other tactics and systems to which China has paid close attention. Having fallen back on land-based support, Beijing can bring the full advantages of its contested zone to bear. U.S. commanders can expect a 360-degree threat environment. As they near Chinese coastlines, moreover, the PLA will assume the exterior lines—making dispersed attack from multiple threat axes possible.

- Target individual vessels or small detachments in an effort to wipe them out. Despite the tenor of Chinese commentary and their own assumptions, U.S. commanders should not automatically assume aircraft carriers would be the prime target for PLA action. Amphibious ships would make tempting targets in a Taiwan contingency, for example. Disabling or sinking a gee-whiz Aegis warship would give Washington pause. Deprived of combat logistics ships, the American fleet cannot easily sustain operations.

- Combine orthodox and unorthodox attacks. The concept of saturation attack implies that cruise missiles will be the dominant implement used by China. This may well be true, but other weaponry like mines and torpedoes are also ideal for use in a contested zone. For instance, antiship missiles could represent the secondary, or unorthodox, element of an orthodox undersea attack. It also bears repeating that Maoist tactics are fluid. Unorthodox attacks morph into unorthodox attacks and back again.

- Merge nonmilitary instruments of national power into the defensive effort. For example, Beijing could convey to Washington the enduring diplomatic and economic repercussions of taking on China over Taiwan or some other object—inducing the United States to hesitate in wartime. Diplomats could try to weaken or pick off U.S. allies, undercutting America's strategic position in Asia. On the operational level, Beijing could trumpet achievements of Chinese arms—say, putting a U.S. carrier or Aegis destroyer out of action—for strategic-communications purposes. Deflating American morale would pay indirect dividends.

How, in more specific terms, will China use its panoply of new hardware for sea denial? Clearly, the PLA has plowed considerable effort and resources into cruise missile procurement and development. One RAND report situates SS-N-22 and SS-N-27 antiship missiles at the heart of China's strategy for a Taiwan contingency, strongly suggesting that the United States would come up on the losing end in an encounter in the Taiwan Strait in 2020.[27] But again, the PLA will probably unleash the raw hitting power of its antiship missiles in concert with other systems.

For instance, Beijing's purchase of (and efforts to reverse engineer) the S-300 Russian air-defense system is suggestive. An indigenous, antiradiation variant of the S-300, the FT-2000 will likely be deployed near the Taiwan Strait to target Taiwanese forces and deter U.S. military intervention in a crossstrait war. Reportedly nearing production, the FT-2000 has earned the nickname "AWACS killer" owing to its mission of attacking the airborne sensors and electronic warfare assets on which U.S. air superiority relies in wartime.

China's newest air-defense warships will be outfitted with similar surface-to-air missiles. In Hughes' terms, the FT-2000 could seriously impair U.S. scouting effectiveness, one of his chief determinants of tactical success. Weapons range means little without the ability to find and target enemy forces at long distances.

U.S. defense planners have ample reason to worry about these systems. The American way of modern warfare—showcased in Afghanistan, the two wars against Iraq, and other conflicts of the past two decades—is predicated on winning the contest over battlefield information at the outset of a conflict. U.S. forces prevailed in large part because superior technology gave them a "common operating picture" of conditions in the battle space that no opponent could match. Airborne sensors detect and target multiple enemy aircraft across long distances, while jammers and antiradiation missiles incapacitate enemy sensors attempting to gather data and target U.S. assets. These tactics effectively paralyze U.S. adversaries during the opening phases of a military campaign, paving the way for an even more important battlefield condition: air supremacy.

Since the dawn of carrier warfare, U.S. naval strategy has viewed command of the air as a prerequisite for surface fleet operations. An operation near Chinese shores would be no different. If Chinese air defenses completely or partially negated the U.S. edge in information warfare, consequently, they would slow down and complicate the efforts of U.S. aircraft to impose dominance in the skies—blunting U.S. offensive action and leaving U.S. warships, including aircraft carriers, vulnerable to air and missile counterstrikes. Robust Chinese air defenses would oblige the United States to devote more energy to securing the skies. Deft use of even an inherently defensive and passive weapon such as the FT-2000 missile, then, would open the way for the Chinese to conduct offensive operations in Mao Zedong's sense.

Beijing would use its air defenses in concert with other forces. If the PLA managed to compel U.S. forces to look skyward, assuming a more defensive posture, it could then pose additional challenges with attack submarines and missile-armed surface vessels. As noted before, a well-designed force package would present U.S. forces with a three-dimensional threat environment featuring multiple threat axes. The more stresses the Chinese can impose, the less likely U.S. forces will be to venture landward of the first island chain. Washington has premised its operational calculus on free access along the Asian mainland. If China can even partially cancel out U.S. technologies that manage the fog of war, it can severely curtail U.S. forces' freedom of maneuver in this littoral milieu—compelling U.S. forces to operate farther from Chinese shores and helping China achieve its goal of sea denial in the near seas.

One caveat is worth stating. Alone or combined, these capabilities do not give China a decisive edge in littoral warfare, let alone outright military superiority over the U.S. military. Rather, as Mao counseled, the PLA will leverage its operational and tactical advantages in an offensive manner, imposing costs sufficient to achieve strategically defensive aims. If Beijing can deny U.S. forces the ability to dictate events, it will have fulfilled the most important goal of its sea-denial strategy, imposing local dominance at sea and aloft. This would be eminently in keeping with the experiences of the past forty years. From Egypt's sinking of the Israeli destroyer *Eilat* with Styx missiles to the Iraqi Exocet attack on USS *Stark* to Hezbollah's crippling of the Israeli corvette *Spear* with a C-802 surface-to-surface missile, experience shows how much havoc a determined yet inferior power can wreak.

In each case a single missile hit scored a mission kill, disabled the stricken vessel, or, in the case of the *Eilat*, sank it altogether. For Chinese naval planners, this promises a handsome return on modest investments. It only makes sense for the PLA to employ such tactics that accord with sound tactical principles while conforming to Chinese strategic and operational traditions. How should U.S. commanders prepare for the eventuality of Chinese antiship missile warfare? In part by heeding Wayne Hughes' prescriptions for tactical success:

- Washington must work with allies. More assets and bases in theater always help. Furthermore, the U.S. and Japanese fleets can make use of the Japanese archipelago, using sea mines, submarines, and portable antiship missiles emplaced in the Ryukyus to impede PLAN egress through the first island chain.

- Hughes urges ship designers to extend the range of U.S. missiles and improve U.S. Navy expeditionary groups' detection and targeting ability, in turn letting commanders refine their tactics to preserve or regain the advantage over prospective adversaries. Continuing work on systems is imperative. So is continuously improving tactics such as emissions control, or EMCON, in a combat environment, and waging aggressive electronic warfare.

- They also need to think in terms of mutual support. Chances are, the balance will shift increasingly to the PLA as Chinese forces increase and refine their arsenal and figure out how best to exploit their contested zone. It only makes sense for the U.S. Navy to mass its defenses to offset these Chinese advantages.

- Naval officers should rethink their entrenched assumption that high-tech warships can strike down the archer before he looses the arrow. Past generations of naval architects designed combatants with just the oppo-site assumption in mind—that U.S. warships *would* suffer battle damage. It might be worth rediscovering this philosophy of naval architecture.

- Some of Hughes's recommendations cannot be speedily implemented. Improving the capacity of U.S. warships to withstand punishment would reduce the likelihood of their becoming mission kills after one enemy missile leaked through their defenses. Better staying power is in large measure a function of designing more rugged warships. As recent experience with platforms like the ill-fated DDG-1000 project has shown, modifying material capabilities takes time, involves steep costs, and incurs considerable uncertainty.

The sooner the navy starts hardening its fleet and reconsidering its tacti-cal and operational practices, the better. Finally, naval officers should not let themselves be entranced by net assessment—by the size and specifications of the Chinese arsenal. They must step up their efforts to understand the ways prospective adversaries like China may wage war. U.S. mariners must school themselves in foreign history and culture, identify alternative futures for mari-time Asia, and prepare accordingly.

Notes

1. Wayne P. Hughes Jr., *Fleet Tactics and Coastal Combat*, 2nd ed. (Annapolis: Naval Institute Press, 2000), 266.

2. Ibid., 268–74.

3. Carl von Clausewitz, *On War*, ed. and trans. Michael Howard and Peter Paret (Princeton, NJ: Princeton University Press, 1976), 605.

4. Hughes, *Fleet Tactics*, 244.

5. Dean Acheson, "Remarks by the Secretary of State (Acheson) before the National Press Club, Washington, January 12, 1950," in Raymond Dennett and Robert K. Turner, eds., *Documents on American Foreign Relations*, vol. 12: *January 1–December 31, 1950* (Princeton, NJ: Princeton University Press, 1951), 431.

6. Quoted in Courtney Whitney, *MacArthur: His Rendezvous with History* (New York: Knopf, 1956), 378–79.

7. Quoted in Samuel Eliot Morison, *The Two-Ocean War: A Short History of the United States Navy in the Second World War* (Boston: Little, Brown, 1963), 476.

8. Alfred Thayer Mahan, *The Influence of Sea Power upon History, 1660–1783* (1890; repr. New York: Dover Publications, 1987), 25, 71.

9. Ibid., 25.

10. Alfred Thayer Mahan, *The Problem of Asia* (1900; repr. Port Washington: Kennikat Press, 1970), 124.

11. Ibid.

12. Mahan, *Influence of Sea Power upon History*, 138.

13. Alfred Thayer Mahan, "Considerations Governing the Disposition of Navies," *National Review*, July 1902, 706.

14. References to U.S. "encirclement" and "containment" are ubiquitous in the Chinese press. See, for example, Willy Wo-Lap Lam, "Hu's Central Asian Gamble to Counter the U.S. 'Containment Strategy,'" *China Brief* 5, no. 15 (5 July 2005): 7–8.

15. Ni Lexiong, "Sea Power and China's Development," *Liberation Daily*, 17 April 2005, 1–2, available at U.S.-China Economic and Security Review Commission Website, http://www.uscc.gov/researchpapers/translated_articles/2005/05_07_18_Sea_Power_and_Chinas_Development.pdf.

16. Ibid., 4.

17. Ibid., 5.

18. Mao, "Strategy in China's Revolutionary War," in *Selected Writings of Mao Tse-Tung*, vol. 1 (Beijing: Foreign Languages Press, 1966), 207, 224.

19. Ibid.

20. Ibid., 220, 234.

21. Ibid., 208, 211, 217, 234.

22. Milan N. Vego, *Naval Strategy and Operations in Narrow Seas*, 2nd rev. ed. (London: Frank Cass, 2003), 85–88.

23. Mao Zedong, "Problems of Strategy in Guerrilla War," in *Selected Writings of Mao Tse-Tung*, vol. 2 (Beijing: Foreign Languages Press, 1966), 83.

24. Ibid., 82–84.

25. Mao Zedong, "On Protracted War," in *Selected Works of Mao Tse-tung*, vol. 2 (Beijing: Foreign Languages Press, 1966), http://www.marxists.org/reference/archive/mao/selected-works/volume-2/mswv2_09.htm.

26. Jiang Shiliang, "The Command of Communications," *Zhongguo Junshi Kexue*, 2 October 2002, 106–14, FBIS-CPP20030107000189.

27. Wendell Minnick, "RAND Study Suggests U.S. Loses War with China," *Defense News*, 16 October 2008, http://www.defensenews.com/story.php?i=3774348&c=ASI&s=AIR.

Larry M. Wortzel

Deterrence and Presence after Beijing's Aerospace Revolution

AT THE 18TH CONGRESS of the Communist Party of China in 2012, a fifth generation of leadership will assume power. People's Liberation Army (PLA) military theorists will spend the months leading up to this transition wrestling with how aerospace power fits into the Communist Party's demands to conduct missions around China's periphery and requirements for greater global reach for China. They will seek to reconcile a military transformation aimed at "preparations to win high-technology localized wars," envisioned to involve Taiwan and mainland China's maritime periphery, with the growing recognition that China has wider geographical interests that military theorists and Chinese Communist Party (CCP) political leaders increasingly recognize require capabilities to operate beyond the local region.[1]

PLA doctrine demonstrates that China's military theorists and planners understand that activities in the domains of warfare (air, space, cyber or electronic, maritime, and land) must be integrated. However, it is not clear that there are firm plans regarding how aviation (the PLA Air Force, PLAAF; and PLAN Navy, PLAN aviation) will fit into this picture of integrated military operations applied to the maritime domain. Even though the 2008 China Defense White Paper designated the PLAAF, PLAN, and Second Artillery as "strategic services (or arms)," how they operate strategically rather than operationally was not specified.[2] The white paper categorizes the government's intent on the use of these services without discussing specific roles. In terms of expenditures, however, it seems that space operations, the strategic rocket forces, and the PLAN are getting the emphasis today. The Department of Defense's 2010 report to Congress on China's military power discusses improved space-based intelligence and military support from space as one of the rapidly improving areas in China's asymmetric capabilities. Generally speaking, thinking in the PLA about how space capabilities and ballistic missiles affect the maritime domain is more developed than are specific ideas about air power. This chapter will examine these issues with a view toward an understanding of how China's integrated aerospace operations affect the maritime domain and U.S. forces.

The contrast between the PLA and U.S. armed forces could not be starker. When General Gordon Sullivan, then chief of staff of the United States Army, landed in Australia in 1992, he gave a speech to the Australian Army that discussed America's "global reach." Sullivan told the audience that he had just landed on a U.S. Air Force C-141 transport that had flown directly from Washington, DC, refueling twice over the Pacific Ocean en route to Australia. He told the Australians that despite the distances between our two countries, our alliance was strong and was backed up by America's global reach. Just as quickly as he had arrived, Sullivan added, a reinforced battalion from the 82nd Airborne Division could be in Australia, or anywhere else, followed rapidly by the rest of the combat brigade. Sullivan did not mention the space and the command, control, communications, computers, intelligence, surveillance, and reconnaissance (C4ISR) architecture supporting the mission. Nor did he discuss the follow-on forces and logistics infrastructure that the Navy and Marine Corps would deploy to support such missions. The point, however, is that the United States routinely executes such missions while the PLA and its Communist Party leaders are only thinking about whether such missions fit how China intends to focus its military in the future.

The PLA cannot conduct such a mission today. However, it is clear that some in the PLA are thinking about these things. That is the thesis of Jiang Yamin, in his 2007 Academy of Military Science text *Long-Distance Operations*.[3] Jiang explores the history of long-distance operations in war and speculates about how the PLA may integrate such missions into its future battlefield operations. But speculation about a more active future and these excursions into future doctrine, roles, and missions requires decisions from the CCP Politburo and Central Military Commission (CMC) before they become reality. Jiang's theorizing is not an isolated instance. There are other officers thinking about the future in similar terms. Discussing the "leap" from brainstorming and theory to actual "military development," three PLA officers argue that the first requirement is to clarify the question of "what to transform and how to transform it."[4] However, they argue, although exploratory thinking is needed, the current task is to "launch training in complex electronic environments, and emphasize the training of the naval, air force, second artillery and other technical branches and specialized units."[5]

A recent article in *Modern Navy* discussed the need for a navy that can respond to air strikes from enemy carriers; carry out long-distance, accurate strikes; and carry out "long distance interception."[6] In the longer term, however, the authors state, "the Navy should gradually strengthen the capability of joint naval formations in charging to the rear of the enemy and striking the enemy's capabilities in taking off and landing aircrafts, as well as warships leaving ports. The Navy should also develop means to smash the enemy's airports and piers, and to destroy its maintenance guidance, and fueling capabilities related to long distance accurate strikes."[7]

This picture of an evolution in military missions suggests a navy that is able to operate at long distances and carry out integrated, offensive strike missions. Such capabilities would involve the aerospace domain and the air force. CCP and CMC chairman Hu Jintao has provided broad guidance that justifies the exploratory approaches to military theory, new defense roles and missions, and the development and procurement of new equipment that we see in PLA and defense-related literature. In his address to the 17th CCP Congress on 15 October 2007, Hu emphasized the importance of "safeguarding China's interests in terms of sovereignty, security and development."[8] In discussing the armed forces, Hu Jintao made four major points, focusing on implementing "the military strategy for the new period," educating the military in its "historical missions," building "computerized armed forces and winning IT-based warfare," and conducting "People's War under new historical conditions." This characterization of the PLA as having a series of historical missions is important. The formulation provides the ideological basis for future defense research and development and acquisition of new systems. More importantly, from the perspective of this chapter, the formulation provides for a broader use of the armed forces outside the region and beyond the near periphery of the nation in a justifiable and transparent justification for the defense of a wider concept of national interests.

The "historic missions" are

- To reinforce the armed forces' loyalty to the CCP and to have them help to consolidate the Party's ruling position in Chinese society,

- To ensure China's sovereignty, territorial integrity, and domestic security in order to continue its national development, particularly during a "strategic window of opportunity" between now and approximately 2020,

- To help safeguard China's expanding national interests, and

- To "play an important role in safeguarding world peace and promoting common development."[9]

These historic missions establish a formal ideological framework that permits the central leadership organs of China to use the military in a regional context and at least justify expanding the scope of PLA operations beyond the region to address critical national interests. PLA and other Chinese national security thinkers increasingly make reference to expanded contingency and force presence missions for the PLA. In one text for the PLA National Defense University, Senior Colonel Wang Lidong expressed the view that as the PLA strengthens to carry out its external missions, it will need to develop a stronger maritime capacity as part of China's "comprehensive national security."[10] In a similar vein, Academy of Military Science theorist Jiang Yamin reminds students of warfare in the PLA that "in the 21st century, Hu Jintao's charge to provide a firm national defense for China means that the PLA must have a strong capability to counter attacks at long distances and defend distant lines of communication."[11]

A great deal of thought in contemporary military and national security texts in China is devoted to maritime operations and how they support broader Chinese national security interests. Three PLA officers writing in the journal *China Military Science* argue that in "naval building," going back to thinking by Mao Zedong, the navy was conceived of as a "strategic armed service," both to face "hegemonic and strong navies" for offshore defense as well as to safeguard maritime rights and interests.[12] Still, the main emphasis on joint operations appears to focus on the space domain. In an interview published in the journal *Modern Navy*, PLA National Defense University's Li Daguang said that modern maritime operations must be "informatized," or information technology–enabled and networked, and will require the use of "military space information resources to be broad-based."[13]

Many texts discuss maritime operations as a domain of war that is supported by aerospace operations that must be integrated to be effective. The general focus, however, is on "integrated operations," which include aerospace effects on the maritime domain. Aerospace power is viewed as providing improved command-and-control, reconnaissance, and early-warning systems across the domains of war. Writing for the PLAAF in 2004, Cai Fengzhen and Tian Anping do not distinguish between attacks on ground targets or maritime targets and see both as simply requiring precise strikes on surface targets.[14] Few texts, in fact, have explicit discussions of PLAAF or PLAN aviation operations and how they will be integrated in the maritime domain in the near future. Two exceptions to this are Jiang Yamin's *Long-Distance Operations*, and Wang Lidong's *On National Maritime Interests*.

Wang Lidong is a graduate of the Dalian Military Academy, the Nanjing Political Academy, and the Central Party School. He is one of the editors at PLA National Defense University Press and has written twelve other books on Party-Army issues discussing such topics as Deng Xiaoping's strategic thinking and how Jiang's "three represents" theory affects the military. Thus, what Wang may lack in operational experience, he makes up for credibility in the General Political Department and the CCP.

In the context of American efforts to secure sea lanes and the air after the terrorist attack on the United States on 11 September 2001, Wang makes explicit the linkages between the security of "strategic maritime passages" and "comprehensive security" on the ocean's surface, on land, and in the air.[15] The author also comments that it is important to recognize the relationship between U.S. Marine Corps aviation and ground forces and how they are used in securing maritime areas, critical islands, and nearby land, implying that such capabilities would be useful to China.[16]

Wang also sees carrier strike groups as important for executing amphibious operations and long-distance expeditionary operations, noting that such expeditionary operations need to be integrated with strategic air power operations.[17] Indeed, China's development of J-15 aircraft and apparent continued interest in purchasing Su-33 fighter aircraft configured to allow the PLA to begin training for carrier-based operations suggests that, at some point, aircraft carrier operations will be part of the PLA's capabilities. Major General Qian Lihua, of the People's Republic of China (PRC) Ministry of Defense's Foreign Affairs Office, said as much in the *Financial Times* on 17 November 2008, noting that although China would have aircraft carriers at some point in the future, the PLA did not contemplate global presence operations. Rather, he implied limited roles for an aircraft carrier in the region.[18]

In the longer term, however, Wang Lidong says that as China moves toward network centric operations, it will also be necessary to "control the seas" with "platform centric operations" that will involve space assets and other platforms to facilitate information exchange if operations are to achieve the ability to exercise sea control.[19] In the introductory parts of the text, Wang emphasized that between the Law of the Sea Treaty and China's own territorial law, China has added more than 3 million square kilometers of sovereign maritime territory, the protection of which is a major component of China's national interest.[20] Wang also characterizes the military challenges and the scope of maritime operations in the twenty-first century as global and involving missiles, electronics, and information technologies "so that maritime operations will now span the surface, subsurface, air, and space domains of war as well as the electronic spectrum."[21]

An introductory text on PLAAF thinking acknowledges that air power can play a decisive role in offensive and defensive operations against maritime objectives, including affecting the outcome of maritime warfare.[22] It is noteworthy, however, that the text spends more time discussing the effects of network centric operations (the uses of aircraft and satellites to enhance networked command and control, improve the psychological impact of operations on enemy morale, and improve electronic warfare) than it does other applications of air power.[23] In fact, the authors of the text argue at one point that the effects of the space component of aerospace power (and especially ballistic missiles and space warfare) are valuable against all forms of surface targets, whether on land or on the sea.[24] There is scant specific discussion of long-distance air power, the use of air-to-air refueling, or long-range bombers, although the text advances the view that an advantage of aerospace power and missiles is that they can be used in operations "anywhere, anytime, [and] accurately, including in outer space."[25] The authors of this text are clear, however, that one must really think of integrated land, maritime, air and space operations, since warfare has been transformed by aircraft, missiles, satellites, and aircraft that can operate in the outer reaches of the atmosphere.[26] Reflecting official PLAAF thinking about implementing the 15th Five-Year Plan, the text supports the concept of long-distance operations and allowing a force to strike the enemy before the enemy mounts an attack, thereby affecting the "scale" and "scope" of operations and permitting a military to "seize" air control and "command of the seas."[27] Another important point in this text is that the authors make the argument that "control of the air" allows the attacker to "paralyze the enemy's ground and naval forces," again making no distinction between ground and maritime surface targets.[28] For the PLAAF, at least, operations in these two domains of war are equal and there is not a great deal of separate thought given to the way that air forces and naval air forces can work in an integral manner.

Li Daguang, in an interview with a reporter from *Modern Navy*, argues that "large scope, large scale" maritime operations will depend on satellite

communications to provide "ample sea communications assistance."[29] Li fore-
sees space assets playing a major role in the "discovery, tracking, guidance,
and attack of targets by main combat weapons and equipment."[30] "Round-
the-clock, all-weather, smooth communications" between "surface ships, submarines, coastal missile combat platforms, and space, air and surface early
warning systems" are required for effective joint maritime operations, according to Li. Indeed, he sees "network-centric warfare" as having expanded the
PLA's traditional five domains of war to a sixth. For Li, "integrated combat
action" includes the areas of "sea, land, air, space, electromagnetic space, and
network space."[31] If Li Daguang's views permeate the PLA, then we can expect
to see a broader role for the PLA's space forces and the elements of the General
Staff Department that manage electronic countermeasures, technical reconnaissance, and communications.

Satellites, Radar, and Jamming: Integrating Advanced Electronic Warfare Technologies

In implementing an effective aerospace warfare strategy, the PLA is emphasizing the role that advanced forms of electronic warfare and electronic countermeasures can play. Li Daguang's work suggests this course of action. Among
the areas currently receiving emphasis in the PLA's electronic warfare journals
are techniques such as digital radio frequency memory (DRFM), and direct
digital synthesis (DDS). The new F-12 DRFM system, for example, still under
development, digitizes a received signal and retransmits it, deceiving the original transmitting radar and creating false targets. This technology can be effective against spacecraft and satellites and is useful for aircraft, ships, and ground
systems. DDS systems allow fast frequency hopping or tuning and can generate signals with less power. This can help in jamming countermeasures and
antijamming analysis.[32] The important point is that PLA theoretical journals
are exploring advanced information and electronic warfare measures independent of any foreign assistance. These measures and the associated technologies can be used throughout any of the domains of war. Broadly speaking,
DRFM and DDS technologies make advanced jamming systems more effective, including in or against satellites, meaning that in the future the PLA likely
will incorporate these technologies into its information warfare programs. The
technologies also contribute to phased-array radar design and effectiveness.
This means that they improve aircraft, naval, space-based, and ground radars.
The PLA also appears to be exercising more regularly in what is now called

a "complex electromagnetic environment," putting these new technologies to the test.

China's Maritime Interests

An exploratory text from a CCP-controlled publisher sketches out how PLA strategists and senior leaders are framing factors that will drive future drive missions for the PLA that address maritime interests.[33] The text outlines ideas about a military force capable of responding to domestic problems, securing China's sovereign territory, defending China's economic and political interests at long distances, patrolling vital sea lines of communication, denying potential adversaries the freedom to coerce China with impunity, and limiting proximity to the coast, from which potential adversaries can conduct strike operations against the Chinese mainland.

Like Wang's book discussed earlier, in his PLA National Defense University text, Wang Lidong takes this matter further, defining China's maritime interests as

- Securing sovereign territorial waters;
- Securing internal waters and the economic zone;
- Gaining access to maritime passages around the globe;
- Securing maritime defensive zones such as the Northwest Pacific Ocean and the Philippine Sea;
- Gaining access to the maritime passages of the South Pacific;
- Gaining access to Indian Ocean maritime passages;
- [Sharing] access to the seabed and natural resources in the common seas; and
- Gaining access to deep ocean strategic areas for nuclear submarine operations and strategic deterrence.[34]

This last point seems to indicate that at least some in the PLA are thinking about long-distance nuclear submarine operations. In the future, once a ballistic missile submarine is operational, it may well leave the waters of the South China Sea and move into the South Pacific. Moving those submarines into patrol areas in deep waters in the South Pacific, if done quietly and professionally, would effectively flank any limited antiballistic missile systems the United States may construct to defend against launches that depend on routes over the North Pole. A recent article by Agence France Presse cites a scholar from the Federation of American Scientists, Hans Kristensen, who notes that there was a significant increase in Chinese attack submarine patrols in 2008, and that although new submarine bases in Hainan offer better access deep water, "China has yet to conduct a single patrol by a ballistic missile submarine."[35] In the late 1970s, in preparation for the long-distance test of the CSS-4 ICBM, the PLA did extensive bathymetric surveys in the deep waters of the South Pacific. The deep waters there could yet become operating areas for the PLA submarine force.

The Domains of War—Maritime and Aerospace Power

Contemporary military theory in China focuses on warfare across a five-dimensional battlefield. These "domains or realms" of war, as they are called in PLA military literature, are land, sea (or maritime, including undersea), air, space, and the electromagnetic spectrum (some authors refer to the "information realm or domain" instead of the electromagnetic spectrum).

Addressing the integrated nature of the air and space domains, one of the major proponents of integrated aerospace power for the PLA, Major General Cai Fengzhen, believes that "control of portions of outer space is a natural extension of other forms of territorial control" such as sea or air control.[36] In one sense, Cai also views the maritime domain as part of this continuum, noting in a different book that space control is a natural extension of other forms of territorial control such as sea control and control of a nation's airspace.[37] In *China Military Science*, writing with Deng Pan, Cai emphasizes that the aerospace battlefield is really the main area for coordinating "attacks" in any domain of war and for information exchange and coordination.[38] As for *The Aerospace Battlefield and China's Air Force*, the authors do not distinguish between air raids or surprise attacks on ground-based or maritime targets, classifying both as "surface attacks" from air or space.[39]

Space operations and warfare in space, therefore, are components of what the PLA calls "informatized," or information age, warfare. In general, PLA strategists are convinced that the air and space domains will merge, that space will be one of the natural domains of war, and that war in space will be an integral part of other military operations. Indeed, in his discussion of joint maritime operations, Li Daguang, a space warfare expert at the PLA National Defense University, focuses almost exclusively on how space operations contribute to maritime operations.[40] Moreover, PLA authors are convinced that "future enemy military forces will depend heavily on information systems in military operations"; therefore, they believe China needs to break through the technological barriers and develop information system countermeasures in space.[41] Two authors in *China Military Science*, the PLA's premier military theory journal, believe that "it is in space that information age warfare will come to its more intensive points. Future war must combine information, firepower, and mobility."[42] They believe that future latent military threats will primarily come in aerospace.

There is no question that PLAAF officers view regional war in space as integrated with the air war. In an article in *China Military Science*, Zhang Jiali and Min Zengfu declare, "in future information age warfare, the integration of war in the air and war in space is a historical necessity. This will be true in limited wars and in major wars."[43] They add that "future war must combine information, firepower, and mobility. Reconnaissance and space systems will be the core of future war."[44] Two researchers at the Nanjing Army Command Academy reinforced this view that the PLA must be prepared to fight across domains and to think about aerospace operations holistically. Writing in *China Military Science*, they state "integrated air and space operations are a logical extension of humankind's struggle for survival and developments in military struggles."[45] Unfortunately, at no point do these authors address how aerospace operations play out in the maritime domain. The reader must infer that when they talk about "being prepared to fight across domains," the concepts apply to land and maritime operations. This implies that PLA planners and strategists understand the implications of such capabilities for military operations and are thinking through concepts to employ the capabilities effectively. However, they are probably not yet at the stage of fielding and training with the technologies.

The Focus on Weapons Platforms

Pan Youmu, in his discussion of integrated aerospace operations and national strategy, shifts the focus from theories of operations and doctrine to weapons platforms and what systems they carry. In Pan's view, "air and space have become places for the maneuver of weapons platforms" in integrated operations.[46] That said, Pan still believes that, even though military operations in space support or affect the other domains of war, "space is really an independent domain of competition."[47] *Long-Distance Operations*, by far the most exploratory text aimed at long-term operational concepts, platforms, and technologies still in the research and development stage, takes a similar approach to Pan's.[48]

The PLA is modernizing some older systems, improving weapons systems on platforms, methodically striving toward new development, buying technology and components globally, and buying new weapons systems from Russia. This is the most salient feature of the "platform-centric approach" to modernization. Given this approach and the weapons and platforms in the inventory, what can it do today to defend the national interests it has been charged to protect? This section will address this question. Subsequently the chapter will discuss what we might expect in the near term (by 2020) and in the longer term, by mid-century, to fulfill expanded missions to protect Chinese interests.

This "road map" for the future sketched out in the PLA publications cited in this chapter is anchored in the military legacies of Deng Xiaoping and Jiang Zemin. Hu Jintao has put his own imprimatur on the plans, however. In his report to the 17th Chinese Communist Party National Congress, Hu endorsed the basic goal to "attain the strategic objective of building computerized armed forces and building and winning IT-based warfare."[49] Hu's speech reinforced the emphasis on methodically building a strong, modern armed force capable of defending China and its interests with technology and tactics supported by China's economy and level of economic development.

The CMC set out "The Three Step Development Strategy" to greater military strength and operational effectiveness for the PLA stretching from the late twentieth century to the mid-twenty-first century.[50] The first phase, a ten-to-twenty-year process to build a firm base of military technology and modernization, is essentially over. The second phase is a decade-long effort to increase budgets and build a stronger military "in accordance with China's national economic power." Third, after "30 years or so of work," toward the middle of the twenty-first century, the PLA is to "complete the process of building a modern, strong military."[51]

A recent article by Chen Zhou, a PLA strategist, published in the Central Party School journal *Xuexi Shibao* explained this approach. Chen characterized the three steps as "laying a solid foundation by 2010, making major progress by 2020, and basically reaching the strategic goal of building an informatized army and becoming capable of winning informatized wars by the mid-21st century."[52] Thus, we cannot expect to see dramatic changes in either the posture or the capabilities of the PLA to integrate aerospace and maritime operations over the near term (e.g., five to ten years). Instead, observers will probably see an evolution of new operational doctrine and the equipment and forces to implement them over time.

The PLA's posture and the improvements in doctrine and weapons are supported by changes in training. According to an article in the 13 October 2008 edition of *Liberation Army Daily*, an evolving understanding of the military strategic guidelines has changed how the military is responding to operations under "informatized conditions," leading to new missions and "multi-service training," including exercises in the maritime domain.[53] The article cites the exercise 联合-2008 (Joint 2008) in the Bohai Gulf as a Jinan Military Region response to the need for joint campaigns, including coordinating surface combat ships and shore-based aircraft. At this time, however, what is the foundation for PLA deterrence and presence?

China's military today is still not a uniformly high-technology force. PLA leaders and planners understand how to organize and coordinate forces on a digitized battlefield and the advantages of doing so. A number of PLA systems operate at sophisticated levels, capable of cooperative target engagement between surface and air platforms. Across the spectrum of its military systems, however, the PLA cannot field or operate a fully digitized and integrated force. The PLA understands and is working to apply "network-centric warfare" concepts but lacks a comprehensive set of much of the data transfer systems necessary to field and maintain a modern force that employs these concepts in warfare in a uniform way.

The PLA has probably fielded a C4ISR architecture than can support an integrated maritime-aerospace campaign to about 2,000 km from the Chinese coast. It has fielded a redundant, automated command-and-control system linking national, regional frontal, and deployed warfighting headquarters. Its major naval combatants, support ships, and a good deal of its aircraft can use air-breathing platforms, surface ships, or satellites for data exchange. Also, the PLA believes that it can effectively bring concentrated fires to bear on deployed enemy naval task groups from maneuvering ballistic missile warheads and air- or surface-launched antiship cruise missiles.

Two researchers from the Second Artillery Engineering College believe that terminal guidance will allow up to 100 km of maneuverability on reentry during an antiship ballistic missile attack, and that a carrier "cannot effectively escape an attack within a short period of time."[54] Simulations led them to conclude that because a carrier strike group can project force out to about 2,500 km, the PLA must reduce its missile warhead circular error probability to attack maneuvering targets at sea outside the carrier's strike range.

There is a basic data-exchange and target-locating architecture to support the PLAN and PLAAF and to ensure connectivity with national and regional C4ISR networks. According to Indian military analysts and statements by a U.S. congressman, the PLA theater-level automated command-and-control system, Qu Dian, is a redundant, military-region or frontal (war front) network linking the General Staff Department headquarters and the PLA's arms and services with regional combat headquarters' and their subordinate major organizations. The Qu Dian system uses fiber-optic cable, high-frequency radio communications, microwave systems, and satellites to enable the CMC, the General Staff Department, and commanders to communicate with forces in their theater of war on a real-time or near-real-time basis. It is comparable to the U.S. Joint Tactical Information Distribution System, a secure network.

Other PLA combat systems have a more limited capability to act as an airborne command post and assist with combat data exchange. The PLAAF has one regiment of airborne early warning/airborne warning and control system (AEW/AWACS) aircraft. The regiment has one Russian Beriev A-50, designated the Kong Jing-2000 (KJ-2000). It is equipped with Chinese-made phased-array radar and has a data-link capability; a data processing system; friendly, hostile, and unidentified Identification Friend-or-Foe system; and a command, control, communications, and intelligence capability. The KJ-2000 can exchange data with other aircraft and naval ships equipped with compatible data links. The aircraft loiter time on station, however, is only about ninety minutes. Also in the regiment are four of China's own Y-8, four-engine turbo-prop aircraft.

The AWACS systems have been data-linked to the F-8 Finback fighter, produced by the Shenyang aircraft factory, and to the Zhi-9 helicopter. The Zhi-9 is a Chinese version of the French Dauphin 2 Eurocopter, the AS 365N, produced under license. In the case of the Zhi-9, a data link passes targeting information to ship-based helicopters, thus some of China's indigenously produced destroyers presumably also have a data-link capability. The system permits data and communications transfer among virtually all destroyers and other properly equipped PLAN surface warfare ships. They also have the Band Stand data link or the C-802 antiship missile and SS-N-22 Moskit supersonic antiship missile. According to the Armed Forces Communications Electronics Association journal *Signal*, China's destroyers are all now capable to data-link with AWACS systems, each other, their onboard helicopters, and their antiship missiles.[55] The *Sovremenny* Ka-25 helicopters are equipped with the A-346Z secure data link, and other Chinese ships have the HN-900 data link, which incorporates other foreign technologies.

The PLAN aviation arm and the PLAAF have a total of thirteen H6-U (Tu-16) tankers and ten Il-78M tankers on order with Russia. If or when they are finally delivered, the newer tankers will extend the range of the Su-30s. This modest air-to-air refueling capability, like the data-link systems described earlier, permit air support to maritime operations and surveillance in limited areas for several days duration. Thus, at this time, presence and deterrence out to about 2,500 km from the coast are getting—and will further receive—vital support from aerospace operations and capabilities.

In the near term (e.g., between now and 2020), then, the United States and its allies are looking at a PLA that will improve weapons, avionics, guidance, and sensor systems but will lack many of the components that would make China a truly global aerospace power able to conduct presence and deterrence operations out of area. Cai Fengzhen and Tian Anping expect that the PLAAF will continue to lag behind the more modern air forces of stronger powers for "some time to come."[56] To make up for this and advance more rapidly, they argue that China must "leap over" historical stages of air force development and experimentation. They see work on advanced weapons moving more quickly than work on advanced air platforms.[57] Over time, however, if PLAAF planners are to achieve the kinds of objectives outlined in Jiang Yamin's *Long-Distance Operations*, the PLAAF will need long-range, stealthy supersonic bombers; unmanned aerial vehicles; and significantly more air-to-air refueling and AEW/AWACS aircraft. Cai and Tian discuss the relationship between sea power and aerospace power as important parts of China's nuclear deterrence and nuclear attack capabilities.[58] Moreover, such capabilities in the maritime domain depend on missiles. They see naval platforms as dependent on aerospace assets for these types of missions and for antimissile, air-defense, and antisubmarine warfare operations.[59]

Contemporary Thoughts on Deterrence

In the PLA National Defense University text *The Science of Military Strategy*, the editors define warfighting and deterrence as "two major basic functions of the armed forces."[60] They see operations and deterrence as interactive and "dialectically unified," with operations designed to secure objectives on the battlefield and deterrence designed to prevent the outbreak of fighting, limit its scope, or contain the scale of a conflict.[61] For the PLA, deterrence requires some real capability, the will to employ the deterrent force, and the ability to take measures to ensure that the opponent can perceive both the capability and the willingness to use the deterrent force (or measures).[62]

On nuclear deterrence, there are no indications that the PLA will depart from the current strategy of maintaining a limited but credible second-strike (retaliatory) capability. However, between developing the new submarine base in Hainan and building new ballistic missile submarines, the PLA will probably make that retaliatory capability more secure when it is finally able to perfect and deploy a submarine-launched ballistic missile.

Of course, the PLA has not always been good at managing enemy perceptions of its deterrence efforts. In the weeks preceding the entry of PLA "volunteers" into the Korea War, various signals were sent to the United States and its allies, which Washington and General Douglas MacArthur either ignored or failed to perceive correctly. Prior to the Sino-Indian War and in the weeks preceding the Chinese attack into Vietnam in 1979, there were also a number of signals sent by Beijing to get the other side to change its posture, but these did not work either. And sometimes deterrent measures can backfire. For instance, the dazzling of a U.S. satellite by a ground-based laser from China and the PLA shoot-down of its own weather satellite are both examples of "space deterrence" that were perceived quite negatively on the part of the United States and the international community. The two most prolific authors in the PLA on aerospace operations, Cai Fengzhen and Tian Anping, advance the idea that deterrence complements diplomatic measures in advancing one's interests and preventing an enemy from taking action. One means of doing so, they suggest, is "making a loud noise to threaten an opponent and create fear."[63] A second means is "to use a demonstration of force to compel an opponent or change the situation."[64] But this method must be public and open if it is to be effective. A third means of effective deterrence, according to the authors, is to actually sacrifice some of one's own forces or create an incident that damages enemy forces. They call this "killing one," a shortened version of the aphorism "execute one as a warning to a hundred."[65]

Using these examples, the long-range, open-ocean test of a PRC CSS-4 intercontinental ballistic missile in 1981 in the South Pacific can be viewed not only a test but also a notice to Moscow and Washington that the PLA Second Artillery had attained a new level of deterrence. Surfacing a submarine in close proximity to the *Kitty Hawk* in 2006 may have served as a notice that the PLA has the capability to get a submarine in position undetected to engage a carrier battle group. The series of articles the PLA has published about maneuvering warheads on ballistic missiles and targeting naval battle groups or aircraft carriers takes has a deterrent effect, and that effect will be magnified as China's DF-21D antiship ballistic missile moves beyond the equivalent of initial operational capability.

Finally, the intercept and collision between a PLA fighter aircraft and the U.S. EP-3 reconnaissance aircraft can be reinterpreted as a deterrent measure against the American peacetime aerial reconnaissance program, even if the intent was not to have the two aircraft collide. The incident with the U.S.

Naval Ship *Impeccable*, however, on 8 March 2009 off Hainan Island, is a perfect example of creating an incident and using it for deterrent purposes. This action is similar to the way that the PLAN harassed the survey ship USS *Bowditch*, a survey ship, in the East China Sea on 23 March 2001. Chinese aircraft also harassed the *Bowditch* in the Yellow Sea. This demonstrates a series of incidents all apparently designed to deter the United States and other countries from conducting military activities or surveys inside the PRC exclusive economic zone. Peter Dutton characterizes these kinds of activities as "signaling and gatekeeping," suggesting that some of China's naval and air activities are designed not only to gather information but are part of a larger access denial and deterrence strategy.[66]

In a discussion of noncombat operations such as China's naval deployment into the Gulf of Aden, Shen Jinlong makes the point that "fast and flexible deployments of naval forces and their ability to reach anywhere in the world can have a role in effectively deterring actions and intentions that encroach upon the country's maritime interests."[67]

Presence

For some years now, the PLAN has been capable of what we in U.S. military parlance would call "presence missions." Its support ships may be limited in number, and PLAN experience at underway replenishment operations is far from extensive, but still there are sufficient ships and experience to permit presence operations on the scale of a deployed squadron in a contested area or region important to China's national interests. The PLAN has been quite capable of conducting missions of the scale that Japan did in support of the Gulf War or that India and France appear to have in the region now. Providing a submarine in support of a surface-action group mission would challenge the PLA but would not be impossible.

Conducting such a mission, however, is a sensitive political decision that clearly requires CMC and Party Politburo approval. Such missions have the potential to elicit reactions from neighbors India and other Southeast Asian nations, and perhaps the United States. The PLA also has no means to support limited presence operations at long distances with fixed-wing aircraft at this time unless they begin long-range navigation and refueling training for the PLAAF or PLAN aviation. Of course, Beijing could seek landing and refueling rights with friends of allies in the affected region, but political considerations have limited such actions as much as operational and ideological matters.

Taking this kind of action differs significantly from the types of "show the flag" and "friendship" operations the PLAN or PLAAF have conducted to date. The decision to conduct these out-of-area operations has been made, but whether they become routine is a matter for further study.

As this volume went to press, a seventh set of Chinese destroyers and a support ship had deployed to the Gulf of Aden for escort duties in response to the threat of piracy in the area; the first naval task force was deployed on 26 December 2008. By all accounts, the PLAN has acquitted itself well and has coordinated with the existing task forces in the region. In addition to attacks on Chinese vessels by Somali pirates, there have been threats and kidnappings of Chinese workers in Africa and in Pakistan. Now that the CCP Politburo has "crossed the rubicon" of authorizing such out-of-area missions for the PLA, we may yet see other PLA deployments in other regions. The PLA task force in the Gulf of Aden has some special operations forces embarked, suggesting that the PLA understands that when such missions are undertaken, there may be a need for forced entry.

China has a permanent presence in the South China Sea around the Spratly and Paracel Islands. There are regular maritime patrols in the East China Sea and Yellow Sea, including around the contested Senkaku/Diaoyu Islands. It would not take much of a shift in policy to make presence missions in area more common, and the PLA's C4ISR structure today supports such operations.

Conclusions

As China develops new capabilities, it will affect how the United States and its allies deploy forces, protect bases and forces, and conduct operations. Already bases in Hawaii, Guam, Japan, Korea, and the West Coast of the United States are within range of Chinese ballistic missiles. Ballistic missile defenses are not yet perfected and are not adequate to protect all these places. As noted earlier, operations within 1,500 mi. (2,414 km) of China's coast are now subject to an integrated, space, air, and navy presence by the PLA for finite periods of time (probably forty-eight to seventy-two hours of persistent presence). China's ships and submarines have hypersonic cruise missiles and land-attack cruise missiles (LACMs). The United States may be able to defend against LACMs, but there is still no reliable defense against a hypersonic cruise missile and especially against massed fires of such cruise missiles. Meanwhile, the PLA is continuing its phased development. Right now the PLA seems to be aiming at a military force capable of responding to domestic problems, securing China's sovereign territory, defending China's economic and political interests at long distances, patrolling vital sea lines of communication, denying potential adversaries the freedom to coerce China with impunity, and limiting proximity to the coast, from which potential adversaries can conduct.

The PLA's space architecture is adequate to support such operations and is improving all the time. Supporting these types of operations with any form of airpower, other than rotary wing, is a problem for the PLA at this time. There are no operational aircraft carriers yet, although an increasing number of statements by a variety of PLA commentators suggest that a development program may already have been started, or is at least under very serious consideration. We will see longer-range air operations, unmanned aerial vehicles operating off ships, more regular air-to-air refueling operations, and the use of friendly airfields to support operations before the PLA increases its capabilities to conduct deterrence or presence operations in the maritime domain supported by air. Again, however, these are perhaps five to ten years off. There is serious thinking in the PLA about long-range bombers and attacking naval and air bases, as mentioned in *Long-Distance Operations*. Actually procuring and fielding such weapon systems seems at least a decade away, although illicit technology transfer may provide useful shortcuts.

Thus, the main aerospace support for maritime operations today, and probably for the next five to ten years, will come from the missiles of the Second Artillery Corps and from the space and space warfare programs in the PLA. In the meantime, the PLA will pursue third- and fourth-generation naval weapons, improving education and training, and firepower coordination.

The space architecture for China will also improve, especially as tracking and data-relay satellites are deployed, giving a more persistent, real-time surveillance presence in space to the PLA. The U.S. Navy seems already to have scrapped plans for one new destroyer, reportedly because it could not defend against ballistic missile warheads. Progress is slow on ballistic missile defense and we do not know how the Obama administration and Congress will approach the matter. Also, there have been no rapid breakthroughs on lasers or other forms of directed energy weapons by the United States that would counter the cruise missile threat from China. The effect of all this is that the U.S. Navy and U.S. Air Force will likely be hindered in carrying out some of its missions in the Western Pacific, particularly within proximity of China, especially in the case of contingencies on the Korean peninsula, around Japan, and involving Taiwan.

Notes

1. Qui Guijin, Wu Jifeng, and Zhang Liang, "On the Transformation of the Basic Points of Military Struggle Preparations," *China Military Science*, no. 1 (January 2008): 85–90, OSC CPP20080619436001.

2. Information Office of the State Council, People's Republic of China, "China's National Defense in 2008," January 2009, http://www.china.org.cn/government/central_gov ernment/2009-01/20/content_17155577.htm.

3. 蒋亚民 [Jiang Yamin], 远战 [*Long-Distance Operations*] (Beijing: Military Science Press, 2007).

4. Qiu et al., "On the Transformation," 6.

5. Ibid.

6. Liu Jianping and Zhui Yue, "Management of the Sea in the 21st Century: Wither the Chinese Navy?" *Modern Navy* (1 June 2007): 6–9, OSC CPP 20070628436012.

7. Ibid.

8. Hu Jintao, "Hu Jintao's Report at the 17th Party Congress," 15 October 2007, http://www.china.org.cn/english/congress/229611.htm.

9. Hu Jintao, "Understanding the New Historic Missions of our Military in the New Period of the New Century," 14 December 2004; and Daniel M. Hartnett, China Analyst, CNA, "The PLA's Domestic and Foreign Activities and Orientation," Testimony before the U.S.-China Economic and Security Review Commission, "China's Military and Security Activities Abroad," Washington, D.C., 4 March 2009, http://www.uscc.gov/hearings/2009hearings/written_testimonies/09_03_04_wrts/09_03_04_hartnett_statement.pdf.

10. 王立东 [Wang Lidong], 国家海上利益论 [*On National Maritime Interests*] (Beijing: National Defense University Press, 2007), 248. See also 巴忠谈 [Ba Zhongtan] et al., eds., 中国国际安全战略问题研究 [*Study of Issues on China's National Security Strategy*] (Beijing: Military Science Press, 2003); 29–51, 128–61, especially 143–46.

11. Jiang, *Long-Distance Operations*, 231.

12. Fang Yonggang, Xu Mingshan, and Wang Shumei, "On Creative Development in the Party's Guiding Theory for Naval Building," *China Military Science*, no. 4 (August 2007): 66–77, OSC CPP20080623436001.

13. Jiang Feng, "What Will Take the Lead Role in Joint Maritime Operations in the Future?" *Modern Navy* (November 2008).

14. Cai Fengzhen and Tian Anping, 空天战杨与中国空军 [*The Aerospace Battlefield and China's Air Force*] (Beijing: Liberation Army Press, 2004), 154–55.

15. Wang, *On National Maritime Interests*, 178.

16. Ibid., 181.

17. Ibid., 203

18. See Wendell Minnick, "Chinese Carrier Comments Spur Speculation on Plans," *Defense News*, 1 December 2008, 30.

19. Wang, *On National Maritime Interests*, 204.

20. Ibid., 13.

21. Ibid., 205.

22. 闵增富 [Min Zengfu], ed., 空军军事思想概论 [*An Introduction to PLA Air Force Military Thinking*] (Beijing: Liberation Army Press, 2006).

23. Ibid., 175–76.

24. Ibid., 173 and 175.

25. Ibid., 172.

26. Ibid., 178.

27. Ibid., 35, 37, and 42.

28. Ibid. 175.

29. Jiang, "What Will Take the Lead Role."

30. Ibid.

31. Ibid. Li is the only PLA author that I have seen refer to network centric warfare as a sixth domain of war.

32. An example of this regarding chip systems can be found in 张新勋, 张兵, 李广强 [Zhang Xinxun, Zhang Bing, and Li Guangqiang], "一种调频调相混合调制信号及抗干扰性能分析" ["Co-Modulated Signal and Anti-Jamming Analysis"], 指挥控制与仿真 [*Command, Control and Simulation*] (January–February 2007): 63–66.

33. 刘静波 [Liu Jingbo], ed., 21 世纪初中国国家安全战略 [*Chinese National Security Strategy in the Early 21st Century*] (Beijing: Current Affairs Press, 2006), 150.

34. Wang, *On National Maritime Interests*, 111–12.

35. "China Doubled Attack Submarine Patrols in 2008," *Agence France Presse*, 3 February 2008, available at www.afp.com. See also Hans Kristensen, "Chinese Submarine Patrols Doubled in 2008," *FAS Strategic Security blog*, http://www.fas.org/blog/ssp/2009/02/patrols.php.

36. 蔡风震 与 田安平 [Cai Fengzhen and Tian Anping], 空天一体作战学 [*A Study of Integrated Aerospace Operations*] (Beijing: Liberation Army Press, 2004), 58.

37. Cai and Tian, *Aerospace Battlefield and China's Air Force*, 207–12.

38. 蔡风震, 邓攀 [Cai Fengzhen and Deng Pan] "空天战场与国家安全体系初探" ["Exploration into Air-Space Battlefields and National Air-Space Security Systems"], 中国军事科学 [*China Military Science*] 19, no. 2 (February 2006): 45.

39. Cai and Tian, *Aerospace Battlefield and China's Air Force*, 154. This is consistent with their views in the 2006 volume, *Study of Integrated Aerospace Operations*, and appears to be the prevailing view in the PLA Air Force. See 常显奇 [Chang Xianqi], 军事航天学 [*Military Astronautics*] (Beijing: National Defense University Press, 2005), 129–39.

40. Jiang, "What Will Take the Lead Role."

41. Yang Jinhui and Chang Xianqi, "Kongjian Xinxi Duikang Wenti Yanjiu" ["Research on Problems of Space Information Warfare"], *Wuxiandian Gongcheng* [*Radio Engineering*] 36, no. 11 (2006): 9.

42. 张加力, 闵增富 [Zhang Jiali and Min Zengfu], "试论局部战争空天中化," ["On Extending the Regional War into the Air and Space"], 中国军事科学 [*China Military Science*] 18, no. 1 (January 2005): 41.

43. Ibid., 37.

44. Ibid., 41.

45. Zhang Zhiwei and Feng Zhuanjiang, "Analysis of Future Integrated Air and Space Operations," *China Military Science* 19, no. 2 (2006), OSC CPP20061208478002.

46. 潘友木 [Pan Youmu], "着眼空天一体化探索国家空天安全战略" ["Focus on Air-Space Integration and Study National Air-Space Security Strategy"], 中国事科学 [*China Military Science*] 19, no. 2 (February 2006), 60.

47. Ibid., 61.

48. Jiang, *Long-Distance Operations*, 192–214.

49. Hu Jintao, "Hold High the Great Banner of Socialism with Chinese Characteristics and Strive for New Victories in Building a Moderately Prosperous Society in All Respects," Report to the Seventeenth National Congress of the Communist Party of China, *Xinhua News Agency*, 24 October 2007, http://news.xinhuanet.com/english/2007-10/24/content_6938749.htm.

50. Jiang Zemin, *Jiang Zemin Wenxuan* [*Selected Works of Jiang Zemin*] (Beijing: People's Press, 2006), 162, 563. See also 张伊宁 [Zhang Yining], et. al., eds., 中国现代军事思想研究 [*Research on Contemporary Chinese Military Thought*] (Beijing: National Defense University Press, 2006), 580, 581.

51. Ibid., 581–82.

52. Chen Zhou, "Xin Shiqi de Jiji Fangyu Junshi Zhanlue" ["A Strategy of Active Defense for the New Period"], *Xuexi Shibao* [*Study Times*], no. 1 (18 August 2008), available at www.studytimes.com.cn, OSC CPP20080818436001001.

53. "Three Transformations Bring Continuous Development to Military Training," 解放军报 [*Liberation Army Daily*], 13 October 2008, 3, OSC CPP20081013708003.

54. Tan Shoulin and Zhang Daqiao, "Effective Range for Terminal Guidance Ballistic Missile Attacking Aircraft Carrier," in *Qingbao zhihui kongzhi yu fangzhen jishu* [*Information Command and Control Systems and Simulation Technology*] 28, no. 4 (August 2006): 6–9.

55. James C. Bussert, "China Debuts Aegis Destroyers," *Signal*, July 2005, http://www.afcea.org/signal/articles/templates/SIGNAL_Article_Template.asp?articleid=992&zoneid=.

56. Cai and Tian, *Aerospace Battlefield and China's Air Force*, 285–87.

57. Ibid., 32–321.

58. Cai and Tian, *Study of Integrated Aerospace Operations*, 73.

59. Ibid.

60. Peng Guangqian and Yao Youzhi, eds., *The Science of Military Strategy* (Beijing: Military Science Press, 2005), 213, 216.

61. Ibid.

62. Ibid., 214.

63. Cai and Tian, *Study of Integrated Aerospace Operations*, 289.

64. Ibid., 289–90.

65. Ibid., 290.

66. Peter Dutton, *Scouting, Signaling and Gatekeeping: Chinese Naval Operations in Japanese Waters and the International Law Implications*, China Maritime Study No. 2 (Newport, RI: China Maritime Studies Institute, Naval War College, February 2009), 2, 6, 21–22.

67. 沈金龙 [Shen Jinlong], "海军非战争军事行动—面临的挑战及对策" ["Naval Non-Combat Military Operations—Challenges Faced and Countermeasures"], 人民海军 [*People's Navy*], 1 December 2008, 4.

Xiaoming Zhang and Sean D. McClung

Challenges in Assessing China's Aerospace Capabilities and Intentions

THE ANCIENT WARRIOR Sun Zi (Sun Tzu) admonished military strategists to "know your enemies." But exactly how does one come to know his enemies or even if they truly are enemies? Some would view this as merely the sum of fact-gathering and analysis, but it is more. Understanding and knowledge of potential adversaries are imbedded in the art of military discovery. The art of discovery, as defined by Sir Francis Bacon, involves first seeking out and setting before you "all that has been said about it by others." This is accomplished in military circles, although not well, through the academic exercises of research, exchange of thoughts and ideas, and debate in areas of military analysis, political and cultural awareness, history, and personal experience. Following these, one is left to what Bacon calls "evoking the spirit to provide oracles," or in more modern language, seeking inspiration for original thought and insight into an issue.[1] This chapter attempts to use Bacon's methods regarding the art of "military discovery" concerning Chinese air and space power and its implications for the U.S. Air Force (USAF) while simultaneously analyzing the current methods of military discovery employed by the Department of Defense (DoD) and the USAF community.

Since 2001, the U.S. military has been facing great challenges in the long war against terrorism while continuing to prepare for potential conventional threats, including war with one or more near-peers. The rise of China, the most important change in the global economic and political balance of recent years, raises concerns about Chinese military modernization that might enable Beijing to dominate Asia or challenge U.S. hegemony. Many military planners and defense thinkers view China as the next potential large-scale threat to the United States, and the USAF is no exception as the People's Liberation Army Air Force (PLAAF) evolves rapidly into an offensive air and space power. A recent Congressional Research Service Report observes that "the question of how the U.S. should respond to China's military modernization effort(s) . . . has emerged as a key issue in defense planning."[2]

However, what methods of assessment and discovery are military planners using to base future strategies upon? A general lack of indigenous USAF research and assessment capabilities regarding Chinese aerospace power development has caused the service to rely heavily on outsourced and narrowly focused open-source research. There have been few critical analyses of how the USAF has assessed China's progress in the air and space realm. With debates raging about the focus of the U.S. military and the USAF's future in it, these analyses may have a substantial impact on acquisition requirements, systems, and strategies. It is therefore imperative to examine critically the methodology associated with the USAF's military discovery process and to understand the implications this may have on contending with a near-peer competitor. This chapter will first examine some current studies on Chinese air and space power. Second, it will comment on contemporary assessments by the Department of Defense and individual researchers. Third, it will offer an extensive assessment of actual Chinese progress and the problems of the PLAAF. Finally, it will review both the USAF's efforts and the associated challenges in maintaining air and space power superiority in the Asia-Pacific region.

Since the end of the Cold War, there have been some notable efforts to study Chinese air power. Highly representative is a USAF-sponsored RAND study in 1995 on the history and capabilities of China's air force. This study opined that the PLAAF professed no coherent strategic doctrine, lacked funds for a comprehensive modernization program, flew outmoded equipment, had ill-trained pilots and ground personnel, possessed no midair refueling capabilities, and could not rely on domestic Chinese manufacturers to develop and produce advanced airpower weapon systems. RAND concluded that China's air force would be unable to mount a credible offensive threat over the next decade due to challenges in five areas: leadership and strategy; manpower; technology and infrastructure; budgets; and competition from other service branches.[3] Today, more than fifteen years later, the RAND study continues to be viewed as a benchmark in understanding China's air and space power and its development. For military discovery to have enduring usefulness, it is essential to understand the extent to which the RAND study remains true and to what extent China has progressed in overcoming the problems that it identified. Regardless, it is clear the RAND monograph was not immune to the challenges of predicting the future; its authors did not foresee the emergence of new security challenges during the second half of the 1990s, which prompted China to accelerate its air force modernization endeavors.

Current Studies on Chinese Air and Space Power

The predominant role played by air and space power in the conflicts since the 1991 Gulf War has been well recognized in Chinese military writings and appears to have forced the PLAAF to reevaluate its strategy and procurement policies. Beijing's concern about a possible conflict in the Taiwan Strait has also intensified as the PLA debates its air force missions and modernization programs. John Wilson Lewis and Xue Litai argue that China's failures in the past decades to create a modern air force lead to uncertainty that China's future efforts will succeed in building credible air power to deter foreign threats and combat Taiwan's continuing course of separatism.[4] Their propositions found support in some official analyses of China's air and space capabilities published since the late 1990s.

Contemporary Assessments by DoD and Individuals

Department of Defense analysts use a "net assessment" approach, taking into account China's strategic goals, doctrines, operational concepts, and fundamental military capabilities. This encompasses a comparative analysis of military, technological, political, economic, and other factors governing relative military capabilities designed to yield an understanding of China's motivations for its evolving military modernization programs. In 2005 the congressionally directed report started to be published in a relatively standardized format that begins with an appraisal of Chinese grand strategy, including how China perceives national power, and incorporates ideas on how China is pursuing its security strategies with prominent emphasis on Taiwan and the Asia-Pacific region. The report focuses on new developments in Chinese military doctrine for modern warfare that address reforms at its military institutions and personnel systems, improved exercises and training standards, and the acquisition of advanced weapons systems. Other areas of emphasis include China's prepa-rations to fight and win short-duration, high-intensity conflicts along China's periphery. The 2005 report characterized China's "active defense" as "distinc-tively offensive" and asserts that deception has a major role within its military strategy.[5] The increasing concern about China's lack of transparency and its missing clarity of intent has prompted DoD's analysts to doubt many of China's stated strategic intentions.

In his evaluation of DoD's 2007 report, Dennis Blasko criticized it as failing to "provide a thorough analysis of PLA modernization" because of its exces-sively broad attempt to discuss "all elements of the [congressional] tasking." As a result, the report leaves "many components of Chinese military strategy and organization" underaddressed.[6] For example, the DoD report focuses mainly on PLAAF's acquisition of third- and fourth-generation aircraft and long-range and precision capabilities as well as China's efforts to develop antisatellite (ASAT) weapons and computer network operations.[7] However, the assessment of these developments illustrates that the PLA is shifting from a strategy of providing point defense of key military, industrial, and political targets to a new joint antiair/antiaccess strategy based on a modern, integrated air-defense system capable of offensive and defensive counterair operations.[8] Because this was not a complete assessment, it reflects only a fraction of emerging PLA capabilities. In addition, China's successful test of a direct-ascent ASAT missile against a Chinese weather satellite in early 2007 convinced DoD's analysts that "the PLA's interest in counterpace systems is more than theoretical" and that this capability could potentially negate the United States' current asymmetrical advantage in space. The 2008 report postulated that China's military capabili-ties are expanding beyond the dimensions of the traditional battlefield into the space and cyberspace domains.[9]

Although the DoD reports contains much beneficial information about Chinese air and space power, some aspects are faulty and misleading while other key elements are not presented. For those who are concerned about how Chinese military modernization may pose a threat to Taiwan and America's interests in the region, criticism of the 2007 report is justified. Indeed, the report fails to address or assess the antiballistic missile implications of the January 2007 ASAT test, which could lead to an erosion of U.S. advantages in ballistic missile technology. Further, it fails to mention the threat to Taiwan posed by China's fast growing precision missile/munitions inventory and the emergent long-range air-defense capability of the PLA, a trend that may have serious implications for U.S. airpower in the region.[10] In addition to these sins of omission, factual inaccuracies in the assessment raise doubts about the quality of the assessment. For example, the 2005 report lists FB-7 and FBC-1 as two different Chinese-developed aircraft, but these are in fact the same air-craft, designated by the Chinese as JH-7/7A.[11]

Another significant factual error was also seen in the 2007 reporting of China's acquisition of Su-27 (J-11/11A) fighters.[12] These aircraft had been a focal point of PLAAF modernization for many years, and in actuality China had stopped production of J-11s under a licensed coproduction agreement with Russia by the end of 2006 when it began to produce an indigenous version of the multirole J-11B, which entered service with PLAAF 1st Division in late 2007.[13] Unfortunately, and perhaps indicative of a lapse in attention, the 2008 report does not give any indication of this development. As if omissions and inaccuracies were not enough, no assessment has ever been included in this report about the fundamental structure of the PLAAF, which is transforming from its overland, limited territorial focus to a more flexible and agile force that is also able to operate offshore in both offensive and defensive roles. It is unclear if this transformation is considered out of scope for the assessment, whether this fact has not been recognized or acknowledged, or whether it is not con-sidered significant. Other deficiencies include a failure to address pilot train-ing, proficiency, tactics, and maintenance for China's advanced aircraft, all of which would seem to be important to informing its assessments. If this report was limited to an attempt to justify regional policies, it might be more under-standable; however, because its primary focus is on elements of PLA modern-ization that are believed to be potentially threatening to U.S. interests, these issues should be better explained. As a document produced by DoD that claims to represent a factual assessment, it appears to fall well short of a forth-coming and comprehensive appraisal. A fiscal year 2010 amendment to the FY2000 National Defense Authorization Act "requires additional information in [this] annual report concerning military and security development involv-ing the PRC, including U.S. engagement and cooperation with China on secu-rity matters, military-to-military contacts and U.S. strategy for engagement and cooperation in the future."[14] Time will determine whether this adjustment will improve the quality and scope of thinking applied to this annual document, but thus far the art of military discovery calls into question whether the appropri-ate measure of thought is being applied to DoD reports provided to Congress.

U.S. policy since 2006 has been to encourage China to make positive stra-tegic choices while hedging against the possibility that Beijing might choose a confrontational strategy. It is possible that this hedging strategy drove the authors of the DoD report toward equating PLA "modernization" with "expan-sion," and therefore dismissed the "possibility of alternate analysis of the same information that might result in different policy options."[15] Under the influence of this policy there have been an increasing number of monographic publications and literature on China's military and its possible immediate, intermediate, and long-term impact on the United States and international community. Unfortunately, many of these assessments have themselves used DoD's reports as primary sources and found their analysis encapsulated within potentially politicized analyses. For example, the *Air and Space Power Journal* fall 2007 issue carries a study by a USAF author who explores the PLAAF's air warfare capabilities and elucidates the nature of offensive Chinese airpower.[16] Although he argues that the PLAAF does not possess any long-range bombers for projecting airpower beyond the Pacific, the author maintains that the development of an offensive airpower doctrine by the Chinese should nonetheless be alarming for American forces in the region. While the PLAAF's heavy emphasis on the use of tactical aircraft to attack traditional targets such as command and control, industrial, and leadership infrastructure is a strategy common to most air forces with regional enemies, the author recommends that the U.S. government take action to curb the PLAAF's ability to wage longer-range offensive air operations by further limiting the transfer of military technology to China, continuing a deterrence and embargo policy, constraining engagement with the Chinese military, and implementing forward deployment of USAF assets to Guam.[17]

U.S. Air Force officers have consistently expressed interest in studying Chinese air and space power. Much of this study is done during their professional military education at a variety of colleges at Air University, Maxwell AFB, Alabama. Here an increasing number of unpublished research reports address Chinese efforts to modernize PLAAF capabilities, which include deployment of fourth-generation fighters, AWACS, and refueling aircraft.[18] These research reports attribute most PLAAF weaknesses to inexperience in combat and, correspondingly, to a lack of critical air competencies, which would be significantly disadvantageous for China in an armed conflict against experienced enemy forces.[19] Even in a relatively "close-fought" war scenario against Taiwan, Colonel Jon T. Thomas' 2006 study points out the PLAAF will have problems addressing the challenges of survivability, availability, and sustainability of airpower assets against enemy air defenses due to limited logistic capabilities and the absence of air refueling and command and control and intelligence, surveillance, and reconnaissance (ISR) assets. Amplifying the author's doubts about the PLAAF's combat capabilities is the fact that Chinese military tradition and doctrine has long been dominated by PLA ground elements. The extent to which the Chinese military has thoroughly considered "how it would conduct an independent air campaign" is unclear.[20] It appears that the implications of independent studies by USAF officers focused on PLAAF culture, strategy, and tactics differ significantly from those of research on the advanced weapons that the PLAAF has recently procured. The focus on how these weapon systems will be employed by Chinese soldiers in the context of Chinese military doctrine and institutional tradition lapses into inconsistencies in logic and belies the fact that the U.S. military has no internal coherent, comprehensive, or substantiated agreement concerning the PLA and its intentions. The process of military discovery finds that the inconsistencies produced by these differing approaches highlight gaps in U.S. military understanding.

In addition to air power issues, some U.S. analysts express growing trepidation over the potential exploitation of U.S. security dependencies and vulnerabilities on space systems. China's space accomplishments in recent years have spurred USAF officers to examine China's military space doctrine, civilian and military space organizations, and military space capabilities. In many cases their studies acknowledge that any efforts to analyze China's space programs are hampered by lack of transparency in Chinese space programs. Lieutenant Colonel Carol Welsch, in her award-winning Air War College research paper "Protecting the Heavens: Implications of China's Antisatellite Programs," urges caution when referencing existing English translations of Chinese publications for analysis. She points out these analyses are always subject to the selectivity of the passages translated, the manner of translation, and the unknown authoritativeness of many Chinese writings.[21] Unlike many studies that argue the Chinese are preparing to fight in space, research reports by USAF officers at the Air War College find minimal evidence to suggest that China has the capability to execute a space warfare doctrine or is developing organizational and management structures to perform such space operations. What is articulated in Chinese military writings, according to Lieutenant Colonel Welsch, is "only a *desired* capability."[22] Lieutenant Colonel Steven Smith expands on the potential advantages of these desired capabilities by pointing out that *if* China developed and deployed an electronic intelligence satellite system, it *could* enable China's long-range antiship missile systems to pose much more effective threat to U.S. Navy ships in the region.[23] Recognizing China's long-term desire for space warfare capabilities is different from attributing an ability to fight space wars. As such, China's posture regarding space may mirror that of the United States—*a desire* to fully exploit the domain for enhanced warfighting, as opposed to executing space warfare itself. Despite these illuminating observations, a preponderance of thinking acknowledges that the nation cannot afford to lower its guard regarding Chinese space programs due to increased U.S. dependencies and vulnerabilities in the space domain.

How should the United States respond to Chinese air and space modernization? Research by individual USAF officers does not paint a common picture. Unfortunately, many of the inconsistencies stem from source documents themselves. Not only is access to Chinese sources limited but much U.S. analysis is incomplete and speculative. Yet the PLAAF could well become a near-peer competitor in air and space by 2020. What seems truly problematic is not the lack of a common position nor the conclusions derived by these USAF officers—among whom analytical variance is expected—but rather the method of discovery that determines how they arrive at their assessments of Chinese air and space power development.

Assessment of Chinese Air and Space Research Issues

The lack of Chinese transparency has historically been a major impediment to the assessment of their military power. This transparency has improved markedly in written media over the last decade, and more Chinese information on the PLA is available through official and unofficial channels than could have been imagined a decade ago. However, due to lack of language capability, few individual assessments by USAF officers, published or unpublished, are actually made based on these Chinese sources. As a result, studies by individual USAF officers have relied on secondary sources and reinterpretations of existing analyses. One of the major sources for individual research on Chinese air and space has been DoD's annual report on Chinese military power, which, as already noted, may be inadvertently influenced by political judgments, evaluations, and intentions and may not be supported by a complete and comprehensive basis in fact. As China continues to emerge in the global arena, it will likely choose to significantly improve its military capabilities. In light of this, should DoD revisit the methods of military discovery that lead to the creation of flawed—or at least questionable—analysis? DoD's propensity to pursue additional defense capabilities has been facilitated by China's lack of transparency. As observed, rather than using primary, open-source analysis, the favored defense methodology has been to project Chinese motivations and intentions for military modernization based on an examination of only a fraction of the information available. Defaulting to a preconception of China as a potential or even likely adversary from the viewpoint of the worst-case scenario, DoD's assessments should certainly give both the researcher and analyst pause. This methodology creates analysis that appears less objective and probably does not provide the necessary information to make honest and accurate appraisals. Trustworthy appraisals lead to the last stage of military discovery, which generates insights to the true nature of things and original thinking about the issues at hand.

Even when using original Chinese sources in analyses, unique Chinese writing style can create misunderstandings. For example, Chinese monographs generally do not cite sources, nor do they include footnotes to provide distinctions between the author's own opinions and the contributions of others to the ideas being presented. As mentioned, within the past a few years there has been an increase in the availability of Chinese writings on air and space power by PLAAF authors. The most notable among these are two books by former deputy chief of the PLAAF, Major General Cai Fengzhen.[24] Perhaps what is most alarming about these publications is not the content per se, but rather the cyclical nature of the research process as it relates to Chinese doctrine and capabilities. For example, these documents borrow most of their terminology and concepts directly from U.S. air and space doctrine while giving little credit to the American thinkers who developed the original concepts. Iterative U.S. analysis of these books and Chinese air and space capabilities in general ends up being a cyclic U.S. self-critique of its own doctrine and China's ability to imitate and rearticulate this doctrine as their own. Major General Cai uses U.S. air and space capabilities, as demonstrated in conflicts since the 1991 Gulf War, to build and elucidate air and space strategy and concepts of operations. He then proceeds to argue for PLAAF development and implementation of similar air and space capabilities. According to Cai and his colleagues, the Chinese air force faces a long path of modernization due to four challenges, including outdated concepts, backward weapon systems, deficient force structures, and shortages of educated personnel in science and technology.[25] Former PLAAF commander Qiao Qingchen wrote prefaces for both of Cai's books, noting that the first book represents a forward-looking effort to explore the theory of air and space warfare, and the second book has laid the theoretical foundations for a future study of air and space operations.[26] Using these two books—which again are based on U.S. air and space doctrine—along with other Chinese publications, Larry Wortzel declares that what makes General Cai's analysis impressive is "how rapidly the PLA has developed advanced capabilities to engage in warfare in space."[27] While it is perhaps true that China has shown great interest in transforming the PLAAF into a capable air and space force, examination of the sources indicates that China continues to borrow heavily from the language and rhetoric in U.S. concepts while continuing to struggle in the development of its own theories and strategies for space warfare and counter-space operations, lagging even further behind in their ability to implement them.

Another challenge to contemporary assessment of China's air and space power is the burgeoning Chinese publication of magazines and periodicals from a variety of institutions and sources. This has created a progressively more complex and confusing situation for Western analysts. Some are popular specialized magazines such as *Aerospace Knowledge, Naval and Merchant Ships, Modern Weaponry, Modern Military Affairs,* and *Shipborne Weapons.* These publications are sponsored by either state-owned defense enterprises or Chinese defense industry associations. The question is to what extent these magazines illuminate the PLA's development of its military capabilities. The articles found in these magazines are often sensational and written by non-authoritative writers, using eye-catching illustrations or photography to better attract continued investment by advertisers and popular readership. Therefore, the usage of these publications requires researchers to be careful about the nature of the sources to the extent that they are authentic and reliable.

Even so, the principal dilemma for American analysts is how to address and evaluate specialized Chinese science and technology journals on air and space. Their contributors are civilian and military faculty members, researchers, and graduate students affiliated with PLA academic institutions and research institutes. These journals report on theoretical research, basic research, and applied research into the areas of air and space weapons and electronic warfare. The difficulty is determining whether the writings represent only the authors' personal views—as much of U.S. research does, whether it reflects the official views of the PLA, or whether this research should be considered as part of ongoing, officially endorsed Chinese government programs within particular areas of interest, such as space warfare. Using common DoD analytical methods that are often based heavily on worst-case assumptions rather than available primary information, conclusions generally default to the latter, where speculations and inaccurate references can inadvertently and easily be made. For example, in his recent article reporting on PLA's space warfare programs, Wortzel cited a number of Chinese studies in which authorship was attributed to PLA officers, implying official direction.[28] On further examination, not all of the authors were affiliated with the PLA, and only one of the four was associated with the PLA's Second Artillery Command College, an organization with authority on the subject. As with many individual USAF publications, the purpose of these specialized periodicals is to disseminate research results, showcase theories, and stir academic debate. Instead, these studies tend to be collectively treated as evidence of the PLA's ongoing space warfare efforts and effectively contribute to confusion regarding actual Chinese military programs. One can readily see how cyclical references, iterative academic exchanges, and a predisposition to address worst-case scenarios converge to produce misleading—and at times fallacious—conclusions that may lead analyses away from the discovery of China's true directions.

Assessment of Actual Progress and Problems of the PLAAF

One thing is clear: Chinese air and space power is being transformed. According to China's 2008 Defense White Paper, Beijing is adopting a three-step development strategy with the goal of modernizing the PLA into "mechanized and informatized" forces by the mid-twenty-first century with different milestones to be achieved in 2010 and 2020.[29] This development effort is focusing on troop training reform (to include conducting training in complex electromagnetic environments), integration of logistics support systems, building three-dimensional weaponry platforms with integrated sea-air-space capabilities, improving military information systems, and strengthening officer training with an emphasis on joint operations. These efforts also include enhanced ideological and political training, and "perfecting" the military legal system.[30] The white paper specifically maintains that the PLAAF has begun transforming itself from a territorial air-defense force to one with both offensive and defensive capabilities, including "certain capabilities to execute long-range precision strikes and strategic projection operations."[31] Several key issues deserve attention in order to understand China's own claims about the development of the PLAAF and air and space power, for the present and the near future, and as it concerns the USAF. These issues include strategy, force structure, the officer corps and enlisted force, unit training, and logistic and maintenance.

During 2004 the PLAAF introduced for the first time a new strategic vision calling for the development of a strategic air force with long-range capabilities and the active involvement of "integrated air and space" operations with "information and firepower systems integration."[32] Despite being modeled in concept on U.S. practices, this strategic vision is different from USAF doctrine on counter-space operations for the purpose of space superiority. In the midst of its discussion about how to integrate air and space power from a broad perspective, the PLAAF continues to face constraints that make it a challenge to operate at a near-peer level against the USAF. The most critical constraint, perhaps, is the fact that the PLAAF does not possess any of its own space assets or strategic missiles. Instead, these systems remain under the control of the General Armament Department and the Second Artillery Corps, respectively. Not only has this been the case in the past but apparently the PLAAF has lost a variety of debates as to whether these capabilities should be placed under its control—though that may be changing of late. Nonetheless, the PLAAF's study of warfare in the United States and Russia has caused Chinese air force theorists to conclude that space systems will continue to play a support role in operations for at least forty years. Given the PLAAF's limited ownership and control of space assets, Chinese military theorists have recommended that the service concentrate on building facilities and institutions to receive satellite services for communication, weather, navigation, and global positioning. This will allow the PLAAF to transition from a traditional air force to one enabled by space-based information (communications, positioning, navigation, and timing, and ISR) capabilities.

China has been making efforts to streamline and optimize the PLAAF's force structure since 2003. These efforts include the retirement of earlier generations of aircraft, a reduction in the number of troops, and the deployment of third-generation combat aircraft and ground-to-air missiles. Although the PLAAF has become modernized and its force size has been significantly reduced, it is still facing substantial replacement problems. While the older J-7 and J-8 fighters remain in service, the initially purchased Su-27s and lately the Chinese assembled J-11s appear to be incapable of fully supporting the mission requirements of the PLAAF, which now places an increased emphasis on offensive vice defensive roles. Currently, the PLAAF has three and a half regiments of Su-30, one regiment of J-11B, five and a half regiments of J-10, and three regiments of JH-7A aircraft. The size of the PLAAF and its offensive capabilities will continue to be limited until a significant number of J-10s and J-11Bs enter into service in the next five years. Even so, the PLAAF will continue to rely on upgrading second-generation aircraft to maintain a sizeable air force. Based on these projections and known aircraft performance, there appears to be no way that the PLAAF will match the capabilities of the USAF, particularly with the combination of speed and stealth seen in the fifth-generation U.S. fighter, the F-22 Raptor.

In 2005 the PLAAF established an additional transport division and one special aircraft division to enhance its long-range airlift and airborne early-warning capabilities. Russia's failure to deliver thirty IL-76MDS will keep this newly created transport division underequipped for years to come, with a limited number of Y-7s and Y-8s constituting the majority of airframes in the interim. There is also slow progress in the integration of support systems such as airborne early-warning/airborne warning and control system, aerial refueling tankers, intelligence collection platforms, and signal jamming aircraft, which are all necessary to increase the effectiveness of combat aircraft and augment warfighting capability. China's 2008 Defense White Paper describes the PLAAF as remaining a mixed force of aviation, ground air defense, airborne, signal, radar, electronic countermeasures, technical reconnaissance, and chemical defense.[33] This mixed force structure will continue to complicate China's air and space decisions, particularly with regard to training and in allocating roles and missions among services and branches and influencing resource allocations for PLAAF modernization.

The PLAAF regards the implementation of its 1999 "Strategic Project for Talented People" as a key to transforming the Chinese air force into a force able to fight high-tech wars under informatized conditions. This project emphasizes recruiting, educating, training, and retaining qualified and capable personnel. Unlike the USAF, whose officers all have college degrees (more than half hold advanced degrees), only one-third of Chinese air force officers are college or university graduates and only 5 percent possess masters' degrees. To facilitate its transformation, the PLAAF reorganized the officer corps of the units in receipt of new-generation aircraft and equipment to include more highly educated personnel. These personnel were transferred from air force headquarters, research institutes, and universities, and they filled up to 80 percent of leadership and technical positions in these units. In addition to improving the quality of next-generation flying units, the introduction of the 1999 National Defense Student Program will for the first time enable the PLAAF to recruit 60 percent of all new officers from civilian colleges and universities. Unfortunately for the PLAAF, although these measures will improve the quality of the force, the PLA still does not have an effective assignment system to rotate officers both across and within their specialties periodically. Likewise, Chinese officer promotions are still implemented at the unit level, where fraternization and departmentalism influence individual initiative and organizational success. Major challenges remain for the PLAAF in retaining highly educated personnel, encouraging capable officers to serve longer, finding those with the special expertise necessary to fulfill key technical positions, and recruiting young talent to join the service.

As previously discussed, Chinese aviation units are transitioning from older generational aircraft to new aircraft with significantly improved capabilities. The PLAAF is also enhancing its training with new systems and methods that increase the importance associated with technical and tactical training in complex environments, combined arms and aircraft type training, and joint training under mission-oriented and confrontational conditions. In April 2002 the PLAAF chose a new "Outline of Military Training and Evaluation" to modernize flight training, and one year later the PLAAF created its own "Red Flag" training base modeled after the U.S. program at Nellis Air Force Base. Despite these changes, Chinese fighter pilots only fly an average of 130 hours per year while their U.S. counterparts average 250–300 hours per year. Still other discrepancies are shown in training requirements, where USAF fighter pilots will fly around 50 hours of air refueling, AWAC command and control, dissimilar air combat training, and night training before being declared combat ready. Although Chinese flight training requirements are not clearly understood, current flight training manuals seem to require several times the 50 hours that a U.S. pilot requires to receive only air refueling training. This suggests that even though the PLAAF has adopted a new guide for pilot training, its equipment, overall requirements, procedures, and methods are still not comparable to U.S. standards and quality of training.

The PLAAF has reportedly begun reorganizing its air logistics and maintenance systems to support deployed units for the conduct of mobile offensive operations, but many areas are still weak. At a recent field-station work conference in December 2008, the PLAAF logistics department acknowledged that most PLAAF field stations were not built to support the multiple types of aircraft deploying into their airfields. A plan has been adopted to modernize airfields in batches with new equipment that can more efficiently move supplies from depots to the field and with integrating computers that can track spare parts and logistics and maintenance support for individual weapons systems and units as a whole. In addition, PLAAF airfields are moving toward microwave landing systems, automated meteorological observation and sounding systems, and secondary radar systems to increase their capabilities to support a variety of aircraft types under all weather conditions. One major PLAAF challenge is a shortage of qualified logistics and maintenance personnel with the knowledge and skills to serve in a variety of positions. While the PLAAF has also begun to convert some junior officer maintenance billets to noncommissioned officer billets, it is not yet clear whether these actions have helped or hindered the PLAAF's overall maintenance capabilities. A second major logistics and maintenance challenge is that reform is still at the initial stages of experimentation, and at local levels. This means that new systems do not yet appear to be standardized across the PLAAF. The final PLAAF challenge in logistics support is that its limited resources will primarily be focused on development units and new units receiving new equipment. Currently, the PLAAF enjoys the benefits of a favorable military spending policy, but budget challenges are likely. As long as the General Logistics Department continues to control military finance, a funding shortfall for the air force is likely for years to come.

China has adopted a three-step strategy to transform its air force. These steps include developing advanced aircraft and integrating them with effective support systems, conducting offensive and defensive operations against ground- and sea-based targets, and relying heavily on informatized systems to employ air and space power effectively. The speed of Chinese air and space modernization has caused concern in the West but is likely to be constrained by the current technological limitations in China's defense industry and by the resources needed to support modernization. Perhaps even more true is that the Chinese air and space transformation will continue to be tempered by inherent differences in the institutional cultures of the PLA ground forces and the PLAAF. While the PLA as a whole is transforming with the introduction of new advanced weapons, the real struggle it faces is against traditional concepts, obsolete practices, outdated organizational structures, and limited funding. In the PLA's own assessment, there has been repeated concern about limitations for the force. These have been identified in official publications as the "three incompatibles," which specifically refer to commanding officers' capabilities, troops' knowledge in science and technology, and training and education, which together are not viewed as sufficiently synchronized to win modern informatized wars.

China recognizes many of these weaknesses and has made addressing them a high priority, so a more rapid than anticipated transformation may still be possible. The remaining challenge to the U.S. Air Force is what Chinese air force modernization means to the USAF mission in the Asia-Pacific region.

USAF Efforts and Issues in Maintaining Air and Space Power Superiority in the Pacific

Until now this chapter has focused on issues related to the process of discovery with regard to current Chinese air and space power. This study has identified some of the challenges associated with making useful assessments and has presented actual problems and progress within the PLAAF. Finally, this chapter contemplates current issues for the USAF in maintaining air and space power for regional superiority; issues that are informed and impacted by the analysis of Chinese air and space strategy and capabilities, which as shown are perhaps imperfectly connected. As discussed earlier, decisions for the USAF are complicated by a lack of indigenous research capabilities dedicated to Chinese air and space power development, and by the lack of a unified DoD position on China in addressing air and space matters.

In truth, the U.S. posture in the Pacific is influenced, but not driven, by the methods of assessment of Chinese military development and what details are included or excluded from the assessment. The United States has long been a Pacific nation as well as an air, space, and, more recently, a cyberspace nation. These national characteristics naturally cause the USAF to perceive an inexorable linkage between its role in protecting U.S. interests in the Asia-Pacific region and its air, space, and cyberspace capabilities. This linkage exists for the USAF in the region regardless of how Chinese capabilities unfold. During the earlier days of the USAF, General Carl A. Spaatz, the first Air Force chief of staff who had commanded strategic air forces in the Pacific, stated that "the argument has been advanced that the Air Force should be concerned with land objectives, and the Navy with objectives on and over the water. That distinction is to deny the peculiar quality of the air medium, the third dimension. The air is indivisible; it covers land and sea."[34] It is clear that General Spaatz recognized the need for airpower to complement existing land and seapower capabilities. While pursuing airpower dominance, the USAF also developed a strong offensive culture with the emphasis of air superiority and strategic striking. Bringing Spaatz's ideas as well as the air force strategic culture forward, the USAF finds it imperative to apply them to the domains of space and cyberspace in today's security environment. With its existing threats and emerging near-peer competitors, the Asia-Pacific region has the potential to present a true challenge for USAF's air, space, and cyberspace capabilities.

Despite the U.S. military's current irregular warfare involvement in Iraq and Afghanistan, the USAF cannot lower its guard in deterring potential conventional/advanced warfare adversaries, extending global freedoms, and maintaining regional peace and prosperity. From an air force Asia-Pacific perspective, challenges in these areas come from North Korea's nuclear proliferation and the high-end military competition that involves both China and Russia. Among these, the most troublesome for the USAF are (1) the emerging threat of modern integrated air defenses to the Air Force's ability to maintain the dominance in modern air warfare; (2) competition for access to, use of, and preeminence in space; and (3) security vulnerabilities resulting from America's dependence on cyberspace. While not unique to the Asia-Pacific regional challenge, all of these issues are clearly associated with a potential confrontation between the United States and China over Taiwan. U.S.-Taiwan military cooperation under the guidance of the Taiwan Relations Act continues to serve a source of tension between China and the United States.

The development and maintenance of capabilities for "Global Reach, Global Power, and Global Vigilance" are keys for the Air Force to confront emerging challenges. So far the USAF has made efforts to optimize command and control and enhance ISR capabilities in the Pacific, redeploy C-17s and KC-135s to Alaska and Hawaii, place three of its seven programmed F-22 squadrons to the Pacific, and rotate the presence of B-1, B-2, and B-52s aircraft at Guam while advocating the need to develop the next-generation, long-range bombers by 2018. However, with the global economic recession, there are likely to be large reductions in the U.S. defense budget, as Defense Secretary Robert Gates has recently recommended. If true, the USAF must prepare to make adjustments to include low-cost alternatives to meet the challenges in the Asia-Pacific region. An objective assessment of regional military situation will be vital for the USAF to respond accordingly.

It is clear that the ongoing Chinese innovation and transformation will affect the USAF's regional posture. Despite the imperfect coverage in the DoD report to Congress on Chinese military development, the rapidly growing precision missile/munitions inventory and the long-range air-defense capabilities of the PLA will be expected to pose significant challenges to both the U.S. Air Force and the U.S. Navy and will have implications for operations and force structure. As stated in Joint Forces Command's 2008 publication, "The Joint Operating Environment" (JOE): "In the long-term, the primary purpose of the military forces of the United States must be deterrence."[35] The forging of Air-Sea Battle doctrine through the Pacific Vision 2008 exercised by the Pacific Air Force and the Navy was an important step in building more appropriate deterrence capabilities needed to deal with a transformed and potentially hostile China. The AirSea Battle also recognizes the essential nature of synchronized air-sea operations against a potential near-peer competitor. Much has been written with regard to potential USAF strategies to safeguard international transit through the Malacca Strait and whether Chinese economically centered strategies should be of concern to future USAF operations. These operational scenarios are further complicated by the expectation that China will develop an active aircraft carrier capability within the next five to ten years. While this chapter will not address those issues in detail, it bears repeating that addressing basing and airfield access issues with allied and friendly nations for forward deployment is essential to maximize USAF effectiveness and progress towards a sustainable USAF and DOD deterrent capability.

As discussed previously, U.S. Air Force research shows that China has little true capability to conduct space warfare, and that Chinese publications likely reflect a "desired capability." However, divisions created between the domains of space and cyberspace are superficial at best. While not all cyber operations are space operations, the opposite may be said to be true. Nearly 100 percent of product from satellites is information, and information is processed through a variety of networks, computers and communications—the cyber domain— a domain in which the Chinese are already capable peer competitors. The USAF has made a profound acknowledgment of this understanding by placing the cyber mission as a numbered air force subordinate to Air Force Space Command. DoD also activated the United States Cyber Command in May 2010 as a subunified command subordinate to USSTRATCOM—the combatant command responsible for the operation of all DoD space assets. These actions recognize the critical connection between the space and cyber domains and will continue to be essential in providing the USAF with an initial ability to protect global access and project American military power if needed.

While this reorganization is a positive step, it may not move quickly enough to adjust to the new paradigms of military operations with a capable peer competitor. The USAF has a relatively brief window of opportunity to rethink its present culture and abilities, which still reflect "an industrial age, mobilization-based . . . paradigm" and to adjust to ways that are "consistent with the intellectual requirements of the future joint force."[36] Space and cyber operations are critical to the U.S. Air Force, but they are inherently joint and connected to interagency and civilian interests. How capabilities are developed to operate effectively in these domains will be important to USAF and DoD operations in the Asia-Pacific region as well as against potential competitors worldwide, including a resurgent Russia, terrorists, and even criminals.

Conclusion

While no intelligence sources were used in the preparation of this study, open-source military discovery indicates that fears of a conventional war with China may be overstated. While the USAF must make adjustments to create a more effective deterrent and protect U.S. interests in the Asia-Pacific region and around the world, DoD assessments of Chinese military power, particularly air and space power, appear inadequately addressed and may not justify established U.S. policy as stated in 2006 Quadrennial Defense Review report that "China has the greatest potential to compete militarily with the United

States and field disruptive military technologies that could over time, off-set traditional U.S. military advantages."[37] If China is to be viewed as a potential adversary, the USAF and DoD must pursue effective open-source (as well as intelligence-based) discovery of its strategies and capabilities that lead to reports, which in turn inform Congress. Congressional trust will lead to the development of more effective avenues and capabilities for cooperation or confrontation, as appropriate.

Creation of indigenous USAF research and discovery capabilities, to include undergraduate- and graduate-level Chinese study programs, is necessary for improved military discovery and decision making. In particular, an enhanced understanding of Chinese air and space power development will enable the USAF to more accurately assess, proactively prepare for and, as appropriate, respond to China's progress in the air and space realm. Because current analyses are relatively ad hoc and limited in their temporal scope, they tend to be less than impartial and reflect incomplete interpretations based on selected and nonauthoritative sources. These limitations call into question the objectivity and thoroughness of the general body of current DoD analysis and may not provide accurate representations. As stated in the JOE, "The defining element in military effectiveness in war lies in the ability to recognize when prewar visions and understanding of war are wrong and must change."[38]

Although conventional arms and strategies have created an effective U.S. deterrent capability, it appears that China's conventional air and space capabilities have not yet reached the level that some allege, and still face significant challenges. Beijing's capabilities in other areas such as cyberspace are only beginning to be explored and understood. Effective and complete military discovery, as it pertains to China or anything else, is an art that is accomplished not by meekly repackaging questionable information but through deep study, contemplation, and professional discussion.

Notes

1. Sir Francis Bacon, *The New Organon or True Directions Concerning the Interpretations of Nature*, "Aphorisms, Book 1," sec. LXXXII (1620), http://www.constitution.org/bacon/nov_org.htm.

2. Ronald O'Rourke, *China Naval Modernization: Implications for U.S. Naval Capabilities—Background and Issues for Congress* (Washington, DC: Congressional Research Service, 10 June 2010), "Summary," i.

3. Kenneth W. Allen, Glenn Krumel, and Jonathan D. Pollack, *China's Air Forces Enters the 21st Century* (Santa Monica, CA: RAND, 1995), 181–88.

4. John Wilson Lewis and Xue Litai, "China's Search for a Modern Air Force," *International Security* 24, no. 1 (Summer 1999): 94.

5. Ibid., 15.

6. Dennis J. Blasko, "The 2007 Report on the Chinese Military: The Top 10 List of Missing Topics," *Joint Force Quarterly*, no. 47 (2007): 48.

7. The United States and China do not use the same terminology when discussing generations of aircraft: using U.S. nomenclature, aircraft produced from 1970 to 1990 constitute the "fourth generation" while China refers to them as "third generation."

8. Office of the Secretary of Defense (DoD), *Annual Report on the Military Power of the People's Republic of China* (Washington, DC: DoD, 2008), 31, http://www.defenselink.mil/pubs/pdfs/China_Military_Report_08.pdf.

9. Ibid., 1, 19–20.

10. Richard Fisher Jr., "Two Cheers for the 2007 PLA Report," 20 June 2007, International Assessment and Strategy Center, http://www.strategycenter.net/printVersion/print_pub.asp?pubID=162.

11. *Chinese Military Aviation* webpage, http://cnair.top81.cn/J-10_J-11_FC-1.htm.

12. Office of the Secretary of Defense (DoD), *Annual Report on the Military Power of the People's Republic of China* (Washington, DC: DoD, 2007), 4, http://www.defenselink.mil/pubs/pdfs/070523-China-Military-Power-final.pdf.

13. *Chinese Military Aviation* webpage, http://cnair.top81.cn/J-10_J-11_FC-1.htm.

14. H.R. 2647, National Defense Authorization Act FY2010, Sec. 1246, http://74.86.203.130/bill/111-h2647/show.

15. Dennis J. Blasko, "Rumsfeld's Take on the Chinese Military: A Dissenting View," *Current History* (September 2006): 264.

16. Eric Lin-Greenberg, "Offensive Airpower with Chinese Characteristics: Development, Capabilities, and Intentions," *Air and Space Power Journal* (Fall 2007): 67–77.

17. Ibid., 72–75.

18. The best one is Jon T. Thomas, "The Wings of the Dragon PLA Air Force Rapid Conventional Force Projection: Beyond Taiwan?" Research Report, Air University, 2006.

19. See, for example, Jerome T. Traughber, "Near Peer Competitors: The Growth of Chinese Military Capabilities," Research Report, Air University, 2008, 14.

20. Thomas, "Wings of the Dragon," 43–48.

21. Carol P. Welsch, "Protecting the Heavens: Implications of China's Antisatellite Programs," Research Report, Air University, 2008, ii.

22. Ibid., emphasis added.

23. Steven A. Smith, "Chinese Space Superiority? China's Military Space Capabilities and the Impact of their Use in a Taiwan Conflict," Research Report, Air University, 2006, 27.

24. Cai Fengzhen, Tian Anping, et al., *Kongtian zhanchang yu Zhongguo kongjun* [*The Aerospace Battlefield and China's Air Force*] (Beijing: PLA Press, 2004); and Cai Fengzhen, Tian Anping, et al., *Kongtian yiti zuozhan xue* [*Study of Integrated Aerospace Operations*] (Beijing: PLA Press, 2006).

25. Cai et al., *Aerospace Battlefield*, 259–83.

26. Ibid., 1–3, and Cai et al., *Study of Integrated Aerospace Operations*, 1–3.

27. Larry Wortzel, "The Chinese People's Liberation Army and Space Warfare," *Astropolitics*, no. 2 (2008): 114.

28. Ibid., 123–25, 135–36.

29. Information Office of State Council of People's Republic of China, *China's National Defense in 2008* (Beijing: Foreign Languages Press, 2009), 8–9.

30. Ibid., 13–26.

31. Ibid., 35–36.

32. Dai Xu, "再见, 老六 h" ["Goodbye, Old J-6 Fighters: A Complete Examination of the Service History of the Last Meritorious Fighter in the Chinese Air Force with Combat Victory Record"],国际展望 [*World Outlook*], no. 19 (2005): 21.

33. Information Office of the PRC, *China's National Defense in 2008*, 26.

34. USAF, "Countersea Operations, Air Force Doctrine Document 2-1.4," 4 June 1999, 5, http://www.fas.org/man/dod-101/usaf/docs/afdd/afdd2-1-4.pdf.

35. United States Joint Forces Command (USJFCOM), "The Joint Operating Environment, 2008: Challenges and Implications for the Future Joint Force," 43, http://www.jfcom.mil/newslink/storyarchive/2008/JOE2008.pdf.

36. Ibid., 50.

37. DoD, "Quadrennial Defense Review Report," 6 February 2006, 29, http://www.defenselink.mil/qdr/report/Report20060203.pdf.

38. USJFCOM, "Joint Operating Environment," 51.

Jeff Hagen

The U.S. Air Force and the Chinese Aerospace Challenge

AS CHINA CONTINUES to modernize its military at a pace commensurate with its growing economic power, it is important for U.S. decision makers to regularly evaluate the balance between observed Chinese capabilities and U.S. forces. Although armed conflict between the United States and China is extremely unlikely and would likely be mutually destructive, there are important shaping, deterrence, and stability reasons for ensuring that the United States is well prepared for contingencies involving China. A conflict over Taiwan has been a long-standing concern but is not the only scenario where the United States and China could become militarily involved. For instance, territorial disputes in the South and East China seas could be sources of future conflict, and other issues involving nations in South or Southeast Asia are also plausible. With the various countries and competing claims that may be involved, these situations could become even more complex than a China–Taiwan scenario.

Key Elements of Modernization

As outlined in the by the U.S. Department of Defense (DoD) in its 2010 report, China is simultaneously modernizing several aspects of its military capabilities.[1] For the U.S. military, three particular areas of this modernization hold the most potential to affect traditional means of power projection and the types of operations on which it has come to rely. These three modernization thrusts are antiaccess threats to U.S. basing, state-of-the-art surface-to-air missile (SAM) defenses, and a fourth-generation air force with precision air-to-ground and air-to-air capabilities.

Before discussing each modernization effort, it is important to recall that simply purchasing equipment does not give a military force an operational capability. Effective testing, ongoing and realistic training, peacetime support, sufficient wartime maintenance, and robust connections to supporting elements such as targeting information and command and control must accompany that equipment. This is particularly critical for forces that must operate at long ranges and interoperate with other services. In an environment like the Taiwan Strait, multiple branches of the Chinese military would be operating simultaneously in a small area, creating opportunities for confusion, uncertainty, and fratricide. However, China appears to have recognized at least some of these difficulties and may be making efforts to address them. The 2010 DoD report refers to enhanced training for strike aircraft, electronic warfare, carrier air, and ground forces. It also discusses exercises occurring across military regions for joint and combined arms operations and the existence of a dedicated adversary force. Despite these efforts, it is interesting to note large Chinese investments in systems such as ballistic missiles, which do not require "interoperability" per se and which can be quite effective even when operating with a preset plan and little communication from higher headquarters.

Antiaccess Threats to U.S. Basing

In the last several years, multiple authors have highlighted the antiaccess threat that China is creating through its procurement of tactical ballistic missiles (TBM) and ground-launched cruise missiles (GLCM). These two systems may soon be joined by air-launched cruise missiles (ALCM) and an air force capable of precision air-to-ground strikes. If we examine the six main U.S. Air Force (USAF) bases in the region against the nonnuclear threats listed in the 2010 DoD report (excluding the 700–750 shorter-range CSS-7 missiles), we see that Osan and Kunsan airbases in South Korea (400 km from the closest point in China) could face up to 480 TBM and 350 GLCM; Kadena (650 km from China), Misawa (850 km, or 1000 km if overflight of Russia is avoided), and Yokota (1,100 km from China) airbases on Japan could face 80 TBM and 350 GLCM; but Andersen AFB (3,000 km from China) on Guam is currently free from threat. However, there appear to be signs of long-range cruise missiles being fitted to H-6 bombers that could soon allow ALCMs to reach Andersen. China clearly possesses the technology to produce conventional ballistic missiles that could reach Andersen as well. The report also discusses possible antiship ballistic missiles under development, which could be used to threaten U.S. aircraft carriers.

RAND has looked at the effects of various TBM and cruise missile warheads against airbase targets, and numbers on the order of thirty to fifty TBM per base appear to be sufficient to overload and kill air defenses, cover all of the open parking areas with submunitions to destroy aircraft parked there, and crater runways such that aircraft cannot take off or land. If thirty to fifty cruise missiles were fired along with the TBMs, they would complicate the air defense problem and could damage or destroy a squadron's worth of aircraft shelters. There would likely also be damage to other critical airbase systems such as fuel storage and handling or maintenance facilities and equipment. Following such an attack, U.S. forces would have to extinguish burning aircraft, clear the airfield of debris and unexploded ordnance, repair runway craters, and fly in replacement aircraft and support equipment before the base could generate useful combat sorties.

If we compare the numbers of missile required to close bases with the numbers that China is currently fielding, clearly the U.S. could face extended periods of time where few, if any, of our bases near China are operating. RAND analysis has estimated that in the near future, even with conservative estimates on TBM production, Kadena could be kept closed to fighter operations for at least a week and kept closed to heavy aircraft such as tankers, bombers, and intelligence, surveillance, and reconnaissance (ISR) aircraft (which require longer runways and hence more crater repairs) for much longer. Alternatively, some of these missiles could be used to close multiple bases for shorter periods, although hundreds of GLCM are also available to contribute to that task.

These antiaccess concerns are sometimes dismissed as too escalatory or counterproductive for China to undertake. The argument is that attacking U.S. bases in South Korea or Japan would fully bring those countries into the conflict, resulting in a net negative for China's ambitions in the region. Similarly, attacking the Andersen airbase on Guam, which is a U.S. territory, would force the United States to fully react and bring much more force to bear than it otherwise would consider using in a conflict with China. Although these arguments have merit, there are several reasons why this viewpoint should not dominate U.S. planning. First, given the mismatch in capabilities between U.S. and Chinese forces, China simply cannot allow the United States to operate freely from bases near Taiwan and expect to achieve its objectives. Since attacking basing appears to be prerequisite for success, and China appears to recognize this fact, U.S. military planners should assume that such attacks might occur. Second, Chinese writings and equipment procurements are clearly becoming oriented to attacking not only Taiwan but also targets further afield. If China saw no self-interest in attacking bases in Japan and beyond, it is difficult to see the need for conventional CSS-5 TBMs, long-range GLCMs and ALCM on bombers. It is unlikely that China would consider these locations to be a priori off limits after having invested so much in the ability to attack them. And finally, even if the United States became convinced of Chinese unwillingness to attack regional bases, the mere existence of potential threats to these bases should cause planners to create robust alternatives to their use.

Surface-to-Air Missiles and Fourth-Generation Air Force

The upgrades of SAMs and fighter aircraft are often grouped together under the term "area denial" to capture the sense of portions of battle space being made too risky for U.S. operations. Indeed, the 2010 DoD report highlights that the air defense over Chinese territory is becoming quite saturated with modern SAMs and defensive fighters. In the case of a mainland China–Taiwan scenario, a key element of this area denial capability is that the threatened airspace is not only over Chinese territory but is being extended over the Taiwan Strait and soon over Taiwan as well by long-range land- and ship-based SAMs and fourth-generation air-to-air fighters. A 200-km-range S-300PMU2 SAM on the Chinese mainland has coverage reaching from Taiwan's western coast 50 km into the island's interior. A *Luzhou*-class DDG with an SA-N-20 SAM in the middle of the strait could engage airborne targets over most of Taiwan. In terms of fighters, there appear to be approximately fifteen Chinese military airbases within 600 km of Taipei (there are 40 within 1,000 km), and it appears China will soon be able to employ between five hundred and one thousand aircraft in a campaign against Taiwan, 20–30 percent of them with modern fourth-generation capabilities such as precision air-to-ground weapons. Within five to ten years this fraction could easily exceed 50 percent with reasonable production rates.

Although the USAF is well trained and equipped to deal with fourth-generation fighters and modern SAMs, the combination of capabilities that China appears to be creating could cause significant additional risk. For example, an isolated, well-located modern SAM does not pose a major challenge to the United States, but two or three operating in range of each other, with one or more of them unlocated and with threat fighters in the area, is a very different story. Similarly, a four-ship formation of Su-27 Flankers is quite a bit more challenging for today's USAF when they are equipped with active radar missiles and effective electronic warfare and are supported by an airborne command-and-control aircraft and long-range SAMs. This challenge would obviously be compounded if the threat were twenty-four Flankers instead of four, and if the U.S. command-and-control aircraft were forced to leave the area for its own safety. As this type of defense expands to cover more of Chinese territory, U.S. military options are constrained. If China can extend these capabilities over Taiwan as well, the U.S. ability to defend Taiwan also becomes circumscribed and other regional contingencies could also be hampered.

Effect of Modernization on U.S. Air Operations

In the recent past, the United States responded to contingencies with rapid deployments of large numbers of fighters to bases and on aircraft carriers close to the conflict. Smaller numbers of bombers, tankers, and ISR aircraft would be deployed to somewhat more distant locations in support. The fighters, which would at least match in number and greatly exceed in capability those of any adversary, would quickly gain air superiority over friendly territory, thereby allowing heavy use of ISR and tankers close to the enemy. With the U.S. Air Force and U.S. Navy's overwhelming advantage in air-to-air and the suppression of enemy air defenses (SEAD), this air superiority could then be extended over the enemy's territory and allow virtually any target or ground force to come under rapid and heavy attack by fighters and bombers flying around the clock.

Interlocking Challenges

The ongoing improvement in Chinese SAMs, air-to-air and air-to-ground fighters and antiaccess missile capabilities, if accompanied by appropriate training and support, could soon create a series of interlocking challenges for this paradigm of air operations. The root of the issue is the looming mismatch between U.S. basing options in the region and Chinese base attack capabilities. If aircraft carriers near Taiwan and airbases in Japan and South Korea can be attacked (or threatened to the degree that the United States is politically unable to use them) to the extent that sorties generated from them are significantly limited, operations from more distant locations such as Guam become the only remaining option. Furthermore, as discussed earlier, threats to bases at these longer ranges appear to be emerging as well, particularly to larger aircraft such as tankers, bombers, and ISR aircraft that require long runways. If basing at Guam could be damaged and sortie generation limited or halted, the United States would be left with few, if any, options for providing land-based fighter sorties.

Sortie Limitations: Larger Consequences

The limit on sorties that the antiaccess threat creates has several second-order effects. For instance, one of the primary USAF missions in a conflict is likely to be the maintenance of air sovereignty. Whereas in the past the United States could match Chinese numbers and exceed Chinese capability, in the near future, if U.S. basing is attacked, China is likely to be able to exceed the sortie numbers that U.S. forces can generate and is likely to begin to approach the capability of the fourth-generation fighters making up the bulk of U.S. forces. This situation is exacerbated by the SAM threat, which reaches close to Taiwan from the mainland and can be pushed farther forward by ship-based air defenses. To avoid the SAMs, nonstealthy fourth-generation fighters would either be forced to remain behind Taiwan or operate at lower altitudes, which puts them at a further disadvantage in air-to-air combat. Although the United States is in process of modernizing its fighter fleet to regain a capability edge, the small size of the F-22 force and the delayed entry of the F-35 mean that the overall gap is unlikely to close in the near term.

The shortage of fighter sorties also makes it difficult to conduct attack operations and protect the vulnerable bomber, ISR, and tanker aircraft that enable them. Since the key threats are China's force of strike aircraft and short-range ballistic missiles, finding and killing targets such as airbases, air defenses, and ballistic missile launchers and infrastructure could be high priority U.S. missions. Although cruise missile strikes from ships and submarines would play an important role, the numbers and types of missiles currently available are not likely to be sufficient to degrade Chinese attacks significantly. Attacks on well-protected targets generally require large force "packages" of aircraft to provide the mutual support necessary to find targets, survive and suppress defenses, and employ sufficient weapons. This is particularly true when facing the modern SAMs and aircraft that China is fielding, which can relocate and mutually protect each other. Attacking mobile targets requires persistence in the target area and survivable ISR. Even cruise missile strikes against fixed targets, which are typically conducted by bombers operating from stand-off ranges, will require fighter protection from long-range interceptors such as the Su-27 (although longer-range weapons could reduce this demand). Hard and buried targets require attacks by weapons generally carried by bombers to within close range of the target. With distant and damaged basing, these packages of attack and support aircraft become difficult to form, difficult to refuel, and difficult to keep on-station.

Traditional Operations Threatened

Perhaps even more concerning than these practical effects, however, is the destabilizing nature of the Chinese threat matched against traditional air force operations. The typical U.S. response to rising tensions anywhere in the world is to begin to deploy forces, especially naval and land-based airpower, into the theater to dissuade, deter, and, if necessary, coerce an adversary. Since these forces have operated from near sanctuary, this strategy has worked to U.S. advantage. If the United States were left alone to operate from bases near China, this would likely be the case in the Pacific as well. Thus, China may feel that its only hope for victory is to attack U.S. forces as they deploy into theater. The very effectiveness of U.S. airpower, coupled with its vulnerability in this theater, has created an incentive for attack, not stability.

Options for Improvement

Despite the rather significant obstacles to military operations in the Pacific that are looming on the horizon, there are several steps the DoD can take to mitigate them and in turn improve deterrence and stability in the region. Although none can be accomplished without investment, most would cost far less than purchasing a new platform. With a focus on providing secure basing for fighters and improving operational flexibility, analyses at RAND and other institutions have brought to light several high-leverage areas:

- Increase the number of airbases and their hardness
- Solidify regional basing arrangements
- Improve long-range strike capability
- Increase operational coordination between the U.S. Air Force and U.S. Navy
- Continue modernization of fighter force
- To the greatest extent possible, encourage Taiwan and other partners to pursue defensive systems that are more survivable and effective against attack.

Increase and Harden Air Bases

The first measure, improved basing, would consist of two types of activities. First, the number of operating surfaces at locations near Guam could be expanded. There are several nearby islands—such as Saipan, Tinian, Rota, Yap, and Palau—that could accommodate smaller bases with a moderate number of support facilities. If tensions with China escalated, personnel, fighters, and support equipment would flow to these dispersed operating locations. Second, bases in this region need to be made more survivable against rapid and comprehensive destruction of aircraft parked in the open, runways, and fuel storage. Thus, current and new airbases need to be equipped with some type of shelter for fighters and their fuel to offer protection against light submunitions. Active defenses could also play a significant role at these ranges since they are less likely to be overwhelmed with numbers.

Together these measures would make a Chinese antiaccess strategy much more difficult to execute. Since the United States would be operating at 3,000 km from China, threats to these locations would be quite expensive, and hence less numerous. Having multiple operating locations directly multiplies the number of threat missiles required, as does survivable aircraft parking and operating surfaces. However, these efforts will not be effective at protecting large aircraft, such as tankers and bombers. These aircraft remain critical to U.S. operations to refuel fighters operating at long ranges and to provide strike capability.

Enhance Regional Basing Options

Because the United States is unlikely to be able to keep runways open to operate large aircraft from inside the threat ring, the need for expanding and clarifying basing options with regional allies is magnified. To take one example, expanded basing options with a nation such as Australia could allow the United States to fly fighters from expanded basing options on or near Guam and refuel them with tankers flying from bases in Northern Australia from outside most threats. There may be similar opportunities with other nations in the region, particularly for noncombat missions such as ISR and refueling. Arrangements such as this would obviously require long and delicate negotiations involving many arms of the U.S. government, and hence cannot be delayed until tensions rise.

Improve Long-Range Strike Capability

The third improvement, increasing the capability of long-range strike, would allow the United States to exploit the expanded but still distant basing options just discussed. Greater use of long-range strike with standoff munitions also reduces the tanker burden, employs more munitions per sortie, and reduces the need for SEAD as compared to conducting strikes with fighters. Although the DoD has been examining future needs for long-range strike for several years, it is not likely that a new platform would be available in the near- or midterm time frames. Thus, more rapid and less expensive options should be considered. These include increasing the weapons carriage capacity of B-52 bombers and exploring options for allowing bomber-training aircraft to temporarily deploy and support combat operations.

Most importantly, however, the United States will need to expand the quantities and capabilities of long-range cruise missiles. As outlined earlier, critical targets such as airbases will be very difficult to attack directly with current fighters and bombers. Analysis by RAND has indicated a need for several thousand long-range cruise missiles with antiship, unitary, penetrating, and submunition warhead variants. The primary USAF cruise missile is envisioned to be the joint air-to-surface standoff missile (JASSM), but its range does not allow access to many targets in a country as large as China. The baseline JASSM might be particularly useful in an antiship variant where the longest range is not needed. The procurement plan for the extended-range variant (JASSM-ER) is for relatively small quantities. Air-launched AGM-86C and ship- and submarine-based Tomahawk missiles would be available in the theater as well but in quantities of hundreds, not thousands. The Tomahawks are also good candidates for an antiship variant since their launchers are continually on-station and could react quickly to Chinese ship movements.

Strengthen Air Force–Navy Operational Coordination

As highlighted by the cruise missile situation, increased cooperation between the U.S. Air Force and U.S. Navy could pay high dividends, given the level of threat and diversity of missions likely to be needed. For many missions, such as air superiority over Taiwan, maritime interdiction, and SEAD, elements from both services will be needed. For this to happen, it will be critical that the services integrate at several different levels. For instance, ISR platforms from one service may need to be able to target weapons for the other, assets from one will likely need to contribute to force protection for the other, and both will likely need to take on less-traditional missions such as maritime interdiction by the U.S. Air Force and airbase defense by the U.S. Navy.

Continue Fighter Force Modernization

The U.S. Air Force is currently modernizing from a fourth-generation (primarily F-15 and F-16 aircraft) to a fifth-generation (F-22 and F-35) fighter force. Although the threat to bases in the region might seem to call into question large investments in relatively short-range fighters, the reality is somewhat more complicated. Because there are several missions that appear to be most effectively accomplished in the foreseeable future by fighters, air-to-air, and SEAD, to take two examples, fighter demand is unlikely to disappear. The advantages of moving from fourth-generation to fifth-generation fighters are several. The latter's stealth characteristics obviously make them more survivable, reducing the need for large support packages. Their modern and integrated sensor suites are more resistant to jamming and reduce the need for offboard ISR assets that require their own basing and support. This combination of high survivability and high effectiveness means that fewer are needed to accomplish the same missions, which is exactly what is needed in antiaccess scenarios. Although heavier reliance on long-range strike may eventually reduce the number of fighters required, operations from longer ranges also increases the requirement, making it difficult to forecast an ideal future mix of fighters and bombers.

Encourage Security Partners to Pursue Survivable Systems

Providing proper support and equipment to regional partners could reduce many of the demands placed on the United States. For example, improved Taiwanese capabilities in survivable air defenses, antiship missiles, and indirect fires would go a long way to reducing current vulnerabilities while limiting possibilities for escalation, given their defensive nature. Mobile SAMs that relocate once or twice a day and limit their radar emissions could cause quite a challenge to Chinese forces. Mobile antiship and short-range surface-to-surface missiles are a survivable approach to blunt an invasion force. These could be supported by small tactical hand- or vehicle-launched unmanned aerial vehicles to provide targeting information. Defense planning in the region is obviously the responsibility of each military, but the United States should encourage the most appropriate and useful capabilities when possible.

Conclusion

Although many believe that the likelihood of armed conflict between the United States and China is low, the recently completed Quadrennial Defense Review states clearly that, "U.S. forces must be able to deter, defend against, and defeat aggression by potentially hostile nation-states" in an antiaccess environment.[2] If the United States wishes to remain relevant in the Pacific, it is likely to need to respond to Chinese modernization in an intelligent and effective way. Any U.S. response should be focused on increasing the deterrent effect of its force posture and providing commanders a broader set of stabilizing options in the face of increasing tensions. Given current fiscal pressures, ongoing counterinsurgencies, and the need to consider requirements in other possible scenarios, the overall expense of these responses must also be considered carefully. If addressed properly, important U.S. military shortcomings can be bolstered at reasonable cost and with positive effects on overall stability in the Western Pacific.

Notes

The opinions and conclusions expressed in this chapter are the author's alone and should not be interpreted as representing those of RAND or any of the sponsors of its research. The RAND Corporation is a nonprofit research organization providing objective analysis and effective solutions that address the challenges facing the public and private sectors around the world. RAND's publications do not necessarily reflect the opinions of its research clients and sponsors.

This chapter is based on Jeff Hagen, "Potential Effects of Chinese Aerospace Capabilities on U.S. Air Force Operations," Hearing on "China's Emergent Military Aerospace and Commercial Aviation Capabilities," U.S.–China Economic and Security Review Commission, Washington, DC, 20 May 2010. This testimony is available for free download at http://www.rand.org/pubs/testimonies/CT347/. This testimony stems from work conducted in RAND Project Air Force and in RAND National Security Research Division. This product is part of the RAND Corporation testimony series. RAND testimonies record testimony presented by RAND associates to federal, state, or local legislative committees; government-appointed commissions and panels; and private review and oversight bodies. For related publications and research by the author, please see http://www.rand.org/pubs/authors/h/hagen_jeff.html.

1. Office of the Secretary of Defense (DoD), *Military and Security Developments Involving the People's Republic of China 2010*, Annual Report to Congress (Washington, DC: Office of the Secretary of Defense, 16 August 2010), http://www.defense.gov/pubs/pdfs/2010_CMPR_Final.pdf.

2. *Quadrennial Defense Review Report (QDR) 2010* (Washington, DC: U.S. Department of Defense, 1 February 2010), http://www.defense.gov/qdr/QDR%20as%20of%20 26JAN10%200700.pdf.

Eric A. McVadon

The U.S. Navy and the Chinese Aerospace Challenge

THE CORE OF THE December 2008 China Maritime Studies Institute conference has been covered by the preceding chapters, based on papers presented. This chapter is not an exhaustive summary of those chapters but rather an elaboration of aspects beyond those that were presented encompassing matters raised in the question-and-answer periods of the conference and especially issues and themes worthy of further exploration that have developed or emerged since the conference.

The chapter additionally includes an examination of the current state of the military relationship and suggests that U.S.–China relations are sufficiently important that we cannot afford simply to point to Chinese intransigence and live with the repeated disruptions. We must at least strive to resolve or circumvent the problem, and we must achieve habits of cooperation rather than those of confrontation. A prescription is offered of a nuanced U.S. policy path: a winding, dual road, one lane for the U.S. government overall, and another for the U.S. Navy. This journey is taken under increasingly complex—even unpromising—current circumstances in order to cope with the heightened challenge resulting from China's aerospace developments and the matter of where the various layers of U.S.–China relations are headed. If this proposed policy path is not the right one, it could at least start a conversation about such a policy. The bilateral relationship is far too important to accept stagnation, waiting for change, and blaming the other side.

Engaging and Hedging

In a keynote speech addressing policy issues related to the rise of China, retired U.S. Navy captain Gerry Roncolato, who serves as deputy director of strategy and policy in the Office of the Chief of Naval Operations, pointed out that even the organizational coffee cups with the logo of the commander of the U.S. Pacific Fleet bear the ubiquitous words "Made in China," continually reminding the Pacific Fleet staff, whether drinking coffee or tea, of the fact of China's emergence.

As to the matter of whether China is a potential partner or adversary, he explained the widely accepted notion that the U.S. wants to engage China but must, as it is popularly expressed, hedge against the prospect of conflict while emphasizing the goal of deterring conflict and emphasizing that conflict is neither inevitable nor likely, despite the robust modernization of the People's Liberation Army (PLA). It was suggested that future maritime economic cooperation between the United States and China has great promise. Achieving and maintaining the right balance of engagement and hedging is difficult, requiring flexibility, agility, adapting to Chinese power, and developing a comprehensive understanding of China as a country that must be allowed to grow yet must be discouraged from acting aggressively.

The Obama administration, at the outset, has had other priority concerns, notably including the global economic downturn. However, China policy was not relegated to the "back burner." Despite attempts to build a more stable foundation on the concept of "strategic assurance," the road continues to be rocky and the destination remains uncertain. As this volume went to press, military relations were once again on the mend after a hiatus.

It may be helpful to think a bit more about how we consider it altogether plausible that forces from the two countries might be involved in conflict, or engaged in cooperative operations. One can readily imagine a scenario in which U.S. Navy F-18s from carriers are in air-to-air combat with PLA Navy (PLAN) Su-30s over the Taiwan Strait. One can just as readily imagine those same F-18s along with U.S. Navy P-3Cs providing air cover and search capability, respectively, for PLAN and other ships of an international naval force protecting sea lanes from pirates and terrorists in the Gulf of Aden or even the Pacific Ocean sea-lanes as oil bound for China is imperiled by some future development. It is a bit harder to imagine a PLAN carrier and its aircraft entering into a "war at sea" with a U.S. Navy carrier strike group (CSG). It is easier to envision that some day in the future a moderate-sized PLAN carrier may seem a better fit than a U.S. Navy behemoth to provide fixed-wing air to an international antipiracy task group somewhere in the East, South, or Southwest Asian littoral.

Can Hedging Be Caused to Wither While Engagement Flourishes?

Decades of ambiguity or duality employed in characterizing the bilateral relationship have, through experience and habit, made it seem normal to sustain a relationship where the terms "potential adversary" and "potential partner" are somehow strangely compatible. The further point is that, if we can so candidly describe the contradiction—must be ready to fight and to engage in cooperative efforts—we should be able to intuitively move away from the perceived need to hedge toward the benefits of fuller engagement and cooperation.

The PLA Air Force (PLAAF) and PLAN aviation have come a long way since 1995, but China's underachievement in fighter aircraft development means the Chinese aircraft most comparable to U.S. top fighters are Russian Su-27s and Su-30s, which have been limited in numbers and are widely believed to be flown less skillfully than are the opposing U.S. Air Force and U.S. Navy fighter aircraft. The indigenous J-10 fighter, after decades of painfully incorporating foreign technologies, is not of the same caliber as these other aircraft. Missiles are thus the core coercive factor that Beijing brings to most conflict scenarios. These missiles are no longer the desperate resort of a poor and technologically backward China—so inaccurate that they were often dubbed terror weapons. Improved accuracy and increased numbers are making the ballistic missiles not only intimidating to the Taiwan populace but also militarily effective weapons.

Much the same can be said about long-range land-attack, various air-launched, and antiship cruise missiles (ASCMs) that complement the ballistic missiles and make possible simultaneous attacks from space and from below the radar horizon—and from different axes. Today's very diverse and lethal arsenal of Chinese cruise missiles and unmanned aerial vehicles (UAVs) has been neglected in our intense focus on ballistic missiles.

The combination of ballistic and cruise missiles (to include UAVs) to attack ships, assault Taiwan, or attempt to neutralize U.S. bases in the region is a new and profoundly serious problem. The uncertainty of the outcome and the risk of escalation suggest that avoidance of conflict by both sides has become all the more important. To ensure that we do not veer into conflict, our high-level dialogue with China, begun in the administration of President George W.

Bush, should continue to be treated by the administration of President Barack Obama as strategic in nature and conducted at high levels of seniority, seriousness, sophistication, and candor, as was first hinted at by Secretary of State Hillary Clinton as she argued in early 2009 for conversion of largely economic talks with China in the Bush administration into a "comprehensive dialogue" with a "broader agenda."[1] In 2010 Washington sent the largest U.S. delegation ever to visit China (with more than two hundred people), led by the secretaries of state and treasury, to conduct the second round of the Obama version of the talks, now called the Strategic and Economic Dialogue (S&ED).[2] Both sides put a positive spin on bilateral relations but did not overcome the tension over arms sales to Taiwan. The S&ED is a work in progress.

A New Administration in Taiwan Has Eased Tensions

With cross-strait tensions now markedly eased, as reflected in China's 2008 Defense White Paper and the U.S. Department of Defense (DoD) annual report to Congress on Chinese military power (using remarkably similar words), the Chinese aspirations are seen by many as a less pressing threat and more of a reminder that we should be working hard to decrease our vulnerability in space and increase the odds of keeping space from becoming the battlefield of the future. We must indeed take China seriously in the domain of space warfare but keep Chinese accomplishments and activities in perspective. In January 2010 China conducted a successful midcourse intercept of a ballistic missile.[3] This was a significant step, but only a step, toward an antiballistic missile (ABM) capability. Much remains to be done to establish first a rudimentary system that would provide some defense against ballistic missiles from a small arsenal such as that of India, and then a great deal more to develop and deploy the components of a comprehensive system that would have significant utility against the ballistic missile arsenals of the United States and Russia. The enormous effort that has gone into the development of the limited-capability American ABM system serves as a useful gauge of the scope of effort needed. It is noteworthy that the currently deployed U.S. ABM system is very far short of being adequate to defend against China's intercontinental and submarine-launched ballistic missiles and that China, simply by building more DF-31A ICBMs and incorporating imaginative decoys and other penetration aids, can stay ahead of U.S. ballistic missile defenses.

Avoiding an Arms Race in Space

If we have been able to manage six decades without a second use of nuclear weapons in war, can we not aspire to many more decades without a first use of weapons in space? We do not want an arms race in space centered on whether China can find simple means to disrupt our complex systems and networks. That race would resemble what we have in recent years been referring to as the global war on terrorism—a conflict where the less advanced entity can simply keep trying until it succeeds, no matter how many times and ways the terrorists must make their attempts and the enormous cost and effort that have been employed to defend against their attacks. The remedy is, I believe, not found in determining which side is able to exhaust or bankrupt the other but rather in the establishment of sufficient trust and confidence so that hedging no longer predominates and cooperation prevails. China's 2008 Defense White Paper reaffirms Beijing's declared opposition to weaponization of space. It states:

> The Chinese government has all along advocated the peaceful use of outer space, and opposed the introduction of weapons and an arms race in outer space. The existing international legal instruments concerning outer space are not sufficient to effectively prevent the spread of weapons to outer space. The international community should negotiate and conclude a new international legal instrument to close the loopholes in the existing legal system concerning outer space.
>
> In February 2008 China and Russia jointly submitted to the [UN Conference on Disarmament] a draft Treaty on the Prevention of the Placement of Weapons in Outer Space and the Threat or Use of Force against Outer Space Objects. China hopes that the [Conference on Disarmament] will start substantial discussions on the draft as soon as possible, and negotiate and conclude the Treaty at an early date.[4]

Whether we accept all this at face value is another matter, but at least at some level the Chinese have offered, and senior levels of the U.S. government have largely ignored, their rationale for this very disconcerting and irresponsible ASAT test, which illustrates something I have long argued: China is always thinking about Taiwan and is capable, where the issue is Taiwan, of making an ill-advised decision. If this someday escalates to unprecedented hostilities between two major nuclear powers, history is likely to report that the Chinese said "we told you so" and that Washington said "told us what?"

China may feel at such a disadvantage in force capabilities that it will conclude that seemingly inordinate risks must be taken to disable, even for a short time, the systems that could permit the United States to conduct devastatingly effective precision attacks to neutralize key elements of Chinese operations. This is not to suggest that such attacks on U.S. command, control, communications, computers, intelligence, surveillance, and reconnaissance (C4ISR) are likely to be effective, but it is to suggest that China may feel the need, if sorely threatened, to abandon constraints that we might imagine as lines not to be crossed.

Chinese Naval Aviation: Projecting Power?

The employment of shipboard aviation by the PLAN is unlikely to resemble the profile of U.S. naval aviation. Chinese naval strategists do not contemplate the conduct of major strikes against distant nations employing carrier-based air or "war at sea" battles pitting Chinese carriers against American carriers. However, the advantages, even the necessity, of having organic naval aviation capabilities are clear in providing surface action groups with air cover and additional combat options and in using helicopters in various roles. China is not emphasizing fixed-wing air antisubmarine warfare, shipboard or land-based, but is seeking other means to sidestep the daunting American submarine force.

Aircraft Carrier Acquisition—Remembering the Basics of Carrier Aviation

There is an obviously important yet little discussed aspect of melding things aeronautical and naval that is likely to emerge for China as a consequence of the much-discussed prospective incorporation of aircraft carriers into the PLAN. It is not just the inherent combining of naval and air platforms—ships and airplanes—but rather the potential realization by China of the remarkable advantages of a navy with sea-based aircraft. Of course, the ships of a force that includes an aircraft carrier are less vulnerable to enemy attacks, more capable because the force can now "see" much farther, strike at greater range, and employ a different family of weapon systems—without placing the central force at direct risk. Moreover, combat air power, airborne surveillance and reconnaissance, and an over-the-horizon deterrent force can be placed where desired over much of the globe—without having to obtain permission from other nations for basing and overflight—and can be moved to avoid attack, close a target, gain operational or weather advantage, demonstrate support for a friend or ally, or go home intact and ready to go to another place.

A Chinese navy with even a modest organic fixed-wing tactical aviation capability is a markedly different, more versatile, and more potent navy than one reliant on surface combatants. The same thing might be said of adding submarines to a navy, as China has done fulsomely. With a carrier force (nominally three or four carriers), the PLAN would move into an exclusive club of fully capable navies. The U.S. Navy is possibly making it even harder to be a full-fledged member of the club with the pending development of maritime UAVs such as the land-based broad-area maritime surveillance (BAMS) UAV- and carrier-based unmanned combat air system (UCAS). The prospect is that UCAS could add new dimensions to carrier warfare. The PLAN is simply not in competition with the U.S. Navy with respect to the capabilities of its future carrier(s).

As I and others have long argued, and as was discussed at the conference, Chinese aircraft carrier acquisition is likely to be driven by understandable and defensible needs to have an organic or integral combat air capability when PLAN forces are operating too far from bases in China to be supported by land-based aircraft. Aircraft carriers do not fit any apparent PLA need in a Taiwan scenario, where unsinkable nearby airfields in great number are available. Moreover, dispatch of one or more PLAN carriers in a Taiwan conflict against the world's best and most experienced carrier navy seems highly imprudent. As has often been said, a Chinese carrier in a cross-strait conflict would be a target, not an asset.

A carrier "with Chinese characteristics," which would probably mean smaller, simpler, slower, more economical to build and operate, and less potent than U.S. Navy carriers, could be an asset for other PLAN missions far from home. Were the threats just a bit different in the Gulf of Aden, the PLAN might not have felt comfortable in January 2009 to have two destroyers and a replenishment ship operating in a hostile environment without air cover. The experience there is likely to lead to the conclusion that it is highly desirable to be able to quickly search large areas of water and deliver weapons hundreds of kilometers from the ships of the force—as aircraft can do.

PLAN Aviation Helicopter Operations Reveal Practical Problems

I recall vividly my first face-to-face encounter with a PLAN frigate commanding officer in the early 1990s. The officer was receptive to conversation with both me, then the defense and naval attaché in Beijing, and my assistant naval attaché—a U.S. Marine Corps helicopter pilot. The frigate commanding officer proudly related that in his several years in command of the ship he had operated helicopters four times. The conversation likewise demonstrated in other ways that he and his crew had minimal experience with helicopter operations.

China has repeatedly, if inadvertently, revealed that in a wide range of fundamental areas of aviation skills proficiency or even basic competence, it has been slow to reach the standards routinely met by the pilots of modern air forces—and may still not measure up. These areas include night flight, formation flight, low-altitude and overwater flight, instrument weather flight, edge-of-the-envelope air combat maneuvers, long-range air navigation, air defense operations involving surface-to-air missiles (SAMs) and friendly aircraft, aerial refueling, and now, as has been described, helicopter shipboard landings at night and in poor weather.

Air ASW—Universally Neglected

Antisubmarine warfare, and especially the airborne component of ASW, is an example of an area of significant weakness in China's naval modernization effort. It is a warfare specialty that has simply been too hard to do for the PLA—at least too hard to attain a requisite level of excellence. In addition to the fundamental complexities of acoustic detection of submarines, the PLAN's primary targets, U.S. nuclear-powered submarines, are so quiet as to be essentially undetectable using passive acoustic methods.

It may seem, then, that for the immediate future a Taiwan conflict would involve three navies all sorely lacking in antisubmarine warfare. The PRC and Taiwan do indeed have minimal ASW capability, but the United States has merely let its air ASW slip. That capability is already being recouped to a significant degree, as I learned from a March 2009 panel of the U.S. Navy officers most directly concerned with P-3, P-8, and BAMS issues. Rejuvenation of air ASW will not allow maritime patrol aircraft to operate near China where air defense is present, but CSGs needing protection from submarines would not be in those areas. China's impressive new submarine force presents a daunting challenge to an intervening U.S. Navy, demanding the most from air and submarine ASW forces in areas where it is feasible for each to operate—a challenge the U.S. Navy seems to be meeting.

A combination of air ASW and submarine ASW techniques intended to detect quiet Chinese submarines during periods when they are emitting noise would permit attrition of those submarines in prospective carrier operating areas—even if time consuming. Thus by virtue of air ASW support and more advanced technologies, superior operational skills and experience, better intelligence support, and a big ocean, the advantage likely goes to the U.S. submarine force. The PLAN submarine force is closing the gap but in my judgment is not yet in the same league as the U.S. Navy submarine force.

All this means that U.S. submarines could operate in areas well east of Taiwan and even in the vicinity of Taiwan with at least acceptable levels of risk, while the very important Chinese submarine force would be highly vulnerable to these U.S. attack submarines and increasingly at risk of detection by U.S. air ASW assets that could once more become highly effective. The PLAN cannot mount such an effective combination of forces.

It appears that China has developed a remedy for this lack of antisubmarine capability against U.S. submarines in the form of a new antiship ballistic missile (ASBM). More will be said about this novel capability in the following, but with respect to the shortcomings of the PLAN in the area of air ASW, a missile of this sort means that the lack of long-range capability to detect and attack U.S. submarines is circumvented by simply lobbing land-based medium-range ballistic missiles from a thousand kilometers or more away, overflying any of the feared U.S. submarines and other threats to the attacking Chinese forces. It is not too great a stretch to suggest that the PLAN is substituting a missile capability for a capability it has not succeeded in attaining—in this case, air ASW.

Concerning Chinese air attack capabilities, there is no doubt that both the PLAN and the PLAAF now have significant forces conceivably armed with very lethal air-launched ASCMs: about 280 Su-27s and Su-30s, 150 J-10s, 120 JH-7s, and 20 H-6Hs. The pertinent question is whether these forces could penetrate the air defenses of U.S. Navy CSGs consisting of Aegis-equipped cruisers and destroyers with SAMs, early-warning aircraft, and the fighter aircraft of the embarked air wing—plus shipboard close-in weapon systems to defend as a last resort against any air-launched missiles that have penetrated the other defenses.

Chinese initial attacks using aircraft at low altitude from several directions, as described in Chinese military newspapers, are a tactic with little chance of achieving surprise and a very big chance of extremely large losses and little success. To have a reasonable chance of success, the PLA would prudently open the attack with the ballistic missiles now under development that are designed to hit ships, as discussed extensively elsewhere in this chapter. Until those MaRVed MRBMs (maneuvering reentry vehicles on medium-range ballistic missiles) are operational, ASCMs launched from the submerged *Kilo*-class submarines at ranges approaching one hundred miles are available now as a substitute.

The expectation is that these ballistic and cruise missiles, while not likely to destroy or sink major warships, are capable of degrading the U.S. air defense systems and disrupting these defenses long enough to deliver air attacks with

precision maritime-strike ASCMs. Vulnerable essential air defense components include the shipboard radars, data and communication links, missile
launchers, carrier flight decks, and aircraft. The air-launched ASCMs, then, are
suitable for follow-on attacks—not the initial strikes.

Ballistic Missile Attack

As mentioned previously, another development that warrants special interest is
the much-discussed Chinese effort to be able to hit ships with ballistic missiles.
The 2010 DoD report offers an exceedingly clear and comprehensive explanation of the Chinese antiship ballistic missile system under development. I
first discovered the Chinese technical writing on this MARVed MRBM half
a decade ago. I brashly said in 2005 at the National Press Club in Washington
that China's development of an ASBM and the means to target those missiles
would, if achieved, be comparable to China's 1964 test of a nuclear weapon. It is
appropriate to repeat that assertion. More recently, a lively debate has ensued,
a significant part of it appearing in various issues in 2010 of the U.S. Naval
Institute *Proceedings*.

Cause for the Americans to Pause?

China's ducks need not all be in a row to threaten U.S. carrier forces and
regional bases. This complicates the decision on CSG intervention—precisely
what China seeks to accomplish. If China's navy and missile forces are able
to achieve a capability to attack U.S. Navy CSGs at a thousand kilometers or
more from China, a major means to intervene in an attack on Taiwan or other
regional conflict will be jeopardized. Several years after I and others noted the
potential implications, the 2010 DoD report stated: "The PLA is acquiring
conventional MRBMs to increase the range at which it can conduct precision
strikes against land targets and naval ships, including aircraft carriers, operating far from China's shores out to the first island chain."[5] U.S. leaders will pause
in calling for prompt dispatch of the carriers if China can threaten the CSGs
with, for example, conventional warhead MaRVed MRBMs. China's asymmetric approach in this case may cause the military-strategic balance of power in
the Pacific to change fundamentally as a result.

Guam: A Valuable Asset or a Vulnerable Target?

Much has been said in recent years about Guam's being outside of the
range of Chinese cruise and ballistic missiles (except of some nuclear-armed

ballistic missiles). I fear that this may have reinforced the long-standing American notion that its forces and bases that are not in immediate proximity to combat are in sanctuary, as was the case with bases and forces in Japan during the Korean and Vietnam wars, and for forces and bases in the Philippines and even at sea at Yankee Station (where U.S. aircraft carriers operated off the coast of North Vietnam) for the Vietnam War.

A hypothetical conflict with China is likely to present a radically different situation, especially if Chinese leaders feel that Taiwan will be lost, China's sovereignty and territorial integrity are challenged, or the conflict is otherwise going very badly for the PLA and Beijing. Under these circumstances, Chinese leaders may lose their apprehension about striking U.S. (and Japanese) territory, especially if Chinese territory is being struck by U.S. forces. Certainly China has remedied or will soon remedy the lack of conventional warhead missiles able to reach Guam. Other U.S. bases in the region, including in Korea, are already within range. It is important that we should not unwittingly adopt a sanctuary mindset. The PLA does not view it that way.

According to one authoritative survey, as early as the end of 2010 China "seeks to have a rudimentary 1,500 to 2,000 km range ASBM capability" and "to a range of 3,000 km by 2015." Efforts would then "focus on a conventional precision strike capability out to 8,000 km" by 2020, and then to global precision strike by 2025.[6] The sanctuary mindset must be relegated to the category of anachronisms. U.S. Navy and Air Force assets in the Western Pacific at sea and ashore are potentially at risk from formidable ballistic and cruise missile attacks with conventional warheads.

Where Do We Go from Here?

Clearly, China's use of space, ranging from ballistic missiles to antisatellite systems, has become more than an astute way to threaten to terrorize Taiwan and harry the United States. Among other things, it holds promise as a key means to complement and safeguard China's sea power. We must now watch for a new form of jointness in the PLA: doctrinal theorizing and operational coordination between the PLAN and the Second Artillery (China's ballistic missile forces) to effect the targeting of ships for attack by ballistic missiles. This could signal other forms of coordination to permit the PLAN and the missile forces to conduct joint attacks or multiaxis attacks by diverse forms of missiles. The PLAN, supported by a tailored ballistic missile force, could become an order of magnitude more effective and less vulnerable because of Chinese missile and space advances as well as other means to disrupt American C4ISR.

This is not a forecast of a conflict between the United States and China. Our policies toward each other continue to lessen the chances of armed conflict; China and the United States are not destined to go to war—contrary to the convictions of some. With respect to China's nuclear arsenal and conventionally armed missiles, the PLA's Second Artillery is not spoiling for a fight and is not expecting to use the weapons. Rather it wants to force Washington in a crisis to take into account that China is a nuclear-weapon nation and, with the ASBM, to show that it might temporarily offset the U.S. advantage of vastly superior naval power, including air defenses that Chinese aircraft cannot penetrate and submarines that the PLAN cannot detect. As explained, ASBMs overfly all this and just might be effective in putting U.S. Navy carriers and cruisers at risk. In any case, it is a threat the United States cannot ignore.

In 2010 Washington took a giant step forward on the matter of countering Chinese advances—of hedging. The latest Quadrennial Defense Review envisions a new Air-Sea Battle plan in response to threats such as China's persistent military buildup, with the U.S. Air Force and Navy pursuing better means to preserve access to the East Asian waters and cope with developing threats to U.S. forces and facilities in the region.[7] Joint Air Force–Navy efforts would combine the strengths of each service to carry out distant strikes with new bombers, a new cruise missile and remote-piloted aircraft launched from aircraft carriers—as explained earlier. All this serves the purpose of making it manifestly clear to Beijing that, even if China obtains a short-term advantage and can render Taiwan nearly void of effective defenses, the PLA cannot achieve a victory over U.S. forces. This step emphasizes that the two militaries are not even in the same league, whether measured in terms of conventional global capabilities or in the area of strategic deterrence—to employ a euphemism to avoid even mention by name of escalatory potential that should not become part of this discussion. In a conflict, China undoubtedly loses in the long run—economically, in the community of nations, and militarily. The new U.S. Air–Sea battle concept helps make that point vividly.

We can only guess at China's real intentions or how those intentions might change as China changes. However, at a minimum, China with its ASAT shot and ABM test has clouded the issue so that those Americans who advocate that the United States should proceed aggressively in space can maneuver behind the clouds. The Obama administration's new national security strategy appears to make it clear that decisions in this arena will not come from those darting around in the clouds. The pertinent sentence from this May 2010 document reads: "To promote security and stability in space, we will pursue activities consistent with the inherent right of self-defense, deepen cooperation with allies and friends, and work with all nations toward the responsible and peaceful use of space."[8]

More Engaging and Less Hedging

We now face what appears to be a profound contradiction: simultaneous hedging and engagement. Somehow in the Sino-U.S. context the combination of these two seems less contradictory and more simply a bit of geopolitical reality.

The widely publicized March 2009 confrontation in the South China Sea between USNS *Impeccable* and Chinese government ships emphasizes this point. On the surface, this incident might be seen as a disagreement between the United States and China concerning interpretation of rules about permissible activities in the two-hundred-mile exclusive economic zone (EEZ) of another country—with China opposing the presence of an intelligence collection ship, as it opposes surveillance flights. The United States treats an EEZ essentially as international waters with respect to the operation of its ships and aircraft.

However, the real basis for the dispute is that China wants to keep the intelligence collectors away, and the United States insists on conducting such operations because it wants to be more effective in the event of hostilities. Just as this confrontation seemed on the brink of escalation (both sides announcing reinforcements), senior people in both governments brought it to a halt, apparently because the United States and China were faced with more important and pressing matters: working together to resolve the global economic downturn and dealing with a newly intransigent North Korea, among other things. The work of *Impeccable* in collecting acoustic intelligence on new PLAN nuclear submarines epitomizes hedging, and the decision to give priority to major aspects of bilateral cooperation to benefit the world epitomizes engagement.

The challenge, worth reemphasizing, for the U.S. Air Force and the U.S. Navy is to find how best, first viewed from a narrow military perspective, to neutralize the threat from Chinese antiship ballistic and cruise missiles and anti-C4ISR techniques and weapons. Then, more broadly, the task is how in the political and strategic arena to attain the right balance between cooperation and hedging, and how to have the cooperation serve to make hedging increasingly unnecessary: engaging and edging away from hedging.

The Task Has Grown Harder, so Washington and Beijing Must Try Harder

Ominous developments in 2010 have made this effort even more complex. As one authority commented recently, "DoD and other observers believe that China's military modernization effort, including its naval modernization effort, is increasingly oriented toward pursuing additional goals [beyond a Taiwan situation], such as asserting or defending China's claims in maritime territorial disputes, protecting China's sea lines of communications, displacing U.S. influence in the Pacific, and asserting China's status as a major world power."[9] As reflected specifically in Beijing's repeated disruptions of military relations with the United States and more generally in a newly assertive attitude in relations with the United States, the route to achieving greater trust and confidence in the bilateral relationship and seeing the need for hedging diminished by cooperative efforts is not obvious. It may be as simple as that the PLA or an influential very senior faction in the PLA, profoundly distrustful of Washington, has been successful in asserting its views.

Positive aspects of the overall relationship persist, as reflected in the "Strategic and Economic Dialogue" conducted in the spring of 2010. However, a preponderance of discussion of cooperation on global issues has not submerged the deep opposition in China to Taiwan arms sales and two other issues. General Ma Xiaotian, PLA deputy chief of general staff, said at the April 2010 Shangri-la Dialogue that continuing U.S. arms sales to Taiwan, congressional restrictions on bilateral military exchanges, and regular surveillance operations by U.S. warships and warplanes were the reasons for the lack of progress in Sino-U.S. military relations.[10] He emphasized the issue of arms sales to Taiwan, stating that "U.S. arms sales to Taiwan are not just an ordinary issue."[11] The Washington summit meeting between President Obama and President Hu Jintao in January 2011 has brought about a significant improvement in bilateral relations. Many of the Chinese complaints were silenced. I was told by Chinese interlocutors that this could persist, but this will be an interesting thing to pursue after the summit has concluded and problems remain.

The recurrence over the decades of disruptions in the bilateral military relationship and the persistence of the current disruption, including the snubbing for several months of U.S. Secretary of Defense Robert Gates' expectation to visit China in 2010 (which occurred in January 2011), understandably arouse concerns about how the United States, especially the U.S. Navy, should respond with respect to both the navy-to-navy relationship and the more ominous concerns that stem from the rebukes, lack of communication, and added tension.

Renewed urgent attention by Washington is unquestionably warranted to counter these important developments, which could be decisive in timely and effective U.S. intervention in the region, including especially the threat to U.S. CSGs posed by capable submarines armed with lethal ASCMs and by the ASBMs with maneuvering reentry vehicles described earlier. The Chinese effort to be able to disrupt U.S. C4ISR assets is logical and expected under the current circumstances. The United States faces an enormously important challenge in denying China the opportunity to partially blind and silence it or significantly degrade the enormous advantages the United States has in promptly turning surveillance discoveries to items of confirmed intelligence and then rapidly into destroyed targets.

Ranking Priorities

A careful assessment should be undertaken of the implications of China's having deployed far in excess of a thousand missiles, many of which are very accurate. Before we permanently move additional forces with specific capabilities to the region, we should ask three questions: (1) Are there forces that can do the job but that do not require basing in the region? (2) Will we have the freedom to use those forces as we wish? (3) Will the forces and bases be acceptably safe?

Concern has been expressed as well about the broader geopolitical aspects of this modernization of the PLA. There is fear by some of a potential erosion of regional nations' confidence in the United States so that they tend to be supportive of China—a country seen as close, huge, prosperous, and increasingly intimidating militarily as well as economically. The United States has no reasonable option other than striving to achieve readiness to cope with this threat militarily. In this regard, however, while China is no match for U.S. military might across the spectrum of warfare, it can pose specific threats that could make more likely Chinese success in achieving limited goals—such as complicating timely U.S. intervention. Beijing has certain advantages as to proximity, strategic depth, and astute choice of weapon systems (missiles that are hard to defend against and sufficiently accurate to pose a new form of threat). The United States cannot assume with confidence that it can simply overwhelm China's ability to both attack Taiwan and make things troublesome for an intervening America. China may prove inept in using its forces, but the United States cannot rely on that as a strategy.

Discouraging Developments Are a Signal to Start a New Dialogue, Not to End the Dialogue

Despite the attention warranted by these threats posed by China, full and urgent attention is required to attempt to move the U.S.–PRC relationship beyond this situation where the two sides see each other as potential adversaries as well as partners in managing other major issues. Given the nature and scope of national differences and specific disputes, this is clearly a daunting task. However, the United States has not, in my view, "pulled out the stops" in dealing with the politico-military aspects of relations with China. We tend to end the conversation each time we prove anew that the PLA is intransigent; that is where, instead, new conversation should start—with both sides required by the most senior people in their respective governments to move beyond, circumvent, or shelve the disagreements and eventually bury them under years of cooperative activity. The situation cries out for candor and maturity.

The importance of the bilateral relationship demands that both sides make a greater effort at a higher level to look beyond the differences, resolving them where possible, suppressing irresolvable issues where appropriate, and employing new forms of candor in dealing with others. In short, the likely most valuable and comprehensive counter to the threats China poses is to determine how best to use cooperation, candor, and new ideas to build trust and confidence. We need to employ these means to gain understanding and to influence each other in establishing the relationship the world needs between its two most important nations. This is a small thing to ask, given the implications of failing to do so.

Notes

1. Glenn Kessler, "China Is at the Heart of Clinton's First Trip," *Washington Post*, 15 February 2009, A6.

2. Andrew Browne, Andrew Batson, and Aaron Back, "Summit Shows Superpowers' Shifting Dynamic," *Wall Street Journal*, 25 May 2010, http://online.wsj.com/article/SB10001424052748703341904575266291812173592.html?KEYWORDS=%22Summit+Shows+Superpowers%E2%80%99+Shifting+Dynamic%22.

3. "China Conducts Test on Ground-Based Midcourse Missile Interception," *Xinhua*, 11 January 2010, http://news.xinhuanet.com/english/2010-01/11/content_12792329.htm.

4. Information Office of the State Council of the PRC, "China's National Defense in 2008," January 2009, 80, http://merln.ndu.edu/whitepapers/China_English2008.pdf.

5. Office of the Secretary of Defense (DoD), *Military and Security Developments Involving the People's Republic of China 2010*, Annual Report to Congress (Washington, DC: Office of the Secretary of Defense, 16 August 2010), http://www .defense.gov/pubs/pdfs/2010_CMPR_Final.pdf, 31.

6. Mark Stokes, *China's Evolving Conventional Strategic Strike Capability*, Project 2049 Institute, 12 September 2009, 2, http://project2049.net/documents/chinese_anti_ship_ ballistic_missile_asbm.pdf.

7. Christopher P. Cavas, "For the USN, QDR Stays the Course," *Defense News*, 27 January 2010, http://www.defensenews.com/story.php?i=4473484.

8. *National Security Strategy* (Washington, DC: The White House, May 2010), 31, http:// www.whitehouse.gov/sites/default/files/rss_viewer/national_security_strategy.pdf.

9. Ronald O'Rourke, *China Naval Modernization: Implications for U.S. Navy Capabilities—Background and Issues for Congress*, Congressional Research Service, 7-5700, available at www.crs.gov, RL33153, 3 February 2011, in "Summary" on unnumbered page following title page.

10. Ma was referring to the constraints legislated in the National Defense Authorization Act of FY 2000, and he was complaining about the U.S. intelligence collection operations in China's EEZ.

11. As reported in an International Institute for Strategic Studies commentary on the 4–6 April 2010 Shangri-La Dialogue, http://www.iiss.org/whats-new/iiss-in-the-press/ june-2010/china-overplays-taiwan-arms/.

China's Military Aerospace Forces: A Visual Overview

Medium and Intercontinental Range Ballistic Missiles

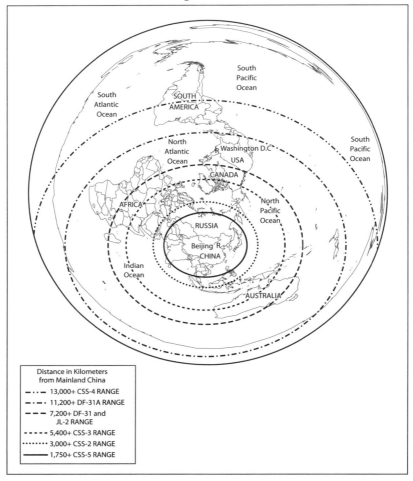

China is capable of targeting its nuclear forces throughout the region and most of the world, including the continental United States. Newer systems, such as the DF-31, DF-31A, and JL-2, will give China a more survivable nuclear force.

Source: Office of the Secretary of Defense (DoD), *Military and Security Developments Involving the People's Republic of China 2010*, Annual Report to Congress (Washington, DC: Office of the Secretary of Defense, 16 August 2010), 35.

Conventional Antiaccess Capabilities

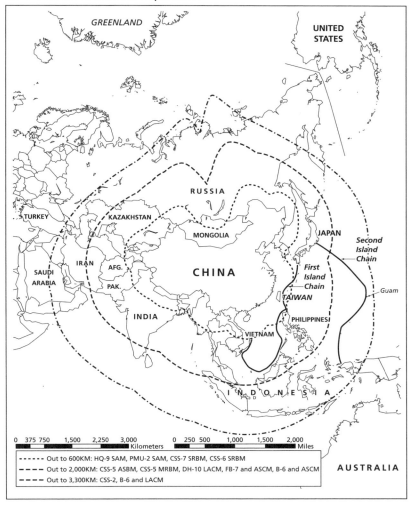

The PLA's conventional forces are currently capable of striking targets well beyond China's immediate periphery. Not included are ranges for naval surface- and subsurface-base weapons, whose employment at distances from China would be determined by doctrine and the scenario in which they are employed.

Source: Office of the Secretary of Defense (DoD), *Military and Security Developments Involving the People's Republic of China 2010*, Annual Report to Congress (Washington, DC: Office of the Secretary of Defense, 16 August 2010), 32.

Taiwan Strait SRBM and SAM Coverage

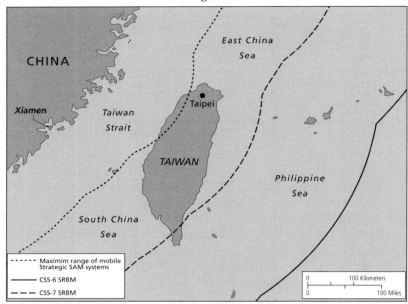

This map depicts notional coverage based on the range of the CSS-6 and CSS-7 SRBMs and the Russian-designed SA-20 PMU2 SAM system. Actual air defense coverage would be noncontiguous and dependent upon precise deployment sites. If deployed near the Taiwan Strait, the PMU2's extended range provides the PLA's SAM force with an offensive capability against Taiwan aircraft.

Source: Office of the Secretary of Defense (DoD), *Military and Security Developments Involving the People's Republic of China 2010*, Annual Report to Congress (Washington, DC: Office of the Secretary of Defense, 16 August 2010), 50.

China's Missile Force

BALLISTIC AND CRUISE MISSILES			
China's Missile Inventory	Missiles	Launchers	Estimated Range
CSS-2	15–20	5–10	3,000+ km
CSS-3	15–20	10–15	5,400+ km
CSS-4	20	20	13,000+ km
DF-31	<10	<10	7,200+ km
DF-31A	10–15	10–15	11,200+ km
CSS-5	85–95	75–85	1,750+ km
CSS-6	350–400	90–110	600 km
CSS-7	700–750	120–140	300 km
DH-10	200–500	45–55	1,500+ km
JL-2	Developmental	Developmental	7,200+ km

Note: China's Second Artillery maintains at least five operational SRBM brigades; an additional two brigades are subordinate to PLA ground forces—one garrisoned in the Nanjing MR and the other in the Guangzhou MR. All SRBM units are deployed to locations near Taiwan.

Source: Office of the Secretary of Defense (DoD), *Military and Security Developments Involving the People's Republic of China 2010*, Annual Report to Congress (Washington, DC: Office of the Secretary of Defense, 16 August 2010), 66.

China's Major Air Units

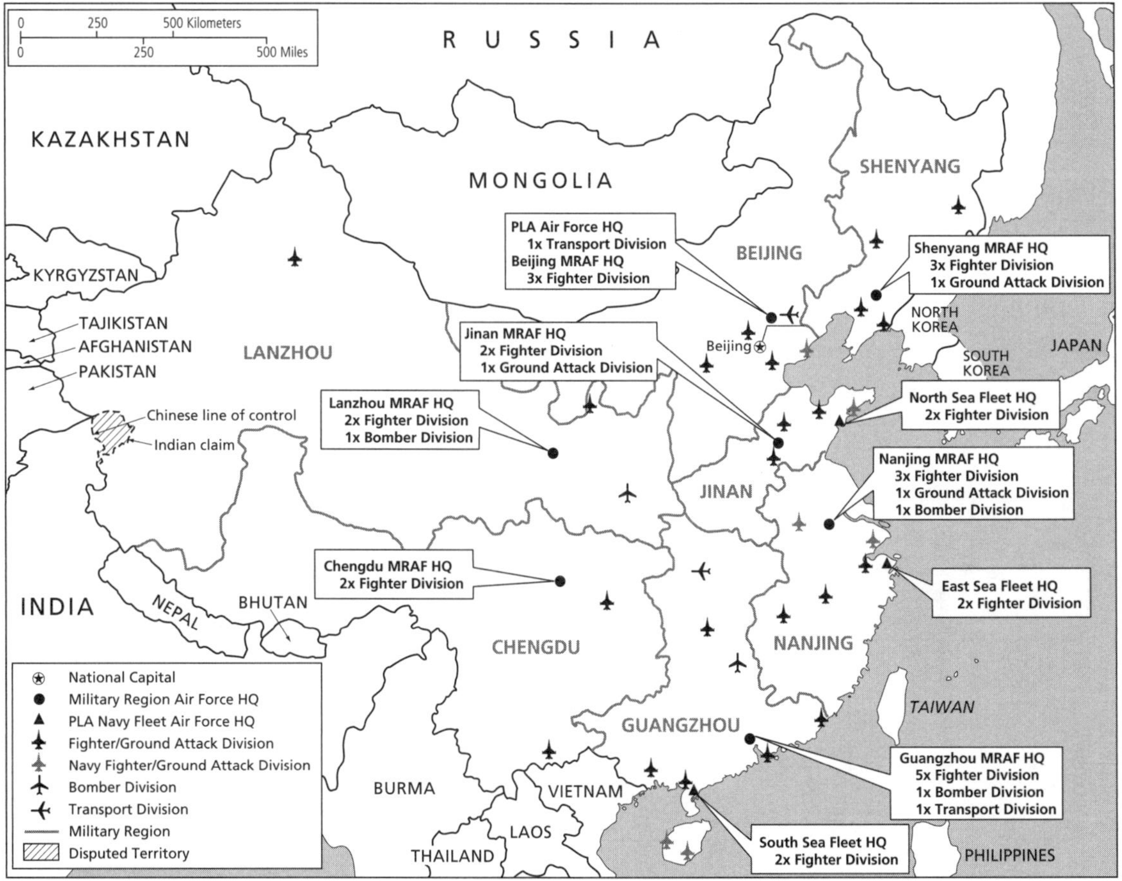

China bases 490 combat aircraft within unrefueled operational range of Taiwan, and has the airfield capacity to expand that number by hundreds. Many of these aircraft are upgrades of older models; however, newer and more advanced aircraft make up a growing percentage of the inventory. It is likely that the PLAAF's primary focus for the coming decade will remain on building the capabilities required to pose a credible military threat to Taiwan and U.S. forces in East Asia, deter Taiwan independence, or influence Taiwan to settle the dispute on Beijing's terms. In a conflict scenario, the PLAAF would use Russian-built and indigenously produced fourth-generation aircraft (e.g., Su-27 and Su-30 variants, and the indigenous F/J-10 multirole fighter) to compete for local air dominance. PLAN aviation would employ Russian Su-30MK2 fighters and FB-7 fighter-bombers for maritime interdiction. Acquisition of an air refueling platform like the Russian IL-78 would extend operational ranges for PLAAF and PLAN strike aircraft armed with precision munitions, thereby increasing the threat to opposing surface and air forces, bases, and logistics nodes distant from China's coast.

Source: Office of the Secretary of Defense (DoD), *Military and Security Developments Involving the People's Republic of China 2010,* Annual Report to Congress (Washington, DC: Office of the Secretary of Defense, 16 August 2010), 3–4, 25, 33, 63.

Taiwan Strait Military Balance, Air Forces

| Aircraft | CHINA | | TAIWAN |
	Total	Within Range of Taiwan	Total
Fighters	1,680	330	388
Bombers/Attack	620	160	22
Transport	450	40	21

Note: The PLAAF and the PLAN have approximately 2,300 operational combat aircraft. These consist of air defense and multirole fighters, ground-attack aircraft, fighter-bombers, and bombers. An additional 1,450 older fighters, bombers, and trainers are employed for training and research and development. The two air arms also possess approximately 450 transports and more than 100 surveillance and reconnaissance aircraft with intelligence, surface search, and airborne early-warning capabilities. The majority of PLAAF and PLAN aircraft are based in the eastern half of the country. Currently, 490 aircraft could conduct combat operations against Taiwan without refueling. However, this number could be significantly increased through any combination of aircraft forward deployment, decreased ordnance loads, or altered mission profiles.

Source: Office of the Secretary of Defense (DoD), *Military and Security Developments Involving the People's Republic of China 2010*, Annual Report to Congress (Washington, DC: Office of the Secretary of Defense, 16 August 2010), 62.

Acronyms

A2/AD	antiaccess/area denial
ADIZ	air defense identification zone
AEW	airborne early warning
AEW&C	airborne early warning and control
ALCM	air-launched cruise missile
AR	air refueling
ARM	antiradiation missile
ASAT	antisatellite
ASBM	antiship ballistic missile
ASCM	antiship cruise missile
ASW	antisubmarine warfare
BMD	ballistic missile defense
BUAA	Beijing University of Aeronautics and Astronautics
BVR	beyond visual range
C4	command, control, communications, and computers
C4I	command, control, communications, computers, and intelligence
C4ISR	command, control, communications, computers, intelligence, surveillance, and reconnaissance
CASC	China Aerospace Science and Technology Corporation

CASIC	China Aerospace Science and Industry Corporation
CATOBAR	catapult-assisted takeoff but arrested recovery
CCP	Chinese Communist Party
CMC	Central Military Commission
CMSI	China Maritime Studies Institute
CSG	carrier strike group
DoD	Department of Defense
DRFM	digital radio frequency memory
ECM	electronic countermeasures
ED	electronic defense
EEZ	exclusive economic zone
ELINT	electronic intelligence
GAD	General Armaments Department
GLCM	ground-launched cruise missile
HA/DR	humanitarian assistance and disaster relief
HALE	high-altitude, long-endurance
ICBM	intercontinental ballistic missile
INF	Intermediate-Range Nuclear Forces (Treaty)
IRBM	intermediate-range ballistic missile
ISR	intelligence, surveillance, and reconnaissance
ITU	International Telecommunications Union
JMSDF	Japan Maritime Self-Defense Force
LACM	land-attack cruise missile
MALE	medium-altitude, long-endurance
MR	military region
MRBM	medium-range ballistic missile
MTCZ	military training coordination zone
nav/pos	navigation-positioning
nm	nautical miles
NUAA	Nanjing University of Aeronautics and Astronautics
ONI	Office of Naval Intelligence
OTH	over-the-horizon
PGM	precision-guided munition
PLA	People's Liberation Army

PLAAF	PLA Air Force
PLAN	PLA Navy
PRC	People's Republic of China
QDR	Quadrennial Defense Review
ROCAF	Republic of China Air Force
SAC	Second Artillery Corps
SAC	Shenyang Aircraft Company
SAM	surface-to-air missile
SAR	search and rescue
SAR	synthetic aperture radar
SIGINT	signals intelligence
SLOC	sea line of communication
SOA	State Oceanic Administration
SRBM	short-range ballistic missile
STOBAR	short takeoff but arrested recovery
TBM	tactical ballistic missile
UAV	unmanned aerial vehicle
UCAS	unmanned combat air system
UCAV	unmanned combat aerial vehicle
UNCLOS	United Nations Convention on the Law of the Sea
USAF	U.S. Air Force
USN	U.S. Navy
V/STOL	vertical/short takeoff and landing
VTOL	vertical takeoff and landing
VTUAV	vertical takeoff UAVs

About the Contributors

Lieutenant Colonel Dennis J. Blasko, USA (Ret.), served twenty-three years as a military intelligence officer and foreign area officer specializing in China.

Dr. Michael S. Chase is an associate research professor and director of the Mahan Scholars Program in the Warfare Analysis and Research Department at the U.S. Naval War College in Newport, Rhode Island.

Mr. David Chen is a principal research analyst at CENTRA Technology, Inc., where he contributes primarily to China-related analytical products.

Mr. Ron Christman is currently the senior intelligence officer and was formerly the division chief (acting), for the Strategic Missile Forces Division of the Defense Intelligence Agency's Office for Military Forces Analysis.

Dr. Roger Cliff is a senior political scientist in the Washington office of the RAND Corporation.

Mr. Gabriel Collins is a private-sector commodity market analyst focusing on China and Russia.

Prof. Peter A. Dutton is a professor of strategic studies in the China Maritime Studies Institute at the U.S. Naval War College.

Mr. Ian Easton is a research affiliate at the Project 2049 Institute, where he conducts primary source Chinese-language research and analysis focused on aerospace and security-related issues in the Asia-Pacific region.

Mr. Richard D. Fisher Jr. is a senior fellow with the International Assessment and Strategy Center.

Mr. Paul S. Giarra leads Global Strategies and Transformation, a professional services firm and consultancy providing national security strategic analysis, defense concept development, military transformation expertise, and applied history as a planning tool.

Mr. Jeff Hagen is a senior engineer at the RAND Corporation. His research areas include technological systems analysis and strategic policy and decision making.

Mr. Eric Hagt is the director of the China program at the World Security Institute in Washington, DC, and chief editor of *China Security Quarterly*.

Mr. Garth Hekler is an analyst with SGIS focusing on China foreign policy issues.

Dr. James R. Holmes is an associate professor of strategy at the Naval War College.

Mr. Daniel J. Kostecka is a senior analyst for the U.S. Navy.

Colonel Kevin Lanzit, USAF (Ret.), is a program manager and senior analyst with CENTRA Technology.

Dr. Nan Li is an associate professor in the Strategic Research Department of the U.S. Naval War College and a member of the department's China Maritime Studies Institute.

Miguel Martinez is a lieutenant commander in the U.S. Navy.

Lieutenant Colonel Anthony J. Mastalir, USAF, is Deputy Group Commander of the 595th Space Group, Space Innovation and Development Center, Schriever AFB, Colorado.

COLONEL SEAN D. MCCLUNG, USAF (RET.), is currently employed at Millennium Engineering and Integration Company in Aegis ballistic missile defense.

COLONEL MICHAEL MCGAUVRAN, USAF (RET.), is a professor of joint military operations at the Naval War College, Newport, Rhode Island.

REAR ADMIRAL ERIC A. MCVADON, USN (RET.), concluded thirty-five years of naval service as the U.S. defense and naval attaché at the American embassy in Beijing, 1990–92.

PROF. WILLIAM S. MURRAY is an associate research professor in the Warfare Analysis and Research Department in the U.S. Naval War College's Center for Naval Warfare Studies.

MR. KEVIN POLLPETER is the China program manager at Defense Group, Inc.

LIEUTENANT COLONEL MARK A. STOKES, USAF (RET.), is executive director of the Project 2049 Institute.

MR. WAYNE A. ULMAN is the China issue manager at the National Air and Space Intelligence Center, Dayton, Ohio.

MR. CHRISTOPHER WEUVE is a naval analyst working for the U.S. Department of Defense.

COLONEL TIMOTHY WHITE, USAF, is a professor of joint military operations at the Naval War College.

DR. LARRY M. WORTZEL is a retired U.S. Army colonel who spent twelve of his thirty-two-year military career in the Asia-Pacific region, including two tours of duty as a military attaché at the American embassy in China.

MR. DAVID D. YANG is an associate political scientist at the RAND Corporation.

DR. TOSHI YOSHIHARA is an associate professor in the Strategy and Policy Department at the Naval War College.

DR. JINGDONG YUAN is associate professor in international security at the Centre for International Security Studies, University of Sydney.

DR. XIAOMING ZHANG is associate professor in the Department of Leadership and Strategy at the Air War College.

The Editors

DR. ANDREW S. ERICKSON is an associate professor in the Strategic Research Department at the U.S. Naval War College and a founding member of the department's China Maritime Studies Institute.

DR. LYLE J. GOLDSTEIN is an associate professor in the Strategic Research Department of the U.S. Naval War College and the founding director of the Naval War College's China Maritime Studies Institute.

Index